McGraw-Hill's
Premium Content

Access Premium Resources
to Help You Study

To gain access to these online resources

1 **USE** your web browser to go to the text's website

2 **CLICK** on "First Time User"

3 **ENTER** the Registration Code printed below

4 After you have entered your registration code, click on "Register"

5 **FOLLOW** the instructions to setup your personal UserID and Password

6 **WRITE** your UserID and Password down for future reference. Keep it in a safe place.

You'll be able to use this code to access Premium McGraw-Hill content to help you study.

To gain access to the content simply log onto the text's website. Enter the registration code exactly as it appears below when prompted by the system.

These instructions are specifically for student access. Instructors are not required to register via the above instructions.

Enter the code below exactly as it appears. Include all dashes.

MXU8-N6VJ-PMBX-FTPG-HKH9

Registration Code

HERE IS YOUR REGISTRATION CODE TO ACCESS MCGRAW-HILL PREMIUM CONTENT AND MCGRAW-HILL ONLINE RESOURCES

For key premium online resources you need **THIS CODE** to gain access. Once the code is entered, you will be able to use the web resources for the length of your course.

Having trouble using your Registration Code?
Visit http://www.mhhe.com/support

 McGraw-Hill Irwin

ISBN 978-0-07-729920-0
MHID 0-07-729920-5

The McGraw-Hill Companies

 McGraw-Hill Higher Education

Business Driven Information Systems

Paige Baltzan

Daniels College of Business, University of Denver

Amy Phillips

Daniels College of Business, University of Denver

Business Driven Information Systems

SECOND EDITION

McGraw-Hill
Irwin

Boston   Burr Ridge, IL   Dubuque, IA   New York   San Francisco   St. Louis
Bangkok   Bogotá   Caracas   Kuala Lumpur   Lisbon   London   Madrid   Mexico City
Milan   Montreal   New Delhi   Santiago   Seoul   Singapore   Sydney   Taipei   Toronto

BUSINESS DRIVEN INFORMATION SYSTEMS

Published by McGraw-Hill/Irwin, a business unit of The McGraw-Hill Companies, Inc., 1221 Avenue of the Americas, New York, NY, 10020. Copyright © 2009, 2008 by The McGraw-Hill Companies, Inc. All rights reserved. No part of this publication may be reproduced or distributed in any form or by any means, or stored in a database or retrieval system, without the prior written consent of The McGraw-Hill Companies, Inc., including, but not limited to, in any network or other electronic storage or transmission, or broadcast for distance learning.

Some ancillaries, including electronic and print components, may not be available to customers outside the United States.

This book is printed on acid-free paper.

1 2 3 4 5 6 7 8 9 0 CCI/CCI 0 9 8

ISBN 978-0-07-128524-7
MHID 0-07-128524-5

To Tony, Hannah, Sophie, and Gus:
What do you always remember?
That I Love You!
That I'm Proud of You!

Paige

To Deborah and Stacy: Thanks for all your
wonderful support throughout the years.
Here's to many, many road trips!

Amy

BRIEF CONTENTS

CONTENTS

Business Driven Information Systems discusses various business initiatives first and how technology supports those initiatives second. The premise for this unique approach is that business initiatives should drive technology choices. Every discussion first addresses the business needs and then addresses the technology that supports those needs. This text provides the foundation that will enable students to achieve excellence in business, whether they major in operations management, manufacturing, sales, marketing, finance, human resources, accounting, or virtually any other business discipline. *Business Driven Information Systems* is designed to give students the ability to understand how information technology can be a point of strength for an organization.

Common business goals associated with information technology projects include reducing costs, improving productivity, improving customer satisfaction and loyalty, creating competitive advantages, streamlining supply chains, global expansion, and so on. Achieving these results is not easy. Implementing a new accounting system or marketing plan is not likely to generate long-term growth or reduce costs across an entire organization. Businesses must undertake enterprisewide initiatives to achieve broad general business goals such as reducing costs. Information technology plays a critical role in deploying such initiatives by facilitating communication and increasing business intelligence. Any individual anticipating a successful career in business whether it is in accounting, finance, human resources, or operation management must understand the basics of information technology that can be found in this text.

We have found tremendous success teaching MIS courses by demonstrating the correlation between business and IT. Students who understand the tight correlation between business and IT understand the power of this course. Students learn 10 percent of what they read, 80 percent of what they personally experience, and 90 percent of what they teach others. The business driven approach takes the difficult and often intangible MIS concepts, brings them to the student's level, and applies them using a hands-on approach to reinforce the concepts. Teaching MIS with a business driven focus helps:

- Add credibility to IT.
- Open student's eyes to IT opportunities.
- Attract majors.
- Engage students.

FORMAT, FEATURES, AND HIGHLIGHTS

Business Driven Information Systems is state-of-the-art in its discussions, presents concepts in an easy-to-understand format, and allows students to be active participants in learning. The dynamic nature of information technology requires all students, more specifically business students, to be aware of both current and emerging technologies. Students are facing complex subjects and need a clear, concise explanation to be able to understand and use the concepts throughout their careers. By engaging students with numerous case studies, exercises, projects, and questions that enforce concepts, *Business Driven Information Systems* creates a unique learning experience for both faculty and students.

- **Audience.** *Business Driven Information Systems* is designed for use in undergraduate or introductory MBA courses in Management Information Systems, which are required in many Business Administration or Management programs as part of the common body of knowledge for all business majors.

- **Logical Layout.** Students and faculty will find the text well organized with the topics flowing logically from one chapter to the next. The definition of each term is provided before it is covered in the chapter and an extensive glossary is included at the back of the text. Each chapter offers a comprehensive opening case study, introduction, learning outcomes, closing case studies, key terms, and making business decision questions. The plug-ins follow the same pedagogical elements with the exception of the exclusion of opening case and closing case studies.

- **Thorough Explanations.** Complete coverage is provided for each topic that is introduced. Explanations are written so that students can understand the ideas presented and relate them to other concepts.

- **Solid Theoretical Base.** The text relies on current theory and practice of information systems as they relate to the business environment. Current academic and professional journals cited throughout the text are found in the Notes at the end of the book—a road map for additional, pertinent readings that can be the basis for learning beyond the scope of the chapters or plug-ins.

- **Material to Encourage Discussion.** All chapters contain a diverse selection of case studies and individual and group problem-solving activities as they relate to the use of information technology in business. Three comprehensive cases at the end of each chapter reinforce content. These cases encourage students to consider what concepts have been presented and then apply those concepts to a situation they might find in an organization. Different people in an organization can view the same facts from different points of view and the cases will force students to consider some of those views.

- **Flexibility in Teaching and Learning.** While most textbooks that are "text only" leave faculty on their own when it comes to choosing cases, *Business Driven Information Systems* goes much further. Several options are provided to faculty with case selections from a variety of sources including *CIO, Harvard Business Journal, Wired, Forbes, Business 2.0,* and *Time,* to name just a few. Therefore, faculty can use the text alone, the text and a complete selection of cases, or anything in between.

- **Integrative Themes.** Several integrative themes recur throughout the text which adds integration to the material. Among these themes are value added techniques and methodologies, ethics and social responsibility, globalization, and gaining a competitive advantage. Such topics are essential to gaining a full understanding of the strategies that a business must recognize, formulate, and in turn implement. In addition to addressing these in the chapter material, many illustrations are provided for their relevance to business practice.

WALKTHROUGH

Learning Outcomes and Introduction

Introduction. Located after the opening case study, the introduction familiarizes students with the overall tone of the chapters. Thematic concepts are also broadly defined.

INTRODUCTION

Decision-making and problem-solving abilities are now the most sought-after traits in up-and-coming executives, according to a recent survey of 1,000 executives by Caliper Associates, as reported in *The Wall Street Journal*. To put it mildly, decision makers and problem solvers have limitless career potential.[2]

Decision making and problem solving in today's electronic world encompass large-scale, opportunity-oriented, strategically focused solutions. The traditional "cookbook" approach to decision making simply will not work. This chapter focuses on technology to help make decisions, solve problems, and find new innovative opportunities. The chapter also highlights how to bring people together with the best IT processes and tools in complete, flexible solutions that can seize business opportunities and combat business challenges (see Figure 2.1).

Learning Outcomes. These outcomes focus on what students should learn and be able to answer upon completion of the chapter.

section 3.1 BUSINESS AND THE INTERNET

LEARNING OUTCOMES

3.1. Compare disruptive and sustaining technologies.

3.2. Explain how the Internet caused disruption among businesses.

3.3. Define the relationship between the Internet and the World Wide Web.

3.4. Describe the different methods an organization can use to access information.

3.5. Compare the three different types of service providers.

Chapter Opening Case Study and Opening Case Questions

Chapter Opening Case Study. To enhance student interest, each chapter begins with an opening case study that highlights an organization that has been time-tested and value proven in the business world. This feature serves to fortify concepts with relevant examples of outstanding companies. Discussion of the case is threaded throughout the chapter.

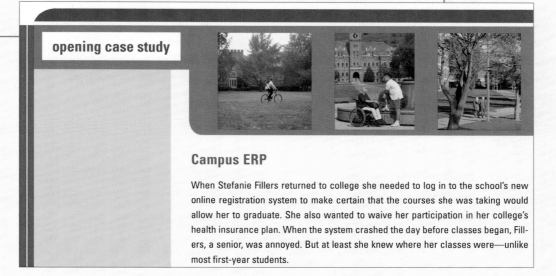

opening case study

Campus ERP

When Stefanie Fillers returned to college she needed to log in to the school's new online registration system to make certain that the courses she was taking would allow her to graduate. She also wanted to waive her participation in her college's health insurance plan. When the system crashed the day before classes began, Fillers, a senior, was annoyed. But at least she knew where her classes were—unlike most first-year students.

Opening Case Questions. Located at the end of each section, poignant questions connect the chapter opening case with important chapter concepts.

OPENING CASE QUESTIONS
Campus ERP

1. How could core ERP components help improve business operations at your college?
2. How could extended ERP components help improve business operations at your college?
3. How can integrating SCM, CRM, and ERP help improve business operations at your college?

Projects and Case Studies

Case Studies. This text is packed with 48 case studies illustrating how a variety of prominent organizations and businesses have successfully implemented many of this text's concepts. All cases are timely and promote critical thinking. Company profiles are especially appealing and relevant to your students, helping to stir classroom discussion and interest. For a full list of cases explored in *Business Driven Information Systems,* turn to the inside back cover.

Apply Your Knowledge. At the end of each chapter you will find several Apply Your Knowledge projects that challenge students to bring the skills they have learned from the chapter to real business problems. There are also 35 Apply Your Knowledge projects on the OLC that accompanies this text (www.mhhe.com/baltzan) that ask students to use IT tools such as Excel, Access, and Dreamweaver to solve business problems. These projects help to develop the application and problem-solving skills of your students through challenging and creative business-driven scenarios.

Project 35:

Sticky Wiki

Wiki (Hawaiian for "quick") is software that allows users to freely create and edit web page content using any web browser. The most common wiki is Wikipedia. Wikis offer a powerful yet flexible collaborative communication tool for developing websites. The best part of a wiki is that it grows and evolves by the collaborative community adding content—the owner of the wiki does not have to add all of the content as is typical in a standard webpage.

Many sites offer free wiki software such as Socialtext, a group-editable website. As one of the first wiki companies, Socialtext wikis are designed for anyone that wants to accelerate team communications, better enable knowledge sharing, foster collaboration, and build online communities. Socialtext also offers WikiWidgets, which make it easy for nontechnical business users to create rich, dynamic wiki content. Today, over 3,000 organizations use Socialtext, including Symantec, Nokia, IKEA, Conde Nast, Ziff-Davis, Kodak, University of Southern California, Boston College, and numerous others.

Project Focus

Create your own wiki. Wikis can address a variety of needs from student involvement, fraternities and sororities, group activities, sport team updates, local band highlights, etc.

Making Business Decisions. Each chapter includes small scenario-driven projects that help students focus individually on decision making as they relate to the topical elements in the chapter.

MAKING BUSINESS DECISIONS

1. **Leveraging the competitive value of the Internet**

   Physical inventories have always been a major cost component of business. Linking to suppliers in real time dramatically enhances the classic goal of inventory "turn." The Internet provides a multitude of opportunities for radically reducing the costs of designing, manufacturing, and selling goods and services. E-mango.com, a fruit emarketplace, must take advantage of these opportunities or find itself at a significant competitive disadvantage. Identify the disadvantages that confront E-mango.com if it does not leverage the competitive value of the Internet.

End-of-Chapter Elements

Each chapter contains complete pedagogical support in the form of:

Key Terms. With page numbers referencing where they are discussed in the text.

KEY TERMS

Application programming interface 94	Electronic catalog 108	Online service provider (OSP) 99
Application service provider (ASP) 99	Electronic check 107	Personalization 106
Associate program (affiliate program) 106	Electronic data interchange (EDI) 107	Podcasting 106
Banner ad 111	Electronic marketplace (emarketplace) 103	Pop-under ad 106
	Encryption 109	Pop-up ad 106
		Portal 97

Three Closing Case Studies. Reinforcing important concepts with prominent examples from businesses and organizations. Discussion questions follow each case study.

CLOSING CASE TWO

Innovative Business Managers

BusinessWeek magazine recognized several innovative managers who have demonstrated talent, vision, and the ability to identify excellent opportunities (see Figure 1.24).

Business Driven Best Sellers. Facilitates learning and demonstrates the relevance of the MIS concepts being taught. Provides a high-level overview of a few of the top-selling business books concentrating on the material covered in the chapter.

BUSINESS DRIVEN BEST SELLERS

The Innovator's Solution. By Clayton Christensen and Michael Raynor (Harvard Business School Publishing, 2003).

Roughly one company in every 10 is able to sustain the kind of growth that translates into an above-average increase in shareholder returns over more than a few years. Once a company's core business has matured, the pursuit of new platforms for growth entails daunting risk. To put it simply, most companies have no idea how to grow, and pursuing growth the wrong way can be worse than no growth.

About the Plug-Ins

Located on the OLC that accompanies this text (www.mhhe.com/baltzan), the overall goal of the plug-ins is to provide an alternative for faculty who find themselves in the situation of having to purchase an extra book to support Microsoft Office. The plug-ins presented here offer integration with the core chapters and provide critical knowledge using essential business applications, such as Microsoft Excel, Microsoft Access, DreamWeaver, and Microsoft Project. Each plug-in uses hands-on tutorials for comprehension and mastery.

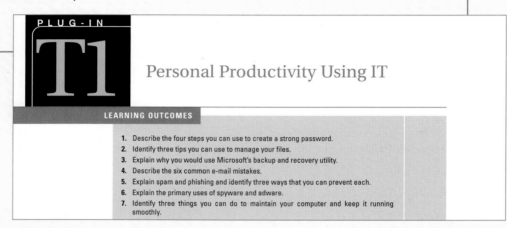

PLUG-IN

T1

Personal Productivity Using IT

LEARNING OUTCOMES

1. Describe the four steps you can use to create a strong password.
2. Identify three tips you can use to manage your files.
3. Explain why you would use Microsoft's backup and recovery utility.
4. Describe the six common e-mail mistakes.
5. Explain spam and phishing and identify three ways that you can prevent each.
6. Explain the primary uses of spyware and adware.
7. Identify three things you can do to maintain your computer and keep it running smoothly.

End-of-Plug-In Elements

Each plug-in contains complete pedagogical support in the form of:

Plug-In Summary. Revisits the plug-in highlights in summary format.

Making Business Decisions. Small scenario-driven projects that help students focus individually on decision making as they relate to the topical elements in the chapters.

★ PLUG-IN SUMMARY

Microsoft Excel is a general-purpose electronic spreadsheet used to organize, calculate, and analyze data. The tasks you can perform with Excel range from preparing a simple invoice to managing an accounting ledger for a business.

Six areas in Excel were covered in this plug-in:

1. Workbooks and worksheets.
2. Working with cells and cell data.
3. Printing worksheets.
4. Formatting worksheets.
5. Formulas.
6. Working with charts and graphics.

★ MAKING BUSINESS DECISIONS

1. Stock Watcher

Mark Martin has created a basic stock watcher worksheet that he uses to report on gains or losses from when he purchased the stock and the last recorded date and price. Mark has given you a snapshot of his spreadsheet (see Figure T2.29) that you can use to recreate this spreadsheet for yourself. Here are some basic steps to follow:

1. Create a new workbook.
2. Enter all the information provided in Figure T2.29.
3. Apply the currency format to the respective columns.

Support and Supplemental Material

All of the supplemental material supporting *Business Driven Information Systems* was developed by the author team to ensure you receive accurate, high-quality, and in-depth content. Included are a complete set of materials that will assist students and faculty in accomplishing course objectives.

For a complete author-narrated overview of the support and supplemental materials of this text, please visit the Online Learning Center (www.mhhe.com/baltzan).

Online Learning Center (www.mhhe.com/baltzan) The McGraw-Hill website for *Business Driven Information Systems* includes support for students and faculty. All supplements will be available exclusively on the OLC. This will allow the authors to continually update and add to the instructor support materials. The following materials will be available on the OLC:

Video Exercises. Each of the videos that accompany the text is supported by detailed teaching notes on how to turn the videos into classroom exercises where your students can apply the knowledge they are learning after watching the videos.

Test Bank. This computerized package allows instructors to custom design, save, and generate tests. The test program permits instructors to edit, add, or delete questions from the test banks; analyze test results; and organize a database of tests and students results. In addition to the traditional test bank material, a new test bank will offer Excel and Access questions for testing purposes.

Instructor's Manual (IM). The IM, written by the authors, includes suggestions for designing the course and presenting the material. Each chapter is supported by answers to end-of-chapter questions and problems, and suggestions concerning the discussion topics and cases.

PowerPoint Presentations. A set of PowerPoint slides, created by the authors, accompanies each chapter that features bulleted items that provide a lecture outline, plus key figures and tables from the text, and detailed teaching notes on each slide.

Classroom Exercises. Choose from over 30 detailed classroom exercises that engage and challenge students. For example, if you are teaching systems development, start the class with the "Skyscraper Activity" where the students build a prototype that takes them through each phase of the systems development life cycle. All classroom exercises can be found in the IM.

Business Driven Teaching Notes. The Business Driven Teaching Notes is a comprehensive Excel spreadsheet containing over 150 additional classroom activities, discussion questions, and video clips. You can also turn any of the classroom activities into additional assignments and use the discussion questions for your online courses. You can use the business driven teaching notes to customize your lectures. Each topic in the text is represented by a tab in the workbook. Simply choose the activities you wish to use, reorder based on your lecture, and hide any you do not want. Then you can easily print your detailed lecture notes straight from the worksheet.

Image Library. Text figures and tables, as permission allows, are provided in a format by which they can be imported into PowerPoint for class lectures.

Project Files. The authors have provided files for all projects that need further support, such as data files.

Captivate Files. A complete set of narrated solution files for all Excel, Access, and web development projects provide narrated step-by-step detail for each project. These are a great aid to help instructors quickly understand questions and can be posted for students to review, saving instructor time with case reviews.

Cohesion Case. The Broadway Cafe is a running case instructors can use to reinforce core material such as customer relationship management, supply chain management, business intelligence, and decision making. The case has 15 sections that challenge students to develop and expand their grandfather's coffee shop. Students receive hands-on experience in business and learn technology's true value of enabling business. Please note that the Cohesion Case is not a McGraw-Hill product but a Baltzan and Phillips direct product. The case can be found at www.cohesioncase.com.

Media Content

MP3 Content. Harness the power of one of the most popular technology tools students use today—the MP3 player. Our innovative approach allows students to download audio and video presentations right into their MP3 players and take learning materials with them wherever they go. MP3 content icons are placed throughout the text highlighting when we recommend watching the content. The content is also available in Shockwave files so you can watch it on a computer if you choose not to use an MP3 player. This text offers more than 40 MP3 downloads with MP3 IMs to help the instructors turn the MP3s into classroom discussions and exercises.

Video Content. Twenty videos accompany this text and cover topics from entrepreneurship to disaster recovery. Video content icons are placed throughout the text highlighting where we recommend watching the videos. Video IMs are also available so you can turn the videos into engaging classroom activities.

Use our EZ Test Online to help your students prepare to succeed with Apple iPod® iQuiz. Using our EZ Test Online you can make test and quiz content available for a student's Apple iPod®. Students must purchase the iQuiz game application from Apple for 99¢ in order to use the iQuiz content. It works on fifth generation iPods and better. Instructors only need EZ Test Online to produce iQuiz-ready content. Instructors take their existing tests and quizzes and export them to a file that can then be made available to the student to take as a self-quiz on their iPods.

Apply Your Knowledge

Business Driven Information Systems contains 35 projects that focus on student application of core concepts and tools. All productivity tool projects come with Captivate solution file that walks students step by step through the solution, which saves instructors valuable time. These projects can be found on the OLC at www.mhhe.com/baltzan.

Project Number	Project Name	Project Type	Plug-In	Focus Area	Project Level	Skill Set
1	Financial Destiny	Excel	T2	Personal Budget	Introductory	Formulas
2	Cash Flow	Excel	T2	Cash Flow	Introductory	Formulas
3	Technology Budget	Excel	T1, T2	Hardware and Software	Introductory	Formulas
4	Tracking Donations	Excel	T2	Employee Relationships	Introductory	Formulas
5	Convert Currency	Excel	T2	Global Commerce	Introductory	Formulas
6	Cost Comparison	Excel	T2	Total Cost of Ownership	Introductory	Formulas
7	Time Management	Excel or Project	T12	Project Management	Introductory	Gantt Charts
8	Maximize Profit	Excel	T2, T4	Strategic Analysis	Intermediate	Formulas or Solver
9	Security Analysis	Excel	T3	Filtering Data	Intermediate	Conditional Formatting, Autofilter, Subtotal
10	Gathering Data	Excel	T3	Data Analysis	Intermediate	Conditional Formatting, PivotTable
11	Scanner System	Excel	T2	Strategic Analysis	Intermediate	Formulas
12	Competitive Pricing	Excel	T2	Profit Maximization	Intermediate	Formulas
13	Adequate Acquisitions	Excel	T2	Break-Even Analysis	Intermediate	Formulas
14	Customer Relations	Excel	T3	CRM	Intermediate	PivotTable
15	Shipping Costs	Excel	T4	SCM	Advanced	Solver
16	Formatting Grades	Excel	T3	Data Analysis	Advanced	If, LookUp
17	Moving Dilemma	Excel	T2, T3	SCM	Advanced	Absolute versus Relative Values
18	Operational Efficiencies	Excel	T3	SCM	Advanced	PivotTable

(*Continued*)

Project Number	Project Name	Project Type	Plug-In	Focus Area	Project Level	Skill Set
19	Too much Information	Excel	T3	CRM	Advanced	PivotTable
20	Turnover Rates	Excel	T3	Data Mining	Advanced	PivotTable
21	Vital Information	Excel	T3	Data Mining	Advanced	PivotTable
22	Breaking Even	Excel	T4	Business Analysis	Advanced	Goal Seek
23	Profit Scenario	Excel	T4	Sales Analysis	Advanced	Scenario Manager
24	Electronic Résumés	HTML	T9, T10, T11	Electronic Personal Marketing	Introductory	Structural Tags
25	Gathering Feedback	Dreamweaver	T9, T10, T11	Data Collection	Intermediate	Organization of Information
26	Daily Invoice	Access	T5, T6, T7, T8	Business Analysis	Introductory	Entities, Relationships, and Databases
27	Billing Data	Access	T5, T6, T7, T8	Business Intelligence	Introductory	Entities, Relationships, and Databases
28	Inventory Data	Access	T5, T6, T7, T8	SCM	Intermediate	Entities, Relationships, and Databases
29	Call Center	Access	T5, T6, T7, T8	CRM	Intermediate	Entities, Relationships, and Databases
30	Sales Pipeline	Access	T5, T6, T7, T8	Business Intelligence	Advanced	Entities, Relationships, and Databases
31	Second Life—Virtual Networking	N/A	N/A	Collaboration	Introductory	The Digital Economy
32	Creating a Podcast	N/A	N/A	Collaboration	Introductory	The Digital Economy
33	Google Earth—Geographic Information	N/A	N/A	Geographic Web	Intermediate	The Digital Economy
34	Photo Story 3—Show-n-Tell	N/A	N/A	Electronic Personal Marketing	Intermediate	The Digital Workforce
35	Sticky Wiki	N/A	N/A	Collaboration	Intermediate	The Digital Workforce

Empowered Instruction

Classroom Performance System
Engage students and assess real-time lecture retention with this simple yet powerful wireless application.You can even deliver tests that instantly grade themselves.

MIS Case Videos
Choose from our library of original video cases to illustrate important concepts or generate class discussion.

PowerPoint Presentations
Robust, detailed, and designed to keep students engaged. Detailed teaching notes are also included on every slide.

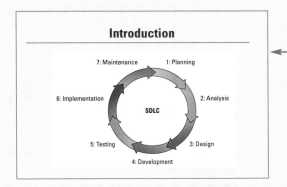

Introduction

7: Maintenance 1: Planning

6: Implementation 2: Analysis

SDLC

5: Testing 3: Design

4: Development

Introduction

Business value

Reporting
Customer identification

Analyzing
Customer segmentation

Predicting
Customer prediction

Time

OFFSHORE OUTSOURCING

Key
Leaders
Up-and-Comers
Rookies

■ Walk the students through the systems development life cycle:
  ■ *Planning phase*—involves establishing a high-level plan of the intended project and determining project goals
  ■ *Analysis phase*—involves analyzing end-user business requirements and refining project goals into defined functions and operations of the intended system
  ■ *Design phase*—involves describing the desired features and operations of the system including screen layouts, business rules, process diagrams, pseudo code, and other documentation
  ■ *Development phase*—involves taking all of the detailed design documents from the design phase and transforming them into the actual system
  ■ *Testing phase*—involves bringing all the project pieces together into a special testing environment to test for errors, bugs, and interoperability, in order to verify that the system meets all the business requirements defined in the analysis phase
  ■ *Implementation phase*—involves placing the system into production so users can begin to perform actual business operations with the system
  ■ *Maintenance phase*—involves performing changes, corrections, additions, and upgrades to ensure the system continues to meet the business goals

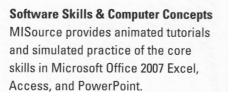

Software Skills & Computer Concepts
MISource provides animated tutorials and simulated practice of the core skills in Microsoft Office 2007 Excel, Access, and PowerPoint.

Spend less time reviewing software skills and computer literacy.

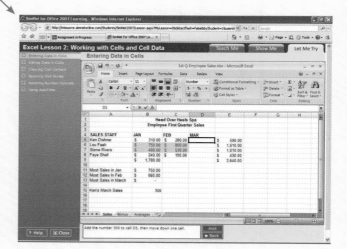

ACKNOWLEDGMENTS

Compiling the second edition of *Business Driven Information Systems* has been a tremendous undertaking and there are numerous people whom we want to heartily thank for their hard work, enthusiasm, and dedication.

This text draws from the efforts of a number of people at McGraw-Hill/Irwin. Paul Ducham, our Publisher, thank you for your insight, your intellect, and your continuous support and belief in our abilities—we simply could not have succeeded without you! Trina Hauger, our Development Editor, thank you for making all of those lists that keep us on track and focused. Mary Conzachi, our Lead Project Manager, thank you for making the difficult production process smooth and effortless.

In addition we would like to thank Brent Gordon (Editorial Director), Natalia Zook (Marketing Manager), Matt Diamond (Designer), Gregory Bates (Media Producer), Kerry Bowler (Media Project Manager), Gina Hangos (Production Supervisor), and Jeremy Cheshareck (Photo Coordinator), for your support and dedication to the success of this text.

Last, but certainly not least, we offer our sincerest gratitude and deepest appreciation to our valuable reviewers whose feedback was instrumental in successfully compiling this text.

Kamal Nayan Agarwal
Howard University

Marvin Albin
University of Southern Indiana

David Bahn
Metropolitan State University

Sunny Baker
California State University—
San Bernardino

Cynthia Barnes
Lamar University

Ozden Bayazit
Central Washington University

Jack Becker
University of North Texas

John Benamati
Miami University

Harry Benham
Montana State University

Henry Bojack
Farmingdale State University

Queen Booker
Minnesota State University—
Mankato

Ralph Caputo
Manhattan College

Judith Carlisle
Dowling College

John Carlson
Baylor University

Jerry Carvalho
Montana State University

Casey Cegielski
Auburn University

Jason Chen
Gonzaga University

Joselina Cheng
University of Central Oklahoma

Robert Chi
California State University—
Long Beach

Richard Christensen
Metropolitan State University

Ta-Tao Chuang
Gonzaga University

Tony Coulson
California State University—
San Bernardino

Steven Creason
Metropolitan State University

Peter DeVries
University of Houston—Downtown

David Dulany
Aurora University

Lauren Eder
Rider University

Roger Finnegan
Metropolitan State University

Frederic Fisher
Florida State University—
Tallahassee

Linda Fried
University of Colorado—Denver

James Frost
Idaho State University

John Gerdes
University of California—
Riverside

Rajni Goel
Howard University

Robert Gordon
Hofstra University

Lorraine Greenwald
SUNY—Farmingdale

John Gudenas
Aurora University

Roslin Hauck
Illinois State University

Rui Huang
State University of Binghamton

Bashorat Ibragimova
University of North Texas

Beata Jones
Texas Christian University

Donald Kalmey
Indiana University Southeast

Rex Karsten
University of Northern Iowa

Chung Kim
Southwest Missouri State

Virginia Kleist
West Virginia University

Mary Beth Klinger
University of Mary Washington

Chang Koh
University of North Texas

Al Lederer
University of Kentucky

Mark Lewis
Regis College

Stephen Loy
Eastern Kentucky University

Joan Lumpkin
Wright State University

Jane Mackay
Texas Christian University

Gary Margot
Ashland University

Don McCubbrey
University of Denver

Nina McGarry
George Washington University

Bernard Merkle
California Lutheran University

Phillip Musa
University of Alabama—
Birmingham

Bijayananda Naik
University of South Dakota

Fred Niederman
Saint Louis University

Michael Pangburn
University of Oregon

Barry Pasternack
California State University—
Fullerton

Alan Graham Peace
West Virginia University

Richard Peterson
Montclair State University

Floyd Ploeger
Texas State University—San Marcos

John Powell
University of South Dakota

Leonard Presby
William Patterson University

Mahesh Raisinghani
Texas Women's University

Frederick Rodammer
Michigan State University

I. Michael Romanov
Metropolitan State University

Kirsten Rosacker
University of South Dakota

Marcos Schniederjans
University of Nebraska—Lincoln

Sheryl Schoenacher
Farmingdale State College

Ken Sears
University of Texas—Arlington

Richard Segall
Arkansas State University

Shanti Shah
Metropolitan State University

Ganesan Shankaranarayanan
Boston University

Stephen Shao
Tennessee State University

K. David Smith
Cameron University

Ray Tsai
St. Cloud State University

Richard Turley
University of Northern Colorado

Robin Wakefield
Baylor University

Shimon Walner
Metropolitan State University

Bin Wang
University of Texas—Pan American

Karen Williams
University of Texas—San Antonio

James Yao
Montclair State University

Myung Yoon
Northeastern Illinois University

Randall Young
University of North Texas

Yue Zhang
California State University—
Northridge

Paige Baltzan

Paige Baltzan teaches in the Department of Information Technology and Electronic Commerce at the Daniels College of Business at the University of Denver. She holds a B.S.B.A specializing in Accounting/MIS from Bowling Green State University and an M.B.A. specializing in MIS from the University of Denver. Paige also teaches online at Strayer University. She is a coauthor of several books including *Business Driven Technology, Essentials of Business Driven Information Systems, I-Series,* and a contributor to *Management Information Systems for the Information Age.*

Before joining the Daniels College faculty in 1999, Paige spent several years working for a large telecommunications company and an international consulting firm where she participated in client engagements in the United States as well as South America and Europe. Paige lives in Lakewood, Colorado, with her husband, Tony, and daughters Hannah and Sophie.

Amy Phillips

Amy Phillips teaches in the Department of Information Technology and Electronic Commerce in the Daniels College of Business at the University of Denver. Amy's main teaching and research areas involve Internet and mobile technologies. With her MCT certification, Amy works with developing training material for Microsoft's Web Services platform, .NET. Amy has been teaching for 25 years and has coauthored several textbooks, including *Business Driven Technology, Management Information Systems for the Information Age 6e, Internet Explorer 6.0, and PowerPoint 2003.*

Business Driven Information Systems

MOST ORGANIZATIONS TODAY rely heavily on the use of information technologies to run various aspects of their businesses. Whether it is to order and ship goods, interact with customers, or conduct other business functions, information technology is often the underlying infrastructure used to perform such activities. Information technology enables companies to perform a variety of tasks both efficiently and effectively. Moreover, information technology allows an organization to remain competitive in today's fast-paced world. This is especially true when one considers the burgeoning popularity of conducting business over the Internet.

Organizations that fail to take advantage of information technology run the risk of falling behind others that adopt information technology solutions. Organizations must adapt to technological advances and innovations to keep pace with today's rapidly changing environment. Their competitors certainly will!

Though technology can be an exciting phenomenon on its own, as a business student you should understand that successful organizations do not utilize technology simply for the sake of technology itself. There must be a solid business reason for implementing technology. Using a technological solution just because it is available is not a good business strategy.

The purpose of Module One is to raise awareness of the vast opportunities that occur when you understand the tight correlation between business and technology. Business strategies and processes should always drive your technology choices. Although sometimes awareness of an emerging technology can lead to new strategic directions, the role of information technology, for the most part, is to support business strategies and process. Understanding business strategies and determining technology support structures is an important discussion and is covered thoroughly throughout this module.

MODULE ONE:
Business Driven
Information Systems

MODULE TWO:
Essentials of Information
Systems

MODULE THREE:
Enterprise Information
Systems

MODULE FOUR:
Developing Information
Systems

Module 1: BUSINESS DRIVEN INFORMATION SYSTEMS

CHAPTER 1: Information Systems in Business

CHAPTER 2: Strategic Decision Making

CHAPTER 3: Ebusiness

1 CHAPTER

Information Systems in Business

What's in IT for me?

This chapter sets the stage for the textbook. It starts from ground zero by providing a clear description of what information technology is and how it fits into business strategies and organizational activities. It then provides an overview of how organizations operate in competitive environments and must continually define and redefine their business strategies to create competitive advantages. Doing so allows organizations to survive and thrive. Importantly, information technology is shown as a key enabler to help organizations operate successfully in such competitive environments.

You, as a business student, must understand the tight correlation between business and technology. You must first understand information technology's role in daily business activities, and then understand information technology's role in supporting and implementing enterprisewide initiatives and global business strategies. After reading this chapter, you should have acquired a solid understanding of business driven information systems, technology fundamentals, and business strategy.

Apple—Merging Technology, Business, and Entertainment

Apple Computer Inc., back from near oblivion, is setting the pace in the digital world with innovation and creativity that has been missing from the company for the past 20 years. The introduction of the iPod, a brilliant merger of technology, business, and entertainment, catapulted Apple back into the mainstream.

Capitalizing on New Trends

In 2000, Steve Jobs was fixated on developing video editing software for the Macintosh. But then he realized millions of people were using computers and CD burners to make audio CDs and to download digital songs called MP3s from illegal online services like Napster. Jobs was worried that he was looking in the wrong direction and had missed the MP3 bandwagon.

Jobs moved fast. He began by purchasing SoundStep from Jeff Robbin, a 28-year-old software engineer and former Apple employee. SoundStep was developing software that simplified the importing and compression of MP3 songs. Robbin and a couple of other programmers began writing code from scratch and developed the first version of iTunes for the Mac in less than four months. This powerful and ingenious database could quickly sort tens of thousands of songs in a multitude of ways and find particular tracks in nanoseconds.

Jobs next challenged the team to make iTunes portable. He envisioned a Walkman-like player that could hold thousands of songs and be taken anywhere. The idea was to modify iTunes and build a tiny new system for what was basically a miniature computer, along with a user interface that could sort and navigate music files with the same sophistication as iTunes on the Mac. The iPod was born nine months later.

Jobs noticed that one last key element was missing, an online store for buying downloadable songs. Such a store would need an ebusiness infrastructure that could automatically deliver songs and track billing and payments for conceivably millions of purchases. In the spring of 2003, 18 months after the launch of the iPod, Apple's iTunes Music Store opened for business. The company's goal was to sell 1 million songs in the first six months. It hit this goal in six days.

Capitalizing on the iPod

With millions of iPods in the hands of consumers, other companies are noticing the trend and finding ways to capitalize on the product. John Lin created a prototype of a remote control for the iPod. Lin took his prototype to *Macworld* where he found success. A few months later, Lin's company had Apple's blessing and a commitment for shelf space in its retail stores. "This is how Apple supports the iPod economy," Lin said.

In the iPod-dominated market, hundreds of companies have been inspired to develop more than 500 accessories—everything from rechargers for the car to $1,500 Fendi bags. Eric Tong, vice president at Belkin, a cable and peripheral manufacturer, believes that 75 percent of all iPod owners purchase at least one accessory—meaning that 30 million accessories have been sold. With most of the products priced between $10 and $200, that puts the iPod economy well over $300 million and perhaps as high as $6 billion. Popular iPod accessories include:

- Altec Lansing Technologies—iPod speakers and recharger dock ($150).
- Belkin—TuneCast mobile FM transmitter ($40).
- Etymotic Research—high-end earphones ($150).
- Griffin Technology—iTrip FM transmitter ($35).
- Kate Spade—Geneva faux-croc mini iPod holder ($55).
- Apple—socks set in six colors, green, purple, blue, orange, pink, and gray ($29).
- Apple—digital camera connector ($29).

Capitalizing on the Future

The latest iPod packs music, audiobooks, podcasts, photos, video, contacts, calendars, games, clocks, and locks in a design up to 45 percent slimmer than the original iPod. It also boasts stamina (up to 20 hours of battery life), generous capacity (30GB or 60GB of storage), a great personality (intuitive, customizable menus), and a touch of genius (the Apple Click Wheel). The latest features include:

- **Videos**—Choose from over 2,000 music videos at the iTunes Music Store or purchase ad-free episodes of a favorite ABC or Disney television show and watch them on the go.
- **Podcasts**—The iTunes Podcast Directory features thousands of free podcasts, or radio-style shows, including favorites from such big names as ABC News, Adam Curry, ESPN, KCRW, and WGBH.
- **Audiobooks**—The digital shelves of the iTunes Music Store are stocked with more than 11,000 audiobooks, including such exclusives as the entire Harry Potter series.
- **Photos**—With storage for up to 25,000 photos, iPod users can view photo slide shows—complete with music—on an iPod or on a TV via the optional video cable.

Capitalizing on the iPhone

The Apple iPhone is a revolutionary new mobile phone that allows customers to make a call by simply touching a name or number in an address book, a favorites list, or a call log. It also automatically syncs all contacts from a PC, Mac, or Internet services, and it allows customers to select voice-mail messages in any order—just like email.

Customers can easily construct a favorites list for frequently made calls and can quickly merge calls to create conference calls.

The iPhone's most impressive feature is a rich email client. With its advanced Safari browser, one of the most advanced web browsers to be offered on a portable device, iPhone lets customers see web pages the way they were designed to be seen, then easily zoom in by simply tapping on the multi-touch display with a finger. Safari also includes built-in Google and Yahoo! search capabilities. The iPhone can multitask, allowing customers to read a web page while downloading email in the background over wireless networks. Expect the iPhone accessory business to be as powerful and vast as the iPod accessory business. A few of the new iPhone accessories include:

- iPhone Bluetooth headset—$149.
- iPhone doc—$49.
- iPhone stereo headset—$29.
- Apple Doc Connector to USB—$29.

iPod's Impact on the Music Business

In the digital era, the unbundling of CDs through the purchase of individual tracks lets consumers pay far less to get a few of their favorite songs rather than buying an entire album. Many analysts predicted that the iPod's success coupled with the consumer's ability to choose individual song downloads would lead to increased revenues for music businesses. However, the industry is seeing individual downloads cannibalizing album profits and failing to attract new music sales. "I've still never bought a download," said Eneka Iriondo-Coysh, a 21-year-old graphic-design student in London who has owned a 10,000 song-capacity iPod for more than two years. "I do it all from my CDs," mostly hip-hop and soul.

The global music industry has been under siege for years amid declining sales. Record companies suffer from piracy, including billions of dollars in lost revenue due to bootlegged CDs. At the same time, music faces new competition for consumer time and money from video games, DVDs, and mobile phones. At traditional record stores, DVDs and games are taking an increasing amount of shelf space, squeezing out CDs. The music download numbers suggest that the iPod's iconic success is not translating into new music sales the way the evolution from vinyl albums to cassettes and then CDs did. For many users, the portable devices are just another way of stocking and listening to music, not an incentive to buy new music.

iPod Security Leaks

Nike and Apple partnered to create a unique iPod accessory, the Nike iPod SportKit. The Kit consists of two components—a wireless *sensor* that fits into Nike + Air Zoom Moire sneakers and a small white *receiver* that plugs in to an iPod Nano—that communicate using wireless radio protocols. The University of Washington's Department of Science and Engineering recently discovered that customers who use the kit while exercising are subject to an invasion of privacy by becoming a surveillance target. Researchers revealed that security flaws in the new radio-frequency

ID-powered device make it easy for tech-savvy stalkers, thieves, and corporations to track every movement an unsuspecting SportKit customer makes. With a simple surveillance tool, a malicious individual could track SportKit owners while they are working out, as well as when they are casually walking around town, a parking lot, or a college campus. With just a few hundred dollars and a little know-how, someone could even plot a SportKit customer's running routes on a Google map without the runner's knowledge. The tracked individuals do not even need to have their iPods with them, just the RFID device.[1]

INTRODUCTION

nformation is everywhere. Most organizations value information as a strategic asset. Consider Apple and its iPod, iPod accessories, and iTunes Music Store. Apple's success depends heavily on information about its customers, suppliers, markets, and operations for each of these product lines. For example, Apple must be able to predict the number of people who will purchase an iPod to help estimate iPod accessory and iTunes sales within the next year. Estimating too many buyers will lead Apple to produce an excess of inventory; estimating too few buyers will potentially mean lost sales due to lack of product (resulting in even more lost revenues from iTunes downloads).

Understanding the direct impact information has on an organization's bottom line is crucial to running a successful business. This text focuses on information, business, technology, and the integrated set of activities used to run most organizations. Many of these activities are the hallmarks of business today—supply chain management, customer relationship management, enterprise resource planning, outsourcing, integration, ebusiness, and others.

section 1.1 INFORMATION SYSTEMS IN BUSINESS

LEARNING OUTCOMES

1.1. Describe the functional areas of a business and why they must work together for the business to be successful.

1.2. Explain information technology's role in business and how you measure success.

1.3. Compare management information systems (MIS) and information technology (IT), and define the relationships among people, information technology, and information.

1.4. Compare the responsibilities of a chief information officer (CIO), chief technology officer (CTO), chief security officer (CSO), chief privacy officer (CPO), and chief knowledge officer (CKO).

1.5. Explain the gap between IT and the business, along with the primary reason this gap exists.

Opportunities
for Knowledge
Workers

INFORMATION TECHNOLOGY'S ROLE IN BUSINESS

Students frequently ask, "Why do we need to study information technology?" The answer is simple: Information technology is everywhere in business. Understanding information technology provides great insight to anyone learning about business.

It is easy to demonstrate information technology's role in business by reviewing a copy of popular business magazines such as *BusinessWeek*, *Fortune*, or *Fast Company*. Placing a marker (such as a Post-it Note) on each page that contains a technology-related article or advertisement indicates that information technology is everywhere in business (see Figure 1.1). These are *business* magazines, not *technology* magazines, yet they are filled with technology. Students who understand technology have an advantage in business.

These magazine articles typically discuss such topics as databases, customer relationship management, web services, supply chain management, security, ethics, business intelligence, and so on. They also focus on companies such as Siebel, Oracle, Microsoft, and IBM. This text explores these topics in detail, along with reviewing the associated business opportunities and challenges.

Information Technology's Impact on Business Operations

Figure 1.2 highlights the business functions receiving the greatest benefit from information technology, along with the common business goals associated with information technology projects, according to *CIO* magazine.[2]

FIGURE 1.1

Technology in *BusinessWeek*
and Fortune

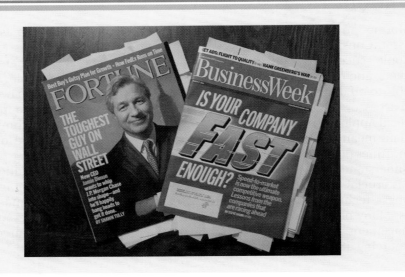

FIGURE 1.2

Business Benefits and Information Technology Project
Goals

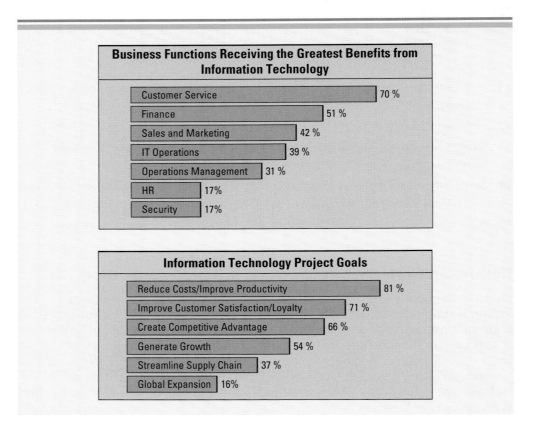

Achieving the results outlined in Figure 1.2, such as reducing costs, improving productivity, and generating growth, is not easy. Implementing a new accounting system or marketing plan is not likely to generate long-term growth or reduce costs across an entire organization. Businesses must undertake enterprisewide initiatives to achieve broad general business goals such as reducing costs. Information technology plays a critical role in deploying such initiatives by facilitating communication and increasing business intelligence. For example, instant messaging and WiMax allow people across an organization to communicate in new and innovative ways.[3]

Understanding information technology begins with gaining an understanding of how businesses function and IT's role in creating efficiencies and effectiveness across the organization. Typical businesses operate by functional areas (often called functional silos). Each area undertakes a specific core business function (see Figure 1.3).[4]

FIGURE 1.3

Departmental Structure of a
Typical Organization

COMMON DEPARTMENTS IN AN ORGANIZATION

ACCOUNTING		MARKETING	OPERATIONS MANAGEMENT
	HUMAN RESOURCES	PRODUCTION MANAGEMENT	
FINANCE		SALES	MANAGEMENT INFORMATION SYSTEMS

Information
Technology

- **Accounting** provides quantitative information about the finances of the business including recording, measuring, and describing financial information.

- **Finance** deals with the strategic financial issues associated with increasing the value of the business, while observing applicable laws and social responsibilities.

- **Human resources (HR)** includes the policies, plans, and procedures for the effective management of employees (human resources).

- **Sales** is the function of selling a good or service and focuses on increasing customer sales, which increases company revenues.

- **Marketing** is the process associated with promoting the sale of goods or services. The marketing department supports the sales department by creating promotions that help sell the company's products.

- **Operations management (OM)** The management of systems or processes that convert or transform resources (including human resources) into goods and services.

- **Management information systems (MIS)** is a general name for the business function and academic discipline covering the application of people, technologies, and procedures— collectively called information systems—to solve business problems.

Functional areas are anything but independent in a business. In fact, functional areas are *interdependent* (see Figure 1.4). Sales must rely on information from operations to understand inventory, place orders, calculate transportation costs, and gain insight into product availability based on production schedules. For an organization to succeed, every department or functional area must work together sharing common information and not be a "silo." Information technology can enable departments to more efficiently and effectively perform their business operations.

Individuals anticipating a successful career in business, whether it is in accounting, finance, human resources, or operation management, must understand information technology including:

- Information technology basics.
- Roles and responsibilities in information technology.
- Measuring information technology's success.

FIGURE 1.4

Marketing Working with
Other Organizational
Departments

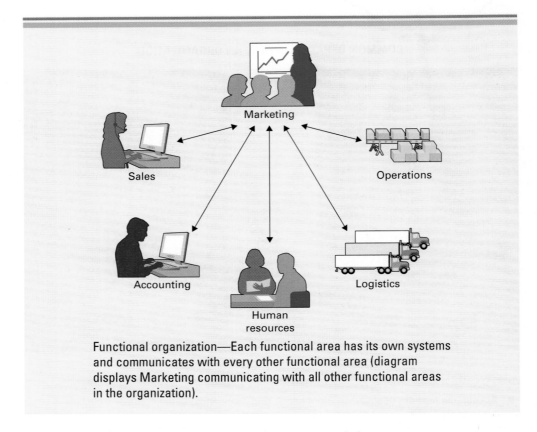

Functional organization—Each functional area has its own systems
and communicates with every other functional area (diagram
displays Marketing communicating with all other functional areas
in the organization).

INFORMATION TECHNOLOGY BASICS

Information technology (IT) is a field concerned with the use of technology in managing and processing information. Information technology can be an important enabler of business success and innovation. This is not to say that IT *equals* business success and innovation or that IT *represents* business success and innovation. Information technology is most useful when it leverages the talents of people. Information technology in and of itself is not useful unless the right people know how to use and manage it effectively.

Management information systems is a business function just as marketing, finance, operations, and human resources management are business functions. Formally defined, *management information systems (MIS)* is a general name for the business function and academic discipline covering the application of people, technologies, and procedures—collectively called information systems—to solve business problems. To perform the MIS function effectively, almost all organizations today, particularly large and medium-sized ones, have an internal IT department, often called Information Technology (IT), Information Systems (IS), or Management Information Systems (MIS). When beginning to learn about information technology it is important to understand[5]

- Data, information, and business intelligence
- IT resources
- IT cultures

Data, Information, and Business Intelligence

It is important to distinguish between data and information. *Data* are raw facts that describe the characteristics of an event. Characteristics for a sales event could include the date, item number, item description, quantity ordered, customer name, and shipping details. *Information* is data converted into a meaningful and useful context. Information from sales events could include best-selling item, worst-selling

FIGURE 1.5

Data in an Excel Spreadsheet

Rows of data in an Excel spreadsheet.

FIGURE 1.6

Data Turned into Information

Data features, such as Autofilter, turn data into information.
This view shows all of Roberta Cross's chicken sales.

item, best customer, and worst customer. ***Business intelligence*** refers to applications and technologies that are used to gather, provide access to, and analyze data and information to support decision-making efforts. Business intelligence helps companies gain a more comprehensive knowledge of the factors affecting their business, such as metrics on sales, production, and internal operations that help companies make better business decisions (see Figures 1.5, 1.6, 1.7).

IT Resources

The plans and goals of the IT department must align with the plans and goals of the organization. Information technology can enable an organization to increase efficiency in manufacturing, retain key customers, seek out new sources of supply, and introduce effective financial management.

It is not always easy for managers to make the right choices when using IT to support (and often drive) business initiatives. Most managers understand their business initiatives well, but are often at a loss when it comes to knowing how to use

FIGURE 1.7

Information Turned into
Business Intelligence

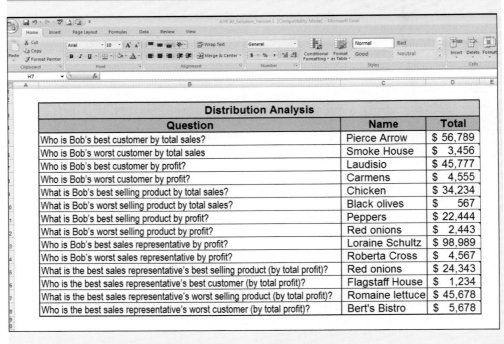

Distribution Analysis		
Question	**Name**	**Total**
Who is Bob's best customer by total sales?	Pierce Arrow	$ 56,789
Who is Bob's worst customer by total sales	Smoke House	$ 3,456
Who is Bob's best customer by profit?	Laudisio	$ 45,777
Who is Bob's worst customer by profit?	Carmens	$ 4,555
What is Bob's best selling product by total sales?	Chicken	$ 34,234
What is Bob's worst selling product by total sales?	Black olives	$ 567
What is Bob's best selling product by profit?	Peppers	$ 22,444
What is Bob's worst selling product by profit?	Red onions	$ 2,443
Who is Bob's best sales representative by profit?	Loraine Schultz	$ 98,989
Who is Bob's worst sales representative by profit?	Roberta Cross	$ 4,567
What is the best sales representative's best selling product (by total profit)?	Red onions	$ 24,343
Who is the best sales representative's best customer (by total profit)?	Flagstaff House	$ 1,234
What is the best sales representative's worst selling product (by total profit)?	Romaine lettuce	$ 45,678
Who is the best sales representative's worst customer (by total profit)?	Bert's Bistro	$ 5,678

*Advanced analytical tools, such as Pivot Tables, uncover business
intelligence in the data. For example, best customer, worst
customer, and best sales representative's best-selling product.*

and manage IT effectively in support of those initiatives. Managers who understand what IT is, and what IT can and cannot do, are in the best position for success. In essence,

- *People* use
- *information technology* to work with
- *information* (see Figure 1.8).

Those three key resources—people, information, and information technology (in that order of priority)—are inextricably linked. If one fails, they all fail. Most important, if one fails, then chances are the business will fail.

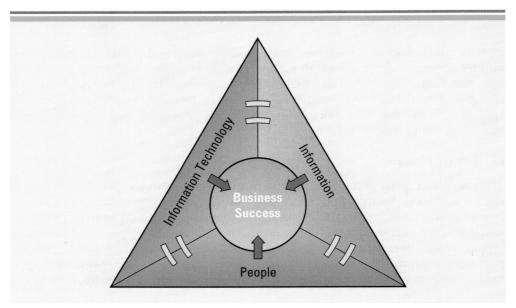

FIGURE 1.9

Different Information Cultures
Found in Organizations

Organizational Information Cultures	
Information-Functional Culture	Employees use information as a means of exercising influence or power over others. For example, a manager in sales refuses to share information with marketing. This causes marketing to need the sales manager's input each time a new sales strategy is developed.
Information-Sharing Culture	Employees across departments trust each other to use information (especially about problems and failures) to improve performance.
Information-Inquiring Culture	Employees across departments search for information to better understand the future and align themselves with current trends and new directions.
Information-Discovery Culture	Employees across departments are open to new insights about crisis and radical changes and seek ways to create competitive advantages.

[handwritten margin notes: "mine", "lets work together", "lets see whats out there", "look what I found"]

IT Cultures

An organization's culture plays a large role in determining how successfully it will share information. Culture will influence the way people use information (their information behavior) and will reflect the importance that company leaders attribute to the use of information in achieving success or avoiding failure. Four common information-sharing cultures exist in organizations today: information-functional, information-sharing, information-inquiring, and information-discovery (see Figure 1.9).[6]

An organization's IT culture can directly affect its ability to compete in the global market. If an organization operates with an information-functional culture, it will have a great degree of difficulty operating. Getting products to market quickly and creating a view of its end-to-end (or entire) business from sales to billing will be a challenge. If an organization operates with an information-discovery culture it will be able to get products to market quickly and easily see a 360-degree view of its entire organization. Employees will be able to use this view to better understand the market and create new products that offer a competitive advantage.

ROLES AND RESPONSIBILITIES IN INFORMATION TECHNOLOGY

Employees across the organization must work closely together to develop strategic initiatives that create competitive advantages. Understanding the basic structure of a typical IT department including titles, roles, and responsibilities will help an organization build a cohesive enterprisewide team. Information technology is a relatively new functional area, having been around formally in most organizations only for about 40 years. Job titles, roles, and responsibilities often differ from organization to organization. Nonetheless, clear trends are developing toward elevating some IT positions within an organization to the strategic level.

Most organizations maintain positions such as chief executive officer (CEO), chief financial officer (CFO), and chief operations officer (COO) at the strategic level. Recently there are more IT-related strategic positions such as chief information officer (CIO), chief technology officer (CTO), chief security officer (CSO), chief privacy officer (CPO), and chief knowledge officer (CKO).

J. Greg Hanson is proud to be the first CIO of the U.S. Senate. Contrary to some perceptions, the technology found in the Senate is quite good, according to Hanson. Hanson's responsibilities include creating the Senate's technology vision, leading the IT department, and deploying the IT infrastructure. Hanson must work with everyone from the 137 network administrators to the senators themselves to ensure that everything is operating smoothly.[7]

FIGURE 1.10

Average CIO Compensation
by Industry

Industry	Average CIO Compensation
Wholesale/Retail/Distribution	$243,304
Finance	$210,547
Insurance	$197,697
Manufacturing	$190,250
Medical/Dental/Health Care	$171,032
Government	$118,359
Education	$93,750

FIGURE 1.11

What Concerns CIOs the
Most?

CIO's Concerns	Percentage
Enchancing customer satisfaction	94%
Security	92
Technology evaluation	89
Budgeting	87
Staffing	83
ROI analysis	66
Building new applications	64
Outsourcing hosting	45

The ***chief information officer (CIO)*** is responsible for (1) overseeing all uses of information technology and (2) ensuring the strategic alignment of IT with business goals and objectives. The CIO often reports directly to the CEO (see Figure 1.10 for average CIO compensation). CIOs must possess a solid understanding of every aspect of an organization coupled with tremendous insight into the capability of IT. Broad roles of a CIO include:

- *Manager*—ensure the delivery of all IT projects, on time and within budget.
- *Leader*—ensure the strategic vision of IT is in line with the strategic vision of the organization.
- *Communicator*—advocate and communicate the IT strategy by building and maintaining strong executive relationships.[8]

Although CIO is considered a position within IT, CIOs must be concerned with more than just IT. According to a recent survey (see Figure 1.11), most CIOs ranked "enhancing customer satisfaction" ahead of their concerns for any specific aspect of IT. We should applaud CIOs who possess the broad business view that customer satisfaction is more crucial and critical than specific aspects of IT.[9]

The ***chief technology officer (CTO)*** is responsible for ensuring the throughput, speed, accuracy, availability, and reliability of an organization's information technology. CTOs have direct responsibility for ensuring the efficiency of IT systems throughout the organization. Most CTOs possess well-rounded knowledge of all aspects of IT, including hardware, software, and telecommunications. CTOs typically report to the CIO. The role of CTO is similar to CIO, except that CIO must take on the additional responsibility of ensuring that IT aligns with the organization's strategic initiatives.

The **chief security officer (CSO)** is responsible for ensuring the security of IT systems and developing strategies and IT safeguards against attacks from hackers and viruses. The role of a CSO has been elevated in recent years because of the number of attacks from hackers and viruses. Most CSOs possess detailed knowledge of networks and telecommunications because hackers and viruses usually find their way into IT systems through networked computers.

The **chief privacy officer (CPO)** is responsible for ensuring the ethical and legal use of information within an organization. CPOs are the newest senior executive position in IT. Recently, 150 of the Fortune 500 companies added the CPO position to their list of senior executives. Many CPOs are lawyers by training, enabling them to understand the often complex legal issues surrounding the use of information.[10]

The **chief knowledge officer (CKO)** is responsible for collecting, maintaining, and distributing the organization's knowledge. The CKO designs programs and systems that make it easy for people to reuse knowledge. These systems create repositories of organizational documents, methodologies, tools, and practices, and they establish methods for filtering the information. The CKO must continuously encourage employee contributions to keep the systems up-to-date. The CKO can contribute directly to the organization's bottom line by reducing the learning curve for new employees or employees taking on new roles.

Danny Shaw was the first CKO at Children's Hospital in Boston. His initial task was to unite information from disparate systems to enable analysis of both the efficiency and effectiveness of the hospital's care. Shaw started by building a series of small, integrated information systems that quickly demonstrated value. He then gradually built on those successes, creating a knowledge-enabled organization one layer at a time. Shaw's information systems have enabled administrative and clinical operational analyses.[11]

All the above IT positions and responsibilities are critical to an organization's success. While many organizations may not have a different individual for each of these positions, they must have leaders taking responsibility for all these areas of concern. The individuals responsible for enterprisewide IT and IT-related issues must provide guidance and support to the organization's employees. Figure 1.12 displays the personal skills pivotal for success in an executive IT role.

The Gap Between Business Personnel and IT Personnel

One of the greatest challenges today is effective communication between business personnel and IT personnel. Figure 1.12 clearly demonstrates the importance of communication for IT executives. Business personnel possess expertise in functional areas such as marketing, accounting, sales, and so forth. IT personnel have the technological expertise. Unfortunately, a communications gap often exists

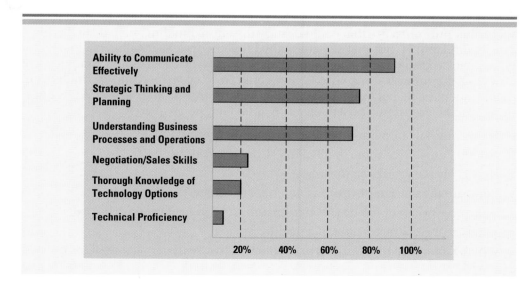

FIGURE 1.12

Skills Pivotal for Success in Executive IT Roles

between the two. Business personnel have their own vocabularies based on their experience and expertise. IT personnel have their own vocabularies consisting of acronyms and technical terms. Effective communication between business and IT personnel should be a two-way street with each side making the effort to understand each other (including written and oral communication).

Improving Communication Business personnel must seek to increase their understanding of IT. Although they do not need to know every technical detail, it is beneficial to understand what IT can and cannot accomplish. Business managers and leaders should read business-oriented IT magazines, such as *InformationWeek* and *CIO*, to increase their IT knowledge.

At the same time, an organization must develop strategies for integrating its IT personnel into the various business functions. Too often, IT personnel are left out of strategy meetings because of the belief they do not understand the business so they will not add any value. That is a dangerous position to take. IT personnel must understand the business if the organization is going to determine which technologies can benefit (or hurt) the business. With a little effort to communicate, IT personnel might provide information on the functionality available in an information system, which could add tremendous value to a meeting about how to improve customer service. Working together, business and IT personnel have the potential to create competitive advantages, reduce costs, and streamline business processes.

It is the CIO's responsibility to ensure effective communications between business and IT personnel. While the CIO assumes the responsibility on an enterprise-wide level, it is each employee's responsibility to communicate effectively on a personal level.

MEASURING INFORMATION TECHNOLOGY'S SUCCESS

IT has become an important part of organizations' strategy, competitive advantage, and profitability. There is management pressure to build systems faster, better, and at minimum cost. The return on investment that an organization can achieve from the money it spends on IT has come under increased scrutiny from senior business executives and directors. Consequently, IT now has to operate like other parts of the organization, being aware of its performance and its contribution to the organization's success and opportunities for improvement. So what is it that managers need to know about measuring the success of information technology?

The first thing managers need to understand about IT success is that it is incredibly difficult to measure. Determining the return on investment (ROI) of new computer equipment is difficult. For example, what is the ROI of a fire extinguisher? If the fire extinguisher is never used, the return on the investment is low. If the extinguisher puts out a fire that could destroy the entire building, then its ROI is high. This is similar to IT systems. If a company implements a $5,000 firewall to prevent virus attacks on the computer systems and it never stops a virus, the company lost $5,000. If the firewall stops viruses that could have cost the company millions of dollars, then the ROI of that firewall is significantly greater than $5,000. A few questions executives recently raised regarding their IT systems include:

- Is the internal IT operation performing satisfactorily?
- Should I outsource some or all of the IT operations?
- How is my outsourcer performing?
- What are the risk factors to consider in an IT project?
- What questions should be asked to ensure an IT project proposal is realistic?
- What are the characteristics of a healthy project?
- Which factors are most critical to monitor to ensure the project remains on track?[12]

To offer detailed information to all layers of management, General Electric Co. (GE) invested $1.5 billion in employee time, hardware, software, and other technologies to implement a real-time operations monitoring system. GE's executives use the new system to monitor sales, inventory, and savings across the company's 13 global business operations every 15 minutes. This allows GE to respond to changes, reduce cycle times, and improve risk management on an hourly basis instead of waiting for monthly or quarterly reports. GE estimates the $1.5 billion investment will provide a 33 percent return over five years.[14]

IT professionals know how to install and maintain information systems. Business professionals know how to run a successful business. But how does a company decide if an information system helps make a business successful? Peter Drucker, a famous management guru, once stated that if you cannot measure it, you cannot manage it. Managers need to ask themselves how they are going to manage IT projects when it is so incredibly difficult to measure IT projects.[13]

The answer lies in the metrics. Designing metrics requires an expertise that neither IT nor business professionals usually possess. Metrics are about neither technology nor business strategy. The questions that arise in metrics design are almost philosophical: How do you define success? How do you apply quantifiable measures to business processes, especially qualitative ones such as customer service? What kind of information best reflects progress, or the lack of it?

Key performance indicators (KPIs) are the measures that are tied to business drivers. Metrics are the detailed measures that feed those KPIs. Performance metrics fall into a nebulous area of business intelligence that is neither technology- nor business-centered, but this area requires input from both IT and business professionals to find success. Cisco Systems implemented a cross-departmental council to create metrics for improving business process operations. The council developed metrics to evaluate the efficiency of Cisco's online order processing and discovered that due to errors, more than 70 percent of online orders required manual input and were unable to be automatically routed to manufacturing. By changing the process and adding new information systems, within six months the company doubled the percentage of orders that went directly to manufacturing.[15]

Effective Business

Efficiency and Effectiveness Metrics

Organizations spend enormous sums of money on IT to compete in today's fast-paced business environment. Some organizations spend up to 50 percent of their total capital expenditures on IT. To justify these expenditures, an organization must measure the payoff of these investments, their impact on business performance, and the overall business value gained.

Efficiency and effectiveness metrics are two primary types of IT metrics. *Efficiency IT metrics* measure the performance of the IT system itself such as throughput, speed, and availability. *Effectiveness IT metrics* measure the impact IT has on business processes and activities including customer satisfaction, conversion rates, and sell-through increases. Peter Drucker offers a helpful distinction between efficiency and effectiveness. Drucker states that managers "Do things right" and/or "Do the right things." Doing things right addresses efficiency—getting the most from each resource. Doing the right things addresses effectiveness—setting the right goals and objectives and ensuring they are accomplished.[16]

Efficiency focuses on the extent to which an organization is using its resources in an optimal way, while effectiveness focuses on how well an organization is achieving its goals and objectives. The two—efficiency and effectiveness—are definitely interrelated. However, success in one area does not necessarily imply success in the other.

Benchmarking—Baseline Metrics

Regardless of what is measured, how it is measured, and whether it is for the sake of efficiency or effectiveness, there must be *benchmarks,* or baseline values the system seeks to attain. *Benchmarking* is a process of continuously measuring system

FIGURE 1.13

Egovernment Ranking for
Efficiency and Effectiveness

Efficiency	Effectiveness
1. United States (3.11)	1. Canada
2. Australia (2.60)	2. Singapore
3. New Zealand (2.59)	3. United States
4. Singapore (2.58)	4. Denmark
5. Norway (2.55)	5. Australia
6. Canada (2.52)	6. Finland
7. United Kingdom (2.52)	7. Hong Kong
8. Netherlands (2.51)	8. United Kingdom
9. Denmark (2.47)	9. Germany
10. Germany (2.46)	10. Ireland

results, comparing those results to optimal system performance (benchmark values), and identifying steps and procedures to improve system performance.

Consider online government services (egovernment) as an illustration of benchmarking efficiency IT metrics and effectiveness IT metrics (see survey results in Figure 1.13). From an effectiveness point of view, Canada ranks number one in terms of egovernment satisfaction of its citizens. (The United States ranks third.) The survey, sponsored by Accenture, also included such attributes as customer-service vision, initiatives for identifying services for individual citizen segments, and approaches to offering egovernment services through multiple-service delivery channels. These are all benchmarks at which Canada's government excels.[17]

In contrast, the *United Nations Division for Public Economics and Public Administration* ranks Canada sixth in terms of efficiency IT metrics. (The United States ranked first.) This particular ranking, based purely on efficiency IT metrics, includes benchmarks such as the number of computers per 100 citizens, the number of Internet hosts per 10,000 citizens, and the percentage of the citizen online population. Therefore, while Canada lags in IT efficiency, it is the premier egovernment provider in terms of effectiveness.[18]

Governments hoping to increase their egovernment presence would benchmark themselves against these sorts of efficiency and effectiveness metrics. There is a high degree of correlation between egovernment efficiency and effectiveness, although it is not absolute.

The Interrelationship Between Efficiency and Effectiveness IT Metrics

Efficiency IT metrics focus on the technology itself. Figure 1.14 highlights the most common types of efficiency IT metrics.

While these efficiency metrics are important to monitor, they do not always guarantee effectiveness. Effectiveness IT metrics are determined according to an organization's goals, strategies, and objectives. Here, it becomes important to consider the strategy an organization is using, such as a broad cost leadership strategy (Wal-Mart, for example), as well as specific goals and objectives such as increasing new customers by 10 percent or reducing new-product development cycle times to six months. Figure 1.15 displays the broad, general effectiveness IT metrics.

In the private sector, eBay constantly benchmarks its information technology efficiency and effectiveness. Maintaining constant website availability and optimal throughput performance is critical to eBay's success.[19]

FIGURE 1.14

Common Types of Efficiency
IT Metrics

Efficiency IT Metrics	
Throughput	The amount of information that can travel through a system at any point in time.
Transaction speed	The amount of time a system takes to perform a transaction.
System availability	The number of hours a system is available for users.
Information accuracy	The extent to which a system generates the correct results when executing the same transaction numerous times.
Web traffic	Includes a host of benchmarks such as the number of page views, the number of unique visitors, and the average time spent viewing a web page.
Response time	The time it takes to respond to user interactions such as a mouse click.

Jupiter Media Metrix ranked eBay as the website with the highest visitor volume (efficiency) for the fourth year in a row, with an 80 percent growth from the previous year. The auction website averaged 8 million unique visitors during each week of the holiday season with daily peaks exceeding 12 million visitors. To ensure constant availability and reliability of its systems, eBay implemented ProactiveNet, a performance measurement and management-tracking tool. The tool allows eBay to monitor its environment against baseline benchmarks, which helps the eBay team keep tight control of its systems. The new system has resulted in improved system availability with a 150 percent increase in productivity as measured by system uptime.[20]

Be sure to consider the issue of security while determining efficiency and effectiveness IT metrics. When an organization offers its customers the ability to purchase products over the Internet, it must implement the appropriate security. It is actually inefficient for an organization to implement security measures for Internet-based transactions as compared to processing nonsecure transactions. However, an organization will probably have a difficult time attracting new customers and increasing web-based revenue if it does not implement the necessary security measures. Purely from an efficiency IT metric point of view, security generates

FIGURE 1.15

Common Types of
Effectiveness IT Metrics

Effectiveness IT Metrics	
Usability	The ease with which people perform transactions and/or find information. A popular usability metric on the Internet is degrees of freedom, which measures the number of clicks required to find desired information.
Customer satisfaction	Measured by such benchmarks as satisfaction surveys, percentage of existing customers retained, and increases in revenue dollars per customer.
Conversion rates	The number of customers an organization "touches" for the first time and persuades to purchase its products or services. This is a popular metric for evaluating the effectiveness of banner, pop-up, and pop-under ads on the Internet.
Financial	Such as return on investment (the earning power of an organization's assets), cost-benefit analysis (the comparison of projected revenues and costs including development, maintenance, fixed, and variable), and break-even analysis (the point at which constant revenues equal ongoing costs).

FIGURE 1.16

The Interrelationships
Between Efficiency and
Effectiveness

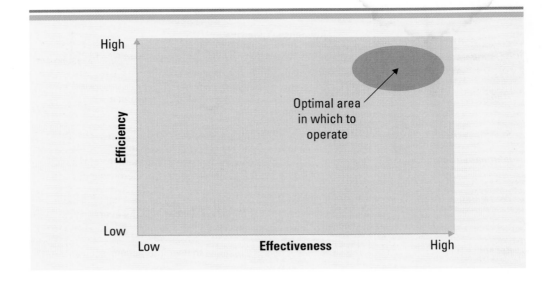

some inefficiency. From an organization's business strategy point of view, however, security should lead to increases in effectiveness metrics.

Figure 1.16 depicts the interrelationships between efficiency and effectiveness. Ideally, an organization should operate in the upper right-hand corner of the graph, realizing both significant increases in efficiency and effectiveness. However, operating in the upper left-hand corner (minimal effectiveness with increased efficiency) or the lower right-hand corner (significant effectiveness with minimal efficiency) may be in line with an organization's particular strategies. In general, operating in the lower left-hand corner (minimal efficiency and minimal effectiveness) is not ideal for the operation of any organization.

OPENING CASE QUESTIONS

Apple—Merging Technology, Business, and Entertainment

1. What might have happened to Apple if its top executives had not supported investment in iPods?

2. Formulate a strategy for how Apple can use efficiency IT metrics to improve its business.

3. Formulate a strategy for how Apple can use effectiveness IT metrics to improve its business.

4. Why would it be unethical for Apple to sell its iTunes customer information to other businesses?

5. Evaluate the effects on Apple's business if it failed to secure its customer information and all of it was accidentally posted to an anonymous website.

section 1.2 BUSINESS STRATEGY

LEARNING OUTCOMES

1.6. Explain why competitive advantages are typically temporary.

1.7. List and describe each of the five forces in Porter's Five Forces Model.

1.8. Compare Porter's three generic strategies.

1.9. Describe the relationship between business processes and value chain analysis.

IDENTIFYING COMPETITIVE ADVANTAGES

To survive and thrive, an organization must create a competitive advantage. A ***competitive advantage*** is a product or service that an organization's customers place a greater value on than similar offerings from a competitor. Unfortunately, competitive advantages are typically temporary because competitors often seek ways to duplicate the competitive advantage. In turn, organizations must develop a strategy based on a new competitive advantage.

When an organization is the first to market with a competitive advantage, it gains a first-mover advantage. The ***first-mover advantage*** occurs when an organization can significantly impact its market share by being first to market with a competitive advantage. FedEx created a first-mover advantage by creating its customer self-service software, which allows people and organizations to request parcel pickups, print mailing slips, and track parcels online. Other parcel delivery companies quickly began creating their own online services. Today, customer self-service on the Internet is a standard for doing business in the parcel delivery business.

As organizations develop their competitive advantages, they must pay close attention to their competition through environmental scanning. ***Environmental scanning*** is the acquisition and analysis of events and trends in the environment external to an organization. Information technology has the opportunity to play an important role in environmental scanning.

Frito-Lay, a premier provider of snack foods such as Cracker Jacks and Cheetos, does not just send its representatives into grocery stores to stock shelves; they carry handheld computers and record the product offerings, inventory, and even product locations of competitors. Frito-Lay uses this information to gain business intelligence on everything from how well competing products are selling to the strategic placement of its own products.

Organizations use three common tools to analyze and develop competitive advantages: (1) Five Forces Model, (2) three generic strategies, and (3) value chain analysis.

Panera
Bread

THE FIVE FORCES MODEL—EVALUATING BUSINESS SEGMENTS

Michael Porter's Five Forces Model is a useful tool to aid organizations facing the challenging decision of entering a new industry or industry segment. The ***Five Forces Model*** helps determine the relative attractiveness of an industry and includes:

1. Buyer power.
2. Supplier power.
3. Threat of substitute products or services.
4. Threat of new entrants.
5. Rivalry among existing competitors (see Figure 1.17).

Buyer Power

Buyer power in the Five Forces Model is high when buyers have many choices of whom to buy from and low when their choices are few. To reduce buyer power (and create a competitive advantage), an organization must make it more attractive for customers to buy from it instead of its competition. One of the best IT-based examples is the loyalty programs that many organizations offer.

Loyalty programs reward customers based on the amount of business they do with a particular organization. The travel industry is famous for its loyalty programs such as frequent-flyer programs for airlines and frequent-guest programs for hotels. Keeping track of the activities and accounts of many thousands or millions of customers covered by loyalty programs is not practical without large-scale IT systems. Loyalty programs are a good example of using IT to reduce buyer power; because of

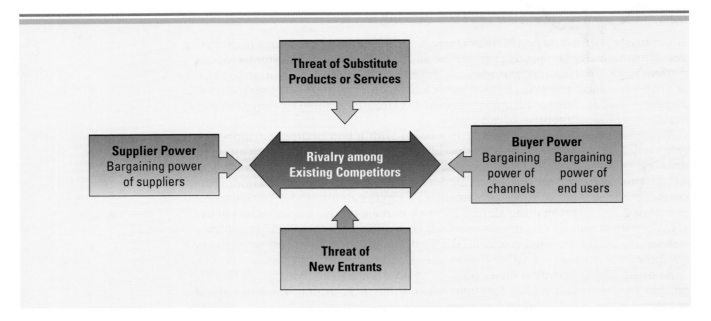

FIGURE 1.17

Porter's Five Forces Model

Competitive
Advantage

the rewards (e.g., free airline tickets, upgrades, or hotel stays) travelers receive, they are more likely to be loyal to or give most of their business to a single organization.

Supplier Power

Supplier power in the Five Forces Model is high when buyers have few choices of whom to buy from and low when their choices are many. Supplier power is the converse of buyer power: A supplier organization in a market will want buyer power to be low. A ***supply chain*** consists of all parties involved, directly or indirectly, in the procurement of a product or raw material. In a typical supply chain, an organization will probably be both a supplier (to customers) and a customer (of other supplier organizations) (see Figure 1.18).

As a buyer, the organization can create a competitive advantage by locating alternative supply sources. IT-enabled business-to-business (B2B) marketplaces can help. A ***business-to-business (B2B) marketplace*** is an Internet-based service that brings together many buyers and sellers (discussed in detail in Chapter 3). One important variation of the B2B marketplace is a private exchange. A ***private exchange*** is a B2B marketplace in which a single buyer posts its needs and then opens the bidding to any supplier who would care to bid. Bidding is typically carried out through a reverse auction. A ***reverse auction*** is an auction format in which increasingly lower bids are solicited from organizations willing to supply the desired product or service at an increasingly lower price. As the bids get lower and lower, more and more suppliers drop out of the auction. Ultimately, the organization with the lowest bid wins. Internet-based reverse auctions are an excellent example of the way that information technology can reduce supplier power for an organization and create a competitive advantage.

FIGURE 1.18

An Organization within the
Supply Chain

Threat of Substitute Products or Services

The ***threat of substitute products or services*** in the Five Forces Model is high when there are many alternatives to a product or service and low when there are few alternatives from which to choose. Ideally, an organization would like to be in a market in which there are few substitutes for the products or services it offers. Of course, that is seldom possible today, but an organization can still create a competitive advantage by using switching costs.

Switching costs are costs that can make customers reluctant to switch to another product or service. A switching cost need not have an associated *monetary* cost. Amazon.com offers an example. As customers purchase products at Amazon.com over time, Amazon develops a profile of their shopping and purchasing habits, enabling Amazon to offer products tailored to a particular customer based on the customer's profile. If the customer decides to shop elsewhere, there is an associated switching cost because the new site will not have the profile of the customer's past purchases. In this way, Amazon.com has reduced the threat of substitute products or services by creating a "cost" to the consumer to switch to another online retailer.

The cell phone industry offers another good example of switching costs. Cell phone providers want to keep their customers as long as possible. Many cell phone providers offer their customers free phones or unlimited minutes if they will sign a one- or two-year contract. This creates a switching cost for the customers if they decide to change providers because they will be required to pay a penalty for breaking their contract. Another switching cost for the cell phone customer was losing the actual cell phone number; however, this switching cost has been removed with the implementation of *local number portability (LNP)* or the ability to "port" cell phone numbers to new providers. Within the context of Porter's Five Forces Model, eliminating this switching cost creates a greater threat of substitute products or services for the supplier. That is, customers can now expect to see more new cell phone providers cropping up over the next several years. They will compete on price, quality, and services with the big-name cell phone providers such as AT&T and Verizon because cell phone numbers can be moved from one provider to another. When businesses reduce or eliminate switching costs, the consumer gains more power.

Threat of New Entrants

The ***threat of new entrants*** in the Five Forces Model is high when it is easy for new competitors to enter a market and low when there are significant entry barriers to entering a market. An entry barrier is a product or service feature that customers have come to expect from organizations in a particular industry and must be offered by an entering organization to compete and survive. For example, a new bank must offer its customers an array of IT-enabled services, including ATM use, online bill paying, and account monitoring. These are significant barriers to entering the banking market. At one time, the first bank to offer such services gained a valuable first-mover advantage, but only temporarily, as other banking competitors developed their own IT systems.

Rivalry Among Existing Competitors

Rivalry among existing competitors in the Five Forces Model is high when competition is fierce in a market and low when competition is more complacent. Although competition is always more intense in some industries than in others, the overall trend is toward increased competition in almost every industry.

The retail grocery industry is intensively competitive. While Kroger, Safeway, and Albertsons in the United States compete in many different ways, essentially they try to beat or match the competition on price. Most of them have loyalty programs that give shoppers special discounts. Customers get lower prices while the store gathers valuable information on buying habits to create pricing strategies. In the future, expect to see grocery stores using wireless technologies to track customer movement throughout the store and match it to products purchased to determine product placement and pricing strategies. Such a system will be IT-based and a huge competitive advantage to the first store to implement it.

Since margins are low in the retail grocery market, grocers build efficiencies into their supply chains, connecting with their suppliers in IT-enabled information partnerships such as the one between Wal-Mart and its suppliers. Communicating with suppliers over telecommunications networks rather than using paper-based systems makes the procurement process faster, cheaper, and more accurate. That equates to lower prices for customers and increased rivalry among existing competitors.

THE THREE GENERIC STRATEGIES—CREATING A BUSINESS FOCUS

Strategy

Once the relative attractiveness of an industry is determined and an organization decides to enter that market, it must formulate a strategy for entering the new market. An organization can follow Porter's three generic strategies when entering a new market: (1) broad cost leadership, (2) broad differentiation, or (3) focused strategy. Broad strategies reach a large market segment, while focused strategies target a niche market. A focused strategy concentrates on either cost leadership or differentiation. Trying to be all things to all people, however, is a recipe for disaster, since it is difficult to project a consistent image to the entire marketplace. Porter suggests that an organization is wise to adopt only one of the three generic strategies illustrated in Figure 1.19.

To illustrate the use of the three generic strategies, consider Figure 1.20. The matrix shown demonstrates the relationships among strategies (cost leadership versus differentiation) and market segmentation (broad versus focused).

■ **Hyundai** is following a broad cost leadership strategy. Hyundai offers low-cost vehicles, in each particular model stratification, that appeal to a large audience.

■ **Audi** is pursuing a broad differentiation strategy with its Quattro models available at several price points. Audi's differentiation is safety, and it prices its various Quattro models (higher than Hyundai) to reach a large, stratified audience.

■ **Kia** has a more focused cost leadership strategy. Kia mainly offers low-cost vehicles in the lower levels of model stratification.

■ **Hummer** offers the most focused differentiation strategy of any in the industry (including Mercedes-Benz).

FIGURE 1.19

Porter's Three Generic Strategies

Cost Leadership strategy — Differentiation strategy

Hyundai | **Audi**

Kia | **Hummer**

Broad market

Focused market

FIGURE 1.20

Porter's Three Generic
Strategies in the Auto
Industry

VALUE CHAIN ANALYSIS—TARGETING BUSINESS PROCESSES

Once an organization enters a new market using one of Porter's three generic strategies, it must understand, accept, and successfully execute its business strategy. Every aspect of the organization contributes to the success (or failure) of the chosen strategy. The business processes of the organization and the value chain they create play an integral role in strategy execution. Figure 1.21 combines Porter's Five Forces and his three generic strategies creating business strategies for each segment.[21]

Value Creation

A *business process* is a standardized set of activities that accomplish a specific task, such as processing a customer's order. To evaluate the effectiveness of its business processes, an organization can use Michael Porter's value chain approach. An organization creates value by performing a series of activities that Porter identified as the value chain. The *value chain* approach views an organization as a series of processes, each of which adds value to the product or service for each customer. To create a competitive advantage, the value chain must enable the organization to provide unique value to its customers. In addition to the firm's own value-creating activities, the firm operates in a value system of vertical activities including those of upstream suppliers and downstream channel members. To achieve a competitive advantage, the firm must perform one or more value-creating activities in a way that creates more overall value than do competitors. Added value is created through lower costs or superior benefits to the consumer (differentiation).

Organizations can add value by offering lower prices or by competing in a distinctive way. Examining the organization as a value chain (actually numerous distinct but inseparable value chains) leads to identifying the important activities that add value for customers and then finding IT systems that support those activities. Figure 1.22 depicts a value chain. Primary value activities, shown at the bottom of the graph, acquire raw materials and manufacture, deliver, market, sell, and provide after-sales services. Support value activities, along the top of the graph, such as firm infrastructure, human resource management, technology development, and procurement, support the primary value activities.

	Generic Strategies		
Industry Force	**Cost Leadership**	**Differentiation**	**Focused**
Entry Barriers	Ability to cut price in retaliation deters potential entrants.	Customer loyalty can discourage potential entrants.	Focusing develops core competencies that can act as an entry barrier.
Buyer Power	Ability to offer lower price to powerful buyers.	Large buyers have less power to negotiate because of few close alternatives.	Large buyers have less power to negotiate because of few alternatives.
Supplier Power	Better insulated from powerful suppliers.	Better able to pass on supplier price increases to customers.	Suppliers have power because of low volumes, but a differentiation-focused firm is better able to pass on supplier price increases.
Threat of Substitutes	Can use low price to defend against substitutes.	Customers become attached to differentiating attributes, reducing threat of substitutes.	Specialized products and core competency protect against substitutes.
Rivalry	Better able to compete on price.	Brand loyalty to keep customers from rivals.	Rivals cannot meet differentiation-focused customer needs.

FIGURE 1.21

Generic Strategies and
Industry Forces

The goal is to survey the customers and ask them the extent to which they believe each activity adds value to the product or service. This generates a quantifiable metric, displayed in percentages in Figure 1.22, for how each activity adds value (or reduces value). The competitive advantage decision then is to (1) target high value-adding activities to further enhance their value, (2) target low value-adding activities to increase their value, or (3) perform some combination of the two.

Organizations should attempt to use information technology to add value to both primary and support value activities. One example of a primary value activity facilitated by IT is the development of a marketing campaign management system that could target marketing campaigns more efficiently, thereby reducing marketing costs. The system would also help the organization better pinpoint target market needs, thereby increasing sales. One example of a support value activity facilitated by IT is the development of a human resources system that could more efficiently reward employees based on performance. The system could also identify employees who are at risk of leaving their jobs, allowing the organization to find additional challenges or opportunities that would help retain these employees and thus reduce turnover costs.

FIGURE 1.22

The Value Chain

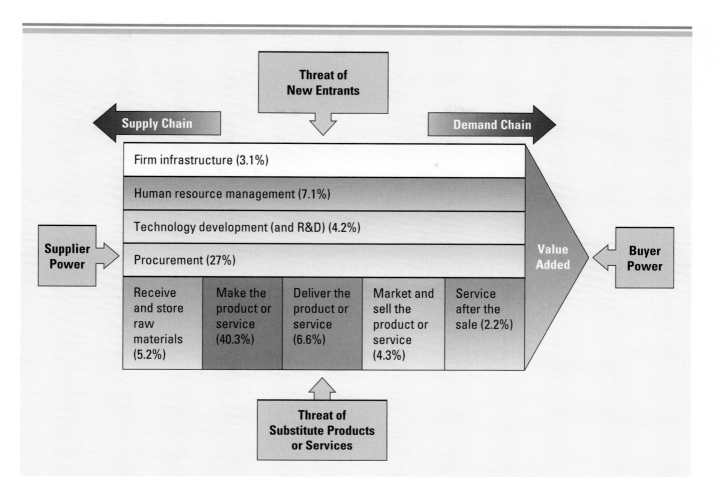

FIGURE 1.23

The Value Chain and Porter's Five Forces

Value chain analysis, a highly useful tool, provides hard and fast numbers for evaluating the activities that add value to products and services. An organization can find additional value by analyzing and constructing its value chain in terms of Porter's Five Forces (see Figure 1.23). For example, if an organization wants to decrease its buyer's or customer's power, it can construct its value chain activity of "service after the sale" by offering high levels of quality customer service. This will increase the switching costs for its customers, thereby decreasing their power. Analyzing and constructing its support value activities can help an organization decrease the threat of new entrants. Analyzing and constructing its primary value activities can help an organization decrease the threat of substitute products or services.

A company can implement its selected strategy by means of programs, budgets, and procedures. Implementation involves organization of the firm's resources and motivation of the employees to achieve objectives. How the company implements its chosen strategy can have a significant impact on its success. In a large company, the personnel implementing the strategy are usually different from those formulating the strategy. For this reason, proper communication of the strategy is critical. Failure can result if the strategy is misunderstood or if lower-level managers resist its implementation because they do not understand the process for selecting the particular strategy.

An organization must continually adapt to its competitive environment, which can cause its business strategy to change. To remain successful, an organization should use Porter's Five Forces, the three generic strategies, and value chain analysis to adopt new business strategies.

6. Did Apple gain a competitive advantage from its decision to invest in an online music business?

7. How can Apple use environmental scanning to gain business intelligence?

8. Using Porter's Five Forces Model, analyze Apple's buyer power and supplier power.

9. Which of the three generic strategies is Apple following?

10. Which of Porter's Five Forces did Apple address through its introduction of the iPhone?

SUMMARY OF KEY THEMES

The purpose of this chapter was twofold:

1. To provide you with an introduction to business driven information systems.

   - By explaining the basics of information technology.
   - By defining roles and responsibilities when addressing information technology in an organization.
   - By analyzing ways to measure information technology's success.

2. To raise awareness of information technology's ability to enable companies to sustain competitive advantages.

   - Businesses must be aware of the various forces that determine whether organizations should enter a new industry or segment and how information technology can be used to reduce or enhance the strength of those forces.
   - Firms need to set strategies and recognize how information technology can be used to add value to those activities that help organizations reach their strategic goals.

KEY TERMS

Benchmarking 17
Benchmarks 17
Business intelligence 11
Business process 25
Business-to-business (B2B) marketplace 22
Buyer power 21
Chief information officer (CIO) 14
Chief knowledge officer (CKO) 15
Chief privacy officer (CPO) 15
Chief security officer (CSO) 15
Chief technology officer (CTO) 14

Competitive advantage 21
Data 10
Effectiveness IT metrics 17
Efficiency IT metrics 17
Environmental scanning 21
First-mover advantage 21
Five Forces Model 21
Information 10
Information accuracy 19
Information technology (IT) 10
Key performance indicators (KPIs) 17
Loyalty program 21
Management information systems (MIS) 10

Private exchange 22
Response time 19
Reverse auction 22
Rivalry among existing competitors 23
Supplier power 22
Supply chain 22
Switching cost 23
System availability 19
Threat of new entrants 23
Threat of substitute products or services 23
Throughput 19
Transaction speed 19
Value chain 25
Web traffic 19

Business 2.0: Bad Business Decisions

Business 2.0 magazine looked at the top 100 bad business decisions of all time including bungled layoffs, customer-service snafus, executive follies, and other madness. Five of the top 10 bad business decisions of all time were made because business personnel did not understand information technology; these five are highlighted below. Perhaps one good reason to pay attention in this course is so that you will not end-up on Business 2.0's bad business decisions![22]

Bad Business Decision 3 of 10: Starbucks

Winner: Dumbest Moment—Marketing

Starbucks directs baristas in the Southeastern United States to email a coupon for a free iced coffee to friends and family members. But email knows no geographic boundaries and, worse, can be printed repeatedly.

After the email spreads to every corner of the country and is reproduced en masse, Starbucks yanks the offer, leading disgruntled customer Kelly Coakley to file a $114 million class-action lawsuit.

Bad Business Decision 4 of 10: Radioshack

Winner: Dumbest Moment—Human Resources

From: RadioShack
To: RadioShack employees
Subject: Your former job
RadioShack fires 400 staffers via email. Affected employees receive a message that reads, "The work force reduction notification is currently in progress. Unfortunately your position is one that has been eliminated."

Bad Business Decision 7 of 10: AOL

Winner: Dumbest Moment—Data Security

In an "attempt to reach out to the academic community with new research tools," AOL releases the search queries of 657,000 users.

Though AOL insists that the information contains no personally identifiable data, *The New York Times* and other news outlets promptly identify a number of specific users, including searcher No. 4417749, soon-to-be-ex-AOL-subscriber Thelma Arnold of Lilburn, Georgia, whose queries include "women's underwear" and "dog that urinates on everything."

The gaffe leads to the resignation of AOL's chief technology officer and a half-billion-dollar class-action lawsuit.

Bad Business Decision 8 of 10: UCLA

Winner: Dumbest Moment—Ecommerce

On the morning of April 3, 2006, Amazon.com sends an email headed "UCLA Wins!" to virtually everyone to whom it has ever sold a sports-related item, attempting to hawk a cap celebrating the Bruins' stirring victory in college basketball's championship game.

Just one problem: The game isn't scheduled to be played until later that night. When it is, UCLA is trounced by Florida, 73–57.

Bad Business Decision 9 of 10: Bank of America

Winner: Dumbest Moment—Outsourcing

After Bank of America announces plans to outsource 100 tech support jobs from the San Francisco Bay Area to India, the American workers are told that they must train their own replacements in order to receive their severance payments.

Here are a few other bad ones that did not make the top 10, but are worth mentioning.

Bad Business Decision: McDonald's

Guess the translator took the phrase "viral marketing" a bit too literally. McDonald's runs a promotional contest in Japan in which it gives away 10,000 Mickey D's-branded MP3 players.

The gadgets come preloaded with 10 songs—and, in some cases, a version of the QQPass family of Trojan horse viruses, which, when uploaded to a PC, seek to capture passwords, user names, and other data and then forward them to hackers.

Bad Business Decision: General Motors

Then again, viral marketing can be messed up in English too. As part of a cross promotion with the NBC-TV show *The Apprentice,* GM launches a contest to promote its Chevy Tahoe SUV. At Chevyapprentice.com, viewers are given video and music clips with which to create their own 30-second commercials.

Among the new Tahoe ads that soon proliferate across the web are ones with taglines like "Yesterday's technology today" and "Global warming isn't a pretty SUV ad—it's a frightening reality."

Bad Business Decision: New York Times Co.

We were wondering how Billy the paperboy could afford that gold-plated Huffy. News carriers and retailers in Worcester, Massachusetts, get an unexpected bonus with their usual shipment of the *Telegram & Gazette:* the credit and debit card numbers of 240,000 subscribers to the paper and its sister publication, the *Boston Globe,* both owned by the New York Times Co.

The security breach is the result of a recycling program in which paper from the *Telegram & Gazette*'s business office is reused to wrap bundles of newspapers.

Bad Business Decision: Sony

PC-B-Q. Defects in batteries made by Sony for portable computing cause a handful of notebooks to burst into spectacular photogenic flames.

The end result is the biggest computer-related recall ever, as Dell replaces the batteries in more than 4 million laptops. In short order, Apple (1.8 million), Lenovo/IBM (500,000), and others do the same.[23]

Question

1. Explain why understanding information technology and management information systems can help you achieve business success—or more importantly, help you avoid business disasters—regardless of your major.

Innovative Business Managers

BusinessWeek magazine recognized several innovative managers who have demonstrated talent, vision, and the ability to identify excellent opportunities (see Figure 1.24).

Jeffrey Immelt, General Electric (GE)

When Jeffrey Immelt took over as CEO of General Electric, he had big shoes to fill. The former CEO, Jack Welch, had left an unprecedented record as one of the top CEOs of all time. Immelt proved his ability to run the company by creating a customer-driven global culture that spawns innovation and embraces technology. The company was forecasting earnings to increase 17 percent in 2005.

Steven Reinemund, PepsiCo

Steven Reinemund turned PepsiCo into a $27 billion food and beverage giant. "To be a leader in consumer products, it's critical to have leaders who represent the population we serve," said Reinemund, who created a diverse leadership group that defined the strategic vision for the company. Reinemund also took a major role in mentoring and teaching his employees and demanded that all senior executives do the same. The payoff: consistent double-digit earnings

FIGURE 1.24

Innovative Business Managers

Innovative Managers	
Jeffrey Immelt, General Electric (GE)	■ Repositioned GE's portfolio with major acquisitions in health care, entertainment, and commercial finance ■ Created a more diverse, global, and customer-driven culture
Steven Reinemund, PepsiCo	■ Developed strong and diverse leadership that helped PepsiCo tap new markets ■ Attained consistent double-digit growth through product innovation and smart marketing
Steven Spielberg, Jeffrey Katzenberg, and David Geffen, DreamWorks SKG	■ Computer-animated *Shrek 2* set a record with a gross of $437 million ■ IPO pulled in $812 million
Robert Nardelli, Home Depot	■ Turned a $46 billion company focused on big stores into a $70 billion chain with urban, suburban, and international outlets ■ Drive for efficiency, such as centralizing purchasing and investing in technology, pushed margins above 30 percent
John Henry, Boston Red Sox	■ Broke the most fabled curse in sports, when the Boston Red Sox won the team's first World Series since 1918 ■ Sold out all 81 home games for the first time in team history
Phil Knight, Nike	■ Transformed a volatile, fad-driven marketing and design icon into a more shareholder-friendly company

and solid sales at a time when many of the company's staple products—potato chips and soft drinks—were under attack for fears about childhood obesity and health concerns.

Steven Spielberg, Jeffrey Katzenberg, and David Geffen, DreamWorks

DreamWorks, founded in 1994 by Steven Spielberg, Jeffrey Katzenberg, and David Geffen, suffered through its share of early bombs. Finally, the studio discovered a green ogre named Shrek and quickly became the hottest studio this side of Pixar Animation. DreamWorks Animation turned a $187 million loss in 2003 into a $196 million profit in 2004, with revenues of $1.1 billion. DreamWorks plans to release two animation films per year, each taking almost four years to produce.

Robert Nardelli, Home Depot

Robert Nardelli took several risks when he became CEO of Home Depot. First, he allocated $14 billion into upgrading merchandise, renovating outdated stores, and investing in new technology such as self-checkout lanes and cordless scan guns. Second, Nardelli expanded into Mexico, China, and other regions, tapping the growing homeowner market. Finally, Nardelli bet big on carrying products for aging baby boomers who wanted to spruce up their empty nests. The moves are paying off. The company sits on $3.4 billion in cash. With 2005 revenues near $80 billion, Home Depot is the number two U.S. retailer after Wal-Mart.

John Henry, Boston Red Sox

John Henry earned his fortune in the global futures market by developing a proprietary futures-trading system that consistently produced double-digit returns. Henry's new system, Sabermetrics, helped him reverse the most fabled curse in sports history by leading the Boston Red Sox to the team's first World Series Championship since 1918. Sabermetrics mines baseball statistics to find undervalued players while avoiding long contracts for aging stars whose performance is likely to decline. With the help of Sabermetrics, Henry built one of the most effective teams in baseball.

Philip Knight, Nike

Philip Knight, who got his start by selling Japanese sneakers from the trunk of his car, built the $12 billion sports behemoth Nike. Knight and his team transformed high-performance sports equipment into high-fashion gear and forever changed the rules of sports marketing with huge endorsement contracts and in-your-face advertising. Then, just as suddenly, Nike lost focus. In early 2000, kids stopped craving the latest sneaker, the company's image took a huge hit from its labor practices, sales slumped, and costs soared.

Thus began Knight's second act. He revamped management and brought in key outsiders to oversee finances and apparel lines. Knight devoted more energy to developing new information systems. Today, Nike's earnings are less volatile and less fad-driven. In 2004, Nike's earnings increased $1 billion.[24]

Questions

1. Choose one of the companies listed above and explain how it could use a chief information officer (CIO), chief technology officer (CTO), and chief privacy officer (CPO) to improve business.
2. Why is it important for all of DreamWork's functional business areas to work together? Provide an example of what might happen if the DreamWorks marketing department failed to work with its sales department.
3. Why is information technology important to an organization like the Boston Red Sox?
4. Which of Porter's Five Forces is most important to Home Depot's business?
5. Which of the three generic strategies is PepsiCo following?
6. Explain the value chain and how a company like GE can use it to improve operations.

The World Is Flat—Thomas Friedman

In his book, *The World is Flat,* Thomas Friedman describes the unplanned cascade of technological and social shifts that effectively leveled the economic world, and "accidentally made Beijing, Bangalore, and Bethesda next-door neighbors." Chances are good that Bhavya in Bangalore will read your next X-ray, or as Friedman learned first-hand, "Grandma Betty in her bathrobe" will make your JetBlue plane reservation from her Salt Lake City home.

Friedman believes this is Globalization 3.0. "In Globalization 1.0, which began around 1492, the world went from size large to size medium. In Globalization 2.0, the era that introduced us to multinational companies, it went from size medium to size small. And then around 2000 came Globalization 3.0, in which the world went from being small to tiny. There is a difference between being able to make long-distance phone calls cheaper on the Internet and walking around Riyadh with a PDA where you can have all of Google in your pocket. It is a difference in degree that's so enormous it becomes a difference in kind," Friedman stated. Figure 1.25 displays Friedman's list of "flatteners."

Friedman writes these flatteners converged around the year 2000 and "created a flat world: a global, web-enabled platform for multiple forms of sharing knowledge and work, irrespective of time, distance, geography, and increasingly, language." At the very moment this platform emerged, three huge economies materialized—those of India, China, and the former Soviet Union—"and 3 billion people who were out of the game, walked onto the playing field." A final convergence may determine the fate of the United States in this chapter of globalization. A "political perfect storm," as Friedman describes it—the dot-com bust, the attacks of 9/11, and

Friedman's 10 Forces That Flattened the World	
1. Fall of the Berlin Wall	The events of November 9, 1989, tilted the worldwide balance of power toward democracies and free markets.
2. Netscape IPO	The August 9, 1995, offering sparked massive investment in fiber-optic cables.
3. Work flow software	The rise of applications from PayPal to VPNs enabled faster, closer coordination among far-flung employees.
4. Open sourcing	Self-organizing communities, such as Linux, launched a collaborative revolution.
5. Outsourcing	Migrating business functions to India saved money *and* a Third World economy.
6. Offshoring	Contract manufacturing elevated China to economic prominence.
7. Supply chaining	Robust networks of suppliers, retailers, and customers increased business efficiency.
8. In-sourcing	Logistics giants took control of customer supply chains, helping mom-and-pop shops go global.
9. Informing	Power searching allowed everyone to use the Internet as a "personal supply chain of knowledge."
10. Wireless	Wireless technologies pumped up collaboration, making it mobile and personal.

FIGURE 1.25

Thomas Friedman's 10 Forces That Flattened the World

the Enron scandal—"distract us completely as a country." Just when we need to face the fact of globalization and the need to compete in a new world, "we're looking totally elsewhere."

Friedman believes that the next great breakthrough in bioscience could come from a 5-year-old who downloads the human genome in Egypt. Bill Gates's view is similar: "20 years ago, would you rather have been a B-student in Poughkeepsie or a genius in Shanghai? Twenty years ago you'd rather be a B-student in Poughkeepsie. Today, it is not even close. You'd much prefer to be the genius in Shanghai because you can now export your talents anywhere in the world."[25]

Questions

1. Do you agree or disagree with Friedman's assessment that the world is flat? Be sure to justify your answer.
2. What are the potential impacts of a flat world for a student performing a job search?
3. What can students do to prepare themselves for competing in a flat world?
4. Identify a current flattener not mentioned on Friedman's list.

MAKING BUSINESS DECISIONS

1. **Competitive Analysis**

   Cheryl O'Connell is the owner of a small, high-end retailer of women's clothing called Excelus. Excelus's business has been successful for many years, largely because of Cheryl's ability to anticipate the needs and wants of her loyal customer base and provide them with personalized service. Cheryl does not see any value in IT and does not want to invest any capital in something that will not directly affect her bottom line. Develop a proposal describing the potential IT-enabled competitive opportunities or threats Cheryl might be missing by not embracing IT. Be sure to include a Porter's Five Forces analysis and discuss which one of the three generic strategies Cheryl should pursue.

2. **Applying the Three Generic Strategies**

   This chapter discussed several examples of companies that pursue differentiated strategies so that they are not forced into positions where they must compete solely based on price. In a team, choose an industry and find and compare two companies, one that is competing based on price and another that is pursuing a differentiated strategy enabled by the creative use of IT. Some industries you may want to consider are clothing retailers, grocery stores, airlines, and personal computers. Prepare a presentation for the class on the ways that the company is using IT to help it differentiate and compete against the low-cost provider. Before you begin, spend some class time to make sure each team selects a different industry.

3. **Using Efficiency and Effectiveness Metrics**

   You are the CEO of a 500-bed acute care general hospital. Your internal IT department is responsible for running applications that support both administrative functions (e.g., patient accounting) as well as medical applications (e.g., medical records). You need assurance that your IT department is a high-quality operation in comparison to similar hospitals. What metrics should you ask your CIO to provide to give the assurance you seek? Provide the reasoning behind each suggested metric. Also, determine how the interrelationship between efficiency metrics and effectiveness metrics can drive your business's success.

4. **Building Business Relationships**

   Synergistics Inc. is a start-up company that specializes in helping businesses build successful internal relationships. You have recently been promoted to senior manager of the

Business and IT Relationship area. Sales for your new department have dwindled over the last two years for a variety of reasons including the burst of the technological stock bubble, recent economic conditions, and a poorly communicated business strategy. Your first task on the job is to prepare a report detailing the following:

- Fundamental reasons for the gap between IT and the business.
- Strategies you can take to convince the business this is an area that is critical to success.
- Strategies the business can follow to ensure synergies exist between the two sides.

5. Determining IT Organizational Structures

You are the chief executive officer for a start-up telecommunications company. The company currently has 50 employees and plans to ramp up to 3,000 by the end of the year. Your first task is to determine how you are going to model your organization. You decide to address the IT department's organizational structure first. You need to consider if you want to have a CIO, CPO, CSO, CTO, and CKO and if so, what the reporting structure will look like and why. You also need to determine the responsibilities for each executive position. Once you have compiled this information, put together a presentation describing your IT department's organizational structure.

6. The Five Forces Model

Your team is working for a small investment company that specializes in technology investments. A new company, Geyser, has just released an operating system that plans to compete with Microsoft's operating systems. Your company has a significant amount of capital invested in Microsoft. Your boss, Jan Savage, has asked you to compile a Porter's Five Forces analysis for Microsoft to ensure that your company's Microsoft investment is not at risk.

APPLY YOUR KNOWLEDGE

1. Capitalizing on Your Career

Business leaders need to be involved in information technology—any computer-based tool that people use to work with information and support the information and information-processing needs of an organization—for the following (primary) reasons:

- The sheer magnitude of the dollars spent on IT must be managed to ensure business value.
- Research has consistently shown that when business leaders are involved in information technology, it enables a number of business initiatives, such as gaining a competitive advantage, streamlining business processes, and even transforming entire organizations.
- Research has consistently shown that when business leaders are not involved in IT, systems fail, revenue is lost, and even entire companies can fail as a result of poorly managed IT.

One of the biggest challenges facing organizations is, "How do we get general business leaders involved in IT?" Research has shown that involvement is highly correlated with personal experience with IT and IT education, including university classes and IT executive seminars. Once general business leaders understand IT through experience and education, they are more likely to be involved in IT, and more likely to lead their organizations in achieving business success through IT.

Project Focus

1. Search the Internet to find examples of the types of technologies that are currently used in the field or industry that you plan to pursue. For example, if you are planning on a career in accounting or finance, you should become familiar with financial systems such as Oracle Financials. If you are planning a career in logistics or distribution, you should research supply chain management systems. If you are planning a career in marketing, you should research customer relationship management systems, blogs, and emarketing.

2. IT is described as an enabler/facilitator of competitive advantage, organizational effectiveness, and organizational efficiency. As a competitive tool, IT can differentiate an organization's products, services, and prices from its competitors by improving product quality, shortening product development or delivery time, creating new IT-based products and services, and improving customer service before, during, and after a transaction. Search the Internet and find several examples of companies in the industry where you plan to work that have achieved a competitive advantage through IT.

3. Create a simple report of your findings; include a brief overview of the type of technologies you found and how organizations are using them to achieve a competitive advantage.

2. Achieving Alignment

Most companies would like to be in the market-leading position of JetBlue, Dell, or Wal-Mart, all of which have used information technology to secure their respective spots in the marketplace. These companies have a relentless goal of keeping the cost of technology down by combining the best of IT and business leadership.

It takes more than a simple handshake between groups to start on the journey toward financial gains; it requires operational discipline and a linkage between business and technology units. Only recently have companies not on the "path for profits" followed the lead of their successful counterparts, requiring more operational discipline from their IT groups as well as more IT participation from their business units. Bridging this gap is one of the greatest breakthroughs a company can make.

Companies that master the art of finely tuned, cost-effective IT management will have a major advantage. Their success will force their competitors to also master the art or fail miserably. This phenomenon has already occurred in the retail and wholesale distribution markets, which have had to react to Wal-Mart's IT mastery, as one example. Other industries will follow. This trend will change not only the face of IT, but also the future of corporate America.

As world markets continue to grow, the potential gains are greater than ever. However, so are the potential losses. The future belongs to those who are perceptive enough to grasp the significance of IT and resourceful enough to synchronize business management and information technology.

Project Focus

1. Use any resource to answer the question, "Why is business-IT alignment so difficult?" Use the following questions to begin your analysis:
   a. How do companies prioritize the demands of various business units as they relate to IT?
   b. What are some of the greatest IT challenges for the coming year?
   c. What drives IT decisions?
   d. Who or what is the moving force behind IT decisions?
   e. What types of efficiency metrics and effectiveness metrics might these companies use to measure the impact of IT?
   f. How can a company use financial metrics to monitor and measure IT investments?
   g. What are some of the issues with using financial metrics to evaluate IT?

3. Market Dissection

To illustrate the use of the three generic strategies, consider Figure AYK.1. The matrix shown demonstrates the relationships among strategies (cost leadership versus differentiation) and market segmentation (broad versus focused).

- Hyundai is following a broad cost leadership strategy. Hyundai offers low-cost vehicles, in each particular model stratification, that appeal to a large audience.

- Audi is pursuing a broad differentiation strategy with its Quattro models available at several price points. Audi's differentiation is safety and it prices its various Quattro models (higher than Hyundai) to reach a large, stratified audience.

- Kia has a more focused cost leadership strategy. Kia mainly offers low-cost vehicles in the lower levels of model stratification.

- Hummer offers the most focused differentiation strategy of any in the industry (including Mercedes-Benz).

Project Focus

Create a similar graph displaying each strategy for a product of your choice. The strategy must include an example of the product in each of the following markets: (1) cost leadership, broad market, (2) differentiation, broad market, (3) cost leadership, focused market, and (4) differentiation, focused market. Potential products include:

- Cereal
- Dog food
- Soft drinks
- Computers
- Shampoo
- Snack foods
- Jeans
- Sneakers
- Sandals
- Mountain bikes
- TV shows
- Movies

FIGURE AYK.1

Porter's Three Generic Strategies

4. Porter's Five Forces

Porter's Five Forces Model is an easy framework to understand market forces. Break into groups and choose two products from the list below to perform a Porter's Five Forces analysis.

- Laptop computer and desktop computer.
- PDA and laptop computer.
- iPod and Walkman.
- DVD player and VCR player.
- Digital camera and Polaroid camera.
- Cell phone and Blackberry PDA.
- Coca-Cola plastic bottle and Coca-Cola glass bottle.
- GPS device and a road atlas.
- Roller skates and Rollerblades.
- Digital books and printed books.
- Digital paper and paper.

5. Measuring Efficiency and Effectiveness

In a group, create a plan to measure the efficiency and effectiveness of this course and recommendations on how you could improve the course to make it more efficient and more effective. You must determine ways to benchmark current efficiency and effectiveness and ways to continuously monitor and measure against the benchmarks to determine if the course is becoming more or less efficient and effective (class quizzes and exams are the most obvious benchmarks). Be sure your plan addresses the following:

- Design of the classroom.
- Room temperature.
- Lighting and electronic capabilities of the classroom.
- Technology available in the classroom.
- Length of class.
- Email and instant messaging.
- Students' attendance.
- Students' preparation.
- Students' arrival time.
- Quizzes and exams (frequency, length, grades).

6. Reorganizing an Organization

The AAA Management Company specializes in the management of rental properties and generates over $20 million in revenues each year and has more than 2,000 employees throughout the United States, Canada, and Mexico. The company has just hired a new CEO, David Paul. David is planning to reorganize the company so that it operates more efficiently and effectively. Next is the new organizational structure that he plans to present to the board of directors on Monday. Break into groups and explain the advantages and disadvantages of such a reporting structure. Reorganize the reporting structure in the way that will be most beneficial to the operations of the company, being sure to justify the new structure.

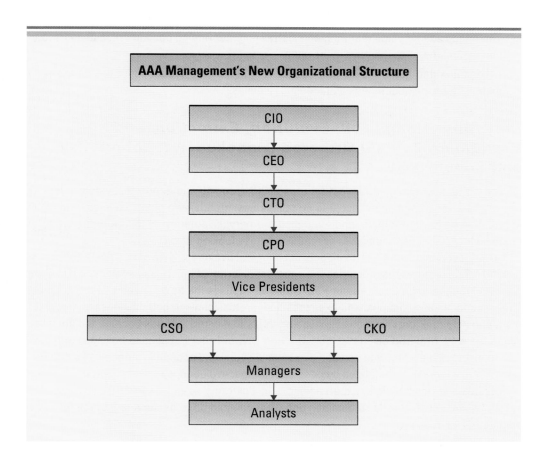

AAA Management's New Organizational Structure

CIO → CEO → CTO → CPO → Vice Presidents → CSO / CKO → Managers → Analysts

The Dumbest Moments in Business History: Useless Products, Ruinous Deals, Clueless Bosses, and Other Signs of Unintelligent Life in the Workplace. By Adam Horowitz and the editors of Business 2.0 (New York: Portfolio, 2004).

In *The Dumbest Moments in Business History,* the editors of Business 2.0 have compiled the best of their first four annual issues plus great (or not so great, if you happen to be responsible) moments from the past. Grouped by theme—bosses gone bad, criminally creative accounting, etc.—*The Dumbest Moments in Business History* is a fun and funny look at the big-time ways that big-time companies have screwed up through the decades. Featuring numerous funny anecdotes, each reveals a person or organization that should have known better, but just did not. If you are interested in learning how not to conduct business take a look at the valuable lessons provided in this book. From New Coke to the Edsel, from *Rosie* magazine to Burger King's "Herb the Nerd," the book's highlights include:

■ A Romanian car plant whose workers banded together to eliminate the company's debt by donating sperm and giving the proceeds to their employer.

■ The Heidelberg Electric Belt, a sort of low-voltage jockstrap sold in 1900 to cure impotence, kidney disorders, insomnia, and many other complaints.

■ The time Beech-Nut sold "100% pure apple juice" that contained nary a drop of apple juice.

■ The Midas ad campaign featuring an elderly customer ripping open her blouse and showing her "mufflers" to the guys in the shop.

■ A London video game maker that sought volunteers who would allow the company to place ads on the headstones of deceased relatives.[26]

Why Most Things Fail: Evolution, Extinction, and Economics. By Paul Ormerod (Hoboken, NJ: John Wiley and Sons, 2005).

Failure is the most fundamental feature of biological, social, and economic systems. Just as species fail—and become extinct—so do companies, brands, and public policies. And while failure may be hard to handle, understanding the pervasive nature of failure in the world of human societies and economies is essential for those looking to succeed.

Linking economic models with models of biological evolution, *Why Most Things Fail* identifies the subtle patterns that comprise the apparent disorder of failure and analyzes why failure arises. Throughout the book, author Paul Ormerod exposes the flaws in some of today's most basic economic assumptions, and examines how professionals in both business and government can help their organizations survive and thrive in a world that has become too complex. Along the way, Ormerod discusses how the Iron Law of Failure applies to business and government, and reveals how you can achieve optimal social and economic outcomes by properly adapting to a world characterized by constant change, evolution, and disequilibrium.

Filled with in-depth insight, expert advice, and illustrative examples, *Why Most Things Fail* will show you why failure is so common and what you can do to become one of the few who succeed.[27]

The Wright Way: 7 Problem-Solving Principles from the Wright Brothers That Can Make Your Business Soar. By Mark Eppler (New York: AMACOM, 2004).

When Wilbur and Orville Wright completed the first successful manned flight on December 17, 1903, they not only astonished everyone in the world with their feat, but they also demonstrated the power of their problem-solving methods. Business teacher and author Mark Eppler has examined these concepts and distilled them into seven principles that managers can use to find solutions to daunting problems.

The Wright Way is a passionate examination of the history of the Wright brothers and the lessons that can be learned from their historic contribution to the modern world. Eppler demonstrates the depth of his outstanding research and analysis by putting the information he has gathered into a usable form from which organizations can glean valuable business insights into innovation, speed-to-market, and hidden opportunities.[28]

2 CHAPTER

Strategic Decision Making

What's In IT for Me?

This chapter describes various types of decision-making information systems used to run basic business processes and facilitate sound and proper decision making. Using decision-making information systems to improve and reengineer businesses processes can significantly help organizations by improving efficiency and effectiveness, and even by redefining industry standards.

You, as a business student, can gain valuable insight into an organization by understanding the types of information systems that exist in and across enterprises. When you understand how to utilize these systems to improve decision making and problem solving you can vastly improve organizational performance. After reading this chapter, you should have gained an appreciation of the various kinds of information systems employed by organizations and how you can use them to help make strategically informed decisions.

Second Life: Succeeding in Virtual Times

Second Life is a virtual world built and owned by its residents. It opened to the public in 2003, and today is inhabited by millions of residents from around the world. The three main parts to Second Life are:

- **The World:** The world of Second Life is constantly changing and growing. It is filled with hundreds of games, from multi-player role-playing games to puzzles and grid-wide contests. There are also dance clubs, shopping malls, space stations, vampire castles, and movie theaters. To find something to do at any time of the day or night, residents simply open the Search menu and click on Events for a listing of discussions, sports, entertainment, games, pageants, education, arts and culture, and charity/support groups.

- **The Creations:** Second Life is dedicated to creativity. Everything in Second Life is resident-created, from the strobe lights in the nightclubs to the cars (or spaceships) in driveways. Imagine tinkering with the steering and handling program of a motorcycle while a friend tweaks the shape of the fuel tank and gives it a wicked flame paint job, in-world and in real-time, before taking it for a spin down a newly created road to look for land to buy. Have you ever wondered what it would be like to have a pair of black leather wings? Build them and give it a go.

- **The Marketplace:** The Marketplace currently supports millions of U.S. dollars in monthly transactions. This commerce is handled with the in-world unit of trade, the Linden dollar, which can be converted to U.S. dollars at several thriving online Linden dollar exchanges. Users can make real money in a virtual world because Second Life has a fully integrated economy designed to reward risk, innovation, and craftsmanship. Residents create their own virtual goods and services. Residents retain the intellectual property rights of their creations and can sell them at various in-world venues. Businesses succeed by the ingenuity, artistic ability, entrepreneurial acumen, and good reputation of their owners. Residents who have amassed lots of Linden dollars are matched with residents who want to buy Linden dollars at LindeX (the official Linden dollar exchange) or at other unaffiliated third-party exchanges.

Businesses on Second Life

Second Life is an exciting new venue for collaboration, business ventures, distance learning, new media studies, and marketing. Business possibilities on Second Life are endless; a few examples include:

- Hold a virtual meeting with sales managers located in Europe and Asia.
- Present new sales initiatives and discuss them with the team real-time.

- Build a new world that allows Second Life residents to interact with company products or services and test new designs and concepts before introducing them to the real world.
- Sell products and services in Second Life by creating an event to promote the product: a concert, a class, a famous speaker, a party, a contest. Many companies are excited about the numerous ways they can use Second Life to support their business. A few companies paving the way on Second Life include:

1-800-flowers.com	H&R Block	Sony
Adidas	IBM	Sprint
Amazon	Intel	Student Travel Association
American Apparel	Kraft Food	Starwood Hotels
American Cancer Society	Lacoste	Sundance Channel
BBC Radio 1	Major League Baseball	Toyota
Best Buy Co. Inc.	Mazda	Universal Motown Records
BMW	Mercedes-Benz	Visa
Calvin Klein	Microsoft	Warner Bros. Music
Circuit City	MTV	Weather Channel
Cisco	NASA	*Wired* magazine
Coca-Cola	National Basketball	Xerox
Coldwell Banker	Association	Yahoo
Comcast	NBC	Yankee Stadium
Crayola	Nissan	
Dell	NPR	

Second Life Success Stories

Virtual Dublin   John Mahon, known as Ham Rambler in Second Life, created the popular city of Dublin. His company, PickSL.net, builds community-based businesses in Second Life. Dublin, as John explains, started with an Irish bar, some great barmen, and plenty of good-spirited conversation. Since then, it has become a destination location in Second Life. "I joined Second Life more than two years ago," John says. "I felt what was missing was a comfortable, easygoing place to meet, talk, and interact. In other words: a good Irish bar. Everyone knows what a good Irish bar is. It needs no marketing. So I built the bar, and it was incredibly successful. I streamed in Irish music. There were lots of friendly people. I didn't start Dublin as a commercial project. It started as a bar where people could gather, hang out, and bring their friends. And then it became clear that people wanted more and that I should build a city around the bar. Build a larger context, in other words. That's where Dublin came from. It's a place people will go," John says.

Infinite Vision Media   The interactive marketing agency Infinite Vision Media specializes in 3D web spaces. Once part of the original team that created the lovely Dublin region, IVM now uses its deep real-world experience in advertising, branding, architecture, and programming to create immersive experiences for Second Life residents.

Neo-Realms Entertainment   As a game and content developer, Neo-Realms Entertainment has hooked the big one in Second Life. The flagship game, Neo-Realms Fishing, can be played at three different fishing camps in-world. "We created the first fishing camp in 2004," says co-founder and designer Steven McCall (known as Sweegy Manilow in Second Life). Steve and his fellow Neo-Realmers, Thanh Ha and Bryan King, were casting in real-world ponds when they realized the dearth of fishing games online. "We thought, 'All MMPGs really need fishing,' " Steve says, laughing. Although it sounded a little esoteric, it turned out that the threesome had their fingers on the pulse of consumer taste. Their little fishing expedition became a huge hit. Featuring various rod and bait types, their system offers fishing quests, reward points redeemable for prizes, and daily multiplayer tournaments for prizes and money. "It's also just a good place to hang out with your friends and socialize," says Steve.

Crescendo Design   In the real world of Wisconsin, architect Jon Brouchoud and his team at Crescendo Design create custom homes and sell plans for Springboard Homes. Their goal is to make energy-efficient, green design features more affordable. Jon and his team have found Second Life to be a great architectural tool. They use Second Life both within their company and among long-distance clients to create virtual designs and structures.

Global Kids   Global Kids is a nonprofit group working to prepare urban youth to become global citizens and community leaders. With help from Main Grid content creators and consultants like The Magicians and the Electric Sheep Company, Global Kids created a program where students in New York City collaborate with Teen Grid Residents from around the world. The teens had to finish the interactive adventure to participate in a real-world essay contest. Winners of the contest received cash prizes (in U.S. dollars) and were part of an awards ceremony co-broadcast into the Teen Grid and on stage in New York City.

American Apparel   American Apparel opened a store in Second Life on Lerappa Island (Lerappa is apparel spelled backward). Resident Aimee Weber was responsible for the build. What makes this opening so special is that it makes an exclusive offer for Second Life residents. Purchasers at the in-world American Apparel store will get a notecard with a promotional code offering a real-life discount at American Apparel's online store.

Sire Records/Regina Spektor   Recently, Sire Records and musician Regina Spektor launched an interactive, virtual listening party for her fourth album, *Begin to Hope,* inside Second Life. Songs from the album were available at six listening posts in a virtual New York City loft in-world.

Marvin the Robot   When Rivers Run Red was asked to create Marvin the Robot for the film *Hitchhikers Guide to the Galaxy*, Justin Bovington headed for Second Life. Rivers Run Red is an innovative marketing and communication firm located in the United Kingdom, and Justin is Fizik Baskerville, a developer in Second Life where he creates his ideas and makes them real. With Marvin, Justin successfully demonstrated Second Life's viability as a development platform—blurring the line between Second Life and real life.[1]

INTRODUCTION

Decision-making and problem-solving abilities are now the most sought-after traits in up-and-coming executives, according to a recent survey of 1,000 executives by Caliper Associates, as reported in *The Wall Street Journal.* To put it mildly, decision makers and problem solvers have limitless career potential.[2]

Decision making and problem solving in today's electronic world encompass large-scale, opportunity-oriented, strategically focused solutions. The traditional "cookbook" approach to decision making simply will not work. This chapter focuses on technology to help make decisions, solve problems, and find new innovative opportunities. The chapter also highlights how to bring people together with the best IT processes and tools in complete, flexible solutions that can seize business opportunities and combat business challenges (see Figure 2.1).

section 2.1 DECISION-MAKING SYSTEMS

LEARNING OUTCOMES

2.1. Explain the difference between transactional information and analytical information. Be sure to provide an example of each.

2.2. Define TPS, DSS, and EIS and explain how an organization can use these systems to make decisions and gain competitive advantages.

2.3. Describe the three quantitative models typically used by decision support systems.

2.4. Describe the relationship between digital dashboards and executive information systems.

2.5. Identify the four types of artificial intelligence systems.

Disney
Imagineering

DECISION MAKING

What is the value of information? The answer to this important question varies. Karsten Solheim would say the value of information is its ability to lower a company's handicap. Solheim, an avid golfer, invented a putter, one with a "ping," that led to a successful golf equipment company and the Ping golf clubs. Ping Inc., a privately held corporation, was the first to offer customizable golf clubs. The company prides itself on being a just-in-time manufacturer that depends on flexible information systems to make informed production decisions. Ping's production systems scan large amounts of information and pull orders that meet certain criteria such as order date (this week), order priority (high), and customer type (Gold). Ping then manufactures the appropriate products, allowing it to carry less than 5 percent of inventory in its warehouse. PING depends on its flexible information systems for production decision support and thanks information technology for the explosion of its business over the past decade.[3]

Business is accelerating at a breakneck pace. The more information a business acquires, the more difficult it becomes to make decisions. The amount of information people must understand to make good decisions is growing exponentially. In the past, people could rely on manual processes to make decisions because they had limited amounts of information to process. Today, with massive volumes of available information it is almost impossible for people to make decisions without the aid of information systems. Highly complex decisions—involving far more information than the human brain can comprehend—must be made in increasingly shorter time frames. Figure 2.2 highlights the primary reasons dependence on information systems to make decisions is growing and will continue to grow.

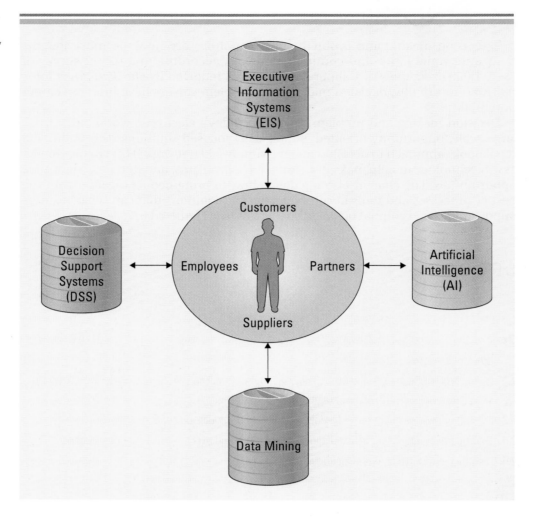

A **model** is a simplified representation or abstraction of reality. Models can be used to calculate risks, understand uncertainty, change variables, and manipulate time. Decision-making information systems work by building models out of organizational information to lend insight into important business issues and opportunities. Figure 2.3 displays three common types of decision-making information systems used in organizations today—transaction processing systems, decision support systems, and executive information systems. Each system uses different models to assist in decision making, problem solving, and opportunity capturing.

FIGURE 2.2

Primary Reasons for Growth
of Decision-Making Information Systems

Reasons for Growth of Decision-Making Information Systems

1. **People need to analyze large amounts of information**—Improvements in technology itself, innovations in communication, and globalization have resulted in a dramatic increase in the alternatives and dimensions people need to consider when making a decision or appraising an opportunity.

2. **People must make decisions quickly**—Time is of the essence and people simply do not have time to sift through all the information manually.

3. **People must apply sophisticated analysis techniques, such as modeling and forecasting, to make good decisions**—Information systems substantially reduce the time required to perform these sophisticated analysis techniques.

4. **People must protect the corporate asset of organizational information**—Information systems offer the security required to ensure organizational information remains safe.

FIGURE 2.3

IT Systems in an Enterprise

Executives — Executive Information Systems (EIS)

Managers — Decision Support Systems (DSS)

Analysts — Transaction Processing Systems (TPS)

Organizational Levels

TRANSACTION PROCESSING SYSTEMS

Transactional information encompasses all of the information contained within a single business process or unit of work, and its primary purpose is to support the performing of daily operational tasks. Examples of transactional information include purchasing stocks, making an airline reservation, or withdrawing cash from an ATM. Organizations use transactional information when performing operational tasks and repetitive decisions such as analyzing daily sales reports to determine how much inventory to carry.

Analytical information encompasses all organizational information, and its primary purpose is to support the performing of managerial analysis tasks. Analytical information includes transactional information along with other information such as market and industry information. Examples of analytical information are trends, sales, product statistics, and future growth projections. Managers use analytical information when making important ad hoc decisions such as whether the organization should build a new manufacturing plant or hire additional sales personnel.

The structure of a typical organization is similar to a pyramid. Organizational activities occur at different levels of the pyramid. People in the organization have unique information needs and thus require various sets of IT tools (see Figure 2.4).

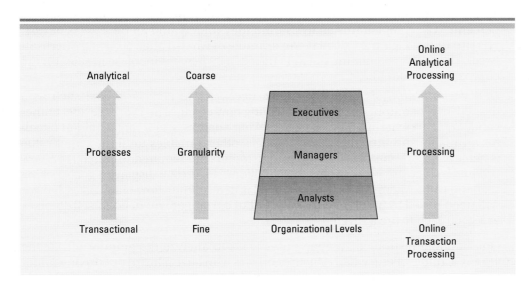

FIGURE 2.4

Enterprise View of Information and Information Technology

At the lower levels of the pyramid, people perform daily tasks such as processing transactions. ***Online transaction processing (OLTP)*** is the capturing of transaction and event information using technology to (1) process the information according to defined business rules, (2) store the information, and (3) update existing information to reflect the new information. During OLTP, the organization must capture every detail of transactions and events. A ***transaction processing system (TPS)*** is the basic business system that serves the operational level (analysts) in an organization. The most common example of a TPS is an operational accounting system such as a payroll system or an order-entry system.

Moving up through the organizational pyramid, people (typically managers) deal less with the details ("finer" information) and more with meaningful aggregations of information ("coarser" information) that help them make broader decisions for the organization. (Granularity means fine and detailed or "coarse" and abstract information.) ***Online analytical processing (OLAP)*** is the manipulation of information to create business intelligence in support of strategic decision making. ***Business intelligence*** is a broad, general term describing information that people use to support their decision-making efforts.

Decision

DECISION SUPPORT SYSTEMS

At limousine and transportation company BostonCoach, managers must dispatch fleets of hundreds of vehicles as efficiently as possible. BostonCoach requires a real-time dispatching system that considers inventory, customer needs, and soft dimensions such as weather and traffic. Researchers at IBM's Thomas J. Watson Research Center built BostonCoach a mathematical algorithm for a custom dispatch system that combines information about weather, traffic conditions, driver locations, and customer pickup requests and determines which cars to assign to which customers. The system is so efficient that, after launching it in Atlanta, BostonCoach experienced a 20 percent increase in revenues.[4]

A ***decision support system (DSS),*** such as BostonCoach's, models information to support managers and business professionals during the decision-making process. Three quantitative models often used by DSS include:

1. ***Sensitivity analysis*** is the study of the impact that changes in one (or more) parts of the model have on other parts of the model. Users change the value of one variable repeatedly and observe the resulting changes in other variables.

2. ***What-if analysis*** checks the impact of a change in an assumption on the proposed solution. For example, "What will happen to the supply chain if a hurricane in South Carolina reduces holding inventory from 30 percent to 10 percent?" Users repeat this analysis until they understand all the effects of various situations. Figure 2.5 displays an example of what-if analysis using Microsoft Excel. The tool is calculating the net effect of a 35 percent increase in sales on the company's bottom line.

3. ***Goal-seeking analysis*** finds the inputs necessary to achieve a goal such as a desired level of output. Instead of observing how changes in a variable affect other variables as in what-if analysis, goal-seeking analysis sets a target value (a goal) for a variable and then repeatedly changes other variables until the target value is achieved. For example, "How many customers are required to purchase a new product to increase gross profits to $5 million?" Figure 2.6 displays a goal-seeking scenario using Microsoft Excel. The model is determining how many bikes Hauger will need to sell to break-even, or a profit of 0. Hauger will need to sell 46 bikes at $3,500 each to break-even.

One national insurance company uses DSSs to analyze the amount of risk the company is undertaking when it insures drivers who have a history of driving under the influence of alcohol. The DSS discovered that only 3 percent of married male

FIGURE 2.5

Example of What-If Analysis in Microsoft Excel

FIGURE 2.6

Example of Goal-Seeking Analysis in Microsoft Excel

homeowners in their forties received more than one DUI. The company decided to lower rates for customers falling into this category, which increased its revenue while mitigating its risk.[5]

Figure 2.7 displays how a TPS is used within a DSS. The TPS supplies transaction-based data to the DSS. The DSS summarizes and aggregates the information from the many different TPS systems, which assists managers in making informed decisions. Burlington Northern and Santa Fe Railroad (BNSF) regularly tests its railroad tracks. Each year hundreds of train derailments result from defective tracks. Using a DSS to schedule train track replacements helped BNSF decrease its rail-caused derailments by 33 percent.[6]

FIGURE 2.7

Interaction Between TPSs
and DSSs

EXECUTIVE INFORMATION SYSTEMS

An *executive information system (EIS)* is a specialized DSS that supports senior-level executives within the organization. An EIS differs from a DSS because an EIS typically contains data from external sources as well as data from internal sources (see Figure 2.8).

Consolidation, drill-down, and slice-and-dice are a few of the capabilities offered in most EISs.

- *Consolidation* involves the aggregation of information and features simple roll-ups to complex groupings of interrelated information. Many organizations track financial information at a regional level and then consolidate the information at a single global level.

- *Drill-down* enables users to view details, and details of details, of information. Viewing monthly, weekly, daily, or even hourly information represents drill-down capability.

- *Slice-and-dice* is the ability to look at information from different perspectives. One slice of information could display all product sales during a given promotion. Another slice could display a single product's sales for all promotions.[7]

Digital Dashboards

A common feature of an EIS is a digital dashboard. *Digital dashboards* integrate information from multiple components and tailor the information to individual preferences. Digital dashboards commonly use indicators to help executives quickly identify the status of key information or critical success factors. Following

FIGURE 2.8

Interaction Between TPSs and EISs

is a list of features included in a dashboard designed for a senior executive of an oil refinery:

- A hot list of key performance indicators, refreshed every 15 minutes.
- A running line graph of planned versus actual production for the past 24 hours.
- A table showing actual versus forecasted product prices and inventories.
- A list of outstanding alerts and their resolution status.
- A graph of crude-oil stock market prices.
- A scroll of headline news from Petroleum Company news, an industry news service.

Digital dashboards, whether basic or comprehensive, deliver results quickly. As digital dashboards become easier to use, more executives can perform their own analysis without inundating IT personnel with questions and requests for reports. According to an independent study by Nucleus Research, there is a direct correlation between use of digital dashboards and companies' return on investment (ROI). Figure 2.9 and Figure 2.10 display two different digital dashboards from Visual Mining.[8]

EIS systems, such as digital dashboards, allow executives to move beyond reporting to using information to directly impact business performance. Digital dashboards help executives react to information as it becomes available and make decisions, solve problems, and change strategies daily instead of monthly.

Verizon Communications CIO Shaygan Kheradpir tracks 100-plus major IT systems on a single screen called "The Wall of Shaygan." Every 15 seconds, a new set of charts communicating Verizon's performance flashes onto a giant LCD screen in Kheradpir's office. The 44 screen shots cycle continuously, all day long, every day.

FIGURE 2.9

Visual Mining NetCharts Corporate Financial Dashboard

FIGURE 2.10

Visual Mining NetCharts Marketing Communications Dashboard

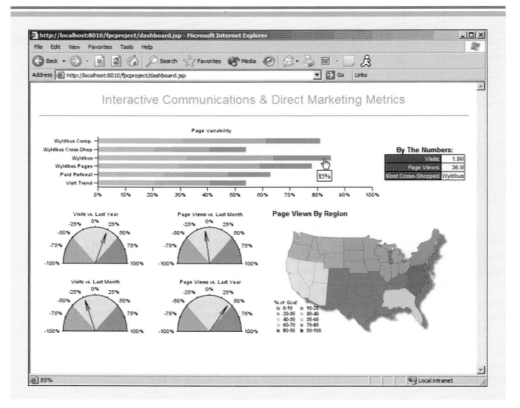

The dashboard includes more than 300 measures of business performance that fall into one of three categories:

1. **Market pulse**—examples include daily sales numbers, market share, and subscriber turnover.

2. **Customer service**—examples include problems resolved on the first call, call center wait times, and on-time repair calls.
3. **Cost driver**—examples include number of repair trucks in the field, repair jobs completed per day, and call center productivity.

Kheradpir has memorized the screens and can tell at a glance when the lines on the charts are not trending as expected. The system informs him of events such as the percentage of customer calls resolved by voice systems, number of repair trucks in the field, and amount of time to resolve an IT system issue. The dashboard works the same way for 400 managers at every level of Verizon.[9]

ARTIFICIAL INTELLIGENCE

Intelligence

Executive information systems are starting to take advantage of artificial intelligence to help executives make strategic decisions. RivalWatch, based in Santa Clara, California, offers a strategic business information service using artificial intelligence that enables organizations to track the product offerings, pricing policies, and promotions of online competitors. Clients can determine the competitors they want to watch and the specific information they wish to gather, ranging from products added, removed, or out of stock to price changes, coupons offered, and special shipping terms. Clients can check each competitor, category, and product either daily, weekly, monthly, or quarterly.

"Competing in the Internet arena is a whole different ballgame than doing business in the traditional brick-and-mortar world because you're competing with the whole world rather than the store down the block or a few miles away," said Phil Lumish, vice president of sales and marketing at RivalWatch.com. "With new products and campaigns being introduced at a breakneck pace, ebusinesses need new tools to monitor the competitive environment, and our service is designed specifically to meet that need."[10]

Intelligent systems are various commercial applications of artificial intelligence. *Artificial intelligence (AI)* simulates human intelligence such as the ability to reason and learn. AI systems can learn or understand from experience, make sense of ambiguous or contradictory information, and even use reasoning to solve problems and make decisions effectively. AI systems can perform such tasks as boosting productivity in factories by monitoring equipment and signaling when preventive maintenance is required. The ultimate goal of AI is the ability to build a system that can mimic human intelligence. AI systems are beginning to show up everywhere:

- At Manchester Airport in England, the Hefner AI Robot Cleaner alerts passengers to security and nonsmoking rules while it scrubs up to 65,600 square feet of floor per day. Laser scanners and ultrasonic detectors keep it from colliding with passengers.
- Shell Oil's SmartPump keeps drivers in their cars on cold, wet winter days. It can service any automobile built after 1987 that has been fitted with a special gas cap and a windshield-mounted transponder that tells the robot where to insert the pump.
- Matsushita's courier robot navigates hospital hallways, delivering patient files, X-ray films, and medical supplies.
- The FireFighter AI Robot can extinguish flames at chemical plants and nuclear reactors with water, foam, powder, or inert gas. The robot puts distance between the human operator and the fire.[11]

AI systems dramatically increase the speed and consistency of decision making, solve problems with incomplete information, and resolve complicated issues that cannot be solved by conventional computing. There are many categories of AI systems; four of the most familiar are: (1) expert systems, (2) neural networks, (3) genetic algorithms, and (4) intelligent agents.

Examples of AI Systems

Expert Systems

Expert systems are computerized advisory programs that imitate the reasoning processes of experts in solving difficult problems. Human expertise is transferred to the expert system, and users can access the expert system for specific advice. Most expert systems reflect expertise from many humans and can therefore perform better analysis than any single expert. Typically, the system includes a knowledge base containing various accumulated experience and a set of rules for applying the knowledge base to each particular situation. The best-known expert systems play chess and assist in medical diagnosis. Expert systems are the most commonly used form of AI in the business arena because they fill the gap when human experts are difficult to find or retain, or are too expensive.

Neural Networks

A *neural network,* also called an *artificial neural network,* is a category of AI that attempts to emulate the way the human brain works. The types of decisions for which neural networks are most useful are those that involve pattern or image recognition because a neural network can learn from the information it processes. Neural networks analyze large quantities of information to establish patterns and characteristics in situations where the logic or rules are unknown.

The finance industry is a veteran in neural network technology and has been relying on various forms of it for over two decades. The industry uses neural networks to review loan applications and create patterns or profiles of applications that fall into two categories: approved or denied. One neural network has become the standard for detecting credit card fraud. Since 1992, this technology has slashed fraud by 70 percent for U.S. Bancorp. Now, even small credit unions are required to use the software in order to qualify for debit-card insurance from Credit Union National Association.[12]

Additional examples of neural networks include:

- Citibank uses neural networks to find opportunities in financial markets. By carefully examining historical stock market data with neural network software, Citibank financial managers learn of interesting coincidences or small anomalies (called market inefficiencies). For example, it could be that whenever IBM stock goes up, so does Unisys stock. Or it might be that a U.S. Treasury note is selling for 1 cent less in Japan than it is in the United States. These snippets of information can make a big difference to Citibank's bottom line in a very competitive financial market.

- In Westminster, California, a community of 87,000 people, police use neural network software to fight crime. With crime reports as input, the system detects and maps local crime patterns. Police say that with this system they can better predict crime trends, improve patrol assignments, and develop better crime prevention programs.

- Fingerhut, the mail-order company based in Minnesota, has 6 million people on its customer list. To determine which customers were and were not likely to order from its catalog, Fingerhut recently switched to neural network software. The company finds that the new software is more effective and expects to generate millions of dollars by fine-tuning its mailing lists.

- Fraud detection widely uses neural networks. Visa, MasterCard, and many other credit card companies use a neural network to spot peculiarities in individual accounts. MasterCard estimates neural networks save it $50 million annually.

- Many insurance companies (Cigna, AIG, Travelers, Liberty Mutual, Hartford) along with state compensation funds and other carriers use neural network software to identify fraud. The system searches for patterns in billing charges, laboratory tests, and frequency of office visits. A claim for which the diagnosis was a sprained ankle but included an electrocardiogram would be flagged for the account manager.

- FleetBoston Financial Corporation uses a neural network to watch transactions with customers. The neural network can detect patterns that may indicate a customer's growing dissatisfaction with the company. The neural network looks for signs such as decreases in the number of transactions or in the account balance of one of FleetBoston's high-value customers.

Neural networks' many features include:

- Learning and adjusting to new circumstances on their own.
- Lending themselves to massive parallel processing.
- Functioning without complete or well-structured information.
- Coping with huge volumes of information with many dependent variables.
- Analyzing nonlinear relationships in information (they have been called fancy regression analysis systems).

The biggest problem with neural networks to date has been that the hidden layers are hidden. It is difficult to see how the neural network is learning and how the neurons are interacting. Newer neural networks no longer hide the middle layers. With these systems, users can manually adjust the weights or connections, giving them more flexibility and control.

Fuzzy logic is a mathematical method of handling imprecise or subjective information. The basic approach is to assign values between 0 and 1 to vague or ambiguous information. The higher the value, the closer it is to 1. The value zero is used to represent nonmembership, and the value one is used to represent membership. For example, fuzzy logic is used in washing machines that determine by themselves how much water to use or how long to wash (they continue washing until the water is clean). In accounting and finance, fuzzy logic allows people to analyze information with subjective financial values (intangibles such as goodwill) that are very important considerations in economic analysis. Fuzzy logic and neural networks are often combined to express complicated and subjective concepts in a form that makes it possible to simplify the problem and apply rules that are executed with a level of certainty.[13]

Genetic Algorithms

A *genetic algorithm* is an artificial intelligence system that mimics the evolutionary, survival-of-the-fittest process to generate increasingly better solutions to a problem. A genetic algorithm is essentially an optimizing system: It finds the combination of inputs that gives the best outputs.

Genetic algorithms are best suited to decision-making environments in which thousands, or perhaps millions, of solutions are possible. Genetic algorithms can find and evaluate solutions with many more possibilities, faster and more thoroughly than a human. Organizations face decision-making environments for all types of problems that require optimization techniques such as the following:

- Business executives use genetic algorithms to help them decide which combination of projects a firm should invest in, taking complicated tax considerations into account.

- Investment companies use genetic algorithms to help in trading decisions.
- Telecommunication companies use genetic algorithms to determine the optimal configuration of fiber-optic cable in a network that may include as many as 100,000 connection points. The genetic algorithm evaluates millions of cable configurations and selects the one that uses the least amount of cable.[14]

Intelligent Agents

An ***intelligent agent*** is a special-purpose knowledge-based information system that accomplishes specific tasks on behalf of its users. Intelligent agents use their knowledge base to make decisions and accomplish tasks in a way that fulfills the intentions of a user. Intelligent agents usually have a graphical representation such as "Sherlock Holmes" for an information search agent.

One of the simplest examples of an intelligent agent is a shopping bot. A ***shopping bot*** is software that will search several retailer websites and provide a comparison of each retailer's offerings including price and availability. Increasingly, intelligent agents handle the majority of a company's Internet buying and selling and handle such processes as finding products, bargaining over prices, and executing transactions. Intelligent agents also have the capability to handle all supply chain buying and selling.

Another application for intelligent agents is in environmental scanning and competitive intelligence. For instance, an intelligent agent can learn the types of competitor information users want to track, continuously scan the web for it, and alert users when a significant event occurs.

By 2010, some 4 million AI robots are expected to populate homes and businesses, performing everything from pumping gas to delivering mail. According to a new report by the United Nations and the International Federation of Robotics, more than half the AI robots will be toys and the other half will perform services. Bots will deactivate bombs, clean skyscraper windows, and vacuum homes.[15]

Multi-Agent Systems and Agent-Based Modeling What do cargo transport systems, book distribution centers, the video game market, a flu epidemic, and an ant colony have in common? They are all complex adaptive systems and thus share some characteristics. By observing parts of the ecosystem, like ant or bee colonies, artificial intelligence scientists can use hardware and software models that incorporate insect characteristics and behavior to (1) learn how people-based systems behave; (2) predict how they will behave under a given set of circumstances; and (3) improve human systems to make them more efficient and effective. This concept of learning from ecosystems and adapting their characteristics to human and organizational situations is called biomimicry.

In the last few years, AI research has made much progress in modeling complex organizations as a whole with the help of multi-agent systems. In a multi-agent system, groups of intelligent agents have the ability to work independently and to interact with each other. The simulation of a human organization using a multi-agent system is called agent-based modeling. Agent-based modeling is a way of simulating human organizations using multiple intelligent agents, each of which follows a set of simple rules and can adapt to changing conditions.

Agent-based modeling systems are being used to model stock market fluctuations, predict the escape routes that people seek in a burning building, estimate the effects of interest rates on consumers with different types of debt, and anticipate how changes in conditions will affect the supply chain, to name just a few. Examples of companies that have used agent-based modeling to their advantage include:

- Southwest Airlines—to optimize cargo routing.
- Procter & Gamble—to overhaul its handling of what the company calls its "supply network" of 5 billion consumers in 140 countries.
- Air Liquide America—to reduce production and distribution costs of liquefied industrial gases.

- Merck & Co.—to find more efficient ways of distributing anti-AIDS drugs in Africa.
- Ford Motor Co.—to build a model of consumer preferences and find the best balance between production costs and customers' demands.
- Edison Chouest Offshore LLC—to find the best way to deploy its service and supply vessels in the Gulf of Mexico.[16]

Data Mining

Wal-Mart consolidates point-of-sale details from its 3,000 stores and uses AI to transform the information into business intelligence. Data-mining systems sift instantly through the information to uncover patterns and relationships that would elude an army of human researchers. The results enable Wal-Mart to predict sales of every product at each store with uncanny accuracy, translating into huge savings in inventories and maximum payoff from promotional spending.[17]

Data-mining software typically includes many forms of AI such as neural networks and expert systems. Data-mining tools apply algorithms to information sets to uncover inherent trends and patterns in the information, which analysts use to develop new business strategies. Analysts use the output from data-mining tools to build models that, when exposed to new information sets, perform a variety of data analysis functions. The analysts provide business solutions by putting together the analytical techniques and the business problem at hand, which often reveals important new correlations, patterns, and trends in information. A few of the more common forms of data-mining analysis capabilities include cluster analysis, association detection, and statistical analysis. Data mining is covered in detail in Chapter 9.

OPENING CASE QUESTIONS

Second Life: Succeeding in Virtual Times

1. How could companies use Second Life for new product or service decision making?

2. How could financial companies use neural networks in Second Life to help their businesses?

3. How could a company such as Nike use decision support systems on Second Life to help its business?

4. How could an apparel company use Second Life to build a digital dashboard to monitor virtual operations?

---

section 2.2 BUSINESS PROCESSES

LEARNING OUTCOMES

2.6. Describe business processes and their importance to an organization.

2.7. Differentiate between customer facing processes and business facing processes.

2.8. Compare business process improvement and business process reengineering.

2.9. Describe the importance of business process modeling (or mapping) and business process models.

2.10. Explain business process management along with the reason for its importance to an organization.

UNDERSTANDING THE IMPORTANCE OF BUSINESS PROCESSES

Businesses gain a competitive edge when they minimize costs and streamline their business processes. Columbia Sportswear Company is a global leader in the design, production, marketing, and distribution of outdoor apparel and footwear. The

Business Process

company is always looking to make the members of its highly mobile workforce more responsive and efficient while also helping them enjoy better work–life balance. Columbia Sportswear wanted new ways to streamline its operations to get up-to-the-minute information to employees working across multiple time zones. The company deployed innovative Microsoft messaging software to give its workers flexible, safeguarded access to messages from anywhere in the world. This helps the company speed every aspect of its business, and gives employees more freedom to enjoy an active lifestyle.[18]

Most organizations pride themselves on providing breakthrough products and services for customers. Unfortunately, if customers do not receive what they want quickly, accurately, and hassle-free even fantastic offerings will not save an organization from annoying its customers and ultimately eroding the firm's financial performance.

The best way an organization can satisfy customers and spur profits is by completely understanding all of its business processes. Waiting in line at a grocery store is a great example of the need for an organization to understand and improve its business processes. In this case, the "process" is called checkout, and the purpose is to pay for and bag groceries. The process begins when a customer steps into line and ends when the customer receives the receipt and leaves the store. The *process steps* are the activities the customer and store personnel do to complete the transaction. A ***business process*** is a standardized set of activities that accomplish a specific task, such as processing a customer's order.[19]

Business processes transform a set of inputs into a set of outputs (goods or services) for another person or process by using people and tools. This simple example describes a customer checkout process. Imagine other business processes: developing new products, building a new home, ordering clothes from mail-order companies, requesting new telephone service from a telephone company, and administering Social Security payments. Making the checkout procedure quick and easy is a great way for grocery stores to increase profits. How long will a customer wait in line to pay for groceries? Automatic checkout systems at grocery stores are an excellent example of business process improvement.

Business Process Reengineering

Examining business processes helps an organization determine bottlenecks, eliminate duplicate activities, combine related activities, and identify smooth-running processes. To stay competitive, organizations must optimize and automate their business processes. Organizations are only as effective as their business processes. Developing logical business processes can help an organization achieve its goals. For example, an automobile manufacturer might have a goal to reduce the time it takes to deliver a car to a customer. The automobile manufacturer cannot hope to meet this goal with an inefficient ordering process or a convoluted distribution process. Sales representatives might be making mistakes when completing order forms, data-entry clerks might not accurately code order information, and dock crews might be inefficiently loading cars onto trucks. All of these errors increase the time it will take to get the car to the customer. Improving any one of these business processes can have a significant effect on the total distribution process, made up of the order entry, production scheduling, and transportation processes. Figure 2.11 displays several sample business processes.[20]

Some processes (such as a programming process) may be contained wholly within a single department. However, most processes (such as ordering a product) are cross-departmental, spanning the entire organization. Figure 2.12 displays the different categories of cross-departmental business processes. ***Customer facing processes*** result in a product or service that is received by an organization's external customer. ***Business facing processes*** are invisible to the external customer but essential to the effective management of the business and include goal setting, day-to-day planning, performance feedback, rewards, and resource allocation.[21]

FIGURE 2.11

Sample Business Processes

ACCOUNTING/FINANCE BUSINESS PROCESSES

Accounts payable
Accounts receivable
Bank account reconciliation
Depreciation, Invoicing
Month-end closing procedures

ENVIRONMENTAL BUSINESS PROCESSES

Environmental protection
Hazardous waste management
Air/water/soil resource management

HUMAN RESOURCES BUSINESS PROCESSES

Disabilities employment policies
Employee hiring policies
Health care benefits
Resignations and terminations
Workplace safety rules and guidelines

MANAGEMENT INFORMATION SYSTEMS BUSINESS PROCESSES

Disaster recovery procedures
Backup/Recovery procedures
Service agreements
Emergency services
Internet use policy
Email policy

Customer Facing Processes	Industry-Specific Customer Facing Processes	Business Facing Processes
Order processing	Banking—Loan processing	Strategic planning
Customer service	Insurance—Claims processing	Tactical planning
Sales process	Government—Grant allocation	Budget forecasting
Customer billing	Hotel—Reservation handling	Training
Order shipping	Airline—Baggage handling	Purchasing raw materials

BUSINESS PROCESS IMPROVEMENT

Improving business processes is paramount to stay competitive in today's electronic marketplace. Organizations must improve their business processes because customers are demanding better products and services; if customers do not receive what they want from one supplier, they can simply click a mouse and have many other choices. ***Business process improvement*** attempts to understand and measure the current process and make performance improvements accordingly.

Figure 2.13 illustrates the basic steps for business process improvement. Organizations begin by documenting what they currently do, and then they establish a way to measure the process, follow the process, measure the performance, and finally identify improvement opportunities based on the collected information. The next step is to implement process improvements and measure the performance of the new improved process. The loop repeats over and over again as it is continuously improved.[22]

Business processes should drive technology choices. Not the other way around. Businesses that choose technology and then attempt to implement business processes based on the technology typically fail. All business processes should be based on business strategies and goals. After determining the most efficient and effective business process, an organization can find the technology that can be used to support the business process. Of course, this does not always happen and often individuals find themselves in the difficult position of changing a business process because the technology cannot support the ideal solution.

This method for improving business processes is effective to obtain gradual, incremental improvement. However, several factors have accelerated the need to radically improve business processes. The most obvious is technology. New technologies (like the Internet and wireless) rapidly bring new capabilities to businesses, thereby raising the competitive bar and the need to improve business processes dramatically. For example, Amazon.com reinvented the supply chain of selling books by using the Internet. Amazon is a book-selling business, yet it fundamentally changed the way customers purchase books.

Another apparent trend is the flattening of the global world through technology bringing more companies and more customers into the marketplace and greatly increasing competition. A customer today can just as easily order a bottle of wine from a winery in France as a wholesaler in the United States. In today's marketplace, major technological and business changes are required just to stay in the game. As a result, companies have requested methods for faster business process improvement. Also, companies want breakthrough performance changes, not just incremental changes, and they want it now. Because the rate of change has increased for

FIGURE 2.13

Business Process Improvement Model

everyone, few businesses can afford a slow change process. One approach for rapid change and dramatic improvement is business process reengineering.

BUSINESS PROCESS REENGINEERING

Business process reengineering (BPR) is the analysis and redesign of workflow within and between enterprises. BPR relies on a different school of thought than business process improvement. *In the extreme*, BPR assumes the current process is irrelevant, does not work, or is broken and must be overhauled from scratch. Such a clean slate enables business process designers to disassociate themselves from today's process and focus on a new process. It is like the designers projecting themselves into the future and asking: What should the process look like? What do customers want it to look like? What do other employees want it to look like? How do best-in-class companies do it? How can new technology facilitate the process?[23]

Figure 2.14 displays the basic steps in a business process reengineering effort. It begins with defining the scope and objectives of the reengineering project, and then goes through a learning process (with customers, employees, competitors, noncompetitors, and new technology). Given this knowledge base, the designers can create a vision for the future and design new business processes by creating a plan of action based on the gap between current processes, technologies, structures, and process vision. It is then a matter of implementing the chosen solution.[24]

FIGURE 2.14

Business Process Reengineering Model

Finding Opportunity Using BPR

Companies frequently strive to improve their business processes by performing tasks faster, cheaper, and better. Figure 2.15 displays different ways to travel the same road. A company could improve the way that it travels the road by moving from foot to horse and then from horse to car. However, true BPR would look at taking a different path. A company could forget about traveling on the same old road and use an airplane to get to its final destination. Companies often follow the same indirect path for doing business, not realizing there might be a different, faster, and more direct way of doing business.[25]

Creating value for the customer is the leading factor for instituting BPR, and information technology often plays an important enabling role. Radical and fundamentally

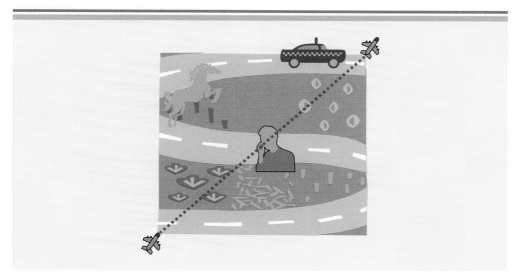

FIGURE 2.15

Better, Faster, Cheaper, or BPR

Company A: Claims Resolution Process

ACME Insurance Agency

Resolution Cycle Time: 3–8 weeks

Progressive Insurance: Claims Resolution Process

Resolution Cycle Time: 30 min–3 hours

FIGURE 2.16

Auto Insurance Claims
Processes

new business processes enabled Progressive Insurance to slash the claims settlement from 31 days to four hours. Typically, car insurance companies follow this standard claims resolution process: The customer gets into an accident, has the car towed, and finds a ride home. The customer then calls the insurance company to begin the claims process, which usually takes over a month (see Figure 2.16).

Progressive Insurance improved service to its customers by offering a mobile claims process. When a customer has a car accident, he or she calls in the claim on the spot. The Progressive claims adjustor comes to the accident and performs a mobile claims process, surveying the scene and taking digital photographs. The adjustor then offers the customer on-site payment, towing services, and a ride home. (see Figure 2.16).[26]

A true BPR effort does more for a company than simply improve it by performing a process better, faster, and cheaper. Progressive Insurance's BPR effort redefined best practices for its entire industry. Figure 2.17 displays the different types of change an organization can achieve, along with the magnitude of change and the potential business benefit.[27]

Selecting a Process for Reengineering

An organization can reengineer its cross-departmental business processes or an individual department's business processes according to its needs. When selecting

FIGURE 2.17

Process Change Spectrum

Process Change Spectrum

Redefine Industry

Define Best Practice

Match Best Practice

Improve Efficiency

No Benefit

Benefit

Strategic
Reengineering

Business Process
Reengineering

Streamline

Automate

Magnitude of Change

a business process to reengineer, wise organizations will focus on those core processes that are critical to their performance, rather than marginal processes that have little impact. Reengineering practitioners can use several criteria to determine the importance of the process:

- Is the process broken?
- Is it feasible that reengineering of this process will succeed?
- Does it have a high impact on the agency's strategic direction?
- Does it significantly impact customer satisfaction?
- Is it antiquated?
- Does it fall far below best-in-class?
- Is it crucial for productivity improvement?
- Will savings from automation be clearly visible?
- Is the return on investment from implementation high and preferably immediate?

Pitfalls of BPR

One hazard of BPR is that the company becomes so wrapped up in fighting its own demons that it fails to keep up with its competitors in offering new products or services. While American Express tackled a comprehensive reengineering of its credit card business, MasterCard and Visa introduced a new product—the corporate procurement card. American Express lagged a full year behind before offering its customers the same service.

BUSINESS PROCESS MODELING

After choosing the processes to reengineer, the organization must determine the most efficient way to begin revamping the processes. To determine whether each process is appropriately structured, organizations should create a cross-functional team to build process models that display input–output relationships among process-dependent operations and departments. They should create business process models documenting a step-by-step process sequence for the activities that are required to convert inputs to outputs for the specific process.

Business process modeling (or *mapping*) is the activity of creating a detailed flowchart or process map of a work process showing its inputs, tasks, and activities, in a structured sequence. A *business process model* is a graphic description of a process, showing the sequence of process tasks, which is developed for a specific purpose and from a selected viewpoint. A set of one or more process models details the many functions of a system or subject area with graphics and text, and its purpose is to:

- Expose process detail gradually and in a controlled manner.
- Encourage conciseness and accuracy in describing the process model.
- Focus attention on the process model interfaces.
- Provide a powerful process analysis and consistent design vocabulary.[28]

A business process model typically displays activities as boxes and uses arrows to represent data and interfaces. Business process modeling usually begins with a functional process representation of *what* the process problem is or an As-Is process model. *As-Is process models* represent the current state of the operation that has been mapped, without any specific improvements or changes to existing processes. The next step is to build a To-Be process model that displays *how* the process problem will be solved or implemented. *To-Be process models* show the results of applying change improvement opportunities to the current (As-Is) process model. This approach ensures that the process is fully and clearly understood before the details of a process solution are decided. The To-Be process model shows *how* the *what* is to be realized. Figure 2.18 displays the As-Is and To-Be process models for ordering a hamburger.[29]

Analyzing As-Is business process models leads to success in business process reengineering since these diagrams are very powerful in visualizing the activities,

FIGURE 2.18

As-Is and To-Be Process
Model for Ordering a
Hamburger

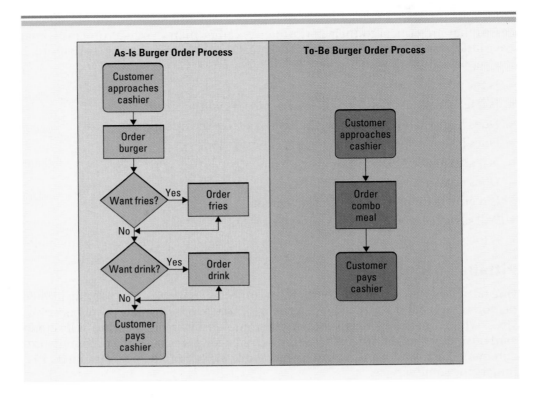

processes, and data flow of an organization. As-Is and To-Be process models are integral in process reengineering projects. Figure 2.19 illustrates an As-Is process model of an order-fulfillment process developed by a process modeling team representing all departments that contribute to the process. The process modeling

FIGURE 2.19

As-Is Process Model for
Order Fulfillment

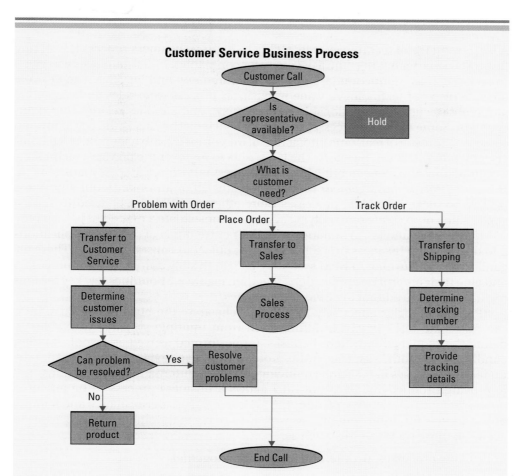

FIGURE 2.20

Customer Service As-Is
Process Model

Customer Service Business Process

team traces the process of converting the input (orders) through all the intervening steps until the final required output (payment) is produced. The map displays the cross-functional departments involved in a typical order-fulfillment process.[30]

It is easy to become bogged down in excessive detail when creating an As-Is process model. The objective is to aggressively eliminate, simplify, or improve the To-Be processes. Successful process improvement efforts result in positive answers to the key process design or improvement question: Is this the most efficient and effective process for accomplishing the process goals? This process modeling structure allows the team to identify all the critical interfaces, overlay the time to complete various processes, start to define the opportunities for process simulation, and identify disconnects (illogical, missing, or extraneous steps) in the processes. Figure 2.20 displays a sample customer service business process As-Is model.[31]

The consulting firm KPMG Peat Marwick uses process modeling as part of its business reengineering practice. Recently the firm helped a large financial services company slash costs and improve productivity in its Manufactured Housing Finance Division. Turnaround time for loan approval was reduced by half, using 40 percent fewer staff members.

Modeling helped the team analyze the complex aspects of the project. "In parts of the loan origination process, a lot of things happen in a short period of time," according to team leader Bob Karrick of KPMG. "During data capture, information is pulled from a number of different sources, and the person doing the risk assessment has to make judgment calls at different points throughout the process. There is often a need to stop, raise questions, make follow-up calls, and so on and then continue with the process modeling effort. Modeling allows us to do a thorough analysis that takes into account all these decision points and variables."[32]

BUSINESS PROCESS MANAGEMENT

A key advantage of technology is its ability to improve business processes. Working faster and smarter has become a necessity for companies. Initial emphasis was given to areas such as production, accounting, procurement, and logistics. The next big areas to discover technology's value in business process were sales and marketing automation, customer relationship management, and supplier relationship management. Some of these processes involve several departments of the company and some are the result of real-time interaction of the company with its suppliers, customers, and other business partners. The latest area to discover the power of technology in automating and reengineering business process is business process management. *Business process management (BPM)* integrates all of an organization's business process to make individual processes more efficient. BPM can be used to solve a single glitch or to create one unifying system to consolidate a myriad of processes.

Many organizations are unhappy with their current mix of software applications and dealing with business processes that are subject to constant change. These organizations are turning to BPM systems that can flexibly automate their processes and glue their enterprise applications together. Figure 2.21 outlines few key reasons organizations are embracing BPM technologies.

BPM technologies effectively track and orchestrate the business process. BPM can automate tasks involving information from multiple systems, with rules to define the sequence in which the tasks are performed as well as responsibilities, conditions, and other aspects of the process. BPM can benefit an organization by updating processes in real-time, reducing expenses, automating key decisions, and improving productivity. BPM not only allows a business process to be executed more efficiently, but it also provides the tools to measure performance and identify opportunities for improvement—as well as to easily make changes in processes to act upon those opportunities such as:

- Bringing processes, people, and information together.
- Breaking down the barriers between business areas and finding owners for the processes.
- Managing business processes within the enterprise and outside the enterprise with suppliers, business partners, and customers.
- Looking at automation horizontally instead of vertically.[33]

Is BPM for Business or Information Technology?

A good BPM solution requires two great parts to work together as one. Since BPM solutions cross application and system boundaries, they often need to be sanctioned and implemented by the IT organization, while at the same time BPM products

FIGURE 2.21

Key Reasons for BPM

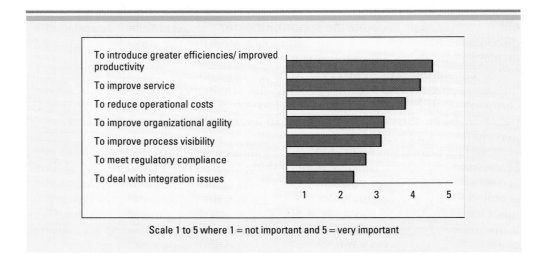

Scale 1 to 5 where 1 = not important and 5 = very important

are business tools that business managers need to own. Therefore, confusion often arises as to whether business or IT managers should be responsible for driving the selection of a new BPM solution.

The key requirement for BPM's success in an organization is the understanding that it is a collaboration of business and IT, and thus both parties need to be involved in evaluating, selecting, and implementing a BPM solution. IT managers need to understand the business drivers behind the processes, and business managers need to understand the impact the BPM solution may have on the infrastructure. Generally, companies that have successfully deployed BPM solutions are those whose business and IT groups have worked together as a cohesive team.

All companies can benefit from a better understanding of their key business processes, analyzing them for areas of improvement and implementing improvements. BPM applications have been successfully developed to improve complex business issues of some medium-to large-sized companies. Like many large-scale implementation projects, BPM solutions are most successful in companies with a good understanding of their technology landscape and management willing to approach business in a new way. BPM solutions are truly driven by the business process and the company's owners.[34]

Effective BPM solutions allow business owners to manage many aspects of the technology through business rules they develop and maintain. Companies that cannot support or manage cultural and organizational changes may lack positive BPM results.

BPM Risks and Rewards

If an organization is considering BPM, it must be aware of the risks involved in implementing these systems. One factor that commonly derails a BPM project has nothing to do with technology and everything to do with people. BPM projects involve cultural and organizational changes that companies must make to support the new management approach required for success. Where 10 area leaders once controlled 10 pieces of an end-to-end process, now a new group is involved in implementing a BPM solution across all these areas. Suddenly the span of control is consolidated and all are accountable to the whole process, not just one piece of the puzzle.

The added benefit of BPM is not only a technology solution, but also a business solution. BPM is a new business architecture and approach to managing the process and enabling proactive, continuous improvement. The new organizational structure and roles created to support BPM help maximize the continuous benefits to ensure success.

An IT director from a large financial services company gave this feedback when asked about his experience in using a BPM solution to improve the company's application help desk process. "Before BPM, the company's application help desk was a manual process, filled with inefficiencies, human error, and no personal accountability. In addition, the old process provided no visibility into the process. There was absolutely no way to track requests, since it was all manual. Business user satisfaction with the process was extremely low. A BPM solution provided a way for the company to automate, execute, manage, and monitor the process in real time. The biggest technical challenge in implementation was ensuring that the user group was self-sufficient. While the company recognized that the IT organization is needed, it wanted to be able to maintain and implement any necessary process changes with little reliance on IT. It views process management as empowering the business users to maintain, control, and monitor the process. BPM goes a long way to enable this process."[35]

Business Process Modeling Examples

A picture is worth a thousand words. Just ask Wayne Kendrick, a system analyst for Mobil Oil Corporation in Dallas, Texas. Kendrick, whose work involves planning and designing complex processes, was scheduled to make a presentation to familiarize top management with a number of projects his group was working on. "I was given 10 minutes for my presentation, and I had 20 to 30 pages of detailed documentation to present. Obviously, I could not get through it all in the time allocated." Kendrick turned to business process models to help communicate his projects. "I think people can relate to pictures better than words," Kendrick said. He applied his thinking to his presentation by using Microsoft's Visio to create business process models and graphs to represent the original 30 pages of text. "It was an effective way to get people interested in my projects and to quickly see the importance of each project," he stated. The process models worked and Kendrick received immediate approval to proceed with all of his projects. Figures 2.22 through 2.27 offer examples of business process models.[36]

FIGURE 2.22

Ebusiness Process Model

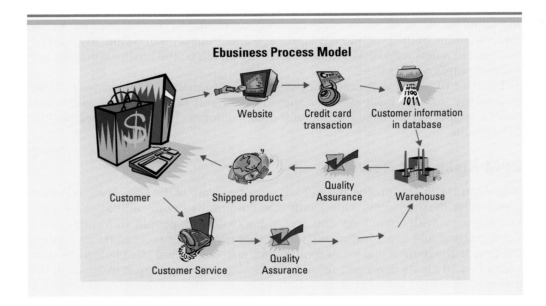

FIGURE 2.23

Online Banking Process Model

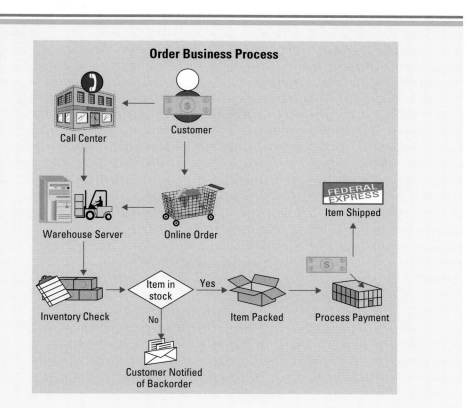

FIGURE 2.24

Customer Order Business
Process Model

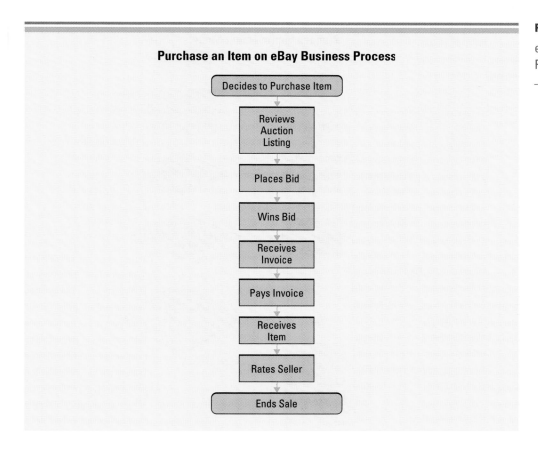

FIGURE 2.25

eBay Buyer Business
Process Model

FIGURE 2.26

eBay Seller Business
Process Model

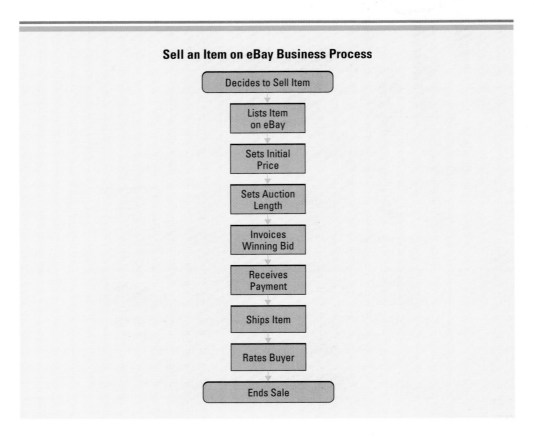

Sell an Item on eBay Business Process

FIGURE 2.27

Business Process
Improvement Model

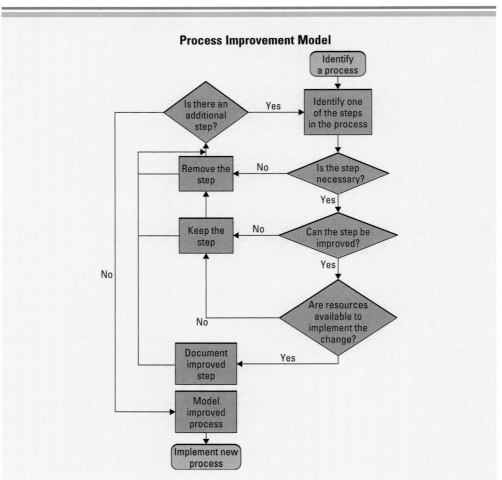

Process Improvement Model

OPENING CASE QUESTIONS

Second Life: Succeeding in Virtual Times

5. How could a company use Second Life to revamp its customer service process?

6. How could a company use Second Life to revamp its order entry process?

7. How could a company use Second Life to reinvent relationships with customers, partners, and employees?

SUMMARY OF KEY THEMES

The purpose of this chapter was to explain the concept of decision making while providing examples of the types of information systems that support decision making. The chapter also showcased the differences between TPS, DSS, and EIS, while introducing business process reengineering and how it can impact an organization.

After reading this chapter you, the business student, should have detailed knowledge of the types of information systems that exist in an organization. You should now have a better understanding of how systems and business processes can improve managerial decision making that affects organizational performance.

Business processes integrate the various systems and improve organization efficiency and effectiveness. Investment in business process improvement, business process reengineering, or business process management is the same as any other technology-related investment. Planning the project properly, setting clear goals, educating those people who have to change their mind-set once the system is implemented, and retaining strong management support will help with a successful implementation generating a solid return on investment.

Organizations must go beyond the basics when implementing business process improvement and realize that it is not a one-time project. Management and improvement of end-to-end business processes is difficult and requires more than a simple, one-time effort. Continuously monitoring and improving core business processes will guarantee performance improvements across an organization.

KEY TERMS

Analytical information   49
Artificial intelligence   55
As-Is process model   65
Business facing process   60
Business intelligence   50
Business process   60
Business process improvement   62
Business process management (BPM)   68
Business process model   65
Business process modeling (or mapping)   65
Business process reengineering (BPR)   63

Consolidation   52
Customer facing process   60
Decision support system (DSS)   50
Digital dashboard   52
Drill-down   52
Executive information system (EIS)   52
Expert system   56
Fuzzy logic   57
Genetic algorithm   57
Goal-seeking analysis   50
Intelligent agent   58
Intelligent system   55
Model   48

Neural network (artificial neural network)   56
Online analytical processing (OLAP)   50
Online transaction processing (OLTP)   50
Sensitivity analysis   50
Shopping bot   58
Slice-and-dice   52
To-Be process model   65
Transaction processing system (TPS)   50
Transactional information   49
What-if analysis   50

Defense Advanced Research Projects Agency (DARPA) Grand Challenge

The DARPA Grand Challenge was designed to leverage American ingenuity to develop autonomous vehicle technologies that can be used by the military. Created in response to a Congressional and U.S. Department of Defense (DoD) mandate with the goal of saving lives on the battlefield, the DARPA Grand Challenge brings together individuals and organizations from industry, the R&D community, government, the armed services, and academia, and includes students, backyard inventors, and automotive enthusiasts.

DARPA Grand Challenge 2004

The DARPA Grand Challenge 2004 field test of autonomous ground vehicles ran from Barstow, California, to Primm, Nevada, and offered a $1 million prize. From the qualifying round at the California Speedway, 15 finalists emerged to attempt the Grand Challenge. However, the prize went unclaimed as no vehicles were able to complete the difficult desert route.

DARPA Grand Challenge 2005

The DARPA Grand Challenge 2005 was held on October 8, 2005, in the Mojave Desert and offered a $2 million prize to the team that completed the course the fastest in under 10 hours. Five teams completed the Grand Challenge course of 132 miles over desert terrain, and Stanley, the Stanford Racing Team's car, garnered the $2 million prize with a winning time of 6 hours, 53 minutes.

The Grand Challenge demonstrated that autonomous ground vehicles can travel long distances across difficult terrain at militarily relevant rates of speed. DARPA Director Dr. Tony Tether said, "When the Wright brothers flew their little plane, they proved it could be done, and just as aviation 'took off' after those achievements, so will the very exciting and promising robotics technologies displayed here today."[37]

Questions

1. How is the DoD using AI to improve its operations and save lives?
2. Why would the DoD use an event, such as the DARPA Grand Challenge, to further technological innovation?
3. Describe how autonomous vehicles could be used by organizations around the world to improve business efficiency and effectiveness.
4. The Ansari X is another technological innovation competition focusing on spacecraft. To win the $10 million Ansari X Prize, a private spacecraft had to be the first to carry the weight equivalent of three people to an altitude of 62.14 miles twice within two weeks. SpaceShipOne, a privately built spacecraft, won the $10 million Ansari X Prize on October 4, 2004. Describe the potential business impacts of the Ansari X competition.

Revving Up Sales at Harley-Davidson

There is a mystique associated with a Harley-Davidson motorcycle. No other motorcycle in the world has the look, feel, and sound of a Harley-Davidson. Demand for Harley-Davidson motorcycles outweighs supply even though the company produces 300,000 motorcycles per year, which generates over $4 billion in revenues. Some models have a two-year waiting list.

The company recently won a number of awards including:

- Rated second in *ComputerWorld's* Top 100 Best Places to Work in IT.
- Rated 51st in *Fortune's* 100 Best Companies to Work For.
- Rated first in *Fortune's* 5 Most Admired Companies in the motor vehicle industry.
- Rated first in the Top 10 Sincerest Corporations by the *Harris Interactive Report.*
- Rated second in the Top 10 Overall Corporations by the *Harris Interactive Report.*

Harley-Davidson's Focus on Technology

Harley-Davidson's technology budget of $50 million is more than 2 percent of its revenue, which is far above the manufacturing industry average. More than 50 percent of this budget is devoted to developing new technologies such as sharing information, gaining business intelligence, and enhancing decision making. Harley-Davidson's commitment to technology is paying off, and by using strategic information systems, the company has reduced operating costs by $40 million.

Talon, Harley-Davidson's proprietary dealer management system, is one of its most successful information systems. Talon handles inventory, vehicle registration, warranties, and point-of-sale transactions for all Harley-Davidson dealerships. The system checks dealer inventory, generates parts orders, and analyzes global organization information. Talon gives Harley-Davidson managers a 360-degree view into enterprisewide information that supports strategic goal setting and decision making throughout all levels of the organization.

Building Supplier Relationships

Harley-Davidson understands and values the importance of building strong relationships with its suppliers, and it invests time, energy, and resources into improving company-to-company information systems. To develop these important relationships, the company deployed Manugistics, a supply chain management (SCM) system that allows it to do business with suppliers in a collaborative, web-based environment. The company uses the SCM software to manage material flows and improve collaboration with key suppliers.

Building Customer Relationships

Each time a customer reaches out to a company, the company has an opportunity to build a trusting relationship with that particular customer. Harley-Davidson realizes that it takes more than just building and selling motorcycles to fulfill the dreams of its customers. For this reason, the company strives to deliver unforgettable experiences along with high-quality products.

Harley-Davidson sells more than $500 million worth of parts and accessories to its loyal followers. Ken Ostermann, Harley-Davidson's manager of electronic commerce and communications, decided the company could increase parts and accessories sales if it could offer the products online. The dilemma facing Ostermann's online strategy was that selling jackets, saddlebags, and T-shirts directly to consumers would bypass Harley-Davidson's 650 dealers, who depend on the high-margin accessories to fuel profits. Ostermann's solution was to build an online store, Harley-Davidson.com, which prompts customers to select a participating Harley-Davidson dealership before placing any online orders. The selected dealership is then responsible for fulfilling the order. The strategy ensures dealers that they will remain the focal point of customers' buying experiences. The company currently receives over 1 million visitors a month to its online store. To guarantee that every customer has a highly satisfying online buying experience, the company asks the dealers to agree to a number of standards including:

- Checking online orders twice daily.
- Shipping online orders within 24 hours.
- Responding to customer inquiries within 24 hours.

Another of Harley-Davidson's customer-centric strategies is its Harley's Owners Group (HOG), which offers an array of events, rides, and benefits to its members. HOG is the largest factory-sponsored motorcycle club in the world with more than 600,000 members and is one of the key drivers helping to build a strong sense of community among Harley-Davidson owners. Harley-Davidson has built a customer following that is extremely loyal, a difficult task to accomplish in any industry.

Harley-Davidson's Corporate Culture

Harley-Davidson employees are the engine behind its outstanding performance and the foundation of the company's overall success. Harley-Davidson believes in a strong sense of corporate ethics and values, and the company's top five core values serve as a framework for the entire corporation:

- Tell the truth.
- Be fair.
- Keep your promises.
- Respect the individual.
- Encourage intellectual curiosity.

The company credits its core values as the primary reason it won the two prestigious awards from the *Harris Interactive Report,* one of the most respected consumer reviews for corporate sincerity, ethics, and standards. Sticking to strong ethics and values is and will continue to be a top priority for the company and its employees.

To enhance its enterprise further, Harley-Davidson plans to keep taking advantage of new technologies and strategies, including a web-based approach to accessing information and an enterprisewide system to consolidate procurement at its eight U.S. facilities.[38]

Questions

1. How does Talon help Harley-Davidson employees improve their decision-making capabilities?
2. Identify a few key metrics a Harley-Davidson marketing executive might want to monitor on a digital dashboard.
3. How can Harley-Davidson benefit from using decision support systems in its business?
4. How can Harley-Davidson use business process improvement to increase customer satisfaction?
5. How can Harley-Davidson use business process reengineering to improve supplier relationships?

Delta Air Lines Plays Catch-Up

The airline industry has a well-deserved reputation for creative use of IT. American Airlines is known as a leader in using IT to drive its business, and United Airlines is known as a fast follower. Delta Air Lines, while highly regarded as a well-run airline, has been a slow follower in IT. However, this has changed. In the past few years, Delta has invested more than $1.5 billion in technology, automating everything from gate and boarding tasks to baggage-handling, inventory control, and revenue accounting.

The airline reservation systems introduced by American Airlines and United Airlines, respectively, Sabre and Apollo, were the earliest examples of significant forays into business driven IT in the airline industry. The programs are inventory control systems that sell and manage available seats on upcoming flights. Travel agents received a special computer terminal from the airline when they signed up for the programs. Usually, a travel agent would sign up for one or the other system, but not both. Airline companies that did not have their own reservation systems (Frontier Airlines, for example) could become "co-hosts" on Sabre or Apollo. A fee was charged to co-hosts for the privilege of listing their flights on the reservation systems.

American and United obtained significant competitive advantages as owners of the reservation systems for several reasons. First, the systems were very profitable. Second, they gave American's and United's IT and operations personnel early and valuable experience with online transaction processing (OLTP) systems. Finally, they gave American and United access to information on the sales volumes of their competitors, such as Frontier, because the information was available in the reservation system's database. For example, if American wanted to consider adding a flight from Denver to Chicago, it could simply examine the historical information in the Sabre system to see if there was enough demand for the new route. It could also see what sort of traffic a competitor such as Frontier was generating on the same route in order to pick the best time to schedule a new flight along with the best price. American and United offered the same competitive intelligence information to their co-host airlines, but charged them for it, and often took weeks to provide it to them.

American and United soon realized they had a gold mine of customer-related information available in their reservation systems. They conceived and rolled out hugely successful frequent-flyer programs, which increased the likelihood that frequent business travelers, their most profitable customers, would fly with them instead of with a competitor. Frequent-flyer programs require sophisticated computer systems to properly account for and manage the flight activity of millions of customers, together with their eligibility for awards—another noteworthy example of business driven IT. Ultimately, frequent-flyer programs became an entry barrier for the industry because all airline companies felt they could not compete for the best customers without having their own frequent-flyer systems.

Follow-on IT Innovations

Yield management systems alter the price of available seats on a flight. The systems operate on a minute-by-minute basis as the date of the flight approaches, depending on the number of seats sold compared to the number expected. This is why an airfare quoted over the phone can be $100 higher if the airfare is quoted again an hour later. Most airlines use yield management systems to sell as many seats as possible at the best price. From the airlines' standpoint, it is better to sell a seat at a lower price than to have a plane take off with a vacant seat. At the same time, airlines want to avoid selling a seat for a price lower than what a passenger is willing to pay. Yield management systems are a great example of solving a business problem with IT because they help business managers maximize the revenue generated by each flight.

American Airlines went so far as to sell some of its systems, such as yield management, to other airlines. When asked why, American's then CIO, Max Hopper, said American might as well recover some of its development costs by selling systems to competitors because eventually competitors would develop their own systems. Besides, Hopper believed that by the time lagging competitors such as Delta figured out how to use the systems, American would have reached the next plateau of IT innovation.

Delta's IT Success

Delta always had a reputation in the industry as a slow follower, being reluctant to give up its paper-based systems for modern IT systems. The company did a turnaround when "CIO for Hire" Charlie Feld, a former Frito-Lay CIO, joined Delta in 1997. Feld quickly addressed some of Delta's most pressing IT issues including projects and people in disarray, departments hiring their own IT consultants to develop systems with no attention given to coordination with other Delta systems, as well as the pending Y2K problem. He established a separate wholly owned subsidiary called Delta Technology, and set out to replace Delta's antiquated IT systems with new applications to run the airline.

Feld began by building the gate and boarding application along with the supporting technical hardware, software, and network infrastructure. The gate and boarding application was chosen because it was most visible to Delta's 104 million passengers. The new system provided gate agents' information on which passengers had checked in, seat assignments, and standby status, and saved an average of 8 to 10 minutes of gate activity per flight. As Chief Technical Officer (CTO) Dean Compton recalled, "I remember when we put in the systems in Jacksonville. I saw an overbooked wide-body 767—where there is normally a lot of confusion around the gate—boarded by two agents on time and ahead of schedule. I'd seen a similar situation in Salt Lake City where we hadn't put in the technology yet, and they had to use nine agents to board the plane, and it still left late."

Delta Technology continued to roll out applications, but by early 2001, the airline industry began to feel the effects of the economic downturn. Delta's board of directors questioned the need to spend additional funds on IT when the airline was under great pressure to reduce its costs. After Delta Technology executives gave an overview of projects they were working on, Vickie Escarra, the chief marketing officer, spoke up in support of the IT initiatives like the gate and boarding application by saying, "Man, we couldn't have done what we're doing today if it wasn't for the technology." The overview from IT coupled with the endorsement from a satisfied business unit customer convinced the board that the IT projects should proceed. They insisted, however, that all projects be supported and justified by a solid business case analysis with emphasis placed on either lowered operating costs or increased revenues.

After September 11, 2001, when traffic fell off even more, Delta began to postpone projects showing a longer payoff (like new HR systems) and to speed up projects showing a faster payoff (like increasing the number of self-service check-in kiosks and replacing call center technology).

Delta processes almost 300 million transactions on its IT infrastructure each month. The company installed SAP software for inventory management, but altered the "flight plan" for Delta's new technology platform. "We're working only on projects that pay off in 12 months and have ongoing impact for at least three years—either building revenue or lowering operating costs," said CIO Curtis Robb. "I see this work going on for another five years. We'll be done when we run out of ideas."

Delta's Problems

Even after making great strides through IT, Delta could not shake financial woes caused by the 9/11 terrorist attacks and high oil prices. By staving off bankruptcy for a year, the carrier thought it was taking the high road. Unfortunately, it has not worked out that way. Delta's then-CEO Gerald Grinstein stood before 1,700 retirees—men and women whose benefits and pensions will be slashed in Chapter 11 proceedings—and swore he shared their pain. "Bankruptcy is beyond strange," he told them in late 2005 at an Atlanta convention center. "I now know why we fought so hard to avoid it."

It is amazing that his remarks did not spark a riot. After all, Chapter 11 has become a last-resort management tool: a way for airlines to slash labor costs, offload pension obligations, dump unwanted jets, and reemerge as moneymakers. United Airlines, for instance, which exited bankruptcy in early 2006 after more than three years, projected more than $1 billion in profits by 2007. Yet Delta's retirees ended up giving the 73-year-old Grinstein, who outlined the airline's financial straits but made no promises about their benefits, a standing ovation. "That took a lot for [him] to be willing to come over and answer our questions," explains Cathy Cone, a retired flight attendant. But the Delta "family," as its workforce still calls itself, evinced plenty of hostility toward Grinstein's predecessor Leo Mullin.

Bankruptcies are notoriously unpredictable, and Delta's is still early in the process. CFO Edward Bastian insists the airline has a leg up on previous legacy carriers in Chapter 11, having entered it "with a transformation plan we've been working on for the past two years." The carrier also has an ace in the hole: GE, the world's biggest aircraft lessor and a major jet-engine maker. Sometimes called the "patron saint of failing airlines," GE knows that liquidations are bad for business. It helped keep US Airways aloft until that carrier finally merged with America West, and it is unlikely to let the third-biggest U.S. carrier disappear. (GE is already the lead provider of Delta's bankruptcy financing.) The real question is whether Delta's management will get its strategy together in time to ensure a post-Chapter 11 existence as a stand-alone carrier or whether Delta will survive only as part of another airline.[39]

Questions

1. What business risks would Delta be taking if it decided not to catch up with industry leaders in using IT to gain a competitive advantage?
2. What competitive advantages can an airline gain by using DSS and EIS?
3. What other industries could potentially benefit from the use of yield management systems?
4. How can American and United use customer information to gain a competitive advantage?
5. What types of metrics would Delta executives want to see in a digital dashboard?

MAKING BUSINESS DECISIONS

1. Making decisions

You are the vice president of human resources for a large consulting company. You are compiling a list of questions that you want each interviewee to answer. The first question on your list is, "How can information technology enhance your ability to make decisions at our organization?" Prepare a one-page report to answer this difficult question.

2. DSS and EIS

Dr. Rosen runs a large dental conglomerate—Teeth Doctors—that staffs more than 700 dentists in six states. Dr. Rosen is interested in purchasing a competitor called Dentix that has 150 dentists in three additional states. Before deciding whether to purchase Dentix, Dr. Rosen must consider several issues:

- The cost of purchasing Dentix.
- The location of the Dentix offices.
- The current number of customers per dentist, per office, and per state.
- The merger between the two companies.
- The professional reputation of Dentix.
- Other competitors.

Explain how Dr. Rosen and Teeth Doctors can benefit from the use of information systems to make an accurate business decision in regard to the potential purchase of Dentix.

3. Finding information on decision support systems

You are working on the sales team for a small catering company that maintains 75 employees and generates $1 million in revenues per year. The owner, Pam Hetz, wants to understand how she can use decision support systems to help expand her business. Pam has an initial understanding of DSS systems and is interested in learning more about what types are available, how they can be used in a small business, and the cost associated with different DSS systems. In a group, research the website www.dssresources.com and compile a presentation that discusses DSS systems in detail. Be sure to answer all Pam's questions on DSS systems in the presentation.

APPLY YOUR KNOWLEDGE

1. Discovering Reengineering Opportunities

In an effort to increase efficiency, your college has hired you to analyze its current business processes for registering for classes. Analyze the current business processes from paying tuition to registering for classes and determine which steps in the process are:

- Broken
- Redundant
- Antiquated

Be sure to define how you would reengineer the processes for efficiency.

2. Dashboard Design

Digital dashboards offer an effective and efficient way to view enterprisewide information at near real time. According to Nucleus Research, there is a direct correlation between use of digital dashboards and a company's return on investment (ROI), hence all executives should be using or pushing the development of digital dashboards to monitor and analyze organizational operations.

Project Focus

Design a digital dashboard for a customer tracking and enterprise operations system. Be sure to address at least 4 of the following indicators with your ideas of how you would measure the indicator such as red, yellow, green status, percentage complete status, etc.:

Customer Tracking System	Enterprise Operations
Customers	Accounting
Marketing	Finance
Order entry	Logistics
Collections	Production
Sales	Distribution
Customer service	Manufacturing
Billing	Human resources
Credit limits	Sales
Transportation	Total Profit

3. Modeling a Business Process

Do you hate waiting in line at the grocery store? Do you find it frustrating when you go to the movie store and cannot find the movie you wanted to rent? Do you get annoyed when the pizza delivery person brings you the wrong order? This is your chance to reengineer the annoying process that drives you crazy. Choose a problem you are currently experiencing and reengineer the process to make it more efficient. Be sure to provide an As-Is and To-Be process model.

4. Revamping Business Processes

The following is the sales order business process for MusicMan. Draw the As-Is process model based on the following narrative:

    a. A customer submits an order for goods to MusicMan, a music retailer, through an online mechanism such as a browser-based order form. The customer supplies his or her name, the appropriate email address, the state to which the order will be shipped, the desired items (IDs and names), and the requested quantities.

    b. The order is received by a processing system, which reads the data and appends an ID number to the order.

    c. The order is forwarded to a customer service representative, who checks the customer's credit information.

    d. If the credit check fails, the customer service representative is assigned the task of notifying the customer to obtain correct credit information, and the process becomes manual from this point on.

    e. If the credit check passes, the system checks a database for the current inventory of the ordered item, according to the item ID, and it compares the quantity of items available with the quantity requested.

    f. If the amount of stock is not sufficient to accommodate the order, the order is placed on hold until new inventory arrives. When the system receives notice of new incoming inventory, it repeats step e until it can verify that the inventory is sufficient to process the order.

    g. If the inventory is sufficient, the order is forwarded simultaneously to a shipping agent who arranges shipment and an accounting agent who instructs the system to generate an invoice for the order.

    h. If the system encounters an error in processing the input necessary to calculate the total price for the invoice, including state sales tax, the accounting agent who initiated the billing process is notified and prompted to provide the correct information.

    i. The system calculates the total price of the order.

    j. The system confirms that the order has been shipped and notifies the customer via email.

    k. At any point in the transaction before shipping, the order can be cancelled by notification from the customer.

5. Revamping Accounts

The accounting department at your company deals with the processing of critical documents. These documents must arrive at their intended destination in a secure and efficient manner. Such documents include invoices, purchase orders, statements, purchase requisitions, financial statements, sales orders, and quotes.

    The current processing of documents is done manually, which causes a negative ripple effect. Documents tend to be misplaced or delayed through the mailing process. Unsecured documents are vulnerable to people making changes or seeing confidential documents. In addition, the accounting department incurs costs such as preprinted forms, inefficient distribution, and storage. Explain BPM and how it can be used to revamp the accounting department.

6. Groove City Process

You have recently purchased a local restaurant, Groove City. The restaurant offers sandwiches, baked goods, and all kinds of imported coffees and teas. You are excited to revamp the business and start making money.

Project Focus

To make your business as efficient and effective as possible you want to redesign processes to remove bottlenecks, reduce redundancies, and streamline workflow. Review the customer ordering process highlighted in the accompanying image and reengineer it to improve your business. After revamping the customer order process compile a list of additional processes you want to analyze for potential reengineering efforts. If you are looking for a real challenge, create your To-Be process diagram using PowerPoint or Visio.

Process Flow:
- (A) Counter A - Food is ordered
- (B) Counter B - Beverages are ordered and food is picked up
- (C) Counter C - Beverages are picked up
- (D) Counter D - Pay for food and beverages
- (E) Counter E - Cream, sugar, lids

BUSINESS DRIVEN BEST SELLERS

Reengineering the Corporation. By Michael Hammer and James Champy (New York: Harper Collins Publishing, 2003).

Business process reengineering reached its heyday in the early 1990s when Michael Hammer and James Champy published their best-selling book, *Reengineering the Corporation*. The authors promoted the idea that radical redesign and reorganization of an enterprise (wiping the slate clean) sometimes was necessary to lower costs and increase quality of service and that information technology was the key enabler for that radical change. Hammer and Champy believed that workflow design in most large corporations was based on invalid assumptions about technology, people, and organizational goals.[40]

The First 90 Days. By Michael Watkins, (Boston: Harvard Business School Press, 2003).

In *The First 90 Days,* Harvard Business School professor Michael Watkins presents a road map for taking charge in your first 90 days in a management job. The first days in a new position are critical because small difference in your actions can have a huge impact on long-term results.

Leaders at all levels are very vulnerable in their first few months in a new job because they lack in-depth knowledge of the challenges they will face and what it will take to succeed with their new company. Failure to create momentum in the first 90 days virtually guarantees an up-hill battle for the rest of an executive's tenure. *The First 90 Days* will equip you with strategies and tools to get up to speed faster and achieve more sooner. It will show you how to diagnose your situation and understand its challenges and opportunities. You will also learn how to assess your own strengths and weaknesses, how to quickly establish priorities, and how to manage key relationships that will help you succeed.[41]

Execution. By Larry Bossidy and Ram Charan (New York: Random House, 2002).

Organizations face many challenges in today's shaky economy—competitive battles, increased costs, decreased margins, and a host of other internal and external forces. To shore up their companies' responses to these factors, today's leaders must be able to take the goals they set for their organizations and turn them into results. Unfortunately, too many companies struggle to bridge the gap between goals and results—they create solid, logical, even bold plans, but are unable to execute properly.

Honeywell CEO Larry Bossidy and management adviser Ram Charan contend that the reason for this gap is that businesspeople do not think about execution as a discipline or a cornerstone of a business' culture—and they must. From middle management all the way up to CEO, a company's leaders must recognize execution as the most important collective set of activities in which they can engage. No more is there room for leaders who rely merely on their vision to get from goals to results; to survive, they must get more involved in the details of execution. There is much work to be done, and *Execution* shows you how to do it.[42]

3

CHAPTER

Ebusiness

SECTION 3.1	SECTION 3.2
Business and the Internet	**Ebusiness**
■ Disruptive Technology	■ Ebusiness Basics
■ Evolution of the Internet	■ Ebusiness Models
■ Accessing Internet Information	■ Organizational Strategies for Ebusiness
■ Providing Internet Information	■ Measuring Ebusiness Success
	■ Ebusiness Benefits and Challenges
	■ New Trends in Ebusiness: Egovernment and Mcommerce

CHAPTER OUTLINE

What's in IT for me?

Managers must understand the importance of doing business on the Internet and how it has revolutionized the way business is performed. Ebusiness offers new opportunities for growth and new ways of performing business activities that were simply not possible before the Internet. More than just giving organizations a means of conducting transactions, ebusiness provides companies with the ability to develop and maintain customer relationships, supplier relationships, and even employee relationships between and within enterprises.

You, as a business student, should understand the fundamental impact of the Internet on business. As future managers and organizational knowledge workers, you need to understand what benefits ebusiness can offer an organization and your career. In addition, you need to understand the challenges that come along with adoption of web technologies and how web 2.0 is impacting communication. You need to be aware of the various strategies organizations can use to deploy ebusiness, as well as recent trends and methods of measuring ebusiness success. This chapter will give you this knowledge and help prepare you for success in today's electronic global marketplace.

Amazon.com—Not Your Average Bookstore

Jeffrey Bezos, CEO and founder of Amazon.com, is running what some people refer to as the "world's biggest bookstore." The story of Bezos's virtual bookstore teaches many lessons about online business. Out of nowhere, this digital bookstore turned an industry upside down. What happened here was more than just creating a website. Bezos conceived and implemented an intelligent, global digital business. Its business is its technology; its technology is its business. Shocking traditional value chains in the bookselling industry, Amazon opened thousands of virtual bookstores in its first few months of operation.

Bezos graduated from Princeton and was the youngest vice president at Banker's Trust in New York. He had to decide if he would stay and receive his 1994 Wall Street bonus or leave and start a business on the Internet. "I tried to imagine being 80 years old, looking back on my life. I knew that I would hardly regret having missed the 1994 Wall Street bonus. But having missed being part of the Internet boom—that would have really hurt," stated Bezos. One evening he compiled a list of 20 products he believed would sell on the Internet. Books, being small-ticket items that are easy and inexpensive to ship, were on the top of the list. It was also apparent that no bookstore could conceivably stock more than a fraction of the 5 million books published annually. Bezos, who had never sold a book in his life, developed a strategic plan for selling books on the Internet. Amazon launched three years later. In the fall of 1994, Amazon filled its first book order—personally packaged by Bezos and his wife.

Amazon's Ebusiness Strategy

Amazon does not operate any physical stores. All of its sales occur through its website. It is consistently pushing the technological envelope in its search to provide a satisfying, personalized experience for its customers. What started as a human-edited list of product suggestions morphed into a sophisticated computer-generated recommendation engine. The company captures the comments and recommendations of buyers for site visitors to read—similar to the friendly salesperson in a store offering advice on which books to buy. The website tracks customer traffic, the number of visitors who access the site, how long they stay, what pages they click on, and so forth. The company uses the information to evaluate buying and selling patterns and the success of promotions. Amazon has quickly become a model success story for ebusinesses around the globe.

Amazon retains customers with website features such as personalized recommendations, online customer reviews, and "1-click ordering"—the creation of a true one-stop shopping establishment where customers can find anything they want to buy online. Through the Amazon.com Auctions, zShops (independent third-party sellers), and more recently the Amazon.com Marketplace (where customers can sell used items), the company is able to offer its customers almost everything.

Shaping Amazon's Future

Amazon released a free web service that enables its business partners (whom Amazon calls "associates") to interact with its website. More specifically, this web service allows its partners to access catalog data, to create and populate an Amazon .com shopping cart, and even to initiate the checkout process. In 16 months, the company has inspired 30,000 associates to invent new ways to extend Amazon's visibility on the Internet. With over 30 million customers, Amazon has become a household brand.[1]

Amazon's New Ventures

Amazon is always looking for new ways to take advantage of ebusiness. Here are a few of its newest creations:

- **Amazon S3:** In March 2006, Amazon launched an online storage service called Amazon Simple Storage Service (Amazon S3). Any type of data, from 1 byte to 5 gigabytes in size, can be stored on the service and the customer is charged monthly fees for data stored and transferred.
- **Unbox:** Released in March 2007, this online video-on-demand service has been criticized for its use of digital rights management.
- **Amazon MP3:** Released in September 2007, the online music store sells downloadable MP3s. Amazon MP3 is selling music from the top four record labels—EMI, Universal, Warner Music, and Sony BMG—as well as many independents; as of January 2008 it was the only store to sell DRM-free music from all top four labels.
- **Vine:** In August 2007, Amazon launched Amazon Vine, which rewards top product reviewers by providing them with free access to products from vendors participating in the program.
- **Kindle:** In November 2007, Amazon launched Amazon Kindle, an ebook reader that downloads content over "Whispernet," a free wireless service on the Sprint Nextel network. Initial offerings include approximately 90,000 books, newspapers, magazines, and blogs. The screen uses E Ink technology to reduce battery consumption.

Global Amazon

Amazon's attempt to become a global presence has been hindered by international laws. For example, Amazon's Canadian ebusiness (Amazon.ca), which operates in both English and French, is forbidden to operate any headquarters, servers, fulfillment centers, or customer service centers in Canada because of laws forbidding foreign-owned booksellers. Instead, Amazon's Canadian site originates in the United States, and Amazon has an agreement with Canada Post to handle distribution within Canada and for the use of the Crown corporation's Mississauga, Ontario, shipping facility. The launch of Amazon.ca generated controversy in Canada. In 2002, the Canadian Booksellers Association and Indigo Books and Music sought a court ruling that Amazon's partnership with Canada Post represented an attempt to circumvent Canadian law, but the litigation was dropped in 2004.

INTRODUCTION

One of the biggest forces changing business is the Internet. By age 21, California vocalist Colbie Caillat swiftly evolved from an aspiring R&B/folk singer to an American pop sensation with the marketing assistance of a little networking tool called MySpace. Caillat recorded a handful of songs, posted them on her MySpace page, and generated virtually no response for the first few months. To her astonishment, when she added the single "Bubbly" to the site, people noticed, and as word of mouth spread her page pulled in a few thousand hits a day. After she had accumulated 6,240 friends, *Rolling Stone* highlighted her as one of the top female artists on MySpace. For four months, she was the number one unsigned artist and garnered over 14 million plays. With such an appealing statistic on her résumé, record labels began courting her and she signed to Universal Republic, as her number of online friends surpassed the 100,000 mark.[2]

Ebusiness is the conducting of business on the Internet, not only buying and selling, but also serving customers and collaborating with business partners. Organizations realize that putting up simple websites for customers, employees, and partners does not create an ebusiness. Ebusiness websites must create a buzz, much as Amazon has done in the bookselling industry. Ebusiness websites must be innovative, add value, and provide useful information. In short, the site must build a sense of community and collaboration, eventually becoming the port of entry for business. Understanding ebusiness begins with understanding:

- Disruptive technology.
- Evolution of the Internet.
- Accessing Internet information.
- Providing Internet information.

section 3.1 BUSINESS AND THE INTERNET

Spawn.com

DISRUPTIVE TECHNOLOGY

Polaroid, founded in 1937, produced the first instant camera in the late 1940s. The Polaroid camera was one of the most exciting technological advances the photography industry had ever seen. By using a Polaroid camera, customers no longer had to depend on others to develop their pictures. The technology was innovative and the product was high-end. The company eventually went public, becoming one of Wall Street's most prominent enterprises, with its stock trading above $60 in 1997. In 2002, the stock was down to 8 cents and the company declared bankruptcy.[3]

How could a company like Polaroid, which had innovative technology and a captive customer base, go bankrupt? Perhaps company executives failed to use Porter's Five Forces to analyze the threat of substitute products or services. If they had, would they have noticed the two threats, one-hour film processing and digital cameras, that eventually stole Polaroid's market share? Would they have understood that their customers, people who want instant access to their pictures without having a third party involved, would be the first to use one-hour film processing and the first to purchase digital cameras? Could the company have found a way to compete with one-hour film processing and the digital camera to save Polaroid?

Most organizations face the same dilemma as Polaroid—the criteria an organization uses to make business decisions for its present business could possibly create issues for its future business. Essentially, what is best for the current business could ruin it in the long term. Some observers of our business environment have an ominous vision of the future—digital Darwinism. ***Digital Darwinism*** implies that organizations which cannot adapt to the new demands placed on them for surviving in the information age are doomed to extinction.[4]

Disruption

Disruptive versus Sustaining Technology

A ***disruptive technology*** is a new way of doing things that initially does not meet the needs of existing customers. Disruptive technologies tend to open new markets and destroy old ones. A ***sustaining technology,*** on the other hand, produces an improved product customers are eager to buy, such as a faster car or larger hard drive. Sustaining technologies tend to provide us with better, faster, and cheaper products in established markets. Incumbent companies most often lead sustaining technology to market, but virtually never lead in markets opened by disruptive technologies. Figure 3.1 displays companies that are expecting future growth to occur from new investments (disruptive technology) and companies that are expecting future growth to occur from existing investments (sustaining technology).

Disruptive technologies typically cut into the low end of the marketplace and eventually evolve to displace high-end competitors and their reigning technologies. Sony is a perfect example of a company that entered the low end of the marketplace and eventually evolved to displace its high-end competitors. Sony started as a tiny company that built portable, battery-powered transistor radios people could carry around with them. The sound quality of Sony's transistor radios was poor because the transistor amplifiers were of lower quality than traditional vacuum tubes, which produce a better sound. But, customers were willing to overlook sound quality for the convenience of portability. With the experience and revenue stream from the portables, Sony improved its technology to produce cheap, low-end transistor amplifiers that were suitable for home use and invested those revenues to improve the technology further, which produced better radios.[5]

FIGURE 3.1

Disruptive and Sustaining Technologies

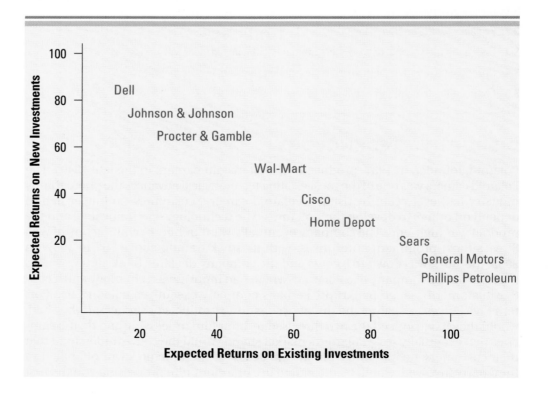

Company	Disruptive Technology
Charles Schwab	Online brokerage
Hewlett-Packard	Microprocessor-based computers; ink-jet printers
IBM	Minicomputers; personal computers
Intel	Low-end microprocessors
Intuit	QuickBooks software; TurboTax software; Quicken software
Microsoft	Internet-based computing; operating system software; SQL and Access database software
Oracle	Database software
Quantum	3.5-inch disks
Sony	Transistor-based consumer electronics

FIGURE 3.2

Companies That Capitalized on Disruptive Technology

The *Innovator's Dilemma,* a book by Clayton M. Christensen, discusses how established companies can take advantage of disruptive technologies without hindering existing relationships with customers, partners, and stakeholders. Xerox, IBM, Sears, and DEC all listened to existing customers, invested aggressively in technology, had their competitive antennae up, and still lost their market-dominant positions. Christensen states that these companies may have placed too much emphasis on satisfying customers' current needs, while neglecting to adopt new disruptive technology that will meet customers' future needs, thus causing the companies to eventually lose market share. Figure 3.2 highlights several companies that launched new businesses by capitalizing on disruptive technologies.[6]

The Internet—Business Disruption

When the Internet was in its early days, no one had any idea how massive it would become. Computer companies did not think it would be a big deal; neither did the phone companies or cable companies. Difficult to access and operate, it seemed likely to remain an arcane tool of the Defense Department and academia. However, the Internet grew, and grew, and grew. It began with a handful of users in the mid-1960s and reached 1 billion by 2005 (see Figure 3.3 and Figure 3.4). Estimates

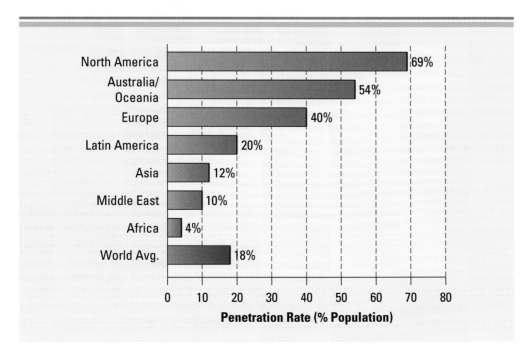

FIGURE 3.3

Internet Penetration by World Region

FIGURE 3.4

World Internet Users

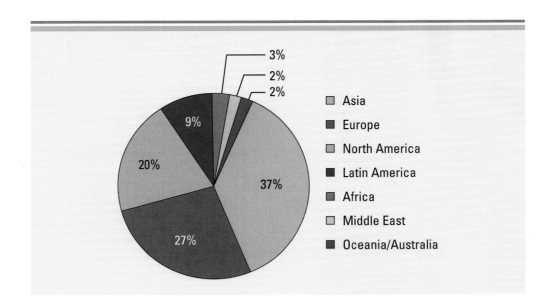

Asia	37%
Europe	27%
North America	20%
Latin America	9%
Africa	3%
Middle East	2%
Oceania/Australia	2%

Industry	Business Changes Due to Technology
Travel	Travel site Expedia.com is now the biggest leisure-travel agency, with higher profit margins than even American Express. Thirteen percent of traditional travel agencies closed in 2002 because of their inability to compete with online travel.
Entertainment	The music industry has kept Napster and others from operating, but $35 billion annual online downloads are wrecking the traditional music business. U.S. music unit sales are down 20 percent since 2000. The next big entertainment industry to feel the effects of ebusiness will be the $67 billion movie business.
Electronics	Using the Internet to link suppliers and customers, Dell dictates industry profits. Its operating margins rose from 7.3 percent in 2002 to 8 percent in 2003, even as it took prices to levels where rivals cannot make money.
Financial services	Nearly every public efinance company makes money, with online mortgage service Lending Tree growing 70 percent a year. Processing online mortgage applications is now 40 percent cheaper for customers.
Retail	Less than 5 percent of retail sales occur online. EBay is on track this year to become one of the nation's top 15 retailers, and Amazon.com will join the top 40. Wal-Mart's ebusiness strategy is forcing rivals to make heavy investments in technology.
Automobiles	The cost of producing vehicles is down because of SCM and web-based purchasing. EBay has become the leading U.S. used-car dealer, and most major car sites are profitable.
Education and training	Cisco saved $133 million in one year by moving training sessions to the Internet.

FIGURE 3.5

The Internet's Impact
on Business

predict there will be more than 3 billion Internet users by 2010. Already, villages in Indonesia and India have Internet access before they have electricity.[7] Figure 3.5 displays several ways the Internet is changing business.

EVOLUTION OF THE INTERNET

During the Cold War in the mid-1960s, the U.S. military decided it needed a bomb-proof communications system, and thus the concept for the Internet was born. The system would link computers throughout the country, allowing messages to get through even if a large section of the country was destroyed. In the early days, the only linked computers were at government think tanks and a few universities. The Internet was essentially an emergency military communications system operated by the Department of Defense's Advanced Research Project Agency (ARPA) and called ARPANET. Formally defined, the **Internet** is a global public network of computer networks that pass information from one to another using common computer protocols. **Protocols** are standards that specify the format of data as well as the rules to be followed during transmission.

In time, every university in the United States that had defense-related funding installed ARPANET computers. Gradually, the Internet moved from a military pipeline to a communications tool for scientists. As more scholars came online, system administration transferred from ARPA to the National Science Foundation. Years later, businesses began using the Internet, and the administrative responsibilities were once again transferred. Today, no one party operates the Internet; however, several entities oversee the Internet and set standards including:

- Internet Engineering Task Force (IETF): The protocol engineering and development arm of the Internet.
- Internet Architecture Board (IAB): Responsible for defining the overall architecture of the Internet, providing guidance and broad direction to the IETF.
- Internet Engineering Steering Group (IESG): Responsible for technical management of IETF activities and the Internet standards process.

Evolution of the World Wide Web

Internet

People often interchange the terms *Internet* and the *World Wide Web,* but these terms are not synonymous. Throughout the 1960s, 1970s, and 1980s, the Internet was primarily used by the Department of Defense to support activities such as email and transferring files. The Internet was restricted to noncommercial activities, and its users included government employees, researchers, university professors, and students. The World Wide Web changed the purpose and use of the Internet.

Some hobbies change the world. In 1994, Stanford Ph.D. students Jerry Yang and David Filo posted a list of their favorite sites on the web. The exact date they posted the links is lost to history, but we do know the list's original name: "Jerry and David's Guide to the World Wide Web." By April 1994, it had a new tongue-in-cheek name: "Yet Another Hierarchical Officious Oracle," or *Yahoo!* for short. Yahoo! represented the first attempt to catalog the web, offering directory-style listings of every site that mattered—with tiny sunglasses marking sites deemed truly cool. When providing exhaustive coverage became impossible, Yahoo! was reborn as a Web portal, combining the directory with search, news headlines, instant messaging, email, photo hosting, job listings, and assorted other services. As other major portals such as Lycos and Excite died off or were consumed by bigger fish, Yahoo! continued to expand. Though surpassed by the Google search juggernaut, Yahoo! remains a true Internet icon.

The **World Wide Web (WWW)** is a global hypertext system that uses the Internet as its transport mechanism. **Hypertext transport protocol (HTTP)** is the Internet standard that supports the exchange of information on the WWW. By defining universal resource locators (URLs) and how they can be used to retrieve resources anywhere on the Internet, HTTP enables web authors to embed hyperlinks in web documents. HTTP defines the process by which a web client, called a browser, originates a request for information and sends it to a web server, a program designed to respond to HTTP requests and provide the desired information. In a hypertext system, users navigate by clicking a hyperlink embedded in the current document. The action displays a second document in the same or a separate browser window. The web has quickly become the ideal medium for publishing information on the Internet and serves as the platform for the electronic economy. Figure 3.6 displays the reasons for the popularity and growth in the WWW.

The WWW remained primarily text-based until 1991 when two events occurred that would forever change the web and the amount and quality of information available (see Figure 3.7). First, Tim Berners-Lee built the first website on August 6, 1991 (http://info.cern.ch/—the site has been archived). The site provided details about the World Wide Web including how to build a browser and set up a web server.

FIGURE 3.6

Reasons for World Wide
Web Growth

Reasons for Growth of the World Wide Web

- The microcomputer revolution made it possible for an average person to own a computer.
- Advancements in networking hardware, software, and media made it possible for business PCs to be inexpensively connected to larger networks.
- Browser software such as Microsoft's Internet Explorer and Netscape Navigator gave computer users an easy-to-use graphical interface to find, download, and display web pages.
- The speed, convenience, and low cost of email have made it an incredibly popular tool for business and personal communications.
- Basic web pages are easy to create and extremely flexible.

FIGURE 3.7

The Internet's Impact on
Information

Internet's Impact on Information	
Easy to compile	Searching for information on products, prices, customers, suppliers, and partners is faster and easier when using the Internet.
Increased richness	*Information richness* refers to the depth and breadth of information transferred between customers and businesses. Businesses and customers can collect and track more detailed information when using the Internet.
Increased reach	*Information reach* refers to the number of people a business can communicate with, on a global basis. Businesses can share information with numerous customers all over the world.
Improved content	A key element of the Internet is its ability to provide dynamic relevant content. Buyers need good content descriptions to make informed purchases, and sellers use content to properly market and differentiate themselves from the competition. Content and product description establish the common understanding between both parties to the transaction. As a result, the reach and richness of that content directly affects the transaction.

It also housed the world's first web directory, since Berners-Lee later maintained a list of other websites apart from his own.[8]

Second, Marc Andreesen developed a new computer program called the NCSA Mosaic (National Center for Supercomputing Applications at the University of Illinois) and gave it away! The browser made it easier to access the websites that had started to appear. Soon websites contained more than just text; they also had sound and video files (see Figure 3.8). These pages, written in the hypertext markup language (HTML), have links that allow the user to quickly move from one document to another, even when the documents are stored in different computers. Web browsers read the HTML text and convert it into a web page.[9]

FIGURE 3.8

File Formats Offered
over the WWW

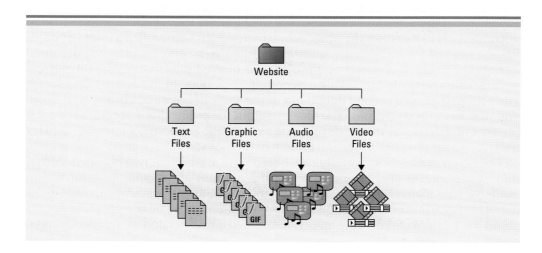

By eliminating time and distance, the Internet makes it possible to perform business in ways not previously imaginable. The ***digital divide*** is when those with access to technology have great advantages over those without access to technology. People living in the village of Siroha, India, must bike five miles to find a telephone. For over 700 million rural people living in India, the digital divide was a way of life, until recently. Media Lab Asia sells telephony and email services via a mobile Internet kiosk mounted on a bicycle, which is known as an "info-thelas." The kiosk has an onboard computer equipped with an antenna for Internet service and a specially designed all-day battery. Over 2,000 villages have purchased the kiosk for $1,200, and another 600,000 villages are interested.[10]

WEB 2.0

Web 2.0's vast disruptive impact is just beginning. ***Web 2.0*** is a set of economic, social, and technology trends that collectively form the basis for the next generation of the Internet—a more mature, distinctive medium characterized by user participation, openness, and network effects. Although the term suggests a new version of the World Wide Web, it does not refer to an update to web technical specifications; instead, it refers to changes in the ways software developers and end users use the web as a platform. According to Tim O'Reilly, "Web 2.0 is the business revolution in the computer industry caused by the move to the Internet as platform, and an attempt to understand the rules for success on that new platform." Figure 3.9 displays the move from web 1.0 to web 2.0, and Figure 3.10 displays the timeline of web 1.0 and web 2.0.[11]

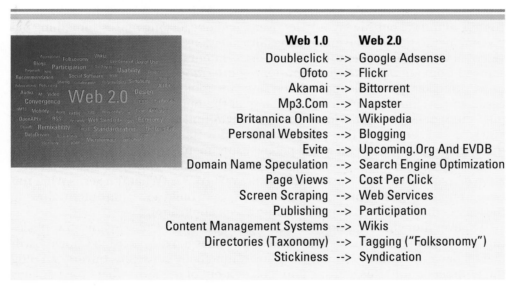

FIGURE 3.9

The Move from Web 1.0 to Web 2.0

FIGURE 3.10

Timeline of Web 1.0

More than just the latest technology buzzword, web 2.0 is a transformative force that is propelling companies across all industries toward a new way of doing business. Those who act on the web 2.0 opportunity stand to gain an early-mover advantage in their markets. What is causing this change? Consider the following raw demographic and technological drivers:

- One billion people around the globe now have access to the Internet.
- Mobile devices outnumber desktop computers by a factor of two.
- Nearly 50 percent of all U.S. Internet access is now via always-on broadband connections.[12]

Combine these drivers with the fundamental laws of social networks and lessons from the web's first decade, and you get web 2.0, the next-generation, user-driven, intelligent web:

- In the first quarter of 2006, MySpace.com signed up 280,000 new users each day and had the second most Internet traffic of any website.
- By the second quarter of 2006, 50 million blogs were created—new ones were added at a rate of two per second.
- In 2005, eBay conducted 8 billion API-based web services transactions.[13]

Mashups

A *web mashup* is a website or web application that uses content from more than one source to create a completely new service. The term is typically used in the context of music; putting Jay-Z lyrics over a Radiohead song makes something old become new. The web version of a mashup allows users to mix map data, photos, video, news feeds, blog entries, and so on. Content used in mashups is typically sourced from an *application programming interface (API)*, which is a set of routines, protocols, and tools for building software applications. A good API makes it easier to develop a program by providing all the building blocks. A programmer puts the blocks together. Most operating environments, such as Microsoft Windows, provide an API so that programmers can write applications consistent with the operating environment. Many people experimenting with mashups are using Microsoft, Google, eBay, Amazon, Flickr, and Yahoo APIs, which has led to the creation of mashup editors. *Mashup editors* are WYSIWYGs (What You See Is What You Get) for mashups. They provide a visual interface to build a mashup, often allowing the user to drag and drop data points into a web application.

Whoever thought technology could help sell bananas? Dole Organic now places three-digit farm codes on each banana and creates a mashup using Google Earth and its banana database. Socially and environmentally conscious buyers can plug the numbers into Dole's website and look at a bio of the farm where the bananas were raised. The site tells the story of the farm and its surrounding community, lists its organic certifications, posts some photos, and offers a link to satellite images of the farm in Google Earth. Customers can personally monitor the production and treatment of their fruit from the tree to the grocer. The process assures customers that their bananas have been raised to proper organic standards on an environmentally friendly, holistically minded plantation.

Corporations from IBM to Google to E*Trade are jumping onboard the trend of mixing and matching software from different sources.[14] Here are a few examples:

- **1001 Secret Fishing Holes:** over a thousand fishing spots in national parks, wildlife refuges, lakes, campgrounds, historic trails, etc. (Google Maps API).
- **25 Best Companies to Work For:** map of the 100 best U.S. companies to work for as rated by *Fortune* magazine (Google Maps API).
- **Album Covers:** uses the Amazon API and an Ajax-style user interface to retrieve CD/DVD covers from the Amazon catalog (Amazon eCommerce API).

- **Gawker:** a handy mashup for keeping up with celebrity sightings in New York City. Readers are encouraged to email as soon as the celeb is spotted (Google Maps API).
- **Gigul8tor:** provides a data entry page where bands can enter information about upcoming gigs and venues. Gigul8tor displays a list of possible locations depending on the venue engine and enters event information right into Eventful in an interface designed just for bands. It shows how different user interfaces could be built in front of Eventful with mashup techniques.
- **GBlinker:** a Google pin wired to a serial port so it flashes when email arrives.
- **OpenKapow:** offers a platform for creating web-based APIs, feeds, and HTML snippets from any website, taking mashup possibilities way beyond the more than 300 APIs offered on ProgrammableWeb.
- **The Hype Machine:** combines blog posts from a set of curated music blogs with Amazon sales data and upcoming events. The Hype Machine tracks songs and discussion posted on the best blogs about music. It integrates with iTunes to take customers right from the web page to the track they are interested in. If the customer prefers buying through Amazon, The Hype Machine figures out what CD page to display.
- **Zillow:** sophisticated home valuation tools with 65 million listings and extensive data on comparables (Microsoft Virtual Earth API).
- **ProgrammableWeb:** the favorite community website of mashup developers; provides comprehensive listings of APIs available on the web and includes forums where developers can discuss how to best use them.[15]

THE FUTURE—WEB 3.0

Web 3.0 is a term that has been coined with different meanings to describe the evolution of web usage and interaction among several separate paths. These include transforming the web into a database, a move toward making content accessible by multiple nonbrowser applications, the leveraging of artificial intelligence technologies, or the semantic web. The ***semantic web*** is an evolving extension of the World Wide Web in which web content can be expressed not only in natural language, but also in a format that can be read and used by software agents, thus permitting them to find, share, and integrate information more easily. It derives from W3C director Sir Tim Berners-Lee's vision of the web as a universal medium for data, information, and knowledge exchange. There is considerable debate as to what the term *web 3.0* means, but many agree it encompasses one or more of the following:

1. Transforming the web into a database.
2. An evolutionary path to artificial intelligence.
3. The realization of semantic web and service-oriented architecture.
4. Evolution toward 3D.[16]

Transforming the Web into a Database

The first step toward a web 3.0 is the emergence of the data-driven web as structured data records are published to the web in formats that are reusable and able to be queried remotely. Because of the recent growth of standardized query language for searching across distributed databases on the web, the data-driven web enables a new level of data integration and application interoperability, making data as openly accessible and linkable as web pages. The data-driven web is the first step on the path toward the full semantic web. In the data-driven web phase, the focus is on making structured data available using databases. The full semantic web stage will widen the scope such that both structured data and even what is traditionally thought of as unstructured or semistructured content (such as web pages, documents, email, etc.) will be widely available in common formats.

An Evolutionary Path to Artificial Intelligence

Web 3.0 has also been used to describe an evolutionary path for the web that leads to artificial intelligence that can reason about the web in a quasi-human fashion. Some skeptics regard this as an unobtainable vision. However, companies such as IBM and Google are implementing new technologies that are yielding surprising information, such as predicting hit songs by mining information on college music websites. There is also debate over whether the driving force behind web 3.0 will be intelligent systems, or whether intelligence will emerge in a more organic fashion, from systems of intelligent people, such as via collaborative filtering services like del.icio.us, Flickr, and Digg that extract meaning and order from the existing web and how people interact with it.[17]

The Realization of the Semantic Web and SOA

Related to the artificial intelligence direction, web 3.0 could be the realization of a possible convergence of the semantic web and service-oriented architecture (SOA). A **service-oriented architecture (SOA)** is a business-driven IT architectural approach that supports integrating a business as linked, repeatable tasks or services. SOA is basically a collection of services that communicate with each other, for example, passing data from one service to another or coordinating an activity between one or more services. Companies have longed to integrate existing systems in order to implement information technology support for business processes that cover the entire business value chain. The main drivers for SOA adoption are that it links computational resources and promotes their reuse. SOA is covered in detail in Chapter 5.

Enterprise architects believe that SOA can help businesses respond more quickly and cost-effectively to changing market conditions. This style of architecture can simplify interconnection to—and usage of—existing IT (legacy) assets.[18]

Evolution Toward 3D

Another possible path for web 3.0 is toward the three-dimensional vision championed by the Web3D Consortium. This would involve the web transforming into a series of 3D spaces, taking the concept realized by Second Life further. This could open up new ways to connect and collaborate using 3D shared spaces.

ACCESSING INTERNET INFORMATION

Many restaurant and franchise experts believe that Cold Stone Creamery's franchisee intranet is what keeps the company on the fast track. Franchisee owners communicate with other owners through Creamery Talk, the company's intranet-based chat room. Since it launched, Creamery Talk has turned into a franchisee's black book, with tips on everything from storefront design to equipment repair. When one owner's freezer broke recently, a post to the chat room turned up an easy fix involving a $21 motor fan.[19]

Four common tools for accessing Internet information include:

- Intranet
- Extranet
- Portal
- Kiosk

Intranet

An **intranet** is an internalized portion of the Internet, protected from outside access, that allows an organization to provide access to information and application software to only its employees. An intranet is an invaluable tool for presenting organizational information as it provides a central location for employees. It can host all kinds of company-related information such as benefits, schedules, strategic directions, and employee directories. At many companies, each department has its own web page on the intranet for departmental information sharing. An intranet is not necessarily open to the external Internet and enables organizations to make internal resources available using familiar Internet clients, such as web browsers, newsreaders, and email.

Intranet publishing is the ultimate in electronic publishing. Companies realize significant returns on investment (ROI) simply by publishing information, such as employee manuals or telephone directories, on intranets rather than printed media.

Citigroup's Global Corporate and Investment Banking division uses an intranet to provide its entire IT department with access to all IT projects including information on project owners, delivery dates, key resources, budget information, and project metrics. Providing this information via an intranet, or one convenient location, has enabled Citigroup to gain a 15 percent improvement in IT project delivery.[20]

Extranet

An **extranet** is an intranet that is available to strategic allies (such as customers, suppliers, and partners). Many companies are building extranets as they begin to realize the benefit of offering individuals outside the organization access to intranet-based information and application software such as order processing. Having a common area where employees, partners, vendors, and customers access information can be a major competitive advantage for an organization.

Wal-Mart created an extranet for its suppliers, which can view detailed product information at all Wal-Mart locations. Suppliers log on to Wal-Mart's extranet and view metrics on products such as current inventory, orders, forecasts, and marketing campaigns. This helps Wal-Mart's suppliers maintain their supply chains and ensure Wal-Mart never runs out of products.[21]

Portal

Portal is a very generic term for what is in essence a technology that provides access to information. A **portal** is a website that offers a broad array of resources and services, such as email, online discussion groups, search engines, and online shopping malls.

Not so long ago, the only way to get any return on the junk in your garage was to hold a yard sale. EBay changed all that. Now tens of thousands of small and medium-size businesses use eBay as their primary storefront, bringing ecommerce to the people. According to eBay lore, the first item auctioned was a broken laser pointer that sold for $14.83, proving that someone somewhere will buy just about anything. Several billion dollars' worth of transactions later, the proof is on firmer ground than ever.

There are general portals and specialized or niche portals. Leading general portals include Yahoo!, Netscape, Microsoft, and America Online. Examples of niche portals include Garden.com (for gardeners), Fool.com (for investors), and Search-Networking.com (for network administrators).

Pratt & Whitney, one of the largest aircraft-engine manufacturers in the world, has saved millions of dollars with its field service portal initiative. Pratt & Whitney's sales and service field offices are geographically scattered around the globe and were connected via expensive dedicated lines. The company saved $2.6 million annually by replacing the dedicated lines with high-speed Internet access to its field service portal. Field staff can find information they need in a fraction of the time it took before. The company estimates this change will save another $8 million per year in "process and opportunity" savings.[22]

Kiosk

A **kiosk** is a publicly accessible computer system that has been set up to allow interactive information browsing. In a kiosk, the computer's operating system has been hidden from view, and the program runs in a full-screen mode, which provides a few simple tools for navigation.

Jason Suker walked into the Mazda showroom in Bountiful, Utah, and quickly found what he was looking for in a car dealership—a web kiosk, one of six stationed around the showroom. Using the kiosk, he could track down the latest pricing information from sites like Kelley Blue Book and Edmunds.com. Suker, eyeing a four-year-old limited-edition Miata in mint condition, quickly pulled up the average retail price on Kelley Blue Book. At $16,000, it was $500 more than the dealer's price. Then, on eBay, Suker checked bids for similar models and found they were going for far less. With a sales representative looking over his shoulder to confirm his findings, the skeptical Suker made a lowball offer and expected the worst: endless haggling over price. However, the sales representative, after commending Suker for his research talent, eventually compromised and offered up the Miata for $13,300.

It was an even better deal for Bountiful Mazda. By using a kiosk to help Suker find the bargain price he wanted, the dealership moved a used car (with a higher profit margin than a new model) and opened the door to the unexpected up-sell with a $1,300, 36,000-mile service warranty.[23]

PROVIDING INTERNET INFORMATION

British Airways, the $11.9 billion airline, outsourced the automation of its FAQ (frequently asked questions) web pages. The airline needed to automatically develop, manage, and post different sets of FAQs for British Airway's loyalty program customers, allowing the company to offer special promotions based on the customer's loyalty program status (gold, silver, bronze). The company outsourced the project to application service provider RightNow Technologies. The new system is helping British Airways create the right marketing programs for the appropriate customer tier.[24]

The three common forms of service providers are:

1. Internet service provider (ISP).
2. Online service provider (OSP).
3. Application service provider (ASP).

Internet Service Provider

An ***Internet service provider (ISP)*** is a company that provides individuals and other companies access to the Internet along with additional related services, such as website building. An ISP has the equipment and the telecommunication line access required to have a point of presence on the Internet for different geographic areas. Larger ISPs have their own high-speed leased lines so they are less dependent on telecommunication providers and can deliver better service to their customers. Among the largest national and regional ISPs are AT&T WorldNet, IBM Global Network, MCI, Netcom, UUNet, and PSINet.

Navigating the different options for an ISP can be daunting and confusing. There are more than 7,000 ISPs in the United States; some are large with household names, and others are literally one-person operations. Although Internet access is viewed as a commodity service, in reality features and performance can differ tremendously among ISPs. Figure 3.11 highlights common ISP features.

Another member of the ISP family is the ***wireless Internet service provider (WISP),*** an ISP that allows subscribers to connect to a server at designated hotspots or access points using a wireless connection. This type of ISP offers access to the Internet and the web from anywhere within the zone of coverage provided by an antenna. This is usually a region with a radius of one mile. Figure 3.12 displays a brief overview of how this technology works.

One example of a WISP is T-Mobile International, a company that provides access to wireless laptop users in more than 2,000 locations including airports, airline clubs, Starbucks coffeehouses, and Borders Books. A wireless service called T-Mobile Hot-Spot allows customers to access the Internet and T-Mobile's corporate intranet via a wireless network from convenient locations away from their home or office. T-Mobile International is the first mobile communications company to extend service on both sides of the Atlantic, offering customers the advantage of using their wireless services when traveling worldwide.[25]

FIGURE 3.11

Common ISP Services

Common ISP Services
■ **Web hosting.** Housing, serving, and maintaining files for one or more websites is a widespread offering.
■ **Hard-disk storage space.** Smaller sites may need only 300 to 500 MB (megabytes) of website storage space, whereas other ebusiness sites may need at least 10 GB (gigabytes) of space or their own dedicated web server.
■ **Availability.** To run an ebusiness, a site must be accessible to customers 24 × 7. ISPs maximize the availability of the sites they host using techniques such as load balancing and clustering many servers to reach 100 percent availability.
■ **Support.** A big part of turning to an ISP is that there is limited worry about keeping the web server running. Most ISPs offer 24 × 7 customer service.

FIGURE 3.12

Wireless Access Diagram

Online Service Provider

An ***online service provider (OSP)*** offers an extensive array of unique services such as its own version of a web browser. The term *online service provider* helps to distinguish ISPs that offer Internet access and their own online content, such as America Online (AOL), from ISPs that simply connect users directly with the Internet, such as EarthLink. Connecting to the Internet through an OSP is an alternative to connecting through one of the national ISPs, such as AT&T or MCI, or a regional or local ISP.

Application Service Provider

An ***application service provider (ASP)*** is a company that offers an organization access over the Internet to systems and related services that would otherwise have to be located in personal or organizational computers. Employing the services of an ASP is essentially outsourcing part of a company's business logic. Hiring an ASP to manage a company's software allows the company to hand over the operation, maintenance, and upgrade responsibilities for a system to the ASP.

One of the most important agreements between the customer and the ASP is the service level agreement. ***Service level agreements (SLAs)*** define the specific responsibilities of the service provider and set the customer expectations. SLAs include such items as availability, accessibility, performance, maintenance, backup/recovery,

Company	Description	Specialty
Appshop www.appshop.com	Application service provider	Oracle 11i ebusiness suite applications
BlueStar Solutions www.bluestarsolutions.com	Application service provider	Managing ERP solutions with a focus on SAP
Concur www.concur.com	Internet service provider	Integrates B2B procurement
Corio www.corio.com	Application service provider	Specializes in Oracle applications
Employease www.employease.com	Online service provider	Human resource applications services
Intacct www.intacct.com	Online service provider	Online general ledger service
LivePerson www.liveperson.com	Online service provider	Real-time chat provider
NetLedger www.netledger.com	Online service provider	Web-based accounting platform
Outtask www.outtask.com	Application service provider	Integration of budgeting, customer service, sales management, and human resources applications
RightNow www.rightnow.com	Online service provider, Internet service provider	Suite of customer service applications
Salesforce.com www.salesforce.com	Online service provider	Suite of customer service applications
Salesnet www.salesnet.com	Online service provider	Suite of sales force automation products and services
Surebridge www.surebridge.com	Application service provider	High-tech manufacturing, distribution, health care applications
UpShot www.upshot.com	Online service provider	Sales force automation products and services
USi www.usinternetworking.com	Application service provider	Ariba, Siebel, Microsoft, and Oracle customer base

FIGURE 3.13

Top ISPs, OSPs, and ASPs

upgrades, equipment ownership, software ownership, security, and confidentiality. For example, an SLA might state that the ASP must have the software available and accessible from 7:00 a.m. to 7:00 p.m. Monday through Friday. It might also state that if the system is down for more than 60 minutes, there will be no charge for that day. Most industry analysts agree that the ASP market is growing rapidly. International Data Corporation (IDC) expected the worldwide ASP market to grow from around $13 billion in 2005 to $23 billion by 2008.[26] Figure 3.13 displays the top ISPs, OSPs, and ASPs.

OPENING CASE QUESTIONS

Amazon.com—Not Your Average Bookstore

1. How has Amazon used technology to revamp the bookselling industry?
2. Is Amazon using disruptive or sustaining technology to run its business?
3. How is Amazon using intranets and extranets to run its business?
4. How could Amazon use kiosks to improve its business?

section 3.2 EBUSINESS

LEARNING OUTCOMES

3.6. Compare the four types of ebusiness models.

3.7. Describe how an organization's marketing, sales, accounting, and customer service departments can use ebusiness to increase revenues or reduce costs.

3.8. Explain why an organization would use metrics to determine a website's success.

3.9. Describe ebusiness along with its benefits and challenges.

3.10. Define mcommerce and explain how an egovernment could use it to increase its efficiency and effectiveness.

Night Agency

EBUSINESS BASICS

In 2003, Tom Anderson and Chris DeWolf started MySpace, a social networking website that offers its members information about the independent music scene around the country representing both Internet culture and teenage culture. Musicians sign up for free MySpace home pages where they can post tour dates, songs, and lyrics. Fans sign up for their own web pages to link to favorite bands and friends. MySpace is now the world's fifth most popular English-language website with over 100 million users.[27]

One of the biggest benefits of the Internet is its ability to allow organizations to perform business with anyone, anywhere, anytime. **Ecommerce** is the buying and selling of goods and services over the Internet. Ecommerce refers only to online transactions. **Ebusiness,** derived from the term ecommerce, is the conducting of business on the Internet, not only buying and selling, but also serving customers and collaborating with business partners. The primary difference between ecommerce and ebusiness is that ebusiness also refers to online exchanges of information, such as a manufacturer allowing its suppliers to monitor production schedules or a financial institution allowing its customers to review their banking, credit card, and mortgage accounts.

In the past few years, ebusiness seems to have permeated every aspect of daily life. Both individuals and organizations have embraced Internet technologies to enhance productivity, maximize convenience, and improve communications globally. From banking to shopping to entertainment, the Internet has become integral to daily life. Figure 3.14 provides examples of a few industries using ebusiness.

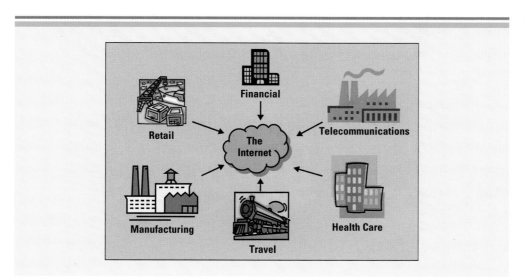

FIGURE 3.14

Overview of Several Industries Using Ebusiness

Ebusiness Term	Definition
Business-to-business (B2B)	Applies to businesses buying from and selling to each other over the Internet.
Business-to-consumer (B2C)	Applies to any business that sells its products or services to consumers over the Internet.
Consumer-to-business (C2B)	Applies to any consumer that sells a product or service to a business over the Internet.
Consumer-to-consumer (C2C)	Applies to sites primarily offering goods and services to assist consumers interacting with each other over the Internet.

	Business	Consumer
Business	B2B	B2C
Consumer	C2B	C2C

FIGURE 3.15

Basic Ebusiness Models

EBUSINESS MODELS

A **ebusiness model** is an approach to conducting electronic business on the Internet. Ebusiness transactions take place between two major entities—businesses and consumers. All ebusiness activities happen within the framework of two types of business relationships: (1) the exchange of products and services between businesses (business-to-business, or B2B) and (2) the exchange of products and services with consumers (business-to-consumer, or B2C) (see Figure 3.15).

The primary difference between B2B and B2C are the customers; B2B customers are other businesses while B2C markets to consumers. Overall, B2B relations are more complex and have higher security needs; plus B2B is the dominant ebusiness force, representing 80 percent of all online business.[28] Figure 3.16 illustrates all

FIGURE 3.16

Ebusiness Models

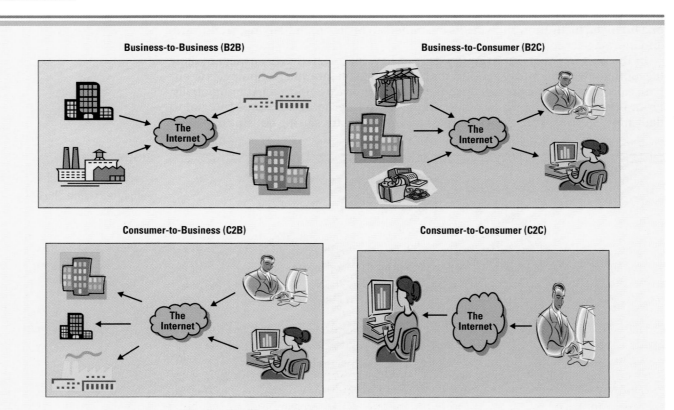

FIGURE 3.17

Business-to-Business
Emarketplace Overview

the ebusiness models: Business-to-business, business-to-consumer, consumer-to-consumer, and consumer-to-business.

Business-to-Business (B2B)

Business-to-business (B2B) applies to businesses buying from and selling to each other over the Internet. Online access to data, including expected shipping date, delivery date, and shipping status, provided either by the seller or a third-party provider is widely supported by B2B models. Electronic marketplaces represent a new wave in B2B ebusiness models. ***Electronic marketplaces,*** or ***emarketplaces,*** are interactive business communities providing a central market where multiple buyers and sellers can engage in ebusiness activities (see Figure 3.17). They present structures for conducting commercial exchange, consolidating supply chains, and creating new sales channels. Their primary goal is to increase market efficiency by tightening and automating the relationship between buyers and sellers. Existing emarketplaces allow access to various mechanisms in which to buy and sell almost anything, from services to direct materials.

Ebusiness

Business-to-Consumer (B2C)

Business-to-consumer (B2C) applies to any business that sells its products or services to consumers over the Internet. Carfax has been in the vehicle history report business for 20 years with an original customer base of used-car dealers. "The Internet was just a new way for us to reach the consumer market," Carfax President Dick Raines said. Carfax spent $20 million on print and TV ads to attract customers to its website. Customers can purchase a Carfax report for $14.95 or six days of reports for $19.95. Carfax has now launched a partnership program for small auto dealers' websites and a cash-back program offering customers 20 percent of revenues received for their referrals. "We continue to look for more and more ways to add value," Raines said.[29] Common B2C ebusiness models include eshops and emalls.

Eshop An ***eshop,*** sometimes referred to as an ***estore*** or ***etailer,*** is a version of a retail store where customers can shop at any hour of the day without leaving their home or office. These online stores sell and support a variety of products and services. The online businesses channeling their goods and services via the Internet only, such as Amazon.com, are called pure plays. The others are an extension of traditional retail outlets that sell online as well as through a traditional physical store. They are generally known as "bricks and clicks" or "click and mortar" organizations, such as the Gap (www.gap.com) and Best Buy (www.bestbuy.com) (see Figure 3.18).

Emall An ***emall*** consists of a number of eshops; it serves as a gateway through which a visitor can access other eshops. An emall may be generalized or specialized depending on the products offered by the eshops it hosts. Revenues for emall operators include membership fees from participating eshops, advertising, and possibly a fee on each transaction if the emall operator also processes payments. Eshops in emalls benefit from brand reinforcement and increased traffic as visiting

FIGURE 3.18

Types of Businesses

Business Types	
Brick-and-mortar business	A business that operates in a physical store without an Internet presence.
Pure-play (virtual) business	A business that operates on the Internet only without a physical store. Examples include Amazon.com and Expedia.com.
Click-and-mortar business	A business that operates in a physical store and on the Internet. Examples include REI and Barnes and Noble.

FIGURE 3.19

Online Auctions

Online Auctions	
Electronic Auction (e-auction)	Sellers and buyers solicit consecutive bids from each other and prices are determined dynamically.
Forward Auction	An auction that sellers use as a selling channel to many buyers and the highest bid wins.
Reverse Auction	An auction that buyers use to purchase a product or service, selecting the seller with the lowest bid.

one shop on the emall often leads to browsing "neighboring" shops. An example of an emall is the Arizona emall www.1az1.com/shopping.

Consumer-to-Business (C2B)

Consumer-to-business (C2B) applies to any consumer that sells a product or service to a business over the Internet. One example of this ebusiness model is Priceline.com where bidders (or customers) set their prices for items such as airline tickets or hotel rooms, and a seller decides whether to supply them. The demand for C2B ebusiness will increase over the next few years due to customers' desire for greater convenience and lower prices.

Consumer-to-Consumer (C2C)

Consumer-to-consumer (C2C) applies to sites primarily offering goods and services to assist consumers interacting with each other over the Internet. EBay, the Internet's most successful C2C online auction website, links like-minded buyers and sellers for a small commission. Figure 3.19 displays the different types of online auctions.

C2C online communities, or virtual communities, interact via email groups, web-based discussion forums, or chat rooms. C2C business models are consumer-driven and opportunities are available to satisfy most consumers' needs, ranging from finding a mortgage to job hunting. They are global swap shops based on customer-centered communication. One C2C community, KazaA, allows users to download MP3 music files, enabling users to exchange files. Figure 3.20 highlights the different types of C2C communities that are thriving on the Internet.

Like many seminal web events, Craigslist started as a quirky side project seemingly devoid of commercial possibilites. In March 1995, Craig Newmark quit his job

FIGURE 3.20

C2C Communities

C2C Communities
■ **Communities of interest**—People interact with each other on specific topics, such as golfing and stamp collecting.
■ **Communities of relations**—People come together to share certain life experiences, such as cancer patients, senior citizens, and car enthusiasts.
■ **Communities of fantasy**—People participate in imaginary environments, such as fantasy football teams and playing one-on-one with Michael Jordan.

as a software architect for Charles Schwab in San Francisco and started a mailing list where subscribers could share information about interesting cultural events in the Bay Area. "I was reflecting on how much people helped each other out on the Net, in those days, on the WELL and usenet news groups," he says via email. As the list grew, people began posting messages looking for apartments, jobs, and other topics. In October 1995, Craig turned his private list into a public website at Cnewmark.com. In September 1997, Craig's list became Craigslist.org. In early 1998, the site began charging a nominal fee for job listings (though the vast majority of ads remain free), and in 1999 Craigslist.org incorporated and began paying its employees. Today, there are 450 local versions of Craigslist in 50 countries, and more than 25 million people visit them each month. The service has been credited with (or blamed for, depending on your point of view) taking the classified ad market away from established newspapers. But Craigslist's greatest contribution may be in proving that, like politics, the greatest global movements are always local.

ORGANIZATIONAL STRATEGIES FOR EBUSINESS

To be successful in ebusiness, an organization must master the art of electronic relationships. Traditional means of customer acquisition such as advertising, promotions, and public relations are just as important with a website. Primary business areas taking advantage of ebusiness include:

- Marketing/sales
- Financial services
- Procurement
- Customer service
- Intermediaries

Marketing/Sales

Direct selling was the earliest type of ebusiness and has proven to be a stepping-stone to more complex commerce operations. Successes such as eBay, Barnes and Noble, Dell Inc., and Travelocity have sparked the growth of this segment, proving customer acceptance of ebusiness direct selling. Marketing and sales departments are initiating some of the most exciting ebusiness innovations (see Figure 3.21).

Cincinnati's WCPO-TV was a ratings blip in 2002 and is now the number three ABC affiliate in the nation. WCPO-TV credits its success largely to digital billboards that promote different programming depending on the time of day. The billboards are updated directly from a website. The station quickly noticed that when current events for the early-evening news were plugged during the afternoon, ratings spiked.

The digital billboards let several companies share one space and can change messages directly from the company's computer. In the morning, a department store can advertise a sale, and in the afternoon, a restaurant can advertise its specials. Eventually customers will be able to buy billboard sign time in hour or minute increments. Current costs to share a digital billboard are $40,000 a month, compared with $10,000 for one standard billboard.[30]

Ebusiness provides an easy way to penetrate a new geographic territory and extend global reach. Large, small, or specialized businesses can use their online sales sites to sell on a worldwide basis with little extra cost. This ability to tap into expanded domestic or even international markets can be an immediate revenue boost to artists, jewelry makers, wineries, and the like, for initial orders and especially for reorders.

The Hotel Gatti (www.hotel-gatti.com) is a small hotel in northern Italy catering primarily to Italian travelers. By introducing its own website with English-language options, it significantly extended its geographic reach. Now, at very little cost, the hotel communicates with and takes reservations from potential customers in the United States and other English-speaking countries. The bottom line is that ebusiness now allows any company to market and sell products globally, regardless of its size.[31]

Marketing and Sales Ebusiness Innovations

- An **online ad** is a box running across a web page that is often used to contain advertisements. The banner generally contains a link to the advertiser's website. Web-based advertising services can track the number of times users click the banner, generating statistics that enable advertisers to judge whether the advertising fees are worth paying. Banner ads are like living, breathing classified ads.

- A **pop-up ad** is a small web page containing an advertisement that appears on the web page outside of the current website loaded in the browser. A **pop-under ad** is a form of a pop-up ad that users do not see until they close the current web browser screen.

- **Associate programs (affiliate programs)** allow businesses to generate commissions or royalties from an Internet site. For example, a business can sign up as an associate of a major commercial site such as Amazon. The business then sends potential buyers to the Amazon site using a code or banner ad. The business receives a commission when the referred customer makes a purchase on Amazon.

- **Viral marketing** is a technique that induces websites or users to pass on a marketing message to other websites or users, creating exponential growth in the message's visibility and effect. One example of successful viral marketing is Hotmail, which promotes its service and its own advertisers' messages in every user's email notes. Viral marketing encourages users of a product or service supplied by an ebusiness to encourage friends to join. Viral marketing is a word-of-mouth type advertising program.

- **Mass customization** is the ability of an organization to give its customers the opportunity to tailor its products or services to the customers' specifications. For example, customers can order M&M's with customized sayings such as "Marry Me."

- **Personalization** occurs when a website can know enough about a person's likes and dislikes that it can fashion offers that are more likely to appeal to that person. Personalization involves tailoring a presentation of an ebusiness website to individuals or groups of customers based on profile information, demographics, or prior transactions. Amazon uses personalization to create a unique portal for each of its customers.

- A **blog** (the contraction of the phrase "web log") is a website in which items are posted on a regular basis and displayed in reverse chronological order. Like other media, blogs often focus on a particular subject, such as food, politics, or local news. Some blogs function as online diaries. A typical blog combines text, images, and links to other blogs, web pages, and other media related to its topic. Since its appearance in 1995, blogging has emerged as a popular means of communication, affecting public opinion and mass media around the world.

- **Real simple syndications (RSS)** is a family of web feed formats used for web syndication of programs and content. RSS is used by (among other things) news websites, blogs, and podcasting, which allows consumers and journalists to have news constantly fed to them instead of searching for it. In addition to facilitating syndication, RSS allows a website's frequent readers to track updates on the site.

- **Podcasting** is the distribution of audio or video files, such as radio programs or music videos, over the Internet to play on mobile devices and personal computers. Podcasting's essence is about creating content (audio or video) for an audience that wants to listen when they want, where they want, and how they want. Podcasters' websites also may offer direct download of their files, but the subscription feed of automatically delivered new content is what distinguishes a podcast from a simple download or real-time streaming. Usually, the podcast features one type of show with new episodes either sporadically or at planned intervals such as daily, weekly, etc.

- **Search engine optimization (SEO)** is a set of methods aimed at improving the ranking of a website in search engine listings. Search engines display different kinds of listings in the search engine results pages (SERPs), including: pay-per-click advertisements, paid inclusion listings, and organic search results. SEO is primarily concerned with advancing the goals of websites by improving the number and position of organic search results for a wide variety of relevant keywords. SEO strategies can increase the number of visitors and the quality of visitors, where quality means visitors who complete the action the site intends (e.g., purchase, sign up, learn something).

    SEO, or "white hat SEO," is distinguished from "black hat SEO," or spamdexing, by methods and objectives. **Spamdexing** uses a variety of deceptive techniques in an attempt to manipulate search engine rankings, whereas legitimate SEO focuses on building better sites and using honest methods of promotion. What constitutes an honest, or ethical, method is an issue that has been the subject of numerous debates.

FIGURE 3.21

Generating Revenue on the Internet through Marketing and Sales Departments

Financial Services

Financial services websites are enjoying rapid growth as they help consumers, businesses, and financial institutions distribute information with greater convenience and richness than is available in other channels. Consumers in ebusiness markets pay for products and services using a credit card or one of the methods outlined in Figure 3.22. Online business payments differ from online consumer payments because businesses tend to make large purchases (from thousands to millions of dollars) and typically do not pay with a credit card. Businesses make online payments using electronic data interchange (EDI) (see Figure 3.23). Transactions between businesses are complex and typically require a level of system integration between the businesses.

Online Consumer Payments	
Financial cybermediary	A *financial cybermediary* is an Internet-based company that facilitates payments over the Internet. PayPal is the best-known example of a financial cybermediary.
Electronic check	An *electronic check* is a mechanism for sending a payment from a checking or savings account. There are many implementations of electronic checks, with the most prominent being online banking.
Electronic bill presentment and payment (EBPP)	An *electronic bill presentment and payment (EBPP)* is a system that sends bills over the Internet and provides an easy-to-use mechanism (such as clicking on a button) to pay the bill. EBPP systems are available through local banks or online services such as Checkfree and Quicken.
Digital wallet	A *digital wallet* is both software and information—the software provides security for the transaction and the information includes payment and delivery information (for example, the credit card number and expiration date).

FIGURE 3.22

Types of Online Consumer Payments

Online Business Payments

Electronic data interchange (EDI) is a standard format for exchanging business data. One way an organization can use EDI is through a value-added network. A *value-added network (VAN)* is a private network, provided by a third party, for exchanging information through a high-capacity connection. VANs support electronic catalogs (from which orders are placed), EDI-based transactions (the actual orders), security measures such as encryption, and EDI mailboxes.

Financial EDI (financial electronic data interchange) is a standard electronic process for B2B market purchase payments. National Cash Management System is an automated clearinghouse that supports the reconciliation of the payments.

FIGURE 3.23

Types of Online Business Payments

Many organizations are now turning to providers of electronic trading networks for enhanced Internet-based network and messaging services. Electronic trading networks are service providers that manage network services. They support business-to-business integration information exchanges, improved security, guaranteed service levels, and command center support (see Figure 3.24). As electronic trading networks expand their reach and the number of Internet businesses continues to grow, so will the need for managed trading services. Using these services allows organizations to reduce time to market and the overall development, deployment, and maintenance costs associated with their integration infrastructures.

Traders at Vanguard Petroleum Corporation spent most days on the phone, patrolling the market for pricing and volume information in order to strike the best possible deal. The process was slow and tied up traders on one negotiation at a time, making it inherently difficult to stay on top of quickly changing prices. One winter, for example, the weather got cold and stayed cold, causing propane prices to increase dramatically. The price was moving so fast that Vanguard was missing opportunities to buy, sell, and execute deals since it was able to complete only one deal at a time.

To bridge these shortcomings and speed the process, Vanguard became one of the first users of Chalkboard, a commodity markets electronic trading network that is now part of ChemConnect, a B2B emarketplace. Vanguard uses Chalkboard to put bids and offers in front of hundreds of traders and complete various trades at multiple delivery points simultaneously. Vanguard now completes deals in real-time and is able to access a broader audience of buyers and sellers.[32]

Procurement

Web-based procurement of maintenance, repair, and operations (MRO) supplies was expected to reach more than $200 billion worldwide by the year 2009. *Maintenance,*

FIGURE 3.24

Diagram of an Electronic
Trading Network

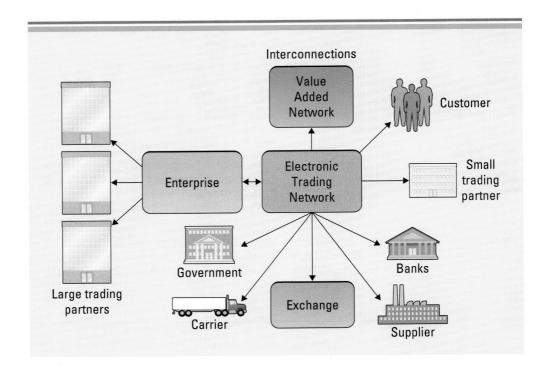

repair, and operations (MRO) materials (also called *indirect materials*) are necessary for running an organization but do not relate to the company's primary business activities. Typical MRO goods include office supplies (such as pens and paper), equipment, furniture, computers, and replacement parts. In the traditional approach to MRO purchasing, a purchasing manager would receive a paper-based request for materials. The purchasing manager would need to search a variety of paper catalogs to find the right product at the right price. Not surprisingly, the administrative cost for purchasing indirect supplies often exceeded the unit value of the product itself. According to the Organization for Economic Cooperation and Development (OECD), companies with more than $500 million in revenue spend an estimated $75 to $150 to process a single purchase order for MRO supplies.[33]

Eprocurement   *Eprocurement* is the B2B purchase and sale of supplies and services over the Internet. The goal of many eprocurement applications is to link organizations directly to preapproved suppliers' catalogs and to process the entire purchasing transaction online. Linking to electronic catalogs significantly reduces the need to check the timeliness and accuracy of supplier information.

   An *electronic catalog* presents customers with information about goods and services offered for sale, bid, or auction on the Internet. Some electronic catalogs manage large numbers of individual items, and search capabilities help buyers navigate quickly to the items they want to purchase. Other electronic catalogs emphasize merchandise presentation and special offers, much as a retail store is laid out to encourage impulse or add-on buying. As with other aspects of ebusiness, it is important to match electronic catalog design and functionality to a company's business goals.

Customer Service

Ebusiness enables customers to help themselves by combining the communications capability of a traditional customer response system with the content richness only the web can provide—all available and operating 24 × 7. As a result, conducting business via the web offers customers the convenience they want while freeing key support staff to tackle more complex problems. The web also allows an organization to provide better customer service through email, special messages, and private password-web access to special areas for top customers.

FIGURE 3.25

Consumer Protection

Issues for Consumer Protection
■ Unsolicited goods and communication
■ Illegal or harmful goods, services, and content
■ Insufficient information about goods or their suppliers
■ Invasion of privacy
■ Cyberfraud

Vanguard manages $690 billion in assets and charges the lowest fees in the industry: 0.26 percent of assets versus an industry average of 0.81 percent. Vanguard keeps fees down by teaching its investors how to better use its website. For good reason: A web log-on costs Vanguard mere pennies, while each call to a service rep is a $9 expense.[34]

Customer service is the business process where the most human contact occurs between a buyer and a seller. Not surprisingly, ebusiness strategists are finding that customer service via the web is one of the most challenging and potentially lucrative areas of ebusiness. The primary issue facing customer service departments using ebusiness is consumer protection.

Consumer Protection An organization that wants to dominate by using superior customer service as a competitive advantage must not only consider how to service its customers, but also how to protect its customers. Organizations must recognize that many consumers are unfamiliar with their digital choices, and some ebusinesses are well aware of these vulnerabilities. For example, 17-year-old Miami high school senior Francis Cornworth offered his "Young Man's Virginity" for sale on eBay. The offer attracted a $10 million phony bid. Diana Duyser of Hollywood, Florida, sold half of a grilled cheese sandwich that resembles the Virgin Mary to the owners of an online casino for $28,000 on eBay. Figure 3.25 highlights the different protection areas for consumers.[35]

Regardless of whether the customers are other businesses or end consumers, one of their greatest concerns is the security level of their financial transactions. This includes all aspects of electronic information, but focuses mainly on the information associated with payments (e.g., a credit card number) and the payments themselves, that is, the "electronic money." An organization must consider such issues as encryption, secure socket layers (SSL), and secure electronic transactions (SET), as explained in Figure 3.26.

Intermediaries

Intermediaries are agents, software, or businesses that bring buyers and sellers together that provide a trading infrastructure to enhance ebusiness. With the introduction of ecommerce there was much discussion about .disintermediation of middle

FIGURE 3.26

Ebusiness Security

Ebusiness Security
Encryption scrambles information into an alternative form that requires a key or password to decrypt the information. Encryption is achieved by scrambling letters, replacing letters, replacing letters with numbers, and other ways.
A *secure socket layer (SSL)* (1) creates a secure and private connection between a client and server computer, (2) encrypts the information, and (3) sends the information over the Internet. SSL is identified by a website address that includes an "s" at the end—http**s**.
A *secure electronic transaction (SET)* is a transmission security method that ensures transactions are secure and legitimate. Similar to SSL, SET encrypts information before sending it over the Internet. However, SET also enables customer authentication for credit card transactions. SETs are endorsed by major ecommerce players including MasterCard, American Express, Visa, Netscape, and Microsoft.

FIGURE 3.27

Types of Intermediaries

Type of Intermediary	Description	Example
Internet service providers	Make money selling a service, not a product	Earthlink.com, Comcast.com, AOL.com
Portals	Central hubs for online content	Yahoo.com, MSN.com, Google.com
Content providers	Use the Internet to distribute copyrighted content	wsj.com, cnn.com, espn.com
Online brokers	Intermediaries between buyers and sellers of goods and services	charlesschwab.com, fidelity.com, datek.com
Market makers	Aggregate three services for market participants: a place, rules, and infrastructure	amazon.com, ebay.com, priceline.com
Online service providers	Extensive online array of services	xdrive.com, lawinfo.com
Intelligent agents	Software applications that follow instructions and learn independently	Sidestep.com, WebSeeker.com, iSpyNOW.com
Application service providers	Sell access to Internet-based software applications to other companies	ariba.com, commerceone.com, ibm.com
Infomediaries	Provide specialized information on behalf of producers of goods and services and their potential customers	autobytel.com, BizRate.com

Ebusiness Success

people/organizations; however, recent developments in ebusiness have seen more reintermediation. *Reintermediation* refers to using the Internet to reassemble buyers, sellers, and other partners in a traditional supply chain in new ways. Examples include New York-based e-Steel Corp. and Philadelphia-based PetroChemNet Inc. bringing together producers, traders, distributors, and buyers of steel and chemicals, respectively, in web-based marketplaces. Figure 3.27 lists intermediaries and their functions.

MEASURING EBUSINESS SUCCESS

Traffic on the Internet retail site for Wal-Mart grew 66 percent in one year. The site receives over 500,000 visitors daily (6.5 million per week), downloads 2 million web pages daily, and averages 60,000 users logged on simultaneously. Wal-Mart's primary concern is maintaining optimal performance for online transactions. A disruption to the website directly affects the company's bottom line and customer loyalty. The company monitors and tracks the hardware, software, and network running the company's website to ensure high quality of service.[36]

The Yankee Group reports that 66 percent of companies determine website success solely by measuring the amount of traffic. Unfortunately, large amounts of website traffic does not necessarily indicate large sales. Many websites with lots of traffic have minimal sales. The best way to measure a site's success is to measure such things as the revenue generated by web traffic, the number of new customers acquired by web traffic, and any reductions in customer service calls resulting from web traffic.[37]

Ashley Qualls is not your average high school student; the 17-year-old is the CEO of a million-dollar business. Ashley is the head of whateverlife.com, a website she started when she was just 14—with $8 borrowed from her mother. Now, just three years later, the website grosses more than $1 million a year, providing Ashley and her working-class family a sense of security they had never really known. This teenage CEO bought her family a four-bedroom house and built herself an office in the basement. It all started with capitalism 101, the law of supply and demand. Ashley became interested in graphic design just as the online social networking craze began to catch fire. When she saw her friends personalizing their MySpace pages, she began

FIGURE 3.28

Website Effectiveness
Metrics

Effectiveness Website Metrics
■ **Cookie**—a small file deposited on a hard drive by a website containing information about customers and their web activities. Cookies allow websites to record the comings and goings of customers, usually without their knowledge or consent.
■ **Click-through**—a count of the number of people who visit one site and click on an advertisement that takes them to the site of the advertiser. Tracking effectiveness based on click-throughs guarantees exposure to target ads; however, it does not guarantee that the visitor liked the ad, spent any substantial time viewing the ad, or was satisfied with the information contained in the ad.
■ **Banner ad**—advertises the products and services of another business, usually another dot-com business. Advertisers can track how often customers click on banner ads resulting in a click-through to their website. Often the cost of the banner ad depends on the number of customers who click on the banner ad. Tracking the number of banner ad clicks is one way to understand the effectiveness of the ad on its target audience.

creating MySpace background designs through Whateverlife. The designs are cheery, colorful, and whimsical, with lots of hearts, Ashley's favorites.

Website Metrics

Figure 3.28 displays a few metrics an organization can use to measure website effectiveness.

To help understand advertising effectiveness, interactivity measures are tracked and monitored. *Interactivity* measures the visitor interactions with the target ad. Such interaction measures include the duration of time the visitor spends viewing the ad, the number of pages viewed, and even the number of repeat visits to the target ad. Interactivity measures are a giant step forward for advertisers, since traditional advertising methods—newspapers, magazines, radio, and television—provide few ways to track effectiveness metrics. Interactivity metrics measure actual consumer activities, something that was impossible to do in the past, and provide advertisers with tremendous amounts of business intelligence.

The ultimate outcome of any advertisement is a purchase. Tying purchase amounts to website visits makes it easy to communicate the business value of the website. Organizations use metrics to tie revenue amounts and new customer creation numbers directly back to the websites or banner ads. Organization can observe through *clickstream data* the exact pattern of a consumer's navigation through a site. Clickstream data can reveal a number of basic data points on how consumers interact with websites. Figure 3.29 displays different types of clickstream metrics.

Marc Barach is the co-inventor and chief marketing officer of Ingenio, a start-up company that specializes in connecting people in real-time. When the Internet first emerged, banner ads were the prevalent marketing tools. Next came pay-per-click where the company pays the search engine each time its website is accessed from a search. Today 35 percent of online spending occurs through pay-per-clicks. Unfortunately, pay-per-clicks are not suitable for all businesses. Roofers, plumbers, auto repair people, and cosmetic surgeons rarely have websites and do not generate business via pay-per-clicks. Barach believes that the next line of Internet advertising will be pay-per-call, and Ingenio has invested five years and $50 million in building the platform to run the business. Here is how pay-per-call works:

■ The user types a keyword into a search engine.

■ The search engine passes the keyword to Ingenio.

■ Ingenio determines the category and sends back the appropriate merchant's unique, traceable 800 telephone number.

■ The 800 number routes through Ingenio's switches, and Ingenio charges the merchant when a customer calls.

A Jupiter Research study discovered that businesses were willing to pay between $2 and $35 for each call lead.[38]

FIGURE 3.29

Clickstream Data Metrics

Clickstream Data Metrics
■ The number of page views (i.e., the number of times a particular page has been presented to a visitor).
■ The pattern of websites visited, including most frequent exit page and most frequent prior website.
■ Length of stay on the website.
■ Dates and times of visits.
■ Number of registrations filled out per 100 visitors.
■ Number of abandoned registrations.
■ Demographics of registered visitors.
■ Number of customers with shopping carts.
■ Number of abandoned shopping carts.

Figure 3.30 provides definitions of common metrics based on clickstream data. To interpret such data properly, managers try to benchmark against other companies. For instance, consumers seem to visit their preferred websites regularly, even checking back to the website multiple times during a given session. Consumers tend to become loyal to a small number of sites, and they tend to revisit those sites a number of times during a particular session.

FIGURE 3.30

Definitions of Website Metrics

Visitor	Visitor Metrics
Unidentified visitor	A visitor is an individual who visits a website. An "unidentified visitor" means that no information about that visitor is available.
Unique visitor	A unique visitor is one who can be recognized and counted only once within a given period of time. An accurate count of unique visitors is not possible without some form of identification, registration, or authentication.
Session visitor	A session ID is available (e.g., cookie) or inferred by incoming address plus browser type, which allows a visitor's responses to be tracked within a given visit to a website.
Tracked visitor	An ID (e.g., cookie) is available that allows a user to be tracked across multiple visits to a website. No information, other than a unique identifier, is available for a tracked visitor.
Identified visitor	An ID is available (e.g., cookie or voluntary registration) that allows a user to be tracked across multiple visits to a website. Other information (name, demographics, possibly supplied voluntarily by the visitor) can be linked to this ID.
Exposure	**Exposure Metrics**
Page exposures (page-views)	The number of times a particular web page has been viewed by visitors in a given time period, without regard to duplication.
Site exposures	The number of visitor sessions at a website in a given time period, without regard to visitor duplication.
Visit	**Visit Metrics**
Stickiness (visit duration time)	The length of time a visitor spends on a website. Can be reported as an average in a given time period, without regard to visitor duplication.
Raw visit depth (total web pages exposure per session)	The total number of pages a visitor is exposed to during a single visit to a website. Can be reported as an average or distribution in a given time period, without regard to visitor duplication.
Visit depth (total unique web pages exposure per session)	The total number of unique pages a visitor is exposed to during a single visit to a website. Can be reported as an average or distribution in a given time period, without regard to visitor duplication.
Hit	**Hit Metrics**
Hits	When visitors reach a website, their computer sends a request to the site's computer server to begin displaying pages. Each element of a requested page (including graphics, text, interactive items) is recorded by the website's server log file as a "hit."
Qualified hits	Exclude less important information recorded in a log file (such as error messages, etc.).

FIGURE 3.31

Ebusiness Benefits

Ebusiness Benefits	
Highly Accessible	Businesses can operate 24 hours a day, 7 days a week, 365 days a year.
Increased Customer Loyalty	Additional channels to contact, respond to, and access customers helps contribute to customer loyalty.
Improved Information Content	In the past, customers had to order catalogs or travel to a physical facility before they could compare price and product attributes. Electronic catalogs and web pages present customers with up-dated information in real-time about goods, services, and prices.
Increased Convenience	Ebusiness automates and improves many of the activities that make up a buying experience.
Increased Global Reach	Business, both small and large, can reach new markets.
Decreased Cost	The cost of conducting business on the Internet is substantially smaller than traditional forms of business communication.

EBUSINESS BENEFITS AND CHALLENGES

According to an NUA Internet Survey, the Internet links more than 1 billion people worldwide. Experts expected global Internet usage to nearly triple between 2006 and 2010, making ebusiness a more significant factor in the global economy. As ebusiness improves, organizations will experience benefits and challenges alike. Figure 3.31 details ebusiness benefits for an organization.

The Internet is forcing organizations to refocus their information systems from the inside out. A growing number of companies are already using the Internet to streamline their business processes, procure materials, sell products, automate customer service, and create new revenue streams. Although the benefits of ebusiness systems are enticing, developing, deploying, and managing these systems is not always easy. Unfortunately, ebusiness is not something a business can just go out and buy. Figure 3.32 details the challenges facing ebusiness.

FIGURE 3.32

Ebusiness Challenges

Ebusiness Challenges	
Protecting Consumers	Consumers must be protected against unsolicited goods and communication, illegal or harmful goods, insufficient information about goods or their suppliers, invasion of privacy, and cyberfraud.
Leveraging Existing Systems	Most companies already use information technology to conduct business in non-Internet environments, such as marketing, order management, billing, inventory, distribution, and customer service. The Internet represents an alternative and complementary way to do business, but it is imperative that ebusiness systems integrate existing systems in a manner that avoids duplicating functionality and maintains usability, performance, and reliability.
Increasing Liability	Ebusiness exposes suppliers to unknown liabilities because Internet commerce law is vaguely defined and differs from country to country. The Internet and its use in ebusiness have raised many ethical, social, and political issues, such as identity theft and information manipulation.
Providing Security	The Internet provides universal access, but companies must protect their assets against accidental or malicious misuse. System security, however, must not create prohibitive complexity or reduce flexibility. Customer information also needs to be protected from internal and external misuse. Privacy systems should safeguard the personal information critical to building sites that satisfy customer and business needs. A serious deficiency arises from the use of the Internet as a marketing means. Sixty percent of Internet users do not trust the Internet as a payment channel. Making purchases via the Internet is considered unsafe by many. This issue affects both the business and the consumer. However, with encryption and the development of secure websites, security is becoming less of a constraint for ebusinesses.
Adhering to Taxation Rules	The Internet is not yet subject to the same level of taxation as traditional businesses. While taxation should not discourage consumers from using electronic purchasing channels, it should not favor Internet purchases over store purchases either. Instead, a tax policy should provide a level playing field for traditional retail businesses, mail-order companies, and Internet-based merchants. The Internet marketplace is rapidly expanding, yet it remains mostly free from traditional forms of taxation. In one recent study, uncollected state and local sales taxes from ebusiness were projected to exceed $60 billion in 2008.

Revenue Models	Advantages	Limitation
Transaction fees	■ Can be directly tied to savings (both process and price savings) ■ Important revenue source when high level of liquidity (transaction volume) is reached	■ If process savings are not completely visible, use of the system is discouraged (incentive to move transactions offline) ■ Transaction fees likely to decrease with time
License fees	■ Creates incentives to do many transactions ■ Customization and back-end integration leads to lock-in of participants	■ Up-front fee is a barrier to entry for participants ■ Price differentiation is complicated
Subscription fees	■ Creates incentives to do transactions ■ Price can be differentiated ■ Possibility to build additional revenue from new user groups	■ Fixed fee is a barrier to entry for participants
Fees for value-added services	■ Service offering can be differentiated ■ Price can be differentiated ■ Possibility to build additional revenue from established and new user groups (third parties)	■ Cumbersome process for customers to continually evaluate new services
Advertising fees	■ Well-targeted advertisements can be perceived as value-added content by trading participants ■ Easy to implement	■ Limited revenue potential ■ Overdone or poorly targeted advertisements can be disturbing elements on the website

A key element of emarketplaces is their ability to provide not only transaction capabilities but also dynamic, relevant content to trading partners. The original ebusiness websites provided shopping cart capabilities built around product catalogs. As a result of the complex emarketplace that must support existing business processes and systems, content is becoming even more critical for emarketplaces. Buyers need good content description to make informed purchases, and sellers use content to properly market and differentiate themselves from the competition. Content and product description establish the common understanding between both parties to the transaction. As a result, the accessibility, usability, accuracy, and richness of that content directly affect the transaction. Figure 3.33 displays the different benefits and challenges of various emarketplace revenue models.

NEW TRENDS IN EBUSINESS: EGOVERNMENT AND MCOMMERCE

Recent business models that have arisen to enable organizations to take advantage of the Internet and create value are within egovernment. *Egovernment* involves the use of strategies and technologies to transform government(s) by improving the delivery of services and enhancing the quality of interaction between the citizen-consumer within all branches of government (refer to Figure 3.34).

One example of an egovernment portal, FirstGov.gov, the official U.S. gateway to all government information, is the catalyst for a growing electronic government. Its powerful search engine and ever-growing collection of topical and customer-focused links connect users to millions of web pages, from the federal government, to local and tribal governments, to foreign nations around the world. Figure 3.35 highlights specific egovernment models.

FIGURE 3.34

Extended Ebusiness Models

	Business	Consumer	Government
Business	B2B conisint.com	B2C dell.com	B2G lockheedmartin.com
Consumer	C2B priceline.com	C2C ebay.com	C2G eGov.com
Government	G2B export.gov	G2C medicare.gov	G2G disasterhelp.gov

FIGURE 3.35

Egovernment Models

Egovernment Models	
Consumer-to-government (C2G)	C2G will mainly constitute the areas where a consumer (or citizen) interacts with the government. It will include areas like elections, when citizens vote for government officials; census, where the consumer provides demographic information to the government; taxation, where the consumer is paying taxes to the government.
Government-to-business (G2B)	This model includes all government interaction with business enterprises whether it is procurement of goods and services from suppliers or information regarding legal and business issues that is transmitted electronically.
Government-to-consumer (G2C)	Governments around the world are now dealing with consumers (or citizens) electronically, providing them with updated information. Governments are also processing applications for visas, renewal of passports and driver's licenses, advertising of tender notices, and other services online.
Government-to-government (G2G)	Governments around the world are now dealing with other governments electronically. Still at an inception stage, this ebusiness model will enhance international trade and information retrieval, for example, on criminal records of new migrants. At the state level, information exchange and processing of transactions online will enable enhanced efficiencies.

Mcommerce

In a few years, Internet-enabled mobile devices will outnumber PCs. **Mobile commerce, or mcommerce,** is the ability to purchase goods and services through a wireless Internet-enabled device. The emerging technology behind mcommerce is a mobile device equipped with a web-ready micro-browser. To take advantage of the mcommerce market potential, handset manufacturers Nokia, Ericsson, Motorola, and Qualcomm are working with telecommunication carriers AT&T Wireless and Sprint to develop smartphones. Using new forms of technology, smartphones offer fax, email, and phone capabilities all in one, paving the way for mcommerce to be accepted by an increasingly mobile workforce. Figure 3.36 gives a visual overview of mcommerce.

FIGURE 3.36

Mcommerce Technology
Overview

Amazon.com has collaborated with Nokia to pioneer a new territory. With the launch of its Amazon.com Anywhere service, it has become one of the first major online retailers to recognize and do something about the potential of Internet-enabled wireless devices. As content delivery over wireless devices becomes faster, more secure, and scalable, mcommerce will surpass landline ebusiness (traditional telephony) as the method of choice for digital commerce transactions. According to the research firm Strategy Analytics, the global mcommerce market was expected to be worth more than $200 billion by 2005, with some 350 million customers generating almost 14 billion transactions annually. Additionally, information activities like email, news, and stock quotes will progress to personalized transactions, "one-click" travel reservations, online auctions, and video-conferencing.[39]

Organizations face changes more extensive and far reaching in their implications than anything since the modern industrial revolution occurred in the early 1900s. Technology is a primary force driving these changes. Organizations that want to survive must recognize the immense power of technology, carry out required organizational changes in the face of it, and learn to operate in an entirely different way.

OPENING CASE QUESTIONS

Amazon.com—Not Your Average Bookstore

5. What is Amazon's ebusiness model?

6. How can Amazon use mcommerce to influence its business?

7. Which metrics could Amazon use to assess the efficiency and effectiveness of Amazon's website?

8. What are some of the business challenges facing Amazon?

SUMMARY OF KEY THEMES

The purpose of this chapter was to provide you with an overview of doing business on the Internet. Understanding how web-based technologies have revolutionized the way organizations conduct business is key to a successful future in business. Internet technologies have not only improved (and sometimes replaced) traditional ways of doing business, but have also introduced new business opportunities and ventures.

By providing this overview, you should now have a better understanding of the benefits and challenges afforded by the Internet channel, recent trends that have and are occurring in the marketplace, and the various strategies and models organizations use to deploy ebusiness. Armed with this knowledge, you, the business student, should be better prepared to place the material presented in the remainder of this textbook in context of the larger ebusiness picture—the global marketplace.

KEY TERMS

Application programming interface 94
Application service provider (ASP) 99
Associate program (affiliate program) 106
Banner ad 111
Blog 106
Brick-and-mortar business 104
Business-to-business (B2B) 103
Business-to-consumer (B2C) 103
Clickstream data 111
Click-and-mortar business 104
Click-through 111
Consumer-to-business (C2B) 104
Consumer-to-consumer (C2C) 104
Cookie 111
Digital Darwinism 88
Digital divide 93
Digital wallet 107
Disruptive technology 88
Ebusiness 87, 101
Ebusiness model 102
Ecommerce 101
Egovernment 114
Emall 103
Eshop (estore, etailer) 103
Electronic bill presentment and payment (EBPP) 107

Electronic catalog 108
Electronic check 107
Electronic data interchange (EDI) 107
Electronic marketplace (emarketplace) 103
Encryption 109
Eprocurement 108
Extranet 97
Financial cybermediary 107
Financial EDI (financial electronic data interchange) 107
Hypertext transport protocol (HTTP) 91
Information reach 92
Information richness 92
Interactivity 111
Intermediary 109
Internet 90
Internet service provider (ISP) 98
Intranet 96
Kiosk 97
Maintenance, repair, and operation (MRO) material (indirect material) 107
Mashup editor 94
Mass customization 106
Mobile commerce, or mcommerce 115
Online ad (banner ad) 106

Online service provider (OSP) 99
Personalization 106
Podcasting 106
Pop-under ad 106
Pop-up ad 106
Portal 97
Protocol 91
Pure-play (virtual) business 104
Real simple syndication (RSS) 106
Reintermediation 110
Search engine optimization (SEO) 106
Secure electronic transaction (SET) 109
Secure socket layer (SSL) 109
Semantic web 95
Service level agreement (SLA) 99
Service-oriented architecture 96
Spamdexing 106
Sustaining technology 88
Value-added network (VAN) 107
Viral marketing 106
Web 2.0 93
Web mashup 94
Wireless Internet service provider (WISP) 98
World Wide Web (WWW) 91

eBay—The Ultimate Ebusiness

Pierre Omidyar was just 28 when he sat down over a long holiday weekend to write the original computer code for what eventually became an Internet super brand—the auction site eBay. Omidyar viewed auctions as a fair mechanism for Internet commerce where sellers could set their minimum prices, and buyers could then determine an item's market value by bidding up to what they were willingly to pay. A novel feedback system could allow buyers and sellers to rate each other, helping minimize fraud by enabling the community to police itself. "I really wanted to give the individual the power to be a producer as well. It was letting the users take responsibility for building the community," Omidyar would later explain.

The site launched on Labor Day, September 4, 1995, under the title of Auction Web, soon to be renamed after the site's domain name—ebay.com (a shortening of Echo Bay, Omidyar's consulting firm). The service was free at first, but started charging to cover Internet service provider costs.

A National Marketplace

Omidyar's auction website, eBay.com, took off. It provided something novel that its users craved: an efficient national marketplace with a strong community built on fairness and trust. A photography student looking for a used camera could choose from models across the nation and trust the timely delivery of the product. The owner of a vintage clothing store could sell to collectors nationwide. The community would expose a deceptive or fraudulent user and ban them from the marketplace.

Entrepreneurs in record numbers began setting up shop on eBay. According to a new survey conducted for eBay by ACNielsen International Research, in 2005 more than 724,000 people supported themselves by selling items on eBay, up from 75,000 in 2002. In addition to these professional eBay sellers, another 1.5 million individuals supplement their income by selling on eBay. In the first six months of 2005, Americans sold merchandise worth about $10.6 billion through eBay.

The stock market value of Omidyar's innovative company grew to $2 billion in just three years, and his site's staying power as an economic engine was evident. Jeffrey Skoll, a Stanford MBA, joined the company in 1996 after the site was already profitable. In March 1998, Meg Whitman took over as president and CEO. In September 1998, eBay launched a successful public offering, making both Omidyar and Skoll billionaires—three years after Omidyar created eBay. In 2005, Omidyar's 214 million eBay shares were worth about $8 billion.

Collaborating with eBay

This ebusiness is collaborating with marketplace, payment, and communication companies that add value for its customers.

Marketplace—The U.S. Postal Service

People who sell items on eBay all have one thing in common: They need to ship their goods to their customers. To support this growing economic force, eBay and the U.S. Postal Service created an innovative economic and educational opportunity.

The Postal Service's bread and butter—first-class mail—is beset by rising costs and falling use. Email and faxes have reduced the amount of mail sent each day, but the Postal Service still bears the cost of delivering to every business and home, six days a week. Package shipping, however, remains a profitable and booming business, as evidenced by the number and earnings of private shippers in the market.

The Postal Service offers free boxes and heavy-duty envelopes for shippers using overnight or priority mail. To make it easier for those in the vanguard of the new, digital economy, the Postal Service will pick up shipments from the sender, and its website sells mailing labels with postage included that can be printed out from a home computer. Over 20 million shipping labels with postage were printed via the eBay/Postal Service link in 2005. Customers can also link to the United Parcel Service site, but eBay does not have a formal relationship with Federal Express.

Payment—PayPal

Founded in 1998, PayPal, an eBay company, enables any individual or business with an email address to securely, easily, and quickly send and receive payments online. PayPal's service builds on the existing financial infrastructure of bank accounts and credit cards and utilizes the world's most advanced proprietary fraud prevention systems to create a safe, global, real-time payment solution.

PayPal has quickly become a global leader in online payment solutions with 96 million account members worldwide. Buyers and sellers on eBay, online retailers, online businesses, as well as traditional off-line businesses are transacting with PayPal, available in 55 countries.

Communication—Skype

Skype, a global Internet communications company, allows people everywhere to make free, unlimited, superior quality voice calls via its innovative peer-to-peer software. Since its launch in August 2003, Skype has been downloaded more than 163 million times in 225 countries and territories. Fifty-four million people are registered to use Skype's free services, with over 3 million simultaneous users on the network at any one time. Skype adds about 150,000 users a day.

In September 2005, eBay acquired Skype for approximately $2.6 billion, anticipating that Skype will streamline and improve communications between buyers and sellers as it is integrated into the eBay marketplace. Buyers will gain an easy way to talk to sellers quickly and get the information they need, and sellers can more easily build relationships. The auction company hopes the acquisition will strengthen its global marketplace and payments platform, while opening several new lines of business and creating significant new opportunities for the company.

Unforeseen Dangers of Collaboration

"Communications is at the heart of ecommerce and community," said Meg Whitman. "By combining the two leading ecommerce franchises, eBay and PayPal, with the leader in Internet voice communications, Skype, we will create an extraordinarily powerful environment for business on the Net."

In October 2005, one month after eBay's acquisition of Skype, a press release discussed two critical flaws in Skype's software, one of which could allow malicious hackers to take control of compromised systems and another that could allow attackers to crash the client software. While fixes for the issues were being addressed, businesses asked their users to refrain from using voice services based on proprietary protocols like Skype while on corporate networks because of network security issues. Perhaps Skype might not be the collaborative tool of choice for eBay.[40]

Questions

1. eBay is one of the only major Internet "pure plays" to consistently make a profit from its inception. What is eBay's ebusiness model and why has it been so successful?

2. Other major websites, like Amazon.com and Yahoo!, have entered the emarketplace with far less success than eBay. How has eBay been able to maintain its dominant position?

3. eBay has long been an emarketplace for used goods and collectibles. Today, it is increasingly a place where major businesses come to auction their wares. Why would a brand-name vendor set up shop on eBay?

4. What are the three different types of online auctions and which one is eBay using?

5. What are the different forms of online payment methods for consumers and business? How might eBay's customer benefit from the different payment methods?

6. Which metrics would you use if you were hired to assess the efficiency and effectiveness of eBay's website?

CLOSING CASE TWO

Ebiz

Amazing things are happening on the Internet, things nobody would believe. Here are two stories that demonstrate how innovation, creativity, and a great idea can turn the Internet into a cash cow.

A Million Dollar Homepage

The Million Dollar Homepage is a website conceived by Alex Tew, a 21-year-old student from Cricklade, Wiltshire, England, to help raise money for his university education. Launched on August 26, 2005, the website is said to have generated a gross income of $1,037,100 and have a Google PageRank of 7.

The index page of the site consists of a 1000 by 1000 pixel grid (1 million pixels), on which he sells image-based links for $1 per pixel, in minimum 10 by 10 blocks. A person who buys one or more of these pixel blocks can design a tiny image that will be displayed on the block, decide which URL the block will link to, and write a slogan that appears when the cursor hovers over the link. The aim of the site was to sell all of the pixels in the image, thus generating $1 million of income for the creator, which seems to have been accomplished. On January 1, 2006, the final 1,000 pixels left were put up for auction on eBay. The auction closed on January 11 with the winning bid of $38,100. This brought the final tally to $1,037,100 in gross income. See the Million Dollar Homepage below.[41]

One Red Paper Clip

The website One Red Paperclip was created by Kyle MacDonald, a Canadian blogger who bartered his way from a single paper clip to a house in a series of trades spanning almost one year. MacDonald began with one red paper clip on July 14, 2005. By July 5, 2006, a chain of bartering had ultimately led to trading a movie role for a two-story farmhouse in Kipling, Saskatchewan. On July 7, 2006—almost exactly one year after MacDonald began his experiment—the deed to the house was signed. In September, at the housewarming party where 12 of the 14 traders were present, he proposed to his girlfriend and she accepted. The wedding ring was made from the original red paper clip he got back from the first woman to have agreed to trade with him.

Following is the timeline, based on the website and as summarized by the BBC:

- On July 14, 2005, MacDonald went to Vancouver and traded the paper clip for a fish-shaped pen.
- MacDonald then traded the pen the same day for a hand-sculpted doorknob from Seattle, Washington, which he nicknamed Knob-T.
- On July 25, 2005, MacDonald traveled to Amherst, Massachusetts, with a friend to trade the Knob-T for a Coleman camp stove (with fuel).
- On September 24, 2005, he went to San Clemente, California, and traded the camp stove for a Honda generator, from a U.S. Marine.
- On November 16, 2005, MacDonald made a second (and successful) attempt (after having the generator confiscated by the New York City Fire Department) in Maspeth, Queens, to trade the generator for an "instant party": an empty keg, an IOU for filling the keg with the beer of the holder's choice, and a neon Budweiser sign.
- On December 8, 2005, he traded the "instant party" to Quebec comedian and radio personality Michel Barrette for a Ski-doo snowmobile.
- Within a week of that, MacDonald traded the snowmobile for a two-person trip to Yahk, British Columbia, in February 2006.
- On or about January 7, 2006, the second person on the trip to Yahk traded MacDonald a cube van for the privilege.
- On or about February 22, 2006, he traded the cube van for a recording contract with Metal Works in Toronto.
- On or about April 11, 2006, MacDonald traded the recording contract to Jody Gnant for a year's rent in Phoenix, Arizona.
- On or about April 26, 2006, he traded the one year's rent in Phoenix, Arizona, for one afternoon with Alice Cooper.
- On or about May 26, 2006, MacDonald traded the one afternoon with Alice Cooper for a KISS motorized snow globe.
- On or about June 2, 2006, he traded the KISS motorized snow globe to Corbin Bernsen for a role in the film *Donna on Demand.*
- On or about July 5, 2006, MacDonald traded the movie role for a two-story farmhouse in Kipling, Saskatchewan.

Questions

1. What other ways could you use the Internet to raise money?
2. What types of businesses could benefit from trading on the Internet?
3. Can you think of any other disruptive or nontraditional ways that you could use the Internet?

How Do You Value Friendster?

Jonathan Abrams is keeping quiet about how he is going to generate revenue from his website, Friendster, which specializes in social networking. Abrams is a 33-year-old Canadian software developer whose experiences include being laid off by Netscape and then moving from one start-up to another. In 2002, Abrams was unemployed, not doing well financially, and certainly not looking to start another business when he developed the idea for Friendster. He quickly coded a working prototype and watched in amazement as his website took off.

The buzz around social networking start-ups has been on the rise. A number of high-end venture capital firms, including Sequoia and Mayfield, have invested more than $40 million into social networking start-ups such as LinkedIn, Spoke, and Tribe Networks. Friendster received over $13 million in venture capital from Kleiner, Perkins, Caufield, Byers, and Benchmark Capital, which reportedly valued the company at $53 million—a startling figure for a company that had yet to generate even a single dime in revenue.

A year after making its public debut, Friendster was one of the largest social networking websites, attracting over 5 million users and receiving more than 50,000 page views per day. The question is how do efficiency metrics, such as web traffic and page views, turn into cash flow? Everyone is wondering how Friendster is going to begin generating revenue.

The majority of Abrams's competitors make their money by extracting fees from their subscribers. Friendster is going to continue to let its subscribers meet for free but plans to charge them for premium services such as the ability to customize their profile page. The company also has plans to extend beyond social networking to an array of value-added services such as friend-based job referrals and classmate searches. Abrams is also looking into using his high-traffic website to tap into the growing Internet advertising market.

Abrams does not appear concerned about generating revenue or about potential competition. "Match.com has been around eight years, has 12 million users, and has spent many millions of dollars on advertising to get them," he said. "We're a year old, we've spent zero dollars on advertising, and in a year or less, we'll be bigger than them—it's a given."

The future of Friendster is uncertain. Google offered to buy Friendster for $30 million in 2003 even though there were signs, both statistical and anecdotal, that Friendster's popularity may have peaked.[42]

Questions

1. How could you use ebusiness metrics to place a value on Friendster?
2. Why would a venture capital company value Friendster at $53 million when the company has yet to generate any revenue?
3. Why would Google be interested in buying Friendster for $30 million when the company has yet to generate any revenue?
4. Identify Friendster's ebusiness model and explain how the company can generate revenue.
5. Explain the ebusiness benefits and challenges facing Friendster.

1. Leveraging the competitive value of the Internet

Physical inventories have always been a major cost component of business. Linking to suppliers in real time dramatically enhances the classic goal of inventory "turn." The Internet provides a multitude of opportunities for radically reducing the costs of designing, manufacturing, and selling goods and services. E-mango.com, a fruit emarketplace, must take advantage of these opportunities or find itself at a significant competitive disadvantage. Identify the disadvantages that confront E-mango.com if it does not leverage the competitive value of the Internet.

2. Implementing an ebusiness model

The Genius is a revolutionary mountain bike with full-suspension and shock-adjustable forks that is being marketed via the Internet. The Genius needs an ebusiness solution that will easily enable internal staff to deliver fresh and relevant product information throughout its website. To support its large audience, the company also needs the ability to present information in multiple languages and serve over 1 million page views per month to visitors in North America and Europe. Explain what ebusiness model you would use to market The Genius on the Internet.

3. Assessing Internet capabilities

Hoover's Rentals is a small privately owned business that rents sports equipment in Denver, Colorado. The company specializes in winter rentals including ski equipment, snowboarding equipment, and snowmobile equipment. Hoover's has been in business for 20 years and, for the first time, it is experiencing a decline in rentals. Brian Hoover, the company's owner, is puzzled by the recent decreases. The snowfall for the last two years has been outstanding, and the ski resorts have opened earlier and closed later than most previous years. Reports say tourism in the Colorado area is up, and the invention of loyalty programs has significantly increased the number of local skiers. Overall, business should be booming. The only reason for the decrease in sales might be the fact that big retailers such as Wal-Mart and Gart Sports are now renting winter sports equipment. Brian would like your team's help in determining how he can use the Internet to help his company increase sales and decrease costs to compete with these big retailers.

4. Online auction sites

You are working for a new Internet start-up company, eMart.com, an online marketplace for the sale of goods and services. The company offers a wide variety of features and services that enable online members to buy and sell their goods and services quickly and conveniently. The company's mission is to provide a global trading platform where anyone can trade practically anything. Suggest some ways that eMart.com can extend its market reach beyond that of its competitor, eBay.com.

5. Everybody needs an Internet strategy

An Internet strategy addresses the reasons businesses want to "go online." "Going online" because it seems like the right thing to do now or because everyone else is doing it is not a good enough reason. A business must decide how it will best utilize the Internet for its particular needs. It must plan for where it wants to go and how best the Internet can help shape that vision. Before developing a strategy a business should spend time on the Internet, see what similar businesses have grown, and what is most feasible, given a particular set of resources. Think of a new online business opportunity and answer the following questions:

a. Why do you want to put your business online?

b. What benefits will going online bring?

c. What effects will being connected to the Internet have on your staff, suppliers, and customers?

6. Searching for disruption

Scheduler.com is a large corporation that develops software that automates scheduling and record keeping for medical and dental practices. Scheduler.com currently holds 48 percent of its market share, has more than 8,700 employees, and operates in six countries.

You are the vice president of product development at Scheduler.com. You have just finished reading *The Innovator's Dilemma* by Clayton Christensen and you are interested in determining what types of disruptive technologies you can take advantage of, or should watch out for, in your industry. Use the Internet to develop a presentation highlighting the types of disruptive technologies you have found that have the potential to give the company a competitive advantage or could cause the company to fail.

7. Finding innovation

Along with disruptive technologies, there are also disruptive strategies. The following are a few examples of companies that use disruptive strategies to gain competitive advantages:

- **Circuit City** and **Best Buy**—These two disrupted the consumer electronics departments of full-service and discount department stores, which has sent them up-market into higher margin goods.
- **Ford**—Henry Ford's Model T was so inexpensive that he enabled a much larger population of people, who historically could not afford cars, to own one.
- **JetBlue**—Whereas Southwest Airlines initially followed a strategy of new-market disruption, JetBlue's approach is low-end disruption. Its long-range viability depends on the major airlines' motivation to run away from the attack, as integrated steel mills and full-service department stores did.
- **McDonald's**—The fast-food industry has been a hybrid disrupter, making it so inexpensive and convenient to eat out that it created a massive wave of growth in the "eating out" industry. McDonald's earliest victims were mom-and-pop diners.

There are numerous other examples of corporations that have used disruptive strategies to create competitive advantages. In a team, prepare a presentation highlighting three additional companies that used disruptive strategies to gain a competitive advantage.

APPLY YOUR KNOWLEDGE

1. Analyzing Websites

Stars Inc. is a large clothing corporation that specializes in reselling clothes worn by celebrities. The company's four websites generate 75 percent of its sales. The remaining 25 percent of sales occur directly through the company's warehouse. You have recently been hired as the director of sales. The only information you can find on the success of the four websites follows:

Website	Classic	Contemporary	New Age	Traditional
Traffic analysis	5,000 hits/day	200 hits/day	10,000 hits/day	1,000 hits/day
Stickiness (average)	20 min.	1 hr.	20 min.	50 min.
Number of abandoned shopping carts	400/day	0/day	5,000/day	200/day
Number of unique visitors	2,000/day	100/day	8,000/day	200/day
Number of identified visitors	3,000/day	100/day	2,000/day	800/day
Average revenue per sale	$1,000	$1,000	$50	$1,300

You decide that maintaining four separate websites is expensive and adds little business value. You want to propose consolidating to one site. Create a report detailing the business value gained by consolidating to a single website, along with your recommendation for consolidation. Be sure to include your website profitability analysis. Please assume that at a minimum 10 percent of hits result in a sale, at an average 30 percent of hits result in a sale, and at a maximum 60 percent of hits result in a sale.

2. Internet Groceries

E-Grocery, founded in 2007, is an online grocery shopping and delivery service. The company caters to thousands of customers in the Phoenix, Seattle, and Denver areas. Established on the idea that people will buy groceries over the Internet, e-Grocery offers over 25,000 items.

Ninety percent of e-Grocery's orders come in via computer; the rest are received by fax. Orders are received at the central office in Lakewood, Colorado, and then distributed by email to a local affiliate store. The store receives the order, the delivery address, and a map to the order location. A store employee designated to online orders will fill, deliver, and collect for the order. E-Grocery members are charged actual shelf prices, plus a per-order charge of $5.00 or 5 percent of the order amount, whichever is greater. Members also receive additional benefits such as electronic coupons, customer discounts, recipes, and tips.

Project Focus

The company is using interactive technology to change the shopping experience. The success of e-Grocery lies within many areas. Analyze the e-Grocery business model using the questions below. Feel free to think outside the box to develop your own analysis of online grocery shopping and ebusiness models.

a. What is e-Grocery's ebusiness model?

b. How does e-Grocery compete with traditional retailers?

c. What value can e-Grocery offer as a true competitive advantage in this marketplace?

d. What is the threat of new entrants in this market segment?

e. How is e-Grocery using technology to change the shopping experience?

f. What are the logistics for making e-Grocery profitable?

g. How does e-Grocery profit from online customer interaction?

h. What kinds of ebusiness strategies can e-Grocery's marketing department use to help grow its business?

i. What are some of the benefits and challenges facing e-Grocery?

3. Getting Personal

Consider Sally Albright, the reigning queen of customization in the movie *When Harry Met Sally.* Take, for example, the scene where she orders pie a la mode: "I'd like the pie heated. And I don't want the ice cream on top; I want it on the side. And I'd like strawberry instead of vanilla if you have it. If not, then no ice cream, just whipped cream, but only if it's real." Particular, yes, but Sally knew what she liked—and was not afraid to ask for it.

Project Focus

A growing number of online retailers are letting you have it your way, too. Choose a company highlighted in Figure AYK.1 and create your own product. Was the website easy to use? Would this service entice you as a customer to make a purchase over a generic product? If you could personalize a product what would it be and how would the website work?

4. Express Yourself

One of the most popular websites among students is MySpace, a site that allows students to express themselves by personalizing their home page. What is your favorite band? Who is your favorite author? What is your favorite movie? You can find out a lot about a person by finding out the answers to these questions.

Project Focus

Build a website dedicated to your favorite band, book, or movie. Your website must contain all of the following:

- An image.
- Two different size headings.
- Different sizes and colors of text.
- Two horizontal rules.
- Text that is bolded, underlined, and/or italicized.
- A textured background.
- A link to a website.
- A link to your email.
- One numbered and one unnumbered list.

5. Creating a Presence

More than 1 billion people are on the Internet. Having an Internet presence is critical for any business that wants to remain competitive. Businesses need their websites to create a "buzz" to attract customers. Ebusiness websites must be innovative, stimulating, add value, and provide useful information. In short, the site must build a sense of community and collaboration, eventually becoming the "port of entry" for business.

Project Focus

You are applying for a job at BagEm, a start-up ebusiness devoted to selling custom book bags that does not have any physical stores and sells bags only over the Internet. You are up against several other candidates for the job. BagEm has asked you to use your business expertise and website development skills to design and build a potential website. The candidate with the best website will be awarded the job. Good luck!

FIGURE AYK.1

Customization Companies

Company	Product
Tommy Hilfiger, custom.tomm.com	Premium-cotton chinos and jeans ($98)
Lands' End, www.landsend.com	Utilitarian jeans and chinos made of luxurious twill in traditional silhouettes ($59)
JCPenney, www.custom.jcpenney.com	Substantial twill pants in classic cuts ($44)
Ralph Lauren Polo, www.polo.com	Everything from basic polos to oxford shirts ($80)
TIMBUK2; www.timbuk2.com	Hip nylon messenger bags ($105)
L.L. Bean, www.llbean.com	Sturdy and colorful books, totes, and messenger bags ($70)
Nike, www.nikeid.com	Full range of athletic shoes and accessories ($90)
VANS, www.vans.com	Classic "Old Skool" lace-up or slip-on sneakers ($50)
Converse, www.converseone.com	Custom Chuck Taylors, the company's most classic style ($60)

The Innovator's Solution. By Clayton Christensen and Michael Raynor (Harvard Business School Publishing, 2003).

Roughly one company in every 10 is able to sustain the kind of growth that translates into an above-average increase in shareholder returns over more than a few years. Once a company's core business has matured, the pursuit of new platforms for growth entails daunting risk. To put it simply, most companies have no idea how to grow, and pursuing growth the wrong way can be worse than no growth.

In *The Innovator's Dilemma,* Clayton Christensen displayed how companies that focus on high-end products for profitable customers can be blindsided by "disruptive technologies" from new competitors—innovations that target low-end customers seeking cheaper products. In *The Innovator's Solution,* Christensen and co-author Michael Raynor show how established companies can create disruptions rather than being destroyed by them and how to turn innovative ideas into new disruptive products that will lead to long-term profitable growth.[43]

Purple Cow. By Seth Godin (New York: Penguin Group, 2003).

Following the traditional rules of marketing is not enough anymore. Consumers are simply inundated with information channels from newspapers and magazines to blogs and email. In today's competitive market, companies must create a remarkable new product to make customers to notice. According to marketing guru Seth Godin, such a product is a Purple Cow, a product or service that is worth making a remark about.

The impact of advertising in newspapers and magazines is fading as people are overwhelmed with information and have stopped paying attention to most media messages. To create a Purple Cow product, Godin advises companies to stop advertising and start innovating. Godin recommends that marketers target a niche, and he explains different ways to spread an idea to consumers who are most likely to purchase the product. Godin claims there is not a shortage of remarkable ideas—every business has opportunities to do great things—but there is a shortage of the will to execute those ideas.[44]

module 2

Essentials of Information Systems

Module Two concentrates on the essential components of information systems. Most people view IT strictly from a technological paradigm, but in fact, IT's power and influence is not so much a factor of its technical nature, but rather of what that technical infrastructure carries, houses, and supports: information. And information is power to an organization. This Module highlights this point and raises awareness of the significance of information to organizational success. Understanding how enterprise architectures support information, how employees access and analyze information to make business decisions, and how wireless and mobile technologies can enable information access 24x7 are the primary learning goals of Module Two. Properly managing information is a key organizational resource and can give a company a definite competitive advantage over competitors. The bottom line is that managers who treat information as a corporate asset yield success in the marketplace.

The module begins by covering information ethics and information security. With the many new governance and compliance regulations, all managers must understand the ethical issues surrounding information. As a key organizational resource, information must be protected from misuse and harm. This involves addressing ethical concerns around the collection, storage, and usage of information; protecting information privacy; and ensuring that information is secure against unauthorized access and attack.

Module 2: ESSENTIALS OF INFORMATION SYSTEMS

Ethics and Information Security

4

CHAPTER

What's in IT for me?

This chapter concerns itself with protecting information from potential misuse. Organizations must ensure they collect, capture, store, and use information in an ethical manner. This could be any type of information they collect and utilize, including information about customers, partners, and employees. Companies must ensure that personal information collected about someone remains private. This is not just a nice thing to do. The law requires it. Perhaps more importantly, information must be physically kept secure to prevent access and possible dissemination and use by unauthorized sources.

You, the business student, must understand ethics and security because they are the top concerns voiced by customers today. These concerns directly influence a customer's likelihood to embrace electronic technologies and conduct business over the web. In this sense, these concerns affect a company's bottom line. You can find evidence in recent news reports about how the stock price of organizations dramatically falls when information privacy and security breaches are made known. Further, organizations face potential litigation if they fail to meet their ethical, privacy, and security obligations concerning the handling of information in their companies.

Sarbanes-Oxley: Where Information Technology, Finance, and Ethics Meet

Congress is cleaning up the way companies do business after accounting and governance scandals rocked investor confidence and damaged the reputation of companies large and small. The Sarbanes-Oxley Act (SOX) of 2002 was enacted in response to the high-profile Enron and WorldCom financial scandals to protect shareholders and the public from accounting errors and fraudulent practices by organizations.

Sarbanes-Oxley

One primary component of the SOX is the definition of which records are to be stored and for how long. For this reason, the legislation not only affects financial departments, but also IT departments whose job it is to store electronic records. SOX states that all business records, including electronic records and electronic messages, "must be saved for not less than five years." The consequences for noncompliance are fines, imprisonment, or both. Three rules of Sarbanes-Oxley affecting the management of electronic records address the following areas:

1. The destruction, alteration, or falsification of records. It states that persons who knowingly alter, destroy, mutilate, conceal, or falsify documents shall be fined or imprisoned for not more than 20 years, or both.

2. The retention period for records storage. Best practices indicate that corporations securely store all business records using the same guidelines set for public accountants. Organizations shall maintain all audit or review work papers for a period of five years from the end of the fiscal period in which the audit or review was concluded.

3. The business records and communications that need to be stored, including electronic communications. IT departments are facing the challenge of creating and maintaining a corporate records archive in a cost-effective fashion that satisfies the requirements put forth by the legislation.

Essentially, any public organization that uses IT as part of its financial business processes must implement IT controls to comply with SOX. The cost of implementing SOX is high at $35 million per year for large companies. William D. Zollars, CEO of Yellow Roadway Corp., the nation's largest trucking firm, said, "It requires an army of people to do the paperwork." Zollars dispatched 200 people to work on SOX compliance, paying more than $9 million for the work—roughly 3 percent of annual profits.

Benefits from Sarbanes-Oxley

Many businesses are promoting the benefits they received from implementing SOX. General Electric Co., which spent about $30 million on SOX compliance, has added controls that boost investors' confidence in the company. United Technologies used SOX to standardize bookkeeping audits in its disparate businesses around the world. The biggest advantage of all, though, may be the greater confidence investors have in financial results.

Some officials expected it to take until 2008 for companies, auditors, and regulators to apply the law efficiently. That might appear to be a long time, and it may seem to be expensive; however, it is a small price to pay to help organizations run smoothly and renew investor confidence.

Implementing Sarbanes-Oxley

Ultimately, Sarbanes-Oxley compliance will require a great deal of work among all departments. Compliance starts with running IT as a business and strengthening IT internal controls. The following are a few practices organizations can follow to ensure compliance with the Sarbanes-Oxley Act.

- Overhaul or upgrade financial systems to meet regulatory requirements for more accurate, detailed, and timely filings.
- Examine the control processes within the IT department and apply best practices to comply with the act's goals. For example, segregation of duties within the systems development staff is a widely recognized best practice that helps prevent errors and outright fraud. The people who code program changes should be different from the people who test them, and a separate team should be responsible for changes in production environments.
- Ensure that information system customizations are not overriding controls by working with internal and external auditors. Homegrown financial systems are fraught with potential information-integrity issues. Although leading enterprise resource planning (ERP) systems offer audit-trail functionality, customizations of these systems often bypass those controls.
- Work with the CIO, CEO, CFO, and corporate attorneys to create a document-retention-and-destruction policy that addresses what types of electronic documents should be saved, and for how long.[1]

INTRODUCTION

Ethics and security are two fundamental building blocks for all organizations. In recent years, such events as the Enron and Martha Stewart scandals along with 9/11 have shed new light on the meaning of ethics and security. When the behavior of a few individuals can destroy billion-dollar organizations, the value of ethics and security should be evident.

section 4.1 ETHICS

Raven
Biotechnologies

LEARNING OUTCOMES

4.1. Explain the ethical issues surrounding information technology.

4.2. Identify the differences between an ethical computer use policy and an acceptable use policy.

4.3. Describe the relationship between an email privacy policy and an Internet use policy.

4.4. Explain the effects of spam on an organization.

4.5. Summarize the different monitoring technologies and explain the importance of an employee monitoring policy.

ETHICS

Ian Clarke, the inventor of a file-swapping service called Freenet, decided to leave the United States for the United Kingdom, where copyright laws are more lenient. Wayne Rosso, the inventor of a file-sharing service called Grokster, left the United States for Spain, again saying goodbye to tough U.S. copyright protections. The U.S. copyright laws, designed decades before the invention of the Internet, make file sharing and many other Internet technologies illegal. Although some individuals use file sharing in unethical manners, such as downloading music and movies illegally, file sharing has many positive benefits, such as improving drug research, software development, and the flow of information.[2]

The ethical issues surrounding copyright infringement and intellectual property rights are consuming the ebusiness world. Advances in technology make it easier for people to copy everything from music to pictures. Technology poses new challenges for our *ethics*—the principles and standards that guide our behavior toward other people. Review Figure 4.1 for an overview of concepts, terms, and ethical issues stemming from advances in technology.

The Securities Exchange Commission (SEC) began inquiries into Enron's accounting practices on October 22, 2001. David Duncan, the Arthur Andersen partner in charge of Enron, instructed his team to begin destroying paper and electronic Enron-related records on October 23, 2001. Kimberly Latham, a subordinate to Duncan, sent instructions on October 24, 2001, to her entire team to follow

FIGURE 4.1

Technology-Related Ethical Issues

Intellectual property	Intangible creative work that is embodied in physical form.
Copyright	The legal protection afforded an expression of an idea, such as a song, video game, and some types of proprietary documents.
Fair use doctrine	In certain situations, it is legal to use copyrighted material.
Pirated software	The unauthorized use, duplication, distribution, or sale of copyrighted software.
Counterfeit software	Software that is manufactured to look like the real thing and sold as such.

Primary Reasons Privacy Issues Reduce Trust for Ebusiness
1. Loss of personal privacy
2. Thirty-seven percent of Internet users are "a lot" more inclined to purchase a product on a website that has a privacy policy
3. Effective privacy and security would convert more Internet users to Internet buyers

FIGURE 4.2

Trust and Ebusiness

Duncan's orders and even compiled a list of computer files to delete. Arthur Andersen blames Duncan for destroying thousands of Enron-related documents. Duncan blames the Arthur Andersen attorney, Nancy Temple, for sending him a memo instructing him to destroy files. Temple blames Arthur Andersen's document deletion policies.[3]

Regardless of who is to blame, the bigger issue is that the destruction of files after a federal investigation has begun is both unethical and illegal. A direct corporate order to destroy information currently under federal investigation poses a dilemma for any professional. Comply, and you participate in potentially criminal activities; refuse, and you might find yourself looking for a new job.

Privacy is one of the largest ethical issues facing organizations. **Privacy** is the right to be left alone when you want to be, to have control over your own personal possessions, and not to be observed without your consent. Privacy is related to **confidentiality,** which is the assurance that messages and information are available only to those who are authorized to view them. Some of the most problematic decisions facing organizations lie in the murky and turbulent waters of privacy. The burden comes from the knowledge that each time employees make a decision regarding issues of privacy, the outcome could potentially sink the company.

Trust between companies, customers, partners, and suppliers is the support structure of ebusiness. One of the main ingredients in trust is privacy. Privacy continues to be one of the primary barriers to the growth of ebusiness. People are concerned their privacy will be violated because of interactions on the web. Unless an organization can effectively address this issue of privacy, its customers, partners, and suppliers might lose trust in the organization, which would hurt its business. In keeping with its mandate to gather intelligence, the CIA is watching YouTube. U.S. spies, now under the Director of National Intelligence (DNI), are looking increasingly online for intelligence; they have become major consumers of social media. "We're looking at YouTube, which carries some unique and honest-to-goodness intelligence," said Doug Naquin, director of the DNI Open Source Center. "We're looking at chat rooms and things that didn't exist five years ago, and trying to stay ahead. We have groups looking at what they call 'Citizens Media': people taking pictures with their cell phones and posting them on the Internet." Figure 4.2 displays the results from a *CIO* survey as to how privacy issues reduce trust for ebusinesses.

INFORMATION ETHICS

Information ethics concerns the ethical and moral issues arising from the development and use of information technologies, as well as the creation, collection, duplication, distribution, and processing of information itself (with or without the aid of computer technologies). Individuals determine how to use information and how information affects them. How individuals behave toward each other, how they handle information and technology, are largely influenced by their ethics. Ethical dilemmas usually arise not in simple, clear-cut situations but out of a clash between competing goals, responsibilities, and loyalties. Inevitably, the decision process has more than one socially acceptable "correct" decision. Figure 4.3 contains examples of ethically questionable or unacceptable uses of information technology.

Examples of Questionable Information Technology Use
Individuals copy, use, and distribute software.
Employees search organizational databases for sensitive corporate and personal information.
Organizations collect, buy, and use information without checking the validity or accuracy of the information.
Individuals create and spread viruses that cause trouble for those using and maintaining IT systems.
Individuals hack into computer systems to steal proprietary information.
Employees destroy or steal proprietary organization information such as schematics, sketches, customer lists, and reports.

Ethics

People make arguments for or against—justify or condemn—the behaviors in Figure 4.3. Unfortunately, there are few hard and fast rules for always determining what is and is not ethical. Knowing the law will not always help because what is legal might not always be ethical, and what might be ethical is not always legal. For example, Joe Reidenberg received an offer for cell phone service from AT&T Wireless. The offer revealed that AT&T Wireless had used Equifax, a credit reporting agency, to identify Joe Reidenberg as a potential customer. Overall, this strategy seemed like good business. Equifax could generate additional revenue by selling information it already owned and AT&T Wireless could identify target markets, thereby increasing response rates to its marketing campaigns.

Unfortunately, the Fair Credit Reporting Act (FCRA) forbids repurposing credit information except when the information is used for "a firm offer of credit or insurance." In other words, the only product that can be sold based on credit information is credit. A representative for Equifax stated, "As long as AT&T Wireless (or any company for that matter) is offering the cell phone service on a credit basis, such as allowing the use of the service before the consumer has to pay, it is in compliance with the FCRA." However, the question remains—is it ethical?[4]

This is a good example of the ethical dilemmas facing organizations. Because technology is so new and pervasive in unexpected ways, the ethics surrounding information are still being defined. Figure 4.4 displays the four quadrants of ethical and legal behavior. The ideal goal for organizations is to make decisions within quadrant I that are both legal and ethical.

Information Has No Ethics

Jerry Rode, CIO of Saab Cars USA, realized he had a public relations fiasco on his hands when he received an email from an irate customer. Saab had hired four Internet

FIGURE 4.4

Acting Ethically and Legally
Are Not Always the Same

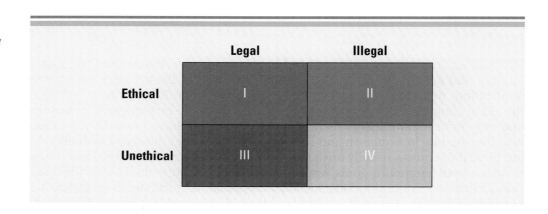

marketing companies to distribute electronic information about Saab's new models to its customers. Saab specified that the marketing campaign be opt-in, implying that it would contact only the people who had agreed to receive promotions and marketing material via email. Unfortunately, one of the marketing companies apparently had a different definition of opt-in and was emailing all customers regardless of their opt-in decision.

Rode fired the errant marketing company and immediately developed a formal policy for the use of customer information. "The customer doesn't see ad agencies and contracted marketing firms. They see Saab USA spamming them," Rode said. "Finger-pointing after the fact won't make your customers feel better."[5]

Information has no ethics. Information does not care how it is used. It will not stop itself from spamming customers, sharing itself if it is sensitive or personal, or revealing details to third parties. Information cannot delete or preserve itself. Therefore, it falls on the shoulders of those who own the information to develop ethical guidelines on how to manage the information. Figure 4.5 provides an overview of some of the important laws that individuals must follow when they are attempting to manage and protect information.

DEVELOPING INFORMATION MANAGEMENT POLICIES

Privacy

Treating sensitive corporate information as a valuable resource is good management. Building a corporate culture based on ethical principles that employees can understand and implement is responsible management. In an effort to provide guidelines for ethical information management, *CIO* magazine (along with over 100 CIOs) developed six principles for ethical information management displayed in Figure 4.6.

Organizations should develop written policies establishing employee guidelines, personnel procedures, and organizational rules for information. These policies set employee expectations about the organization's practices and standards and protect the organization from misuse of computer systems and IT resources. If an organization's employees use computers at work, the organization should, at a minimum, implement epolicies. *Epolicies* are policies and procedures that address the ethical use of computers and Internet usage in the business environment. These policies typically embody the following:

- Ethical computer use policy.
- Information privacy policy.
- Acceptable use policy.
- Email privacy policy.
- Internet use policy.
- Anti-spam policy.

Ethical Computer Use Policy

In a case that illustrates the perils of online betting, a leading Internet poker site reported that a hacker exploited a security flaw to gain an insurmountable edge in high-stakes, no-limit Texas hold-'em tournaments—the ability to see his opponents' hole cards. The cheater, whose illegitimate winnings were estimated at between $400,000 and $700,000 by one victim, was an employee of AbsolutePoker.com, who hacked the system to show that it could be done. Regardless of what business a company operates—even one that many view as unethical—the company must protect itself from unethical employee behavior.

One of the essential steps in creating an ethical corporate culture is establishing an ethical computer use policy. An *ethical computer use policy* contains general principles to guide computer user behavior. For example, the ethical computer use policy might explicitly state that users should refrain from playing computer games during working hours. This policy ensures the users know how

FIGURE 4.5

Established Information-Related Laws

Established Information-Related Laws	
Privacy Act—1974	Restricts what information the federal government can collect; allows people to access and correct information on themselves; requires procedures to protect the security of personal information; and forbids the disclosure of name-linked information without permission.
Family Education Rights and Privacy Act—1974	Regulates access to personal education records by government agencies and other third parties and ensures the right of students to see their own records.
Cable Communications Act—1984	Requires written or electronic consent from viewers before cable TV providers can release viewing choices or other personally identifiable information.
Electronic Communications Privacy Act—1986	Allows the reading of communications by a firm and says that employees have no right to privacy when using their companies' computers.
Computer Fraud and Abuse Act—1986	Prohibits unauthorized access to computers used for financial institutions, the U.S. government, or interstate and international trade.
The Bork Bill (officially known as the Video Privacy Protection Act, 1988)	Prohibits the use of video rental information on customers for any purpose other than that of marketing goods and services directly to the customer.
Communications Assistance for Law Enforcement Act—1994	Requires that telecommunications equipment be designed so that authorized government agents are able to intercept all wired and wireless communications being sent or received by any subscriber. The act also requires that subscriber call-identifying information be transmitted to a government when and if required.
Freedom of Information Act—1967, 1975, 1994, and 1998	Allows any person to examine government records unless it would cause an invasion of privacy. It was amended in 1974 to apply to the FBI, and again in 1994 to allow citizens to monitor government activities and information gathering, and once again in 1998 to access government information on the Internet.
Health Insurance Portability and Accountability Act (HIPAA)—1996	Requires that the health care industry formulate and implement regulations to keep patient information confidential.
Identity Theft and Assumption Deterrence Act—1998	Strengthened the criminal laws governing identity theft making it a federal crime to use or transfer identification belonging to another. It also established a central federal service for victims.
USA Patriot Act—2001 and 2003	Allows law enforcement to get access to almost any information, including library records, video rentals, bookstore purchases, and business records when investigating any act of terrorist or clandestine intelligence activities. In 2003, Patriot II broadened the original law.
Homeland Security Act—2002	Provided new authority to government agencies to mine data on individuals and groups including emails and website visits; put limits on the information available under the Freedom of Information Act; and gave new powers to government agencies to declare national heath emergencies.
Sarbanes-Oxley Act—2002	Sought to protect investors by improving the accuracy and reliability of corporate disclosures and requires companies to (1) implement extensive and detailed policies to prevent illegal activity within the company, and (2) to respond in a timely manner to investigate illegal activity.
Fair and Accurate Credit Transactions Act—2003	Included provisions for the prevention of identity theft including consumers' right to get a credit report free each year, requiring merchants to leave all but the last five digits of a credit card number off a receipt, and requiring lenders and credit agencies to take action even before a victim knows a crime has occurred when they notice any circumstances that might indicate identity theft.
CAN-Spam Act—2003	Sought to regulate interstate commerce by imposing limitations and penalties on businesses sending unsolicited email to consumers. The law forbids deceptive subject lines, headers, return addresses, etc., as well as the harvesting of email addresses from websites. It requires businesses that send spam to maintain a do-not-spam list and to include a postal mailing address in the message.

Six Principles for Ethical Information Management
1. Information is a valuable corporate asset and should be managed as such, like cash, facilities, or any other corporate asset.
2. The CIO is steward of corporate information and is responsible for managing it over its life cycle—from its generation to its appropriate destruction.
3. The CIO is responsible for controlling access to and use of information, as determined by governmental regulation and corporate policy.
4. The CIO is responsible for preventing the inappropriate destruction of information.
5. The CIO is responsible for bringing technological knowledge to the development of information management practices and policies.
6. The CIO should partner with executive peers to develop and execute the organization's information management policies.

to behave at work and the organization has a published standard by which to deal with user infractions. For example, after appropriate warnings, the company may terminate an employee who spends significant amounts of time playing computer games at work.

There are variations in how organizations expect their employees to use computers, but in any approach, the overriding principle when seeking appropriate computer use should be informed consent. The users should be *informed* of the rules and, by agreeing to use the system on that basis, *consent* to abide by the rules.

An organization should make a conscientious effort to ensure all users are aware of the policy through formal training and other means. If an organization were to have only one epolicy, it should be an ethical computer use policy since it is the starting point and the umbrella for any other policies the organization might establish.

Information Privacy Policy

Scott Thompson is the executive vice president of Inovant, the company Visa set up to handle its technology. Thompson errs on the side of caution in regard to Visa's information: He bans the use of Visa's customer information for anything outside its intended purpose—billing.

Visa's customer information details how people are spending their money, in which stores, on which days, and even at what time of day. Sales and marketing departments around the country no doubt are salivating at any prospect of gaining access to Visa's databases. "They would love to refine the information into loyalty programs, target markets, or even partnerships with Visa. There are lots of creative people coming up with these ideas. This whole area of information sharing is enormous and growing. For the marketers, the sky's the limit," Thompson said. Privacy specialists along with Thompson developed a strict credit card information policy, which the company follows.

The question now is can Thompson guarantee that unethical use of his information will not occur? Many experts do not believe that he can. In a large majority of cases, the unethical use of information happens not through the malicious scheming of a rogue marketer, but rather unintentionally. For instance, information is collected and stored for some purpose, such as record keeping or billing. Then, a sales or marketing professional figures out another way to use it internally, share it with partners, or sell it to a trusted third party. The information is "unintentionally" used for new purposes. The classic example of this type of unintentional information reuse is the Social Security number, which started simply as a way to identify government retirement benefits and is now used as a

Creating an Information Privacy Policy

1. **Adoption and implementation of a privacy policy.** An organization engaged in online activities or ebusiness has a responsibility to adopt and implement a policy for protecting the privacy of personal information. Organizations should also take steps that foster the adoption and implementation of effective online privacy policies by the organizations with which they interact, for instance, by sharing best practices with business partners.

2. **Notice and disclosure.** An organization's privacy policy must be easy to find, read, and understand. The policy must clearly state:
   - What information is being collected?
   - The use of information being collected.
   - Possible third-party distribution of that information.
   - The choices available to an individual regarding collection, use, and distribution of the collected information.
   - A statement of the organization's commitment to information security.
   - What steps the organization takes to ensure information quality and access.

3. **Choice and consent.** Individuals must be given the opportunity to exercise choice regarding how personal information collected from them online may be used when such use is unrelated to the purpose for which the information was collected. At a minimum, individuals should be given the opportunity to opt out of such use.

4. **Information security.** Organizations creating, maintaining, using, or disseminating personal information should take appropriate measures to assure its reliability and should take reasonable precautions to protect it from loss, misuse, or alteration.

5. **Information quality and access.** Organizations should establish appropriate processes or mechanisms so that inaccuracies in material personal information, such as account or contact information, may be corrected. Other procedures to assure information quality may include use of reliable sources, collection methods, appropriate consumer access, and protection against accidental or unauthorized alteration.

sort of universal personal ID, found on everything from drivers' licenses to savings accounts.

An organization that wants to protect its information should develop an information privacy policy. An *information privacy policy* contains general principles regarding information privacy. Figure 4.7 highlights a few guidelines an organization can follow when creating an information privacy policy.

Acceptable Use Policy

An *acceptable use policy (AUP)* is a policy that a user must agree to follow in order to be provided access to a network or to the Internet. *Nonrepudiation* is a contractual stipulation to ensure that ebusiness participants do not deny (repudiate) their online actions. A nonrepudiation clause is typically contained in an AUP.

Many businesses and educational facilities require employees or students to sign an acceptable use policy before gaining network access. When signing up with an Internet service provider (ISP), each customer is typically presented with an AUP, which states that they agree to adhere to certain stipulations (see Figure 4.8).

Email Privacy Policy

Email is so pervasive in organizations that it requires its own specific policy. In a recent survey, 80 percent of professional workers identified email as their preferred means of corporate communications. Trends also show a dramatic increase in the adoption rate of instant messaging (IM) in the workplace. While email and IM are common business communication tools, there are risks associated with using them. For instance, a sent email is stored on at least three or four different computers (see Figure 4.9). Simply deleting an email from one computer does not delete it off the other computers. Companies can mitigate many of the risks of

FIGURE 4.8

Acceptable Use Policy
Stipulations

Acceptable Use Policy Stipulations

1. Not using the service as part of violating any law.

2. Not attempting to break the security of any computer network or user.

3. Not posting commercial messages to groups without prior permission.

4. Not performing any nonrepudiation.

5. Not attempting to send junk email or spam to anyone who does not want to receive it.

6. Not attempting to mail bomb a site. A ***mail bomb*** is sending a massive amount of email to a specific person or system resulting in filling up the recipient's disk space, which, in some cases, may be too much for the server to handle and may cause the server to stop functioning.

using electronic messaging systems by implementing and adhering to an email privacy policy.[6]

One of the major problems with email is the user's expectations of privacy. To a large extent, this exception is based on the false assumption that email privacy protection exists somehow analogous to that of U.S. first-class mail. This is simply not true. Take the example of London lawyer Richard Phillips. After his secretary spilled a little ketchup on his pants, Phillips demanded restitution from her—via email—in the amount of a measly £4. The subject line of that email: "Ketchup Trousers." The secretary failed to pay immediately, owing to her mother's sudden death, but quickly made the David versus Goliath matter public, humiliating Phillips. His firm later said Phillips had resigned, but it was careful to note that the departure had nothing to do with the trousers incident.

Generally, the organization that owns the email system can operate the system as openly or as privately as it wishes. That means that if the organization wants to read everyone's email, it can do so. If it chooses not to read any, that is allowable too. Hence, it is up to the organization to decide how much, if any, email it is going to read. Then, when it decides, it must inform the users, so that they can consent to

FIGURE 4.9

Email Is Stored on Multiple
Computers

Deleting an email from the recipient's computer does not delete it from the sender's computer or the provider's computers.

FIGURE 4.10

Email Privacy Policy
Stipulations

Email Privacy Policy Stipulations
1. The policy should be complementary to the ethical computer use policy.
2. It defines who legitimate email users are.
3. It explains the backup procedure so users will know that at some point, even if a message is deleted from their computer, it will still be on the backup tapes.
4. It describes the legitimate grounds for reading someone's email and the process required before such action can be taken.
5. It informs that the organization has no control of email once it is transmitted outside the organization.
6. It explains what will happen if the user severs his or her connection with the organization.
7. It asks employees to be careful when making organizational files and documents available to others.

this level of intrusion. In other words, an ***email privacy policy*** details the extent to which email messages may be read by others.

Organizations must create an email privacy policy. Figure 4.10 displays a few of the key stipulations generally contained in an email privacy policy.

Internet Use Policy

Similar to email, the Internet has some unique aspects that make it a good candidate for its own policy. These include the large amounts of computing resources that Internet users can expend, thus making it essential that such use be legitimate. In addition, the Internet contains numerous materials that some believe are offensive and, hence, some regulation is required. An ***Internet use policy*** contains general principles to guide the proper use of the Internet. Figure 4.11 lists a few important stipulations that might be included in an Internet use policy.

Anti-Spam Policy

Chief technology officer (CTO) of the law firm Fenwick and West, Matt Kesner reduced incoming spam by 99 percent and found himself a corporate hero. Before the spam reduction, the law firm's partners (whose time is worth $350 to $600 an hour) found themselves spending hours each day sifting through 300 to 500 spam messages. The spam blocking engineered by Kesner traps between 5,000 and 7,000 messages a day.[7]

Spam is unsolicited email. An ***anti-spam policy*** simply states that email users will not send unsolicited emails (or spam). Spam plagues all levels of employees within an organization from receptionists to CEOs. Estimates indicate that spam accounts for 40 percent to 60 percent of most organizations' email traffic. Ferris Research says spam cost U.S. businesses over $10 billion in 2005, and Nucleus Research stated that

FIGURE 4.11

Internet Use Policy
Stipulations

Internet Use Policy Stipulations
1. The policy should describe available Internet services because not all Internet sites allow users to access all services.
2. The policy should define the organization's position on the purpose of Internet access and what restrictions, if any, are placed on that access.
3. The policy should complement the ethical computer use policy.
4. The policy should describe user responsibility for citing sources, properly handling offensive material, and protecting the organization's good name.
5. The policy should clearly state the ramifications if the policy is violated.

FIGURE 4.12

Spam Prevention Tips

Spam Prevention Tips

- **Disguise email addresses posted in a public electronic place.** When posting an email address in a public place, disguise the address through simple means such as replacing "jsmith@domain.com" with "jsmith at domain dot com." This prevents spam from recognizing the email address.

- **Opt out of member directories that may place an email address online.** Choose not to participate in any activities that place email addresses online. If an email address is placed online be sure it is disguised in some way.

- **Use a filter.** Many ISPs and free email services now provide spam filtering. While filters are not perfect, they can cut down tremendously on the amount of spam a user receives.

companies forfeit $874 per employee annually in lost productivity from spam alone. Spam clogs email systems and siphons IT resources away from legitimate business projects.[8]

It is difficult to write anti-spam policies, laws, or software because there is no such thing as a universal litmus test for spam. One person's spam is another person's newsletter. End users have to be involved in deciding what spam is because what is unwanted can vary widely not just from one company to the next, but from one person to the next. What looks like spam to the rest of the world could be essential business communications for certain employees.

John Zarb, CIO of Libbey, a manufacturer of glassware, china, and flatware, tested Guenivere (a virus and subject-line filter) and SpamAssassin (an open source spam filter). He had to shut them off after 10 days because they were rejecting important legitimate emails. As Zarb quickly discovered, once an organization starts filtering email, it runs the risk of blocking legitimate emails that look like spam. Avoiding an unacceptable level of "false positives" requires a delicate balancing act. The IT team tweaked the spam filters and today, the filters block about 70 percent of Libbey's spam, and Zarb said the "false positive" rate is far lower, but still not zero. Figure 4.12 highlights a few methods an organization can follow to prevent spam.

ETHICS IN THE WORKPLACE

Concern is growing among employees that infractions of corporate policies—even accidental ones—will be a cause for disciplinary action. The Whitehouse.gov Internet site displays the U.S. president's official website and updates on bill signings and new policies. Whitehouse.com, however, leads to a trashy site that capitalizes on its famous name. A simple mistype from .gov to .com could potentially cost someone her or his job if the company has a termination policy for viewing illicit websites. Monitoring employees is one of the largest issues facing CIOs when they are developing information management policies.

Legal precedents that hold businesses financially responsible for their employees' actions drives the decision of whether to monitor what employees do on company time with corporate resources. Increasingly, employee monitoring is not a choice; it is a risk-management obligation. Michael Soden, CEO of the Bank of Ireland, issued a mandate stating that company employees could not surf illicit websites with company equipment. Next, he hired Hewlett-Packard to run the IT department. A Hewlett-Packard employee soon discovered illicit websites on Soden's computer. Soden resigned.[9]

A survey of workplace monitoring and surveillance practices by the American Management Association (AMA) and the ePolicy Institute showed the degree to which companies are turning to monitoring:

- 82 percent of the study's 1,627 respondents acknowledged conducting some form of electronic monitoring or physical surveillance.
- 63 percent of the companies stated that they monitor Internet connections.
- 47 percent acknowledged storing and reviewing employee email messages.[10]

FIGURE 4.13

Employee Monitoring Effects

Employee Monitoring Effects
1. Employee absenteeism is on the rise, hitting 21 percent in 2004. The lesson here might be that more employees are missing work to take care of personal business. Perhaps losing a few minutes here or there—or even a couple of hours—is cheaper than losing entire days.
2. Studies indicate that electronic monitoring results in lower job satisfaction, in part because people begin to believe the quantity of their work is more important than the quality.
3. Electronic monitoring also induces what psychologists call "psychological reactance": the tendency to rebel against constraints. If you tell your employees they cannot shop, they cannot use corporate networks for personal business, and they cannot make personal phone calls, then their desire to do all these things will likely increase.

Monitoring Technologies

Many employees use their company's high-speed Internet access to shop, browse, and surf the web. Fifty-nine percent of all 2004 web purchases in the United States were made from the workplace, according to ComScore Networks. Vault.com determined that 47 percent of employees spend at least half an hour a day surfing the web.[11]

This research indicates that managers should monitor what their employees are doing with their web access. Most managers do not want their employees conducting personal business during working hours. For these reasons many organizations have increasingly taken the Big Brother approach to web monitoring with software that tracks Internet usage and even allows the boss to read employees' email. Figure 4.13 highlights a few reasons the effects of employee monitoring are worse than the lost productivity from employee web surfing.

This is the thinking at SAS Institute, a private software company consistently ranked in the top 10 on many "Best Places to Work" surveys. SAS does not monitor its employees' web usage. The company asks its employees to use company resources responsibly, but does not mind if they occasionally check sports scores or use the web for shopping.

Many management gurus advocate that organizations whose corporate cultures are based on trust are more successful than those whose corporate cultures are based on distrust. Before an organization implements monitoring technology it should ask itself, "What does this say about how the organization feels about its employees?" If the organization really does not trust its employees, then perhaps it should find new ones. If an organization does trust its employees, then it might want to treat them accordingly. An organization that follows its employees' every keystroke is unwittingly undermining the relationships with its employees.[12]

Information technology monitoring is tracking people's activities by such measures as number of keystrokes, error rate, and number of transactions processed. Figure 4.14 displays different types of monitoring technologies currently available.

Monitoring employee behavior should not just extend to the employee, but to how employees monitor each other. In 2002 a 14-year-old Canadian boy named Ghyslain Raza innocently swung a golf-ball retriever around in a quiet corner of his high school, pretending he was *The Phantom Menace*'s Darth Maul. He videotaped it, and he left the tape at school, where it was found several months later. Not long after, Raza became an Internet sensation, known today as the "Star Wars kid," with fans adding light-saber effects and music, and creating video revisions that number over a hundred. The embarrassing footage has since become one of the Internet's most popular, having been spoofed on TV shows ranging from *American Dad* to *The Colbert Report* to *Arrested Development*. In 2003, Raza sued the individuals who posted the video online, and the case was settled.

FIGURE 4.14

Monitoring Technologies

Common Monitoring Technologies	
Key logger, or key trapper, software	A program that, when installed on a computer, records every keystroke and mouse click.
Hardware key logger	A hardware device that captures keystrokes on their journey from the keyboard to the motherboard.
Cookie	A small file deposited on a hard drive by a website containing information about customers and their web activities. Cookies allow websites to record the comings and goings of customers, usually without their knowledge or consent.
Adware	Software that generates ads that install themselves on a computer when a person downloads some other program from the Internet.
Spyware (sneakware or stealthware)	Software that comes hidden in free downloadable software and tracks online movements, mines the information stored on a computer, or uses a computer's CPU and storage for some task the user knows nothing about.
Web log	Consists of one line of information for every visitor to a website and is usually stored on a web server.
Clickstream	Records information about a customer during a web surfing session such as what websites were visited, how long the visit was, what ads were viewed, and what was purchased.

Employee Monitoring Policies

Women are known to engage in a little private chitchat in the ladies' room, but how would they feel if the conversation was broadcast on CNN during a presidential speech? When newsreader Kyra Phillips made a pit stop, she unfortunately left her microphone on, broadcasting the news that her sister-in-law was a "control freak," among numerous other pronouncements. Phillips later laughed it off and even provided a *Late Show* "Top 10" list of excuses for why it happened. Sample: "How was I supposed to know we had a reporter embedded in the bathroom?" Although this reporter was able to laugh off the incident, an organization must ensure its employees are comfortable with any monitoring it is undertaking, including monitoring the restroom.

The best path for an organization planning to engage in employee monitoring is open communication surrounding the issue. A recent survey discovered that communication about monitoring issues is weak for most organizations. One in five companies did not even have an acceptable use policy and one in four companies did not have an Internet use policy. Companies that did have policies usually tucked them into the rarely probed recesses of the employee handbook, and then the policies tended to be of the vague and legal jargon variety: "XYZ company reserves the right to monitor or review any information stored or transmitted on its equipment." Reserving the right to monitor is materially different from clearly stating that the company does monitor, listing what is tracked, describing what is looked for, and detailing the consequences for violations.

An organization must formulate the right monitoring policies and put them into practice. Employee monitoring policies explicitly state how, when, and where the company monitors its employees. CSOs that are explicit about what the company does in the way of monitoring and the reasons for it, along with actively educating their employees about what unacceptable behavior looks like, will find that employees not only acclimate quickly to a policy, but also reduce the CSO's burden by policing themselves. Figure 4.15 displays several common stipulations an organization can follow when creating an employee monitoring policy.

FIGURE 4.15

Employee Monitoring Policy
Stipulations

Employee Monitoring Policy Stipulations
1. Be as specific as possible.
2. Always enforce the policy.
3. Enforce the policy in the same way for everyone.
4. Expressly communicate that the company reserves the right to monitor all employees.
5. Specifically state when monitoring will be performed.
6. Specifically state what will be monitored (email, IM, Internet, network activity, etc.).
7. Describe the types of information that will be collected.
8. State the consequences for violating the policy.
9. State all provisions that allow for updates to the policy.
10. Specify the scope and manner of monitoring for any information system.
11. When appropriate, obtain a written receipt acknowledging that each party has received, read, and understood the monitoring policies.

OPENING CASE QUESTIONS

Sarbanes-Oxley: Where Information Technology, Finance, and Ethics Meet

1. Define the relationship between ethics and the Sarbanes-Oxley Act.
2. Why is records management an area of concern for the entire organization and not just the IT department?
3. Identify two policies an organization can implement to achieve Sarbanes-Oxley compliance.
4. What ethical dilemmas are being solved by implementing Sarbanes-Oxley?
5. What is the biggest ethical roadblock for organizations attempting to achieve Sarbanes-Oxley compliance?

section 4.2 INFORMATION SECURITY

LEARNING OUTCOMES

4.6. Describe the relationship between information security policies and an information security plan.

4.7. Summarize the five steps to creating an information security plan.

4.8. Provide an example of each of the three primary information security areas: (1) authentication and authorization, (2) prevention and resistance, and (3) detection and response.

4.9. Describe the relationships and differences between hackers and viruses.

HOW MUCH WILL DOWNTIME COST YOUR BUSINESS?

The old business axiom "time is money" needs to be updated to more accurately reflect the crucial interdependence between IT and business processes. To reflect the times, the phrase should state "uptime is money." The leading cause of downtime is a software failure followed by human error, according to Infonetics research. Unplanned downtime can strike at any time from any number of causes, ranging from tornadoes to sink overflows to network failures to power outages. Although natural disasters may appear to be the most devastating causes of IT outages, they are hardly the most frequent or biggest threats to uptime. Figure 4.16 highlights sources of unplanned downtime.

According to Gartner Group, on average, enterprises lose $108,000 of revenue every hour their IT infrastructure is down. Figure 4.17 displays the four categories

FIGURE **4.16**

Sources of Unplanned Downtime

Sources of Unplanned Downtime

Bomb threat	Hacker	Snowstorm
Burst pipe	Hail	Sprinkler malfunction
Chemical spill	Hurricane	Static electricity
Construction	Ice storm	Strike
Corrupted data	Insects	Terrorism
Earthquake	Lightning	Theft
Electrical short	Network failure	Tornado
Epidemic	Plane crash	Train derailment
Equipment failure	Frozen pipe	Smoke damage
Evacuation	Power outage	Vandalism
Explosion	Power surge	Vehicle crash
Fire	Rodents	Virus
Flood	Sabotage	Water damage (various)
Fraud	Shredded data	Wind

FIGURE **4.17**

The Cost of Downtime

Financial Performance

Revenue recognition

Cash flow

Payment guarnatees

Credit rating

Stock price

Revenue

Direct loss

Compensatory payments

Lost future revenue

Billing losses

Investment losses

Lost productivity

$

Know your cost of downtime per hour, per day, per week.

Damaged Reputation

Customers

Suppliers

Financial markets

Banks

Business partners

Other Expenses

Temporary employees

Equipment rentals

Overtime costs

Extra shipping charges

Travel expenses

Legal obligations

associated with downtime, according to the Gartner Group. A few questions companies should ask when determining the cost of downtime include:

- How many transactions can the company afford to lose without significantly impacting business?
- Does the company depend upon one or more mission-critical applications to conduct business?
- How much revenue will the company lose for every hour a critical application is unavailable?
- What is the productivity cost associated with each hour of downtime?
- How will collaborative business processes with partners, suppliers, and customers be affected by an unexpected IT outage?
- What is the total cost of lost productivity and lost revenue during unplanned downtime?

The reliability and resilience of IT systems have never been more essential for success as businesses cope with the forces of globalization, 24×7 operations, government and trade regulations, and overextended IT budgets and resources. Any unexpected IT downtime in today's business environment has the potential to cause both short- and long-term costs with far-reaching consequences. Section 4.2 explains how you can use security to combat the threat of downtime. Understanding how to secure a business network is critical to keeping downtime to a minimum and uptime to a maximum.

PROTECTING INTELLECTUAL ASSETS

Smoking is not just bad for a person's health; it seems that it is also bad for company security. With companies banning smoking inside their offices, smokers are forced outside—usually to specific smoking areas in the back of the building. The doors leading out to them are a major security hole, according to a study undertaken by NTA Monitor Ltd., a U.K.-based Internet security tester.

NTA's tester was able to easily get inside a corporate building through a back door that was left open so smokers could easily and quickly get out and then back in, according to the company. Once inside, the tester asked an employee to take him to a meeting room, claiming the IT department had sent him. Even without a pass, he reportedly gained access unchallenged and was then able to connect his laptop to the company's network.

Organizational information is intellectual capital. Just as organizations protect their assets—keeping their money in an insured bank or providing a safe working environment for employees—they must also protect their intellectual capital. An organization's intellectual capital includes everything from its patents to its transactional and analytical information. With security breaches on the rise and computer hackers everywhere, an organization must put in place strong security measures to survive.

The Health Insurance Portability and Accountability Act (HIPAA) protects the privacy and security of personal health records and has the potential to impact every business in the United States. HIPAA affects all companies that use electronic data interchange (EDI) to communicate personal health records. HIPAA requires health care organizations to develop, implement, and maintain appropriate security measures when sending electronic health information. Most important, these organizations must document and keep current records detailing how they are performing security measures for all transmissions of health information. On April 21, 2005, security rules for HIPAA became enforceable by law.

The Health Information Management Society estimated that 70 percent of all health care providers failed to meet the April 2005 deadline for privacy rule compliance. Health care organizations need to take HIPAA regulations seriously since noncompliance can result in substantial fines and even imprisonment.[13]

Beyond the health care industry, all businesses must understand the importance of information security, even if it is not enforceable by law. **Information security** is a broad term encompassing the protection of information from accidental or intentional misuse by persons inside or outside an organization. Figure 4.18 displays the typical size of an organization's information security budget relative to the organization's overall IT budget from the CSI/FBI Computer Crime and Security Survey.

State Farm Bank

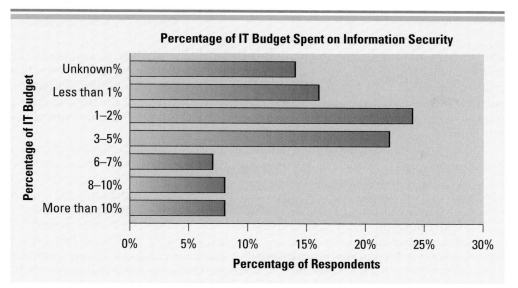

FIGURE 4.18

Organization's Security
Budget

Forty-six percent of respondents indicated that their organization spent between 1 and 5 percent of the total IT budget on security. Only 16 percent indicated that their organization spent less than 1 percent of the IT budget on security.

Figure 4.19 displays the spending per employee on computer security broken down by both public and private industries. The highest average computer security investment per employee was found in the transportation industry.[14]

Security is perhaps the most fundamental and critical of all the technologies/disciplines an organization must have squarely in place to execute its business strategy. Without solid security processes and procedures, none of the other technologies can develop business advantages.

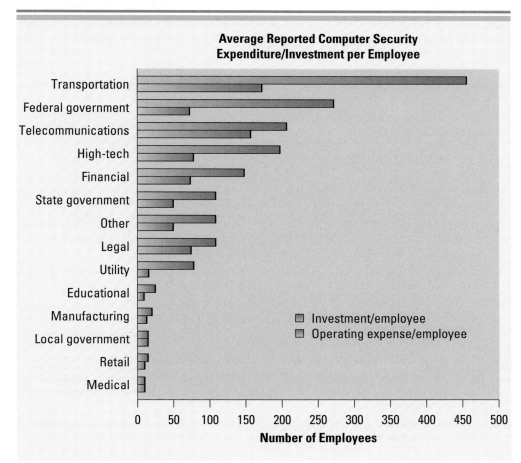

FIGURE 4.19

Security Spending per
Employee

THE FIRST LINE OF DEFENSE—PEOPLE

With current advances in technologies and business strategies organizations are able to determine valuable information such as who are the top 20 percent of the customers that produce 80 percent of all revenues. Most organizations view this type of information as valuable intellectual capital, and they are implementing security measures to prevent the information from walking out the door or falling into the wrong hands. Enterprises can implement information security lines of defense through people first and through technology second.

Adding to the complexity of information security is the fact that organizations must enable employees, customers, and partners to access information electronically to be successful in this electronic world. Doing business electronically automatically creates tremendous information security risks for organizations. Surprisingly, the biggest issue surrounding information security is not a technical issue, but a people issue.

The CSI/FBI Computer Crime and Security Survey reported that 38 percent of respondents indicated security incidents originated within the enterprise. *Insiders* are legitimate users who purposely or accidentally misuse their access to the environment and cause some kind of business-affecting incident. Most information security breaches result from people misusing an organization's information either advertently or inadvertently. For example, many individuals freely give up their passwords or write them on sticky notes next to their computers, leaving the door wide open to intruders.[15]

The director of information security at a large health care company discovered how easy it was to create an information security breach when she hired outside auditors to test her company's security awareness. In one instance, auditors found that staff members testing a new system had accidentally exposed the network to outside hackers. In another, auditors were able to obtain the passwords of 16 employees when the auditors posed as support staff; hackers frequently use such "social engineering" to obtain passwords. *Social engineering* is using one's social skills to trick people into revealing access credentials or other information valuable to the attacker. Dumpster diving, or looking through people's trash, is another way social engineering hackers obtain information.[16]

Information security policies identify the rules required to maintain information security. An *information security plan* details how an organization will implement the information security policies. Figure 4.20 is an example of the University of Denver's Information Security Plan.

FIGURE 4.20

Sample Information
Security Plan

Interim Information Security Plan
This Information Security Plan ("Plan") describes the University of Denver's safeguards to protect information and data in compliance ("Protected Information") with the Financial Services Modernization Act of 1999, also known as the Gramm Leach Bliley Act, 15 U.S.C. Section 6801. These safeguards are provided to: ■ Ensure the security and confidentiality of Protected Information; ■ Protect against anticipated threats or hazards to the security or integrity of such information; and ■ Protect against unauthorized access to or use of Protected Information that could result in substantial harm or inconvenience to any customer.
This Information Security Plan also provides for mechanisms to: ■ Identify and assess the risks that may threaten Protected Information maintained by the University of Denver; ■ Develop written policies and procedures to manage and control these risks; ■ Implement and review the plan; and ■ Adjust the plan to reflect changes in technology, the sensitivity of covered data and information and internal or external threats to information security.
Identification and Assessment of Risks to Customer Information
The University of Denver recognizes that it has both internal and external risks. These risks include, but are not limited to: ■ Unauthorized access of Protected Information by someone other than the owner of the covered data and information

FIGURE 4.20

(continued)

Interim Information Security Plan *(continued)*

- Compromised system security as a result of system access by an unauthorized person
- Interception of data during transmission
- Loss of data integrity
- Physical loss of data in a disaster
- Errors introduced into the system
- Corruption of data or systems
- Unauthorized access of covered data and information by employees
- Unauthorized requests for covered data and information
- Unauthorized access through hardcopy files or reports
- Unauthorized transfer of covered data and information through third parties

The University of Denver recognizes that this may not be a complete list of the risks associated with the protection of Protected Information. Since technology growth is not static, new risks are created regularly. Accordingly, the Information Technology Department and the Office of Student Affairs will actively participate with and seek advice from an advisory committee made up of university representatives for identification of new risks. The University of Denver believes current safeguards used by the Information Technology Department are reasonable and, in light of current risk assessments, are sufficient to provide security and confidentiality to Protected Information maintained by the University.

Information Security Plan Coordinators

The University CIO and the Vice President for Student Affairs, in consultation with an advisory committee, have been appointed as the coordinators of this Plan. They are responsible for assessing the risks associated with unauthorized transfers of covered data and information and implementing procedures to minimize those risks to the University of Denver.

Design and Implementation of Safeguards Program

Employee Management and Training

During employee orientation, each new employee in departments that handle Protected Information will receive proper training on the importance of confidentiality of Protected Information.

Physical Security

- The University of Denver has addressed the physical security of Protected Information by limiting access to only those employees who have a business reason to know such information.

Information Systems

The University of Denver has policies governing the use of electronic resources and firewall and wireless policies. The University of Denver will take reasonable and appropriate steps consistent with current technological developments to make sure that all Protected Information is secure and to safeguard the integrity of records in storage and transmission. The University of Denver will develop a plan to ensure that all electronic Protected Information is encrypted in transit.

Selection of Appropriate Service Providers

Due to the specialized expertise needed to design, implement, and service new technologies, vendors may be needed to provide resources that the University of Denver determines not to provide on its own. In the process of choosing a service provider that will maintain or regularly access Protected Information, the evaluation process shall include the ability of the service provider to safeguard Protected Information. Contracts with service providers may include the following provisions:

- A stipulation that the Protected Information will be held in strict confidence and accessed only for the explicit business purpose of the contract;
- An assurance from the contract partner that the partner will protect the Protected Information it receives.

Continuing Evaluation and Adjustment

This Information Security Plan will be subject to periodic review and adjustment, especially when due to the constantly changing technology and evolving risks. The Coordinators, in consultation with the Office of General Counsel, will review the standards set forth in this policy and recommend updates and revisions as necessary. It may be necessary to adjust the plan to reflect changes in technology, the sensitivity of student/customer data and internal or external threats to information security.

FIGURE 4.21

Creating an Information
Security Plan

Five Steps for Creating an Information Security Plan	
1. **Develop the information security policies**	Identify who is responsible and accountable for designing and implementing the organization's information security policies. Simple, yet highly effective types of information security policies include requiring users to log off of their systems before leaving for lunches or meetings, never sharing passwords with anyone, and changing personal passwords every 60 days. The chief security officer (CSO) will typically be responsible for designing these information security policies.
2. **Communicate the information security policies**	Train all employees on the policies and establish clear expectations for following the policies. For example, let all employees know that they will receive a formal reprimand for leaving a computer unsecured.
3. **Identify critical information assets and risks**	Require the use of user IDs, passwords, and antivirus software on all systems. Ensure any systems that contain links to external networks have the appropriate technical protections such as firewalls or intrusion detection software. A *firewall* is hardware and/or software that guards a private network by analyzing the information leaving and entering the network. *Intrusion detection software (IDS)* searches out patterns in information and network traffic to indicate attacks and quickly responds to prevent any harm.
4. **Test and reevaluate risks**	Continually perform security reviews, audits, background checks, and security assessments.
5. **Obtain stakeholder support**	Gain the approval and support of the information security polices from the board of directors and all stakeholders.

The first line of defense an organization should follow is to create an information security plan detailing the various information security policies. A detailed information security plan can alleviate people-based information security issues. Figure 4.21 displays the five steps for creating an information security plan.

Businesses consider desktop users to be the biggest security risk to their networks, despite increased concern over outsourced labor and remote users. Figures from a recent Sophos network security survey indicated that businesses still see office-bound employees as those most likely to expose their networks to IT threats. Such users were considered the greatest threat to security by 44 percent of respondents. Mobile employees, are considered to be a greater security threat by 31 percent of respondents. Other users considered to be a threat to network security include contractors and outsourced labor, at 14 percent, and guests, at 11 percent. Sophos's head of technology, Paul Ducklin, said, "This is a representation of how common telecommuting and remote working has become," to the extent that half of those in the office are also remote workers. "The obvious thing we can draw from the results is that administrators haven't become complacent about desktop security," Ducklin said. He also pointed out that while some organizations employ a "stricter regimen for outside than inside," the physical risks to equipment associated with mobile users—such as the loss of or damage to a laptop—are unavoidable.

Figure 4.22 provides the top 10 questions from Ernst & Young that managers should ask to ensure their information is secure.

THE SECOND LINE OF DEFENSE—TECHNOLOGY

Arkansas State University (ASU) recently completed a major network upgrade that brought gigabit-speed network capacity to every dorm room and office on its campus. The university was concerned that the new network would be a tempting playground for hackers. To reduce its fear, the university installed intrusion detection software (IDS) from Cisco Systems to stay on top of security and potential network abuses. Whenever the IDS spots a potential security threat, such as a virus or

Top 10 Questions Managers Should Ask Regarding Information Security
1. Does our Board of Directors recognize information security is a board-level issue that cannot be left to the IT department alone?
2. Is there clear accountability for information security in our organization?
3. Do our Board members articulate an agreed-upon set of threats and critical assets? How often do we review and update these?
4. How much is spent on information security and what is it being spent on?
5. What is the impact on the organization of a serious security incident?
6. Does our organization view information security as an enabler? (For example, by implementing effective security, could we enable our organization to increase business over the Internet?)
7. What is the risk to our business of getting a reputation for low information security?
8. What steps have we taken to ensure that third parties will not compromise the security of our organization?
9. How do we obtain independent assurance that information security is managed effectively in our organization?
10. How do we measure the effectiveness of our information security activities?

a hacker, it alerts the central management system. The system automatically pages the IT staff, who deal with the attack by shutting off access to the system, identifying the hacker's location, and calling campus security.[17]

Once an organization has protected its intellectual capital by arming its people with a detailed information security plan, it can begin to focus its efforts on deploying the right types of information security technologies such as the IDS installed at Arkansas State.

Organizations can deploy numerous technologies to prevent information security breaches. When determining which types of technologies to invest in, it helps to understand the three primary information security areas:

1. Authentication and authorization.
2. Prevention and resistance.
3. Detection and response.[18]

Authentication and Authorization

Authentication is a method for confirming users' identities. Once a system determines the authentication of a user, it can then determine the access privileges (or authorization) for that user. *Authorization* is the process of giving someone permission to do or have something. In multiple-user computer systems, user access or authorization determines such things as file access, hours of access, and amount of allocated storage space. Authentication and authorization techniques are broken down into three categories, and the most secure type involves a combination of all three:

1. Something the user knows such as a user ID and password.
2. Something the user has such as a smart card or token.
3. Something that is part of the user such as a fingerprint or voice signature.

Something the User Knows Such As a User ID and Password   The first type of authentication, using something the user knows, is the most common way to identify individual users and typically consists of a unique user ID and password. However, this is actually one of the most *ineffective* ways for determining authentication because passwords are not secure. All it typically takes to crack a password is enough time. More than 50 percent of help-desk calls are password related, which can cost an organization significant money, and passwords are vulnerable to being coaxed out of somebody by a social engineer.

FIGURE 4.23

Examples of Identity Theft

Identity Theft Examples
An 82-year-old woman in Fort Worth, Texas, discovered that her identity had been stolen when the woman using her name was involved in a four-car collision. For 18 months, she kept getting notices of lawsuits and overdue medical bills that were really meant for someone else. It took seven years for her to get her financial good name restored after the identity thief charged over $100,000 on her 12 fraudulently acquired credit cards.
A 42-year-old retired Army captain in Rocky Hill, Connecticut, found that an identity thief had spent $260,000 buying goods and services that included two trucks, a Harley-Davidson motorcycle, and a time-share vacation home in South Carolina. The victim discovered his problem only when his retirement pay was garnished to pay the outstanding bills.
In New York, members of a pickpocket ring forged the driver's licenses of their victims within hours of snatching the women's purses. Stealing a purse typically nets around $200, if not less. But stealing the person's identity can net on average between $4,000 and $10,000.
A crime gang took out $8 million worth of second mortgages on victims' homes. It turned out the source of all the instances of identity theft came from a car dealership.
The largest identity-theft scam to date in U.S. history was broken up by police in 2002 when they discovered that three men had downloaded credit reports using stolen passwords and sold them to criminals on the street for $60 each. Many millions of dollars were stolen from people in all 50 states.

Identity theft is the forging of someone's identity for the purpose of fraud. The fraud is often financial fraud, to apply for and use credit cards in the victim's name or to apply for a loan. By 2003, online banking was not yet ubiquitous but everyone could see that, eventually, it would be. Everyone includes Internet criminals, who by then had already built software capable of surreptitiously grabbing personal information from online forms, like the ones used for online banking. The first of these so-called form-grabbing viruses was called Berbew and was wildly effective. Lance James, a researcher with Secure Science Corp., believes it operated undetected for as long as nine months and grabbed as much as 113GB of data—millions of personal credentials. Like all exploits, Berbew was eventually detected and contained, but, as is customary with viruses, strands of Berbew's form-grabbing code were stitched into new viruses that had adapted to defenses. The process is not unlike horticulturalists' grafting pieces of one plant onto another in order to create hardier mums. Figure 4.23 displays several examples of identity theft.

Phishing is a common way to steal identities online. *Phishing* is a technique to gain personal information for the purpose of identity theft, usually by means of fraudulent email. One way to accomplish phishing is to send out email messages that look as though they came from legitimate businesses such as AOL, MSN, or Amazon. The messages appear to be genuine with official-looking formats and logos. These emails typically ask for verification of important information like passwords and account numbers. The reason given is often that this personal information is required for accounting or auditing purposes. Since the emails look authentic, up to one in five recipients respond with the information, and subsequently becomes a victim of identity theft and other fraud.

Something the User Has Such As a Smart Card or Token The second type of authentication, using something that the user has, offers a much more effective way to identify individuals than a user ID and password. Tokens and smart cards are two of the primary forms of this type of authentication. *Tokens* are small electronic devices that change user passwords automatically. The user enters his or her user ID and token-displayed password to gain access to the network. A *smart card* is a device that is around the same size as a credit card, containing embedded technologies that can store information and small amounts of software to perform some limited processing. Smart cards can act as identification instruments, a form of digital cash, or a data storage device with the ability to store an entire medical record.

Something That Is Part of the User Such As a Fingerprint or Voice Signature The third kind of authentication, using something that is part of the user, is by far the best and most effective way to manage authentication. *Biometrics* (narrowly defined) is the identification of a user based on a physical characteristic, such as a fingerprint, iris, face, voice, or handwriting. Unfortunately, biometric authentication can be costly and intrusive. For example, iris scans are expensive and considered intrusive by most people. Fingerprint authentication is less intrusive and inexpensive but is also not 100 percent accurate. Biometrics are being used to help clear airport security in about four minutes. The Clear Card is a preregistered form of ID that lets travelers bypass airport security lines. The card works by storing biometrics of iris and fingerprint inside a microchip on the card. At the airport, the user swipes the card at a security kiosk and the computer matches the biometrics on the card with the fingerprint or iris. If it matches, the user is ready for takeoff. The card is available for $100 along with a $28 fee for a Transportation Security Administration background check.

Prevention and Resistance

Prevention and resistance technologies stop intruders from accessing intellectual capital. A division of Sony Inc., Sony Pictures Entertainment (SPE), defends itself from attacks by using an intrusion detection system to detect new attacks as they occur. SPE develops and distributes a wide variety of products including movies, television, videos, and DVDs. A compromise to SPE security could cost the company valuable intellectual capital as well as millions of dollars and months of time. The company needed an advanced threat management solution that would take fewer resources to maintain and require limited resources to track and respond to suspicious network activity. The company installed an advanced intrusion detection system allowing it to monitor all of its network activity including any potential security breaches.[19]

The cost of downtime or network operation failures can be devastating to any business. For example, eBay experienced a 22-hour outage in June 2000 that caused the company's market cap to plunge an incredible $5.7 billion. Downtime costs for businesses can vary from $100 to $1 million per hour. An organization must prepare for and anticipate these types of outages resulting most commonly from hackers and viruses. Technologies available to help prevent and build resistance to attacks include content filtering, encryption, and firewalls.[20]

Content Filtering

Content filtering occurs when organizations use software that filters content to prevent the transmission of unauthorized information. Organizations can use content filtering technologies to filter email and prevent emails containing sensitive information from transmitting, whether the transmission was malicious or accidental. It can also filter emails and prevent any suspicious files from transmitting such as potential virus-infected files. Email content filtering can also filter for spam, a form of unsolicited email. Organizational losses from spam were expected to be about $198 billion in 2007 (see Figure 4.24).[21]

Sean Lane's purchase was supposed to be a surprise for his wife. Then it appeared as a news headline, "Sean Lane bought 14k White Gold 1/5 ct Diamond Eternity Flower Ring from overstock.com," on the social networking website Facebook. Without Lane's knowledge, the headline was visible to everyone in his online network, including 500 classmates from Columbia University and 220 other friends, co-workers, and acquaintances. And his wife. The wraps came off his Christmas gift thanks to an advertising feature called Beacon, which shares news of Facebook members' online purchases with their friends. The idea, according to the company,

2003	$20.5
2007	$198

is to allow merchants to effectively turn millions of Facebook users into a word-of-mouth promotion service. Lane called it "Christmas ruined," and more than 50,000 other users signed a petition calling on Facebook to stop broadcasting people's transactions without their consent.

Encryption

Security

Encryption scrambles information into an alternative form that requires a key or password to decrypt the information. If there is an information security breach and the information was encrypted, the person stealing the information will be unable to read it. Encryption can switch the order of characters, replace characters with other characters, insert or remove characters, or use a mathematical formula to convert the information into some sort of code. Companies that transmit sensitive customer information over the Internet, such as credit card numbers, frequently use encryption.

Some encryption technologies use multiple keys like public key encryption. *Public key encryption (PKE)* is an encryption system that uses two keys: a public key that everyone can have and a private key for only the recipient (see Figure 4.25). When implementing security using multiple keys, the organization provides the public key to all of its customers (end consumers and other businesses). The customers use the public key to encrypt their information and send it along the Internet. When it arrives at its destination, the organization would use the private key to unscramble the encrypted information.

Firewalls

One of the most common defenses for preventing a security breach is a firewall. A *firewall* is hardware and/or software that guards a private network by analyzing the information leaving and entering the network. Firewalls examine each message that wants entrance to the network. Unless the message has the correct markings, the firewall prevents it from entering the network. Firewalls can even detect computers communicating with the Internet without approval. As Figure 4.26 illustrates, organizations typically place a firewall between a server and the Internet.

FIGURE 4.25

Public Key Encryption (PKE)
System

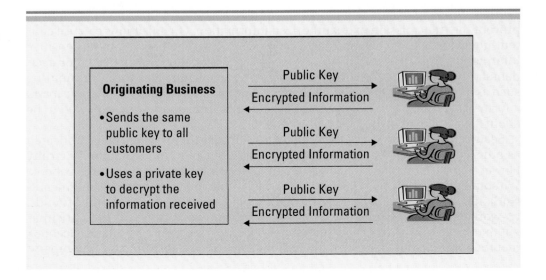

Originating Business

• Sends the same public key to all customers

• Uses a private key to decrypt the information received

Public Key
Encrypted Information

Public Key
Encrypted Information

Public Key
Encrypted Information

FIGURE 4.26

Sample Firewall Architecture Connecting Systems Located in Chicago, New York, and Boston

Detection and Response

The final area where organizations can allocate resources is in detection and response technologies. If prevention and resistance strategies fail and there is a security breach, an organization can use detection and response technologies to mitigate the damage. The most common type of defense within detection and response technologies is antivirus software.

A single worm can cause massive damage. In August 2003, the "Blaster worm" infected over 50,000 computers worldwide and was one of the worst outbreaks of the year. Jeffrey Lee Parson, 18, was arrested by U.S. cyber investigators for unleashing the damaging worm on the Internet. The worm replicated itself repeatedly, eating up computer capacity, but did not damage information or programs. The worm generated so much traffic that it brought entire networks down.

The FBI used the latest technologies and code analysis to find the source of the worm. Prosecutors said that Microsoft suffered financial losses that significantly exceeded $5,000, the statutory threshold in most hacker cases. Parson, charged with intentionally causing or attempting to cause damage to a computer, was sentenced to 18 months in prison, three years of supervised release, and 100 hours of community service. "What you've done is a terrible thing. Aside from injuring people and their computers, you shook the foundation of technology," U.S. District Judge Marsha Pechman told Parson.

"With this arrest, we want to deliver a message to cyber-hackers here and around the world," said U.S. Attorney John McKay in Seattle. "Let there be no mistake about it, cyber-hacking is a crime. We will investigate, arrest, and prosecute cyber-hackers."[22]

Typically, people equate viruses (the malicious software) with hackers (the people). While not all types of hackers create viruses, many do. Figure 4.27 provides an overview of the most common types of hackers and viruses.

Some of the most damaging forms of security threats to ebusiness sites include malicious code, hoaxes, spoofing, and sniffers (see Figure 4.28).

Implementing information security lines of defense through people first and through technology second is the best way for an organization to protect its vital intellectual capital. The first line of defense is securing intellectual capital by creating an information security plan detailing the various information security policies. The second line of defense is investing in technology to help secure information through authentication and authorization, prevention and resistance, and detection and response.

FIGURE 4.27

Hackers and Viruses

Hackers—people very knowledgeable about computers who use their knowledge to invade other people's computers.

- **White-hat hackers**—work at the request of the system owners to find system vulnerabilities and plug the holes.
- **Black-hat hackers**—break into other people's computer systems and may just look around or may steal and destroy information.
- **Hactivists**—have philosophical and political reasons for breaking into systems and will often deface the website as a protest.
- **Script kiddies** or **script bunnies**—find hacking code on the Internet and click-and-point their way into systems to cause damage or spread viruses.
- **Cracker**—a hacker with criminal intent.
- **Cyberterrorists**—seek to cause harm to people or to destroy critical systems or information and use the Internet as a weapon of mass destruction.

Viruses—software written with malicious intent to cause annoyance or damage.

- **Worm**—a type of virus that spreads itself, not only from file to file, but also from computer to computer. The primary difference between a virus and a worm is that a virus must attach to something, such as an executable file, in order to spread. Worms do not need to attach to anything to spread and can tunnel themselves into computers.
- **Denial-of-service attack (DoS)**—floods a website with so many requests for service that it slows down or crashes the site.
- **Distributed denial-of-service attack (DDoS)**—attacks from multiple computers that flood a website with so many requests for service that it slows down or crashes. A common type is the Ping of Death, in which thousands of computers try to access a website at the same time, overloading it and shutting it down.
- **Trojan-horse virus**—hides inside other software, usually as an attachment or a downloadable file.
- **Backdoor programs**—viruses that open a way into the network for future attacks.
- **Polymorphic viruses and worms**—change their form as they propagate.

FIGURE 4.28

Security Threats to Ebusiness

Security Threats to Ebusiness

Elevation of privilege is a process by which a user misleads a system into granting unauthorized rights, usually for the purpose of compromising or destroying the system. For example, an attacker might log onto a network by using a guest account, and then exploit a weakness in the software that lets the attacker change the guest privileges to administrative privileges.

Hoaxes attack computer systems by transmitting a virus hoax, with a real virus attached. By masking the attack in a seemingly legitimate message, unsuspecting users more readily distribute the message and send the attack on to their co-workers and friends, infecting many users along the way.

Malicious code includes a variety of threats such as viruses, worms, and Trojan horses.

Spoofing is the forging of the return address on an email so that the message appears to come from someone other than the actual sender. This is not a virus but rather a way by which virus authors conceal their identities as they send out viruses.

Spyware is software that comes hidden in free downloadable software and tracks online movements, mines the information stored on a computer, or uses a computer's CPU and storage for some task the user knows nothing about. According to the National Cyber Security Alliance, 91 percent of the study had spyware on their computers that can cause extremely slow performance, excessive pop-up ads, or hijacked home pages.

A **sniffer** is a program or device that can monitor data traveling over a network. Sniffers can show all the data being transmitted over a network, including passwords and sensitive information. Sniffers tend to be a favorite weapon in the hacker's arsenal.

Packet tampering consists of altering the contents of packets as they travel over the Internet or altering data on computer disks after penetrating a network. For example, an attacker might place a tap on a network line to intercept packets as they leave the computer. The attacker could eavesdrop or alter the information as it leaves the network.

Sarbanes-Oxley: Where Information Technology, Finance, and Ethics Meet

6. What information security dilemmas are being solved by implementing Sarbanes-Oxley?

7. How can Sarbanes-Oxley help protect a company's information security?

8. What impact does implementing Sarbanes-Oxley have on information security in a small business?

9. What is the biggest information security roadblock for organizations attempting to achieve Sarbanes-Oxley compliance?

SUMMARY OF KEY THEMES

The purpose of this chapter was to highlight the need for organizations to protect information from misuse. Discussion first centered on the concept of information ethics and how organizations need to be aware of the moral issues surrounding the development and use of information and information technology. Information privacy was examined with an emphasis placed on understanding the legal obligations and general expectations on organizations in terms of how personal information is collected, shared, and stored. Information security includes the two levels of defense that organizations have to protect their information resources: people and technology.

You, the business student, must understand that ethics and security of information and information technology are of paramount importance in organizations today. Organizations that fail to meet these obligations not only face legal repercussions, but also the wrath of consumers who have high expectations on how their personal information is handled by companies.

KEY TERMS

Acceptable use policy (AUP)   138
Adware   143
Anti-spam policy   140
Authentication   151
Authorization   151
Backdoor program   156
Biometrics   153
Black-hat hacker   156
Clickstream   143
Confidentiality   133
Content filtering   153
Cookie   143
Copyright   132
Counterfeit software   132
Cracker   156
Cyberterrorist   156
Denial-of-service attack (DoS)   156
Distributed denial-of-service attack (DDoS)   156
Elevation of privilege   156
Email privacy policy   140
Encryption   154

Epolicies   135
Ethical computer use policy   135
Ethics   132
Fair use doctrine   132
Firewall   150, 154
Hacker   156
Hactivist   156
Hardware key logger   143
Hoaxes   156
Identity theft   152
Information privacy policy   138
Information security   146
Information security plan   148
Information security policies   148
Information technology monitoring   142
Insider   148
Intellectual property   132
Internet use policy   140
Intrusion detection software (IDS)   150
Key logger software (key trapper)   143
Mail bomb   139

Malicious code   156
Nonrepudiation   138
Packet tampering   156
Phishing   152
Pirated software   132
Polymorphic virus and worm   156
Privacy   133
Public key encryption (PKE)   154
Script kiddies or script bunnies   156
Smart card   152
Sniffer   156
Social engineering   148
Spam   140
Spoofing   156
Spyware (sneakware or stealthware)   143, 156
Token   152
Trojan-horse virus   156
Virus   156
Web log   143
White-hat hacker   156
Worm   156

Banks Banking on Security

Bank of America, Commerce Bancorp, PNC Financial Services Group, and Wachovia were victims of a crime where a person tried to obtain customer data and sell it to law firms and debt-collection agencies. New Jersey police seized 13 computers from the alleged master-mind with 670,000 account numbers and balances. There is no indication the data were used for identity theft, but it highlights how increasingly difficult it is to protect information against such schemes as the market value of personal information grows. In the past, banks were wary of the cost or customer backlash from adopting network security technologies. Today, banks are beefing up network security as more customers begin to view security as a key factor when choosing a bank.

Bank of America

Bank of America is moving toward a stronger authentication process for its 13 million online customers. Bank of America's SiteKey service is designed to thwart scams in which customers think they are entering data on the bank's website, when they are actually on a thief's site built to steal data. This occurs when a worm tells a computer to reroute the bank's URL into a browser to another site that looks exactly like the bank's.

SiteKey offers two-factor authentication. When enrolling in SiteKey, a customer picks an image from a library and writes a brief phrase. Each time the customer signs on, the image and phrase are displayed, indicating that the bank recognizes the computer the customer is using and letting the customer know that he is in fact at the bank's official website. The customer then enters a password and proceeds. When signing on from a different computer than usual the customer must answer one of three prearranged questions.

Wells Fargo & Company

"Out-of-wallet" questions contain information that is not found on a driver's license or ATM card. Wells Fargo is implementing a security strategy that operates based on "out-of-wallet" questions as a second factor for network password enrollment and maintenance. It is also offering network security hardware such as key fobs that change passwords every 60 seconds, and launching a two-factor authentication pilot in which small businesses making electronic funds transfers will need a key fob to complete transactions.

E-Trade Financial Corporation

E-Trade Financial Corporation provides customers with account balances exceeding $50,000 a free Digital Security ID for network authentication. The device displays a new six-digit code every 60 seconds, which the customer must use to log on. Accounts under $50,000 can purchase the Digital Security ID device for $25.

Barclay's Bank

Barclay's Bank instituted online-transfer delays of between several hours and one day. The delays, which apply the first time a transfer is attempted between two accounts, are intended to give the bank time to detect suspicious activity, such as a large number of transfers from multiple accounts into a single account. The online-transfer delay was adopted in response to a wave of phishing incidents in which thieves transferred funds from victims' bank accounts into accounts owned by "mules." Mules are people who open bank accounts based on an email solicitation, usually under the guise of a business proposal. From the mule accounts, the thieves withdraw cash, open credit cards, or otherwise loot the account.

Barclay's also offers account monitoring of customer's actions to compare them with historical profile data to detect unusual behavior. For instance, the service would alert the bank to contact the customer if the customer normally logs on from England and suddenly logs on from New York and performs 20 transactions.[23]

Questions

1. What reason would a bank have for not wanting to adopt an online-transfer delay policy?
2. What are the two primary lines of security defense and why are they important to financial institutions?
3. Explain the differences between the types of security offered by the banks in the case. Which bank would you open an account with and why?
4. What additional types of security, not mentioned in the case above, would you recommend a bank implement?
5. Identify three policies a bank should implement to help it improve information security.
6. Describe monitoring policies along with the best way for a bank to implement monitoring technologies.

CLOSING CASE TWO

Hacker Hunters

Hacker hunters are the new breed of crime fighter. They employ the same methodology used to fight organized crime in the 1980s—informants and the cyberworld equivalent of wiretaps. Daniel Larking, a 20-year veteran who runs the FBI's Internet Crime Complaint Center, taps online service providers to help track down criminal hackers. Leads supplied by the FBI and eBay helped Romanian police round up 11 members of a gang that set up fake eBay accounts and auctioned off cell phones, laptops, and cameras they never intended to deliver.

On October 26, 2004, the FBI unleashed Operation Firewall, targeting the ShadowCrew, a gang whose members were schooled in identity theft, bank account pillage, and selling illegal goods on the Internet. ShadowCrew's 4,000 gang members lived in a dozen countries and across the United States. For months, agents had been watching their every move through a clandestine gateway into their website, shadowcrew.com. One member turned informant and called a group meeting, ensuring the members would be at home on their computers during a certain time, when the Secret Service issued orders to move in on the gang. The move was synchronized around the globe to prevent gang members from warning each other via instant messages. Twenty-eight gang members in eight states and six countries were arrested, most still at their computers. Authorities seized dozens of computers and found 1.7 million credit card numbers and more than 18 million email accounts.

ShadowCrew's Operations

The alleged ringleaders of ShadowCrew included Andres Mantovani, 23, a part-time community college student in Arizona, and David Appleyard, 45, a former New Jersey mortgage broker. Mantovani and Appleyard allegedly were administrators in charge of running the website and recruiting members. The site created a marketplace for over 4,000 gang members who bought and sold hot information and merchandise. The website was open for business 24 hours a day, but since most of the members held jobs, the busiest time was from 10 p.m. to 2 a.m. on Sundays. Hundreds of gang members would meet online to trade credit card information, passports, and even equipment to make fake identity documents. Platinum credit cards cost more than gold ones and discounts were offered for package deals. One member known as "Scarface" sold 115,695 stolen credit card numbers in a single trade. Overall, the gang made more than $4 million in credit card purchases over two years. ShadowCrew was equivalent to an eBay for the underworld. The site even posted crime tips on how to use stolen credit cards and fake IDs at big retailers.

The gang stole credit card numbers and other valuable information through clever tricks. One of the favorites was sending millions of phishing emails—messages that appeared to be from legitimate companies such as Yahoo!—designed to steal passwords and credit card numbers. The gang also hacked into corporate databases to steal account data. According to sources familiar with the investigation, the gang cracked the networks of 12 unidentified companies that were not even aware their systems had been breached.

Police Operations

Brian Nagel, an assistant director at the Secret Service, coordinated the effort to track the ShadowCrew. Allies included Britain's national high-tech crimes unit, the Royal Canadian Mounted Police, and the Bulgarian Interior Ministry. Authorities turned one of the high-ranking members of the gang into a snitch and had the man help the Secret Service set up a new electronic doorway for ShadowCrew members to enter their website. The snitch spread the word that the new gateway was a more secure way to the website. It was the first-ever tap of a private computer network. "We became shadowcrew.com," Nagel said. Mantovani and Appleyard were slated for trial in late 2005. Authorities anticipated using case evidence to make additional arrests.[24]

Questions

1. What types of technology could big retailers use to prevent identity thieves from purchasing merchandise?
2. What can organizations do to protect themselves from hackers looking to steal account data?
3. Authorities frequently tap online service providers to track down hackers. Do you think it is ethical for authorities to tap an online service provider and read people's email? Why or why not?
4. Do you think it was ethical for authorities to use one of the high-ranking officials to trap other gang members? Why or why not?
5. In a team, research the Internet and find the best ways to protect yourself from identity theft.

CLOSING CASE THREE

Executive Dilemmas in the Information Age

The vast array of business initiatives from supply chain management, customer relationship management, business process reengineering, and enterprise resource planning makes it clear that information technology has evolved beyond the role of mere infrastructure to the support of business strategy. Today, in more and more industries, IT is a business strategy and is quickly becoming a survival issue.

Board and executive team agendas are increasingly peppered with, or even hijacked by, a growing range of IT issues from compliance to ethics and security. In most companies today, computers are key business tools. They generate, process, and store the majority of critical business information. Executives must understand how IT can affect a business by successfully addressing a wide range of needs—from large electronic discovery projects to the online review of document collections by geographically dispersed teams. A few examples of executive IT issues follow.

Stolen Proprietary Information

A computer company investigated to determine if an executive who accepted a job with a competitor stole proprietary information. The hard drive from the executive's laptop and desktop machine were forensically imaged. The analysis established that the night before the executive left, he downloaded all of the company's process specifications and distributor agreements, which he then zipped and emailed to the competitor. Additionally, reconstruction of deleted files located emails between the executive and the competitor discussing his intent to provide the proprietary information if he was offered additional options in the new company.

Sexual Harassment

A woman employed by a large defense contractor accused her supervisor of sexual harassment. The woman was fired from her job for poor performance and subsequently sued her ex-boss and the former employer.

A computer company was retained by the plaintiff's attorneys to investigate allegations of the former supervisor's harassing behavior. After making a forensic image backup of the ex-boss's hard drive, the forensic company was able to recover deleted electronic messages that showed the ex-boss had a history of propositioning women under his supervision for "special favors." A situation that might have been mired in a "he said/she said" controversy was quickly resolved; the woman got her job back, and the real culprit was terminated.

Stolen Trade Secrets

The board of directors of a technical research company demoted the company's founder and CEO. The executive, disgruntled because of his demotion, was later terminated. It was subsequently determined that the executive had planned to quit about the same time he was fired and establish a competitive company. Upon his termination, the executive took home two computers; he returned them to the company four days later, along with another company computer that he had previously used at home. Suspicious that critical information had been taken, the company's attorneys sent the computers to a computer forensic company for examination.

After making a forensic image backup of the hard drives, the forensic analysis identified a file directory that had been deleted during the aforementioned four-day period that had the same name as the competing company the executive had established. A specific search of the deleted files in this directory identified the executive's "to do list" file. This file indicated the executive planned to copy the company's database (valued at $100 million) for his personal use. Another item specified the executive was to "learn how to destroy evidence on a computer."

The computer forensic company's examination also proved that the executive had been communicating with other competing companies to establish alliances, in violation of the executive's nondisclosure agreement with the company. It was also shown that numerous key company files were located on removable computer storage media that had not been turned over by the executive to the company.[25]

Questions

1. Explain why understanding technology, especially in the areas of security and ethics, is important for a CEO. How do a CEO's actions affect the organizational culture?
2. Identify why executives in nontechnological industries need to worry about technology and its potential business ramifications.
3. Describe why continuously learning about technology allows an executive to better analyze threats and opportunities.
4. Identify three things that a CTO, CPO, or CSO could do to prevent the above issues.

1. Firewall decisions

You are the CEO of Inverness Investments, a medium-sized venture capital firm that specializes in investing in high-tech companies. The company receives over 30,000 email messages per year. On average, there are two viruses and three successful hackings against the company each year, which result in losses to the company of about $250,000 per year. Currently, the company has antivirus software installed but does not have any firewalls.

Your CIO is suggesting implementing 10 firewalls for a total cost of $80,000. The estimated life of each firewall is about three years. The chances of hackers breaking into the system with the firewalls installed are about 3 percent. Annual maintenance costs on the firewalls is estimated around $15,000. Create an argument for or against supporting your CIO's recommendation to purchase the firewalls. Are there any considerations in addition to finances?

2. Preventing identity theft

The FBI states that identity theft is one of the fastest-growing crimes. If you are a victim of identity theft, your financial reputation can be ruined, making it impossible for you to cash a check or receive a bank loan. Learning how to avoid identity theft can be a valuable activity. Research the following websites and draft a document stating the best ways to prevent identity theft.

- The Federal Trade Commission Consumer Information on ID theft at www.consumer.gov/idtheft.
- The Office of the Comptroller of the Currency at www.occ.treas.gov/chcktfd.idassume.htm.
- The Office of the Inspector General at www.ssa.gov/oig/when.htm.
- U.S. Department of Justice at www.usdoj.gov/criminal/fraud/idtheft.html.

3. Discussing the three areas of information security

Great Granola Inc. is a small business operating out of northern California. The company specializes in selling homemade granola, and its primary sales vehicle is through its website. The company is growing exponentially and expects its revenues to triple this year to $12 million. The company also expects to hire 60 additional employees to support its growing number of customers. Joan Martin, the CEO, is aware that if her competitors discover the recipe for her granola, or who her primary customers are, it could easily ruin her business. Joan has hired you to draft a document discussing the different areas of information security, along with your recommendations for providing a secure ebusiness environment.

4. Information privacy

A study by the Annenberg Public Policy Center at the University of Pennsylvania shows that 95 percent of people who use the Internet at home think they should have a legal right to know everything about the information that websites collect from them. Research also shows that 57 percent of home Internet users incorrectly believe that when a website has an information privacy policy it will not share personal information with other websites or companies. In fact, the research found that after showing the users how companies track, extract, and share website information to make money, 85 percent found the methods unacceptable, even for a highly valued site. Write a short paper arguing for or against an organization's right to use and distribute personal information gathered from its website.

5. Spying on email

Technology advances now allow individuals to monitor computers that they do not even have physical access to. New types of software can capture an individual's incoming and outgoing email and then immediately forward that email to another person. For example, if you are at work and your child is home from school and she receives an email from John at 3:00 pm, at

3:01 pm you will receive a copy of that email sent to your email address. A few minutes later, if she replies to John's email, within seconds you will again receive a copy of what she sent to John. Describe two scenarios (other than the above) for the use of this type of software: (1) where the use would be ethical, (2) where the use would be unethical.

6. **Stealing software**

The software industry fights against pirated software on a daily basis. The major centers of software piracy are in places like Russia and China where salaries and disposable income are comparatively low. People in developing and economically depressed countries will fall behind the industrialized world technologically if they cannot afford access to new generations of software. Considering this, is it reasonable to blame someone for using pirated software when it could potentially cost him or her two months' salary to purchase a legal copy? Create an argument for or against the following statement: "Individuals who are economically less fortunate should be allowed access to software free of charge in order to ensure that they are provided with an equal technological advantage."

7. **Acting ethically**

Assume you are an IT manager and one of your projects is failing. You were against the project from the start; however, the project had powerful sponsorship from all of the top executives. You know that you are doomed and that the project is doomed. The reasons for the failure are numerous including the initial budget was drastically understated, the technology is evolving and not stable, the architecture was never scaled for growth, and your resources do not have the necessary development skills for the new technology. One of your team leads has come to you with a plan to sabotage the project that would put the project out of its misery without assigning any blame to the individuals on the project. Create a document detailing how you would handle this situation.

APPLY YOUR KNOWLEDGE

1. Grading Security

Making The Grade is a nonprofit organization that helps students learn how to achieve better grades in school. The organization has 40 offices in 25 states and more than 2,000 employees. The company wants to build a website to offer its services online. Making The Grade's online services will provide parents seven key pieces of advice for communicating with their children to help them achieve academic success. The website will offer information on how to maintain open lines of communication, set goals, organize academics, regularly track progress, identify trouble spots, get to know their child's teacher, and celebrate their children's successes.

Project Focus

You and your team work for the director of information security. Your team's assignment is to develop a document discussing the importance of creating information security polices and an information security plan. Be sure to include the following:

- The importance of educating employees on information security.
- A few samples of employee information security policies specifically for Making The Grade.
- Other major areas the information security plan should address.
- Signs the company should look for to determine if the website is being hacked.
- The major types of attacks the company should expect to experience.

2. Eyes Everywhere

The movie *Minority Report* chronicled a futuristic world where people are uniquely identifiable by their eyes. A scan of each person's eyes gives or denies them access to rooms, computers, and anything else with restrictions. The movie portrayed a black market in new eyeballs to help people hide from the authorities. (Why did they not just change the database entry instead? That would have been much easier, but a lot less dramatic.)

The idea of using a biological signature is entirely plausible since biometrics is currently being widely used and is expected to gain wider acceptance in the near future because forging documents has become much easier with the advances in computer graphics programs and color printers. The next time you get a new passport, it may incorporate a chip that has your biometric information encoded on it. Office of Special Investigations agents with fake documents found that it was relatively easy to enter the United States from Canada, Mexico, and Jamaica, by land, sea, and air.

The task of policing the borders is daunting. Some 500 million foreigners enter the country every year and go through identity checkpoints. More than 13 million permanent-resident and border-crossing cards have been issued by the U.S. government. Also, citizens of 27 countries do not need visas to enter this country. They are expected to have passports that comply with U.S. specifications that will also be readable at the border.

In the post-9/11 atmosphere of tightened security, unrestricted border crossing is not acceptable. The Department of Homeland Security is charged with securing the nation's borders, and as part of this plan, new entry/exit procedures were instituted at the beginning of 2003. An integrated system, using biometrics, will be used to identify foreign visitors to the United States and reduce the likelihood of terrorists entering the country.

Early in 2003, after 6 million biometric border-crossing cards had been issued, a pilot test conducted at the Canadian border detected more than 250 imposters. The testing started with two biometric identifiers: photographs for facial recognition and fingerprint scans. As people enter and leave the country, their actual fingerprints and facial features are compared to the data on the biometric chip in the passport.[26]

Project Focus

In a group, discuss the following:

a. How do you feel about having your fingerprints, facial features, and perhaps more of your biometric features encoded in documents like your passport? Explain your answer.

b. Would you feel the same way about having biometric information on your driver's license as on your passport? Why or why not?

c. Is it reasonable to have different biometric identification requirements for visitors from different nations? Explain your answer. What would you recommend as criteria for deciding which countries fall into what categories?

d. The checkpoints U.S. citizens pass through upon returning to the country vary greatly in the depth of the checks and the time spent. The simplest involves simply walking past the border guards who may or may not ask you your citizenship. The other end of the spectrum requires that you put up with long waits in airports where you have to line up with hundreds of other passengers while each person is questioned and must produce a passport to be scanned. Would you welcome biometric information on passports if it would speed the process, or do you think that the disadvantages of the reduction in privacy, caused by biometric information, outweigh the advantages of better security and faster border processing? Explain your answer.

3. Setting Boundaries

Even the most ethical people sometimes face difficult choices. Acting ethically means behaving in a principled fashion and treating other people with respect and dignity. It is simple to say, but not so simple to do since some situations are complex or ambiguous. The important role of ethics in our lives has long been recognized. As far back as 44 B.C., Cicero said that ethics are indispensable to anyone who wants to have a good career. Having said that, Cicero, along with some of the greatest minds over the centuries, struggled with what the rules of ethics should be.

Our ethics are rooted in our history, culture, and religion, and our sense of ethics may shift over time. The electronic age brings with it a new dimension in the ethics debate—the amount of personal information that we can collect and store, and the speed with which we can access and process that information.[27]

Project Focus

In a group, discuss how you would react to the following situations:

a. A senior marketing manager informs you that one of her employees is looking for another job and she wants you to give her access to look through her email.

b. A vice president of sales informs you that he has made a deal to provide customer information to a strategic partner, and he wants you to burn all of the customer information onto a DVD.

c. You are asked to monitor your employee's email to discover if he is sexually harassing another employee.

d. You are asked to install a video surveillance system in your office to watch if employees are taking office supplies home with them.

e. You are looking on the shared network drive and discover that your boss's entire hard drive has been copied to the network for everyone to view. What do you do?

f. You have been accidentally copied on an email from the CEO, which details who will be the targets of the next round of layoffs. What would you do?

4. Contemplating Sharing

Bram Cohen is the creator of one of the most successful peer-to-peer (P2P) programs ever developed, BitTorrent. BitTorrent allows users to quickly upload and download enormous amounts of data, including files that are hundreds or thousands of times bigger than a single MP3. BitTorrent's program is faster and more efficient than traditional P2P networking.

Cohen showed his code to the world at a hacker conference, as a free, open source project aimed at computer users who need a cheap way to swap software online. But the real audience turns out to be TV and movie fanatics. It takes hours to download a ripped episode of *Alias* or *Monk* off Kazaa, but BitTorrent can do it in minutes. As a result, more than 20 million people have downloaded the BitTorrent application. If any one of them misses a favorite TV show, no worries. Surely, someone has posted it as a "torrent." As for movies, if you can find it at Blockbuster, you can probably find it online somewhere—and use BitTorrent to download it. "Give and ye shall receive" became Cohen's motto, which he printed on T-shirts and sold to supporters.[28]

Project Focus

There is much debate surrounding the ethics of peer-to-peer networking. Do you believe BitTorrent is ethical or unethical? Justify your answer.

BUSINESS DRIVEN BEST SELLERS

The Smartest Guys in the Room, By Bethany McLean and Peter Elkind (New York: Penguin Group, 2003).

The biggest and most shocking business story of our time is the Enron debacle, and Fortune's senior writers Bethany McLean and Peter Elkind have dug up the full story of the players and the plays that created the scandal of the century. *The Smartest Guys in the Room* details the rise and fall of the Enron empire as well as its cast of intriguing characters in a gripping narrative that is based on a wide range of private documents and exclusive sources.[29]

Career Warfare. By David D'Alessandro (New York: McGraw-Hill, 2004).

What does it really take to make it to the top? Unfortunately, hard work and big accomplishments will only get you so far. Competing at the top levels where the competition is ferocious—where everybody is hardworking and accomplished—you need a much more subtle advantage. You need to build a reputation or "personal brand" that convinces people to trust you!

The primary problem is that it is difficult to build trust and a great personal brand. First, you must understand that you will be judged on everything including the most insignificant moments. Then, you have to become conscious of the personal impression you are making every single day. Next, you have to be noticed—and noticed for the right qualities. Ultimately, a big career requires everything from the right kind of manners, to the right style of handling your detractors, to the right instincts about when to leave a job and when to stick with it. *Career Warfare* offers the unwritten rules of organizational life, the real truths you need to know in order to build an incredible personal brand and trust.[30]

Leadership Sopranos Style: Lessons from a Fictional Mob Boss. By Deborrah Himsel (Chicago: Dearborn, 2004).

As a successful leadership development executive at Avon, Deborrah Himsel understands what it takes to become an effective business leader. Using the central character from the HBO series *The Sopranos* as a reference point and example of a leader who embraces the right leadership qualities, she describes a variety of business scenarios where Tony Soprano's wisdom and skills actually pay off. With insight, style, and wit, Himsel presents memorable leadership lessons that are timely and inspirations. By using such a well-developed (and well-written) character to epitomize the lessons she imparts, she is able to capture the depth and intensity of the tasks leaders must master to become more effective in their pivotal roles.

Himsel describes how blunt, Soprano-style forthrightness has helped her deal with her subordinates as well as consultants. Using 360-degree feedback, seeking self-awareness, and coaching underlings are relevant leadership skills Tony demonstrates season after season. Himsel has distilled these skills and methods into a leadership plan that is both full of valuable lessons and easy to grasp.[31]

Enterprise Architectures

What's in IT for me?

Why do you, as a business student, need to understand the underlying technology of any business? Isn't this technical stuff something that businesses hire nerds and geeks for? Every manager in the 21st century must have a base-level appreciation of what technology can and cannot do for the business. The information presented in this chapter attempts to create a more level playing field between managers and IT staff, who are already ingrained in technology terms and acronyms.

If you understand the concepts of planning and development of information systems, you can think about how information technology can be used to support business decisions. This is a critical skill for any businessperson, no matter if they are just starting out or a seasoned Fortune 500 employee. Learning about information architectures will give you a competitive advantage because understanding how information systems work can provide you with feedback on overall business performance.

After reading this chapter, you should have many of the skills needed to become directly involved in analyzing current business systems, in recommending needed changes in business processes, in evaluating alternative hardware and software options, and in judging the technical feasibility of a project.

Virgin Mobile

Virgin Mobile USA is a joint venture between Richard Branson's Virgin Group and Sprint. Launched nationally in July 2002, Virgin Mobile USA has set the pace as the fastest growing wireless carrier in the United States while redefining the entire prepaid market. As the nation's first mobile virtual network operator (MVNO) and the first wireless service to solely target the youth market, Virgin Mobile has attracted nearly 2 million wireless users to its pay-as-you-go service with no contracts and no hidden fees. Virgin Mobile also provides customers with innovative, personalized voice and data offerings tailored to the lifestyle and preferences of today's young consumers.

As an MVNO, Virgin Mobile faces the unique challenge of owning the customer relationship, including call management, without owning the mobile network. This requires extensive application and systems integration between Virgin Mobile's information technology architecture and the legacy systems that power the Sprint PCS network.

Virgin Mobile has also faced intense time-to-market pressure since its inception as the wireless industry grows more cluttered every day. Virgin Mobile targeted and successfully executed its public launch just seven months from the date the company was founded. This was an extremely aggressive timeline in an industry where businesses often take years to get off the ground. Since going live, the time-to-market pressure has not subsided. To stay fresh and maintain a competitive advantage, Virgin Mobile must roll out new features continually.

To address these imposing challenges, and implement a world-class mobile service with reliability and scalability, Virgin Mobile made a strategic decision to rely on a team of technology partners to provide key capabilities. This was a classic "buy versus build" strategy. However, Virgin Mobile still had to deploy (and manage) its own IT infrastructure—the "glue" holding everything together and ensuring flawless operation. After all, with no contracts to sign or long-term obligations, prepaid customers who are dissatisfied can abandon Virgin Mobile at any time. This is a key business pressure that traditional mobile service providers do not face.

Virgin Mobile's architecture is based on a service-oriented architecture that enables the company to build functionality as web services and then expose the services via multiple channels (e.g., handsets from Audiovox and Kyocera). The architecture links a customer relationship system, a prepaid billing solution, and value-added services from a variety of content providers. In addition, Virgin Mobile built 26 application interfaces for core business functions such as point-of-sale order entry, order management, product fulfillment, and mobile service provisioning. Most of these interfaces were built as web services.

The scope of the integration work was a major driver behind the decision to utilize a service oriented architecture and web services. Because web services are open and standards-based, Virgin Mobile is able to create and expose the services much faster than would have been possible using traditional development and integration techniques. In addition, the reuse of services eliminates wasteful, redundant development projects, which lowers integration costs and accelerates project completion substantially.

On an ongoing basis, the carrier releases new functionality and features every four to six weeks. The Virgin Mobile infrastructure handles more than 2 million web services transactions per day. Virgin Mobile phones and accessories are available at over 12,000 retail locations, including Amazon. com, Best Buy, CompUSA, Media Play, Rite Aid, Safeway, Sam Goody, Sprint stores, Target, Wal-Mart, Virgin Megastores, and select college bookstores.[1]

INTRODUCTION

Enterprise architecture lies at the heart of most companies' operating capabilities. Changes in IT lead therefore to fundamental changes in how businesses operate. Since many companies depend on these technologies, no longer is IT simply nice to have; no longer is IT just value-adding. It has become vital.

Recent advances have led to major changes in how IT services are delivered. Low-cost computing power has driven a shift toward more distributed processing. Internetworking technologies, which provide a low-cost way to connect virtually everyone on the same network, present new possibilities for addressing business computing needs. The operational mechanisms at the heart of many businesses continue to evolve. New technologies add to, improve, and interconnect older systems to yield architectures with complex operational characteristics.

More importantly, new approaches to system design and development now enable large, complex applications to be built from reusable modules linked through shared services and common interfaces. This approach dramatically increases the ability to reuse data, information, and applications and to share a common infrastructure, which further increases the flexibility and speed with which new value-creating IT-enabled business initiatives can be launched and globally deployed.

While enterprise architecture alone cannot convey sustainable proprietary advantage, businesses that remain chained to a legacy of incompatible and inflexible proprietary architectures find themselves at a significant strategic disadvantage as they attempt to keep pace with increasingly shorter cycles of innovation, productivity, and return on investments. This chapter covers the basics of enterprise architecture including terminology, characteristics, and associated managerial responsibilities for building a solid enterprise architecture.

section 5.1 MANAGING ENTERPRISE ARCHITECTURES

LEARNING OUTCOMES

5.1 Explain the three components of an enterprise architecture.

5.2 Describe how an organization can implement a solid information architecture.

5.3 List and describe the five-ilities in an infrastructure architecture.

5.4 Compare web services and open systems.

Hurricane
Katrina Video

ENTERPRISE ARCHITECTURES

A 66-hour failure of an FBI database that performed background checks on gun buyers was long enough to allow criminals to buy guns. The database failed at 1:00 p.m. on a Thursday and was not restored until 7:30 a.m. Sunday. The FBI must complete a gun check within three days; if it fails to do so, a merchant is free to make the sale. During this outage, any gun checks that were in progress were not finished, allowing merchants to complete those gun sales at their own discretion.[2]

To support the volume and complexity of today's user and application requirements, information technology needs to take a fresh approach to enterprise architectures by constructing smarter, more flexible environments that protect from system failures and crashes. **Enterprise architectures (EA)** include the plans for how an organization will build, deploy, use, and share its data, processes, and IT assets. A unified enterprise architecture will standardize enterprisewide hardware and software systems, with tighter links to the business strategy. A solid enterprise architecture can decrease costs, increase standardization, promote reuse of IT assets, and speed development of new systems. The right enterprise architecture can make IT cheaper, strategic, and more responsive. The primary business goals of enterprise architectures are displayed in Figure 5.1.

FIGURE 5.1

Primary Business Goals of
Enterprise Architectures

Experts liken an EA plan to a blueprint. Just like you would never build a house without a blueprint, enterprise architecture gives a company a look into its processes, down to its data and technology, and how they are supporting the goals of the company, to make the processes more efficient and more effective, and to reduce costs. To be successful, however, an EA program must address more than just technology. With enterprise architecture, the subject is the business, and must be looked at with up to four different lenses: business, data, applications, and technology architecture. Trying to line those up is what enterprise architecture is all about. Therefore, enterprise architectures are never static; they continually change. Organizations use enterprise architects to help manage change. An ***enterprise architect*** is a person grounded in technology, fluent in business, and provides the important bridge between IT and the business. T-Mobile International's enterprise architects review projects to ensure they are soundly designed, meet the business objectives, and fit with the overall enterprise architecture. One T-Mobile project was to create software that would let subscribers customize the ring sounds on their cell phones. The project group assumed it would have to create most of the software from scratch. However, T-Mobile's EAs found software already written elsewhere at T-Mobile that could be reused to create the new application. The reuse reduced the development cycle time by eight months, and the new application was available in less than six weeks.[3]

Companies that have created solid enterprise architectures, such as Virgin Mobile and T-Mobile, are reaping huge rewards in savings, flexibility, and business alignment. Basic enterprise architectures contain three components (see Figure 5.2).

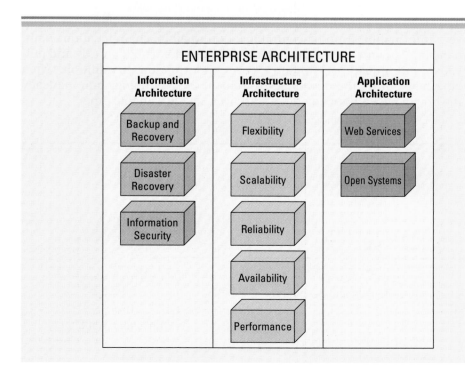

FIGURE 5.2

Three Components of
Enterprise Architecture

1. *Information architecture* identifies where and how important information, such as customer records, is maintained and secured.

2. *Infrastructure architecture* includes the hardware, software, and telecommunications equipment that, when combined, provides the underlying foundation to support the organization's goals.

3. *Application architecture* determines how applications integrate and relate to each other.

INFORMATION ARCHITECTURE

Information architecture identifies where and how important information, such as customer records, is maintained and secured. A single backup or restore failure can cost an organization more than time and money; some data cannot be re-created, and the business intelligence lost from that data can be tremendous. Chief information officers (CIO) should have enough confidence in their backup and recovery systems that they could walk around and randomly pull out cables to prove that the systems are safe. The CIO should also be secure enough to perform this test during peak business hours. If the thought of this test makes the CIO cringe, then the organization's customers should be cringing also. Figure 5.3 shows the three primary areas an enterprise information architecture should focus on:

Architecture

1. Backup and recovery
2. Disaster recovery
3. Information security

Backup and Recovery

Each year businesses lose time and money because of system crashes and failures. One way to minimize the damage of a system crash is to have a backup and recovery strategy in place. A *backup* is an exact copy of a system's information. *Recovery* is the ability to get a system up and running in the event of a system crash or failure and includes restoring the information backup. Many different types of backup and recovery media are available, including redundant storage servers, tapes, disks, and even CDs and DVDs. All the different types of backup and recovery media are reliable; their primary differences are the speed and associated costs.

A chain of more than 4,000 franchise locations, 7-Eleven Taiwan uploads backup and recovery information from its central location to all its chain locations daily. The company implemented a new technology solution that could quickly and reliably download and upload backup and recovery information. In addition, when a connection fails during the download or upload, the technology automatically resumes the download without having to start over, saving valuable time.[4]

FIGURE 5.3

Information Architecture

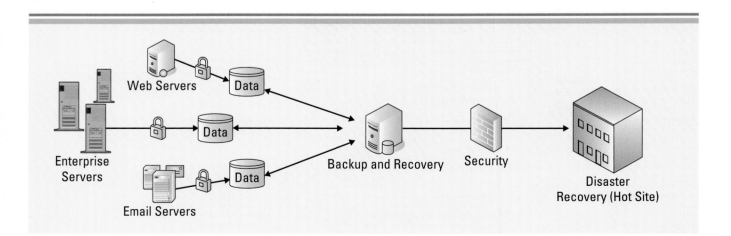

Organizations should choose a backup and recovery strategy that is in line with its business goals. If the organization deals with large volumes of critical information, it will require daily backups, perhaps even hourly backups, to storage servers. If the organization deals with small amounts of noncritical information, then it might require only weekly backups to external hard drives, tapes, CDs, or DVDs. Deciding how often to back up information and what media to use is a critical business decision. If an organization decides to back up on a weekly basis, then it is taking the risk that, if a total system crash occurs, it could lose a week's worth of work. If this risk is acceptable, then a weekly backup strategy will work. If this risk is unacceptable, then the organization needs to move to a daily backup strategy. Some organizations find the risk of losing a day's worth of work too high and move to an hourly backup strategy.

Two techniques used to help in case of system failure are fault tolerance and failover. **Fault tolerance** is a computer system designed that in the event a component fails, a backup component or procedure can immediately take its place with no loss of service. Fault tolerance can be provided via software, embedded in hardware, or provided by some combination. **Failover** is a backup in which the functions of a computer component (such as a processor, server, network, or database) are assumed by secondary system components when the primary component becomes unavailable through either failure or scheduled downtime. A failover procedure involves automatically offloading tasks to a standby system component so that the procedure is as seamless as possible to the end user. Used to make systems more fault tolerant, failover is typically an integral part of mission-critical systems that must be constantly available, such as systems used in the financial industry.[5]

Disaster Recovery

A northern Ohio power company, FirstEnergy, missed signs that there were potential problems in its portion of North America's electrical grid. The events that followed left an estimated 50 million people in the Northeast and Canada in the dark. The failings are laid out in the widely reported findings of a joint U.S./Canadian task force that investigated the causes of the blackout and recommended what to do to avoid big-scale outages in the future. The report detailed many procedures and best practices including:

- Mind the enterprise architectures.
- Monitor the quality of computer networks that provide data on power suppliers and demand.
- Make sure the networks can be restored quickly in the case of downtime.
- Set up disaster recovery plans.
- Provide adequate staff training, including verbal communication protocols so that operators are aware of any IT-related problems that may be affecting their situational awareness of the power grid.

Disasters such as power outages, floods, and even harmful hacking strike businesses every day. Organizations must develop a disaster recovery plan to prepare for such occurrences. A **disaster recovery plan** is a detailed process for recovering information or an IT system in the event of a catastrophic disaster such as a fire or flood. Spending on disaster recovery is rising worldwide among financial institutions (see Figure 5.4).

A comprehensive disaster recovery plan considers the location of the backup information. Many organizations store backup information in an off-site facility. StorageTek, a worldwide technology company that delivers a broad range of data storage offerings, specializes in providing off-site information storage and disaster recovery solutions. A comprehensive disaster recovery plan also foresees the possibility that not only the computer equipment but also the building where employees work may be destroyed. A **hot site** is a separate and fully equipped facility where the company can move immediately after a disaster and resume business. A **cold site** is a separate facility that does not have any computer equipment, but is a place where employees can move after a disaster.

Hardware

A **disaster recovery cost curve** charts (1) the cost to the organization of the unavailability of information and technology and (2) the cost to the organization of recovering from a disaster over time. Figure 5.5 displays a disaster recovery cost curve and shows that where the two lines intersect is the best recovery plan in terms of cost and time. Creating an organization's disaster recovery cost curve is no small task. It must consider the cost of losing information and technology within each department or functional area, and the cost of losing information and technology across the whole enterprise. During the first few hours of a disaster, those costs will be low but become increasingly higher over time. With those costs in hand, an organization must then determine the costs of recovery. Cost of recovery during the first few hours of a disaster is exceedingly high and diminishes over time.

On April 18, 1906, San Francisco was rocked by an earthquake that destroyed large swathes of the city and claimed the lives of more than 3,000 inhabitants of the Bay area. More than a century later, a bigger, bolder, rebuilt, and more resilient San Francisco is more important than ever. Now it serves as the heart of the global IT industry and a major world financial center. However, San Francisco remains well aware of the terrible potential that exists along the San Andreas fault.

The vast skyscrapers downtown may now be built to withstand huge pressures, but what about the infrastructure and the systems that keep modern business ticking—and the people who must be able to access them? **Business continuity planning (BCP)** is a plan for how an organization will recover and restore partially or completely interrupted critical function(s) within a predetermined time after a disaster or extended disruption. Business continuity and disaster recovery are serious issues for all organizations in the Bay area, including the Union Bank of California, which is based in the heart of downtown San Francisco.[6]

FIGURE 5.5

The Disaster Recovery Cost
Curve

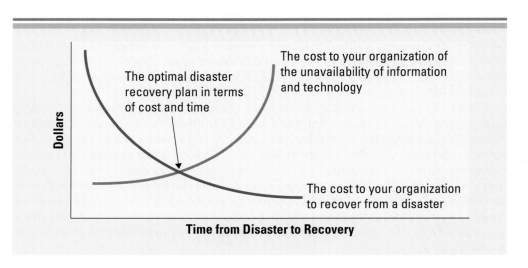

Barry Cardoza, head of business continuity planning and disaster recovery at Union Bank of California, said, "You have disasters that you can see coming and you've got disasters that you can't see coming and an earthquake is an example of [the latter]. And you don't know how bad it's going to be until it hits."[7]

As such, the bank must have processes in place ahead of such an event to mitigate the threat. Simply reacting is not a strategy. The continuity department must also understand every aspect of the business and weigh downtime for each in terms of financial and reputational damage. Union Bank of California has created a disaster recovery plan that includes multiple data centers in diverse locations, mirrored sites that can take over at the flick of a switch, hot sites where staff can walk in and start working exactly as they would if they were in their normal location, and a vast amount of redundancy. In addition, the bank has created real-time mirroring between data centers. It is now a matter of minutes not hours for Union Bank of California to be up and running in the event of a disaster.

Information Security

Security professionals are under increasing pressure to do the job right and cost-effectively as networks extend beyond organizations to remote users, partners, and customers, and to cell phones, PDAs, and other mobile devices. Regulatory requirements to safeguard data have increased. Concerns about identity theft are at an all-time high. Hacking and other unauthorized access contribute to the approximately 10 million instances of identity theft each year, according to the Federal Trade Commission. Good information architectures include a strong information security plan, along with managing user access and up-to-date antivirus software and patches.[8]

Managing User Access Managing user access to information is a critical piece of the information architecture. Passwords may still be the weakest link in the security chain. At Vitas Healthcare Corporation, with a workforce of 6,000 and operations across 15 states, authorized employees enter as many as a half-dozen passwords a day to access multiple systems. While it is important to maintain password discipline to secure customers' health care data, maintaining and managing the situation creates a drag on the IT department. "Our help desk spends 30 percent of their time on password management and provisioning," said John Sandbrook, senior IT director.

The company began using Fischer International Corporation's Identity Management Suite to manage passwords and comply with data-access regulations such as the Sarbanes-Oxley Act. The ID-management product includes automated audit, reporting, and compliance capabilities, plus a common platform for password management, provisioning, and self-service. With the software, the company can enforce stronger passwords with seven, eight, or nine characters, numbers, and capital letters that frequently change. The company anticipates curbing help-desk password time by 50 percent.[9]

Up-to-Date Antivirus Software and Patches Security is a top priority for business managers, regardless of the size of their company. Among Fortune 500 companies, more than 80 percent of those surveyed described updating security procedures, tools, and services as a key business priority. That desire holds true for small, midsize, or large companies and for IT managers and corporate managers.

The main focus for most managers is preventing hackers, spammers, and other malcontents from entering their networks, and nearly two-thirds are looking to enhance their network-security-management, intrusion-detection, content-filtering, and anti-spam software. More than half also plan to upgrade their encryption software.

Microsoft issues patches for its software on the second Tuesday of every month. These patches must be downloaded and installed on all systems across the entire enterprise if the company wants to keep its systems protected. At OMD, a media buying and planning subsidiary of Omnicom Group Inc., the network administrator had to manually install critical patches on all 100 servers, taking more than a week to deploy the patch across the company. Now, OMD uses automated installation software for patches and upgrades. The company purchased software that lets it move ahead with applying patches without taking down entire systems and balancing patch-deployment timing among servers so that all departments were not down at once during a patch install. Given everything else that security professionals need to think about, automated installation software is a welcome relief.[10]

INFRASTRUCTURE ARCHITECTURE

Gartner Inc. estimates that the typical web application goes down 170 hours per year. At Illinois-based online brokerage OptionsXpress, application performance problems can have a serious impact on livelihoods. Nearly 7,000 options traders visit the OptionsXpress website at any given time, completing nearly 20,000 transactions a day. With all this online traffic, the brokerage's IT administrators were always up against the clock when re-creating troublesome applications offline in the development environment. The company struggled to unlock the mystery behind a problematic trading application that was forcing traders to resubmit orders. Sometimes the application would just die and then restart itself for no apparent reason.[11]

Infrastructure architecture includes the hardware, software, and telecommunications equipment that, when combined, provides the underlying foundation to support the organization's goals (see Figure 5.6). As an organization changes, its systems must be able to change to support its operations. If an organization grows by 50 percent in a single year, its systems must be able to handle a 50 percent growth rate. Systems that cannot adapt to organizational changes can severely hinder the organization's ability to operate. The future of an organization depends on its ability to meet its partners and customers on their terms, at their pace, any time of the day, in any geographic location. The following are the five primary characteristics of a solid infrastructure architecture:

1. Flexibility
2. Scalability

FIGURE 5.6

Infrastructure Architecture Characteristics

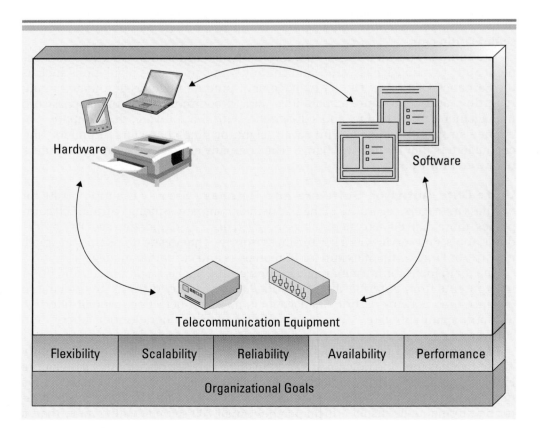

176   **Chapter 5** Enterprise Architectures

3. Reliability
4. Availability
5. Performance

Flexibility

Organizations must watch today's business, as well as tomorrow's, when designing and building systems. Systems must be flexible enough to meet all types of business changes. For example, a system might be designed to include the ability to handle multiple currencies and languages, even though the company is not currently performing business in other countries. When the company starts growing and performing business in new countries, the system will already have the flexibility to handle multiple currencies and languages. If the company failed to recognize that its business would someday be global, it would need to redesign all its systems to handle multiple currencies and languages, not easy once systems are up and running.

Scalability

Estimating organizational growth is a challenging task. Growth can occur in a number of different forms including more customers and product lines and expansion into new markets. *Scalability* refers to how well a system can adapt to increased demands. A number of factors can create organizational growth including market, industry, and economy factors. If an organization grows faster than anticipated, it might experience all types of performance degradations, ranging from running out of disk space to a slowdown in transaction speeds. Anticipating expected—and unexpected—growth is key to building scalable systems that can support that growth.

MSNBC's website typically received moderate traffic. On September 11, 2001, the site was inundated with more than 91 million page views as its customers were trying to find out information about the terrorist attacks. Fortunately, MSNBC had anticipated this type of surging demand and built scalable systems accordingly, allowing it to handle the increased page view requests.[12]

ilities

Capacity planning determines the future IT infrastructure requirements for new equipment and additional network capacity. Performing a capacity plan is one way to ensure the IT infrastructure is scalable. It is cheaper for an organization to implement an IT infrastructure that considers capacity growth at the beginning of a system launch than to try to upgrade equipment and networks after the system has been implemented. Not having enough capacity leads to performance issues and hinders the ability of employees to perform their jobs. If 100 workers are using the Internet to perform their jobs and the company purchases bandwidth that is too small and the network capacity is too small, the employees will spend a great deal of time just waiting to get information from the Internet. Waiting for an Internet site to return information is not very productive.

Web 2.0 is driving demand for capacity planning. Delivering entertainment-grade video over the Internet poses significant challenges as service providers scale solutions to manage millions of users, withstand periods of peak demand, and deliver a superior quality of experience while balancing network capacity and efficient capital investment. Given the success of YouTube and the likelihood of similar video experiences, the bandwidth required to transport video services will continue to increase and the possibility of video degradation will become more challenging. Since video cannot tolerate packet loss (e.g., blocks of data lost), congestion due to overuse is not acceptable—admitting just one more stream to a network near peak capacity could degrade the video and broadcast quality for all users.

Reliability

Reliability ensures all systems are functioning correctly and providing accurate information. Reliability is another term for accuracy when discussing the correctness of systems within the context of efficiency IT metrics. Inaccurate information processing occurs for many reasons, from the incorrect entry of data to information corruption. Unreliable information puts the organization at risk when making decisions based on the information.

Availability

Availability (an efficiency IT metric) addresses when systems can be accessed by users. *High availability* refers to a system or component that is continuously operational for a desirably long length of time. Availability is typically measured relative to "100 percent operational" or "never failing." A widely held but difficult-to-achieve standard of availability for a system or product is known as "five 9s" (99.999 percent) availability. Some companies have systems available 24 × 7 to support business operations and global customer and employee needs. With the emergence of the web, companies expect systems to operate around the clock. A customer who finds that a website closes at 9:00 p.m. is not going to be a customer long.

Systems, however, must come down for maintenance, upgrades, and fixes. One challenge organizations face is determining when to schedule system downtime if the system is expected to operate continually. Exacerbating the negative impact of scheduled system downtime is the global nature of business. Scheduling maintenance during the evening might seem like a great idea, but the evening in one city is the morning somewhere else in the world, and global employees may not be able to perform their jobs if the system is down. Many organizations overcome this problem by having redundant systems, allowing the organization to take one system down by switching over to a redundant, or duplicate, system.

Performance

Performance measures how quickly a system performs a certain process or transaction (in terms of efficiency IT metrics of both speed and throughput). Not having enough performance capacity can have a devastating, negative impact on a business. A customer will wait only a few seconds for a website to return a request before giving up and moving on to another website. To ensure adaptable systems performance, capacity planning helps an organization determine future IT infrastructure requirements for new equipment and additional network capacity. It is cheaper for an organization to design and implement an IT infrastructure that envisions performance capacity growth than to update all the equipment after the system is already operational.

Abercrombie & Fitch (A&F) uses the Internet to market its distinctive image of being a fashion trendsetter to one of its largest customer segments, college students. The company designed its enterprise architecture with the help of IBM, which ensured www.abercrombie.com paralleled the same sleek but simple design of *A&F Quarterly*, the company's flagship magazine. Abercrombie & Fitch knew that its website had to be accessible, available, reliable, and scalable to meet the demands of its young customers. Young customers tend to be Internet savvy, and their purchasing habits vary from customers who only shop for sale items at midnight to customers who know exactly what they want immediately. The highly successful website gives customers not only an opportunity to shop online, but also a taste of the Abercrombie & Fitch lifestyle through downloadable MP3s, calendars, and desktop accessories.[13]

APPLICATION ARCHITECTURE

Gartner Inc. research indicates that application problems are the single largest source of downtime, causing 40 percent of annual downtime hours and 32 percent of average downtime costs. *Application architecture* determines how applications integrate and relate to each other. Advances in integration technology—primarily web services and open systems—are providing new ways for designing more agile, more responsive enterprise architectures that provide the kind of value businesses need. With these new architectures, IT can build new business capabilities faster, cheaper, and in a vocabulary the business can understand.[14]

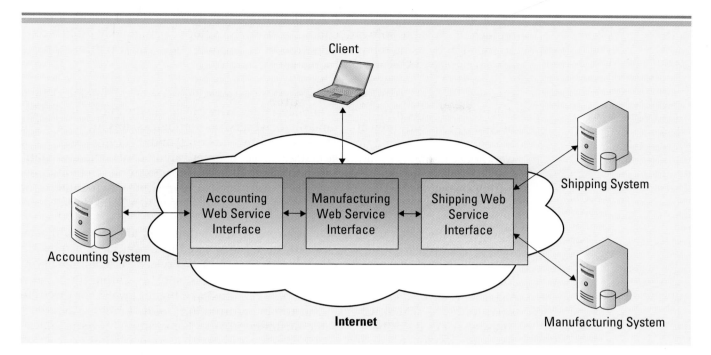

FIGURE 5.7

Web Service Architecture

Web Services

Web services are quickly becoming the next major frontier in computing. **Web services** contain a repertoire of web-based data and procedural resources that use shared protocols and standards permitting different applications to share data and services. The major application of web services is the integration among different applications (refer to Figure 5.7). Before web services, organizations had trouble with interoperability. **Interoperability** is the capability of two or more computer systems to share data and resources, even though they are made by different manufacturers. If a manufacturing system can talk to (share information with) a shipping system, interoperability exists between the two systems. The traditional way that organizations achieved interoperability was to build integrations. Now, an organization can use web services to perform the same task.

Verizon's massive enterprise architecture includes three different companies—GTE, Bell Atlantic, and NYNEX—each with its own complex systems. To find a customer record in any of the three companies' systems, Verizon turns to its search engine, called Spider. Spider is Verizon's version of Google, and it is helping Verizon's business to thrive.

Spider contains a vital customer information web service that encapsulates Verizon's business rules, which help it to access the correct data repository when looking for customer information. Whenever a new system is built that needs to link to customer information, all the system developer has to do is reuse the web service that will link to the customer records. Because Verizon has the web service in place as part of its enterprise architecture, development teams can build new applications within a month, as opposed to six months.

Web services encompass all the technologies that are used to transmit and process information on and across a network, most specifically the Internet. It is easiest to think of an individual web service as software that performs a specific task, with that task being made available to any user who needs its service. For example, a "Deposit" web service for a banking system might allow customers to perform the task of depositing money to their accounts. The web service could be used by a bank teller, by the customer at an ATM, and/or by the customer performing an online transaction through a web browser.

The "Deposit" web service demonstrates one of the great advantages of using the web service model to develop applications. Developers do not have to reinvent the wheel every time they need to incorporate new functionality. A web service is really a piece of reusable software code. A software developer can quickly build a new application by using many of these pieces of reusable code. The two primary parts of web services are events and services.

Events Events are the eyes and ears of the business expressed in technology—they detect threats and opportunities and alert those who can act on the information. Pioneered by telecommunication and financial services companies, this involves using IT systems to monitor a business process for events that matter—a stock-out in the warehouse or an especially large charge on a consumer's credit card—and automatically alert the people best equipped to handle the issue. For example, a credit monitoring system automatically alerts a credit supervisor and shuts down an account when the system processes a $7,000 charge on a credit card with a $6,000 limit.

Services Services are more like software products than they are coding projects. They must appeal to a broad audience, and they need to be reusable if they are going to have an impact on productivity. Early forms of services were defined at too low a level in the architecture to interest the business, such as simple "Print" and "Save" services. The new services are being defined at a higher level; they describe such things as "Credit Check," "Customer Information," and "Process Payment." These services describe a valuable business process. For example, "Credit Check" has value not just for programmers who want to use that code in another application, but also for businesspeople who want to use it across multiple products, such as auto loans and mortgages, or across multiple business.

The trick to building services is finding the right level of granularity. T-Mobile builds services starting at the highest level and then works its way down to lower levels, helping to ensure it does not build services that no one uses. The company first built a "Send Message" web service and then built a "Send SMS Message" web service that sends messages in special formats to different devices such as cell phones and pagers.

Lydian Trust's enterprise architects designed a web service called "Get Credit" that is used by several different business units for loan applications. "Get Credit" seeks out credit ratings over the Internet from the major credit bureaus. One day, one of the credit bureau's web servers crashed, and Lydian Trust's "Get Credit" web service could not make a connection. Since the connection to the server was loosely linked, the system did not know what to do. "Get Credit" was not built to make more than one call. So, while it waited for a response, hundreds of loan applications sat idle.

Lydian Trust's loan officers had to work overnight to ensure that all of the applications were completed within 24 hours as promised by the company. Fortunately, Lydian Trust's customers never felt the pain; however, its employees did. Systems must be designed to deal with the existence of certain events, or the lack of an event, in a way that does not interrupt the overall business. The "Get Credit" web service has been modified to include an automatic email alert to a supervisor whenever the web service encounters a delay.[15]

Open Systems

Microsoft Internet Explorer (MSIE) is very much the incumbent in the web browser arena. Before the arrival of open source Mozilla Firefox, MSIE had an estimated 97 percent of market share. Firefox has cut into MSIE's niche, dipping MSIE usage below 90 percent in the United States and down to about 60 percent in Germany. Firefox has an open source team of developers and testers. The Mozilla Firefox project's launch by Netscape in 1998 was a defining moment for the open source movement. Firefox is a leader in the open source developments that provide low cost and a lot of options for technology. Developers of Firefox interact through newsgroups, mailing lists, IRC channels, and various websites.[16]

An ***open system*** is a broad, general term that describes nonproprietary IT hardware and software made available by the standards and procedures by which their products work, making it easier to integrate them. In general, ***open source*** refers to any program whose source code is made available for use or modification as users or other developers see fit. Historically, the makers of proprietary software have generally not made source code available. Open source software is usually developed as a public collaboration and made freely available. Amazon.com embraced open source technology, converting from Sun's proprietary operating system to Linux. The switch to an open source operating system, such as Linux, is simplifying the process by which Amazon.com associates can build links to Amazon.com applications into their websites.

The designs of open systems allow for information sharing. In the past, different systems were independent of each other and operated as individual islands of control. The sharing of information was accomplished through software drivers and devices that routed data allowing information to be translated and shared between systems. Although this method is still widely used, its limited capability and added cost are not an effective solution for most organizations. Another drawback to the stand-alone system is it can communicate only with components developed by a single manufacturer. The proprietary nature of these systems usually results in costly repair, maintenance, and expansion because of a lack of competitive forces. On the other hand, open system integration is designed to:

- Allow systems to seamlessly share information. The sharing of information reduces the total number of devices, resulting in an overall decrease in cost.

- Capitalize on enterprise architectures. This avoids installing several independent systems, which creates duplication of devices.

- Eliminate proprietary systems and promote competitive pricing. Often a sole-source vendor can demand its price and may even provide the customer with less than satisfactory service. Utilization of open systems allows users to purchase systems competitively.[17]

OPENING CASE QUESTIONS

Virgin Mobile

1. How can an organization use an information architecture to protect its IT investment in electronic devices outlined in the case?

2. How can an organization use the architectures mentioned in this section to protect information security?

3. Identify the five-ilities and rank them in order of importance for a cell phone (1 highest, 5 lowest).

4. Describe the importance of web services and open systems to companies such as Virgin Mobile.

---

section 5.2 ARCHITECTURE TRENDS

LEARNING OUTCOMES

5.5 Describe the business value in deploying a service oriented architecture.

5.6 Explain the need for interoperability and loose coupling in building today's IT systems.

5.7 Identify the logical functions used in a virtualized environment.

5.8 Explain the business benefits of grid computing.

ARCHITECTURE TRENDS

To keep business systems up-and-running $24 \times 7 \times 365$ while continuing to be flexible, scalable, reliable, and available is no easy task. Organizations today must continually watch new architecture trends to ensure they can keep up with new and

FIGURE 5.8

The Service Oriented Architecture

disruptive technologies. This section discusses three architecture trends that are quickly becoming requirements for all businesses including:

- Service Oriented Architectures
- Virtualization
- Grid Computing

SERVICE ORIENTED ARCHITECTURE

Service oriented architecture (SOA) is a business-driven IT architectural approach that supports integrating a business as linked, repeatable tasks or services. SOA helps today's businesses innovate by ensuring that IT systems can adapt quickly, easily, and economically to support rapidly changing business needs. It helps businesses increase the flexibility of their processes, strengthen their underlying IT architecture, and reuse their existing IT investments by creating connections among disparate applications and information sources.

SOA is not a concrete architecture: It is something that leads to a concrete architecture (as illustrated in Figure 5.8). It might be described as a style, paradigm, concept, perspective, philosophy, or representation. That is, SOA is not a concrete tool or framework to be purchased. It is an approach, a way of thinking, a value system that leads to certain concrete decisions when designing a concrete architecture.

Crutchfield, in Charlottesville, Virginia, sells electronics through three channels: the web, a call center, and two retail shops. With a service oriented architecture, a single application now handles the initial order processing from all three sales channels, with fraud checking and the workflow encapsulated using a series of messages. Although simple to build, Crutchfield's SOA is rigorous, averaging 3,800 daily orders that book on average $1.1 million daily in revenues.[18]

SOA Business Benefits

The reality in IT enterprises is that architectures are heterogeneous across operating systems, applications, system software, and application infrastructure. Some existing applications are used to run current business processes, so starting from scratch to build a new architecture is not an option. Enterprises should quickly respond to business changes with agility; leverage existing investments in applications and application infrastructure to address newer business requirements; and support new channels of interactions with customers, partners, and suppliers. SOA with its loosely coupled nature allows enterprises to plug in new services or upgrade existing services in a granular fashion. This enables businesses to address the new business requirements, provides the option to make the services consumable across different channels, and exposes the existing enterprise and legacy applications as services, thereby safeguarding existing IT infrastructure investments (see Figure 5.9). The key technical concepts of SOA are:

- *Services*—a business task
- *Interoperability*—the capability of two or more computer systems to share data and resources, even though they are made by different manufacturers

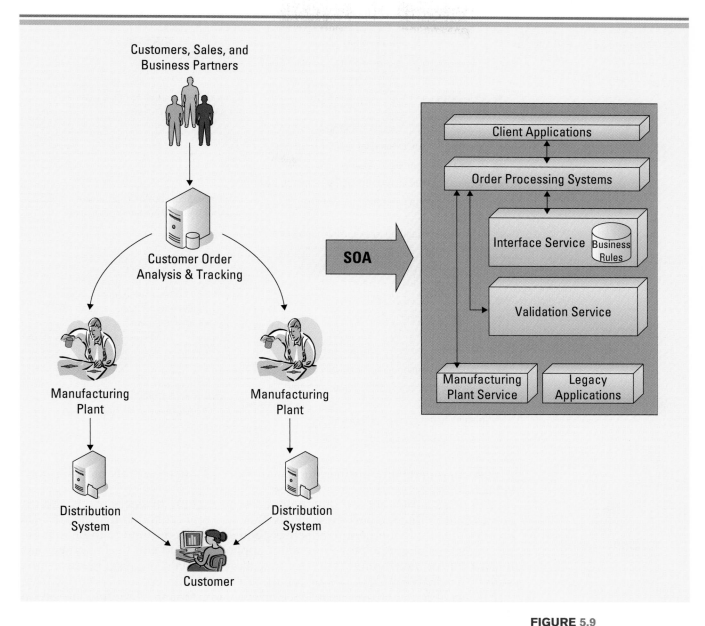

FIGURE 5.9

SOA Integration

■ *Loose coupling*—the capability of services to be joined together on demand to create composite services, or disassembled just as easily into their functional components[19]

Service

Service oriented architecture begins with a service—an SOA *service* being simply a business task, such as checking a potential customer's credit rating when opening a new account. It is important to stress that this is part of a business process. As mentioned in the previous section, services are "like" software products, however, when describing SOA, do not think about software or IT. Think about what a company does on a day-to-day basis, and break up those business processes into repeatable business tasks or components.

SOA provides the technology underpinnings for working with services that are not just software or hardware, but rather business tasks. It is a pattern for developing a more flexible kind of software application that can promote loose coupling among software components while reusing existing investments in technology in new, more valuable ways across the organization. SOA is based on standards that

FIGURE 5.10

Business Issues and SOA
Solutions

Business Issues	SOA Solutions
■ Agents unable to see policy coverage information remotely ■ Calls/faxes used to get information from other divisions ■ Clinical patient information stored on paper ■ Complex access to supplier design drawings	Integrate information to make it more accessible to employees.
■ High cost of handling customer calls ■ Reconciliation of invoice deductions and rebates ■ Hours on hold to determine patient insurance eligibility ■ High turnover leading to excessive hiring and training costs	Understand how business processes interact to better manage administrative costs.
■ Decreasing customer loyalty due to incorrect invoices ■ Customers placed on hold to check order status ■ Inability to quickly update policy endorsements ■ Poor service levels	Improve customer retention and deliver new products and services through reuse of current investments.
■ Time wasted reconciling separate databases ■ Manual processes such as handling trade allocations ■ Inability to detect quality flaws early in cycle ■ High percentage of scrap and rework	Improve people productivity with better business integration and connectivity.

Software

enable interoperability, business agility, and innovation to generate more business value for those who use these principles.

SOA helps companies become more agile by aligning business needs and the IT capabilities that support these needs. Business drives requirements for IT; SOA enables the IT environment to effectively and efficiently respond to these requirements. SOA is about helping companies apply reusability and flexibility that can lower cost (of development, integration, maintenance), increase revenue, and obtain sustainable competitive advantage through technology.

It is very important to note that SOA is an evolution. Although its results are revolutionary, it builds on many technologies used in the marketplace, such as web services, transactional technologies, information-driven principles, loose coupling, components, and object-oriented design. The beauty of SOA is that these technologies exist together in SOA through standards, well-defined interfaces, and organizational commitments to reuse key services instead of reinventing the wheel. SOA is not just about technology, but about how technology and business link themselves for a common goal of business flexibility.

Businesses have become increasingly complex over the past couple of decades. Factors such as mergers, regulations, global competition, outsourcing, and partnering have resulted in a massive increase in the number of applications any given company might use. These applications were implemented with little knowledge of the other applications with which they would be required to share information in the future. As a result, many companies are trying to maintain IT systems that coexist but are not integrated.

SOA can help provide solutions to companies that face a variety of business issues; Figure 5.10 lists some of those.[20]

Interoperability

As defined in the previous section, interoperability is the capability of two or more computer systems to share data and resources, even though they are made by different manufacturers. Businesses today use a variety of systems that have resulted in a heterogeneous environment. This heterogeneity has inundated businesses with the lack of interoperability. However, since SOA is based on open standards, businesses can create solutions that draw upon functionality from these existing, previously isolated systems that are portable and/or interoperable, regardless of the environment in which they exist.

A web service was defined earlier as an open standards way of supporting interoperability. Web services are frequently application programming interfaces (API) that can be accessed over a network, such as the Internet, and executed on a remote system hosting the requested services. SOA is a style of architecture that enables the creation of applications that are built by combining loosely coupled and interoperable services. These services interoperate based on a formal definition that is independent of the underlying platform and programming language. In SOA, since the basic unit of communication is a message rather than an operation, web services are usually loosely coupled. Although SOA can exist without web services, the best-practice implementation of SOA for flexibility always involves web services.

Technically, web services are based on *Extensible Markup Language (XML),* a markup language for documents containing structured information. The technical specifics of XML's capabilities go beyond the scope of this book, but for our purposes, they support things such as ebusiness transactions, mathematical equations, and a thousand other kinds of structured information. XML is a common data representation that can be used as the medium of exchange between programs that are written in different programming languages and execute different kinds of machine instructions. In simple terms, think about XML as the official translator for structured information. Structured information is both the content (word, picture, and so on) and the role it plays. XML is the basis for all web service technologies and the key to interoperability; every web service specification is based on XML.

Loose Coupling

Part of the value of SOA is that it is built on the premise of loose coupling of services. *Loose coupling* is the capability of services to be joined on demand to create composite services or disassembled just as easily into their functional components.

Loose coupling is a way of ensuring that the technical details such as language, platform, and so on are decoupled from the service. For example, look at currency conversion. Today all banks have multiple currency converters, all with different rate refreshes at different times. By creating a common service "conversion of currency" that is loosely coupled to all banking functions that require conversion, the rates, times, and samplings can be averaged to ensure floating the treasury in the most effective manner possible. Another example is common customer identification. Most businesses lack a common customer ID and, therefore, have no way to determine who the customers are and what they buy for what reason. Creating a common customer ID that is independent of applications and databases allows loosely coupling the service "Customer ID" to data, and applications without the application or database ever knowing who it is or where it is.

The difference between traditional, tightly bound interactions and loosely coupled services is that, before the transaction occurs, the functional pieces (services) operating within the SOA are dormant and disconnected. When the business process initiates, these services momentarily interact with each other. They do so for just long enough to execute their piece of the overall process, and then they go back to their dormant state, with no long-standing connection to the other services with which they just interacted. The next time the same service is called, it could be as part of a different business process with different calling and destination services.

A great way to understand this is through the analogy of the telephone system. At the dawn of widespread phone usage, operators had to physically plug in a wire to create a semipermanent connection between two parties. Callers were "tightly bound" to each other. Today you pick up your cell phone and put it to your ear, and there's no dial tone—it's disconnected. You enter a number, push "Talk," and only then does the process initiate, establishing a loosely coupled connection just long enough for your conversation. Then when the conversation is over, your cell phone goes back to dormant mode until a new connection is made with another party. As a result, supporting a million cell phone subscribers does not require that the cell phone service provider support a million live connections; it requires supporting only the number of simultaneous conversations at any given time. It allows for a much more flexible and dynamic exchange.[21]

VIRTUALIZATION

Virtualization is a framework of dividing the resources of a computer into multiple execution environments. It is a way of increasing physical resources to maximize the investment in hardware. Generally, this process is done with virtualization software, running on the one physical unit that emulates multiple pieces of hardware.

In a virtualized environment, the logical functions of computing, storage, and network elements are separated from their physical functions. Functions from these resources can then be manually or automatically allocated to meet the changing needs and priorities of a business. These concepts can be applied broadly across the enterprise, from data-center resources to PCs and printers.

Through virtualization, people, processes, and technology work together more efficiently to meet increased service levels. Since capacity can be allocated dynamically, chronic over-provisioning is eliminated and an entire IT architecture is simplified (see Figure 5.11).

FIGURE 5.11

Virtualization Architecture

Even something as simple as partitioning a hard drive is considered virtualization because you take one drive and partition it to create two separate hard drives. Devices, applications, and users are able to interact with the virtual machines as if it were a real single logical resource.

What Are Virtual Machines?

System virtualization (often referred to as "server virtualization" or "desktop virtualization," depending on the role of the virtualized system) is the ability to present the resources of a single computer as if it is a collection of separate computers ("virtual machines"), each with its own virtual CPUs, network interfaces, storage, and operating system.

Virtual machine technology was first implemented on mainframes in the 1960s to allow the expensive systems to be partitioned into separate domains and used more efficiently by more users and applications. As standard PC servers became more powerful in the past decade, virtualization has been brought to the desktop and notebook processors to provide the same benefits.[22]

Virtual machines appear both to the user within the system and the world outside as separate computers, each with its own network identity, user authorization and authentication capabilities, operating system version and configuration, applications, and data. The hardware is consistent across all virtual machines: While the number or size of them may differ, devices are used that allow virtual machines to be portable, independent of the actual hardware type on the underlying systems.

Figure 5.12 shows an overview of what a system virtualization framework looks like.

Virtualization Business Benefits

Virtualization is by no means a new technology. As previously mentioned, mainframe computers have offered the ability to host multiple operating systems for over 30 years. However, several trends have moved virtualization into the spotlight, such as hardware being underutilized, data centers running out of space, energy costs increasing, and system administration costs mounting. The U.S. Environmental Protection Agency recently proclaimed that data centers consumed 61 billion

FIGURE 5.12

System Virtualization

kilowatt-hours of electricity. That is roughly 1.6 percent of total U.S. electricity consumption and is worth about $4.5 billion. Assuming current trends continue, by 2011 the national energy consumption by data centers is expected to nearly double, making energy efficiency a top priority.[23]

The first major virtualization trend highlights hardware being underutilized. In the April 1965 issue of *Electronics* magazine, Gordon Moore first offered his observation about processor computing power, which has come to be known as Moore's law. In describing the increasing power of computing power, Moore stated: "The complexity for minimum component costs has increased at a rate of roughly a factor of two per year." What he means is that each year (actually, most people estimate the time frame at around 18 months), for a given size processor, twice as many individual components can be squeezed onto a similarly sized piece of silicon. Put another way, every new generation of chip delivers twice as much processing power as the previous generation—at the same price.

Moore's law demonstrates increasing returns—the amount of improvement itself grows over time because there's an exponential increase in capacity for every generation of processor improvement. That exponential increase is responsible for the mind-boggling improvements in computing—and the increasing need for virtualization.[24]

Today, many data centers have machines running at only 10 to 15 percent of total processing capacity, which translates to 85 to 90 percent of the machine's power being unused. In a way, Moore's law is no longer relevant to most companies because they are not able to take advantage of the increased power available to them.

Moore's law not only enables virtualization, but also effectively makes it mandatory. Otherwise, increasing amounts of computing power will go to waste each year.

A second virtualization trend concentrates on data centers running out of space. The business world has undergone an enormous transformation over the past 20 years. In 1985, the vast majority of business processes were paper based. Computerized systems were confined to so-called backroom automation: payroll, accounting, and the like. That has all changed, thanks to the steady march of Moore's law. Business process after business process has been captured in software and automated, moving from paper to computers.[25]

The rise of the Internet has exponentially increased this transformation. Companies want to communicate with customers and partners in real time, using the worldwide connectivity of the Internet. Naturally, this has accelerated the move to computerized business processes.

Boeing's latest airliner, the 787 Dreamliner, is being designed and built in a radically new way. Boeing and each of its suppliers use computer-aided design (CAD) software to design their respective parts of the plane. All communication about the project uses the CAD designs as the basis for discussion. Use of CAD software enables testing to be done in computer models rather than the traditional method of building physical prototypes, thereby speeding completion of the plane by a year or more.

The Dreamliner project generates enormous amounts of data. Just one piece of the project—a data warehouse containing project plans—runs to 19 terabytes of data. The net effect of all this and similar projects at other companies is that huge numbers of servers have been put into use over the past decade, which is causing a real-estate problem—companies are running out of space in their data centers.[26]

Virtualization, by offering the ability to host multiple guest systems on a single physical server, helps organizations to reclaim data center territory, thereby avoiding the expense of building out more data center space. This is an enormous benefit of virtualization because data centers cost in the tens of millions of dollars to construct.

Rapidly escalating energy costs are also furthering the trend toward virtualization. The cost of running computers, coupled with the fact that many of the machines filling up data centers are running at low utilization rates, means that virtualization's ability to reduce the total number of physical servers can significantly reduce the overall cost of energy for companies. Data center power is such an issue that energy companies are putting virtualization programs into place to address it.

These trends reveal why virtualization is a technology whose time has come. The exponential power growth of computers, the substitution of automated processes for manual work, the increasing cost to power the multitude of computers, and the high personnel cost to manage that multitude all cry out for a less expensive way to run data centers. In fact, a newer, more efficient method of running data centers is critical because, given the trends mentioned above, the traditional methods of delivering computing are becoming cost prohibitive.

Virtualization enables data center managers to make far better use of computer resources than in nonvirtualized environments, and it enables an enterprise to maximize its investment in hardware. Underutilized hardware platforms and server sprawl—today's norm—can become things of the past. By virtualizing a large deployment of older systems on a few highly scalable, highly reliable, enterprise-class servers, businesses can substantially reduce costs related to hardware purchases, provisioning, and maintenance.

Additional Virtualization Benefits

Virtualization offers more than server consolidation benefits as described in the previous section. Rapid application deployment, dynamic load balancing, and streamlined disaster recovery top the list of additional benefits. Virtualization technologies can reduce application test and deployment time from days or weeks to a matter of hours by enabling users to test and qualify software in isolation but also in the same environment as the production workload.

Virtualization, in all its forms, is a highly disruptive yet clearly beneficial technology. Enterprises are deploying virtualization for a number of real and significant benefits. The strongest driver—business continuity—is surprising, but many of the other drivers, such as flexibility and agility, server consolidation, and reduced administration costs, are fully expected.

Other advantages of virtualization include a variety of security benefits (stemming from centralized computing environments); improved service-level management (i.e., the ability to manage resource allocation against service levels for specific applications and business users); the ability to more easily run legacy systems; greater flexibility in locating staff; and reduced hardware and software costs.

In its 620-acre facility in Lafayette, Indiana, Subaru of Indiana produces cars and SUVs for its parent company, Fuji Heavy Industries, and Camry vehicles for Toyota. It has the capacity to produce 21,800 vehicles a month, using the just-in-time method of manufacturing. This method requires a streamlined production line, with highly accurate and reliable inventory controls. A lack of any one component can stop the assembly line and trigger problems up and down the supply chain.

The facility suffered from several problems. Some of its applications had reliability issues, but the IT staff faced compatibility issues when it tried to use newer servers as standbys for older models. However, expanding the number of servers would necessitate a major upgrade of the data center's power needs and the associated cooling system. To reduce complexity and increase capacity and reliability, the IT staff installed a virtualization architecture to increase flexibility and system reliability, as well as reduce downtime, system administration workload, power consumption, and the overall number of physical servers by more than two-thirds.[27]

GRID COMPUTING

When you turn on the light, the power grid delivers exactly what you need, instantly. Computers and networks can now work that way using grid computing. ***Grid computing*** is an aggregation of geographically dispersed computing, storage, and network resources, coordinated to deliver improved performance, higher quality of service, better utilization, and easier access to data.

Grid computing enables the virtualization of distributed computing and data resources such as processing, network bandwidth, and storage capacity to create a single system image, granting users and applications seamless access to vast IT

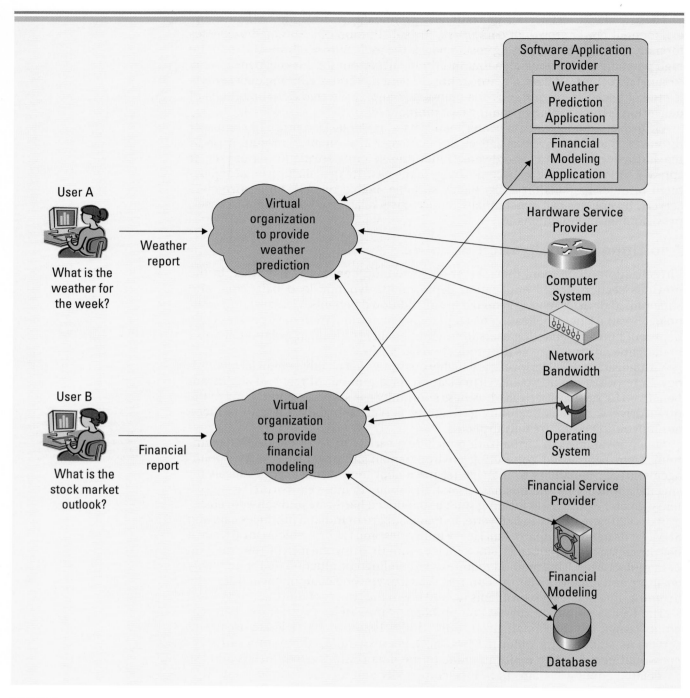

FIGURE 5.13

Virtual Organizations Using
Grid Computing

capabilities. Virtualizing these resources yields a scalable, flexible pool of processing and data storage that the enterprise can use to improve efficiency. Moreover, it will help create a sustainable competitive advantage by streamlining product development and allowing focus to be placed on the core business. Over time, grid environments will enable the creation of virtual organizations and advanced web services as partnerships and collaborations become more critical in strengthening each link in the value chain (see Figure 5.13).

Grid Computing Business Benefits

At its core, grid computing is based on an open set of standards and protocols (e.g., Open Grid Services Architecture) that enable communication across heterogeneous, geographically dispersed environments, as shown in Figure 5.14. With grid computing, organizations can optimize computing and data resources, pool them for large-capacity workloads, share them across networks, and enable collaboration.

Google, the secretive, extraordinarily successful $6.1 billion global search engine company, is one of the most recognized brands in the world. Yet it selectively discusses its innovative information management architecture—which is based on one of the largest grid computing systems in the world. Google runs on hundreds of thousands of servers—by one estimate, in excess of 450,000—racked up in thousands of clusters in dozens of data centers around the world. It has data centers in Ireland, Virginia, and California. It recently opened a new center in Atlanta and is currently building two football-field-sized centers in The Dalles, Oregon. By having its servers and data centers distributed geographically, Google delivers faster performance to its worldwide audience.[28]

Grid computing goes far beyond sheer computing power. Today's operating environments must be resilient, flexible, and integrated as never before. Organizations around the world are experiencing substantial benefits by implementing grids in critical business processes to achieve both business and technology benefits. These business benefits include:

- Improving productivity and collaboration of virtual organizations and respective computing and data resources.
- Allowing widely dispersed departments and businesses to create virtual organizations to share data and resources.
- Building robust and infinitely flexible and resilient operational architectures.

FIGURE 5.14

Virtualization of Grid Computing

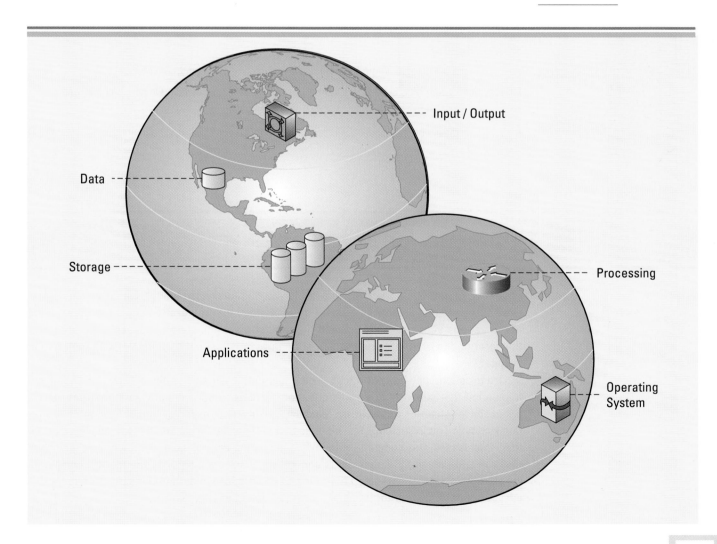

- Providing instantaneous access to massive computing and data resources.
- Leveraging existing capital investments, which in turn help to ensure optimal utilization and costs of computing capabilities.[29]

Many organizations have started identifying the major business areas for grid computing business applications. Some examples of major business areas include:

- Life sciences, for analyzing and decoding strings of biological and chemical information.
- Financial services, for running long, complex financial models and arriving at more accurate decisions.
- Higher education for enabling advanced, data- and computation-intensive research.
- Engineering services, including automotive and aerospace, for collaborative design and data-intensive testing.
- Government, for enabling seamless collaboration and agility in both civil and military departments and other agencies.
- Collaborative games for replacing the existing single-server online games with more highly parallel, massively multiplayer online games.

In this pervasive need of information anytime and anywhere, the explosive grid computing environments have now proven to be so significant that they are often referred to as being the world's single and most powerful computer solutions.

OPENING CASE QUESTIONS

Virgin Mobile

5. Explain the advantages Virgin Mobile has using a service oriented architecture.

6. Why does Virgin Mobile need to use interoperability and loose coupling in its architecture?

7. Explain the business drivers for Virgin Mobile using virtualization.

8. What business benefits would Virgin Mobile experience deploying grid computing?

SUMMARY OF KEY THEMES

The purpose of this chapter was to provide you, the business student, with a detailed overview of the various enterprise architectures found in an organization and an understanding of the various activities that surround the regular maintenance and upkeep of an organization information architect and the primary characteristics that comprise a solid information architecture.

Organizations pay special attention to computing basics since these form the underlying foundation that supports a firm's information systems. A solid underlying infrastructure is a necessity for ensuring the security, reliability, quality, and responsiveness of a firm's information systems. These systems are the tools that companies utilize and heavily rely upon to run their businesses and compete in today's competitive environment. As such, it is important that you understand the components and activities surrounding an organization's computing infrastructure so that you may be attuned to what is involved and take steps to ensure this infrastructure is kept up-to-date and running as smoothly as possible.

CLOSING CASE ONE

Chicago Tribune's Server Consolidation a Success

The *Chicago Tribune* is the seventh-largest newspaper in the country. Overhauling its data center and consolidating servers was a difficult task; however, the payoff was tremendous. The *Chicago Tribune* successfully moved its critical applications from a mishmash of mainframes and older servers to a new dual-site enterprise architecture, which has resulted in lower costs and increased reliability throughout the company.

The paper's new enterprise architecture clustered its servers over a two-mile distance, lighting up a 1 Gbps dark-fiber link—an optical fiber that is in place but not yet being used—between two data centers. This architecture lets the newspaper spread the processing load between the servers while improving redundancy and options for disaster recovery. The transfer to the new architecture was not smooth. A small piece of software written for the transition contained a coding error that caused the *Tribune's* editorial applications to experience intermittent processing failures. As a result, the paper was forced to delay delivery to about 40 percent of its 680,000 readers and cut 24 pages from a Monday edition, costing the newspaper nearly $1 million in advertising revenue.

After editorial applications were stabilized, the *Tribune* proceeded to migrate applications for operations—the physical production and printing of the newspaper—and circulation to the new enterprise architecture. "As we gradually took applications off the mainframe, we realized that we were incurring very high costs in maintaining underutilized mainframes at two different locations," said Darko Dejanovic, vice president and CTO of the Tribune Co., which owned the *Chicago Tribune,* the *Los Angeles Times,* Long Island's *Newsday,* and about a dozen other metropolitan newspapers. "By moving from two locations to one, we've achieved several million dollars in cost savings. There's no question that server consolidation was the right move for us."

The Tribune Co. is excited about its new enterprise architecture and is now looking to consolidate software across its newspapers. Currently, each newspaper maintains its own applications for classified advertising and billing, which means the parent company must support about 10 billing packages and the same number of classified-ad programs. The Tribune Co. has found that most of the business processes can be standardized. So far, it has standardized about 95 percent of classified-ad processes and about 90 percent of advertising-sales processes. The Tribune Co. plans to replace the disparate billing and ad applications across the company with a single package that will be used by all business units. The different newspapers will not necessarily share the same data, but they will have the same processes and the same systems for accessing them. Over time, that will allow some of the call centers to handle calls for multiple newspapers; East Coast centers will handle the early-morning calls, and West Coast centers the late-day and evening calls.

The Tribune Co. is looking at a few additional projects including the implementation of hardware that will allow its individual applications to run on partial CPUs, freeing processor power and making more efficient use of disk space.[30]

Questions

1. Review the five characteristics of infrastructure architecture and rank them in order of their potential impact on the Tribune Co.'s business.
2. What is the disaster recovery cost curve? Where should the Tribune Co. operate on the curve?
3. Define backups and recovery. What are the risks to the Tribune Co.'s business if it fails to implement an adequate backup plan?
4. Why is a scalable and highly available enterprise architecture critical to the Tribune Co.'s current operations and future growth?
5. Identify the need for information security at the Tribune Co.
6. How could the Tribune Co. use a "Classified Ad" web service across its different businesses?

CLOSING CASE TWO

The U.S. Open Supports SOA

The U.S. Open is a tennis event sponsored by the United States Tennis Association (USTA), a not-for-profit organization with more than 665,000 members. It devotes 100 percent of its proceeds to the advancement of tennis. At last count, more than 5 million viewers checked out the U.S. Open online.

The USTA created an integrated scoring system for the U.S. Open. This scoring system helps collect data from all tennis courts and then stores and distributes the information to USOpen.org, the official website of the U.S. Open. The ability to immediately and simultaneously distribute scoring information, supporting more than 156 million scoring updates, illustrates how the USTA leverages SOA to support its business goals. SOA helped the USTA use its existing computing systems to become more responsive and more closely aligned with the needs of its customers and partners.

For example, umpires officiating at each of the U.S. Open matches hold a device they use to keep score. These devices feed into a database that holds the collective tournament scores. From there, the constantly changing scoring information is fed to numerous servers that can be accessed through the U.S. Open website. When visitors go to USOpen.org and click the "Live Scores" link, they see the scoreboards for all 18 courts that are updated before the visitors' eyes. This is then used to present visitors with instantly updated scoring information that is presented on the site's On Demand Scoreboards and the "matches in progress" pages.

Scores and statistics can also be instantly viewed on the website and compared with past U.S. Open events and similar competitions. Additionally, SOA is helping support the integration of information and statistics related to the tournament, such as individual scores and how they compare with current and past performance of the players and competitors.

Linking all of the tournament's information and delivering scores in real time requires a sophisticated information technology infrastructure that can be easily accessed and understood by USTA subscribers, many of whom are not IT professionals. The USTA is at the beginning stages of an SOA, and the USOpen.org website will be able to accommodate a growing audience of tennis fans worldwide.

The U.S. Open is the world's largest annually attended sporting event, and USOpen.org is among the top five most-trafficked sports event websites. The site has seen a 62 percent year-over-year traffic increase, with 5 million unique users, 27 million visits, and 79,000 concurrent real-time scoreboards. Since SOAs are scalable and flexible, they can easily meet the demands of the constantly changing USOpen.org website and the anticipated heavy site traffic produced by 27 million visits—with each visitor spending nearly an hour and a half per visit.[31]

Questions

1. Review the five characteristics of infrastructure architecture and rank them in order of their potential impact on the USOpen.org.
2. What are the USTA security concerns regarding interoperability between the tournament database and its website?
3. How could the USTA benefit from virtualization?
4. Identify the value of integrating the tournament information with the USTA website, USOpen.org.
5. Why would a sudden surge in server utilization during the middle of the U.S. Open spell disaster for the USTA?
6. Why is loose coupling a critical business component to the USTA architecture?

CLOSING CASE THREE

eBay's Grid

eBay Inc. is using grid computing to deliver online auction services to millions of users. The biggest technology issue facing eBay is managing its shared grid infrastructure, which currently spreads across more than 15,000 servers. Instead of managing individual servers, eBay wants its systems administrators to manage aggregations of servers, a process that would be eased considerably with grid standards.

With 222 million registered users at the last count, 610 million listings each quarter, and 6 million new items added every day, it takes a lot of computing power to keep eBay operating as fast and reliably as users have come to expect. However, eBay experienced a major outage in 1999 that resulted in a total loss of service. The architecture of the system made it vulnerable: Bid information was maintained in a single massive database that was both a point of contention and a single point of failure. The business logic for all except one application was also centralized.

Following the disastrous outage of 1999, eBay launched an overhaul of its IT infrastructure, rebuilding its data centers around a grid-type architecture. The first task was to eliminate the single point of failure in the huge system. Then eBay needed to reconstruct the application to ensure that it had fault isolation and that processes and tasks of like size and cost weren't congesting and competing with each other. Basically, eBay had to disaggregate the monolithic system and ensure scale and fault tolerance.

The auction site abandoned its one huge back-end system and four or five very large search databases. Search used to update in 6 to 12 hours from the time in which someone would place a bid or an item for sale. Today, updates are usually less than 90 seconds. At present, eBay has 200 back-end databases, all of them in the 6- to 12-processor range. Not all those are necessary to run the site; many are for disaster recovery and for data replication.

The extra redundancy built into the system allows eBay to be run $24 \times 7 \times 365$; it is never brought down for scheduled maintenance as was required with the old implementation.

The operating results are exceptional: Although system usage went up by about an order of magnitude, downtime went down from about 15 days per year to just a few hours.

eBay also ensures that security is built in to every piece of its infrastructure and architecture. To date, it has never been hacked. In addition, eBay believes this infrastructure will allow it to scale nearly indefinitely.[32]

Questions

1. Review the five characteristics of infrastructure architecture and rank them in order of their potential impact on eBay's business.
2. What are the business benefits that eBay enjoys thanks to grid computing?
3. What precautions would eBay take to ensure 100 percent security?
4. How can eBay take advantage of implementing SOA?
5. Explain how eBay uses fault tolerance.
6. Describe the potential value of eBay using virtualization.
7. What ethical and security concerns should eBay be aware of to ensure its business operates properly?

MAKING BUSINESS DECISIONS

1. Purchasing a computer

Dell is considered the fastest company on earth and specializes in computer customization. Connect to Dell's website at www.dell.com. Go to the portion of Dell's site that allows you to customize either a laptop or a desktop computer. First, choose an already prepared system and note its price and capability in terms of CPU speed, RAM size, monitor quality, and storage capacity. Now, customize that system to increase CPU speed, add more RAM, increase monitor size and quality, and add more storage capacity. What is the difference in price between the two? Which system is more in your price range? Which system has the speed and capacity you need?

2. Web-enabled cell phones

Computers categorized by size for personal needs include PDAs, laptops, and desktop computers. Other variations include web-enabled cell phones that include instant text messaging and web computers. For this project, you will need a group of four people, which you will then split into two groups of two. Have the first group research web-enabled cell phones, their capabilities and costs. Have that group make a purchase recommendation based on price and capability. Have the second group do the same for web computers. What is your vision of the future? Will we ever get rid of clunky laptops and desktops in favor of more portable and cheaper devices such as web-enabled cell phones and web computers? Why or why not?

3. Small-business computers

Many different types of computers are available for small businesses. Use the Internet to find three different vendors of laptops or notebooks that are good for small businesses. Find the most expensive and the least expensive that the vendor offers and create a table comparing the different computers based on the following:

- CPU
- Memory
- Hard drive
- Optical drive
- Operating system
- Utility software
- Application software
- Support plan

Determine which computer you would recommend for a small business looking for an inexpensive laptop. Determine which computer you would recommend for a small business looking for an expensive laptop.

4. Planning for disaster recovery

You are the new senior analyst in the IT department at Beltz, a large snack food manufacturing company. The company is located on the beautiful shoreline in Charleston, North Carolina. The company's location is one of its best and also worst features. The weather and surroundings are beautiful, but the threat of hurricanes and other natural disasters is high. Compile a disaster recovery plan that will minimize any risks involved with a natural disaster.

5. Comparing backup and recovery systems

Research the Internet to find three different vendors of backup and recovery systems. Compare and contrast the three systems and determine which one you would recommend if you were installing a backup and recovery system for a medium-sized business with 3,500 employees that maintains information on the stock market. Compile your findings in a presentation that you can give to your class that details the three systems' strengths and weaknesses, along with your recommendation.

APPLY YOUR KNOWLEDGE

1. Ranking the *-ilities*

In a group, review the list of IT infrastructure qualities and rank them in order of their impact on an organization's success. Use a rating system of 1 to 7, where 1 indicates the biggest impact and 7 indicates the least impact.

IT Infrastructure Qualities	Business Impact
Availability	
Accessibility	
Reliability	
Scalability	
Flexibility	
Performance	
Capacity Planning	

2. Designing an enterprise architecture

Components of a solid enterprise architecture include everything from documentation to business concepts to software and hardware. Deciding which components to implement and how to implement them can be a challenge. New IT components are released daily, and business needs continually change. An enterprise architecture that meets your organization's needs today may not meet those needs tomorrow. Building an enterprise architecture that is scalable, flexible, available, accessible, and reliable is key to your organization's success.

You are the enterprise architect (EA) for a large clothing company called Xedous. You are responsible for developing the initial enterprise architecture. Create a list of questions you will need answered to develop your architecture. Below is an example of a few of the questions you might ask.

- What are the company's growth expectations?
- Will systems be able to handle additional users?

- How long will information be stored in the systems?
- How much customer history must be stored?
- What are the organization's business hours?
- What are the organization's backup requirements?

3. Back on Your Feet

You are working for GetSmart, a document creation company for legal professionals. Due to the highly sensitive nature of the industry, employees must store all work on the network drive and are not allowed to backup the data to a CD, flash drive, or any other type of external storage including home computers. The company has been following this policy for the last three years without any issues. You return to work Monday morning after a long weekend to find that the building was struck by lightning destroying several servers. Unfortunately, the backup strategy failed and all of the data from your department has been lost.

When the head of the company demanded an explanation as to why they did not have any individual backups, he was shown the company policy he had signed not once but three times. The end result was the head of IT along with four of his cronies that had developed this ridiculous policy were fired.

Project Focus

You have been placed on a committee with several of your peers to revamp the backup and recovery policies and create a new disaster recovery plan. You must create policies and procedures that will preserve the sensitive nature of the documents, while ensuring the company is safe from disasters. Be sure to address a worst case scenario where the entire building is lost.

4. Growing, Growing, Gone

You are the founder of Black Pearl, a small comic book start-up. The good news is Black Pearl has found tremendous success. You have 34 employees in a creative, yet functional, office in downtown Chicago. The comics you produce are of extremely high quality. The artwork is unmatched and the storylines are compelling, gripping, and addictive, according to your customers. Your comics are quickly becoming a cult classic and Black Pearl customers are extremely loyal. You produce all of the comics and sell them in your store and via the Internet to individuals all over the United States.

Project Focus

You had vision when you started Black Pearl. You knew the potential of your business model to revamp the comic industry. You purchased high-end computers and customizable software to support your operations. Now, you are faced with a new dilemma. You have a large international following and you have decided to pursue international opportunities. You would like to open stores in Japan, France, and Brazil over the next year. To determine if this is possible you need to evaluate your current systems to see if they are flexible and scalable enough to perform business internationally. You know that you are going to run into many international business issues. Create a list of questions you need to answer to determine if your systems are capable of performing international business.

The New Language of Business: SOA & Web 2.0, By Sandy Carter (Indianapolis: IBM Press, 2007).

There is now a direct, provable link between an organization's flexibility and business performance. To optimize flexibility, companies must achieve unprecedented levels of integration and automation of key processes and infrastructure, both internally and externally. At the same time, they must learn to manage their processes far more dynamically and responsively.

Until recently, technology stood in the way of achieving these goals. Thanks to the emergence of service oriented architecture (SOA), web 2.0, and open standards, technology now enables companies to achieve those goals. In *The New Language of Business,* one of IBM's top SOA strategists demonstrates how business leaders can use innovations in technology to drive dramatic process improvements and support accelerating change.

Sandy Carter shows how to deconstruct a business into a "componentized" business model, then support that model with linked, repeatable IT services that can adapt quickly, easily, and economically. These techniques will help both IT professionals and business leaders reach new levels of operational excellence to deliver the market-focused innovations that matter most.[33]

Does IT Matter? By Nicholas G. Carr (Boston: Harvard Business School Publishing, 2004).

Every year, companies spend more than $2 trillion on computer and communications equipment and services. Underlying these enormous expenditures is one of modern business's most deeply held assumptions—that information technology is increasingly critical to competitive advantage and strategic success.

In this explosive and engaging book, Nicholas G. Carr calls the common wisdom into question, contending that IT's strategic importance has actually dissipated as its core functions have become available and affordable to all. Expanding on the controversial *Harvard Business Review* article that provoked a storm of debate around the world, *Does IT Matter?* shows that IT–like earlier infrastructural technologies, such as railroads and electric power, is steadily evolving from a profit-boosting proprietary resource to a simple cost of doing business.

Carr draws on convincing historical and contemporary examples to explain why innovations in hardware, software, and networking are rapidly replicated by competitors, neutralizing their strategic power to set one business apart from the pack. But more important, he shows why IT's emergence as a shared and standardized infrastructure is a natural and necessary process that may ultimately deliver huge economic and social benefits.[34]

6

CHAPTER

Databases and Data Warehouses

SECTION 6.1 **Database Fundamentals**	**SECTION 6.2** **Data Warehouse Fundamentals**
■ Organizational Information ■ Storing Organizational Information ■ Relational Database Fundamentals ■ Relational Database Advantages ■ Database Management Systems ■ Integrating Information Among Multiple Databases	■ Accessing Organizational Information ■ History of Data Warehousing ■ Data Warehouse Fundamentals ■ Data Mining and Business Intelligence

CHAPTER OUTLINE

What's in IT for me?

This chapter introduces the concept of information and its relative importance to organizations. It distinguishes between data stored in transactional databases and information housed in enterprisewide data warehouse systems. The chapter also provides an overview of database fundamentals and the steps required to integrate various bits of data stored across multiple, operational data stores into a comprehensive and centralized repository of summarized information, which can be turned into powerful business intelligence.

You, as a business student, must understand the difference between transactional data and summarized information and the different types of questions you would use a transactional database or enterprise data warehouse to answer. You need to be aware of the complexity of storing data in databases and the level of effort required to transform operational data into meaningful, summarized information. You need to realize the power of information and the competitive advantage a data warehouse brings an organization in terms of facilitating business intelligence. Understanding the power of information will help you prepare to compete in a global marketplace. Armed with the power of information you will make smart, informed, and data-supported managerial decisions.

It Takes a Village to Write an Encyclopedia

The concept of gathering all the world's knowledge in a single place goes back to the ancient Library of Alexandria, but the modern concept of a general-purpose, widely distributed, printed encyclopedia dates from shortly before the 18th century. The Internet has expanded on the concept with the development of Wikipedia. Founded by Jimmy Wales, Wikipedia is a project to produce a free content encyclopedia that can have thousands of contributors and be edited by anyone, and it now contains millions of articles and pages worldwide. Wikipedia ranks among the top 15 online destinations worldwide.

A wiki is a type of website connected to a database that allows users to easily add and edit content and is especially suited for collaborative writing. The name is based on the Hawaiian term *wiki,* meaning quick, fast, or to hasten. In essence, wiki is a simplification of the process of creating web pages combined with a database that records each individual change, so that at any time, a page can be reverted to any of its previous states. A wiki system may also provide tools that allow users to easily monitor the constantly changing state of the wiki and discuss the issues that emerge in trying to achieve a general consensus about wiki content.

Wikipedia Tightens the Reins

Wikipedia is exploding with information. The site originally allowed unrestricted access so that people could contribute without registering. As with any database management system, governance is a key issue. Without governance, there is no control over how information is published and maintained.

When you research Wikipedia, you find stories about how competing companies are removing and editing each other's entries in Wikipedia to gain market share. The *Washington Post* reported that Capitol Hill is playing "WikiPolitics" by editing representatives' and senators' biographies and speeches. Wikipedia had to temporarily block certain Capitol Hill web addresses from altering entries.

Wikipedia recently began tightening its rules for submitting entries following the disclosure that it ran a piece falsely implicating a man in the Kennedy assassinations. John Seigenthaler Sr., who was Robert Kennedy's administrative assistant in the early 1960s, wrote an article revealing that Wikipedia had run a biography claiming Seigenthaler had been suspected in the assassinations of the former attorney general and his brother, President John F. Kennedy. Wikipedia now requires users to register before they can create and edit articles.

Wikipedia has grown into a storehouse of pieces on topics ranging from medieval art to nanotechnology. The volume of content is possible because the site relies on volunteers, including many experts in their fields, to submit entries and edit previously submitted articles. The website hopes that the registration requirement will limit the number of stories being created. "What we're hopeful to see is that by slowing that down to 1,500 a day from several thousand, the people who are monitoring this will have more ability to improve the quality," Wales said. "In many cases the types of things we see going on are impulse vandalism."

The Future of Wiki

Can the wisdom of crowds trump the genius of Google? Wales believes that it not only can, but it will. Wales plans to launch a new search engine called Wikiasari and hopes that it could someday overtake Google as the web search leader.

Like Wikipedia, Wikiasari will rely on the support of a volunteer community of users. The idea is that web surfers and programmers will be able to bring their collective intelligence to bear, to fine-tune search results and make the experience more effective for everyone. "If you search in Google, a lot of the results are very, very good and a lot of the results are very, very bad," Wales says. What that shows, Wales says, is that mathematical formulas alone do not produce consistently relevant results. "Human intelligence is still a very important part of the process," he says.

People can contribute to Wikiasari in one of two ways. The first is by enabling ordinary computer users to rerank search results. When a user performs a search on Wikiasari, the engine will return results based on a formula akin to Google's Page-Rank system, which determines relevance by counting the number of times other web pages link to a specific page, among other things. Unlike Google, however, users will then be able to reorder the results based on which links they find most useful by selecting an edit function. Wikiasari's servers will then store the new results along with the original query. When the same query is made in the future, Wikiasari will return the results in the order saved by most users.

Potential web users with programming knowledge have a second way to contribute. Wikiasari's technology is based on Apache's open source web search software Lucene and Nutch, and Wales plans to unveil all the company's computer code to the outside world. This kind of open source development is in sharp contrast to the approach of the leading search engines, which do not release their search ranking formulas. Yet Wales contends that his open approach will ultimately prevail, because anyone any place in the world can weigh in with tweaks to Wikiasari's code to help return more relevant results.

A Fly in the Wiki

Wikipedia will fail soon, crushed under the weight of an automated assault by marketers and others seeking online traffic. So says law professor Eric Goldman, who predicts Wikipedia's downfall. Goldman, a professor at the Santa Clara University School of Law, argues that Wikipedia will see increasingly vigorous efforts to subvert its editorial process, much as Digg.com has seen. As marketers become more determined and turn to automated tools to alter Wikipedia entries to generate online traffic, Goldman predicts Wikipedians will burn out trying to keep entries clean.

"Thus, Wikipedia will enter a death spiral where the rate of junkiness will increase rapidly until the site becomes a wasteland," Goldman writes. "Alternatively, to prevent this death spiral, Wikipedia will change its core open-access architecture, increasing the database's vitality by changing its mission somewhat."

As precedent, Goldman cites the fate of the Open Directory Project, a user-edited web directory, which he says "is now effectively worthless." "I love Wikipedia," Goldman concludes. "I use it every day. Based on the stats from my Google personalized search, Wikipedia is the number one site I click on from Google search results. So I'm not rooting for it to fail. But the very architecture of Wikipedia contains the seeds of its own destruction. Without fame or fortune, I don't think Wikipedia's incentive system is sustainable."[1]

INTRODUCTION

Information is powerful. Information is useful in telling an organization how its current operations are performing and estimating and strategizing how future operations might perform. New perspectives open up when people have the right information and know how to use it. The ability to understand, digest, analyze, and filter information is key to success for any professional in any industry. This chapter demonstrates the value an organization can uncover and create by learning how to manage, access, and analyze organizational information.

It is important to distinguish between data and information. *Data* are raw facts that describe the characteristics of an event. Characteristics for a sales event could include the date, item number, item description, quantity ordered, customer name, and shipping details. *Information* is data converted into a meaningful and useful context. Information from sales events could include best-selling item, worst-selling item, best customer, and worst customer.

section 6.1 DATABASE FUNDAMENTALS

LEARNING OUTCOMES

6.1 List, describe, and provide an example of each of the five characteristics of high quality information.

6.2 Define the relationship between a database and a database management system.

6.3 Describe the advantages an organization can gain by using a database.

6.4 Define the fundamental concepts of the relational database model.

6.5 Describe the two primary methods for integrating information across multiple databases.

6.6 Compare relational integrity constraints and business-critical integrity constraints.

6.7 Describe the benefits of a data-driven website.

ORGANIZATIONAL INFORMATION

Google recently reported a 200 percent increase in sales of its new Enterprise Search Appliance tool. Companies use the tool within an enterprise information portal (EIP) to search corporate information for answers to customer questions and to fulfill sales orders. Hundreds of Google's customers are already using the tool—Xerox, Hitachi Data Systems, Nextel Communications, Procter & Gamble, Discovery Communications, Cisco Systems, and Boeing. The ability to search, analyze, and comprehend information is vital for any organization's success. The incredible 200 percent growth in sales of Google's Search Appliance tool is a strong indicator that organizations are coveting technologies that help organize and provide access to information.[2]

Information is everywhere in an organization. When addressing a significant business issue, employees must be able to obtain and analyze all the relevant information so they can make the best decision possible. Organizational information comes at different levels and in different formats and "granularities." *Information granularity* refers to the extent of detail within the information (fine and detailed or coarse and abstract). Employees must be able to correlate the different levels, formats, and granularities of information when making decisions. For example, if employees are using a supply chain management system to make decisions, they might find that their suppliers send information in different formats and granularity at different levels. One supplier might send detailed information in a spreadsheet, another supplier might send summary information in a Word document, and still another might send aggregate information from a database.

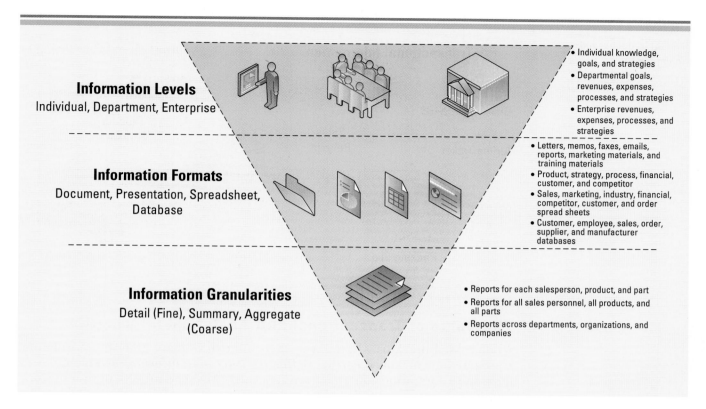

Information Levels
Individual, Department, Enterprise

- Individual knowledge, goals, and strategies
- Departmental goals, revenues, expenses, processes, and strategies
- Enterprise revenues, expenses, processes, and strategies

Information Formats
Document, Presentation, Spreadsheet, Database

- Letters, memos, faxes, emails, reports, marketing materials, and training materials
- Product, strategy, process, financial, customer, and competitor
- Sales, marketing, industry, financial, competitor, customer, and order spread sheets
- Customer, employee, sales, order, supplier, and manufacturer databases

Information Granularities
Detail (Fine), Summary, Aggregate (Coarse)

- Reports for each salesperson, product, and part
- Reports for all sales personnel, all products, and all parts
- Reports across departments, organizations, and companies

Employees will need to compare these different types of information for what they commonly reveal to make strategic decisions. Figure 6.1 displays types of information found in organizations.

Successfully collecting, compiling, sorting, and finally analyzing information from multiple levels, in varied formats, exhibiting different granularity can provide tremendous insight into how an organization is performing. Taking a hard look at organizational information can yield exciting and unexpected results such as potential new markets, new ways of reaching customers, and even new ways of doing business.

Samsung Electronics took a detailed look at over 10,000 reports from its resellers to identify "lost deals" or orders lost to competitors. The analysis yielded the enlightening result that 80 percent of lost sales occurred in a single business unit, the health care industry. Furthermore, Samsung was able to identify that 40 percent of its lost sales in the health care industry were going to one particular competitor. Before performing the analysis, Samsung was heading into its market blind. Armed with this valuable information, Samsung is changing its selling strategy in the health care industry by implementing a new strategy to work more closely with hardware vendors to win back lost sales.[3]

Not all companies are successful at managing information. Staples, the office-supplies superstore, opened its first store in 1986 with state-of-the-art technology. The company experienced rapid growth and soon found itself overwhelmed with the resulting volumes of information. The state-of-the-art technology quickly became obsolete, and the company was unable to obtain any insight into its massive volumes of information. A simple query such as identifying the customers who purchased a computer, but not software or peripherals, took hours. Some queries required several days to complete and by the time the managers received answers to their queries it was too late for action.[4]

After understanding the different levels, formats, and granularities of information, it is important to look at a few additional characteristics that help determine the value of information. These characteristics are type (transactional and analytical), timeliness, and quality.

FIGURE 6.1

Levels, Formats, and Granularities of Organizational Information

Information

FIGURE 6.2

Transactional versus
Analytical Information

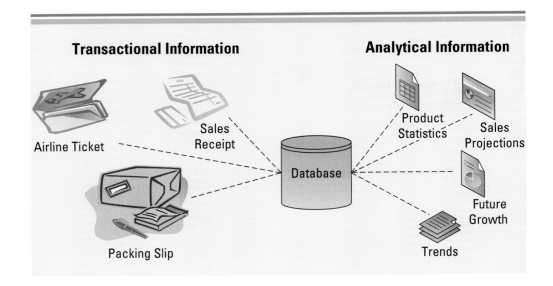

The Value of Transactional and Analytical Information

As discussed previously in the text, there are two primary types of information, transactional and analytical. Recall that *transactional information* encompasses all of the information contained within a single business process or unit of work, and its primary purpose is to support the performing of daily operational tasks. Organizations capture and store transactional information in databases, and they use it when performing operational tasks and repetitive decisions such as analyzing daily sales reports and production schedules to determine how much inventory to carry.

Recall that *analytical information* encompasses all organizational information, and its primary purpose is to support the performing of managerial analysis tasks. Analytical information is used when making important ad hoc decisions such as whether the organization should build a new manufacturing plant or hire additional sales personnel. Figure 6.2 displays different types of transactional and analytical information.

The Value of Timely Information

The need for timely information can change for each business decision. Some decisions require weekly or monthly information while other decisions require daily information. Timeliness is an aspect of information that depends on the situation. In some industries, information that is a few days or weeks old can be relevant while in other industries information that is a few minutes old can be almost worthless. Some organizations, such as 911 centers, stock traders, and banks, require consolidated, up-to-the-second information, 24 hours a day, seven days a week. Other organizations, such as insurance and construction companies, require only daily or even weekly information.

Real-time information means immediate, up-to-date information. *Real-time systems* provide real-time information in response to query requests. Many organizations use real-time systems to exploit key corporate transactional information. In a survey of 700 IT executives by Evans Data Corp., 48 percent of respondents said they were already analyzing information in or near real-time, and another 25 percent reported plans to add real-time systems.[5]

The growing demand for real-time information stems from organizations' need to make faster and more effective decisions, keep smaller inventories, operate more efficiently, and track performance more carefully. But timeliness is relative. Organizations need fresh, timely information to make good decisions. Information also needs to be timely in the sense that it meets employees' needs—but no more. If employees can absorb information only on an hourly or daily basis, there is no need to gather real-time information in smaller increments. For example, MBIA Insurance Corp. uses overnight updates to feed its real-time systems. Employees use this information to make daily risk decisions for mortgages, insurance policies, and other services. The company found that overnight updates were sufficient, as long as users could gain immediate access to the information they needed to make business decisions during the day.[6]

Most people request real-time information without understanding one of the biggest pitfalls associated with real-time information—continual change. Imagine the following scenario: Three managers meet at the end of the day to discuss a business problem. Each manager has gathered information at different times during the day to create a picture of the situation. Each manager's picture may be different because of this time discrepancy. Their views on the business problem may not match since the information they are basing their analysis on is continually changing. This approach may not speed up decision making, and may actually slow it down.

The timeliness of the information required must be evaluated for each business decision. Organizations do not want to find themselves using real-time information to make a bad decision faster.

The Value of Quality Information

Westpac Financial Services (WFS), one of the four major banks in Australia, serves millions of customers from its many core systems, each with its own database. The databases maintain information and provide users with easy access to the stored information. Unfortunately, the company failed to develop information-capturing standards, which led to inconsistent organizational information. For example, one system had a field to capture email addresses while another system did not. Duplicate customer information among the different systems was another major issue, and the company continually found itself sending conflicting or competing messages to customers from different operations of the bank. A customer could also have multiple accounts within the company, one representing a life insurance policy and one representing a credit card. WFS had no way to identify that the two different customer accounts were for the same customer.

WFS had to solve its information quality problems immediately if it was to remain competitive. The company purchased NADIS (Name & Address Data Integrity Software), a software solution that filters customer information, highlighting missing, inaccurate, and redundant information. Customer service ratings are on the rise for WFS now that the company can operate its business with a single and comprehensive view of each one of its customers.[7]

Business decisions are only as good as the quality of the information used to make the decisions. Figure 6.3 reviews five characteristics common to high quality

		FIGURE 6.3
Accuracy	Are all the values correct? For example, is the name spelled correctly? Is the dollar amount recorded properly?	Five Common Characteristics of High Quality Information
Completeness	Are any of the values missing? For example, is the address complete including street, city, state, and zip code?	
Consistency	Is aggregate or summary information in agreement with detailed information? For example, do all total fields equal the true total of the individual fields?	
Uniqueness	Is each transaction, entity, and event represented only once in the information? For example, are there any duplicate customers?	
Timeliness	Is the information current with respect to the business requirements? For example, is information updated weekly, daily, or hourly?	

FIGURE 6.4

Low Quality Information Example

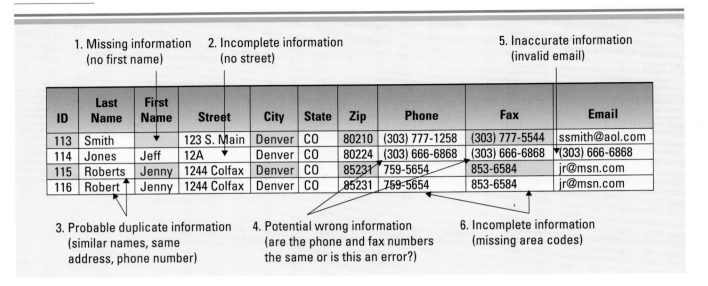

1. Missing information (no first name)
2. Incomplete information (no street)
5. Inaccurate information (invalid email)

ID	Last Name	First Name	Street	City	State	Zip	Phone	Fax	Email
113	Smith		123 S. Main	Denver	CO	80210	(303) 777-1258	(303) 777-5544	ssmith@aol.com
114	Jones	Jeff	12A	Denver	CO	80224	(303) 666-6868	(303) 666-6868	(303) 666-6868
115	Roberts	Jenny	1244 Colfax	Denver	CO	85231	759-5654	853-6584	jr@msn.com
116	Robert	Jenny	1244 Colfax	Denver	CO	85231	759-5654	853-6584	jr@msn.com

3. Probable duplicate information (similar names, same address, phone number)
4. Potential wrong information (are the phone and fax numbers the same or is this an error?)
6. Incomplete information (missing area codes)

information: accuracy, completeness, consistency, uniqueness, and timeliness. Figure 6.4 highlights several issues with low quality information including:

1. The first issue is *missing* information. The customer's first name is missing. (See #1 in Figure 6.4.)
2. The second issue is *incomplete* information since the street address contains only a number and not a street name.
3. The third issue is a probable *duplication* of information since the only slight difference between the two customers is the spelling of the last name. Similar street addresses and phone numbers make this likely.
4. The fourth issue is potential *wrong* information because the customer's phone and fax numbers are the same. Some customers might have the same number for phone and fax line, but the fact that the customer also has this number in the email address field is suspicious.
5. The fifth issue is definitely an example of *inaccurate* information since a phone number is located in the email address field.
6. The sixth issue is *incomplete* information since there is not a valid area code for the phone and fax numbers.

Recognizing how low quality information issues occur will allow organizations to begin to correct them. The four primary sources of low quality information are:

1. Online customers intentionally enter inaccurate information to protect their privacy.
2. Different systems have different information entry standards and formats.
3. Call center operators enter abbreviated or erroneous information by accident or to save time.
4. Third-party and external information contains inconsistencies, inaccuracies, and errors.[8]

Addressing the above sources of information inaccuracies will significantly improve the quality of organizational information and the value that can be extracted from the information.

Understanding the Costs of Poor Information Using the wrong information can lead to making the wrong decision. Making the wrong decision can cost time, money, and even reputations. Every business decision is only as good as the information used to make the decision. Bad information can cause serious business ramifications such as:

- Inability to accurately track customers, which directly affects strategic initiatives.
- Difficulty identifying the organization's most valuable customers.
- Inability to identify selling opportunities and wasted revenue from marketing to nonexisting customers and nondeliverable mail.
- Difficulty tracking revenue because of inaccurate invoices.
- Inability to build strong relationships with customers—which increases buyer power.

Understanding the Benefits of Good Information High quality information can significantly improve the chances of making a good decision and directly increase an organization's bottom line. Lillian Vernon Corp., a catalog company, used web analytics to discover that men preferred to shop at Lillian Vernon's website instead of looking through its paper catalog. Based on this information, the company began placing male products more prominently on its website and soon realized a 15 percent growth in sales to men.[9]

Another company discovered that Phoenix, Arizona, is not a good place to sell golf clubs, even with its high number of golf courses. An analysis revealed that typical golfers in Phoenix are either tourists or conventioneers. These golfers usually bring their clubs with them while visiting Phoenix. The analysis further revealed that two of the best places to sell golf clubs in the United States are Rochester, New York, and Detroit, Michigan.[10]

There are numerous examples of companies that have used their high quality information to make solid strategic business decisions. High quality information does not automatically guarantee that every decision made is going to be a good one, since people ultimately make decisions. But such information ensures that the basis of the decisions is accurate. The success of the organization depends on appreciating and leveraging the true value of timely and high quality information.

STORING ORGANIZATIONAL INFORMATION

Organizational information is stored in a database. Applications and programs, such as supply chain management systems, and customer relationship management systems, access the data in the database so the program can consult it to answer queries. The records retrieved in answer to questions become information that can be used to make decisions. The computer program used to manage and query a database is known as a database management system (DBMS). The properties and design of database systems are included in the study of information science.

The central concept of a database is that of a collection of records, or pieces of information. Typically, a given database has a structural description of the type of facts held in that database: This description is known as a schema. The schema describes the objects that are represented in the database and the relationships among them. There are a number of different ways of organizing a schema, that is, of modeling the database structure. These are known as database models (or data models). The most commonly used model today is the relational model, which represents all information in the form of multiple related tables each consisting of rows and columns. This model represents relationships by the use of values common to more than one table. Other models, such as the hierarchical model, and the network model, use a more explicit representation of relationships.

Many professionals consider a collection of data to constitute a database only if it has certain properties; for example, if the data are managed to ensure integrity and quality, if it allows shared access by a community of users, if it has a schema, or if it supports a query language. However, there is no definition of these properties that is universally agreed upon.[11]

RELATIONAL DATABASE FUNDAMENTALS

There are many different models for organizing information in a database, including the hierarchical database, network database, and the most prevalent—the relational database model. Broadly defined, a **database** maintains information about various types of objects (inventory), events (transactions), people (employees), and places (warehouses). In a **hierarchical database model,** information is organized into a tree-like structure that allows repeating information using parent/child relationships in such a way that it cannot have too many relationships. Hierarchical structures were widely used in the first mainframe database management systems. However, owing to their restrictions, hierarchical structures often cannot be used to relate to structures that exist in the real world. The **network database model** is a flexible way of representing objects and their relationships. Where the hierarchical model structures data as a tree of records, with each record having one parent record and many children, the network model allows each record to have multiple parent and child records, forming a lattice structure. The **relational database model** is a type of database that stores information in the form of logically related two-dimensional tables. This text focuses on the relational database model.

Consider how the Coca-Cola Bottling Company of Egypt (TCCBCE) implemented an inventory-tracking database to improve order accuracy by 27 percent, decrease order response time by 66 percent, and increase sales by 20 percent. With over 7,400 employees, TCCBCE owns and operates 11 bottling plants and 29 sales and distribution centers, making it one of the largest companies in Egypt.

Traditionally, the company sent distribution trucks to each customer's premises to take orders and deliver stock. Many problems were associated with this process including numerous information entry errors, which caused order-fulfillment time to take an average of three days. To remedy the situation, Coca-Cola decided to create presales teams equipped with handheld devices to visit customers and take orders electronically. On returning to the office, the teams synchronized orders with the company's inventory-tracking database to ensure automated processing and rapid dispatch of accurate orders to customers.[12]

Database

Entities and Attributes

Figure 6.5 illustrates the primary concepts of the relational database model—entities, entity classes, attributes, keys, and relationships. An **entity** in the relational database model is a person, place, thing, transaction, or event about which information is stored. A table in the relational database model is a collection of similar entities. The tables of interest in Figure 6.5 are *CUSTOMER, ORDER, ORDER LINE, PRODUCT,* and *DISTRIBUTOR.* Notice that each entity class (the collection of similar entities) is stored in a different two-dimensional table. **Attributes,** also called fields or columns, are characteristics or properties of an entity class. In Figure 6.5 the attributes for *CUSTOMER* include *Customer ID, Customer Name, Contact Name,* and *Phone.* Attributes for *PRODUCT* include *Product ID, Product Description,* and *Price.* Each specific entity in an entity class (e.g., Dave's Sub Shop in the *CUSTOMER* table) occupies one row in its respective table. The columns in the table contain the attributes.

Keys and Relationships

To manage and organize various entity classes within the relational database model, developers must identify primary keys and foreign keys and use them to create logical relationships. A **primary key** is a field (or group of fields) that uniquely identifies a given entity in a table. In *CUSTOMER,* the *Customer ID* uniquely identifies each entity (customer) in the table and is the primary key. Primary keys are important because they provide a way of distinguishing each entity in a table.

A **foreign key** in the relational database model is a primary key of one table that appears as an attribute in another table and acts to provide a logical relationship between the two tables. Consider Hawkins Shipping, one of the distributors appearing

FIGURE 6.5

Potential Relational Database for Coca-Cola Bottling Company of Egypt (TCCBCE)

		Order Number: 34562	
Coca-Cola Bottling Company of Egypt **Sample Sales Order**			

| Customer:
 Dave's Sub Shop | Date:
 8/6/2008 | | |

Quantity	Product	Price	Amount
100	Vanilla Coke	$0.55	$55

Distributor Fee $12.95

Order Total $67.95

CUSTOMER

Customer ID	Customer Name	Contact Name	Phone
23	Dave's Sub Shop	David Logan	(555)333-4545
43	Pizza Palace	Debbie Fernandez	(555)345-5432
765	T's Fun Zone	Tom Repicci	(555)565-6655

ORDER

Order ID	Order Date	Customer ID	Distributor ID	Distributor Fee	Total Due
34561	7/4/2008	23	DEN8001	$22.00	$145.75
34562	8/6/2008	23	DEN8001	$12.95	$67.95
34563	6/5/2008	765	NY9001	$29.50	$249.50

ORDER LINE

Order ID	Line Item	Product ID	Quantity
34561	1	12345AA	75
34561	2	12346BB	50
34561	3	12347CC	100
34562	1	12349EE	300
34563	1	12345AA	100
34563	2	12346BB	100
34563	3	12347CC	50
34563	4	12348DD	50
34563	5	12349EE	100

DISTRIBUTOR

Distributor ID	Distributor Name
DEN8001	Hawkins Shipping
CHI3001	ABC Trucking
NY9001	Van Distributors

PRODUCT

Product ID	Product Description	Price
12345AA	Coca-Cola	$0.55
12346BB	Diet Coke	$0.55
12347CC	Sprite	$0.55
12348DD	Diet Sprite	$0.55
12349EE	Vanilla Coke	$0.55

in the *DISTRIBUTOR* table. Its primary key, *Distributor ID,* is DEN8001. Notice that *Distributor ID* also appears as an attribute in the ORDER table. This establishes the fact that Hawkins Shipping (*Distributor ID* DEN8001) was responsible for delivering orders 34561 and 34562 to the appropriate customer(s). Therefore, *Distributor ID* in the *ORDER* table creates a logical relationship (who shipped what order) between *ORDER* and *DISTRIBUTOR.*

RELATIONAL DATABASE ADVANTAGES

From a business perspective, database information offers many advantages, including:

- Increased flexibility.
- Increased scalability and performance.
- Reduced information redundancy.
- Increased information integrity (quality).
- Increased information security.

Increased Flexibility

Databases tend to mirror business structures, and a good database can handle changes quickly and easily, just as any good business needs to be able to handle changes quickly and easily. Equally important, databases provide flexibility in allowing each user to access the information in whatever way best suits his or her needs. The distinction between logical and physical views is important in understanding flexible database user views. The ***physical view*** of information deals with the physical storage of information on a storage device such as a hard disk. The ***logical view*** of information focuses on how users logically access information to meet their particular business needs. This separation of logical and physical views is what allows each user to access database information differently. That is, while a database has only one physical view, it can easily support multiple logical views. In the previous database illustration, for example, users could perform a query to determine which distributors delivered shipments to Pizza Palace last week. At the same time, another person could perform some sort of statistical analysis to determine the frequency at which Sprite and Diet Coke appear on the same order. These represent two very different logical views, but both views use the same physical view.

Consider another example—a mail-order business. One user might want a report presented in alphabetical format, in which case last name should appear before first name. Another user, working with a catalog mailing system, would want customer names appearing as first name and then last name. Both are easily achievable, but different logical views of the same physical information.

Increased Scalability and Performance

The official website of The American Family Immigration History Center, www.ellisisland.org, generated over 2.5 billion hits in its first year of operation. The site offers easy access to immigration information about people who entered America through the Port of New York and Ellis Island between 1892 and 1924. The database contains over 25 million passenger names correlated to 3.5 million images of ships' manifests.[13]

Only a database could "scale" to handle the massive volumes of information and the large numbers of users required for the successful launch of the Ellis Island website. ***Scalability*** refers to how well a system can adapt to increased demands. ***Performance*** measures how quickly a system performs a certain process or transaction. Some organizations must be able to support hundreds or thousands of online users including employees, partners, customers, and suppliers, who all want to access and share information. Databases today scale to exceptional levels, allowing all types of users and programs to perform information-processing and information-searching tasks.

Reduced Information Redundancy

Redundancy is the duplication of information, or storing the same information in multiple places. Redundant information occurs because organizations frequently capture and store the same information in multiple locations. The primary problem with redundant information is that it is often inconsistent, which makes it difficult to determine which values are the most current or most accurate. Not having correct information is confusing and frustrating for employees and disruptive to an organization. One primary goal of a database is to eliminate information redundancy by recording each piece of information in only one place in the database. Eliminating information redundancy saves space, makes performing information updates easier, and improves information quality.

Increased Information Integrity (Quality)

Information integrity is a measure of the quality of information. Within a database environment, *integrity constraints* are rules that help ensure the quality of information. Integrity constraints can be defined and built into the database design. The database (more appropriately, the database management system, which is discussed below) ensures that users can never violate these constraints. There are two types of integrity constraints: (1) relational integrity constraints and (2) business-critical integrity constraints.

Relational integrity constraints are rules that enforce basic and fundamental information-based constraints. For example, an operational integrity constraint would not allow someone to create an order for a nonexistent customer, provide a markup percentage that was negative, or order zero pounds of raw materials from a supplier. *Business-critical integrity constraints* enforce business rules vital to an organization's success and often require more insight and knowledge than relational integrity constraints. Consider a supplier of fresh produce to large grocery chains such as Kroger. The supplier might implement a business-critical integrity constraint stating that no product returns are accepted after 15 days past delivery. That would make sense because of the chance of spoilage of the produce. These types of integrity constraints tend to mirror the very rules by which an organization achieves success.

The specification and enforcement of integrity constraints produce higher quality information that will provide better support for business decisions. Organizations that establish specific procedures for developing integrity constraints typically see a decline in information error rates and an increase in the use of organizational information.

Increased Information Security

Information is an organizational asset. Like any asset, the organization must protect its information from unauthorized users or misuse. As systems become increasingly complex and more available over the Internet, security becomes an even bigger issue. Databases offer many security features including passwords, access levels, and access controls. Passwords provide authentication of the user who is gaining access to the system. Access levels determine who has access to the different types of information, and access controls determine what type of access they have to the information. For example, customer service representatives might need read-only access to customer order information so they can answer customer order inquiries; they might not have or need the authority to change or delete order information. Managers might require access to employee files, but they should have access only to their own employees' files, not the employee files for the entire company. Various security features of databases can ensure that individuals have only certain types of access to certain types of information.

Databases can increase personal security as well as information security. The Chicago Police Department (CPD) has relied on a crime-fighting system called Citizen and Law Enforcement Analysis and Reporting (CLEAR). CLEAR electronically streamlines the way detectives enter and access critical information to help them solve crimes, analyze crime patterns, and ultimately promote security in a proactive manner. The CPD enters 650,000 new criminal cases and 500,000 new arrests into CLEAR each year.[14]

DATABASE MANAGEMENT SYSTEMS

Ford's European plant manufactures more than 5,000 vehicles a day and sells them in over 100 countries worldwide. Every component of every model must conform to complex European standards, including passenger safety standards and pedestrian and environmental protection standards. These standards govern each stage of Ford's manufacturing process from design to final production. The company needs to obtain many thousands of different approvals each year to comply with the standards. Overlooking just one means the company cannot sell the finished vehicle, which brings the production line to a standstill and could potentially cost Ford up to 1 million euros per day. Ford built the Homologation Timing System (HTS), based on a relational database, to help it track and analyze these standards. The reliability and high performance of the HTS have helped Ford substantially reduce its compliance risk.[15]

A database management system is used to access information from a database. A **_database management system (DBMS)_** is software through which users and application programs interact with a database. The user sends requests to the DBMS and the DBMS performs the actual manipulation of the information in the database. There are two primary ways that users can interact with a DBMS: (1) directly and (2) indirectly, as displayed in Figure 6.6. In either case, users access the DBMS and the DBMS accesses the database.

Data-Driven Websites

FIGURE 6.6

Interacting Directly and Indirectly with a Database through a DBMS

The pages on a website must change according to what a site visitor is interested in browsing. Consider for example, a company selling sports cars. A database is created with information on each of the currently available cars (e.g., make, model, engine details, year, a photograph, etc.). A visitor to the website clicks on Porsche, for example, enters the price range he or she is interested in, and hits "Go." The visitor is presented with information on available cars within the price range and an invitation to purchase or request more information from the company. Via a secure administration area on the website, the company has the ability to modify, add, or remove cars to the database.[16]

① Search Query

③ Results

② Database

FIGURE 6.7

Wikipedia—Data-Driven
Website

A **data-driven website** is an interactive website kept constantly updated and relevant to the needs of its customers through the use of a database. Data-driven websites are especially useful when the site offers a great deal of information, products, or services. Website visitors are frequently angered if they are buried under an avalanche of information when searching a site. A data-driven website invites visitors to select and view what they are interested in by inserting a query. The website analyzes the query and then custom builds a web page in real-time that satisfies the query. Figure 6.7 displays a Wikipedia user querying business intelligence and the database sending back the appropriate web page that satisfies the user's request.[17]

Data-Driven Website Business Advantages

When building a website, ask two primary questions to determine if the site needs a database:

1. How often will the content change?
2. Who will be making the content changes?

For a general informational website with static information, it is best to build a "static" website—one that a developer can update on an as-needed basis, perhaps a few times a year. A static website is less expensive to produce and typically meets business needs.

For a website with continually changing information—press releases, new product information, updated pricing, etc.—it is best to build a data-driven website. Figure 6.8 displays the many advantages associated with a data-driven website.[18]

Data-Driven Business Intelligence

Companies can gain business intelligence by viewing the data accessed and analyzed from their website. Figure 6.9 displays how running queries or using analytical tools, such as a Pivot Table, on the database that is attached to the website can offer insight into the business, such as items browsed, frequent requests, items bought together, etc.

FIGURE 6.8

Data-Driven Website Advantages

Data-Driven Website Advantages
■ **Development:** Allows the website owner to make changes any time—all without having to rely on a developer or knowing HTML programming. A well-structured, data-driven website enables updating with little or no training.
■ **Content management:** A static website requires a programmer to make updates. This adds an unnecessary layer between the business and its web content, which can lead to misunderstandings and slow turnarounds for desired changes.
■ **Future expandability:** Having a data-driven website enables the site to grow faster than would be possible with a static site. Changing the layout, displays, and functionality of the site (adding more features and sections) is easier with a data-driven solution.
■ **Minimizing human error:** Even the most competent programmer charged with the task of maintaining many pages will overlook things and make mistakes. This will lead to bugs and inconsistencies that can be time consuming and expensive to track down and fix. Unfortunately, users who come across these bugs will likely become irritated and may leave the site. A well-designed, data-driven website will have "error trapping" mechanisms to ensure that required information is filled out correctly and that content is entered and displayed in its correct format.
■ **Cutting production and update costs:** A data-driven website can be updated and "published" by any competent data-entry or administrative person. In addition to being convenient and more affordable, changes and updates will take a fraction of the time that they would with a static site. While training a competent programmer can take months or even years, training a data-entry person can be done in 30 to 60 minutes.
■ **More efficient:** By their very nature, computers are excellent at keeping volumes of information intact. With a data-driven solution, the system keeps track of the templates, so users do not have to. Global changes to layout, navigation, or site structure would need to be programmed only once, in one place, and the site itself will take care of propagating those changes to the appropriate pages and areas. A data-driven infrastructure will improve the reliability and stability of a website, while greatly reducing the chance of "breaking" some part of the site when adding new areas.
■ **Improved stability:** Any programmer who has to update a website from "static" templates must be very organized to keep track of all the source files. If a programmer leaves unexpectedly, it could involve re-creating existing work if those source files cannot be found. Plus, if there were any changes to the templates, the new programmer must be careful to use only the latest version. With a data-driven website, there is peace of mind, knowing the content is never lost—even if your programmer is.

FIGURE 6.9

BI in a Data-Driven Website

① Web Page

② Database

③ PivotTable

INTEGRATING INFORMATION AMONG MULTIPLE DATABASES

Until the 1990s, each department in the United Kingdom's Ministry of Defense (MOD) and Army headquarters had its own systems, each system had its own database, and sharing information among the departments was difficult. Manually inputting the same information multiple times into the different systems was also time consuming and inefficient. In many cases, management could not even compile the information it required to answer questions and make decisions.

The Army solved the problem by integrating its systems, or building connections between its many databases. These integrations allow the Army's multiple systems to automatically communicate by passing information between the databases, eliminating the need for manual information entry into multiple systems because after entering the information once, the integrations send the information immediately to all other databases. The integrations not only enable the different departments to share information, but have also dramatically increased the quality of the information. The army can now generate reports detailing its state of readiness and other vital issues, nearly impossible tasks before building the integrations among the separate systems.[19]

An *integration* allows separate systems to communicate directly with each other. Similar to the UK's army, an organization will maintain multiple systems, with each system having its own database. Without integrations, an organization will (1) spend considerable time entering the same information in multiple systems and (2) suffer from the low quality and inconsistency typically embedded in redundant information. While most integrations do not eliminate all redundant information, they can ensure the consistency of it across multiple systems.

An organization can choose from two integration methods. The first is to create forward and backward integrations that link processes (and their underlying databases) in the value chain. A *forward integration* takes information entered into a given system and sends it automatically to all downstream systems and processes. A *backward integration* takes information entered into a given system and sends it automatically to all upstream systems and processes.

Figure 6.10 demonstrates how this method works across the systems or processes of sales, order entry, order fulfillment, and billing. In the order entry system, for example, an employee can update the information for a customer. That information, via the integrations, would be sent upstream to the sales system and downstream to the order fulfillment and billing systems.

Ideally, an organization wants to build both forward and backward integrations, which provide the flexibility to create, update, and delete information in any of the systems. However, integrations are expensive and difficult to build and maintain and most organizations build only forward integrations (sales through billing in

FIGURE 6.10

A Forward and Backward Customer Information Integration Example

FIGURE 6.11

Integrating Customer
Information among
Databases

Figure 6.10). Building only forward integrations implies that a change in the initial system (sales) will result in changes occurring in all the other systems. Integration of information is not possible for any changes occurring outside the initial system, which again can result in inconsistent organizational information. To address this issue, organizations can enforce business rules that all systems, other than the initial system, have read-only access to the integrated information. This will require users to change information in the initial system only, which will always trigger the integration and ensure that organizational information does not get out of sync.

The second integration method builds a central repository for a particular type of information. Figure 6.11 provides an example of customer information integrated using this method across four different systems in an organization. Users can create, update, and delete customer information only in the central customer database. As users perform these tasks on the central customer database, integrations automatically send the new and/or updated customer information to the other systems. The other systems limit users to read-only access of the customer information stored in them. Again, this method does not eliminate redundancy—but it does ensure consistency of the information among multiple systems.

OPENING CASE QUESTIONS

It Takes a Village to Write an Encyclopedia

1. Determine if an entry in Wikipedia is an example of transactional information or analytical information.

2. What is the impact to Wikipedia if the information contained in its database is of low quality?

3. Review the five common characteristics of high quality information and rank them in order of importance to Wikipedia.

4. How is Wikipedia resolving the issue of poor information?

5. Identify the different types of entities that might be stored in Wikipedia's database.

6. Why is database technology so important to Wikipedia's business model?

6.8. Describe the roles and purposes of data warehouses and data marts in an organization.

6.9. Compare the multidimensional nature of data warehouses (and data marts) with two-dimensional nature of databases.

6.10. Identify the importance of ensuring cleanliness of information throughout an organization.

6.11. Explain the relationship between business intelligence and a data warehouse.

ACCESSING ORGANIZATIONAL INFORMATION

Applebee's Neighborhood Grill & Bar posts annual sales in excess of $3.2 billion and is actively using information from its data warehouse to increase sales and cut costs. The company gathers daily information for the previous day's sales into its data warehouse from 1,500 restaurants located in 49 states and seven countries.

Understanding regional preferences, such as patrons in Texas preferring steaks more than patrons in New England, allows the company to meet its corporate strategy of being a neighborhood grill appealing to local tastes. The company has found tremendous value in its data warehouse by being able to make business decisions about customers' regional needs. The company also uses data warehouse information to perform the following:

- Base its labor budgets on actual number of guests served per hour.
- Develop promotional sale item analysis to help avoid losses from overstocking or understocking inventory.
- Determine theoretical and actual costs of food and the use of ingredients.[20]

HISTORY OF DATA WAREHOUSING

In the 1990s as organizations began to need more timely information about their business, they found that traditional operational information systems were too cumbersome to provide relevant information efficiently and quickly. Operational systems typically include accounting, order entry, customer service, and sales and are not appropriate for business analysis for the following reasons:

- Information from other operational applications is not included.
- Operational systems are not integrated, or not available in one place.
- Operational information is mainly current—does not include the history that is required to make good decisions.
- Operational information frequently has quality issues (errors)— the information needs to be cleansed.
- Without information history, it is difficult to tell how and why things change over time.
- Operational systems are not designed for analysis and decision support.

During the latter half of the 20th century, the numbers and types of databases increased. Many large businesses found themselves with information scattered across multiple platforms and variations of technology, making it almost impossible for any one individual to use information from multiple sources. Completing reporting requests across operational systems could take days or weeks using antiquated reporting tools that were designed more or less to execute the business rather than run the business. From this idea, the data warehouse was born as a place where relevant information could be held for completing strategic reports for management. The key here is the word *strategic* as most executives were less concerned with the day-to-day operations than they were with a more overall look at the model and business functions.

A key idea within data warehousing is to take information from multiple platforms/technologies (as varied as spreadsheets, databases, and word files) and place them in a common location that uses a common querying tool. In this way operational databases could be held on whatever system was most efficient for the operational business, while the reporting/strategic information could be held in a common location using a common language. Data warehouses take this a step further by giving the information itself commonality by defining what each term means and keeping it standard. An example of this would be gender, which can be referred to in many ways (Male, Female, M/F, 1/0), but should be standardized on a data warehouse with one common way of referring to each sex (M/F).

This design makes decision support more readily available without affecting day-to-day operations. One aspect of a data warehouse that should be stressed is that it is *not* a location for *all* a business's information, but rather a location for information that is interesting, or information that will assist decision makers in making strategic decisions relative to the organization's overall mission.

Data warehousing is about extending the transformation of data into information. Data warehouses offer strategic level, external, integrated, and historical information so businesses can make projections, identify trends, and decide key business issues. The data warehouse collects and stores integrated sets of historical information from multiple operational systems and feeds them to one or more data marts. It may also provide end-user access to support enterprisewide views of information.

DATA WAREHOUSE FUNDAMENTALS

Data
Warehouse

A ***data warehouse*** is a logical collection of information—gathered from many different operational databases—that supports business analysis activities and decision-making tasks. The primary purpose of a data warehouse is to aggregate information throughout an organization into a single repository in such a way that employees can make decisions and undertake business analysis activities. Therefore, while databases store the details of all transactions (for instance, the sale of a product) and events (hiring a new employee), data warehouses store that same information but in an aggregated form more suited to supporting decision-making tasks. Aggregation, in this instance, can include totals, counts, averages, and the like.

The data warehouse modeled in Figure 6.12 compiles information from internal databases or transactional/operational databases and external databases through ***extraction, transformation, and loading (ETL),*** which is a process that extracts information from internal and external databases, transforms the information using a common set of enterprise definitions, and loads the information into a data warehouse. The data warehouse then sends subsets of the information to data marts. A ***data mart*** contains a subset of data warehouse information. To distinguish between data warehouses and data marts, think of data warehouses as having a more organizational focus and data marts having focused information subsets particular to the needs of a given business unit such as finance or production and operations.

Lands' End created an organizationwide data warehouse so all its employees could access organizational information. Lands' End soon discovered that there could be "too much of a good thing." Many of its employees would not use the data warehouse because it was simply too big, too complicated, and had too much irrelevant information. Lands' End knew there was valuable information in its data warehouse, and it had to find a way for its employees to easily access the information. Data marts were the perfect solution to the company's information overload problem. Once the employees began using the data marts, they were ecstatic at the wealth of information. Data marts were a huge success for Lands' End.[21]

Multidimensional Analysis

A relational database contains information in a series of two-dimensional tables. In a data warehouse and data mart, information is multidimensional, meaning it

FIGURE 6.12

Model of a Typical Data Warehouse

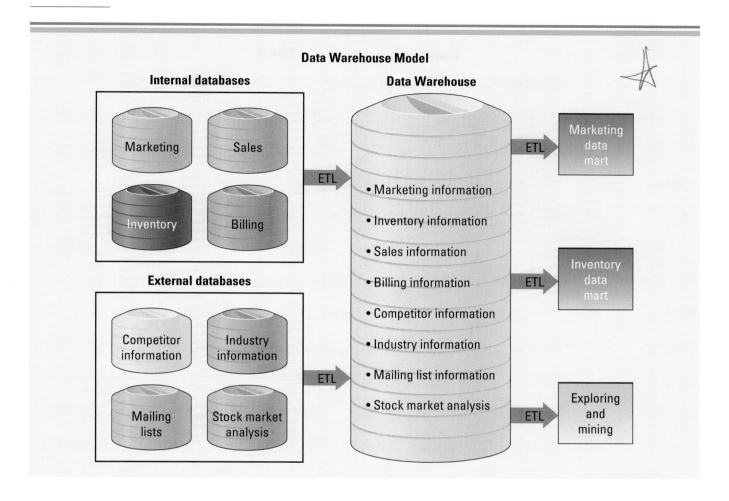

Data Warehouse Model

contains layers of columns and rows. For this reason, most data warehouses and data marts are *multidimensional databases*. A *dimension* is a particular attribute of information. Each layer in a data warehouse or data mart represents information according to an additional dimension. A **cube** is the common term for the representation of multidimensional information. Figure 6.13 displays a cube (cube a) that represents store information (the layers), product information (the rows), and promotion information (the columns).

Once a cube of information is created, users can begin to slice-and-dice the cube to drill down into the information. The second cube (cube b) in Figure 6.13 displays a slice representing promotion II information for all products at all stores. The third cube (cube c) in Figure 6.13 displays only information for promotion III, product B, at store 2. By using multidimensional analysis, users can analyze information in a number of ways and with any number of dimensions. Users might want to add dimensions of information to a current analysis including product category, region, and even forecasted versus actual weather. The true value of a data warehouse is its ability to provide multidimensional analysis that allows users to gain insights into their information.

Data warehouses and data marts are ideal for off-loading some of the querying against a database. For example, querying a database to obtain an average of sales for product B at store 2 while promotion III is under way might create a considerable processing burden for a database, essentially slowing down the time it takes another person to enter a new sale into the same database. If an organization performs numerous queries against a database (or multiple databases), aggregating that information into a data warehouse will be beneficial.

FIGURE 6.13

A Cube of Information for Performing a Multidimensional Analysis on Three Stores for Five Products and Four Promotions

Information Cleansing or Scrubbing

Maintaining quality information in a data warehouse or data mart is extremely important. The Data Warehousing Institute estimates that low-quality information costs U.S. businesses $600 billion annually. That number may seem high, but it is not. If an organization is using a data warehouse or data mart to allocate dollars across advertising strategies, low-quality information will definitely have a negative impact on its ability to make the right decision.[22]

To increase the quality of organizational information and thus the effectiveness of decision making, businesses must formulate a strategy to keep information clean. This is the concept of *information cleansing or scrubbing,* a process that weeds out and fixes or discards inconsistent, incorrect, or incomplete information.

Specialized software tools exist that use sophisticated algorithms to parse, standardize, correct, match, and consolidate data warehouse information. This is vitally important because data warehouses often contain information from several different databases, some of which can be external to the organization. In a data warehouse, information cleansing occurs first during the ETL process and second on the information once it is in the data warehouse. Companies can choose information cleansing software from several different vendors including Oracle, SAS, Ascential Software, and Group 1 Software. Ideally, scrubbed information is error-free and consistent.

Dr Pepper/Seven Up, Inc., was able to integrate its myriad databases in a data warehouse (and subsequently data marts) in less than two months, giving the company access to consolidated, clean information. Approximately 600 people in the company regularly use the data marts to analyze and track beverage sales across multiple dimensions, including various distribution routes such as bottle/can sales, fountain food-service sales, premier distributor sales, and chain and national accounts. The company is now performing in-depth analysis of up-to-date sales information that is clean and error-free.[23]

Looking at customer information highlights why information cleansing is necessary. Customer information exists in several operational systems. In each system all details of this customer information could change from the customer ID to contact information (see Figure 6.14). Determining which contact information is accurate and correct for this customer depends on the business process that is being executed.

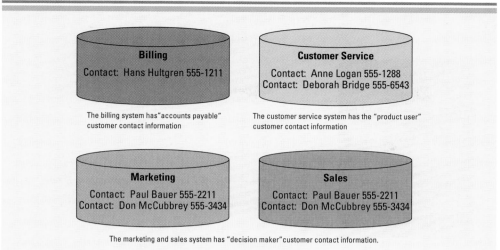

FIGURE 6.14

Contact Information in
Operational Systems

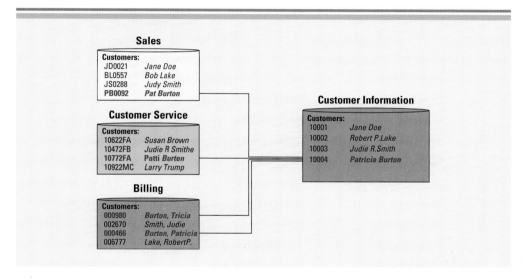

FIGURE 6.15

Standardizing Customer
Name from Operational
Systems

Figure 6.15 displays a customer name entered differently in multiple operational systems. Information cleansing allows an organization to fix these types of inconsistencies and cleans the information in the data warehouse. Figure 6.16 displays the typical events that occur during information cleansing.

Achieving perfect information is almost impossible. The more complete and accurate an organization wants its information to be, the more it costs. The trade-off for perfect information lies in accuracy versus completeness. Accurate information means it is correct, while complete information means there are no blanks. A birth date of 2/31/10 is an example of complete but inaccurate information (February 31 does not exist). An address containing Denver, Colorado, without a zip code is an example of incomplete information that is accurate. For their information, most organizations determine a percentage high enough to make good decisions at a reasonable cost, such as 85 percent accurate and 65 percent complete.

DATA MINING AND BUSINESS INTELLIGENCE

Data mining is the process of analyzing data to extract information not offered by the raw data alone. Data mining can also begin at a summary information level (coarse granularity) and progress through increasing levels of detail (drilling down), or the reverse (drilling up).

FIGURE 6.16

Information Cleansing
Activities

To perform data mining, users need data-mining tools. ***Data-mining tools*** use a variety of techniques to find patterns and relationships in large volumes of information and infer rules from them that predict future behavior and guide decision making. Data-mining tools for data warehouses help users uncover business intelligence in their data. Data mining and business intelligence are covered in detail in Chapter 9.

OPENING CASE QUESTIONS

It Takes a Village to Write an Encyclopedia

7. How could Wikipedia use a data warehouse to improve its business operations?

8. Why must Wikipedia cleanse or scrub the information in its data warehouse?

9. How could a company use information from Wikipedia to gain business intelligence?

SUMMARY OF KEY THEMES

The purpose of this chapter was to provide you, the business student, with a detailed discussion concerning data, information, and business intelligence. Databases contain data, and data warehouses and data-mining tools help users extract information and business intelligence from the data. The chapter provided you with a robust description of database fundamentals and how data in various data stores are extracted, transferred, and loaded into central data warehouses and data marts. Treating data and information as key organizational assets offers companies several advantages, namely the ability to make sound decisions based on accurate and reliable information and ultimately to uncover business intelligence.

CLOSING CASE ONE

Searching for Revenue—Google

Google founders Sergey Brin and Larry Page are on *Forbes* magazine's list of world billionaires. Google, famous for its highly successful search engine, experienced 850 percent revenue growth in 2005.

How Google Works

Figure 6.17 displays the life of an average Google query. The web server sends the query to the index servers. The content inside the index server is similar to the index at the back of a book;

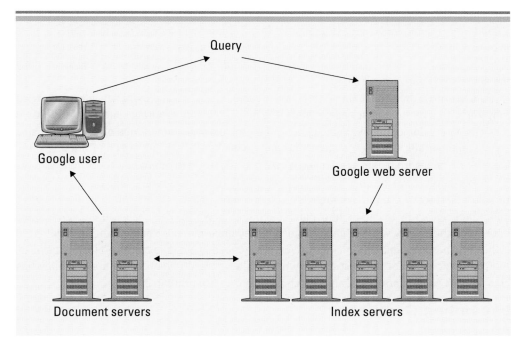

FIGURE 6.17

Sample Google Architecture

Query

Google user

Google web server

Document servers

Index servers

it tells which pages contain the words that match any particular query term. Then the query travels to the document servers, which actually retrieve the stored documents and generate snippets to describe each search result. Finally, the search engine returns the results to the user. All these activities occur within a fraction of a second.

Google consists of three distinct parts:

1. The web crawler, known as Googlebot, finds and retrieves web pages and passes them to the Google indexer. Googlebot functions much like a web browser. It sends a request for a web page to a web server, downloads the entire page, and then hands it off to Google's indexer. Googlebot can request thousands of different web pages simultaneously.

2. The indexer indexes every word on each page and stores the resulting index of words in a huge database. This index is sorted alphabetically by search term, with each index entry storing a list of documents in which the term appears and the location within the text where it occurs. Indexing the full text of web pages allows Google to go beyond simply matching single search terms. Google gives more priority to pages that have search terms near each other and in the same order as the query. Google can also match multi-word phrases and sentences.

3. The query processor compares the search query to the index and recommends the documents that it considers most relevant. Google considers more than a hundred factors in determining which documents are most relevant to a query, including the popularity of the page, the position and size of the search terms within the page, and the proximity of the search terms to one another. The query processor has several parts, including the user interface (search box), the "engine" that evaluates queries and matches them to relevant documents, and the results formatter.

Selling Words

Google's primary line of business is its search engine; however, the company does not generate revenue from people using its site to search the Internet. It generates revenue from the marketers and advertisers that are paying to place their ads on the site.

About 200 million times each day, people from all over the world access Google to perform searches. AdWords, a part of the Google site, allows advertisers to bid on common search terms. The advertisers simply enter in the keywords they want to bid on and the maximum amounts they want to pay per click, per day. Google then determines a price and a search ranking for those keywords based on how much other advertisers are willing to pay for the same terms. Pricing for keywords can range from 5 cents to $3 a click. A general search term like *tropical vacation* costs less than a more specific term like *Hawaiian vacation*. Whoever bids the most for a term appears in a sponsored advertisement link either at the top or along the side of the search-results page.

Paid search is the ultimate in targeted advertising because consumers type in exactly what they want. One of the primary advantages of paid search web programs such as AdWords is that customers do not find it annoying, as is the problem with some forms of web advertising such as banner ads and pop-up ads. According to the Interactive Advertising Bureau, overall industry revenues from paid search surpassed banner ads in the third quarter of 2003.

"A big percentage of queries we get are commercial in nature," said Salar Kamangar, Google's director of product management. "It is a marketplace where the advertisers tell us about themselves by telling us how much each lead is worth. They have an incentive to bid how much they really want to pay, because if they underbid, their competitors will get more traffic." Kamangar came up with the AdWords concept and oversees that part of the business. AdWords accounts for the vast majority of Google's annual revenue, and the company has over 150,000 advertisers in its paid-search program, up from zero in 2002.

Expanding Google

Google has a secret weapon working for its research and development department—hackers. Hackers actually develop many of the new and unique ways to expand Google. The company elicits hacker ideas through its application program interface (API), a large piece of the Google code. The API enables developers to build applications around the Google search engine. By making the API freely available, Google has inspired a community of programmers that are extending Google's capabilities. "It's working," said Nelson Minar, who runs the API effort. "We get clever hacks, educational uses, and wacky stuff. We love to see people do creative things with our product." A few of the successful developed applications include:

Banana Slug, www.bananaslug.com. For customers who hit a dead end with Google search, the site adds a random word to search text that generates surprising results.

Cookin' with Google, www.researchbuzz.org. Enter the ingredients that are in the fridge and the site returns potential recipes for those ingredients.

Google Alert, www.googlealert.com. Google Alert automatically searches the web for information on a topic and returns the results by email.

RateMyProfessors.com, www.ratemyprofessors.com. The goal of this site was to create a place where students could rank their teachers. However, too many jokesters typing in false professor names such as "Professor Harry Leg" and "Professor Ima Dog" left the information on the site questionable. The developers turned to the Google API to create an automatic verification tool. If Google finds enough mentions in conjunction with a professor or university then it considers the information valid and posts it to the website.

Froogle, www.froogle.com. Google launched a beta version of a new shopping search tool called Froogle that the company claims is the most comprehensive product search engine available. Froogle has 15 product categories in its directory. Similar to the Google Directory, customers can view products either by using a keyword search or by drilling down through a particular category and its subcategories.

Stopping Google

As part of its Google Print Library Project, the company is scanning all or parts of the book collections of the University of Michigan, Harvard University, Stanford University, the New York Public Library, and Oxford University. It intends to make those texts searchable on Google and to sell advertisements on the web pages.

The Authors Guild filed a lawsuit against search engine Google, alleging that its scanning and digitizing of library books constitutes a "massive" copyright infringement. "This is a plain and brazen violation of copyright law," Nick Taylor, president of the New York-based Authors Guild, said in a statement about the lawsuit, which is seeking class action status. "It's not up to Google or anyone other than the authors, the rightful owners of these copyrights, to decide whether and how their works will be copied."

In response, Google defended the program in a company blog posting. "We regret that this group chose to sue us over a program that will make millions of books more discoverable to the world—especially since any copyright holder can exclude their books from the program," wrote Susan Wojcicki, vice president of product management. "Google respects copyright. The use we make of all the books we scan through the Library Project is fully consistent with both the fair use doctrine under U.S. copyright law and the principles underlying copyright law itself, which allow everything from parodies to excerpts in book reviews."[24]

Questions

1. How did the website RateMyProfessors.com solve its problem of low-quality information?
2. Review the five common characteristics of high-quality information and rank them in order of importance to Google's business.
3. What would be the ramifications to Google's business if the search information it presented to its customers was of low quality?
4. Describe the different types of database. Why should Google use a relational database?

5. Identify the different types of entities, attributes, keys, and relationships that might be stored in Google's AdWords relational database.
6. How could Google use a data warehouse to improve its business operations?
7. Why would Google need to scrub and cleanse the information in its data warehouse?
8. Identify a data mart that Google's marketing and sales department might use to track and analyze its AdWords revenue.

Mining the Data Warehouse

According to a Merrill Lynch survey in 2006, business intelligence software and data-mining tools were at the top of CIOs' technology spending list. Following are a few examples of how companies are using data warehousing and data-mining tools to gain valuable business intelligence.

Ben & Jerry's

These days, when we all scream for ice cream, Ben & Jerry's cuts through the din by using integrated query, reporting, and online analytical processing technology from business intelligence (BI) software vendor Business Objects. Through an Oracle database and with BI from Business Objects, Ben & Jerry's tracks the ingredients and life of each pint. If a consumer calls in with a complaint, the consumer affairs staff matches the pint with which supplier's milk, eggs, cherries, or whatever did not meet the organization's near-obsession with quality.

The BI tools let Ben & Jerry's officials access, analyze, and act on customer information collected by the sales, finance, purchasing, and quality-assurance departments. The company can determine what milk customers prefer in the making of the ice cream. The technology helped Ben & Jerry's track more than 12,500 consumer contacts in 2005. The information ranged from comments about the ingredients used in ice cream to queries about social causes supported by the company.

California Pizza Kitchen

California Pizza Kitchen (CPK) is a leading casual dining chain in the premium pizza segment with a recognized consumer brand and an established, loyal customer base. Founded in 1985, there are currently more than 130 full-service restaurants in over 26 states, the District of Columbia, and five foreign countries.

Before implementing its BI tool, Cognos, CPK used spreadsheets to plan and track its financial statements and line items. The finance team had difficulty managing the volume of information, complex calculations, and constant changes to the spreadsheets. It took several weeks of two people working full time to obtain one version of the financial statements and future forecast. In addition, the team was limited by the software's inability to link cells and calculations across multiple spreadsheets, so updating other areas of corporate records became a time-consuming task. With Cognos, quarterly forecasting cycles have been reduced from eight days to two days. The finance team can now spend more time reviewing the results rather than collecting and entering the information.

Noodles & Company

Noodles & Company has more than 70 restaurants throughout Colorado, Illinois, Maryland, Michigan, Minnesota, Texas, Utah, Virginia, and Wisconsin. The company recently purchased Cognos BI tools to help implement reporting standards and communicate real-time operational information to field management throughout the United States.

Before implementing the first phase of the Cognos solution, IT and finance professionals spent days compiling report requests from numerous departments including sales and marketing, human resources, and real estate. Since completing phase one, operational Cognos reports are being accessed on a daily basis through the Noodles & Company website. This provides users with a single, 360-degree view of the business and consistent reporting throughout the enterprise.

Noodles & Company users benefit from the flexible query and reporting capabilities, allowing them to see patterns in the information to leverage new business opportunities. Cognos tools can pull information directly from a broad array of relational, operational, and other systems.[25]

Questions

1. How is Ben & Jerry's using business intelligence to remain successful and competitive in a saturated market?
2. Why is information cleansing critical to California Pizza Kitchen's success?
3. Why is 100 percent accurate and complete information impossible for Noodles & Company to obtain?
4. Describe how each of the companies above is using BI from its data warehouse to gain a competitive advantage.

CLOSING CASE THREE

Harrah's—Gambling Big on Technology

The large investment made by Harrah's Entertainment Inc. in its information technology strategy has been tremendously successful. The results of Harrah's investment include:

- 10 percent annual increase in customer visits.
- 33 percent increase in gross market revenue.
- Yearly profits of over $208 million.
- Highest three-year ROI (return on investment) in the industry.
- A network that links over 42,000 gaming machines in 26 casinos across 12 states.
- Rated number six of the 100 best places to work in IT for 2003 by *ComputerWorld* magazine.
- Recipient of 2000 Leadership in Data Warehousing Award from the Data Warehousing Institute (TDWI), the premier association for data warehousing.

The casino industry is highly competitive (rivalry among existing competitors is fierce). Bill Harrah was a man ahead of his time when he opened his first bingo parlor in 1937 with the commitment of getting to know each one of his customers. In 1984, Phil Satre, president and CEO of Harrah's, continued that commitment to customers. In search of its competitive advantage, Harrah's invested in an enterprisewide technology infrastructure to maintain Bill Harrah's original conviction: "Serve your customers well and they will be loyal."

Harrah's Commitment to Customers

Harrah's recently implemented its patented Total Rewards™ program to help build strong relationships with its customers. The program rewards customers for their loyalty by tracking their gaming habits across its 26 properties and currently maintains information on over 19 million customers, information the company uses to analyze, predict, and maximize each customer's value.

One major reason for the company's success is Harrah's implementation of a service-oriented strategy. Total Rewards allows Harrah's to give every customer the appropriate amount of personal attention, whether it's leaving sweets in the hotel room or offering free meals. Total Rewards works by providing each customer with an account and a corresponding card that the player swipes each time he or she plays a casino game. The program collects information on the amount of time the customers gamble, their total winnings and losses, and their betting strategies. Customers earn points based on the amount of time they spend gambling, which they can then exchange for comps such as free dinners, hotel rooms, tickets to shows, and even cash.

Total Rewards helps employees determine which level of service to provide each customer. When a customer makes a reservation at Harrah's, the service representative taking the call can view the customer's detailed information including the customer's loyalty level, games typically played, past winnings and losses, and potential net worth. If the service representative notices that the customer has a Diamond loyalty level, the service representative knows that customer should never have to wait in line and always receive free upgrades to the most expensive rooms.

"Almost everything we do in marketing and decision making is influenced by technology," says Gary Loveman, Harrah's chief operating officer. "The prevailing wisdom in this business is that the attractiveness of property drives customers. Our approach is different. We stimulate demand by knowing our customers. For example, if one of our customers always vacations at Harrah's in April, they will receive a promotion in February redeemable for a free weekend in April."

Gaining Business Intelligence with a Data Warehouse

Over 90 million customers visit Harrah's each year, and tracking a customer base larger than the population of Australia is a challenge. To tackle this challenge Harrah's began developing a system called WINet (Winner's Data Network). WINet links all Harrah's properties, allowing the company to collect and share customer information on an enterprisewide basis. WINet collects customer information from all the company transactions, game machines, and hotel management and reservations systems and places the information in a central data warehouse. Information in the data warehouse includes both customer and gaming information recorded in hourly increments. The marketing department uses the data warehouse to analyze customer information for patterns and insights, which allows it to create individualized marketing programs for each customer based on spending habits. Most important, the data warehouse allows the company to make business decisions based on information, not intuition.

Casinos traditionally treat customers as though they belong to a single property, typically the place the customer most frequently visits. Harrah's was the first casino to realize the potential of rewarding customers for visiting more than one property. Today, Harrah's has found that customers who visit more than one of its properties represent the fastest growing revenue segment. In the first two years of the Total Rewards program, the company received a $100 million increase in revenue from customers who gambled at more than one casino.

Harrah's also uses business intelligence to determine gaming machine performance. Using the data warehouse, Harrah's examines the performance and cost structure of each individual gaming machine. The company can quickly identify games that do not deliver optimal operational performance and can make a decision to move or replace the games. The capability to assess the performance of each individual slot machine has provided Harrah's with savings in the tens of millions of dollars. CIO Tim Stanley stated, "As we leverage more data from our data warehouse and increase the use and sophistication of our decision science analytical tools, we expect to have many new ways to improve customer loyalty and satisfaction, drive greater revenues, and decrease our costs as part of our ongoing focus on achieving sustainable profitability and success."

Security and Privacy

Some customers have concerns about Harrah's information collection strategy since they want to keep their gambling information private. The good news for these customers is that casinos are actually required to be more mindful of privacy concerns than most companies. For example, casinos cannot send marketing material to any underage persons. To adhere to strict government regulations, casinos must ensure that the correct information security and restrictions are in place. Many other companies actually make a great deal of money by selling customer information. Harrah's will not be joining in this trend since its customer information is one of its primary competitive advantages.

The Future of Harrah's

Harrah's current systems support approximately $140,000 in revenue per hour (that's almost $25 million weekly). In the future, Harrah's hopes to become device-independent by allowing employees to access the company's data warehouse via PDAs, handheld computers, and even cell phones. "Managing relationships with customers is incredibly important to the health of our business," Stanley says. "We will apply whatever technology we can to do that."[26]

Questions

1. Identify the effects poor information might have on Harrah's service-oriented business strategy.

2. How does Harrah's use database technologies to implement its service-oriented strategy?

3. Harrah's was one of the first casino companies to find value in offering rewards to customers who visit multiple Harrah's locations. Describe the effects on the company if it did not build any integrations among the databases located at each of its casinos. How could Harrah's use a data warehouse to synchronize customer information?

4. Estimate the potential impact to Harrah's business if there is a security breach in its customer information.

5. Identify three different types of data marts Harrah's might want to build to help it analyze its operational performance.

6. What might occur if Harrah's fails to clean or scrub its information before loading it into its data warehouse?

MAKING BUSINESS DECISIONS

1. **Explaining relational databases**

   You have been hired by Vision, a start-up recreational equipment company. Your manager, Holly Henningson, is unfamiliar with databases and their associated business value. Holly has asked you to create a report detailing the basics of databases. Holly would also like you to provide a detailed explanation of relational databases along with their associated business advantages.

2. **Entities and attributes**

   Martex Inc. is a manufacturer of athletic equipment, and its primary lines of business include running, tennis, golf, swimming, basketball, and aerobics equipment. Martex currently supplies four primary vendors including Sam's Sports, Total Effort, The Underline, and Maximum Workout. Martex wants to build a database to help it organize its products. In a group, identify the different types of entities, attributes, keys, and relationships Martex will want to consider when designing its database.

3. **Integrating information**

   You are currently working for the Public Transportation Department of Chatfield. The department controls all forms of public transportation including buses, subways, and trains. Each department has about 300 employees and maintains its own accounting, inventory, purchasing, and human resource systems. Generating reports across departments is a difficult task and usually involves gathering and correlating the information from the many different databases. It typically takes about two weeks to generate the quarterly balance sheets and profit and loss statements. Your team has been asked to compile a report recommending what the Public Transportation Department of Chatfield can do to alleviate its information and system issues. Be sure that your report addresses the various reasons departmental reports are presently difficult to obtain as well as how you plan to solve this problem.

4. Information timeliness

Information timeliness is a major consideration for all organizations. Organizations need to decide the frequency of backups and the frequency of updates to a data warehouse. In a team, describe the timeliness requirements for backups and updates to a data warehouse for each of the following:

- Weather tracking systems.
- Car dealership inventories.
- Vehicle tire sales forecasts.
- Interest rates.
- Restaurant inventories.
- Grocery store inventories.

5. Improving information quality

HangUps Corporation designs and distributes closet organization structures. The company operates five systems—order entry, sales, inventory management, shipping, and billing. The company has severe information quality issues including missing, inaccurate, redundant, and incomplete information. The company wants to implement a data warehouse containing information from the five different systems to help maintain a single customer view, drive business decisions, and perform multidimensional analysis. Identify how the organization can improve its information quality when it begins designing and building its data warehouse.

APPLY YOUR KNOWLEDGE

1. Determining Information Quality Issues

Real People is a magazine geared toward working individuals that provides articles and advice on everything from car maintenance to family planning. *Real People* is currently experiencing problems with its magazine distribution list. Over 30 percent of the magazines mailed are returned because of incorrect address information, and each month it receives numerous calls from angry customers complaining that they have not yet received their magazines. Below is a sample of *Real People's* customer information. Create a report detailing all of the issues with the information, potential causes of the information issues, and solutions the company can follow to correct the situation.

ID	First Name	Middle Initial	Last Name	Street	City	State	Zip Code
433	M	J	Jones	13 Denver	Denver	CO	87654
434	Margaret	J	Jones	13 First Ave.	Denver	CO	87654
434	Brian	F	Hoover	Lake Ave.	Columbus	OH	87654
435	Nick	H	Schweitzer	65 Apple Lane	San Francisco	OH	65664
436	Richard	A		567 55th St.	New York	CA	98763
437	Alana	B	Smith	121 Tenny Dr.	Buffalo	NY	142234
438	Trevor	D	Darrian	90 Fresrdestil	Dallas	TX	74532

2. Mining the Data Warehouse

Alana Smith is a senior buyer for a large wholesaler that sells different types of arts and crafts to greeting card stores such as Hallmark. Alana's latest marketing strategy is to send all of her customers a new line of handmade picture frames from Russia. All of Alana's information supports her decision for the new line. Her analysis predicts that the frames should sell an average of 10 to 15 per store, per day. Alana is excited about the new line and is positive it will be a success.

One month later Alana learns that the frames are selling 50 percent below expectations and averaging between five to eight frames sold daily in each store. Alana decides to access the company's data warehouse information to determine why sales are below expectations. Identify several different dimensions of information that Alana will want to analyze to help her decide what is causing the problems with the picture frame sales.

3. Cleansing Information

You are working for BI, a start-up business intelligence consulting company. You have a new client that is interested in hiring BI to clean up its information. To determine how good your work is, the client would like your analysis of the following spreadsheet.

CUST ID	First Name	Last Name	Address	City	State	Zip	Phone	Last Order Date
233620	Christopher	Lee	12421 W Olympic Blvd	Los Angeles	CA	75080-1100	(972)680-7848	4/18/2010
233621	Bruce	Brandwen	268 W 44th St	New York	PA	10036-3906	(212)471-6077	5/3/2010
233622	Glr	Johnson	4100 E Dry Creek Rd	Littleton	CO	80122-3729	(303)712-5461	5/6/2010
233623	Dave	Owens	466 Commerce Rd	Staunton	VA	24401-4432	(540)851-0362	3/19/2010
233624	John	Coulbourn	124 Action St	Maynard	MA	1754	(978)987-0100	4/24/2010
233629	Dan	Gagliardo	2875 Union Rd	Cheektowaga	NY	14227-1461	(716)558-8191	5/4/2010
23362	Damanceee	Allen	1633 Broadway	New York	NY	10019-6708	(212)708-1576	
233630	Michael	Peretz	235 E 45th St	New York	NY	10017-3305	(212)210-1340	4/30/2010
233631	Jody	Veeder	440 Science Dr	Madison	WI	53711-1064	(608)238-9690 X227	3/27/2010
233632	Michael	Kehrer	3015 SSE Loop 323	Tyler	TX	75701	(903)579-3229	4/28/2010
233633	Erin	Yoon	3500 Carillon Pt	Kirkland	WA	98033-7354	(425)897-7221	3/25/2010
233634	Madeline	Shefferly	4100 E Dry Creek Rd	Littleton	CO	80122-3729	(303)486-3949	3/33/2010
233635	Steven	Conduit	1332 Enterprise Dr	West Chester	PA	19380-5970	(610)692-5900	4/27/2010
233636	Joseph	Kovach	1332 Enterprise Dr	West Chester	PA	19380-5970	(610)692-5900	4/28/2010
233637	Richard	Jordan	1700 N	Philadelphia	PA	19131-4728	(215)581-6770	3/19/2010
233638	Scott	Mikolajczyk	1655 Crofton Blvd	Crofton	MD	21114-1387	(410)729-8155	4/28/2010
233639	Susan	Shragg	1875 Century Park E	Los Angeles	CA	90067-2501	(310)785-0511	4/29/2010
233640	Rob	Ponto	29777 Telegraph Rd	Southfield	MI	48034-1303	(810)204-4724	5/5/2010
233642	Lauren	Butler	1211 Avenue Of The Americas	New York	NY	10036-8701	(212)852-7494	4/22/2010
233643	Christopher	Lee	12421 W Olympic Blvd	Los Angeles	CA	90064-1022	(310)689-2577	3/25/2010
233644	Michelle	Decker	6922 Hollywood Blvd	Hollywood	CA	90028-6117	(323)817-4655	5/8/2010
233647	Natalia	Galeano	1211 Avenue Of The Americas	New York	NY	10036-8701	(646)728-6911	4/23/2010
233648	Bobbie	Orchard	4201 Congress St	Charlotte	NC	28209-4617	(704)557-2444	5/11/2010
233650	Ben	Konfino	1111 Stewart Ave	Bethpage	NY	11714-3533	(516)803-1406	3/19/2010
233651	Lenee	Santana	1050 Techwood Dr NW	Atlanta	GA	30318-KKRR	(404)885-2000	3/22/2010
233652	Lauren	Monks	7700 Wisconsin Ave	Bethesda	MD	20814-3578	(301)771-4772	3/19/2005
233653	Mark	Woolley	10950 Washington Blvd	Culver City	CA	90232-4026	(310)202-2900	4/20/2010

4. Different Dimensions

The focus of data warehousing is to extend the transformation of data into information. Data warehouses offer strategic level, external, integrated, and historical information so businesses can make projections, identify trends, and make key business decisions. The data warehouse collects and stores integrated sets of historical information from multiple operational systems and feeds them to one or more data marts. It may also provide end-user access to support enterprisewide views of information.

Project Focus

You are currently working on a marketing team for a large corporation that sells jewelry around the world. Your boss has asked you to look at the following dimensions of data to determine which ones you want in your data mart for performing sales and market analysis (see Figure AYK.1). As a team, categorize the different dimensions ranking them from 1 to 5, with 1 indicating that the dimension offers the highest value and must be in your data mart and 5 indicating that the dimension offers the lowest value and does not need to be in your data mart.

FIGURE AYK.1

Data Warehouse Data

Dimension	Value (1–5)	Dimension	Value (1–5)
Product number		Season	
Store location		Promotion	
Customer net worth		Payment method	
Number of sales personnel		Commission policy	
Customer eating habits		Manufacturer	
Store hours		Traffic report	
Salesperson ID		Customer language	
Product style		Weather	
Order date		Customer gender	
Product quantity		Local tax information	
Ship date		Local cultural demographics	
Current interest rate		Stock market closing	
Product cost		Customer religious affiliation	
Customer's political affiliation		Reason for purchase	
Local market analysis		Employee dress code policy	
Order time		Customer age	
Customer spending habits		Employee vacation policy	
Product price		Employee benefits	
Exchange rates		Current tariff information	
Product gross margin			

5. Understanding Search

Pretend that you are a search engine. Choose a topic to query. It can be anything such as your favorite book, movie, band, or sports team. Search your topic on Google, pick three or four pages from the results, and print them out. On each printout, find the individual words from your query (such as "Boston Red Sox" or "The Godfather") and use a highlighter to mark each word with color. Do that for each of the documents that you print out. Now tape those documents on a wall, step back a few feet, and review your documents. If you did not know what the rest of a page said and could only judge by the colored words, which document do you think would be most relevant? Is there anything that would make a document look more relevant? Is it better to have the words be in a large heading or to occur several times in a smaller font? Do you prefer it if the words are at the top or the bottom of the page? How often do the words need to appear? Come up with two or three things you would look for to see if a document matched a query well. This exercise mimics search engine processes and should help you understand why a search engine returns certain results over others.

BUSINESS DRIVEN BEST SELLERS

Business @ The Speed of Thought. **By Bill Gates (Grand Central Publishing, 1999).**

Business @ the Speed of Thought was written by Bill Gates to inspire you to demand—and get—more from technology, enabling you and your company to respond faster to your customers, adapt to changing business demands, and prosper in the digital economy. "How you gather, manage, and use information will determine whether you win or lose" is Bill Gates' simple message. *Business @ the Speed of Thought* is not a technical book. It shows how business and technology are now inextricably linked. Each chapter is structured around a business or management issue, showing how digital processes can dramatically improve your results.[27]

Why Smart Executives Fail. **By Sydney Finkelstein**

In *Why Smart Executives Fail,* Sydney Finkelstein, a professor of management at Dartmouth's Tuck School of Business, explains why leadership fails and how company leaders can get back on track. This book shows examples from GM, Mattel, Motorola, Rite Aid, Webvan, and other companies as well as the results of six years of research on the issue of leadership failure. Finkelstein explains that the causes of failed management are surprisingly few, and they are not ineptitude or greed. Even the brightest executives fail because:

- They choose not to cope with innovation, change, and management.
- They misread the competition.
- They brilliantly fulfill the wrong vision.
- They cling to an inaccurate view of reality.
- They ignore vital information.
- They identify too closely with the company.[28]

7
CHAPTER

Networks, Telecommunications, and Mobile Technology

What's in IT for Me?

The pace of technological change never ceases to amaze. What only a few years ago would have been considered *Star Trek* technology is becoming normal. What used to take hours to download over a dial-up modem connection can now transfer in a matter of seconds through an invisible, wireless network connection from a computer thousands of miles away. We are living in an increasingly wireless present and hurtling ever faster toward a wireless future. The tipping point of ubiquitous, wireless, handheld, mobile computing is not far away.

As a business student, you must understand the concepts of network architecture and mobile technology to be able to understand how information technology can be used to support your business decisions. This is a critical skill for business executives, regardless if you are a novice or a seasoned Fortune 500 employee. By learning about the various concepts discussed in this chapter, you will develop a better understanding of how business can leverage technologies to compete in today's mobile world.

In addition, after reading this chapter, you should have many of the skills needed to become directly involved in analyzing current networking architectures, in recommending needed changes in mobile business processes, and in evaluating alternative networking options.

The Ironman

Florida-based World Triathlon Corporation (WTC), owner of the Ironman Triathlon World Championship, is in the business of fulfilling dreams—the dreams of endurance athletes to complete one of the world's most grueling events. The Ironman Triathlon World Championship brings more than 1,700 of the world's top endurance athletes to rugged Kailua-Kona, Hawaii, for a world championship race every fall. Athletes attempt to swim 2.4 miles, cycle 112 miles, and run a full 26.2 mile marathon—all in a single day. The event features a remote course that threads around the side of an active volcano and offers breathtaking vistas, but also rough terrain, shimmering heat, and shifting trade winds.

In the past, it wasn't easy for family and friends to know how their son, sister, friend, or colleague was faring in the contest. Even those who could afford the trip to Hawaii were in the dark about their athletes' progress. "As a spectator, you'd see the start, and then the athletes would disappear, and that was pretty much it until the finish line," recalls Dave Scott, who ran his first triathlon in 1976. The Ironman Triathlon World Championship has changed all that. Using mobile technology, long-range WiMAX networks, and wi-fi enabled hotspots, the Ironman is transforming the way audiences and athletes experience the race. By using WiMAX to enable remote cameras at locations along the course, Ironman raised the bar for professional sports broadcasting. It also spotlighted a technology many say will help bring the next billion users into the Internet community.

People worldwide now can look at any athlete and find out where he is on the course and what speed he is running. WTC makes this possible by using WiMAX to provide high-speed broadband connections in various locations along the 140-mile course. The company uses radio frequency identification (RFID) to track the athlete's progress and high-bandwidth communications to transmit professional-quality video and other data, and makes the information accessible over the Ironmanlive.com website.

Networking the course was a challenge because of the same factors that make the race challenging for the athletes. "We're on a very rough, rugged course on an island with an active volcano," explains Dan Gerson, Ironmanlive.com production manager. "It's hot, it's windy, and there's no infrastructure. If you can deploy WiMAX here, you can probably deploy it pretty much anywhere." Airspan Networks provided the WiMAX infrastructure, using its high-performance base stations and subscriber stations to create a high-throughput network backbone capable of transmitting data rates required for top-quality video. The team set up its base station atop the hotel that served as the event's starting point and finish line, which also happened to be one of the lowest geographical points of the course. The team was operating in a non-line-of-sight environment and highly porous volcanic rock absorbed the wireless signals more than other types of rock would.

Airspan set up relays on the ridge sides of the volcano, the side of the road, the sides of buildings—anywhere to keep the fidelity of the signals. Some cameras were in locations without power, so they used generators. This was a wireless deployment in every sense of the word, and a great demonstration of the viability of WiMAX technology. Athletes were filmed as they passed by the WiMAX-enabled video stations equipped with network video cameras. That footage was incorporated into the live webcast, along with pre-event interviews, commentary, footage shot from cameras on motorcycles and helicopters, and other content produced by the Ironman team. WTC produced the broadcast at the event site in a live production studio that streamed the video data to the global servers that run the Ironmanlive.com website.

In addition to these video-enabling technologies, Ironman used other wireless technologies to bring the athletes and their fans closer. For example, Ironman employed RFID technology to track each athlete's progress along the event route and maximize accuracy and safety. Each athlete wore an ankle bracelet with an RFID tag, and as a competitor crossed over one of 12 timing mats spread throughout the course, the RFID tag communicated to a reader that captured the athlete's times, and that information was relayed over the wireless network to a database. Seconds later, this information was available on the Ironmanlive.com website, where spectators and viewers at home could see the athlete's pace and timing. Many viewers stayed on the website throughout the event, monitoring their athlete's progress.

WTC also set up eight wireless hotspots, including five along the event course and at the finish line. An Internet cafe was stocked with notebook and handheld computers, providing convenient, wireless access to event information and the Ironmanlive.com site. Two giant-screen displays showed the live program coverage from Ironmanlive.com. Staff used additional notebooks and handheld devices to manage the race and access information on each athlete's progress. For example, if athletes needed medical care, the health care team used a PDA to scan their RFID tags and instantly access medical records and local contact information.

Ironman's transformative use of wireless computing makes sound business success. The compelling programming solidifies the respect WTC earns for its sports broadcasting leadership. It also drives larger audiences and higher advertising revenues for WTC and NBC, which uses WTC's Ironman Triathlon programming in its own broadcast of the event a month or two later. Larger audiences and better experiences for athletes and their families ultimately lead to greater participation in the Ironman Triathlon and its more than two dozen qualifying races and to growing popularity for the sport.[1]

INTRODUCTION

Change is everywhere in the information technology domain, but nowhere is change more evident and more dramatic than in the realm of telecommunications and networking. Most information systems today rely on digital networks to communicate information in the form of data, graphics, video, and voice. Companies large and small from all over the world use networked systems and the Internet to locate suppliers and buyers, to negotiate contracts with them, and to provide bigger, better, and faster services than ever before.

Telecommunication systems enable the transmission of data over public or private networks. A *network* is a communications, data exchange, and resource-sharing system created by linking two or more computers and establishing standards, or protocols, so that they can work together. Telecommunication systems and networks are traditionally complicated and historically inefficient. However, businesses can benefit from today's modern network infrastructures that provide reliable global reach to employees and customers. Businesses around the world are moving to network infrastructure solutions that allow greater choice in how they go to market—solutions with global reach. These alternatives include wireless, voice over Internet protocol (VoIP), and radio frequency identification (RFID). This chapter takes a detailed look at key telecommunication, network, and wireless technologies being integrated into businesses around the world.

section 7.1 NETWORKS AND TELECOMMUNICATIONS

The Motley Fool

LEARNING OUTCOMES

7.1. Compare LANs, WANs, and MANs.

7.2. Describe the business benefits associated with VoIP.

7.3. Explain the difference between a VPN and a VAN.

7.4. Identify the advantages and disadvantages of broadband technology.

7.5. List and describe many of the network security problems.

NETWORK BASICS

Networks range from small two-computer networks to the biggest network of all, the Internet. A network provides two principle benefits: the ability to communicate and the ability to share. Music is the hot product line at coffee retailer Starbucks. In Starbucks stores, customers can shop for music wirelessly through iTunes free, thanks to the company's own increasingly sophisticated in-store network.

Today's corporate digital networks include a combination of local area networks and the Internet. A *local area network (LAN)* is designed to connect a group of computers in close proximity to each other such as in an office building, a school, or a home. A LAN is useful for sharing resources like files, printers, games, or other applications. A LAN in turn often connects to other LANs, and to the Internet or wide area networks. A *wide area network (WAN)* spans a large geographic area, such as a state, province, or country. WANs often connect multiple smaller networks, such as local area networks or metropolitan area networks (MANs). A *metropolitan area network (MAN)* is a large computer network usually spanning a city.

Direct data communication links between a company and its suppliers or customers, or both, have been successfully used to give the company a strategic advantage. The Sabre airline reservation system is a classic example of a strategic information system that depends upon communication provided through a network. Sabre Airline Solutions pioneered technological advances for the industry in areas such as revenue management, pricing, flight scheduling, cargo, flight operations, and crew scheduling. In addition, not only did Sabre help invent ecommerce (now referred to as ebusiness) for the travel industry, but the company also holds claim to progressive solutions that defined—and continue to revolutionize—the travel and transportation marketplace.[2]

The remainder of this chapter assumes a basic understanding of the fundamentals of networks and telecommunications. If you need an introduction or a refresher of these fundamentals please review Appendix C, "Network and Telecommunications."

Using Networks and Telecommunications for Business Advantages

After gaining an understanding of networking and telecommunication fundamentals, it is easy to apply these to competitive advantages for any business including:

- Voice over IP.
- Networking businesses.
- Increasing the speed of business.
- Securing business networks.

VOICE OVER IP

Originally, phone calls made over the Internet had a reputation of offering poor call quality, lame user interfaces, and low call-completion rates. With new and improved technology and IT infrastructures, Internet phone calls now offer similar quality to traditional landline and cellular telephone calls. Today, many consumers are making phone calls over the Internet by using voice over Internet protocol (VoIP). *Voice over IP (VoIP)* uses TCP/IP technology to transmit voice calls over long-distance telephone lines. VoIP transmits over 10 percent of all phone calls in the United States and this number is growing exponentially.

Networks

The telecom industry is experiencing great benefits from combining VoIP with emerging standards that allow for easier development, interoperability among systems, and application integration. This is a big change for an industry that had relied on proprietary systems to keep customers paying for upgrades and new features. The VoIP and open standards combination has produced more choices, lower prices, and new applications.

Many VoIP companies, including Vonage, 8 × 8, and AT&T (CallVantage), typically offer calling within the United States for a fixed fee and a low per-minute charge for international calls. Broadband Internet access (broadband is described in detail later in this chapter) is required, and regular house phones plug in to an analog telephone adapter provided by the company or purchased from a third party (such as DLink or Linksys) as displayed in Figure 7.1.

Since VoIP uses existing network and Internet infrastructure to route telephone calls more efficiently and inexpensively than traditional telephone service, VoIP offers businesses significant cost savings, productivity gains, and service enhancements.

Unfortunately, VoIP routes calls through the same paths used by network and Internet traffic, therefore it has the same vulnerabilities and is subject to the same Internet threats. Much like data, VoIP traffic can be intercepted, captured, or modified. Any threat that slows or degrades service even slightly will disrupt business. As a result, VoIP traffic must be secured.

Skype has long been one of the most popular VoIP options for consumers—largely because of its low cost (free for calls between Skype users and only a few dollars per month to call landlines). Now, it is gaining popularity in the business world as well.

The company has been adding features that make it more business-friendly. Two examples are the Windows Installer/MSI package that makes it easy to roll out the application to multiple machines and the Skype for Business Control Panel that allows administrators to manage all of a company's Skype accounts from a centralized interface. The small-business market is especially amenable to Skype's budget-friendly and feature-rich service.

Rip Curl is one of the greatest surf and snow brands in the world. With more than 1,200 staff members and a retail presence in more than 60 countries, the company

FIGURE 7.1

Diagram of VoIP Connection

Internet
Connection

Cable Modem

Router

VoIP Adapter

Computer

Telephone

faces communications challenges in keeping abreast of global industry trends, sharing global marketing plans, coordinating events, and collaborating on design initiatives across many regions.

Rip Curl's finance and marketing divisions have been using Skype's free instant messaging and video calls for more than two years to track communications with international colleagues. Recently, Rip Curl's head of IT directed all staff to use Skype as their preferred method of communication.[3]

Skype already includes many features that make it attractive to business users, including call forwarding and the ability to filter and block unwanted calls. In addition, Skype's conference calling feature lets users have conversations with multiple people (up to 10 participants), mixing participants who are using Skype, regular landline phones, and mobile phones.

Skype allows users to do more than just place voice calls. For instance, users with computers equipped with web cams can make video calls to get "face time" with coworkers or clients—without the hassle or expense of traveling. In addition to features built into the Skype software, many useful add-in programs are available to download that add functionality and enhance productivity (see Figure 7.2).[4]

Skype also uses a file transfer feature that makes it easier to collaborate with colleagues over the phone; users can send copies of reports, pictures, or other files they need to share—with no limits on file size. This feature can be disabled if an administrator does not want users to be able to transfer files due to security or privacy issues.

Some features available using VoIP solutions include:

- Business application integration (for instance, tying IP telephony to a customer database).
- Calendar integration.
- Call waiting.
- Caller ID.
- Click-of-a-mouse simplicity—employees make or transfer calls right on their computer.
- Conference call capabilities with on-screen document sharing.
- Comprehensive information about each caller.

FIGURE 7.2

Skype Add-In Programs

Add-in	Function
Skype Office Toolbar	This add-on makes calls to names or phone numbers in a Word document, Excel spreadsheet, or PowerPoint presentation. After installing the add-in, users can use it to turn phone numbers in the document into links, which can be clicked to make a voice call or send an SMS message. Users can send the file they are working on in the Office application to a Skype contact.
Skylook	This add-on is an extension to Outlook that records calls and voice-mail to MP3 files and accesses them from Outlook. Users can call Outlook contacts over Skype and have emails read over the phone.
HotRecorder for VoIP	This add-on records Skype calls automatically using a third-party program, such as HotRecorder for VoIP (HR4VoIP). It works with Skype 3.0, as well as other VoIP applications such as Net2Phone, Google Talk, and Yahoo Messenger.
Universal Chat Translator	Today's business world is increasingly international in nature. If a user needs to communicate with people who speak another language, install the Universal Chat Translator to translate Skype chat conversations and read them. The add-on translator supports Arabic, Chinese (simplified and traditional), Dutch, French, German, Greek, Japanese, Italian, Korean, Portuguese, Russian, and Spanish. It translates the messages sent to the other language and translates the received messages to English. The translation takes place in real time for active chats or conversations can be stored in a chat history.
uSeeToo	This add-on shares photos, drawings, maps, and other graphical images. Users can add text captions and other content. It includes a drawing board, and it allows users to create, show, and save multiple boards.
PresenterNet	This add-in conducts interactive web meetings, sales presentations, "webinars," and more, using PowerPoint and Skype teleconferencing. It works with Windows, Windows Mobile, Linux, and Macintosh, and with Internet Explorer, Firefox, and Safari browsers.
Unyte	This add-in shares desktop applications with Skype contacts and others, and will share with multiple users.
TalkandWrite Extra for Skype 3.0	This add-on is a document collaboration program that allows two users to remotely work on the same document and annotate it, add text, and more, with the changes made by either party immediately made available to both.
RemoteCall	This add-in connects to remote desktops during a Skype call by clicking an icon added to the Skype Contacts and Tools menus.

- Desktop application (i.e., Microsoft Outlook) integration.
- Dial-by-name capability.
- Easy navigation.
- Four or five-digit dialing to anyone, regardless of location.
- Mobility—users can work from anywhere.
- Three-way calling.[5]

NETWORKING BUSINESSES

Retailer REI reports that one-third of all customers who buy online and pick up at the store make another purchase while there, spending an average of $90. From a technology perspective, in-store pick up needs to have some level of inventory integration to work effectively. The integration of data is critical in being able to display to the consumer the availability of products at the closest geographic store.[6]

To set up an ebusiness even a decade ago would have required an individual organization to assume the burden of developing the entire network infrastructure. Today, industry-leading companies have developed Internet-based products and services to handle many aspects of customer and supplier interactions. "In today's retail market, you cannot be a credible national retailer without having a robust website," says Dennis Bowman, senior vice president and CIO of Circuit City, who adds that customers now expect seamless retailing between online and in-store

FIGURE 7.3

Business Network
Characteristics

- Provide for the transparent exchange of information with suppliers, trading partners, and customers.
- Reliably and securely exchange information internally and externally via the Internet or other networks.
- Allow end-to-end integration and provide message delivery across multiple systems, in particular, databases, clients, and servers.
- Respond to high demands with scalable processing power and networking capacity.
- Serve as the integrator and transaction framework for both digital businesses and traditional brick-and-mortar businesses that want to leverage the Internet for any type of business.

just as they expect stores that are clean and well stocked. For this reason, retailers are working furiously to integrate their ebusiness sites with their inventory and point-of-sale (POS) systems so that they can accept in-store returns of merchandise bought online and allow customers to buy on the web and pick up in the store.

Some companies, such as Best Buy, Circuit City, Office Depot, and Sears, already have their physical and online stores integrated. These companies have been the fast movers because they already had an area in their stores for merchandise pickup (usually for big, bulky items such as TVs and appliances), and because long before the web they had systems and processes in place that facilitated the transfer of a sale from one store to another. To take on the challenge of business integration, an organization needs a secure and reliable network for mission-critical systems (see Figure 7.3).

A ***virtual private network (VPN)*** is a way to use the public telecommunication infrastructure (e.g., Internet) to provide secure access to an organization's network (see Figure 7.4). A ***valued-added network (VAN)*** is a private network, provided by a third party, for exchanging information through a high-capacity connection.

Organizations engaging in ebusiness have relied largely on VPNs, VANs, and other dedicated links handling electronic data interchange transactions. These traditional solutions are still deployed in the market, and for many companies will likely hold a strategic role for years to come. However, these conventional technologies present significant challenges:

- By handling only limited kinds of business information, these contribute little to a reporting structure intended to provide a comprehensive view of business operations.
- They offer little support for the real-time business process integration that will be essential in the digital marketplace.
- Relatively expensive and complex to implement, conventional technologies make it difficult to expand or change networks in response to market shifts.

FIGURE 7.4

Virtual Private Network
Overview

INCREASING THE SPEED OF BUSINESS

Transmission can occur at different speeds. By speed we do not mean how fast the signal travels in terms such as miles per hour, but rather the volume of data that can be transmitted per unit of time. Terms such as bandwidth, hertz (Hz), and baud are used to describe transmission speeds, whereas a measure such as bits transmitted per second (bits per second, or bps) would be more understandable. **Bandwidth** is the difference between the highest and the lowest frequencies that can be transmitted on a single medium, and it is a measure of the medium's capacity. *Hertz* is cycles per second, and *baud* is the number of signals sent per second. If each cycle sends one signal that transmits exactly one bit of data, which is often the case, then all these terms are identical.

In information technology publications, baud was formerly used for relatively slow speeds such as 2,400 baud (2,400 bits per second) or 14,400 baud (14,400 bps), while hertz (with an appropriate prefix) was used for higher speeds such as 500 megahertz (500 million bps) or 2 gigahertz (2 billion bps). More recently, the term *baud* has fallen into disfavor, but hertz is still widely used. For clarity, we will stick with bps in this chapter.

The notion of bandwidth, or capacity, is important for telecommunications. For example, approximately 50,000 bits (Os and 1s) are required to represent one page of data. To transmit this page over a 128,000 bps (128 Kbps) digital subscriber line (DSL) would take only four-tenths of a second. Graphics require approximately 1 million bits for one page. This would require about 8 seconds over a 128 Kbps DSL. Full-motion video transmission requires the enormous bandwidth of 12 million bps, and thus data compression techniques must be employed to be able to send video over the existing telephone network. The bandwidth determines what types of communication—voice, data, graphics, full-motion video—can reasonably be transmitted over a particular medium. Figure 7.5 outlines the typical transmission speeds found in business today (a few of the technologies mentioned in Figure 7.5 will be discussed in detail in the next section). Figure 7.6 gives an overview of the average time required to download specific Internet functions.[7]

High-speed Internet, once an exotic and expensive service used only by larger companies, is now an inexpensive mainstream offering. The term **broadband** generally refers to high-speed Internet connections transmitting data at speeds greater than 200 kilobytes per second (Kbps), compared to the 56 Kbps maximum speed offered by traditional dial-up connections. While traditional dial-up access (using normal voice telephone line technology) suffices for some consumers, many need or want the much faster connections that technological advances now allow. The right option for Internet access will depend on a company's needs and which services are available. Figure 7.7 lists some of the advantages and disadvantages of current conventional broadband technology available.[8]

FIGURE 7.5

Telecommunications Transmission Speeds

Transmission Medium	Typical Speeds
Twisted pair—voice telephone	14.4 Kbps–56 Kbps
Twisted pair—digital telephone	128 Kbps–1.544 Mbps
Twisted pair—LAN	10 Mbps–100 Mbps
Coaxial cable—LAN	10 Mbps–1 Gbps
Wireless—LAN	6 Mbps–54 Mbps
Microwave—WAN	50 Kbps–100 Mbps
Satellite—WAN	50 Kbps–100 Mbps
Fiber-optic cable—WAN	100 Mbps–100 Gbps

KEY: bps = bits per second
Kbps = thousand bits per second
Mbps = million bits per second
Gbps = billion bits per second

FIGURE 7.6

Internet Function Average
Download Time

Internet Function	Dial-up (56K)	Satellite (512K)	DSL (1M)	Cable (1M)	Wireless (5M)
An email	1 sec.	<1 sec.			
A basic web page (25K)	10 sec.	<1 sec.			
One five-minute song (5M)	15 min.	2 min.	1 min.		40 sec.
One two-hour movie (500M)	20 hrs.	4 hrs.	2 hrs.		70 min.

FIGURE 7.7

Advantages and Disadvantages of Broadband Technology

Technology	Typical Download Speed (Mbps)	Typical Uplink Speed (Mbps)	Advantages	Disadvantages
Digital subscriber line (DSL)	.5–3	1.0	– Good upload rates – Uses existing telephone lines	– Speeds vary depending on distance from telephone company's central office – Slower downloads than less expensive alternatives
Cable	.5–4	.5–1	– Uses existing cable infrastructure – Low-cost equipment	– Shared connections can overload system, slowing upload times
TI/T3 dedicated line	1.5–3	1.5–3	– Uses existing phone wiring	– Performance drops significantly with range – Susceptible to cross talk
Fiber-to-the-home	4.5	10.2	– Fast data speeds – Infrastructure has long life expectancy – Low maintenance – Low power costs	– Not widely available – Significant deployment cost (for company)
Fixed wireless	.5–12	.5	– Typically inexpensive to install, no underground digging	– Weather, topography, buildings, and electronics can cause interference
Satellite	.5–2	.05	– Nearly universal coverage – Available in otherwise inaccessible areas	– Expensive service/equipment – Upload/download delays

SECURING BUSINESS NETWORKS

Networks are a tempting target for mischief and fraud. An organization has to be concerned about proper identification of users and authorization of network access, the control of access, and the protection of data integrity. A firm must identify users before they are granted access to a corporate network, and that access should be appropriate for the given user. For example, an organization may allow outside suppliers access to its internal network to learn about production plans, but the firm must prevent them from accessing other information such as financial records. In addition, the organization should preserve the integrity of its data; users should be allowed to change and update only well-specified data. These problems are exacerbated on the Internet where individuals must be very concerned about fraud, invalid purchases, and misappropriation of credit card information.

Providing network security is a difficult challenge. Almost all networks require some kind of log-on, including user name and password. Many people are casual with their passwords, making them easy to guess. A good password has both letters and numbers along with a few punctuation marks for added security. Most corporate security goes far beyond passwords, however. One common approach is a firewall, a computer that sits between an internal network and the Internet. The firewall allows access to internal data from specified incoming sites but tries to detect unauthorized access attempts and prevent them from occurring.

For highly secure communications, a sender can encrypt data, that is, encode the data so that someone without the "key" to decode them cannot read the message. There are a number of encryption approaches, and controversy exists over how strong the encryption should be. The most secure approaches use longer keys, making it much more difficult for an intruder to compute the key. The U. S. government is concerned about terrorists and criminals who might have access to strong encryption that is beyond the capabilities of law enforcement authorities to decrypt. There are export restrictions on encryption programs.

For Internet commerce, various schemes have been proposed for sending credit card or other payments over the network in a secure manner. Some involve encryption and others various forms of digital certificates or digital cash. Many firms worry that customers will not want to complete transactions on the Internet because of the fear their credit card numbers might be stolen. However, a law limits individual liability for credit card misuse to $50.

Data Sharing

Even more important than the sharing of technology resources is the sharing of data. Either a LAN or a WAN permits users on the network to get data (if they are authorized to do so) from other points on the network. It is very important, for example, for managers to be able to retrieve overall corporate sales forecasts from corporate databases to use in developing spreadsheets (or any other program used for business analysis) to project future activity. To satisfy customers, automobile dealers need to be able to locate particular vehicle models and colors with specific equipment installed. Managers at various points in a supply chain need to have accurate, up-to-date data on inventory levels and locations. Accountants at corporate headquarters need to be able to retrieve summary data on sales and expenses from each of the company's divisional computer centers. The chief executive officer, using an executive information system, needs to be able to access up-to-the-minute data on business trends from the corporate network.

OPENING CASE QUESTIONS

The Ironman

1. How is WTC using telecommunication and network technologies to improve its competitive advantage in the professional sports broadcasting industry?

2. Describe the different types of network architectures WTC is using.

3. Explain the role TCP/IP plays in the broadcast of the Ironman Triathlon World Championship.

4. Identify a new telecommunication or network product that TWC could use to improve its operations.

5. What security issues does WTC need to address?

7.6. Explain the business benefits of using wireless technology.

7.7. Identify the advantages and disadvantage of deploying cellular technology.

7.8. Describe how satellite technology works.

7.9. Explain how LBS, GPS, and GIS help to create business value.

7.10. Describe RFID and how it can be used to help make a supply chain more effective.

7.11. List and discuss the wireless trends that consumers and businesses can benefit from.

BUSINESS DRIVERS FOR A MOBILE WORKFORCE

Dr Pepper/Seven Up Inc., of Plano, Texas, monitors the operation of its vending machines via wireless technology. Dr Pepper/Seven Up Inc. has installed specialized hardware and software along with wireless technology in vending machines. The software collects inventory, sales, and "machine-health" data at each vending machine, and then, on a daily basis, the Dr Pepper/Seven Up Inc. network operations center polls each machine. A dome antenna atop the vending machine allows broadcast and reception via a wireless network. The data are aggregated and stored at a separate facility. With client software installed on their PCs, managers and sales personnel at Dr Pepper/Seven Up Inc. can access the data via a secure website. Management at Dr Pepper/Seven Up Inc. is excited about the business value of the data being collected, both for daily operations and in the potential for data mining (see Chapter 6). Information like this is helpful when considering new placements of vending machines or locations where multivendor machines might be warranted, such as in front of a Target store or high-traffic supermarket. Dr Pepper/Seven Up Inc. can use the data to plan loading of trucks and truck routes.[9]

Rapid and widespread growth of mobile technology in the 21st century has shaped one of the largest technology markets after the PC revolution in the 1980s and 1990s. Untethered connectivity, anytime, anywhere, has fueled a major market and technology disruption, which has permeated almost every consumer market worldwide. The domino effect of the success of mobile technology has resulted in opportunities for innovation and creativity in technology, marketing, and business strategy.

Cirque Du Soleil

Companies worldwide are going mobile to increase productivity, speed delivery to market, and reduce operating costs. Retail, distribution, and manufacturing businesses are no exception. Wireless transmissions rely on radio waves (e.g., cellular technology), microwaves, and satellites to send data across high-frequency radio ranges that later connect to wired media.

United Parcel Service and FedEx have been using mobile technologies for years, making it possible for information about dispatching and deliveries to travel between couriers and central stations. FedEx's famous tracking system, which can find a package's location from its tracking number, uses a wireless courier-management system.

The terms *mobile* and *wireless* are often used synonymously, but actually denote two different technologies. *Mobile* means the technology can travel with the user, but it is not necessarily in real-time; users can download software, email messages, and web pages onto their personal digital assistant (PDA), laptop, or other mobile device for portable reading or reference. Information collected while on the road can be synchronized with a PC or corporate server.

Wireless, on the other hand, refers to any type of electrical or electronic operation that is accomplished without the use of a "hard wired" connection. International Data

FIGURE 7.8

Wireless Drivers

Drivers of Wireless Technology Growth	
Universal access to information and applications	People are mobile and have more access to information than ever before, but they still need to get to the point where they can access all information anytime, anywhere, anyplace.
The automation of business processes	Wireless technologies have the ability to centralize critical information and eliminate redundant processes.
User convenience, timeliness, and ability to conduct business 24373365	People delayed in airports no longer have to feel cut off from the world or their office. Through wireless tools and wireless solutions such as a BlackBerry RIM device, they can access their information anytime, anywhere, anyplace.

Wireless

Corporation expected nearly two-thirds of handheld devices to include integrated wireless networking by 2010. Figure 7.8 displays the factors inspiring the growth of wireless technologies.

State government agencies, such as transportation departments, use wireless devices to collect field information—tracking inventory, reporting times, monitoring logistics, and completing forms—all from a mobile environment. The transportation industry is using mobile devices to help determine current locations and alternate driving routes.

Mobile technologies are transforming how we live, work, and play. Handheld devices continue to offer additional functionality, and cellular networks are advancing rapidly in their increased speed and throughput abilities (cellular networks will be described in detail in the next section). These enabling technologies fuel widespread adoption and creation of new and innovative ways to perform business. The big changes that will re-create workplaces, industries, and organizations are coming from mobile and wireless technologies. Figure 7.9 displays a few common examples of mobile technologies that are changing our world.

The retail industry is fiercely competitive. With the advent of the World Wide Web, nontraditional companies such as Amazon.com have emerged and have made brick-and-mortar companies like Barnes & Noble rethink their strategy. Competition is also driving profit margins down. The success of a retailer depends on inventory management, cost control, and proactive customer service. To gain the competitive advantage, more and more retailers are turning to mobile applications to enhance worker productivity, operational efficiencies, and anytime, anywhere

FIGURE 7.9

Mobile Devices Changing Business

Mobile Devices Changing Business

- **Wireless local area network (wLAN):** uses radio waves rather than wires to transmit information across a local area network.

- **Cellular phones and pagers:** provide connectivity for portable and mobile applications, both personal and business.

- **Cordless computer peripherals:** connect wirelessly to a computer, such as a cordless mouse, keyboard, and printer.

- **Satellite television:** allows viewers in almost any location to select from hundreds of channels.

- **WiMAX wireless broadband:** enables wireless networks to extend as far as 30 miles and transfer information, voice, and video at faster speeds than cable. It is perfect for Internet service providers (ISPs) that want to expand into sparsely populated areas, where the cost of bringing in cable wiring or DSL is too high.

- **Security sensor:** alerts customers to break-ins and errant pop flies. Its dual sensors record vibration and acoustic disturbances—a shattered window—to help avoid false alarms.

FIGURE 7.10

Steps to Take for Deploying Mobile Strategies

Step	Description
Defining risks	Before a realistic assessment of any mobile strategy can be put in place, companies must define evaluation criteria. Many companies look at technology and applications in isolation, without defining any potential risks to the organization: risks both if the project is undertaken and if it is not.
Knowing the limits of technology	It is imperative that companies not only examine the abilities of any technology to provide needed functionality, but also to explore any limits of the chosen technology. Setting realistic expectations for any mobile technology, both to IT resources deploying the solution and to the ultimate users, is a necessary component of any successful mobile strategy.
Protecting data from loss	Companies must take concrete and immediate steps to assure protection of mobile corporate information assets. Security must be a multi-faceted approach and encompass a variety of techniques covering all areas of exposure.
Compliance in the mobile enterprise	The move to mobility, with far more devices "free to roam wild," will cause a major upsurge in occurrences of data breaches, some of which may not even be discovered, or not discovered for a significant period. Companies must formulate a mobile security strategy before the problem becomes overwhelming.
Staying flexible and embracing change	Companies should not assume that once created, a mobile strategy is a fixed and/or finished product. With the high rate of change in the marketplace (e.g., devices, connection types, applications), it is incumbent upon the organization to monitor and modify the policy on a regular basis.

customer service. On the sales floor and in the warehouse, mobile solutions can help track materials and shipments from supplier and distributors to the customers, manage inventory, and support point-of-sales activities. Since vast amounts of data can be collected in an automated fashion, analysis can be done much faster and the results can be used continuously to improve operations and customer service. Figure 7.10 briefly describes several important steps companies should take to formulate an effective mobile strategy.[10]

A relatively small number of enterprises (less than 25 percent) have a specific mobile strategy in place. Most struggle with individual mobile projects or try to link mobility to a broader IT strategy. Companies must focus on building a mobile strategy that addresses the peculiarities inherent in mobile computing. The strategy should leverage a number of uses across a variety of lines of businesses within the company to maximize the ROI (return on investment), standardize on architectures and platforms, and provide the most secure infrastructure available to eliminate (as much as possible) extremely costly data loss and security breaches inherent in mobile business. Understanding the different types of mobile technologies available will help executives determine how to best equip their workforce. These mobile technologies are discussed in the remainder of this section and include:

- Using cellular technologies in business.
- Using satellite technologies in business.
- Using wireless technologies in business.
- Mobile business trends.

USING CELLULAR TECHNOLOGIES IN BUSINESS

Continental Airlines passengers in Houston will be able to board flights using just a cell phone or personal-digital assistant instead of a regular boarding pass at Bush Intercontinental Airport. The program could expand to airlines and airports nationwide. Instead of a paper pass, Continental Airlines and the Transportation Security Administration will let passengers show a code the airline has sent to their cell phone or PDA. The two-dimensional bar code, a jumble of squares and rectangles, stores the passenger's name and flight information. A TSA screener will confirm the bar code's authenticity with a handheld scanner. Passengers still need to show photo identification. The electronic boarding pass also works at airport gates. If a passenger's cell phone or mobile device loses power, the passenger can get a paper boarding pass from a kiosk or a Continental agent. Houston-based Continental, the nation's number four airline, has been working on the new feature for years to increase efficiency, eliminate paperwork, and make travel easier.[11]

In less than 20 years, the mobile telephone has gone from being rare, expensive equipment of the business elite to a pervasive, low-cost personal item. Several countries, including the United Kingdom, now have more mobile phones than people. There are over 500 million active mobile phone accounts in China. Luxembourg has the highest mobile phone penetration rate in the world, at 164 percent. The total number of mobile phone subscribers in the world was estimated at 3.3 billion at the end of 2007, thus reaching an equivalent of over half the planet's population. At present, Africa has the largest growth rate of cellular subscribers in the world, its markets expanding nearly twice as fast as Asian markets. The availability of prepaid or pay-as-you-go services, where the subscriber is not committed to a long-term contract, has helped fuel this growth in Africa as well as in other continents.[12]

Cellular telephones (cell phones) work by using radio waves to communicate with radio antennas (or towers) placed within adjacent geographic areas called cells. A telephone message is transmitted to the local cell by the cellular telephone and then is passed from antenna to antenna, or cell to cell, until it reaches the cell of its destination, where it is transmitted to the receiving telephone. As a cellular signal travels from one cell into another, a computer that monitors signals from the cells switches the conversation to a radio channel assigned to the next cell. In a typical analog cell phone system in the United States, the cell phone carrier receives about 800 frequencies to use across the city. The carrier chops up the city into cells. Each cell is typically 10 square miles. Cells are normally thought of as hexagons on a big hexagonal grid, such as what Figure 7.11 illustrates. Each cell has a base station that consists of a tower and a small building containing the radio equipment.[13]

FIGURE 7.11

Cellular Technology Overview

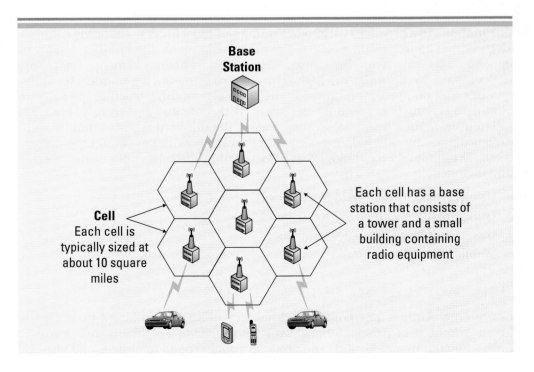

FIGURE 7.12

Cellular Technology Advantages and Disadvantages

Generation	Technology	Advantages and Disadvantages
1G	AMPS (Advanced Mobile Phone Service)	– Analog voice service only
2G	CDMA (Code Division Multiple Access) TDMA (Time Division Multiple Access) GSM (Global Systems for Mobile Communications PDC (Personal Digital Cellular)	– Digital voice service – 9.6 Kbps to 14.4 Kbps data service – Enhanced calling features (such as caller ID) – No always-on data connection
3G	W-CDMA (Wideband Code Division Multiple Access)	– Superior voice quality – Always-on data connection up to 2 Mbps – Broadband data services (such as streaming audio and video)
4G	W-CDMA (Wideband Code Division Multiple Access) MC-CDMA (Multi Carrier CDMA)	– Wi-fi access networks – Always-on data connection 20–100 Mbps – Converged data and voice over IP

Older cellular systems are analog, and newer cellular systems are digital. Personal communication services (PCS) are one popular type of digital cellular service. PCS are entirely digital. They can transmit both voice and data and operate in a higher frequency range (1,900 MHz) than analog cellular telephones (analog cellular service operates in the 800 and 900 MHz bands). These digital cellular systems are capable of sending and receiving short text messages.

PCS are second-generation (2G) mobile communications technology, and analog cellular systems are first generation (1G). Second-generation cellular networks are, circuit-switched digital networks that can transmit data at about 10 kilobits per second (Kbps), which is extremely slow. Third-generation (3G) networks use a newer packet-switched technology that is much more efficient (and hence faster) than dedicated circuit-switched networks. Third-generation networks have speeds ranging from 120 to 144 Kbps for mobile users in, for example, a car, and up to 2 gigabits per second (Gbps) for stationary users. These 3G networks are designed for high-speed transmission of multimedia data and voice. The major network operators are providing 3G services, and some groups and companies have already started working on fourth-generation (4G) mobile phone system. The 4G technology will take mobile communication another step up to integrate radio and television transmissions, and to consolidate the world's phone standards into one high-speed technology. Figure 7.12 displays many of the cellular technologies along with their advantages and disadvantages.

The Finnish government decided that the fastest way to warn citizens of disasters was the mobile phone network. In Japan, mobile phone companies provide immediate notification of earthquakes and other natural disasters to their customers free of charge. In the event of an emergency, disaster response crews can locate trapped or injured people using the signals from their mobile phones. An interactive menu accessible through the phone's Internet browser notifies the company if the user is safe or in distress. In Finland, rescue services suggest hikers carry mobile phones in case of emergency even when deep in the forests beyond cellular coverage, as the radio signal of a cell phone attempting to connect to a base station can be detected by overflying rescue aircraft with special detection gear. In addition, users in the United States can sign up through their provider for free text messages when an Amber Alert goes out for a missing person in their area.[14]

The latest trends in cell phones reflect a convergence of voice, video, and data communications. By blending information with entertainment, cell phones are center-stage in the evolving trend of mobile infotainment. As an example, the Apple iPhone is a revolutionary mobile phone that allows users to make calls, surf the web (Google and Yahoo! are built right in) over a wi-fi connection, email a photo, use a widescreen iPod with touch controls to various content—including music, audiobooks, videos, TV shows, and movies. Technically speaking, the iPhone is a smartphone, discussed in the next section.

Personal Digital Assistants

Personal digital assistants (PDA) are small, handheld computers capable of entirely digital communications transmission. They have built-in wireless telecommunications capabilities as well as work-organization software. PDAs can display, compose, send, and receive email messages, and some models can provide wireless access to the Internet. Unlike mobile phones, PDAs do not require subscription-based network services. They are stand-alone minicomputers, much like PCs before the Internet.

The first generation of successful PDAs were Palm Pilots. They primarily functioned as electronic organizers with support for address books, calendars, email, notes, and so on. The PDA only occasionally needs to connect to a companion PC for synchronization. For instance, a PDA can be synchronized with a PC address book, calendar, and email inbox via a USB cable. Newer PDA models can also connect to PCs wirelessly via Bluetooth (described in the next section), or connect to the Internet via wireless.

A *smartphone* combines the functions of a cellular phone and a PDA in a single device. It differs from a normal cell phone in that it has an operating system and local storage, so users can add and store information, send and receive email, and install programs to the phone as they could with a PDA. A smartphone gives users the best of both worlds—it has much the same capabilities as a PDA and the communications ability of a mobile phone.

As the old saying goes, "timing is everything." Nowhere is that more true than in the real estate business in Hawaii. Real estate agents continue to look for tools that will give them an edge. Real-time access to their area's multiple listing service (MLS) provides one way for agents to take advantage of timing. MLS offers a database of local properties for sale, with the ability to sort them by a variety of criteria. An agent who accesses a home's listing as soon as it hits the MLS gains a key advantage against the competition because the agent can immediately request a viewing or, at a minimum, simply drive by the location with a client.

Real estate agents are rarely in their offices, so they require technology that not only provides real-time access to their local MLS but also enables them to manage contact information, keep their calendars current, send and receive emails, view documents, calculate basic mortgage numbers and more. The lighter the solution, the better, so that they can leave the laptop behind when necessary. In addition, if they can combine that with cell phone functionality, they need only one device to conduct business.

Many real estate agents in Hawaii are using smartphones as a solution to their needs. Easy to carry and dependable, smartphones give them real-time access to their local MLS, enabling them to learn about properties as soon as they are listed for sale.

Bluetooth

Electronic devices can connect to one another in many different ways. The various pieces and parts of computers, entertainment systems, and telephones, make up a community of electronic devices. These devices communicate with each other using a variety of wires, cables, radio signals, and infrared light beams, and an even greater variety of connectors, plugs, and protocols. Bluetooth technology eliminates the need for wires that tangle everyday lives. *Bluetooth* is a telecommunications industry specification that describes how mobile phones, computers, and personal digital assistants (PDAs) can be easily interconnected using a short-range wireless

FIGURE 7.13

Bluetooth Virtual Keyboard

Beams of light, which detect the user's movements, make up this virtual keyboard.

connection. Bluetooth headsets allow users to cut the cord and make calls even while their cell phones are tucked away in a briefcase. Wireless Bluetooth printing allows users of a Bluetooth-enabled PDA or laptop to attach to a printer via a Bluetooth adapter connected to the printer's communication port.

Since Bluetooth's development in 1994 by the Swedish telecommunications company Ericsson, more than 1,800 companies worldwide have signed on to build products to the wireless specification and promote the new technology in the marketplace. The engineers at Ericsson code-named the new wireless technology Bluetooth to honor a 10th century Viking king, Harald Bluetooth, who is credited with uniting Denmark and bringing order to the country.

Bluetooth capability is enabled in a device by means of an embedded Bluetooth chip and supporting software. Although Bluetooth is slower than competing wireless LAN technologies, the Bluetooth chip enables Bluetooth networking to be built into a wide range of devices—even small devices such as cellular phones and PDAs. Bluetooth's maximum range is 30 feet, limiting it to gadget-to-gadget communication.

One challenge to wireless devices is their size. Everyone wants their mobile devices to be small, but many people also curse the tiny, cryptic keyboards that manufacturers squeeze into smart phones and PDAs. The laws of physics have proved a significant barrier to solving this problem, but VKB Inc.'s Bluetooth Virtual Keyboard offers a possible solution (see Figure 7.13). VKB's technology uses a red laser to illuminate a virtual keyboard outline on any surface. Despite its futuristic look, the laser is really just a visual guide to where users put their fingers. A separate illumination and sensor module invisibly tracks when and where each finger touches the surface, translating that into keystrokes or other commands.

USING SATELLITE TECHNOLOGIES IN BUSINESS

A special variation of wireless transmission employs satellite communication to relay signals over very long distances. A communications *satellite* is a big microwave repeater in the sky; it contains one or more transponders that listen to a particular portion of the electromagnetic spectrum, amplifying incoming signals, and retransmitting them back to Earth. A *microwave transmitter* uses the atmosphere (or outer space) as the transmission medium to send the signal to a microwave receiver. The microwave receiver then either relays the signal to another microwave transmitter or translates the signal to some other form, such as digital impulses. Microwave signals follow a straight line and do not bend with the curvature of the

FIGURE 7.14

Satellite Microwave Link

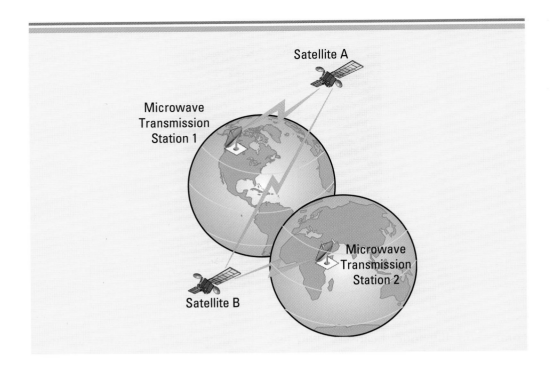

Earth; therefore, long-distance terrestrial transmission systems require that micro-wave transmission stations be positioned about 37 miles apart, making this form of transmission expensive.

This problem can be solved by bouncing microwave signals off communication satellites, enabling them to serve as relay stations for microwave signals transmitted from terrestrial stations (as illustrated in Figure 7.14). Communication satellites are cost effective for transmitting large quantities of data over very long distances. Satellites are typically used for communication in large, geographically dispersed organizations that would be difficult to tie together through cabling media or terrestrial microwave. Originally, this microwave technology was used almost exclusively for satellite and long-range communication. Recently, however, developments in cellular technology allow complete wireless access to networks, intranets, and the Internet via microwave transmission.

Conventional communication satellites move in stationary orbits approximately 22,000 miles above the Earth. A newer satellite medium, the low-orbit satellite, travels much closer to the Earth and is able to pick up signals from weak transmitters. Low-orbit satellites also consume less power and cost less to launch than conventional satellites. With such wireless networks, businesspeople almost anywhere in the world will have access to full communication capabilities, including voice communication via satellite phones, videoconferencing, and multimedia-rich Internet access.

General Motors is serious about satellite radio. Previously, GM made XM satellite radio standard on all Cadillacs, and now the subscription radio service will also be available for all new Buick, Hummer, and Saab models as well. The move enlarges XM's customer base while also giving drivers a chance to test the technology for three months free of charge.

The devices used for satellite communication range from handheld units to mobile base stations to fixed satellite dish receivers. The peak data transmission speeds range from 2.4 Kbps to 2 Mbps, depending on the solution being sought. For the everyday mobile professional, satellite communication does not provide a compelling benefit, but for people requiring voice and data access from remote locations or guaranteed coverage in non-remote locations, satellite technology may be worth while. Also, some satellite service providers offer roaming between existing cellular systems and satellite systems.[15]

FIGURE 7.15

Location-Based Services
Market Segments

Mass Market	
Emergency Services	■ Locate emergency call ■ Roadside assistance
Navigation Services	■ Navigation to point of interest (directions, maps) ■ Etourism ■ Avoidance of traffic jams
Tracking Services	■ Find-a-friend ■ Tracking of children ■ Elderly
Location Advertising	■ Located video push
Gaming	■ N-Gage (allows multiple gamers to play against each other over Bluetooth or wireless phone network connections)
Professional Market	
Workforce Organization	■ Field force management ■ Optimization of routes ■ Logistics ■ Enterprise resource planning
Security	■ Field tracking ■ Worker protection

Satellite-based location will shape the future, creating new applications. Besides emergency call location and navigation in cars and on mobile phones, a range of new services will appear: personal assistance and medical care, localized presence services, finding friends, gaming, localized blogs, and so on. To enable the wide commercial success of each service, several key technological challenges need to be met: accuracy; ubiquity of service, including in dense urban areas and inside buildings; and delivery of information instantaneously.

Location-based services (LBS) are wireless mobile content services that provide location-specific information to mobile users moving from location to location. The market for location-based services is tremendous, with a variety of available and future services in a number of market segments: mobile telephony, enterprise, vertical markets, automotive and consumer devices. Figure 7.15 highlights many of the location-based services market segments that are currently pushing this technology.

Have you ever needed an ATM and not known where to find one? For tourists and businesspeople traveling far from home, that is an all-too-familiar predicament. Each year, 2 million cardholders contact MasterCard via telephone or the website looking for the location of nearby ATMs; some 70 percent of inquiries are received from international travelers venturing outside their home countries.

MasterCard now provides cardholders with a mobile, location-based search and directory service, so they can request the location of the nearest ATM be sent to their mobile phone via SMS (Short Message Service, or text message). The service, which works with all major mobile operators in the United States, is provided by MasterCard to cardholders free of charge (although operator text message rates may apply).

A user that employs location-based services on a regular basis faces a potential privacy problem. Many users consider location information to be highly sensitive and are concerned about a number of privacy issues, including:

■ Target marketing: Mobile users' locations can be used to classify customers for focused marketing efforts.

■ Embarrassment: One customer's knowledge of another's location may lead to embarrassing situations.

■ Harassment: Location information can be used to harass or attack a user.

- Service denial: A health insurance firm might deny a claim if it learned that a user visited a high-risk area.
- Legal restrictions: Some countries regulate the use of personal data.

Unlike other information in cyberspace, location information has the potential to allow an adversary to physically locate a person, and therefore most wireless subscribers have legitimate concerns about their personal safety if such information should fall into the wrong hands. Laws and rules of varying clarity, offering different degrees of protection, have been or are being enacted in the United States, the European Union, and Japan.

Global Positioning System (GPS)

The most popular location-based service used today is Global Positioning System. The **Global Positioning System (GPS)** is a constellation of 24 well-spaced satellites that orbit the Earth and make it possible for people with ground receivers to pinpoint their geographic location. The location accuracy is anywhere from 10 to 100 meters for most equipment. Accuracy can be pinpointed to within one meter with special military-approved equipment. Figure 7.16 illustrates the GPS architecture.

The GPS is owned and operated by the U.S. Department of Defense but is available for general use around the world. In 1993, the Defense Department made this global positioning technology available for commercial use to anyone who has a GPS device. GPS devices have special microprocessors that analyze satellite signals. Sirf Technology specializes in building GPS microprocessors for phones, electronics, and car navigation systems. Since going public in 2004, Sirf Technology has seen revenue climb 60 percent to $117 million with net profits of $30.7 million. With new federal regulation forcing wireless operators to include GPS in their phones and networking equipment, chip demand is exploding. Recently Sirf Technology has developed a golf GPS that helps golfers calculate the distance from the tee to the pin, or to know exactly where they are with relation to features such as hidden bunkers, water hazards, or greens. The United States Golf Association now permits distance-measuring devices for use in tournaments at the discretion of the organizers.[16]

The market for GPS services has grown to more than $5 billion with expectations for demand to double over the next few years. Tracking, navigation, and hardware

GPS

FIGURE 7.16

Global Positioning System Architecture

GPS Enabled Device

GPS Enabled Base Station

promise to be multibillion-dollar markets by 2010. UPS has outfitted 75,000 drivers with GPS-enabled handhelds to help them reach destinations more efficiently. The handhelds will also trigger email alerts if a company vehicle speeds or ventures into unauthorized areas. Steve Wozniak, Apple co-founder, started a company in 2002 named Wheels of Zeus that combines GPS data with local wireless networking. The technology helps parents keep tabs on their children or can alert IT managers when company-owned computers leave the premises. Zingo, in the United Kingdom, uses GPS-enabled cars and text messaging to help subscribers hail cabs.

A *geographic information system (GIS)* is designed to work with information that can be shown on a map. Companies that deal in transportation use GISs combined with database and GPS technology. Airlines and shipping companies can plot routes with up-to-the-second information on the location of all their transport vehicles. Hospitals can keep track of where personnel are located by using a GIS and sensors that pick up the transmission of badges worn by hospital staff.

Automobiles have GPSs linked to maps that display, in a screen on the dashboard, driving directions and exact location of the vehicle. GM offers the OnStar system, which sends a continuous stream of information to the OnStar center about the car's exact location. The OnStar Vehicle Diagnostics automatically performs hundreds of diagnostic checks on four key operating systems—the engine/transmission, antilock brakes, air bags, and OnStar systems—in GM vehicles. The vehicle is programmed to send the results via email to the owner each month. The unique email report also provides maintenance reminders based on the current odometer reading, remaining engine oil life, and other relevant ownership information.[17]

Some cell phone providers equip their phones with GPS chips that enable users to be located to within a geographical location about the size of a tennis court. This allows emergency services such as 911 to find a cell phone user. Marketers are monitoring cell phone GPS development, hoping to be able to call potential customers when they are walking past their store to let them know of a special sale.

American farmers on the leading edge use GPS satellite navigation to map and analyze fields, telling them where to apply the proper amounts of seeds, fertilizer, and herbicides. In the past farmers managed their business on a per-field basis; now they can micromanage. One Illinois farmer found that parts of his fields did not need any fertilizer after monitoring the soil. Less fertilizer lowers costs and reduces pollution from the runoff of water from the fields. One GPS application is to use geographic fixes from the GPS and a computerized counter to record how much grain is being harvested each second from each meter of the field. Then the farmer downloads this information into a personal computer, which produces a contour map that shows variations of, say, more than 60 bushels an acre. Cross-referencing this information to other variables, such as characteristics of the soil, allows the farmer to analyze why some land is less productive. The farmer combines these data with GPS navigational fixes to precisely apply herbicides or fertilizer only where it is really needed.[18]

A GIS is useful for mobile applications, but it offers benefits that go well beyond what is required in a mobile environment. For example, using a GIS, users can decide what information is and is not relevant to them, and formulate their queries based on their personal criteria. Unlike a paper map, a GIS allows for in-depth analysis and problem solving that can make marketing, sales, and planning much more successful. The following are some common GIS uses:

- **Finding what is nearby.** This is the most common use for mobile users. Given a specific location, the GIS finds sources within a defined radius. This may include entertainment venues, medical facilities, restaurants, or gas stations. Users might also use the GIS to locate vendors that sell a specific item they want. This promotes m-commerce by matching buyers with sellers. The results can be provided using a map of the surrounding area or the destination addresses.

- **Routing information.** This is another common use for mobile users. Once users have an idea of where they want to go, a GIS can provide directions on how to get there. Once again, this can be provided graphically using a map or with step-by-step instructions. For mobile applications, it is often helpful to provide routing information in conjunction with search services.

- **Information alerts.** Users may want to be notified when information that is relevant to them becomes available based on their location. For example, a commuter might want to know if he or she is entering a section of the highway that has traffic congestion, or a shopper might want to be notified if his or her favorite store is having a sale on a certain item.

- **Mapping densities.** For business analysis, knowing population densities can be extremely useful. This allows users to find out where high concentrations of a certain population may be. Densities are typically mapped based on a standard area unit, such as hectares or square miles making it easy to see distributions. Examples of density mapping may include the location of crime incidents for police to determine where additional patrolling is required, or of customers to help determine ideal field delivery routes.

- **Mapping quantities.** People map quantities to find out where the most or least of a feature may be. This information could, for example, be used to determine where to locate a new business or service. For example, if someone is interested in opening a Laundromat, it would be prudent to determine how many others are in the area and what the population base is. This type of mapping can be useful for urban planning and environmental studies; for example, for city planners who are trying to determine where to build more parks.[19]

A GIS can provide information and insight to both mobile users and people at fixed locations. This information uses the location coordinates provided by one of the positioning technologies to give details that are relevant to the user at that specific moment. Many of the location-based services discussed earlier in this section would benefit from the information provided from a GIS.

USING WIRELESS TECHNOLOGIES IN BUSINESS

Denver International Airport (DIA) is betting that travelers will like getting something free, and so far, it looks like a good bet. The airport, one of the busiest in the Unites States, switched its public wi-fi offering from paid to advertising-supported. Within a week, and with no public notice of the change, wi-fi use grew tenfold. About 50 million passengers pass through DIA every year, with as many as 165,000 per day during busy times of the year. Now that wi-fi is free, there are 7,000 to 8,000 connections to the network per day. To link all those free users with the Internet, the airport had to increase its bandwidth and network infrastructure to allow 10 Mbps connections just for the wi-fi users.

Wireless fidelity (wi-fi) is a means of linking computers using infrared or radio signals. Wi-fi, or what is sometimes referred to as wireless LANs, represent only a small proportion of LANs in operation today, but a rapidly growing proportion. Wi-fi technology has obvious advantages for people on the move who need access to the Internet in airports, restaurants, and hotels. Wi-fi is also gaining acceptance as a home or neighborhood network, permitting an assortment of laptop and desktop computers to share a single broadband access point to the Internet. Wireless LANs are also moving into the corporate and commercial world, especially in older buildings and confined spaces where it would be difficult or impossible to establish a wired LAN or where mobility is paramount. Even in newer buildings, wireless LANs are often being employed as overlay networks. In such cases, wi-fi is installed in addition to wired LANs so that employees can easily move their laptops from office to office and can connect to the network in places such as lunchrooms and patios.

After years of discussion and delay, U.S. airlines will start offering in-flight Internet connections, instant messaging, and wireless email, thus turning the airplane cabin into a wi-fi hotspot. Helping lead many of the airlines into the new era is AirCell, which in June 2006 won exclusive air-to-ground wi-fi rights by plunking down $31.3 million for 3 MHz of terrestrial digital wireless spectrum at a Federal Communications

FIGURE 7.17

Wi-Fi in the Sky

Commission auction. The company has already inked deals with American Airlines and Virgin America to install its air-to-ground system equipment, which company founder Jimmy Ray has been fine-tuning for the past decade and a half. The system will take to the air as soon as American Airlines retrofits a few of its transcontinental 767-200s. Virgin America will do the same for its 10-plane fleet, in addition to 31 planes on order from Airbus. Figure 7.17 illustrates how this "wi-fi in the sky" will work.[20]

Recently, McDonald's has promised to outfit 14,000 of its locations with upscale coffee bars accompanied by expanded wi-fi service as the fast-food chain inches closer to offering the wireless technology free of charge. Currently, McDonald's provides wi-fi service to 15,000 of its 30,000 U.S. and international locations. The service is available most often through a credit card purchase or through Internet service provider Wayport.[21]

While wi-fi is hot, security is not. With a laptop in the passenger seat of his SUV and a special antenna on the roof, Mike Outmesguine ventured off to sniff out wireless networks between Los Angeles and San Francisco. While en route, he got a big whiff of insecurity.

While his 800-mile drive confirmed that the number of wireless networks is growing explosively, he also found that only a third used basic encryption, a key security measure. In nearly 40 percent of the networks not a single change had been made to the gear's wide-open default settings.

"They took it out of the box, powered it up, and it worked. And they left it alone," said Outmesguine, who owns a technical services company. He frequently goes out on such drives in search of insecure networks. While Outmesguine says he doesn't try to break in, others aren't so benign. If criminals were to target unsecured wireless routers, they could create an attack that could piggyback across thousands of wi-fi networks in urban areas such as Chicago or New York City. A wi-fi attack could take over 20,000 wireless routers in New York City within a two-week period, with most of the infections occurring within the first day.[22]

WiMAX

The main problems with broadband access are that it is expensive and it does not reach all areas. The main problem with wi-fi access is that hotspots are very small, so coverage is sparse. An evolving technology that can solve all of these problems is called WiMAX. *WiMAX,* or Worldwide Interoperability for Microwave Access, is a telecommunications technology aimed at providing wireless data over long distances in a variety of ways, from point-to-point links to full mobile cellular type access. WiMAX can cover a stretch of as much as 3,000 square miles depending on the number of users. In New York City, for example, many base stations will be required around the city to meet the heavy demand, while a sparsely populated region will need fewer.

Sprint Nextel along with Google is developing a new mobile Internet portal using WiMAX wireless technology to offer web search and social networking. Sprint's WiMAX for high-speed wireless and its services for detecting location will be combined with Google tools including email, chat, and other applications. Sprint aims to use the emerging WiMAX technology to better compete with rival wireless and wired broadband networks. Sprint planned to test the WiMAX service in Chicago, Baltimore, and Washington by the end of 2008 with a goal of attaining coverage for 100 million people.[23]

WiMAX offers web access speeds that are five times faster than typical wireless networks, though they are still slower than wired broadband. Higher-end notebook computers will have WiMAX technology built starting in late in 2008, though WiMAX cards that plug into a slot in the computer will also be available. Companies such as Nokia, Motorola, and Samsung Electronics are also making mobile devices and infrastructure with WiMAX technology.

WiMAX could potentially erase the suburban and rural blackout areas that currently have no broadband Internet access because phone and cable companies have not yet run the necessary wires to those remote locations.

A WiMAX system consists of two parts:

- A WiMAX tower. A single WiMAX tower can provide coverage to a very large area—as big as 3,000 square miles.
- A WiMAX receiver. The receiver and antenna could be built into a laptop the way wi-fi access is today.[24]

A WiMAX tower station can connect directly to the Internet using a high-bandwidth, wired connection (for example, a T3 line). It can also connect to another WiMAX tower using a line-of-sight, microwave link. This connection to a second tower (often referred to as a backhaul) is what allows WiMAX to provide coverage to remote rural areas. Figure 7.18 illustrates the WiMAX architecture.

Wi-fi-style access will be limited to a four-to-six mile radius (25 square miles of coverage, which is similar in range to a cell-phone zone). Through the stronger line-of-sight antennas, the WiMAX transmitting station would send data to WiMAX-enabled computers or routers set up within the transmitter's 30-mile radius. This is what allows WiMAX to achieve its maximum range. Figure 7.19 displays many of the benefits of the WiMAX technology.[25]

Radio Frequency Identification (RFID)

Radio frequency identification (RFID) technologies use active or passive tags in the form of chips or smart labels that can store unique identifiers and relay this information to electronic readers. RFID tags, often smaller than a grain of sand, combine

FIGURE 7.18

WiMAX Architecture

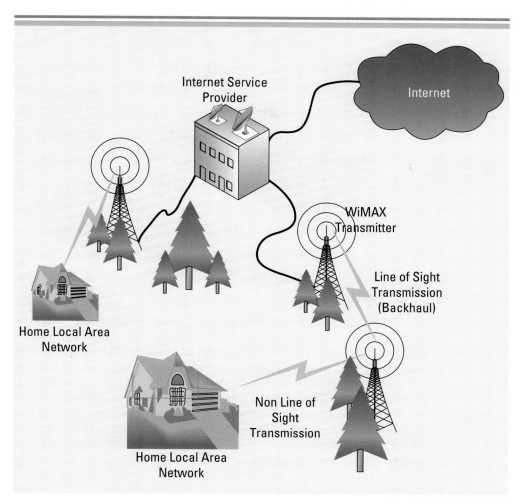

tiny chips with an antenna. When a tag is placed on an item, it automatically radios its location to RFID readers on store shelves, checkout counters, loading bay doors, and shopping carts. With RFID tags, inventory is taken automatically and continuously. RFID tags can cut costs by requiring fewer workers for scanning items; they also can provide more current and more accurate information to the entire supply chain. Wal-Mart saves on average $8.4 billion a year by installing RFID in many of its operations. Figure 7.20 illustrates one example of an RFID architecture.

FIGURE 7.19

WiMAX Benefits

Benefit	Description
Long Range	The most significant benefit of WiMAX compared to existing wireless technologies is the range. WiMAX has a communication range of up to 30 miles, enough to blanket an entire city.
Low Cost	Base stations will cost less than $20,000 but will still provide customers with T1-class connections.
Wireless	By using a WiMAX system, companies/ residents no longer have to rip up buildings or streets or lay down expensive cables.
High Bandwidth	WiMAX can provide shared data rates of up to 70 Mbps. This is enough bandwidth to support more than 60 businesses at once with T1-type connectivity. It can also support over a thousand homes at 1 Mbps DSL-level connectivity.
Service	WiMAX can provide users with two forms of wireless service: 1. Non line of sight operates at 2 to 11 GHz, which at a lower level frequency has the ability to bend around obstacles more easily. A small antenna on a computer connects to the tower and is backward compatible with existing wi-fi technologies. 2. Line of sight can go as high as 66 GHz since the signal is stronger and more stable, which leads to greater bandwidth. A fixed dish antenna points straight at the tower or for communication between tower to tower.

FIGURE 7.20

RFID Architecture

RFID

The advent of RFID has allowed everyone from shipping companies to hospitals to reduce costs and overhead by creating visibility into inefficient business processes. Aberdeen's research shows that 38 percent of enterprises using RFID are doing so to improve the cost, safety, and reliability of managing business processes. Organizations are leveraging RFID to improve the productivity of their workforce all while simplifying the implementation and ongoing management costs of their networks.[26]

When Wal-Mart announced its RFID strategy in 2003, it was just one of many retailers that had become enamored of the technology. By placing RFID tags on cases and pallets shipped from manufacturers to Wal-Mart distribution centers, companies would be able to keep close tabs on their shipments. In turn, that would allow Wal-Mart and its suppliers to streamline their supply chains and ultimately ensure shelves were always fully stocked.

RFID tags represented the next big step forward from bar codes, the ubiquitous stripes on the sides of packages that provide basic product and pricing information. The simplest tags, passive RFID tags, require no internal power supply. Incoming radio frequency signals from RFID readers can transmit a minute electrical current, enough to power the integrated circuit in the tag and transmit a response. The key benefit is that the bar code on a case or pallet no longer needs to be swiped to identify the contents; the tag just needs to come within range of a reader—anywhere from a few feet up to 600 feet. In addition, RFID tags can transmit far more information about a product, including price, serial number, and even when and where it was made.

Much of the recent interest surrounding RFID has arisen from mandates and recommendations by government agencies such as the U.S. Department of Defense (DoD) and the Food and Drug Administration (FDA), and from a few private-sector megacorporations.

RFID technologies offer practical benefits to almost anyone who needs to keep track of physical assets. Manufacturers improve supply chain planning and execution by incorporating RFID technologies. Retailers use RFID to control theft, increase efficiency in their supply chains, and improve demand planning. Pharmaceutical manufacturers use RFID systems to combat the counterfeit drug trade and reduce errors in filling prescriptions. Machine shops track their tools with RFID to avoid misplacing tools and to track which tools touched a piece of work. RFID-enabled smart cards help control perimeter access to buildings. In the last couple of years, owing in large part to Wal-Mart and DoD mandates, many major retail chains and consumer goods manufacturers have begun testing pallet- and case-level merchandise tagging to improve management of shipments to customers.[27]

RFID tags differ from conventional bar code tags in a number of ways. These differences create the benefit of adopting the technology, while simultaneously creating the greatest concern over the privacy issues involved. For example, under today's bar code technology, a pack of Wrigley's gum sold in Houston has the same bar code as a pack sold in New York City. With RFID, however, each pack would have a unique ID code that could be tied to the purchaser of that gum when the buyer uses an "item registration system" such as a frequent shopper card or a credit card.

The purchaser could then be tracked if he or she entered that same store again, or perhaps more frightening, entered any other store with RFID reading capability. Unlike a bar code, RFID tags can be read from much greater distances and the reading of such devices is nondirectional. This means that if someone enters a store with a pack of gum in a pocket or purse, the RFID reader can identify that pack of gum, the time and date it was purchased, where it was purchased, and how frequently the consumer comes into the store. If a credit card or a frequent shopper card was used to purchase the gum, the manufacturer and store could also tie that information to the consumer's name, address, and email and then direct targeted advertisements by gum companies as the shopper walks down the aisles, or send mailings through email or regular mail about other products.

As the technology behind RFID advances, the potential for privacy infringement does as well. RFID already has the capability to determine the distance of a tag from the reader location. With such technology already available, it is not difficult to imagine a situation in which retailers could determine the location of individuals within the store, and thus target specific advertisements to that customer based upon past purchases (as in the gum example used above). In effect, that store would be creating a personal log of past purchases, shopping patterns, and ultimately behavioral patterns. While such information gathering would be considered intrusive enough by many consumers' standards, the danger that such information could be sold to other retailers (similar to the way such profiles are currently sold regarding Internet commerce) could create potentially devastating information vulnerabilities. While some RFID critics have pointed out that the technology could lead to some sort of corporate "Big Brother," concern more widespread that allowing RFID to develop without legal restrictions will eliminate the possibility for consumers to refuse to give such information to retailers.[28]

Some steps are being taken to mitigate these privacy issues. For example, a recent proposal would require that all RFID-tagged products be clearly labeled. This would give consumers the choice to select products without RFID, or at a minimum to recognize that the items they select are being tracked. For those unsatisfied with disclosure, a growing number of products are designed to limit exposure to RFID tagged products. One such product is "Kill Codes," a command that turns off all RFID tags immediately as the consumer comes into contact with them, thus eliminating the effectiveness of the technology. Another countermeasure against RFID privacy invasion is "RSA Blocker Tags," which try to address privacy concerns while maintaining the integrity of the product. Under this technology, the item can be tracked only by that store's authorized reader, meaning customers cannot be tracked outside of the store in which they purchased the item.[29]

With RFID becoming both smarter and smaller, the possibilities for its uses are endless (see Figure 7.21). While RFID poses certain ethical dilemmas for government and commercial operations, it also simplifies life for the common person. As medical benefits are explored further, RFID tags will not only be used for convenience and profit, but also for saving lives.[30]

MOBILE WORKFORCE TRENDS

Airplane seats. Car dashboards. Digital cameras. Kiosks at shopping malls, school campuses, and hotels. Stadium bleachers. Handheld calculators. Kitchen appliances. These are just a few of the mobile devices and locations that are being wired for wireless. The visionary images of yesterday are giving way to a reality in which connectivity is nearly ubiquitous. Real-time information is now the currency of business and the enabler of groundbreaking innovations in education, entertainment, and media. The predictions help identify emerging mobile trends and indicate

RFID Use	Description
Preventing toilets from overflowing	You can purchase a "smart" toilet, one that shuts itself off when it is close to overflowing. According to AquaOne, its RFID-enhanced toilets are not only convenient, but they also prevent health risks in public places such as hospitals and nursing homes.
Identifying human remains	Hurricane Katrina left behind many unclaimed casualties, despite the tireless searches by countless people. Thanks to the VeriChip, RFID tags are now being used to locate bodies in an effort to reunite loved ones. This helps to identify cadavers during transport, and coroners are now able to collect body parts for burial in their rightful places.
Getting into nightclubs	Barcelona's Baja Beach Club is now grafting RFID tags into the arms of patrons who want instant access to the exclusive hangout. The tag also functions as a debit card.
Cooking with robots	Robotic pots and pans with RFID chips in the handles make it almost impossible to botch a meal. With these RFID chips, the cookware can be coordinated with a recipe card that has a similar chip. Then, the cookware will set its temperature and duration to the exact specifications the food calls for.
Timing athletic events	RFID transponders are being used as timing systems in major sporting events all over the world, including the Boston Marathon and Ironman championships (as described in the opening case). With a chip attached to an athlete's shoe, bicycle, etc., timing can begin and end with the utmost accuracy; the timer stops when the person crosses the finishing mat, which contains an antenna that will be signaled by the RFID chip. The technology is especially handy in very close finishes between competitors.
Tracking wheels of cheese	To track cheese through each process and handler until it is sold, RFID tags are being placed just under the edges of the food products. The industry is having problems with theft, loss, and even counterfeit cheese. While the idea of black market cheese may sound ridiculous, consider this—just one wheel of Parmesan cheese can be worth several hundred dollars.
Monitoring casinos	Casinos are already heavily monitored, but the unique betting habits of each player can now be logged, thanks to RFID tags inside betting chips. The chips keep track of high rollers and their spending patterns, and they make it even harder for thieves to counterfeit chips or steal them from other players. All of this technology is used to stack more odds in the house's favor.
Tracking razor blades	Thanks to low-cost RFID tags, Gillette can now afford to place small transponders in each package of its popular razor products. This is done in an attempt to salvage more razors as they make their way through a very convoluted supply chain. Many of the small products are lost or stolen. While it might sound trivial for the company to worry about losing a razor here and there, the problem is really far worse than that. Gillette's Mach 3 razor, retailing at more than $10 each, is one of the most commonly stolen items in a store.
Issuing passports	The U.S. State Department has approved of passports with microchips inside, and the technology is already being tested in trials. While the government maintains that its purpose is to improve communication between law enforcement agencies, others feel there will be more sinister repercussions.

FIGURE 7.21

Unusual Uses of RFID

ways that consumers and businesses will benefit. These trends include widespread use of mobile social networks, greater choice in multifunction devices, and more wireless home entertainment options.

- **Social networking gets mobilized.** Mobility is added to existing Internet business models, services, and behaviors, driving traffic for wireless operators. Those in their teens and twenties accustomed to constant connectivity and habit-forming websites, such as MySpace and Facebook, lead a wave of membership in mobile social networks. Location social networking including friend and event finder services are gaining popularity, even in the professional and over-50 segments. Google, Yahoo!, and Skype are more compelling for users than wireless brands, which are hard-pressed to compete. Social networking applications initially are preloaded on many mobile devices sold and later become downloadable.

- **Mobile TV.** In the short term, wireless users are unlikely to plunk down $5.99 to $9.99 per month for mobile TV service. Instead, look for per-view or per-minute pricing for "sneaking," a consumer tendency to watch key minutes of a sports event or drama while engaged in another activity. Sneaking leads to more regular viewing, and within three to five years, mobile TV will become an indispensable service. Broadcast TV is the primary driver of revenues and consumer adoption, but peer-to-peer video is gaining interest, too. Operators are squaring off with content providers over control of the subscriber relationship and user experience.

- **Multifunction devices become cheaper and more versatile.** Intense competition and margin pressure will continue in the handset market, forcing prices of third-generation (3G) handsets below $90 and making them affordable for a wide range of users. Seeking to replicate the success of camera phones, device manufacturers will produce more multifunction units with music-playing, location, video and other capabilities. Twenty percent of all handsets sold in North America are application specific—built for a usage proposition, such as music or video consumption or business productivity.

- **Location-based services.** GPS is the location technology of choice for the wireless industry. Handset manufacturers will continue to push GPS-enabled handsets as the technology evolves from popular in-car satellite navigation systems like TomTom to a broadly accepted feature in wireless phones. With Nokia having launched its first GPS-enabled handsets in early 2007 and bandwidth available to support new multimedia services, location-based service providers are building critical mass. Since there are 10 to 20 times more mobile phones sold than any other consumer electronics device, wireless is a huge driver for GPS adoption.

- **Mobile advertising.** Major brands are shifting from basic SMS marketing to more sophisticated multimedia advertising. RBC Capital Markets expects mobile marketing revenues to balloon from $45 million in 2005 to $1.5 billion by 2010. With the technological ability to target and measure the effectiveness of mobile advertising, brands are more strategic in their approach. Rich 3G content and video services and accuracy advancements in GPS-based location services deliver further value to brands targeting existing and potential customers in innovative ways.

- **Wireless providers move into home entertainment.** Mobile makes headway against fixed broadband operators, which have dominated Internet and cheaper voice service provision in the home. Wi-fi will remain the primary wireless access technology. The fixed operators may be strengthened by wi-fi capabilities in consumer electronics devices (set-top boxes, game consoles, and MP3 players) that enable cost-effective content downloads.

- **Wireless security moves to the forefront.** There is a monumental need to put strong security measures in place. This could be the year that hackers really start paying attention to millions of wireless devices, the growth in mobile data usage, and vulnerable points between mobile and fixed networks. CIOs consistently cite security as their number one concern in extending network access to wireless devices. Attacks, viruses, and data security now exceed device loss or theft as concerns. Emerging services, such as VoIP and mobile payments, provide additional challenges. Vulnerabilities directly affect the bottom line, corporate image, regulatory compliance, and competitive advantage.

- **Enterprise mobility.** Enterprises can't resist the convenient, reliable, attractively priced, bundled mobile solutions entering the market. Corporations switch from phones to mobile computers for transactions, data collection, and messaging for a wide variety of employees. Many voice communications processes, such as order placement and delivery notifications, dispatch operations, and remote asset monitoring, continue to shift to wireless data to increase information access and field transaction volume across organizations. Many corporations will completely replace their cellular handsets with a combined voice/data device or a data-only device.[31]

SUMMARY OF KEY THEMES

The purpose of this chapter was to provide you, the business student, with a detailed overview of the various telecommunications technologies employed by organizations today. This included discussion on VoIP, business networks, network security, wireless fidelity, and mobile technologies. Organizations are taking advantage of these technologies in the information systems applications they are building. It is important to understand which technologies are available and how businesses can leverage these technologies in their daily and long-term strategic operations.

KEY TERMS

Bandwidth 244
Bluetooth 252
Broadband 244
Geographic information system
  (GIS) 257
Global positioning system
  (GPS) 256
Local area network (LAN) 239
Location-based services
  (LBS) 255

Metropolitan area network
  (MAN) 239
Microwave transmitter 253
Network 239
Radio frequency identification
  (RFID) 260
Satellite 253
Smartphone 252
Telecommunication system 239

Valued-added network
  (VAN) 243
Virtual private network
  (VPN) 243
Voice over IP (VoIP) 240
Wide area network (WAN) 239
WiMAX 260
Wireless fidelity (wi-fi) 258

CLOSING CASE ONE

Public Safety

Located 80 miles northeast of Salt Lake City, Logan, Utah, has a population of over 45,000 residents and spans 16.8 square miles. With 50 officers and additional support personnel, the Logan City Police Department is the primary law enforcement agency for the city, responding to more than 20,000 incidents a year.

The police department was looking for a way to improve communications for officers on patrol. Although the squad cars were already equipped with laptops, they lacked the capability to communicate via the Internet. The department wanted a secure way to provide access to online departmental resources and the benefits of real-time communication that would improve the productivity, efficiency, and safety of officers in the field.

The department had an existing, proprietary 19.2 Kbps wireless network for computer-aided dispatching. The slow speed of this network constrained the department from deploying new applications that required greater bandwidth, so the department implemented a number of wi-fi hotspots throughout the city. However, this created another problem for the users. Officers would need to manually disconnect from the low-speed network and connect to the higher speed wi-fi hotspots to access the department's email and field reporting systems. This added complexity made the new system difficult to use. More importantly, the city's IT department was very concerned about the implications of opening the network to potential hackers, viruses, Internet worms, and other external network security threats.

The Logan police department installed a mobile VPN, meeting the city's three main requirements: security, reliability, and ease of use for the officer in the field. The mobile VPN provides features traditionally found in VPNs—strong encryption and authentication security, based on the industry standard. However, while traditional VPNs are designed for either point-to-point connections or stationary users connecting from remote locations, the mobile VPN solution is designed specifically for the mobile workforce. By using a secured mobile VPN, the City of Logan is able to realize the benefits of new wireless technology without compromising network security.

By providing its officers with better access to information—real-time field reporting, database queries, and bi-directional communication—officers can spend more time protecting the public. In addition to time savings, there was a significant improvement in the flow of information. With real-time communication across any available wireless network connection, reports can be filed immediately after an incident, instead of hours later when an officer returns from patrol. Police officers are more productive and accurate in their work, which in turn creates a safer community.[32]

Questions

1. What business value does the city receive from deploying a wireless network for its police department?
2. Identify and describe the principal telecommunication and network technologies the police department is using.
3. What security risks must the police department be aware of in using wireless technology and what precautions should it be taking to ensure electronic protection?
4. How could the police department use RFID, WiMAX, and some of the other technologies discussed in this chapter to create efficiencies?

CLOSING CASE TWO

UPS versus FedEx: Head-to-Head on Wireless

Federal Express and United Parcel Service are always seeking a competitive edge over one another. And as the two companies are encroaching on each other's primary businesses (UPS on overnight delivery and FedEx on ground delivery), they are concurrently stepping up their wireless deployments as well. The reason: operational efficiency—a critical business requirement aimed at shaving costs, increasing reach, and doing more with the same resources.

Their approaches to deploying wireless technologies over the past 15 years have been markedly different. FedEx has led the way with cutting-edge applications, while UPS has been slower and more deliberate. FedEx deploys new technologies as soon as it can justify the cost and demonstrate improved efficiencies and customer benefit. UPS refreshes its technology base roughly every five to seven years, when it rolls out a unified system in stages that it synchronizes with the life span of the older system. But the goal is the same for both companies:

to use next-generation wireless technologies to better manage the delivery of millions of packages that flow through dozens of sorting facilities every day.

The two companies are exploiting new wireless technologies in their differing attempts at aiding the two main components of their operations: pickup/delivery and packaging/sorting. Both are also looking ahead to potential applications of radio frequency identification and GPS wireless technologies.

	UPS	FedEx
Main hub	Louisville, Kentucky	Memphis, Tennessee
Total packages handled each day	13.6 million	5 million
Number of air deliveries daily	2 million	3.1 million
Wireless devices in field	90,000	80,000
Wireless devices in sorting facilities	55,000	70,000
Wireless access points	9,000	5,000

Seeking New Benefits from Wireless

In addition to their major package-scanning retooling efforts, FedEx and UPS continue to investigate what business benefits they might gain from other wireless technologies. Two have gained particular attention: RFID tags, which could replace bar code scanners, and GPS, which can precisely locate field units.

As UPS and FedEx are showing, wireless technology provides the medium through which dynamic exchange happens. Interconnectedness allows drivers to talk, computers to interact, and businesses to work together. Whether it is wireless routing or fueling of trucks, it is all happening dynamically. Although few companies have the scale of UPS and FedEx, they can adopt many of the wireless technologies scaled to their size, and use devices and network components that fit their operations.[33]

Questions

1. Explain the fundamentals of wireless fidelity.
2. Describe the differences between UPS, and FedEx's use of wi-fi.
3. Identify two types of wireless business opportunities the companies could use to gain a competitive advantage.
4. How could RFID help the companies deal with potential security issues?
5. Develop a Bluetooth, GPS, or satellite product that the parcel delivery business could use to improve efficiencies.

CLOSING CASE THREE

Improving IT's Bedside Manner at Florida Hospital

Florida Hospital is an acute-care health care system providing more than 2,800 beds throughout Florida. With a comprehensive network of 17 hospitals and 12 Centra Care walk-in urgent care centers, Florida Hospital treats more than 1 million patient visits each year. In fact, the Florida Hospital system is the second-busiest in the United States. In addition, Florida Hospital is one of the largest Medicare providers in the country.

The health care organization offers a wide range of health services to the people it serves, including many nationally and internationally recognized programs in cardiology, oncology, gynecology, neurology, the treatment of diabetes, orthopedics, and physical rehabilitation. *U.S. News & World Report* has recognized Florida Hospital as one of "America's Best Hospitals."

Florida Hospital decided to expand its wireless network. For years nurses and doctors had been using the organization's conventional computer network to record and track patient information. However, such things as vital statistics and medication history had to be entered by hand, often at patient bedsides, and then typed into the computer system at nurses' stations or other computer locations away from a patient's room. The process had inherent disadvantages, mainly from retyping errors and difficulty quickly entering and accessing information. Also, doctors or nurses often need such information at the patient's bedside to assess progress and determine further treatment.

To move its advanced information technology systems closer to patients, Florida Hospital wanted to deploy a mobile patient care work cart and application. The mobile computing stations include laptops on specially designed, adjustable carts with electrical outlets and cords. The patient care application delivered over the mobile computing station covers three areas of patient information: intravenous (IV) administration history; vital statistics, such as blood pressure, heart rate and temperature; and X-ray and lab reports for services ordered for the patient.

To make these carts effective, Florida Hospital needed a wireless network. Previously it had been using a proprietary wireless system to bring patient case management files to nurses using laptop computers, but the system had become out-of-date, falling behind the rapid advances in wireless technology standards.

Hospitals could well be the most challenging environments to deploy wireless networks. The lead-lined walls of X-ray rooms, for example, block any radio signals from passing through. In addition, wireless signals must negotiate a phalanx of interference from wired medical diagnostic and monitoring devices.

Network security is an especially important issue for Florida Hospital—or any health care organization—because of the sensitivity of medical records. In addition, government regulations, such as the Health Insurance Portability and Accountability Act of 1996 (HIPAA), require hospitals to meet specific privacy and security safeguards. To ensure the security of its wireless LAN, Florida Hospital has deployed advanced access point detection.

The new wireless system brought other advantages as well. Hospital electrical power systems are highly regulated because of dangers from sparks igniting oxygen or other gases and chemicals used for patient care. Installing new power outlets for each of the 400 wireless access points would have been a major logistical and regulatory burden, greatly slowing the wireless network's deployment. Fortunately, by installing special technology to run electrical power over Ethernet cables, Florida Hospital eliminated the need for additional cabling, as well as avoiding regulatory concerns with power lines.

More than 14,670 total users currently access the wireless network, including bedside clinicians and other health care providers. Seven hundred wireless laptops are currently deployed across seven campuses for clinical purposes, and multiple highly integrated clinical applications are in use throughout the environment. Those hospital employees not using the WLAN for clinical data collection and recording generally use it for email and for other back-office functionality specific to their jobs. Thanks to the workflow advantages provided by the wireless technology, the quality of patient care has improved by allowing and facilitating more time for the clinician to be at the bedside.[34]

Questions

1. Explain how hospitals are using telecommunication and network technologies to improve their operations.

2. Identify a new telecommunication or network product that Florida Hospital could use to improve its operations.

3. Why is real-time information important to hospitals?

4. How is Florida Hospital using wireless technology to improve its operations?
5. Identify several wireless technologies that are changing the way businesses operate and explain how hospitals can use these technologies to improve their operations.

MAKING BUSINESS DECISIONS

1. Wireless fitness

Sandifer's Fitness Club is located in beautiful South Carolina. Rosie Sandifer has owned and operated the club for 20 years. The club has three outdoor pools, two indoor pools, 10 racquetball courts, 10 tennis courts, an indoor and outdoor track, along with a four-story exercise equipment and massage therapy building. Rosie has hired you as a summer intern specializing in information technology. The extent of Rosie's current technology includes a few PCs in the accounting department and two PCs with Internet access for the rest of the staff. Your first assignment is to create a report detailing networks and wireless technologies. The report should explain how the club could gain a business advantage by implementing a wireless network. If Rosie likes your report, she will hire you as the full-time employee in charge of information technology. Be sure to include all of the different uses for wireless devices the club could implement to improve its operations.

2. Secure access

Organizations that have traditionally maintained private, closed systems have begun to look at the potential of the Internet as a ready-made network resource. The Internet is inexpensive and globally pervasive: Every phone jack is a potential connection. However, the Internet lacks security. What obstacles must organizations overcome to allow secure network connections?

3. Integrating wireless worlds

Tele-Messaging is a next-generation integrated Internet and wireless messaging service that offers services to ISPs, telecommunications carriers, and portal companies. According to Tele-Messaging's research, the primary reason that 90 percent of the people go online is for email. However, the challenge for Tele-Messaging is how to successfully attract and retain these customers. Customers want more than free calls to sign up and are looking for a host of additional services with whiz-bang technology to give them the information they want, when they want it, anywhere, and in the method most convenient to them. List the infrastructures needed to deliver the technology with the necessary reliability, availability, and scalability demanded by Tele-Messaging's customers.

4. Shipment routes

Mary Conzachi works in planning for Loadstar, a large trucking company and barge operator in the Midwest. She has looked into a variety of systems to keep track of the location of trucks and barges so that the company can route shipments better and answer customer inquiries faster. Mary's major concern is with the trucks; the barges have commodities and take weeks to move something. She states that it is much harder to keep up with trucking. Mary has collected information on a variety of products that can help track trucks. For example, the GPS service used for air and marine navigation would allow Loadstar to pinpoint the exact location of a truck. Loadstar would need a system that could identify the truck and send the ID and GPS data to headquarters.

Another possibility is to use a cellular phone in each truck and have the driver call in at certain hours. Mary said she didn't need to know that a truck is at a certain latitude and longitude. If the driver says he or she is at milepost 50 on Interstate 80 in Nebraska, that's good enough. What solution do you recommend? Why?

5. Network analysis

Global Manufacturing is considering a new technology application. The company wants to process orders in a central location and then assign production to different plants. Each plant will operate its own production scheduling and control system. Data on work in process and completed assemblies will be transmitted back to the central location that processes orders.

At each plant, Global uses personal computers that perform routine applications such as payroll and accounting. The production scheduling and control systems will be a package program running on a new computer dedicated to this application. Global has a high-level systems design for data transmission from the central computer to the plants and for the plant data to be transmitted back to central planning.

The systems staff at Global has retained you as a consultant to help with further analysis. What kind of computer configuration seems most appropriate? What kind of transmission network is needed? What data should be collected? Prepare a plan showing the information Global must develop in order to establish this telecommunications system. Should Global use a private network or can it accomplish its objectives through the Internet?

APPLY YOUR KNOWLEDGE

1. GoGo Gadgets

Now that wi-fi and other types of high-speed wireless networks are becoming common, devices using that technology are multiplying rapidly. Wireless gadgets run the gamut from cell phones to kitchen appliances and digital cameras. Here are some of the hottest new wireless broadband gadgets.

- Samsung's $3,499 POPCON refrigerator will feature a wi-fi enabled, detachable screen that can function as a TV. The fridge also can be programmed to remember products' expiration dates and generate alerts when the milk is getting old.
- The Nokia 770 Internet Tablet is small enough to fit in a pocket. It comes with a 4.13-inch-wide touch screen that can be used to access the web over a wi-fi network. The $350 device can also access the web via a cell phone with a Bluetooth connection.
- Motorola's latest E815 mobile phone operates over Verizon Wireless's new EVDO (Evolution Data Optimized) wireless network, offering speeds comparable to digital subscriber line (DSL). The phone can even record and play back video clips. It also features a built-in MP3 digital music player.
- Hop-On's HOP 1515 may look like a typical cell phone, but it actually makes calls over wi-fi networks. Typically sold with a $20 to $30 monthly service plan, the phone allows for unlimited over-the-web international and long-distance calling. The $39 HOP 1515 is sold through wi-fi hotspot operators, wireless carriers, and retailers.
- Eastman Kodak's EasyShare-One is a digital camera with wi-fi capabilities, allowing users to share their snapshots wirelessly. You will be able to snap a photo and immediately show it to a friend on a wi-fi-enabled PC or TV.

Project Focus

A dizzying array of new wireless technologies now promises to make today's wi-fi networks seem like poky dial-up connections by comparison. These new technologies will extend the reach of wireless networks, not just geographically but also into new uses in the home and office.

a. Research the Internet and discover new wireless devices that entrepreneurs and established companies can use to improve their business.

b. Explain how businesses can use these devices to create competitive advantages, streamline production, and improve productivity.

2. WAP

Wireless Internet access is quickly gaining popularity among people seeking high-speed Internet connections when they are away from their home or office. The signal from a typical wireless access point (WAP) only extends for about 300 feet in any direction, so the user must find a hotspot to be able to access the Internet while on the road. Sometimes hotspots are available for free or for a small fee.

You work for a sales company, SalesTek, which has a sales force of 25 representatives and customers concentrated in Denver, Colorado; Salt Lake City, Utah; and Santa Fe, New Mexico. Your sales representatives are constantly on the road and they require 24x7 Internet access.

Project Focus

You have been asked to find hotspots for your colleagues to connect while they are on the road. It is critical that your sales force can access the Internet 24x7 to connect with customers, suppliers, and the corporate office. Create a document detailing how your mobile workforce will be able to stay connected to the Internet while traveling. Here are a few tips to get you started:

a. Use websites such as www.wifinder.com and www.jiwire.com to determine which commercial hotspots would be the most appropriate for your sales force and the commercial network service that these hotspots use.

b. Research the websites of two or three commercial networks that seem most appropriate to discover more about pricing and services. (Hint: T-Mobile is one example.)

c. Use www.wifinder.com and www.wififreespot.com to determine how many free public hotspots are available in these cities. Are there enough for your company to rely on them or should you use a commercial wi-fi system. If so, which one?

d. You might also research www.fon.com to see alternative methods of using home broadband connections to stay connected.

3. The Virtualization Opportunity

Virtualization makes good business sense. Organizations recognize the opportunity to use virtualization to break down the silos that keep applications from sharing infrastructure and that contribute to chronic underutilization of IT resources. Virtualization can help an organization simultaneously reduce costs, increase agility, and make IT more responsive to the needs of the business. So for many organizations, the question is not, "Should we virtualize?" Instead, the question is, "How can we transition to a virtualized environment in a predictable, cost-effective manner?"

Project Focus

You are the CFO for Martello's, a food distribution organization with locations in Chicago, New York, and San Francisco. Your CIO, Jeff Greenwald, has given you a proposal for a budget of $2 million to convert the organization to a virtualized environment. You are unfamiliar with virtualization, how it works, and the long-term goals it will satisfy for the company. You have a meeting with Jeff tomorrow and you want to be able to discuss his proposal. Use the Internet to research virtualization to prepare for your meeting. Once you have a solid understanding of virtualization create a report detailing your decision to grant or deny Jeff's budget proposal.

4. Securing Your Home Wireless Network

These days wireless networking products are so ubiquitous and inexpensive that anyone can easily build a wireless network with less than $100 worth of equipment. However, wireless networks are exactly that—wireless—they do not stop at walls. In fact, wireless networks often carry signals more than 300 feet from the wireless router. Living in an apartment, dorm, condominium, or house means that you might have dozens of neighbors who can access your wireless network.

It is one thing to let a neighbor borrow a lawn mower, but it is another thing to allow a neighbor to access a home wireless network. There are several good reasons for not sharing a home wireless network including:

- Slow down Internet performance.
- Allow others to view files on your computers and spread dangerous software such as viruses.
- Allow others to monitor the websites you visit, read your email and instant messages as they travel across the network, and copy your usernames and passwords.
- Allow others to send spam or perform illegal activities with your Internet connection.

Project Focus

Securing a home wireless network is invaluable and allows you to enable security features that can make it difficult for uninvited guests to connect through your wireless network. Create a document detailing all of the features you can use to secure a home wireless network.

5. Weather Bots

Warren Jackson, an engineering graduate student at the University of Pennsylvania, was not interested in the weather until he started investigating how the National Weather Service collected weather data. The weather service has collected most of its information using weather balloons that carry a device to measure items like pressure, wind, and humidity. When the balloon reaches about 100,000 feet and pressure causes it to pop, the device falls and lands a substantial distance from its launch point. The National Weather Service and researchers sometimes look for the $200 device, but of the 80,000 sent up annually, they write-off many as lost.

Convinced there had to be a better way, Jackson began designing a GPS-equipped robot that launches a parachute after the balloon pops, and brings the device back down to Earth, landing it at a predetermined location set by the researchers. The idea is so inventive that the Penn's Weiss Tech House—a university organization that encourages students to innovate and bring their ideas to market—awarded Jackson and some fellow graduate engineering student's first prize in its third annual PennVention Contest. Jackson won $5,000, and access to expert advice on prototyping, legal matters, and branding.

Project Focus

GPS and GIS can be used in all sorts of devices, in many different industries, for multiple purposes. You want to compete, and win first prize, in the PennVention next year. Create a product, using a GPS or GIS, that is not currently in the market today that you will present at the fourth annual PennVention.

6. Wireless Networks and Streetlamps

Researchers at Harvard University and BBN Technologies have designed CitySense, a wireless network capable of reporting real-time sensor data across the entire city of Cambridge, Massachusetts. CitySense is unique because it solves a constraint on previous wireless networks—battery life. The network mounts each node on a municipal streetlamp, where it draws power from city electricity. Researchers plan to install 100 sensors on streetlamps throughout Cambridge by 2011, using a grant from the National Science Foundation. Each node will include an embedded PC running the Linux OS, an 802.11 wi-fi interface, and weather sensors.

One of the challenges in the design was how the network would allow remote nodes to communicate with the central server at Harvard and BBN. CitySense will do that by letting each node form a mesh with its neighbors, exchanging data through multiple-hop links. This strategy allows a node to download software or upload sensor data to a distant server hub using a small radio with only a 1-kilometer range.

Project Focus

You are responsible for deploying a CitySense network around your city. What goals would you have for the system besides monitoring urban weather and pollution? What other benefits could a CitySense network provide? How could local businesses and citizens benefit from the network? What legal and ethical concerns should you understand before deploying the network? What can you do to protect your network and your city from these issues?

BUSINESS DRIVEN BEST SELLERS

The Power Of Mobility, By Russell McGuire (Hoboken, NJ: John Wiley & Sons, 2007).

Over 80 percent of Americans above the age of five own a cell phone, most with digital cameras built in, and bundled with an email service specifically designed for sending those captured moments to friends and family. These consumer applications are just simple examples of mobility being built in to everyday products to create tremendous new value. From a business perspective, a new technology can introduce radical changes—changes so dramatic that they fundamentally shift the nature of the business, the nature of the product, and the reasons customers buy the product. When this happens, the rules of competition change. It is happening now: The age of mobility is upon us. How will it impact you and your business in the months and years to come?

The Power of Mobility shows you how to look forward, envision the power of mobility in your business, and implement the steps required to turn vision into reality. Russell McGuire, one of the telecom industry's leading strategists, details the specific actions you must take to deliver the tremendous value that mobility adds—and win customers' hearts and wallets. He presents a powerful framework for capturing the power of mobility: the seven steps. If you can digitize, connect, evaluate, limit, position, protect, and learn, you will capture the power of mobility in your products, your services, and your processes. He further clarifies the power of the seven steps with illustrative case studies of seven companies that have successfully implemented this framework and redefined the rules of competition in their industries.

The mobility age represents a great opportunity for businesses large and small to capture the power of mobility to create competitive differentiation and to take market share. Stories of businesses that have been crushed by the competition because they have denied the changes brought by technologies in the past will likely be repeated. You have a choice. You can wait for a competitor to lead and define the rules to his benefit and your demise. Or you can lead and set the rules—if you capture the power of mobility now.[35]

Into the Unknown: Leadership Lessons from Lewis and Clark's Daring Westward Expedition. By Jack Uldrich (New York: AMACOM, 2004).

Latching onto the idea that everything old is new again, Jack Uldrich, a former naval officer and author of *The Next Big Thing Is Really Small,* puts forth Lewis and Clark as two shining examples of all that is right with leadership and management. Spotlighting the pair's many strong points, from people skills and future-thinking capabilities to optimism and an ability to see the forest as well as the trees, Uldrich (drawing on what has obviously been years of extensive research) points to modern-day companies such as Coca-Cola, General Electric, and DaimlerChrysler as entities that could all learn something from Lewis and Clark.

Whether the "project" is a westward expedition or a hostile corporate takeover, Uldrich makes the case that the past is not so different from the present—or from the future—especially when concerning new technologies. The parallels between these men and today's leaders are intriguing and well thought out. For corporate types looking for tips, there is certainly plenty to digest. The overriding messages are clear: mentor and be mentored; find a way to balance the task at hand with the overall future vision; maintain a confident and optimistic approach from the beginning.[36]

Enterprise Information Systems

Organizations utilize various types of information systems to help run their daily operations. These are primarily transactional systems that concentrate on the management and flow of low-level data items pertaining to basic business processes such as purchasing and order delivery. The data are often rolled up and summarized into higher-level decision support systems to help firms understand what is happening in their organizations and how best to respond. To achieve seamless handling of the data, organizations must ensure that their enterprise information systems are tightly integrated. Doing so allows organizations to manage and process basic business processes as efficiently and effectively as possible and to make better informed decisions.

This module highlights the various types of enterprise information systems found in organizations and collaborative tools employees can use to facilitate communication and knowledge sharing. The chapters speak to various types of enterprise information systems and their role in helping firms reach their strategic goals. Though each chapter is devoted to specific types of enterprise systems, these systems must work in tandem with each other, giving enterprisewide views or 360-degree views of the business. Organizations that can correlate and summarize enterprisewide information are prepared to meet their strategic business goals and outperform their competitors.

Operations Management and Supply Chain Management

8

CHAPTER

CHAPTER OUTLINE

What's in IT for me?

Information technology can be used to revolutionize and transform operations and supply chain management processes. Information systems enable companies to better manage the flow of information, materials, and financial payments that occurs between and among stages in a supply chain to maximize total supply chain effectiveness and profitability.

You, as a business student, need to know the significance of a supply chain to organizational success and the critical role information technology plays in ensuring smooth operations of a supply chain. A supply chain consists of all direct and indirect parties involved in the procurement of a product or raw material. These parties can be internal groups or departments within an organization or external partner companies and end customers.

This chapter emphasizes the important role information technology plays in providing an underlying infrastructure and coordination mechanisms needed for operations management and supply chains to function as effectively and efficiently as possible. Knowing this you will appreciate and understand the capabilities and limitations of operations management, the benefits and challenges of supply chain management, as well as future trends where information systems will play a critical part.

Dell's Famous Supply Chain

Speed is at the core of everything Dell does. Dell assembles nearly 80,000 computers every 24 hours. The computer manufacturer has done more than any other company when it comes to tweaking its supply chain. About 10 years ago, Dell carried 20 to 25 days of inventory in a sprawling network of warehouses. Today, Dell does not have a single warehouse and carries only two hours of inventory in its factories and a maximum of just 72 hours across its entire operation. Dell's vast, global supply chain is in constant overdrive, making the company one of the fastest, most hyperefficient organizations on the planet.

Disaster Occurs

In 2002, a 10-day labor lockout shut down 29 West Coast ports extending from Los Angeles to Seattle, idled 10,000 union dockworkers, and blocked hundreds of cargo ships from unloading raw materials and finished goods. The port closings paralyzed global supply chains and ultimately cost U.S. consumers and businesses billions of dollars.

Analysts expected Dell, with its just-in-time manufacturing model, would be especially hard hit when parts failed to reach its two U.S.-based factories. Without warehouses filled with motherboards and hard drives, the world's largest PC maker would simply find itself with nothing to sell within a matter of days. Dell knew all too well that its ultra-lean, high-speed business model left it vulnerable to just such a situation. "When a labor problem or an earthquake or a SARS epidemic breaks out, we've got to react quicker than anyone else," said Dick Hunter, the company's supply chain expert. "There's no other choice. We know these things are going to happen; we must move fast to fix them. We just can't tolerate any kind of delay."

Fortunately, the same culture of speed and flexibility that seems to put Dell at the mercy of disruptions also helps it deal with them. Dell was in constant, round-the-clock communication with its parts makers in Taiwan, China, and Malaysia and its U.S.-based shipping partners. Hunter dispatched a "tiger team" of 10 logistics specialists to Long Beach, California, and other ports; they worked with Dell's carrying and freight-forwarding networks to assemble a contingency plan.

When the tiger team confirmed that the closings were all but certain, Dell moved into high gear. It chartered 18 airplanes (747s) from UPS, Northwest Airlines, and China Airlines. A 747 holds the equivalent of 10 tractor-trailers—enough parts to manufacture 10,000 PCs. The bidding for the planes grew fierce, running as high as $1 million for a one-way flight from Asia to the West Coast. Dell got in the bidding early and kept costs around $500,000 per plane. Dell also worked with its Asia-based suppliers to ensure that its parts were always at the Shanghai and Taipei airports in time for its returning charters to land, reload, refuel, and take off. The company was consistently able to get its planes to the United States and back within 33 hours, which kept its costs down and its supply chain moving.

Meanwhile, Dell had people on the ground in every major harbor. In Asia, the freight specialists saw to it that Dell's parts were the last to be loaded onto each cargo ship so they would be unloaded first when the ship hit the West Coast. The biggest test came when the ports reopened and companies scrambled to sort through the backed-up mess of thousands of containers. Hunter's tiger team had anticipated this logistical nightmare. Even though Dell had PC components in hundreds of containers on 50 ships, it knew the exact moment when each component cycled through the harbor, and it was among the first to unload its parts and speed them to its factories in Austin, Texas, and Nashville, Tennessee. In the end, Dell did the impossible: It survived a 10-day supply chain blackout with roughly 72 hours of inventory without delaying a single customer order.

The aftershocks of the port closings reverberated for weeks. Many companies began to question the wisdom of running so lean in an uncertain world, and demand for warehouse space soared as they piled up buffer inventory to insure against labor unrest, natural disasters, and terrorist attacks.

Building a "Dell-like" Supply Chain

Dell's ultimate competitive weapon is speed, which gives the technical giant's bottom line a real boost. Figure 8.1 displays a five-point plan for building a fast supply chain—direct from Dell.[1]

FIGURE 8.1

How to Build a Dell-Like
Supply Chain

Dell-Like Supply Chain Plan
1. **The supply chain starts with the customer.** By cutting out retailers and selling directly to its customers, Dell is in a far better position to forecast real customer demand.
2. **Replace inventory with information.** To operate with close to zero inventory, Dell communicates constantly with its suppliers. It sends out status updates three times a day from its assembly plants; every week it updates its quarterly demand forecasts. By making communication its highest priority, Dell ensures the lowest possible inventory.
3. **If you cannot measure it, you cannot manage it.** Dell knows what works because it measures everything from days in inventory to the time it takes to build a PC. As Dell slashed those numbers, it got more efficient.
4. **Complexity slows you down.** Dell cut the number of its core PC suppliers from several hundred to about 25. It standardized critical PC components, which streamlined its manufacturing. Dell got faster by making things simpler.
5. **Create a watershed mind-set.** Dell is not content with incremental improvement; it demands massive change. Each year, it wants its Austin-based PC-assembly plant—already very fast—to improve production by 30 percent. "You don't get a big result if you do not challenge people with big goals," Dell CEO Kevin Rollins said.

INTRODUCTION

Production is the creation of goods and services using the factors of production: land, labor, capital, entrepreneurship, and knowledge. Production has historically been associated with manufacturing, but the nature of business has changed significantly in the last 20 years. The service sector, especially Internet services, has grown dramatically. The United States now has what is called a service economy—that is, one dominated by the service sector.

Organizations that excel in operations management, specifically supply chain management, perform better in almost every financial measure of success, according to a report from Boston-based AMR Research Inc. When supply chain excellence improves operations, companies experience a 5 percent higher profit margin, 15 percent less inventory, 17 percent stronger "perfect order" ratings, and 35 percent shorter cycle times than their competitors. "The basis of competition for winning companies in today's economy is supply chain superiority," said Kevin O'Marah, vice president of research at AMR Research. "These companies understand that value chain performance translates to productivity and market-share leadership. They also understand that supply chain leadership means more than just low costs and efficiency: It requires a superior ability to shape and respond to shifts in demand with innovative products and services."[2]

Collecting, analyzing, and distributing transactional information to all relevant parties, supply chain management (SCM) systems help all the different entities in the supply chain work together more effectively. SCM systems provide dynamic holistic views of organizations. Users can "drill down" into detailed analyses of supply chain activities to find valuable information on the organizational operations. This chapter explores the details of operations management and supply chain management.

LILL 1154

section 8.1 OPERATIONS MANAGEMENT

LEARNING OUTCOMES

8.1. Define the term operations management.

8.2. Explain operations management's role in business.

8.3. Describe the correlation between operations management and information technology.

8.4. Describe the five characteristics of competitive priorities.

8.5. Explain supply chain management and its role in a business.

OPERATIONS MANAGEMENT FUNDAMENTALS

Books, DVDs, downloaded MP3s, and dental and medical procedures are all examples of goods and services. *Production management* describes all the activities managers do to help companies create goods. To reflect the change in importance from manufacturing to services, the term production often has been replaced by operations to reflect the manufacturing of both goods and services. *Operations management (OM)* is the management of systems or processes that convert or transform resources (including human resources) into goods and services. Operations management is responsible for managing the core processes used to manufacture goods and produce services.

Essentially, the creation of goods or services involves transforming or converting inputs into outputs. Various inputs such as capital, labor, and information are used to create goods or services using one or more transformation processes (e.g., storing, transporting, and cutting). A *transformation process* is often referred to as the technical core, especially in manufacturing organizations, and is the actual conversion of inputs to outputs. To ensure that the desired outputs are obtained, an organization takes measurements at various points in the transformation process (feedback) and

FIGURE 8.2

Operations Involves the Conversion of Inputs into Outputs

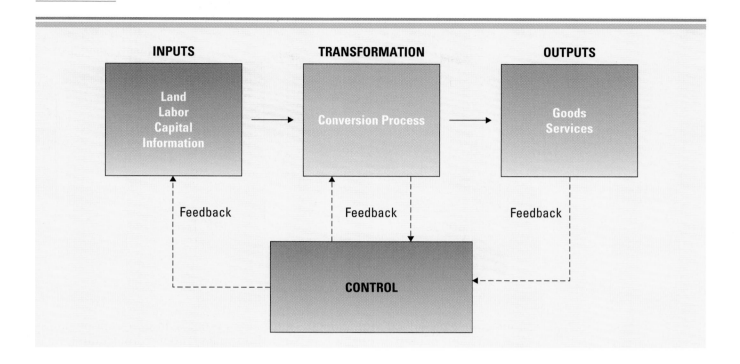

then compares them with previously established standards to determine whether corrective action is needed (control). Figure 8.2 depicts the conversion system.[3]

Figure 8.3 displays examples of inputs, transformation processes, and outputs. Although goods and services are listed separately in Figure 8.2 it is important to note that goods and services often occur jointly. For example, having the oil changed in a car is a service, but the oil that is delivered is a good. Similarly, house painting is a service, but the paint is a good. The goods–service combination is a continuum. It ranges from primarily goods with little service to primarily service with few goods (see Figure 8.4). There are relatively few pure goods or pure services; therefore, organizations typically sell product packages, which are a combination of goods and services. This makes managing operations more interesting, and also more challenging.[4]

Value-added is the term used to describe the difference between the cost of inputs and the value of price of outputs. OM is critical to an organization because of its ability

FIGURE 8.3

Examples of Inputs, Transformation, and Outputs

Inputs	Transformation	Outputs
Restaurant inputs include hungry customers, food, wait staff	Well-prepared food, well served: agreeable environment	Satisfied customers
Hospital inputs include patients, medical supplies, doctors, nurses	Health care	Healthy individuals
Automobile inputs include sheet steel, engine parts, tires	Fabrication and assembly of cars	High-quality cars
College inputs include high school graduates, books, professors, classrooms	Imparting knowledge and skills	Educated individuals
Distribution center inputs include stock keeping units, storage bins, workers	Storage and redistribution	Fast delivery of available products

OM

to increase value-added during the transformation process. In nonprofit organizations, the value of outputs (highway construction, police, and fire protection) is their value to society; the greater the value-added, the greater the effectiveness of the operations. In for-profit organizations, the value of outputs is measured by the prices that customers are willing to pay for those goods or services. Firms use the money generated by value-added for research and development, investment in new facilities and equipment, worker salaries, and profits. Consequently, the greater the value-added, the greater the amount of funds available for these important activities.

OM IN BUSINESS

The scope of OM ranges across the organization and includes many interrelated activities, such as forecasting, capacity planning, scheduling, managing inventories, assuring quality, motivating employees, deciding where to locate facilities, and more.

Reviewing the activities performed in an airline company makes it easy to understand how a service organization's OM team adds value. The company consists of the airplanes, airport facilities, and maintenance facilities, and typical OM activities include:

- **Forecasting:** Estimating seat demand for flights, weather and landing conditions, and estimates for growth or reduction in air travel are all included in forecasting.
- **Capacity planning:** This is the key essential metric for the airline to maintain cash flow and increase revenues. Underestimating or overestimating flights will hurt profits.
- **Scheduling:** The airline operates on tight schedules that must be maintained including flights, pilots, flight attendants, ground crews, baggage handlers, and routine maintenance.
- **Managing inventory:** Inventory of such items as foods, beverages, first-aid equipment, in-flight magazines, pillows, blankets, and life jackets is essential for the airline.
- **Assuring quality:** Quality is indispensable in an airline where safety is the highest priority. Today's travelers expect high-quality customer service during ticketing, check-in, curb service, and unexpected issues where the emphasis is on efficiency and courtesy.

- **Motivating and training employees:** Airline employees must be highly trained and continually motivated, especially when dealing with frustrated airline travelers.
- **Locating facilities:** Key questions facing airlines include which cities to offer services, where to host maintenance facilities, and where to locate major and minor hubs.[5]

Opposite from an airline is a bike factory, which is typically an assembly operation: buying components such as frames, tires, wheels, gears, and other items from suppliers, and then assembling bicycles. A bike factory also does some of the fabrication work itself, forming frames and making the gears and chains. Obviously, an airline company and a bike factory are completely different types of operations. One is primarily a service operation, the other a producer of goods. Nonetheless, these two operations have much in common. The same as the airline, the bike factory must schedule production, deal with components, order parts and materials, schedule and train employees, ensure quality standards are met, and above all satisfy customers. In both organizations, the success of the business depends on short- and long-term planning and the ability of its executives and managers to make informed decisions.[6]

IT'S ROLE IN OM

Managers can use IT to heavily influence OM decisions including productivity, costs, flexibility, quality, and customer satisfaction. One of the greatest benefits of IT on OM is in making operational decisions because operations management exerts considerable influence over the degree to which the goals and objectives of the organization are realized. Most OM decisions involve many possible alternatives that can have varying impacts on revenues and expenses. OM information systems are critical for managers to be able to make well-informed decisions.

Decision support systems and *executive information systems* can help an organization perform what-if analysis, sensitivity analysis, drill-down, and consolidation. Numerous managerial and strategic key decisions are based on OM information systems that affect the entire organization, including:

- **What:** What resources will be needed, and in what amounts?
- **When:** When will each resource be needed? When should the work be scheduled? When should materials and other supplies be ordered? When is corrective action needed?
- **Where:** Where will the work be performed?
- **How:** How will the product or service be designed? How will the work be done (organization, methods, equipment)? How will resources be allocated?
- **Who:** Who will perform the work?

OM Strategic Business Systems

UPS uses package flow information systems at each of its locations. The custom-built systems combine operations strategy and mapping technology to optimize the way boxes are loaded and delivered. The goal is to use the package flow software to cut the distance that delivery trucks travel by more than 100 million miles each year. The project will also help UPS streamline the profitability of each of its facility locations.[7]

Operations strategy is concerned with the development of a long-term plan for determining how to best utilize the major resources of the firm so that there is a high degree of compatibility between these resources and the firm's long-term corporate strategy. Operations strategy addresses very broad questions about how these major resources should be configured to achieve the desired corporate objectives. Some of the major long-term issues addressed in operations strategy include:

- How big to make the facilities?
- Where to locate the facilities?

FIGURE 8.5

Hierarchy of Operational Planning

Type of Planning	Time Frame	Issues	Decisions	Systems
Strategic Planning	Long range	Plant size, location, type of processes	How will we make the products? Where do we locate the facility or facilities? How much capacity do we require? When should we add additional capacity?	Materials requirement planning (MRP) systems
Tactical Planning	Intermediate range	Workforce size, material requirements	How many workers do we need? When do we need them? Should we work overtime or put on a section shift? When should we have material delivered? Should we have a finished goods inventory?	Global inventory management systems
Operational Planning and Control (OP&C)	Short range	Daily scheduling of employees, jobs, and equipment, process management, inventory management	What jobs do we work on today or this week? To whom do we assign what tasks? What jobs have priority?	Inventory management and control systems, transportation planning systems, distribution management systems

- When to build additional facilities?
- What type of process(es) to install to make the products?

Each of these issues can be addressed by OM decision support systems. In developing an operations strategy, management needs to consider many factors. These include (*a*) the level of technology that is or will be available, (*b*) the required skill levels of the workers, and (*c*) the degree of vertical integration, in terms of the extent to which outside suppliers are used.

Today, many organizations, especially larger conglomerates, operate in terms of **strategic business units (SBUs),** which consist of several stand-alone businesses. When companies become really large, they are best thought of as being composed of a number of businesses (or SBUs). As displayed in Figure 8.5, operations strategy supports the long-range strategy developed at the SBU level.[8]

Decisions at the SBU level focus on being effective, that is, "on doing the right things." These decisions are sometimes referred to as **strategic planning,** which focuses on long range planning such as plant size, location, and type of process to be used. The primary system used for strategic planning is a materials requirement planning system. **Materials requirement planning (MRP) systems** use sales forecasts to make sure that needed parts and materials are available at the right time and place in a specific company. The latest version of MRP is enterprise resource planning, which is discussed in detail in Chapter 10.[9]

Strategic decisions impact intermediate-range decisions, often referred to as tactical planning, which focuses on being efficient, that is, "doing things right." **Tactical planning** focuses on producing goods and services as efficiently as possible within the strategic plan. Here the emphasis is on producing quality products, including when material should be delivered, when products should be made to best meet demand, and what size the workforce should be. One of the primary systems used in tactical planning includes global inventory management. **Global inventory management systems** provide the ability to locate, track, and predict the movement of every component or material anywhere upstream or downstream in the production process. This allows an organization to locate and analyze its inventory anywhere in its production process.[10]

Finally, **operational planning and control (OP&C)** deals with the day-to-day procedures for performing work, including scheduling, inventory, and process management. **Inventory management and control systems** provide control and visibility to the status of individual items maintained in inventory. The software maintains inventory record accuracy, generates material requirements for all purchased items, and analyzes inventory performance. Inventory management and control software provides organizations with the information from a variety of sources including:

- Current inventory and order status.
- Cost accounting.
- Sales forecasts and customer orders.
- Manufacturing capacity.
- New-product introductions.[11]

Two additional OP&C systems include transportation planning and distribution management. **_Transportation planning systems_** track and analyze the movement of materials and products to ensure the delivery of materials and finished goods at the right time, the right place, and the lowest cost. **_Distribution management systems_** coordinate the process of transporting materials from a manufacturer to distribution centers to the final customers. Transportation routes directly affect the speed and cost of delivery. An organization will use these systems to help it decide if it wants to use an effectiveness route and ship its products directly to its customers or use an efficiency route and ship its products to a distributor that ships the products to customers.

COMPETITIVE OM STRATEGY

The key to developing a competitive OM strategy lies in understanding how to create value-added goods and services for customers. Specifically, value is added through the competitive priority or priorities that are selected to support a given strategy. Five key competitive priorities translate directly into characteristics that are used to describe various processes by which a company can add value to its OM decisions including:

1. Cost
2. Quality
3. Delivery
4. Flexibility
5. Service[12]

OM Strategy

Cost

Every industry has low-cost providers. However, being the low-cost producer does not always guarantee profitability and success. Products sold strictly on the basis of cost are typically commodity-like products including such goods as flour, petroleum, and sugar. In other words, customers cannot distinguish the products made by one firm from those of another. As a result, customers use cost as the primary determinant in making a purchasing decision.

Low-cost market segments are frequently very large, and many companies are lured by the potential for significant profits, which are associated with large unit volumes of product. As a consequence, the competition in this segment is exceedingly fierce—and so is the failure rate. After all, there can be only one lowest-cost producer, and that firm usually establishes the selling price in the market.

Quality

Quality can be divided into two categories—product quality and process quality. Product quality levels vary as to the particular market that it aims to serve. For example, a generic bike is of significantly different quality than the bike of a world-class cyclist. Higher quality products command higher prices in the marketplace. Organizations must establish the "proper level" of product quality by focusing on the exact requirements of their customers. Overdesigned products with too much quality will be viewed as being prohibitively expensive. Underdesigned products, on the other hand, will lose customers to products that cost a little more but are perceived by the customers as offering greater value.

Process quality is critical in every market segment. Regardless of whether the product is a generic bike or a bike for an international cyclist, customers want products without defects. Thus, the primary goal of process quality is to produce error-free products. The investment in improving quality pays off in stronger customer relationships and higher revenues. Many organizations use modern quality control standards, including:

- **Six sigma quality:** The goal is to detect potential problems to prevent their occurrence and achieve no more than 3.4 defects per million opportunities. That is important to companies like Bank of America, which makes 4 million transactions a day.[13]

- **Malcolm Baldrige National Quality Awards:** In 1987 in the United States, a standard was set for overall company quality with the introduction of the Malcolm Baldrige National Quality Awards, named in honor of the late U.S. secretary of commerce. Companies can apply for these awards in each of the following areas: manufacturing, services, small businesses, education, and health care. To qualify, an organization has to show quality in seven key areas: leadership, strategic planning, customer and market focus, information and analysis, human resources focus, process management, and business results.[14]

- **ISO 900:** The common name given to quality management and assurance standards. Comes from the ***International Organization for Standardization (ISO),*** a nongovernmental organization established in 1947 to promote the development of world standards to facilitate the international exchange of goods and services. ISO is a worldwide federation of national standards bodies from more than 140 countries. ISO 900 standards require a company to determine customer needs, including regulatory and legal requirements. The company must also make communication arrangements to handle issues such as complaints. Other standards involve process control, product testing, storage, and delivery.

- **ISO 14000:** This collection of the best practices for managing an organization's impact on the environment does not prescribe specific performance levels, but establishes environmental management systems. The requirements for certification include having an environmental policy, setting specific improvement targets, conducting audits of environmental programs, and maintaining top management review of processes. Certification in ISO 14000 displays that a firm has a world-class management system in both quality and environmental standards.[15]

- **CMMI:** Capability Maturity Model Integration is a framework of best practices. The current version, CMMI-DEV, describes best practices in managing, measuring, and monitoring software development processes. CMMI does not describe the processes themselves; it describes the characteristics of good processes, thus providing guidelines for companies developing or honing their own sets of processes.[16]

Delivery

Another key factor in purchasing decisions is delivery speed. The ability of a firm to provide consistent and fast delivery allows it to charge a premium price for its products. George Stalk, Jr., of the Boston Consulting Group, has demonstrated that both profits and market share are directly linked to the speed with which a company can deliver its products relative to its competition. In addition to fast delivery, the reliability of the delivery is also important. In other words, products should be delivered to customers with minimum variance in delivery times.[17]

Flexibility

Flexibility, from a strategic perspective, refers to the ability of a company to offer a wide variety of products to its customers. Flexibility is also a measure of how fast a company can convert its process(es) from making an old line of products to producing a new product line. Product variety is often perceived by the customers to be a dimension of quality.

The flexibility of the manufacturing process at John Deere's Harvester Works in Moline, Illinois, allows the firm to respond to the unpredictability of the agricultural industry's equipment needs. By manufacturing such small-volume products as seed planters in "modules," or factories within a factory, Deere can offer farmers a choice of 84 different planter models with such a wide variety of options that farmers can have planters virtually customized to meet their individual needs. Its manufacturing process thus allows Deere to compete on both speed and flexibility.[18]

Currently, there appears to be a trend toward offering environmentally friendly products that are made through environmentally friendly processes. As consumers become more aware of the fragility of the environment, they are increasingly turning toward products that are safe for the environment. Several flexible manufacturers now advertise environmentally friendly products, energy-efficient products, and recycled products.

Service

With shortened product life cycles, products tend to migrate toward one common standard. As a consequence, these products are often viewed as commodities in which price is the primary differentiator. For example, the differences in laptops offered among PC manufactures are relatively insignificant so price is the prime selection criterion. For this reason, many companies attempt to place an emphasis on high-quality customer service as a primary differentiator. Customer service can add tremendous value to an ordinary product.

Businesses are always looking toward the future to find the next competitive advantage that will distinguish their products in the marketplace. To obtain an advantage in such a competitive environment, firms must provide "value-added" goods and services, and the primary area where they can capitalize on all five competitive priorities is in the supply chain.

OM AND THE SUPPLY CHAIN

To understand a supply chain, consider a customer purchasing a Trek bike from a dealer. The supply chain begins when a customer places an order for a Trek bike with the dealer. The dealer purchases the bike from the manufacturer, Trek. Trek purchases the raw materials required to make the bike such as metal, packaging, and accessories from different suppliers. The supply chain for Trek encompasses every activity and party involved in the process of fulfilling the order from the customer for the new bike.

A ***supply chain*** consists of all parties involved, directly or indirectly, in the procurement of a product or raw material. ***Supply chain management (SCM)*** involves the management of information flows between and among stages in a supply chain to maximize total supply chain effectiveness and profitability. The four basic components of supply chain management are:

1. **Supply chain strategy**—the strategy for managing all the resources required to meet customer demand for all products and services.
2. **Supply chain partners**—the partners chosen to deliver finished products, raw materials, and services including pricing, delivery, and payment processes along with partner relationship monitoring metrics.
3. **Supply chain operation**—the schedule for production activities including testing, packaging, and preparation for delivery. Measurements for this component include productivity and quality.
4. **Supply chain logistics**—the product delivery processes and elements including orders, warehouses, carriers, defective product returns, and invoicing.[19]

Dozens of steps are required to achieve and carry out each of the above components. SCM software can enable an organization to generate efficiencies within these steps by automating and improving the information flows throughout and

FIGURE 8.6

A Typical Manufacturing Supply Chain

among the different supply chain components. Figures 8.6 and 8.7 display the typical supply chains for goods and services.

Wal-Mart and Procter & Gamble (P&G) implemented a successful SCM system
that linked Wal-Mart's distribution centers directly to P&G's manufacturing centers. Every time a Wal-Mart customer purchases a P&G product, the system sends
a message directly to the factory alerting P&G to restock the product. The system
also sends an automatic alert to P&G whenever a product is running low at one
of Wal-Mart's distribution centers. This real-time information allows P&G to produce and deliver products to Wal-Mart without having to maintain large inventories
in its warehouses. The SCM system saves time, reduces inventory, and decreases
order-processing costs for P&G, which P&G passes on to Wal-Mart in the form of
discounted prices.[20]

Figure 8.8 diagrams the stages of the SCM system for a customer purchasing a
product from Wal-Mart. The diagram demonstrates how the supply chain is dynamic
and involves the constant flow of information between the different parties. For example, a customer purchases a product from Wal-Mart and generates order information. Wal-Mart supplies the order information to its warehouse or distributor. The
warehouse or distributor transfers the order information to the manufacturer, who
provides pricing and availability information to the store and replenishes the

FIGURE 8.7

A Typical Service Supply Chain

FIGURE 8.8

Supply Chain for a Product Purchased from Wal-Mart

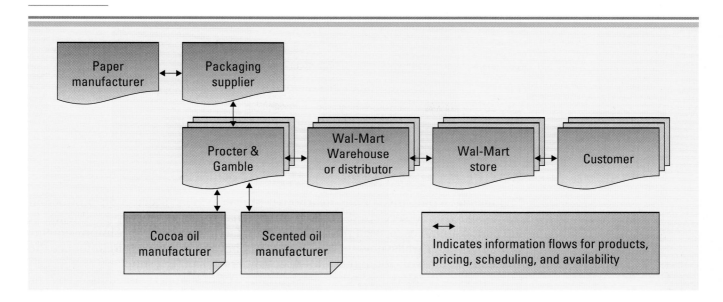

product. Partners transfer all payments electronically. Effective and efficient supply chain management systems can enable an organization to:

- Decrease the power of its buyers.
- Increase its own supplier power.
- Increase switching costs to reduce the threat of substitute products or services.
- Create entry barriers thereby reducing the threat of new entrants.
- Increase efficiencies while seeking a competitive advantage through cost leadership (see Figure 8.9).[21]

FIGURE 8.9

Effective and Efficient Supply Chain Management's Effect on Porter's Five Forces

OPENING CASE QUESTIONS

Dell's Famous Supply Chain

1. How would operations management be a critical component to a company like Dell?

2. How would Dell use each of the three OM planning strategies to improve its operations?

3. How might Dell use each of the five competitive priorities to increase value to its goods and services?

4. Illustrate Dell's potential supply chain management system.

LEARNING OUTCOMES

8.6. List and describe the five components of a typical supply chain.

8.7. Define the relationship between information technology and the supply chain.

8.8. Identify the factors driving supply chain management.

8.9. Summarize the best practices for implementing a successful supply chain management system.

SUPPLY CHAIN FUNDAMENTALS

Greater Chicago
Food Depository

The average company spends nearly half of every dollar it earns on production needs—goods and services it needs from external suppliers to keep producing. In the past, companies focused primarily on manufacturing and quality improvements within their four walls; now their efforts extend beyond those walls to influence the entire supply chain including customers, customers' customers, suppliers, and suppliers' suppliers. Today's supply chain is a complex web of suppliers, assemblers, logistic firms, sales/marketing channels, and other business partners linked primarily through information networks and contractual relationships. SCM systems enhance and manage the relationships. The supply chain has three main links (see Figure 8.10):

1. Materials flow from suppliers and their upstream suppliers at all levels.
2. Transformation of materials into semifinished and finished products—the organization's own production processes.
3. Distribution of products to customers and their downstream customers at all levels.

Organizations must embrace technologies that can effectively manage and oversee their supply chains. SCM is becoming increasingly important in creating organizational efficiencies and competitive advantages. Best Buy checks inventory levels at each of its 750 stores in North America as often as every half hour with its SCM system, taking much of the guesswork out of inventory replenishment. Supply chain management improves ways for companies to find the raw components they

FIGURE 8.10

A Typical Supply Chain

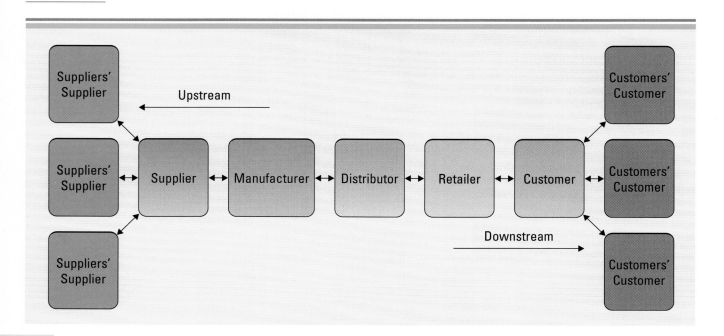

FIGURE 8.11

The Five Basic Supply Chain Management Components

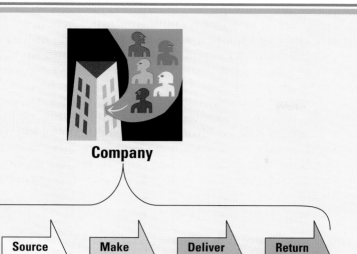

Company

| Plan | Source | Make | Deliver | Return |

THE FIVE BASIC SUPPLY CHAIN MANAGEMENT COMPONENTS
1. **Plan** – This is the strategic portion of supply chain management. A company must have a plan for managing all the resources that go toward meeting customer demand for products or services. A big piece of planning is developing a set of metrics to monitor the supply chain so that it is efficient, costs less, and delivers high quality and value to customers.
2. **Source** – Companies must carefully choose reliable suppliers that will deliver goods and services required for making products. Companies must also develop a set of pricing, delivery, and payment processes with suppliers and create metrics for monitoring and improving the relationships.
3. **Make** – This is the step where companies manufacture their products or services. This can include scheduling the activities necessary for production, testing, packaging, and preparing for delivery. This is by far the most metric-intensive portion of the supply chain, measuring quality levels, production output, and worker productivity.
4. **Deliver** – This step is commonly referred to as logistics. *Logistics* is the set of processes that plans for and controls the efficient and effective transportation and storage of supplies from suppliers to customers. During this step, companies must be able to receive orders from customers, fulfill the orders via a network of warehouses, pick transportation companies to deliver the products, and implement a billing and invoicing system to facilitate payments.
5. **Return** – This is typically the most problematic step in the supply chain. Companies must create a network for receiving defective and excess products and support customers who have problems with delivered products.

need to make a product or service, manufacture that product or service, and deliver it to customers. Figure 8.11 highlights the five basic components of supply chain management.[22]

Technology advances in the five SCM components have significantly improved companies' forecasting and business operations. Businesses today have access to modeling and simulation tools, algorithms, and applications that can combine information from multiple sources to build forecasts for days, weeks, and months in advance. Better forecasts for tomorrow result in better preparedness today.

Mattel Inc. spent the past several years investing heavily in software and processes that simplify its supply chain, cut costs, and shorten cycle times. Using supply chain management strategies, the company cut weeks out of the time it takes to design, produce, and ship everything from Barbies to Hot Wheels. Mattel installed optimization software that measures, tweaks, and validates the operations of its seven distribution centers, seven manufacturing plants, and other facilities that make up its vast worldwide supply chain. Mattel improved forecasting from monthly to weekly. The company no longer produces more inventory than stores require and delivers inventory upon request. Mattel's supply chain moves quickly to make precise forecasts that help the company meet demand.[23]

IT'S ROLE IN THE SUPPLY CHAIN

As companies evolve into extended organizations, the roles of supply chain participants are changing. It is now common for suppliers to be involved in product development and for distributors to act as consultants in brand marketing. The notion of virtually seamless information links within and between organizations is an essential element of integrated supply chains.

Information technology's primary role in SCM is creating the integrations or tight process and information linkages between functions within a firm—such as marketing, sales, finance, manufacturing, and distribution—and between firms, which allow the smooth, synchronized flow of both information and product between customers, suppliers, and transportation providers across the supply chain. Information technology integrates planning, decision-making processes, business operating processes, and information sharing for business performance management (see Figure 8.12). Considerable evidence shows that this type of supply chain integration results in superior supply chain capabilities and profits.[24]

Adaptec, Inc., of California manufactures semiconductors and markets them to the world's leading PC, server, and end-user markets through more than 115 distributors

FIGURE 8.12

The Integrated Supply Chain

FIGURE 8.13

Factors Driving Supply Chain
Management

and thousands of value-added resellers worldwide. Adaptec designs and manufactures products at various third-party locations around the world. The company uses supply chain integration software over the Internet to synchronize planning. Adaptec personnel at the company's geographically dispersed locations communicate in real time and exchange designs, test results, and production and shipment information. Internet-based supply chain collaboration software helped the company reduce inventory levels and lead times.[25]

Although people have been talking about the integrated supply chain for a long time, it has only been recently that advances in information technology have made it possible to bring the idea to life and truly integrate the supply chain. Visibility, consumer behavior, competition, and speed are a few of the changes resulting from advances in information technology that are driving supply chains (see Figure 8.13).

Visibility

Supply chain visibility is the ability to view all areas up and down the supply chain. Making the change to supply chains requires a comprehensive strategy buoyed by information technology. Organizations can use technology tools that help them integrate upstream and downstream, with both customers and suppliers.

To make a supply chain work most effectively, organizations must create visibility in real time. Organizations must know about customer events triggered downstream, but so must their suppliers and their suppliers' suppliers. Without this information, partners throughout the supply chain can experience a bullwhip effect, in which disruptions intensify throughout the chain. The ***bullwhip effect*** occurs when distorted product demand information passes from one entity to the next throughout the supply chain. The misinformation regarding a slight rise in demand for a product could cause different members in the supply chain to stockpile inventory. These changes ripple throughout the supply chain, magnifying the issue and creating excess inventory and costs.[26]

Today, information technology allows additional visibility in the supply chain. Electronic information flows allow managers to view their suppliers' and customers' supply chains. Some organizations have completely changed the dynamics of their industries because of the competitive advantage gained from high visibility in the supply chain. Dell is the obvious example. The company's ability to get product to the customer and the impact of the economics have clearly changed the nature of competition and caused others to emulate this model.

Consumer Behavior

The behavior of customers has changed the way businesses compete. Customers will leave if a company does not continually meet their expectations. They are more demanding because they have information readily available, they know exactly what they want, and they know when and how they want it.

Demand planning systems generate demand forecasts using statistical tools and forecasting techniques. Companies can respond faster and more effectively to consumer demands through supply chain enhancements such as demand planning software. Once an organization understands customer demand and its effect on the supply chain it can begin to estimate the impact that its supply chain will have on its customers and ultimately the organization's performance. The payoff for a successful demand planning strategy can be tremendous.

A study by Peter J. Metz, executive director of the MIT Center for ebusiness, found that companies have achieved impressive bottom-line results from managing demand in their supply chains, averaging a 50 percent reduction in inventory and a 40 percent increase in timely deliveries.[27]

SCM
Advantages

Competition

Supply chain management software can be broken down into (1) supply chain planning software and (2) supply chain execution software. Both increase a company's ability to compete. *Supply chain planning (SCP) systems* use advanced mathematical algorithms to improve the flow and efficiency of the supply chain while reducing inventory. SCP depends entirely on information for its accuracy. An organization cannot expect the SCP output to be accurate unless correct and up-to-date information regarding customer orders, sales information, manufacturing capacity, and delivery capability is entered into the system.

An organization's supply chain encompasses the facilities where raw materials, intermediate products, and finished goods are acquired, transformed, stored, and sold. These facilities are connected by transportation links, where materials and products flow. Ideally, the supply chain consists of multiple organizations that function as efficiently and effectively as a single organization, with full information visibility. *Supply chain execution (SCE) systems* automate the different steps and stages of the supply chain. This could be as simple as electronically routing orders from a manufacturer to a supplier. Figure 8.14 details how SCP and SCE software correlate to the supply chain.

FIGURE 8.14

Supply Chain Planning and Supply Chain Execution Software's Correlation to the Supply Chain

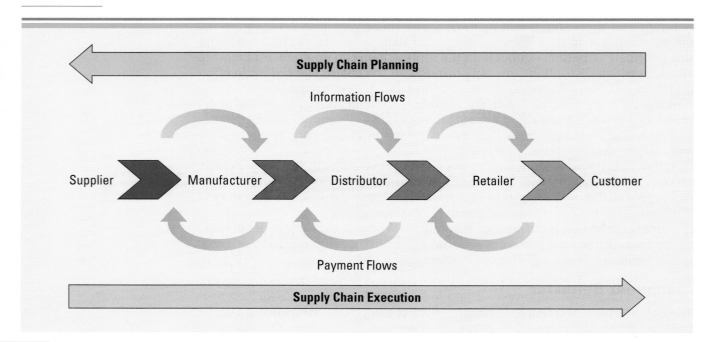

FIGURE 8.15

Factors Fostering Speed

Three Factors Fostering Speed
1. Pleasing customers has become something of a corporate obsession. Serving the customer in the best, most efficient, and most effective manner has become critical, and information about issues such as order status, product availability, delivery schedules, and invoices has become a necessary part of the total customer service experience.
2. Information is crucial to managers' abilities to reduce inventory and human resource requirements to a competitive level.
3. Information flows are essential to strategic planning for and deployment of resources.

General Motors, Ford, and DaimlerChrysler made history when the three automotive giants began working together to create a unified supply chain planning/execution system that all three companies and their suppliers could leverage. Gary Lapidus, Goldman Sachs Group's senior analyst, estimated that Newco, the name of the joint venture, would have a potential market capitalization of between $30 billion and $40 billion, with annual revenues of about $3 billion.

The combined automotive giants' purchasing power is tremendous with GM spending $85 billion per year, Ford spending $80 billion, and DaimlerChrysler spending $73 billion. The ultimate goal of Newco was to process automotive production, from ordering materials and forecasting demand to making cars directly to consumer specifications through the web. The automotive giants understand the impact strategic supply chain planning and execution can have on their competition.[28]

Speed

During the past decade, competition has focused on speed. New forms of servers, telecommunications, wireless applications, and software are enabling companies to perform activities that were once never thought possible. These systems raise the accuracy, frequency, and speed of communication between suppliers and customers, as well as between internal users. Another aspect of speed is the company's ability to satisfy continually changing customer requirements efficiently, accurately, and quickly. Timely and accurate information is more critical to businesses than ever before. Figure 8.15 displays the three factors fostering this change.

SUPPLY CHAIN MANAGEMENT SUCCESS FACTORS

To succeed in today's competitive markets, companies must align their supply chains with the demands of the markets they serve. Supply chain performance is now a distinct competitive advantage for companies proficient in the SCM area. Perdue Farms excels at decision making based on its supply chain management system. Perdue Farms moves roughly 1 million turkeys, each within 24 hours of processing, to reach holiday tables across the nation yearly. The task is no longer as complicated as it was before Perdue Farms invested $20 million in SCM technology. SCM makes Perdue more adept at delivering the right number of turkeys, to the right customers, at the right time.[29]

SCM Success Metrics

Supply chain management metrics can help an organization understand how it's operating over a given time period. Supply chain measurements can cover many areas including procurement, production, distribution, warehousing, inventory, transportation, and customer service. However, a good performance in one part of the supply chain is not sufficient. A supply chain is only as strong as its weakest link. The solution is to measure all key areas of the supply chain. Figure 8.16 displays common supply chain management metrics.[30]

FIGURE 8.16

Supply Chain
Management Metrics

Supply Chain Management Metrics

- **Back order:** An unfilled customer order. A back order is demand (immediate or past due) against an item whose current stock level is insufficient to satisfy demand.

- **Customer order promised cycle time:** The anticipated or agreed upon cycle time of a purchase order. It is a gap between the purchase order creation date and the requested delivery date.

- **Customer order actual cycle time:** The average time it takes to actually fill a customer's purchase order. This measure can be viewed on an order or an order line level.

- **Inventory replenishment cycle time:** Measure of the manufacturing cycle time plus the time included to deploy the product to the appropriate distribution center.

- **Inventory turns (inventory turnover):** The number of times that a company's inventory cycles or turns over per year. It is one of the most commonly used supply chain metrics.

To achieve success such as reducing operating costs, improving asset productivity, and compressing order cycle time, an organization should follow the seven principles of supply chain management outlined in Figure 8.17.

These seven principles run counter to previous built-in functional thinking of how companies organize, operate, and serve customers. Old concepts of supply chains are typified by discrete manufacturing, linear structure, and a focus on buy–sell transactions ("I buy from my suppliers, I sell to my customers"). Because the traditional supply chain is spread out linearly, some suppliers are removed from the end customer. Collaboration adds the value of visibility for these companies. They benefit by knowing immediately what is being transacted at the customer end of the supply chain (the end customer's activities are visible to them). Instead of waiting days or weeks (or months) for the information to flow upstream through the supply chain, with all the potential pitfalls of erroneous or missing information, suppliers can react in near real-time to fluctuations in end-customer demand.

Dell Inc. offers one of the best examples of an extremely successful SCM system. Dell's highly efficient build-to-order business model enables it to deliver customized computer systems quickly. As part of the company's continual effort to improve its supply chain processes, Dell deploys supply chain tools to provide global views of forecasted product demand and materials requirements, as well as improved factory scheduling and inventory management.[31]

FIGURE 8.17

Seven Principles of Supply
Chain Management

Seven Principles of Supply Chain Management

1. Segment customers by service needs, regardless of industry, and then tailor services to those particular segments.

2. Customize the logistics network and focus intensively on the service requirements and on the profitability of the preidentified customer segments.

3. Listen to signals of market demand and plan accordingly. Planning must span the entire chain to detect signals of changing demand.

4. Differentiate products closer to the customer, since companies can no longer afford to hold inventory to compensate for poor demand forecasting.

5. Strategically manage sources of supply, by working with key suppliers to reduce overall costs of owning materials and services.

6. Develop a supply chain information technology strategy that supports different levels of decision making and provides a clear view (visibility) of the flow of products, services, and information.

7. Adopt performance evaluation measures that apply to every link in the supply chain and measure true profitability at every stage.

Organizations should study industry best practices to improve their chances of successful implementation of SCM systems. The following are keys to SCM success.[32]

Make the Sale to Suppliers

The hardest part of any SCM system is its complexity because a large part of the system extends beyond the company's walls. Not only will the people in the organization need to change the way they work, but also the people from each supplier that is added to the network must change. Be sure suppliers are on board with the benefits that the SCM system will provide.

Wean Employees off Traditional Business Practices

Operations people typically deal with phone calls, faxes, and orders scrawled on paper and will most likely want to keep it that way. Unfortunately, an organization cannot disconnect the telephones and fax machines just because it is implementing a supply chain management system. If the organization cannot convince people that using the software will be worth their time, they will easily find ways to work around it, which will quickly decrease the chances of success for the SCM system.

Ensure the SCM System Supports the Organizational Goals

It is important to select SCM software that gives organizations an advantage in the areas most crucial to their business success. If the organizational goals support highly efficient strategies, be sure the supply chain design has the same goals.

Deploy in Incremental Phases and Measure and Communicate Success

Design the deployment of the SCM system in incremental phases. For instance, instead of installing a complete supply chain management system across the company and all suppliers at once, start by getting it working with a few key suppliers, and then move on to the other suppliers. Along the way, make sure each step is adding value through improvements in the supply chain's performance. While a big-picture perspective is vital to SCM success, the incremental approach means the SCM system should be implemented in digestible bites, and also measured for success one step at a time.

Be Future Oriented

The supply chain design must anticipate the future state of the business. Because the SCM system likely will last for many more years than originally planned, managers need to explore how flexible the systems will be when (not if) changes are required in the future. The key is to be certain that the software will meet future needs, not only current needs.[33]

SUPPLY CHAIN MANAGEMENT SUCCESS STORIES

Figure 8.18 depicts the top reasons more and more executives are turning to SCM to manage their extended enterprises. Figure 8.19 lists several companies using supply chain management to drive operations.

Apple Computer initially distributed its business operations over 16 legacy applications. Apple quickly realized that it needed a new business model centered on an integrated supply chain to drive performance efficiencies. Apple devised an implementation strategy that focused on specific SCM functions—finance, sales, distribution, and manufacturing—that would most significantly help its business.

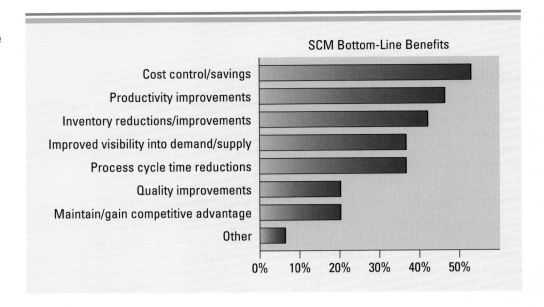

SCM Bottom-Line Benefits

The company decided to deploy leading-edge functionality with a new business model that provided:

- Build-to-order and configure-to-order manufacturing capabilities.
- Web-enabled configure-to-order order entry and order status for customers buying directly from Apple at Apple.com.
- Real-time credit card authorization.
- Available-to-promise and rules-based allocations.
- Integration to advanced planning systems.

Since its SCM system went live, Apple Computer has experienced substantial benefits in many areas including measurable improvements in its manufacturing processes, a decrease by 60 percent in its build-to-order and configure-to-order cycle times, and the ability to process more than 6,000 orders daily.[34]

FIGURE 8.19

Companies Using Supply
Chain Management
Technologies to Drive
Operations

Companies Using Supply Chain to Drive Operations	
Dell	Business grows 17 percent per year with a $40 billion revenue base.
Nokia	Supply chain best practices are turning ideas into profitable businesses.
Procter & Gamble	Consumer-driven supply chain is the defining architecture for large consumer companies. Best practices in product innovation and supply chain effectiveness are tops.
IBM	Hardware supply chain product-development processes overhauled to the tune of 70 percent better, faster, and cheaper.
Wal-Mart Stores	Everyday low prices define the customer demand driving Wal-Mart's partner integrated supply chain.
Toyota Motor	Lean is one of the top three best practices associated with benchmarked supply chain excellence.
The Home Depot	Cutting-edge supply chain management improved logistics and innovative services.
Best Buy	SCM has radically thinned inventories and delivered enviable business positions.
Marks & Spencer	A pioneer in the use of radio frequency identification (RFID) in stores, Marks& Spencer manages to grow and stay lean.

FUTURE SUPPLY CHAIN TRENDS

A television commercial shows a man in a uniform quietly moving through a family home. The man replaces the empty cereal box with a full one just before a hungry child opens the cabinet. He then opens a new sack of dog food as the hungry bulldog eyes him warily, and finally hands a full bottle of shampoo to the man in the shower who had just run out. The next wave in supply chain management will be home-based supply chain fulfillment.

Walgreens is differentiating itself from other national chains by marketing itself as the family's just-in-time supplier. Consumers today are becoming incredibly comfortable with the idea of going online to purchase products when they want, how they want, and at the price they want. Walgreens is developing custom websites for each household that allow families to order electronically and then at their convenience go to the store to pick up their goods at a special self-service counter or the drive-through window. Walgreens is making a promise that goes beyond low prices and customer service and extends right into the home.[35]

The functionality in supply chain management systems is becoming more and more sophisticated as supply chain management matures. Now and in the future, the next stages of SCM will incorporate more functions such as marketing, customer service, and product development. This will be achieved through more advanced communication networks, adoption of more user-friendly decision support systems, and availability of shared information to all participants in the supply chain. SCM is an ongoing development as technology makes it possible to acquire information ever more accurately and frequently from all over the world, and as it introduces new tools to aid in the analytical processes that deal with the supply chain's growing complexity.

SCM Future

According to Forrester Research, Inc., U.S. firms will spend $35 billion over five years to improve business processes that monitor, manage, and optimize their extended supply chains. Figure 8.20 displays the fastest growing SCM components that can have the greatest potential impact on an organization's bottom line.[36]

New technologies are also going to improve the supply chain. Radio frequency identification (RFID) technologies use active or passive tags in the form of chips or smart labels that can store unique identifiers and relay this information to electronic readers. RFID will become an effective tool for tracking and monitoring inventory movement in a real-time SCM environment. The real-time information will provide managers with an instant and accurate view of inventories within the supply chain.

Using current SCM systems, the RFID will check the inventory status and then trigger the replenishment process. Organizations using RFIDs will be able to quickly and

Growing SCM Components	
Supply chain event management (SCEM)	Enables an organization to react more quickly to resolve supply chain issues. SCEM software increases real-time information sharing among supply chain partners and decreases their response time to unplanned events. SCEM demand will skyrocket as more and more organizations begin to discover the benefits of real-time supply chain monitoring.
Selling chain management	Applies technology to the activities in the order life cycle from inquiry to sale.
Collaborative engineering	Allows an organization to reduce the cost and time required during the design process of a product.
Collaborative demand planning	Helps organizations reduce their investment in inventory, while improving customer satisfaction through product availability.

FIGURE 8.20

Fast Growth SCM Components

accurately provide current inventory levels (in real-time) at any point in the supply chain. Reducing inventory levels to their reorder points allows electronic regeneration of replenishment orders. With quick and accurate information about inventories, the use of safety stock levels guarding against uncertainty can also be reduced. Hence, the potential benefits of RFIDs include a reduction of human intervention (or required labor) and holding fewer inventories, which nets a reduction in operating costs.

SCM applications have always been expensive, costing between $1 million and $10 million. As the industry matures and competition increases, vendors will continue adapting their pricing models to attract midsize and smaller companies.[37]

OPENING CASE QUESTIONS

Dell's Famous Supply Chain

5. How might Dell use each of the five basic SCM components?

6. How has Dell influenced visibility, consumer behavior, competition, and speed through the use of IT in its supply chain?

7. Explain the seven principles of SCM in reference to Dell's business model.

SUMMARY OF KEY THEMES

This chapter introduced the concepts of operations management and supply chain management showcasing how information technology can be used to improve fundamental business processes. As this chapter has illustrated, supply chains exist across a variety of sectors and industries. Various examples were given showcasing information technology's ability to help organizations improve their interactions with suppliers, manufacturers, distributors, warehouses, and customers.

As a business student, you should understand this pivotal role that information technology plays in facilitating operations management and supply chain processes and in supporting the basic infrastructure and coordination needed for core business operations to function.

KEY TERMS

Bullwhip effect,   293
Collaborative demand
    planning,   299
Collaborative engineering,   299
Demand planning
    system,   294
Distribution management
    system,   285
Global inventory management
    system,   284
International Organization for
    Standardization (ISO),   286
Inventory management and
    control system,   284
Logistics,   291

Materials requirement
    planning (MRP)
    systems,   284
Operational planning and
    control (OP&C),   284
Operations management
    (OM),   280
Production,   280
Production management,   280
Selling chain
    management,   299
Strategic business unit
    (SBU),   284
Strategic planning,   284
Supply chain,   287

Supply chain event
    management (SCEM),   299
Supply chain execution (SCE)
    system,   294
Supply chain management
    (SCM),   287
Supply chain planning (SCP)
    system,   294
Supply chain visibility,   293
Tactical planning,   284
Transformation process,   280
Transportation planning
    system,   285
Value-added,   281

BudNet

Every time a six-pack moves off the shelf, Anheuser-Busch's top-secret nationwide data network, BudNet, knows. BudNet is Anheuser-Busch's secret weapon and one of the reasons that Anheuser's share (by volume) of the $74.4 billion U.S. beer market inched up to 50.1 percent from 48.9 percent in a single year.

Dereck Gurden, a sales representative for Sierra Beverage, one of about 700 U.S. distributors that work for Anheuser-Busch, manages an 800-square-mile territory in California's Central Valley. His customers include 7-Eleven, Buy N Save, and dozens of liquor marts and restaurants. When Gurden enters one of his customers' stores he already knows what products are selling, which campaigns are successful, and what needs to be done to help the customer's business.

When entering a store, Gurden checks his handheld PC, which displays vital store information. "First, I'll scroll through and check the accounts receivable, make sure everything's current," he says. "Then it'll show me an inventory screen with a four-week history. I can get past sales, package placements—facts and numbers on how much of the sales they did when they had a display in a certain location." Gurden also walks around the store and inputs competitor information into his PC relating to product displays, pricing strategies, and promotions.

How BudNet Works

Information is entered into BudNet nightly from several thousand beer distributors and sales representatives. The information allows Anheuser-Busch managers to constantly adjust production and fine-tune marketing campaigns. The system works as follows:

1. Sales representatives collect new orders and track competitors' marketing efforts on PDAs and laptops.
2. Distributors compile the information and transmit it daily to Anheuser corporate headquarters.
3. Anheuser brand managers analyze the information and make decisions for distributors.
4. Distributors log on to BudNet to get the latest intelligence.
5. Sales representatives rearrange displays and rotate stock based on the recommendations.

Anheuser-Busch uses BudNet's information to constantly change marketing strategies, to design promotions to suit the ethnic makeup of its markets, and as early warning radar that detects where rivals might have an edge. "If Anheuser-Busch loses shelf space in a store in Clarksville, Tennessee, they know it right away," says Joe Thompson, president of Independent Beverage Group, a research and consulting firm. "They're better at this game than anyone, even Coca-Cola."

According to dozens of analysts, beer-industry veterans, and distributor executives, Anheuser has made a deadly accurate science out of determining what beer lovers are buying, as well as when, where, and why. The last time you bought a six-pack of Bud Light at the corner store, Anheuser servers most likely recorded what you paid, when that beer was brewed, whether you purchased it warm or chilled, and whether you could have gotten a better deal down the street. BudNet has not just added efficiency into the beer supply chain; it is changing the dynamics of the industry.[38]

Questions

1. Describe the five competitive priorities of operations management and how Budweiser can use each one to streamline production.
2. How can an SCM system help a distributor such as Anheuser-Busch make its supply chain more effective and efficient?

3. SCM is experiencing explosive growth. Explain why this statement is true using BudNet as an example.
4. Evaluate BudNet's effect on each of the five factors that are driving SCM success.
5. List and describe the components of a typical supply chain along with its ability to help Budweiser make effective decisions.

CLOSING CASE TWO

Listerine's Journey

When you use Listerine antiseptic mouthwash, you are experiencing the last step in a complex supply chain spanning several continents and requiring months of coordination by countless businesses and individuals. The resources involved in getting a single bottle of Listerine to a consumer are unbelievable. As raw material transforms into finished product, what will be Listerine travels around the globe and through multiple supply chains and information systems.

The Journey Begins

A farmer in Australia is harvesting a crop of eucalyptus for eucalyptol, the oil found in its leathery leaves. The farmer sells the crop to an Australian processing company, which spends about four weeks extracting the eucalyptol from the eucalyptus.

Meanwhile, in New Jersey, Warner-Lambert (WL) partners with a distributor to buy the oil from the Australian company and transport it to WL's Listerine manufacturing and distribution facility in Lititz, Pennsylvania. The load will arrive at Lititz about three months after the harvest.

At the same time, in Saudi Arabia, a government-owned operation is drilling deep under the desert for the natural gas that will yield the synthetic alcohol that gives Listerine its 43-proof punch. Union Carbide Corp. ships the gas via tanker to a refinery in Texas, which purifies it and converts it into ethanol. The ethanol is loaded onto another tanker, and then transported from Texas through the Gulf of Mexico to New Jersey, where it is transferred to storage tanks and transported via truck or rail to WL's plant. A single shipment of ethanol takes about six to eight weeks to get from Saudi Arabia to Lititz.

SPI Polyols Inc., a manufacturer of ingredients for the confectionery, pharmaceutical, and oral-care industries, buys corn syrup from farmers in the Midwest. SPI converts the corn syrup into sorbitol solution, which sweetens and adds bulk to the Cool Mint Listerine. The syrup is shipped to SPI's New Castle, Delaware, facility for processing and then delivered on a tank wagon to Lititz. The whole process, from the time the corn is harvested to when it is converted into sorbitol, takes about a month.

By now the ethanol, eucalyptol, and sorbitol have all arrived at WL's plant in Lititz, where employees test them, along with the menthol, citric acid, and other ingredients that make up Listerine, for quality assurance before authorizing storage in tanks. To mix the ingredients, flow meters turn on valves at each tank and measure out the right proportions, according to the Cool Mint formula developed by WL R&D in 1990. (The original amber mouthwash was developed in 1879.)

Next, the Listerine flows through a pipe to fillers along the packaging line. The fillers dispense the product into bottles delivered continuously from a nearby plastics company for just-in-time manufacturing. The bottles are capped, labeled, and fitted with tamper-resistant safety bands, then placed in shipping boxes that each hold one dozen 500-milliliter bottles. During this process, machines automatically check for skewed labels, missing safety bands, and other problems. The entire production cycle, from the delivery via pipe of the Listerine liquid to the point where bottles are boxed and ready to go, takes a matter of minutes. The line can produce about 300 bottles per minute—a far cry from the 80 to 100 bottles that the line produced per minute before 1994.

Each box travels on a conveyor belt to the palletizer, which organizes and shrink-wraps the boxes into 100-case pallets. Stickers with identifying bar codes are affixed to the pallets. Drivers forklift the pallets to the distribution center, located in the same Lititz facility, from which the boxes are shipped around the world.

Finally, the journey is completed when a customer purchases a bottle of Listerine at a local drugstore or grocery store. In a few days, the store will place an order for a replacement bottle of Listerine. And so begins the cycle again.[39]

Questions

1. Explain the role of operations management for Warner-Lambert.
2. Summarize SCM and describe Warner-Lambert's supply chain strategy. Diagram the SCM components.
3. Detail Warner-Lambert's three operations management strategies and identify systems it could use to help make strategic decisions.
4. What would happen to Warner-Lambert's business if a natural disaster in Saudi Arabia depletes its natural gas resources?
5. Assess the impact to Warner-Lambert's business if the majority of the eucalyptus crop was destroyed in a natural disaster.

CLOSING CASE THREE

How Levi's Got Its Jeans into Wal-Mart

People around the world recognize Levi's as an American icon, the cool jeans worn by movie stars James Dean and Marilyn Monroe. However, the company failed to keep up with the fast-changing tastes of American teenagers. In particular, it missed the trend to baggy jeans that caught hold in the mid-1990s. Sales plummeted from $7.1 billion in 1996 to $4.1 billion in 2003, and Levi's U.S. market share dropped from 18.7 percent in 1997 to 12 percent in 2003, a huge decline of almost one-third in both dollars and market share.

Analyzing and Responding to What Happened

Competition hit Levi Strauss on both the high and low ends. Fashion-conscious buyers were drawn to high-priced brands like Blue Cult, Juicy, and Seven, which had more fashion cachet than Levi's. On the low end, parents were buying Wrangler and Lee jeans for their kids because on average they cost about $10 less than Levi's Red Tab brand. Wrangler and Lee were also the brands they found at discount retailers such as Wal-Mart, Target, and T. J. Maxx. David Bergen, Levi's chief information officer (CIO), described the company as "getting squeezed," and "caught in the jaws of death."

Levi Strauss's new CEO, Philip A. Marineau, came to the company from PepsiCo in 1999, a year after he helped PepsiCo surpass Coca-Cola in sales for the first time. Marineau recruited Bergen in 2000 from Carstation.com. Marineau quickly realized that turning Levi Strauss around would entail manufacturing, marketing, and distributing jeans that customers demanded, particularly customers at the low end where the mass market was located.

Bergen was eager to join Marineau's team because of his background in clothing, retailing, and manufacturing with companies such as The Gap and Esprit de Corps in the 1980s. He knew that Marineau's plan to anticipate customer wants would require up-to-date IT applications such as data warehousing, data mining, and customer relationship management (CRM) systems. He also knew that selling to mass market retailers would require upgrades to the supply chain management (SCM) systems, and he understood that globalization would necessitate standardized enterprise resource planning (ERP) systems. Overall, it was a challenge any ambitious CIO would covet. After all, designing and installing IT systems that drive and achieve key business initiatives is what it is all about.

Joining Wal-Mart

Wal-Mart was a pioneer in supply chain management systems, having learned early on that driving costs out of the supply chain would let it offer products to customers at the lowest possible prices, while at the same time assuring that products the customers demanded were always on store shelves. Becoming one of Wal-Mart's 30,000 suppliers is not easy. Wal-Mart insists that its suppliers do business using up-to-date IT systems to manage the supply chain—not just the supply chain between Wal-Mart and its suppliers, but the supply chains between the suppliers and their suppliers as well. Wal-Mart has strict supply chain management system requirements that its business partners must meet.

Wal-Mart's requirements presented Levi Strauss with a serious hurdle to overcome because its supply chain management systems were in bad shape. Levi Strauss executives did not even have access to key information required to track where products were moving in the supply chain. For example, they did not know how many pairs of jeans were in the factory awaiting shipment, how many were somewhere en route, or how many had just been unloaded at a customer's warehouse. According to Greg Hammann, Levi's U.S. chief customer officer, "Our supply chain could not deliver the services Wal-Mart expected."

Bergen created a cross-functional team of key managers from IT, finance, and sales to transform Levi Strauss's systems to meet Wal-Mart's requirements. Their recommendations included network upgrades, modifications to ordering and logistics applications, and data warehouse improvements, among others. Although Bergen realized that about half the changes required to current IT systems to accommodate the state-of-the-art demands of Wal-Mart would be a waste of resources since these systems were being replaced by a new SAP enterprise software system over the next five years, Levi Strauss could not wait for the SAP installation if it wanted Wal-Mart's business now, so it decided to move forward with the changes to the current systems.

The successful transformation of its supply chain management system allowed the company to collaborate with Wal-Mart. The company introduced its new signature line at Wal-Mart, which sells for around $23 and has fewer details in the finish than Levi's other lines, no trademark pocket stitching or red tab, for example. Wal-Mart wants big-name brands to lure more affluent customers into its stores, while still maintaining the low price points all Wal-Mart customers have come to expect. Wal-Mart Senior Vice President Lois Mikita noted that Wal-Mart "continues to tailor its selection to meet the needs of customers from a cross section of income levels and lifestyles." She also stated she is impressed with the level of detail Levi Strauss has put into its systems transformation efforts to "make the execution of this new launch 100 percent."

Achieving Business Success Through IT

Bergen's changes were a success and the percentage of products delivered on time quickly rose from 65 percent to 95 percent primarily because of the updated supply chain management system. Levi's total sales were also up in the third and fourth quarters of 2003, for the first time since 1996. NPD Group's Fashionworld is a research group that tracks apparel and footwear market trends. In 2003, Levi's appeared on NPD Fashionworld's top 10 list of brands preferred by young women, ending an absence of several years. Marshall Cohen, a senior industry analyst at NPD Fashionworld, noted that Levi's "hadn't been close to that for a while. Teens hadn't gravitated toward Levi's in years. That was incredible. A lot of that has to do with having the right style in the right place at the right time." The improved systems, Cohen noted, also helped the company get the right sizes to the right stores.

Another highly successful IT system implemented by Levi Strauss is a digital dashboard that executives can display on their PC screens. The dashboard lets an executive see the status of a product as it moves from the factory floor to distribution centers to retail stores. For example, the dashboard can display how Levi's 501 jeans are selling at an individual Kohl's store compared to forecasted sales. "When I first got here I didn't see anything," Hammann said. "Now I can drill down to the product level."

The digital dashboard alerts executives to trends that under the previous systems would have taken weeks to detect. For example, in 2003 Levi Strauss started to ship Dockers Stain Defender pants. Expected sales for the pants were around 2 million pairs. The digital dashboard quickly notified key executives that the trousers were selling around 2.5 million pairs. This information enabled them to adjust production upward in time to ship more pants, meet the increased demand, and avoid lost sales. Levi Strauss also uses the systems to control supply during key seasonal sales periods such as back-to-school and Christmas.

"If I look overconfident, I'm not," Bergen said. "I'm very nervous about this change. When we trip, we have to stand up real quick and get back on the horse, as they say." As if to reinforce Bergen's point, Gib Carey, a supply chain analyst at Bain, noted, "The place where companies do fail is when they aren't bringing anything new to Wal-Mart. Wal-Mart is constantly looking at 'How can I get the same product I am selling today at a lower price somewhere else?' "[40]

Questions

1. How did Levi Strauss achieve business success through the use of supply chain management?

2. What might have happened to Levi Strauss if its top executives had not supported investments in SCM?

3. David Bergen, Levi's CIO, put together a cross-functional team of key managers from IT, finance, and sales to transform Levi's systems to meet Wal-Mart's requirements. Analyze the relationships between these three business areas and OM and SCM systems. How can OM and an SCM system help support these three critical business areas?

4. Describe the five basic SCM components in reference to Wal-Mart's business model.

5. Explain the future trends of SCM and provide an example of how Levi Strauss could use these technologies to streamline its business operations.

6. Identify any security and ethical issues that might occur for a company doing business with Wal-Mart.

MAKING BUSINESS DECISIONS

1. **Analyzing Dell's supply chain management system**

   Dell's supply chain strategy is legendary. If you want to build a successful SCM system, your best bet is to model your SCM system after Dell's. In a team, research Dell's supply chain management strategy on the web and create a report discussing any new SCM updates and strategies the company is currently using that were not discussed in this text. Be sure to include a graphical presentation of Dell's current supply chain model.

2. Increasing information

Galina's is a high-end auction house located in New York City. Galina's specializes in selling jewelry, art, and antique furniture primarily from estate sales. The owner, Galina Bucrya, would like to begin offering certain items for auction over the Internet. Galina is unfamiliar with the Internet and not quite sure how to pursue her new business strategy. You are working for Information Inc., a small business consulting company that specializes in ebusiness strategies. Galina has hired you to help her create her supply chain ebusiness strategy. Compile a report describing supply chain management, the potential benefits her company can receive from an SCM strategy, your recommendation for an efficient or effective SCM strategy, and your views on the future of SCM.

3. Increasing revenues with SCM

Cold Cream is one of the premier beauty supply stores in the metro New York area. People come from all over to sample the store's unique creams, lotions, makeup, and perfumes. The company receives its products from manufacturers around the globe. The company would like to implement an SCM system to help it better understand its customers and their purchasing habits. Create a report summarizing SCM systems and explain how an SCM system can directly influence Cold Cream's revenues.

APPLY YOUR KNOWLEDGE

1. Operational Mowing

Mary Lou has worked for the same Fortune 500 company for almost 15 years. Although the company had gone through some tough times, things were starting to turn around. Customer orders were up, and quality and productivity had improved dramatically from what they had been only a few years earlier due to a companywide quality improvement program. So it came as a real shock to Mary Lou and about 400 of her co-workers when they were suddenly terminated following the new CEO's decision to downsize the company.

After recovering from the initial shock, Mary Lou tried to find employment elsewhere. Despite her efforts, after eight months of searching she was no closer to finding a job than the day she started. Her funds were being depleted and she was getting more discouraged. There was one bright spot, though: She was able to bring in a little money by mowing lawns for her neighbors. She got involved quite by chance when she heard one neighbor remark that now that his children were on their own, nobody was around to cut the grass. Almost jokingly, Mary Lou asked him how much he'd be willing to pay. Soon Mary Lou was mowing the lawns of 10 neighbors. Other neighbors wanted her to work on their lawns, but she did not feel that she could spare any more time from her job search.

However, as the rejection letters began to pile up, Mary Lou knew she had to make a decision if she would go into business for herself or continue her job search.

Project Focus

By the end of her first year in business, Mary Lou was easily earning a good living. She began performing other services such as fertilizing lawns, weeding gardens, trimming shrubs, and installing sprinkler systems. Business was so good that Mary Lou hired several employees to assist her and believed she could further expand her business. As Mary

Lou begins to plan her expansion, she needs your assistance in answering the following questions:

1. In what ways are Mary Lou's customers most likely to judge the quality of her lawn care services?
2. Mary Lou is the operations manager of her business. Among her responsibilities are forecasting, inventory management, scheduling, quality assurance, and maintenance.
   1. What kinds of things would likely require forecasts?
   2. What inventory items does Mary Lou probably have? Name one inventory decision she has to make periodically.
   3. What scheduling must she do? What things might occur to disrupt schedules and cause Mary Lou to reschedule?
   4. How important is quality assurance to Mary Lou's business?
3. What are some of the trade-offs that Mary Lou probably considered relative to:
   1. Working for a company instead of for herself?
   2. Expanding the business?
   3. Launching a website?
4. The town is considering an ordinance that would prohibit grass clippings at the curb for pickup because local landfills cannot handle the volume. What options might Mary Lou consider if the ordinance is passed?
5. Mary Lou decided to offer her employees a bonus of $250 for ideas on how to improve the business, and they provided several good ideas. One idea that she initially rejected now appears to hold great promise. The employee who proposed the idea has left the company and is currently working for a competitor. Should Mary Lou send the employee a check for the idea?

2. Total Recall

In mid-2000, the Firestone Tire Company issued a recall of some of its tires—those mounted on certain sport-utility vehicles (SUV) of the Ford Motor Company. This was done in response to reports that tire treads on some SUVs separated in use, causing accidents, some of which involved fatal injuries as vehicles rolled over.

At first, Firestone denied there was a problem with its tires, but it issued the recall under pressure from consumer groups and various government agencies. All of the tires in question were produced at the same tire plant, and there were calls to shut down that facility. Firestone suggested that Ford incorrectly matched the wrong tires with its SUVs. There were also suggestions that the shock absorbers of the SUVs were rubbing against the tires, causing or aggravating the problem.

Project Focus

Both Ford and Firestone denied that this had been an ongoing problem. However, there was a public outcry when it was learned that Firestone had previously issued recalls of these tires in South America, and the companies had settled at least one lawsuit involving an accident caused by tread separation several years earlier.

This case raises a number of issues, some related to possible causes and others to ethics. Discuss each of these factors and their actual or potential relevance to what happened:

1. Product
2. Quality control
3. Ethics

3. Building Visibility

Visionary companies are building extended enterprises to best compete in the new Internet economy. An extended enterprise combines the Internet's power with new business structures and processes to eliminate old corporate boundaries and geographic restrictions. Networked supply chains create seamless paths of communication among partners, suppliers, manufacturers, retailers, and customers. Because of advances in manufacturing and distribution, the cost of developing new products and services is dropping, and time to market is speeding up. This has resulted in increasing customer demands, local and global competition, and increased pressure on the supply chain.

To stay competitive, companies must reinvent themselves so that the supply chain—sourcing and procurement, production scheduling, order fulfillment, inventory management, and customer care—is no longer a cost-based back-office exercise, but rather a flexible operation designed to effectively address today's challenges.

The Internet is proving an effective tool in transforming supply chains across all industries. Suppliers, distributors, manufacturers, and resellers now work together more closely and effectively than ever. Today's technology-driven supply chain enables customers to manage their own buying experiences, increases coordination and connectivity among supply partners, and helps reduce operating costs for every company in the chain.[41]

Project Focus

In the past, assets were a crucial component of success in supply chain management. In today's market, however, a customer-centric orientation is key to retaining competitive advantage. Using the Internet and any other resources available, develop a strategic plan for implementing a networked, flexible supply chain management system for a start-up company of your choice. Research Netflix if you are unfamiliar with how start-up companies are changing the supply chain. Be sure that your supply chain integrates all partners—manufacturers, retailers, suppliers, carriers, and vendors—into a seamless unit and views customer relationship management as a key competitive advantage. There are several points to consider when creating your customer-centric supply chain strategy:

- Taking orders is only one part of serving customer needs.
- Businesses must fulfill the promise they make to customers by delivering products and information upon request—not when it is convenient for the company.
- Time to market is a key competitive advantage. Companies must ensure uninterrupted supply, and information about customer demands and activities is essential to this requirement.
- Cost is an important factor. Companies need to squeeze the costs from internal processes to make the final products less expensive.
- Reducing design-cycle times is critical, as this allows companies to get their products out more quickly to meet customer demand.

4. Netflix Your Business

Netflix reinvented the video rental business using supply chain technology. Netflix, established in 1998, is the largest online DVD rental service, offering flat-rate rental-by-mail to customers in the United States. Headquartered in Los Gatos, California, it has amassed a collection of 80,000 titles and over 6.8 million subscribers. Netflix has over 42 million DVDs and ships 1.6 million a day, on average, costing a reported $300 million a year in postage. On February 25, 2007, Netflix announced the delivery of its billionth DVD.

The company provides a monthly flat-fee service for the rental of DVD movies. A subscriber creates an ordered list, called a rental queue, of DVDs to rent. The DVDs are delivered individually via the United States Postal Service from an array of regional warehouses (44 in 29 states). A subscriber keeps a rented DVD as long as desired but has a limit on the number of DVDs (determined by subscription level) that can be checked out at any one time. To rent a new DVD, the subscriber mails the previous one back to Netflix in a prepaid mailing envelope. Upon receipt of the disc, Netflix ships another disc in the subscriber's rental queue.[42]

Project Focus

Netflix's business is video rental, but it used technology to revamp the supply chain to completely disrupt the entire video rental industry. Reinvent IT is a statewide contest where college students can propose a new business that they will reinvent by revamping the supply chain (such as Netflix has done). You want to enter and win the contest. Reinvent a traditional business, such as the video rental business, using supply chain technologies.

5. Finding Shelf Space at Wal-Mart

Wal-Mart's business strategy of being a low-cost provider by managing its supply chain down to the minutia has paid off greatly. Each week, approximately 100 million customers, or one-third of the U.S. population, visit Wal-Mart's U.S. stores. Wal-Mart is currently the world's largest retailer and the second largest corporation behind ExxonMobil. It was founded by Sam Walton in 1962 and is the largest private employer in the United States and Mexico. Wal-Mart is also the largest grocery retailer in the United States, with an estimated 20 percent of the retail grocery and consumables business, and the largest toy seller in the United States, with an estimated 45 percent of the retail toy business, having surpassed Toys "R" Us in the late 1990s.

Wal-Mart's business model is based on selling a wide variety of general merchandise at "always low prices." The reason Wal-Mart can offer such low prices is due to its innovative use of information technology tools to create its highly sophisticated supply chain. Wal-Mart has famously invited its major suppliers to jointly develop powerful supply chain partnerships. These are designed to increase product flow efficiency and, consequently, Wal-Mart's profitability.

Many companies have stepped up to the challenge, starting with the well-known Wal-Mart/Procter & Gamble alliance, which incorporated vendor-managed inventory, category management, and other intercompany innovations. Wal-Mart's CFO became a key customer as P&G's objective became maximizing Wal-Mart's internal profitability. Unlike many other retailers, Wal-Mart does not charge a slotting fee to suppliers for their products to appear in the store. Alternatively, Wal-Mart focuses on selling more popular products and often pressures store managers to drop unpopular products in favor of more popular ones, as well as pressuring manufacturers to supply more popular products.[43]

Project Focus

You are the owner of a high-end collectible toy company. You create everything from authentic sports figure replicas to famous musicians and movie characters including Babe Ruth, Hulk Hogan, Mick Jagger, Ozzy Osbourne, Alien, and the Terminator. It would be a huge win for your company if you could get your collectibles into Wal-Mart. Compile a strategic plan highlighting the steps required to approach Wal-Mart as your supply chain partner. Be sure to address the pros and cons of partnering with Wal-Mart, including the cost to revamp your current supply chain to meet Wal-Mart's tough supply chain requirements.

6. Shipping Problems

Entrepreneurship is in Alyssa Stuart's blood. Alyssa has been starting businesses since she was 10 years old, and she finally has the perfect business of custom-made furniture. Customers who visit Alyssa's shop can choose from a number of different fabrics and 50 different styles of couch and chair designs to create their custom-made furniture. Once the customer decides on a fabric pattern and furniture design, the information is sent to China where the furniture is built and shipped to the customer via the West Coast. Alyssa is excited about her business; all of her hard work has finally paid off as she has over 17,000 customers and 875 orders currently in the pipe.

Project Focus

Alyssa's business is booming. Her high quality products and outstanding customer service have created an excellent reputation for her business. But Alyssa's business is at risk of losing everything and she has come to you for help solving her supply chain issues.

Yesterday, a dockworkers union strike began and shut down all of the West Coast shipping docks from San Francisco to Canada. Work will resume only when the union agrees to new labor contracts, which could take months. Alyssa has asked you to summarize the impact of the dock shutdown on her business and create a strategy to keep her business running, which is especially difficult since Alyssa guarantees 30-day delivery on all products or the product is free. What strategies do you recommend for Alyssa's business to continue working while her supply chain is disrupted by the dockworkers strike?

7. Political Supply Chains

The U.S. government crafted a deal with the United Arab Emirates (UAE) that would let a UAE-based firm, Dubai Ports World (DPW), run six major U.S. ports—New York, New Jersey, Baltimore, New Orleans, Miami, and Philadelphia. Currently, London-based Peninsular and Oriental Steam Navigation Co. (P&O), the fourth largest port operator in the world, runs the six ports. But the $6.8 billion sale of P&O to DPW would effectively turn over North American operations to the government-owned company in Dubai.[44]

Project Focus

Some citizens are worried that the federal government may be outsourcing U.S. port operations to a company prone to terrorist infiltration by allowing a firm from the United Arab Emirates to run port operations within the United States. You have been called in on an investigation to determine the potential effects on U.S. businesses' supply chains if these ports were shut down due to terrorist activities. The United Arab Emirates has had people involved in terrorism. In fact, some of its financial institutions laundered the money for the 9/11 terrorists. Create an argument for or against outsourcing these ports to the UAE. Be sure to detail the effect on U.S. businesses' supply chains if these ports are subjected to terrorist acts.

BUSINESS DRIVEN BEST SELLERS

Built to Last. By Jim Collins (Collins Business Essentials, 1994).

Drawing upon a six-year research project at the Stanford University Graduate School of Business, Jim Collins and Jerry I. Porras took 18 truly exceptional and long-lasting companies and studied each in direct comparison to one of its top competitors. They examined the companies from their very beginnings to the present day—as start-ups, as midsize companies, and as large corporations. Throughout, the authors asked: "What makes the truly exceptional companies different from the comparison companies and what were the common practices these enduringly great companies followed throughout their history?"

Filled with hundreds of specific examples and organized into a coherent framework of practical concepts that can be applied by managers and entrepreneurs at all levels, *Built to Last* provides a master blueprint for building organizations that will prosper long into the 21st century and beyond.[45]

Good to Great. By Jim Collins (Collins Business Essentials, 2001).

Built to Last, the defining management study of the '90s showed how great companies triumph over time and how long-term sustained performance can be engineered into the DNA of an enterprise from the very beginning.

But what about the company that is not born with great DNA? How can good companies, mediocre companies, even bad companies achieve enduring greatness?

- **The study:** For years, this question preyed on the mind of Jim Collins. Are there companies that defy gravity and convert long-term mediocrity or worse into long-term superiority? And if so, what are the universal distinguishing characteristics that cause a company to go from good to great?

- **The standards:** Using tough benchmarks, Collins and his research team identified a set of elite companies that made the leap to great results and sustained those results for at least 15 years. How great? After the leap, the good-to-great companies generated cumulative stock returns that beat the general stock market by an average of seven times in 15 years, better than twice the results delivered by a composite index of the world's greatest companies, including Coca-Cola, Intel, General Electric, and Merck.

- **The findings:** The findings of the good-to-great study will surprise many readers and shed light on virtually every area of management strategy and practice:

- **Level 5 leaders:** The research team was shocked to discover the type of leadership required to achieve greatness.

- **The hedgehog concept:** To go from good to great requires transcending the curse of competence.

- **A culture of discipline:** When you combine a culture of discipline with an ethic of entrepreneurship, you get the magical alchemy of great results.

- **Technology accelerators:** Good to great companies think differently about the role of technology.

- **The flywhere and the doom loop:** Those who launch radical change programs and wrenching restructuring will almost certainly fail to make the leap.[46]

9

CHAPTER

Customer Relationship Management and Business Intelligence

What's in IT for me?

This chapter discusses how information technology can be used to support firms in their interactions with customers. At the simplest level, organizations implement CRM to gain a better understanding of customer needs and behaviors, and information technology provides companies with a new channel to communicate with customers beyond those traditionally used by organizations such as face-to-face or paper-based methods.

Organizations recognize the importance of maintaining and fostering healthy relationships with customers. Doing so has a direct and positive effect on customer loyalty and retention. This greatly adds to a company's profitability and provides an edge over competitors who fail to foster customer relationships.

You, as a business student, must understand the critical relationship your business will have with its customers. You must also understand how to analyze your organizational data to ensure you are not just meeting, but exceeding your customer's expectations. Business intelligence (BI) is the best way to understand your customer's current—and more importantly—future needs. Like never before, enterprises are technologically empowered to reach their goals of integrating, analyzing, and making intelligent business decisions based on their data.

Customer First Awards

Profitable Player Award: Progressive

Fast Company granted Progressive the coveted Profitable Player Customer First Award. Imagine walking into a Circuit City prepared to buy an expensive digital camera and being told you could get it cheaper at Best Buy. Sound crazy? If a customer shopping for car insurance calls Progressive, that is what happens. For years, the company has handed out rivals' rates to potential customers. In 2002, it began scrolling competitors' rates—even when its own were higher—across its website.

It is a bold piece of Progressive's plan to foster long-term customer loyalty. Progressive may lose some customers who opt for lower rates, but CEO Glenn Renwick thinks transparency will keep the rest around. "We hope it establishes a feeling of trust for the company," he said.

Renwick seems to be getting his wish. The third-largest auto insurer in the United States, Progressive has averaged an awe-inducing 75 percent annual profit growth since 2001. Progressive continues to roll out still more customer-focused services, including a test program that lets drivers exchange a totaled vehicle for another of the same or better make, year, and mileage (Progressive does the shopping).

Progressive has long emphasized innovations that transform the customer experience and the efficiency of its operations. Its 2,900-plus immediate response vehicles (IRVs), which the company pioneered 10 years ago, are sent to accident sites or customers' homes to assess damage and in some cases pay claims immediately. Renwick says the IRVs—mobile offices for Progressive's claim representatives—were designed in part to help the customer's "emotional EKG." Reps arrive in the IRVs and quickly take care of the details so the accident victim can get back on the road as soon as possible. But the IRVs are more than just reassuring perks for stressed-out drivers. They save Progressive money by reducing costs of vehicle storage and rental cars on the 10,000 or so claims it handles in a typical day.

This results in happier customers like Dave Meisburger, whose wife was in a car accident a few years ago. Within four hours of her initial call to Progressive, an adjustor had been to their Mobile, Alabama, home, assessed the damage, and cut them a check, right in the driveway. Now Meisburger says he will never leave Progressive. "They could double their rate, and I wouldn't care. Their customer service means more to me than anything," he said.

More recently, Progressive has launched and expanded its Concierge Level claims-service facilities, now available in 18 metropolitan areas. Clients bring in their damaged cars, get a beeper and a rental car, and are notified when repairs are done. In addition to saving the customer time and energy, the centers help streamline communications among Progressive, the customer, and the body shop, increasing productivity of inspections and repairs.

"We're a company that has thought about claims continuously," Renwick said. "Rather than believing that there's one breakthrough that gets you to a new utopia of customer service, we're continuously trying to improve."

High-Tech Achiever Award: Mini USA

Fast Company granted Mini the coveted High-Tech Achiever Customer First Award. Before Angela DiFabio bought her Mini Cooper, she had been dreaming about it for a year. The Philadelphia-based Accenture consultant spent untold hours on Mini's website, playing with dozens of possibilities before coming up with the perfect combination: A chili-pepper-red exterior, white racing stripes on the hood, and a custom rally badge bar on the grill.

When DiFabio placed her order with her dealer, the same build-your-own tool— and all the price and product details it provided—left her feeling as if she were getting a fair deal. "He even used the site to order my car," she said. "That made me feel like I was getting the same information that he was, that I wasn't missing something."

While she waited for her Mini to arrive, DiFabio logged on to Mini's website every day, this time using its "Where's My Baby?" tracking tool to follow her car, like an expensive FedEx package, from the factory in Britain to its delivery. "I think most places you go to for a car, if you order one it's just a big black hole," DiFabio said. "To be able to check the process made the wait exciting. It definitely gave me a feeling of control in the process."

Being in control. Not missing anything. Making the wait, if there must be one, exciting. It's how every customer wants the service experience to be. And it is what Mini USA, whose customers must usually wait two to three months for their cars, is using technology to do. The website does more than just provide information or sell products or services. It keeps customers engaged, and when they are more engaged, they are usually happier, too. "Our ultimate goal was to make waiting fun," said Kerri Martin, Mini USA's marketing manager.

Mini's technology is not groundbreaking; however, it makes an impact on the customer experience because of how it is integrated with the brand: It is fun and makes users feel like part of the clan. Many car websites have build-your-own tools, but few are as customizable as Mini's, where the choices are endless and the on-screen car image changes to your specifications. The tracking service, which is unusual, acknowledges and soothes customers' anxiety and impatience—and perhaps stretches the nervous-parent metaphor a bit. In the "scheduled for production" phase, for example, the tracking tool assures them that their Mini "will begin to move through the 'birth canal' at our Oxford plant. Rest well knowing that your baby is in the best of hands."

The challenge for Mini is meeting the high expectations of such eager customers. Critics note that some dealerships are not as integrated with their website as they should be. And when expectant Mini owners, who it turns out are a fretful bunch, found a way to track their cars through independent shipping companies, some customers were upset that Mini's tool was not updated as quickly as the information they were finding on their own. To try to adjust these customers' expectations, Mini added an online video that explains everything that has to happen in the port and why its online tool might be slower than the independent data. It has not appeased everyone, but it has helped soothe some anxiety.

Some of Mini's technology is just for fun: Stay on the Mini site too long, and a pop-up window tells you to "save your retinas for the road." Owners are emailed birthday cards when their Mini is a year old and sent notices when new features are available on the site. DiFabio looks forward to these messages. "Emails I get from other companies feel more like an ad. This feels more like a club," she said.[1]

INTRODUCTION

*C**ustomer relationship management (CRM)** involves managing all aspects of a customer's relationship with an organization to increase customer loyalty and retention and an organization's profitability. As organizations begin to migrate from the traditional product-focused organization toward customer-driven organizations, they are recognizing their customers as experts, not just revenue generators. Organizations are quickly realizing that without customers, they simply would not exist and it is critical they do everything they can to ensure their customers' satisfaction. In an age when product differentiation is difficult, CRM is one of the most valuable assets a company can acquire. The sooner a company embraces CRM the better off it will be and the harder it will be for competitors to steal loyal and devoted customers.

section 9.1 CUSTOMER RELATIONSHIP MANAGEMENT

Patagonia

LEARNING OUTCOMES

9.1. Compare operational and analytical customer relationship management.

9.2. Explain the formula an organization can use to find its most valuable customers.

9.3. Describe and differentiate the CRM technologies used by sales departments and customer service departments.

9.4. Describe and differentiate the CRM technologies used by marketing departments and sales departments.

9.5. Compare customer relationship management, supplier relationship management, partner relationship management, and employee relationship management.

CUSTOMER RELATIONSHIP MANAGEMENT FUNDAMENTALS

When dealing with sick customers, flexibility is key. That is why Walgreens has made healthy investments in customer service over the past 30 years, originating the drive-through pharmacy and pioneering a network for refilling prescriptions at any location. Walgreens credits much of its growth to an increased investment in customer service. The company has developed new software that can print prescription labels in 14 languages and in large type for older patrons. Besides investing in customer-friendly technology, the 103-year-old chain is not forgetting the human touch. Walgreens spends more on payroll at stores where performance is below average, increasing the clerk-to-customer ratio; and it recently launched an online training program for all employees. With 19 straight quarters of double-digit earnings growth, the prescription appears to be working.

Today, most competitors are simply a mouse-click away. The intense competition in today's marketplace forces organizations to switch from sales-focused strategies to customer-focused strategies. Charles Schwab recouped the cost of a multimillion-dollar customer relationship management system in less than two years. The system, developed by Siebel, allows the brokerage firm to trace each interaction with a customer or prospective customer and then provide services (retirement planning, for instance) to each customer's needs and interests. The system provides Schwab with a complete view of its customers, which it uses to differentiate serious investors from nonserious investors. For example, automated deposits from paychecks are a sign of a serious investor, while stagnant balances signal a nonserious investor. Once Schwab is able to make this determination, the firm allocates its resources accordingly, saving money by not investing time or resources in subsidizing nonserious investors.[2]

Customer relationship management (CRM) involves managing all aspects of a customer's relationship with an organization to increase customer loyalty and retention and an organization's profitability. CRM allows an organization to gain insights into customers' shopping and buying behaviors. Kaiser Permanente undertook a CRM strategy to improve and prolong the lives of diabetics. After compiling CRM information on 84,000 diabetic patients, Kaiser found that only 20 percent were getting their eyes checked routinely. (Diabetes is the leading cause of blindness.) As a result, Kaiser is now enforcing rigorous eye-screening programs for diabetics, along with creating support groups for obesity and stress (two more factors that make diabetes even worse). This CRM-based "preventive medicine" approach is saving Kaiser money and, more importantly, improving the health of diabetic patients.[3]

Figure 9.1 provides an overview of a typical CRM system. Customers contact an organization through various means including call centers, web access, email, faxes, and direct sales. A single customer may access an organization multiple times through many different channels. The CRM system tracks every communication between the customer and the organization and provides access to CRM information across different systems from accounting to order fulfillment. Understanding all customer communications allows the organization to communicate effectively with each customer. It gives the organization a detailed understanding of each customer's products and services regardless of the customer's preferred communication channel. A customer service representative can easily view detailed account

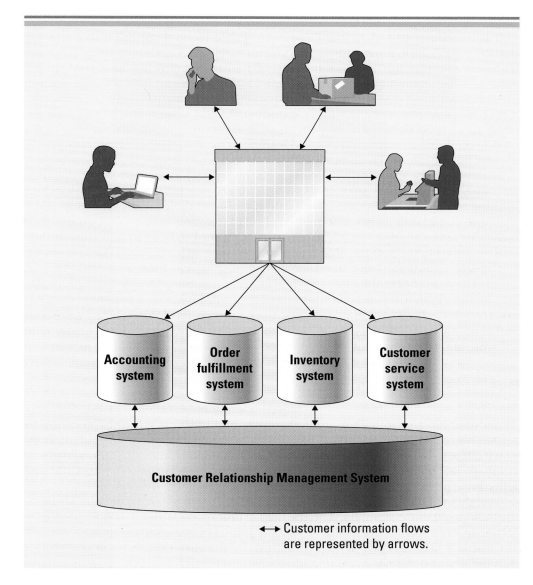

FIGURE 9.1

Customer Relationship
Management Overview

Accounting system

Order fulfillment system

Inventory system

Customer service system

Customer Relationship Management System

◄──► Customer information flows
are represented by arrows.

information and history through a CRM system when providing information to a customer such as expected delivery dates, complementary product information, and customer payment and billing information. Understanding the fundamentals of CRM includes the following:

- CRM as a business strategy.
- Business benefits of CRM.
- Evolution of CRM.
- Operational and analytical CRM.

CRM as a Business Strategy

Eddie Bauer ships 110 million catalogs a year, maintains two websites, and has more than 600 retail stores. The company collects information through customer transactions and analyzes the information to determine the best way to market to each individual customer. Eddie Bauer discovered that customers who shop across all three of its distribution channels—catalogs, websites, and stores—spend up to five times more than customers who shop through only one channel.

Michael Boyd, director of CRM at Eddie Bauer, stated, "Our experience tells us that CRM is in no way, shape, or form a software application. Fundamentally, it is a business strategy to try to optimize profitability, revenue, and satisfaction at an individual customer level. Everything in an organization, every single process, every single application, is a tool that can be used to serve the CRM goal."[4]

It is important to realize that CRM is not just a technology, but also a strategy that an organization must embrace on an enterprise level. Although there are many technical components of CRM, it is actually a process and business goal simply enhanced by technology. Implementing a CRM system can help an organization identify customers and design specific marketing campaigns tailored to each customer, thereby increasing customer spending. A CRM system also allows an organization to treat customers as individuals, gaining important insights into their buying preferences and behaviors and leading to increased sales, greater profitability, and higher rates of customer loyalty.

When a "lucky ambassador" greets a Harrah's guest at a video-poker machine by name, wishes her a happy birthday, and offers free tickets to a show, luck has nothing to do with it. The moment customers insert their loyalty card into a slot machine, the casino giant's $30 million-plus CRM system reveals every move they have ever made at any of its 28 properties. "If you start to have a really unfortunate visit, you start to think, 'Man, that place is really just bad luck,' " said Gary Loveman, Harrah's president and CEO. "If we see that coming, we can intervene" with perks to soothe the pain of gambling losses. While many companies struggle to employ CRM successfully, gathering massive amounts of data without using it to benefit customers, Harrah's is building on its mastery. In the future, its slot machines will spout real-time monetary credits and dinner coupons using new customer-recognition software and hardware, leaving even its losing customers feeling a little luckier.[5]

Business Benefits of CRM

The company 1-800-Flowers.com achieved operational excellence by building customer intimacy to continue to improve profits and business growth. The company turned brand loyalty into brand relationships by using the vast amounts of information it collected to understand customers' needs and expectations. The floral delivery company adopted SAS Enterprise Miner to analyze the information in its CRM systems. Enterprise Miner sifts through information to reveal trends, explain outcomes, and predict results so that businesses can increase response rates and quickly identify their profitable customers. With the help of Enterprise Miner, 1-800-Flowers.com is continuing to thrive, averaging 17 percent annual increases in revenue.[6]

CRM is a business philosophy based on the premise that those organizations that understand the needs of individual customers are best positioned to achieve sustainable competitive advantage in the future. Many aspects of CRM are not new to organizations; CRM is simply performing current business better. Placing customers at the forefront of all thinking and decision making requires significant operational and technology changes.

A customer strategy starts with understanding who the company's customers are and how the company can meet strategic goals. *The New York Times* understands this and has spent the past decade researching core customers to find similarities among groups of readers in cities outside the New York metropolitan area. Its goal is to understand how to appeal to those groups and make *The New York Times* a national newspaper, expanding its circulation and the reach it offers to advertisers. *The New York Times* is growing in a relatively flat publishing market and has achieved a customer retention rate of 94 percent in an industry that averages roughly 60 percent.[7]

As the business world increasingly shifts from product focus to customer focus, most organizations recognize that treating existing customers well is the best source of profitable and sustainable revenue growth. In the age of ebusiness, however, an organization is challenged more than ever before to satisfy its customers. Figure 9.2 displays the benefits derived by an organization from a CRM strategy.

The National Basketball Association's New York Knicks are becoming better than ever at communicating with their fans. Thanks to a CRM solution, New York Knicks' management now knows which season-ticket holders like which players, what kind of merchandise they buy, and where they buy it. Management is finally able to send out fully integrated email campaigns that do not overlap with other marketing efforts.[8]

An organization can find its most valuable customers by using a formula that industry insiders call RFM—Recency, Frequency, and Monetary value. In other words, an organization must track:

- How recently a customer purchased items (recency).
- How frequently a customer purchases items (frequency).
- How much a customer spends on each purchase (monetary value).

Once a company has gathered this initial CRM information, it can compile it to identify patterns and create marketing campaigns, sales promotions, and services to increase business. For example, if Ms. Smith buys only at the height of the season, then the company should send her a special offer during the off-season. If Mr. Jones always buys software but never computers, then the company should offer him free software with the purchase of a new computer.

The CRM technologies discussed in this chapter can help organizations find answers to RFM and other tough questions, such as who are their best customers and which of their products are the most profitable.

CRM
Advantages

Evolution of CRM

Knowing the customer, especially knowing the profitability of individual customers, is highly lucrative in the financial services industry. Its high transactional nature has

CRM Benefits
Provide better customer service
Improve call center efficiency
Cross-sell products more effectively
Help sales staff close deals faster
Simplify marketing and sales processes
Discover new customers
Increase customer revenues

FIGURE 9.2

CRM Benefits

FIGURE 9.3

Evolution of CRM

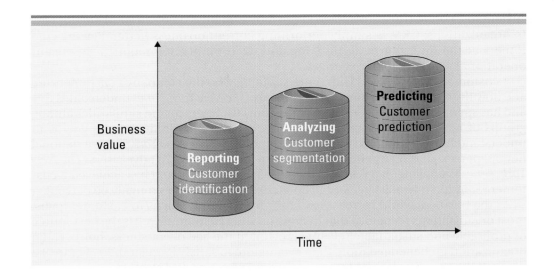

always afforded the financial services industry more access to customer information than other industries have, but it has embraced CRM technologies only recently.

Barclays Bank is a leading financial services company operating in more than 70 countries. In the United Kingdom, Barclays has over 10 million personal customers and about 9.3 million credit cards in circulation, and it serves 500,000 small business customers. Barclays decided to invest in CRM technologies to help it gain valuable insights into its business and customers.

With the new CRM system, Barclays' managers are better able to predict the financial behavior of individual customers and assess whether a customer is likely to pay back a loan in full and within the agreed-upon time period. This helps Barclays manage its profitability with greater precision because it can charge its customers a more appropriate rate of interest based on the results of the customer's risk assessment. Barclays also uses a sophisticated customer segmentation system to identify groups of profitable customers, both on a corporate and personal level, which it can then target for new financial products. One of the most valuable pieces of information Barclays discovered was that about 50 percent of its customers are nonprofitable and that less than 30 percent of its customers provide 90 percent of its profits.[9]

There are three phases in the evolution of CRM: (1) reporting, (2) analyzing, and (3) predicting. ***CRM reporting technologies*** help organizations identify their customers across other applications. ***CRM analysis technologies*** help organizations segment their customers into categories such as best and worst customers. ***CRM predicting technologies*** help organizations make predictions regarding customer behavior such as which customers are at risk of leaving (see Figure 9.3).

Both operational and analytical CRM technologies can assist in customer reporting (identification), customer analysis (segmentation), and customer prediction. Figure 9.4 highlights a few of the important questions an organization can answer using CRM technologies.

Operational and Analytical CRM

Joe Guyaux knows the best way to win customers is to improve service. Under his leadership and with the help of Siebel CRM, the PNC retail banking team increased new consumer checking customers by 19 percent in one year. PNC retained 21 percent more of its consumer checking households as well as improved customer satisfaction by 9 percent.[10]

The two primary components of a CRM strategy are operational CRM and analytical CRM. ***Operational CRM*** supports traditional transactional processing for day-to-day front-office operations or systems that deal directly with the customers. ***Analytical CRM*** supports back-office operations and strategic analysis and includes all systems that do not deal directly with the customers. The primary

FIGURE 9.4

Reporting, Analyzing, and
Predicting Examples

REPORTING "Asking What Happened"	ANALYZING "Asking Why It Happened"	PREDICTING "Asking What Will Happen"
What is the total revenue by customer?	Why did sales not meet forecasts?	What customers are at risk of leaving?
How many units did we manufacture?	Why was production so low?	What products will the customer buy?
Where did we sell the most products?	Why did we not sell as many units as last year?	Who are the best candidates for a mailing?
What were total sales by product?	Who are our customers?	What is the best way to reach the customer?
How many customers did we serve?	Why was customer revenue so high?	What is the lifetime profitability of a customer?
What are our inventory levels?	Why are inventory levels so low?	What transactions might be fraudulent?

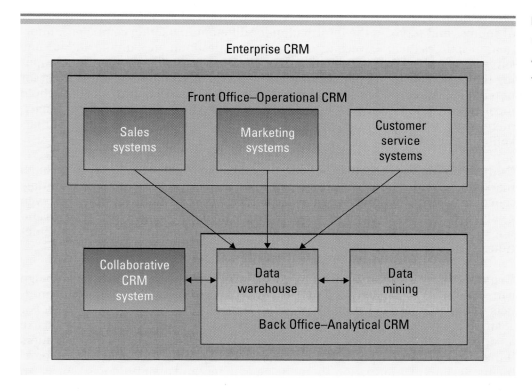

FIGURE 9.5

Operational CRM and
Analytical CRM

difference between operational CRM and analytical CRM is the direct interaction between the organization and its customers. Figure 9.5 provides an overview of operational CRM and analytical CRM.

USING IT TO DRIVE OPERATIONAL CRM

Figure 9.6 displays the different technologies marketing, sales, and customer service departments can use to perform operational CRM.

Marketing and Operational CRM

Companies are no longer trying to sell one product to as many customers as possible; instead, they are trying to sell one customer as many products as possible. Marketing departments are able to transform to this new way of doing business by using CRM technologies that allow them to gather and analyze customer information

Operational CRM Technologies		
Marketing	**Sales**	**Customer Service**
1. List generator	1. Sales management	1. Contact center
2. Campaign management	2. Contact management	2. Web-based self-service
3. Cross-selling and up-selling	3. Opportunity management	3. Call scripting

to deploy successful marketing campaigns. In fact, a marketing campaign's success is directly proportional to the organization's ability to gather and analyze the right information. The three primary operational CRM technologies a marketing department can implement to increase customer satisfaction are:

1. List generator.
2. Campaign management.
3. Cross-selling and up-selling.

List Generator   *List generators* compile customer information from a variety of sources and segment the information for different marketing campaigns. Information sources include website visits, website questionnaires, online and off-line surveys, flyers, toll-free numbers, current customer lists, and so on. After compiling the customer list, an organization can use criteria to filter and sort the list for potential customers. Filter and sort criteria can include such things as household income, education level, and age. List generators provide the marketing department with a solid understanding of the type of customer it needs to target for marketing campaigns.

Campaign Management   *Campaign management systems* guide users through marketing campaigns performing such tasks as campaign definition, planning, scheduling, segmentation, and success analysis. These advanced systems can even calculate quantifiable results for return on investment (ROI) for each campaign and track the results in order to analyze and understand how the company can fine-tune future campaigns.

Cross-Selling and Up-Selling   Two key sales strategies a marketing campaign can deploy are cross-selling and up-selling. *Cross-selling* is selling additional products or services to a customer. *Up-selling* is increasing the value of the sale. For example, McDonald's performs cross-selling by asking customers if they would like an apple pie with their meal. McDonald's performs up-selling by asking customers if they would like to super-size their meals. CRM systems offer marketing departments all kinds of information about their customers and their products, which can help them identify cross-selling and up-selling marketing campaigns.

The California State Automobile Association (CSAA) had to take advantage of its ability to promote and cross-sell CSAA automotive, insurance, and travel services to beat its competition. Accomplishing this task was easy once the company implemented E.piphany's CRM system. The system integrated information from all of CSAA's separate databases, making it immediately available to all employees through a web-based browser. Employees could quickly glance at a customer's profile and determine which services the customer currently had and which services the customer might want to purchase based on her or his needs as projected by the software.[11]

Sales and Operational CRM

Siebel, one of the largest providers of CRM software, had 33,000 subscribers in January 2005. Salesforce.com, provider of on-demand web-based customer relationship management software, added 40,000 subscribers during the first three months of 2005, more than all of Siebel's subscribers. Salesforce.com's total number of subscribers is over 500,000. Merrill Lynch, one of the biggest customers in the sales force market, signed on for 5,000 subscriptions for its global private client division, making the brokerage firm Salesforce.com's largest customer. Salesforce.com's new product, Customforce, includes tools for adding data analysis capabilities, spreadsheet-style mathematical formulas, business processes, and forecasting models.[12]

Sales departments were the first to begin developing CRM systems. Sales departments had two primary reasons to track customer sales information electronically. First, sales representatives were struggling with the overwhelming amount of customer account information they were required to maintain and track. Second, companies were struggling with the issue that much of their vital customer and sales information remained in the heads of their sales representatives. One of the first CRM components built to help address these issues was the sales force automation component. *Sales force automation (SFA)* is a system that automatically tracks all of the steps in the sales process. SFA products focus on increasing customer satisfaction, building customer relationships, and improving product sales by tracking all sales information.

Serving several million guests each year, Vail Resorts Inc. maintains dozens of systems across all seven of its properties. These systems perform numerous tasks including recording lift ticket, lodging, restaurant, conference, retail, and ski rental sales. Since a significant percentage of the company's revenue results from repeat guests, building stronger, more profitable relationships with its loyal customers is Vail Resorts first priority.

To improve its customer service and marketing campaign success, Vail deployed the Ascential CRM system, which integrated the customer information from its many disparate systems. The CRM system is providing Vail Resorts with a detailed level of customer insight, which helps the company personalize its guest offerings and promotions. By using a CRM system that integrates information from across all of its resorts and business lines, the company can determine what, where, and how its guests behave across all of its properties. For example, the company can now offer discounts on lift ticket and ski rentals for customers staying in its resorts. The three primary operational CRM technologies a sales department can implement to increase customer satisfaction are:

1. Sales management CRM systems.
2. Contact management CRM systems.
3. Opportunity management CRM systems.[13]

Sales Management CRM Systems   Figure 9.7 depicts the typical sales process, which begins with an opportunity and ends with billing the customer for the sale. Leads and potential customers are the lifeblood of all sales organizations, whether the products they are peddling are computers, clothing, or cars. How the leads are handled can make the difference between revenue growth or decline. *Sales management CRM systems* automate each phase of the sales process, helping individual sales representatives coordinate and organize all of their accounts. Features include calendars to help plan customer meetings, alarm reminders signaling important tasks, customizable multimedia presentations, and document generation. These systems can even provide an analysis of the sales cycle and calculate how each individual sales representative is performing during the sales process.

Contact Management CRM Systems   A *contact management CRM system* maintains customer contact information and identifies prospective customers for future sales. Contact management systems include such features as maintaining organizational charts, detailed customer notes, and supplemental sales information. For example, a contact management system can take an incoming telephone number and display the caller's name along with notes detailing previous conversations. This allows the sales representative to answer the telephone and say, "Hi Sue, how is your new laptop working? How was your vacation to Florida?" without

FIGURE 9.7

Overview of the Sales Process

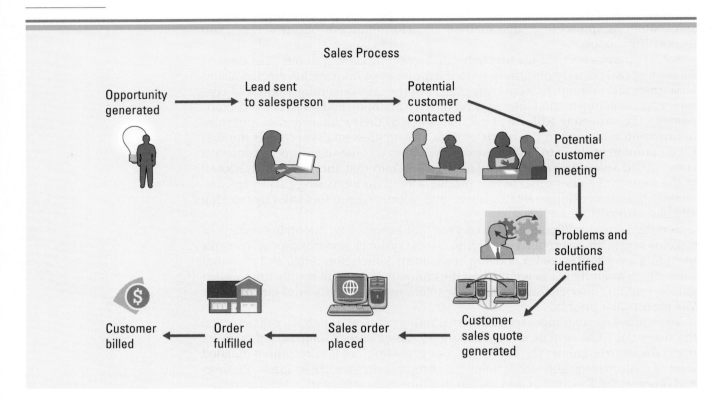

receiving any reminders of such details first from the customer. The customer feels valued since the sales associate knows her name and even remembers details of their last conversation!

A $16 billion technology company, 3M is a leader in health care, safety, electronics, telecommunications, office, and consumer markets. The company began to focus on streamlining and unifying its sales processes with the primary goals of better customer segmentation and more reliable lead generation and qualification. To achieve these goals the company implemented a CRM system and soon found itself receiving the following benefits:

- Cutting the time it takes to familiarize sales professionals with new territories by 33 percent.
- Increasing management's visibility of the sales process.
- Decreasing the time it takes to qualify leads and assign sales opportunities by 40 percent.

One of the more successful campaigns driven by the CRM system allowed 3M to deliver direct mail to targeted government agencies and emergency services in response to the anthrax attacks in 2002. All inquiries to the mail campaign were automatically assigned to a sales representative who followed up with a quote. In little more than a week, the company had received orders for 35,000 respirator masks.[14]

Opportunity Management CRM Systems *Opportunity management CRM systems* target sales opportunities by finding new customers or companies for future sales. Opportunity management systems determine potential customers and competitors and define selling efforts including budgets and schedules. Advanced opportunity management systems can even calculate the probability of a sale, which can save sales representatives significant time and money when attempting to find new customers. The primary difference between contact management and opportunity management is that contact management deals with existing customers

FIGURE 9.8

CRM Pointers for Gaining
Prospective Customers

CRM Pointers for Gaining Prospective Customers	
1. Get their attention	If you have a good prospect, chances are that he or she receives dozens of offers from similar companies. Be sure your first contact is professional and gets your customer's attention.
2. Value their time	When you ask for a meeting, you are asking for the most valuable thing a busy person has—time. Many companies have had great success by offering high-value gifts in exchange for a meeting with a representative. Just be careful because some organizations frown on expensive gifts. Instead, offer these prospective customers a report that can help them perform their jobs more effectively.
3. Overdeliver	If your letter offered a free DVD in exchange for a meeting, bring a box of microwave popcorn along with the movie. Little gestures like these tell customers that you not only keep your word, but also can be counted on to overdeliver.
4. Contact frequently	Find new and creative ways to contact your prospective customers frequently. Starting a newsletter and sending out a series of industry updates are excellent ways to keep in contact and provide value.
5. Generate a trustworthy mailing list	If you are buying a mailing list from a third party be sure that the contacts are genuine prospects, especially if you are offering an expensive gift. Be sure that the people you are meeting have the power to authorize a sale.
6. Follow up	One of the most powerful prospecting tools is a simple thank-you note. Letting people know that their time was appreciated may even lead to additional referrals.

and opportunity management deals with new customers. Figure 9.8 displays six CRM pointers a sales representative can use to increase prospective customers.

Customer Service and Operational CRM

Andy Taylor became president of Enterprise, his father's $76 million rental-car company, in 1980. Today, it is the largest in North America, with $7 billion in revenue. How has he kept customer service a priority? By quantifying it. Enterprise surveys 1.7 million customers a year. If a branch's satisfaction scores are low, employees, even vice presidents, cannot be promoted. The result is self-propagating. Seeking better scores, managers make better hires. And because Enterprise promotes almost solely from within, nearly every executive—including Taylor, who started out washing cars—has a front-line understanding of what it takes to keep customers happy. "The company would never have gotten that 100-fold growth without Andy's knack for putting systems and processes in place so you can deliver consistent service," said Sandy Rogers, senior vice president of corporate strategy.[15]

Sales and marketing are the primary departments that interact directly with customers before a sale. Most companies recognize the importance of building strong relationships during the marketing and sales efforts; however, many fail to realize the importance of continuing to build these relationships after the sale is complete. It is actually more important to build postsale relationships if the company wants to ensure customer loyalty and satisfaction. The best way to implement postsale CRM strategies is through the customer service department.

One of the primary reasons a company loses customers is bad customer service experiences. Providing outstanding customer service is a difficult task, and many CRM technologies are available to assist organizations with this important activity. For example, by rolling out Lotus Instant Messaging to its customers, Avnet Computer Marketing has established an efficient, direct route to push valuable information and updates out to its customers. The company uses Lotus Instant Messaging to provide real-time answers to customer questions by listing its support specialists' status by different colors on its website: green if they are available, red if they are

CRM Future

not, or blue if they are out of the office. The customer simply clicks on a name to begin instant messaging or a chat session to get quick answers to questions.[16]

Before access to Lotus Instant Messaging, customers had to wait in "1-800" call queues or for email responses for answers. The new system has increased customer satisfaction along with tremendous savings from fewer long-distance phone charges. Avnet also estimates that Lotus Instant Messaging saves each of its 650 employees five to 10 minutes a day. The three primary operational CRM technologies a customer service department can implement to increase customer satisfaction are:

1. Contact center.
2. Web-based self-service.
3. Call scripting.[17]

Contact Center   Knowledge-management software, which helps call centers put consistent answers at customer-service representative's fingertips, is often long on promise and short on delivery. The problem? Representatives have to take time out from answering calls to input things they have learned—putting the "knowledge" in knowledge management.

Brad Cleveland, who heads the Incoming Calls Management Institute, said, "Software is just a tool. It doesn't do any good unless people across the organization are using it to its potential." Sharp Electronics is making it happen. Sharp's frontline representatives built the system from scratch. And as Sharp rolled out its network over the past four years, representatives' compensation and promotions were tied directly to the system's use. As a result, the customer call experience at Sharp has improved dramatically: The proportion of problems resolved by a single call has soared from 76 percent to 94 percent.[18]

A *contact center* (or *call center*) is where customer service representatives (CSRs) answer customer inquiries and respond to problems through a number of different customer touchpoints. A contact center is one of the best assets a customer-driven organization can have because maintaining a high level of customer support is critical to obtaining and retaining customers. Numerous systems are available to help an organization automate its contact centers. Figure 9.9 highlights a few of the features available in contact center systems.

Contact centers also track customer call history along with problem resolutions—information critical for providing a comprehensive customer view to the CSR. CSRs who can quickly comprehend and understand all of a customer's products and issues provide tremendous value to the customer and the organization. Nothing makes frustrated customers happier than not having to explain their problems to yet another CSR.

New emotion-detection software called Perform, created by Nice Systems, is designed to help companies improve customer service by identifying callers who are upset. When an elderly man distressed over high medical premiums hung up during his phone call to the Wisconsin Physician Services Insurance Corporation's call center, an IT system detected the customer's exasperation and automatically emailed a supervisor. The supervisor listened to a digital recording of the conversation, called the customer, and suggested ways to lower the premium. The system uses algorithms to determine a baseline of emotion during the first five to 10 seconds of a call, any deviation from the baseline triggers an alert.[19]

FIGURE 9.9

Common Features Included in Contact Centers

Common Features Included in Contact Centers	
Automatic call distribution	A phone switch routes inbound calls to available agents.
Interactive voice response (IVR)	Directs customers to use touch-tone phones or keywords to navigate or provide information.
Predictive dialing	Automatically dials outbound calls and when someone answers, the call is forwarded to an available agent.

Web-Based Self-Service *Web-based self-service systems* allow customers to use the web to find answers to their questions or solutions to their problems. FedEx uses web-based self-service systems to allow customers to track their own packages without having to talk to a CSR. FedEx customers can simply log on to FedEx's website and enter their tracking number. The website quickly displays the exact location of the package and the estimated delivery time.

Another great feature of web-based self-service is *click-to-talk* buttons. Click-to-talk buttons allow customers to click on a button and talk with a CSR via the Internet. Powerful customer-driven features like these add tremendous value to any organization by providing customers with real-time information without having to contact company representatives.[20]

Call Scripting Being a CSR is not an easy task, especially when the CSR is dealing with detailed technical products or services. *Call scripting systems* access organizational databases that track similar issues or questions and automatically generate the details for the CSR who can then relay them to the customer. The system can even provide a list of questions that the CSR can ask the customer to determine the potential problem and resolution. This feature helps CSRs answer difficult questions quickly while also presenting a uniform image so two different customers do not receive two different answers.

Documedics is a health care consulting company that provides reimbursement information about pharmaceutical products to patients and health care professionals. The company currently supports inquiries for 12 pharmaceutical companies and receives over 30,000 customer calls per month. Originally, the company had a data file for each patient and for each pharmaceutical company. This inefficient process resulted in the potential for a single patient to have up to 12 different information files if the patient was a client of all 12 pharmaceutical companies. To answer customer questions, a CSR had to download each customer file, causing tremendous inefficiencies and confusion. The company implemented a CRM system with a call scripting feature to alleviate the problem and provide its CSRs with a comprehensive view of every customer, regardless of the pharmaceutical company. The company anticipated 20 percent annual growth primarily because of the successful implementation of its new system.[21]

Customer Relationship Management (CRM) Metrics

Brother International Corporation experienced skyrocketing growth in its sales of multifunction centers, fax machines, printers, and labeling systems in the late 1990s. Along with skyrocketing sales growth came a tremendous increase in customer service calls. When Brother failed to answer the phone fast enough, product returns started to increase. The company responded by increasing call center capacity, and the rate of returns began to drop. However, Dennis Upton, CIO of Brother International, observed that all the company was doing was answering the phone. He quickly realized that the company was losing a world of valuable market intelligence (business intelligence) about existing customers from all those telephone calls. The company decided to deploy SAP's CRM solution. The 1.8 million calls Brother handled dropped to 1.57 million, which reduced call center staff from 180 agents to 160 agents. Since customer demographic information is now stored and displayed on the agent's screen based on the incoming telephone number, the company has reduced call duration by an average of one minute, saving the company $600,000 per year. A company must continually monitor its efforts to ensure success.[22]

CRM Success

Without understanding CRM's impact, a business will not be able to understand if its CRM practices are adding to its success. Using CRM metrics to track and monitor performance is a best practice for many companies. One rule for managers is to measure and monitor no more than seven (plus or minus two) key CRM metrics out of the hundreds of CRM metrics available. Figure 9.10 displays a few common CRM metrics tracked by organizations.[23]

FIGURE 9.10

CRM Metrics

Sales Metrics	Service Metrics	Marketing Metrics
■ Number of prospective customers	■ Cases closed same day	■ Number of marketing campaigns
■ Number of new customers	■ Number of cases handled by agent	■ New customer retention rates
■ Number of retained customers	■ Number of service calls	■ Number of responses by marketing campaign
■ Number of open leads	■ Average number of service requests by type	■ Number of purchases by marketing campaign
■ Number of sales calls	■ Average time to resolution	■ Revenue generated by marketing campaign
■ Number of sales calls per lead	■ Average number of service calls per day	■ Cost per interaction by marketing campaign
■ Amount of new revenue	■ Percentage compliance with service-level agreement	■ Number of new customers acquired by marketing campaign
■ Amount of recurring revenue	■ Percentage of service renewals	■ Customer retention rate
■ Number of proposals given	■ Customer satisfaction level	■ Number of new leads by product

USING IT TO DRIVE ANALYTICAL CRM

Maturing analytical CRM and behavioral modeling technologies are helping numerous organizations move beyond legacy benefits such as enhanced customer service and retention to systems that can truly improve business profitability. Unlike operational CRM that automates call centers and sales forces with the aim of enhancing customer transactions, analytical CRM solutions are designed to dig deep into a company's historical customer information and expose patterns of behavior on which a company can capitalize. Analytical CRM is primarily used to enhance and support decision making and works by identifying patterns in customer information collected from the various operational CRM systems.

For many organizations, the power of analytical CRM solutions provides tremendous managerial opportunities. Depending on the specific solution, analytical CRM tools can slice and dice customer information to create made-to-order views of customer value, spending, product affinities, percentile profiles, and segmentations. Modeling tools can identify opportunities for cross-selling, up-selling, and expanding customer relationships.

Personalization occurs when a website can know enough about a person's likes and dislikes to fashion offers that are more likely to appeal to that person. Many organizations are now utilizing CRM to create customer rules and templates that marketers can use to personalize customer messages.

The information produced by analytical CRM solutions can help companies make decisions about how to handle customers based on the value of each and every one. Analytical CRM can help reveal information about which customers are worth investing in, which should be serviced at an average level, and which should not be invested in at all.

Data gained from customers can also reveal information about employees. Wachovia Bank surveys customers—25,000 every month—for feedback on their service experience. It asks about individual employees and uses those answers in one-on-one staff coaching. A 20-minute coaching session at a Manhattan branch made clear how this feedback—each customer surveyed rates 33 employee behaviors—can improve

FIGURE 9.11

Analytical CRM Information
Examples

Analytical CRM Information Examples	
1. Give customers more of what they want	Analytical CRM can help an organization go beyond the typical "Dear Mr. Smith" salutation. An organization can use its analytical CRM information to make its communications more personable. For example, if it knows a customer's shoe size and preferred brand it can notify the customer that there is a pair of size 12 shoes set aside to try on the next time the customer visits the store.
2. Find new customers similar to the best customers	Analytical CRM might determine that an organization does a lot of business with women 35 to 45 years old who drive SUVs and live within 30 miles of a certain location. The company can then find a mailing list that highlights this type of customer for potential new sales.
3. Find out what the organization does best	Analytical CRM can determine what an organization does better than its competitors. For example, if a restaurant caters more breakfasts to midsized companies than its competition does, it can purchase a specialized mailing list of midsized companies in the area and send them a mailing that features the breakfast catering specials.
4. Beat competitors to the punch	Analytical CRM can determine sales trends allowing an organization to offer the best customers deals before the competition has a chance to. For example, a clothing store might determine its best customers for outdoor apparel and send them an offer to attend a private sale right before the competition runs its outdoor apparel sale.
5. Reactivate inactive customers	Analytical CRM can highlight customers who have not done any business with the organization in a while. The organization can then send them a personalized letter along with a discount coupon. It will remind them of the company and may help spark a renewed relationship.
6. Let customers know they matter	Analytical CRM can determine what customers want and need, so an organization can contact them with this information. Anything from a private sale to a reminder that the car is due for a tune-up is excellent customer service.

service. The branch manager urged an employee to focus on sincerity rather than on mere friendliness, to "sharpen her antenna" so she would listen to customers more intuitively, and to slow down rather than hurry up. That focus on careful, sincere, intuitive service has paid off: Wachovia has held the top score among banks in the American Customer Satisfaction Index since 2001.[24]

Analytical CRM relies heavily on data warehousing technologies and business intelligence to glean insights into customer behavior (These are covered in detail in Section 9.2). These systems quickly aggregate, analyze, and disseminate customer information throughout an organization. Figure 9.11 displays a few examples of the kind of information insights analytical CRM can help an organization gain.[25]

UPS's data-intensive environment is supported by the largest IBM DB2 database in the world, consisting of 236 terabytes of data related to its analytical CRM tool. The shipping company's goal is to create one-to-one customer relationships, and it is using Quantum View tools that allow it to let customers tailor views of such things as shipment history and receive notices when a package arrives or is delayed. UPS has built more than 500 customer relationship management applications that run off of its data warehouse.[26]

Data warehouses are providing businesses with information about their customers and products that was previously impossible to locate, and the resulting payback can be tremendous. Organizations are now relying on business intelligence to provide them with hard facts that can determine everything from which type of marketing and sales campaign to launch, to which customers to target, at what time. Using CRM along with business intelligence allows organizations to make better, more informed decisions and to reap amazing unforeseen rewards.

Sears, Roebuck and Company is the third-largest U.S. retailer. Even though Sears does not know exactly "who" its customers are (by name and address) since many customers use cash or non-Sears credit cards, it can still benefit from analytical CRM technologies. Sears uses these technologies to determine what its generic customers prefer to buy and when they buy it, which enables the company to predict what they will buy. Using analytical CRM, Sears can view each day's sales by region, district, store, product line, and individual item. Sears can now monitor the precise impact of advertising, weather, and other factors on sales of specific items. For the first time, Sears can even group or "cluster," widely divergent types of items. For example, merchandisers can track sales of a store display marked "Gifts under $25" that might include sweatshirts, screwdrivers, and other unrelated items. The advertising department can then follow the sales of "Gifts under $25" to determine which products to place in its newspaper advertisements.[27]

CRM TRENDS: SRM, PRM, ERM

Organizations are discovering a wave of other key business areas where it is beneficial to take advantage of building strong relationships. These emerging areas include supplier relationship management (SRM), partner relationship management (PRM), and employee relationship management (ERM).

Supplier Relationship Management

Supplier relationship management (SRM) focuses on keeping suppliers satisfied by evaluating and categorizing suppliers for different projects, which optimizes supplier selection. SRM applications help companies analyze vendors based on a number of key variables including strategy, business goals, prices, and markets. The company can then determine the best supplier to collaborate with and can work on developing strong relationships with that supplier. The partners can then work together to streamline processes, outsource services, and provide products that they could not provide individually.

With the merger of the Bank of Halifax and Bank of Scotland, the new company, HBOS, implemented an SRM system to provide consistent information to its suppliers. The system integrates procurement information from the separate Bank of Halifax and Bank of Scotland operational systems, generating a single repository of management information for consistent reporting and analysis. Other benefits HBOS derived from the SRM solution include:

- A single consolidated view of all suppliers.
- Consistent, detailed management information allowing multiple views for every executive.
- Elimination of duplicate suppliers.[28]

Partner Relationship Management

Organizations have begun to realize the importance of building relationships with partners, dealers, and resellers. ***Partner relationship management (PRM)*** focuses on keeping vendors satisfied by managing alliance partner and reseller relationships that provide customers with the optimal sales channel. PRM's business strategy is to select and manage partners to optimize their long-term value to an organization. In effect, it means picking the right partners, working with them to help them be successful in dealing with mutual customers, and ensuring that partners and the ultimate end customers are satisfied and successful. Many of the features of a PRM application include real-time product information on availability, marketing materials, contracts, order details, and pricing, inventory, and shipping information.

PRM is one of the smaller segments of CRM that has superb potential. PRM grew from a $500 million business to a $1 billion business in less than four years. This is a direct reflection of the growing interdependency of organizations in the new economy. The primary benefits of PRM include:

- Expanded market coverage.
- Offerings of specialized products and services.
- Broadened range of offerings and a more complete solution.

Employee Relationship Management

Jim Sinegal runs Costco, one of the largest wholesale club chains, but there are two things he does not discount: employee benefits and customer service. Average hourly wages trounce those of rival Sam's Club, and 86 percent of workers have health insurance (versus a reported 47 percent at Sam's). Sinegal is not just being nice. Happy employees, he believes, make for happier customers. Low prices (he caps per-item profits at 14 percent) and a generous return policy certainly help. Although Wall Street has long been arguing for smaller benefits, a stingier return policy, and bigger profits, Sinegal sides with customers and staff. "We're trying to run Costco in a fashion that is not just going to satisfy our shareholders this year or this month," he said, "but next year and on into the future."[29]

Employee relationship management (ERM) provides employees with a subset of CRM applications available through a web browser. Many of the ERM applications assist the employee in dealing with customers by providing detailed information on company products, services, and customer orders.

At Rackspace, a San Antonio-based web-hosting company, customer focus borders on the obsessive. Joey Parsons, 24, won the Straightjacket Award, the most coveted employee distinction at Rackspace. The award recognizes the employee who best lives up to the Rackspace motto of delivering "fanatical support," a dedication to customers that is so intense it borders on the loony. Rackspace motivates its staff by treating each team as a separate business, which is responsible for its own profits and losses and has its own ERM website. Each month, employees can earn bonuses of up to 20 percent of their monthly base salaries depending on the performance of their units by both financial and customer-centric measurements such as customer turnover, customer expansion, and customer referrals. Daily reports are available through the team's ERM website.[30]

THE UGLY SIDE OF CRM: WHY CRM MATTERS MORE NOW THAN EVER BEFORE

Business 2.0 ranked "You—the customer" as number one in the top 50 people who matter most in business and stated the following: "It has long been said that the customer is always right, but for a long time companies never really meant it. Now, companies have no choice as the power of the customer grows exponentially as the Internet grows. You—or rather, the collaborative intelligence of tens of millions of people, the networked you—continually create and filter new forms of content, anointing the useful, the relevant, and the amusing and rejecting the rest. You do it on websites like Amazon, Flickr, and YouTube, via podcasts and SMS polling, and on millions of self-published blogs.

"In every case, you have become an integral part of the action as a member of the aggregated, interactive, self-organizing, auto-entertaining audience. But the 'You Revolution' goes well beyond user-generated content. Companies as diverse as Delta Air Lines and T-Mobile are turning to you to create their ad slogans. Procter & Gamble and Lego are incorporating your ideas into new products. You constructed open source software and are its customer and its caretaker. None of this should be a surprise, since it was you—your crazy passions and hobbies and obsessions—that built out the web in the first place. And somewhere out there, you are building web 3.0. We do not yet know what that is, but one thing is for sure: It will matter."[31]

You have more power than ever before. A decade ago if you had a complaint against a company you could make a phone call or write a letter. Now you can literally contact hundreds or thousands of people to log your complaint. Figure 9.12 shows examples of you—the customer—taking your power to the people.

FIGURE 9.12

Customer Power

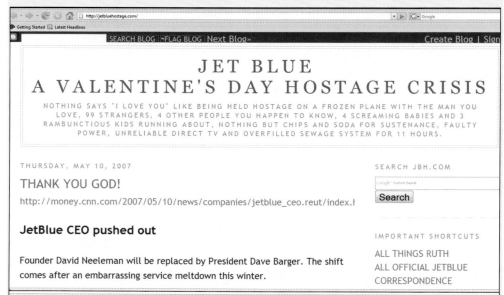

section 9.2 BUSINESS INTELLIGENCE

LEARNING OUTCOMES

9.6. Explain the problem associated with business intelligence. Describe the solution to this business problem.

9.7. Describe the three common forms of data-mining analysis?

9.8. Compare tactical, operational, and strategic BI.

9.9. Explain the organizationwide benefits of BI.

9.10. Describe the four categories of BI business benefits.

MTV

BUSINESS INTELLIGENCE

Business intelligence (BI) refers to applications and technologies that are used to gather, provide access to, and analyze data and information to support decision-making efforts. An early reference to business intelligence occurs in Sun Tzu's book *The Art of War.* Sun Tzu claims that to succeed in war, one should have full knowledge of one's own strengths and weaknesses and full knowledge of the enemy's strengths and weaknesses. Lack of either one might result in defeat. A certain school of thought draws parallels between the challenges in business and those of war, specifically:

- Collecting information.
- Discerning patterns and meaning in the information.
- Responding to the resultant information.[32]

Many organizations today find it next to impossible to understand their own strengths and weaknesses, let alone their enemies', because the enormous volume of organizational data is inaccessible to all but the IT department. Organization data include far more than simple fields in a database; it also includes voice mail, customer phone calls, text messages, video clips, along with numerous new forms of data.

The Problem: Data Rich, Information Poor

As businesses increase their reliance on enterprise systems such as CRM, they are rapidly accumulating vast amounts of data. Every interaction between departments or with the outside world, historical information on past transactions, as well as external market information, is entered into information systems for future use and access. Research from IDC expects businesses to face a data explosion over the next few years as the number of digital images, email in-boxes, and broadband connections doubles by 2010. The amount of data being generated is doubling every year, and some think it will soon begin to double every month. Data are a strategic asset for a business, and if the asset is not used, the business is wasting resources.[33]

An ideal business scenario would be as follows: An account manager, on her way to a client visit, looks up past proposals, as well as the client's ordering, payment, delivery, support, and marketing history. At a glance, she can tell that the client's ordering volumes have dropped lately. A few queries later she understands that the client has a support issue with a given product. The account manager calls her support department and learns that the defective part will be replaced within 24 hours. In addition, the marketing records show that the client recently attended a user conference and expressed interest in the new product line. With this information, the account manager is fully prepared for a constructive sales call. She understands all aspects of her client's relationship with her firm, understands the client's issues, and can confidently address new sales opportunities.

In most organizations, it would take the account manager, in the example above, hours or days to get answers to questions about her client. With all the data available, it is surprising how difficult it is for managers to get a clear picture of fundamental business information, such as inventory levels, orders in the pipeline, or client history. Many organizations contain disparate silos of information. Client orders and payment records are kept in the accounting system; installation and support information is stored in the customer service database; contact management software tracks the proposals and sales call history; and marketing contact history is kept by marketing. Rarely do these systems speak the same language, and there is no simple way for a nontechnical user to get answers quickly.

As a result, information has to be requested from different departments or IT, who must dedicate staff to pull together various reports. Responses can take weeks, by which time the information may be outdated. It has been said that organizations are data rich and information poor. The challenge is to transform data into useful information. With this information, employees gain knowledge that can be leveraged to increase company profitability.

The Solution: Business Intelligence

In every organization, employees make hundreds of decisions each day. They can range from whether to give a customer a discount, whether to start producing a part, whether to launch another direct-mail campaign, whether to order additional materials, and so on. These decisions are sometimes based on facts, but mostly based on experience, accumulated knowledge, and rule of thumb.

That poses a problem because experience, knowledge, and rule of thumb can take years to develop. Some employees never acquire them. Those who do may still fall prey to decision traps or biases in judgment. Improving the quality of business decisions has a direct impact on costs and revenue. For instance, giving a customer a discount may or may not help the bottom line, depending on the profitability of the client over the duration of the relationship. To improve the quality of business decisions, managers can provide existing staff with BI systems and tools that can assist them in making better, more informed decisions. The result creates an agile intelligent enterprise. A few examples of using BI to make informed business decisions include:

- **Retail and sales:** Predicting sales; determining correct inventory levels and distribution schedules among outlets; and loss prevention.
- **Banking:** Forecasting levels of bad loans and fraudulent credit card use, credit card spending by new customers, and which kinds of customers will best respond to (and qualify for) new loan offers.
- **Operations management:** Predicting machinery failures; finding key factors that control optimization of manufacturing capacity.
- **Brokerage and securities trading:** Predicting when bond prices will change; forecasting the range of stock fluctuations for particular issues and the overall market; determining when to buy or sell stocks.
- **Insurance:** Forecasting claim amounts and medical coverage costs; classifying the most important elements that affect medical coverage; predicting which customers will buy new insurance policies.

FIGURE 9.13

BI Data Analysis

Reliable	The data have been documented as the certified or approved data for the enterprise. The business users are confident that the data are the best possible and that they suit the decision-making purposes.
Consistent	The processes that deliver the data to the business community are well documented; there are no surprises such as missing or inaccurate data in the mix, analytics that will not run, response times that are unpredictable.
Understandable	The data have been defined in business terms; calculations and algorithms are easily accessed for comprehension. These are documented in a data dictionary or metadata repository that is easy to access and understand.
Easily manipulated	It is no longer required to have a PhD in statistics to get sophisticated analytics delivered to users' fingertips. And it is just as easy to change the question or set different parameters to twist and turn the data in ways unimaginable just a few years ago.[34]

- **Hardware and software:** Predicting disk-drive failures; forecasting how long it will take to create new chips; predicting potential security violations.
- **Law enforcement:** Tracking crime patterns, locations, and criminal behavior; identifying attributes to assist in solving criminal cases.
- **Government and defense:** Forecasting the cost of moving military equipment; testing strategies for potential military engagements; predicting resource consumption.
- **Airlines:** Capturing data on where customers are flying and the ultimate destination of passengers who change carriers in hub cities; thus, airlines can identify popular locations that they do not service and can check the feasibility of adding routes to capture lost business.
- **Health care:** Correlating demographics of patients with critical illnesses; developing better insights on symptoms and their causes and how to provide proper treatments.
- **Broadcasting:** Predicting what is best to air during prime time and how to maximize returns by interjecting advertisements.
- **Marketing:** Classifying customer demographics that can be used to predict which customers will respond to a mailing or buy a particular product.

The solution of implementing business intelligence systems and tools allows business users to receive data for analysis. (See Figure 9.13.)

Shell Services International's BI solution gave the company access to information about revenues between fuel and nonfuel business. Seeing that 20 percent of products were delivering 80 percent of sales, Shell significantly improved margin and turnover. It also negotiated better deals with suppliers and improved product master file management, which helped reduce working capital.[35]

Figure 9.14 displays how organizations using BI can find the root causes to problems and provide solutions simply by asking "Why?" The process is initiated by analyzing a global report, say of sales per quarter. Every answer is followed by a new question, and users can drill deep down into a report to get to fundamental causes. Once they have a clear understanding of root causes, they can take highly effective action.

Finding the answers to tough business questions by using data that is reliable, consistent, understandable, and easily manipulated allows a business to gain valuable insight into such things as:

- **Where the business has been.** Historical perspective is always important in determining trends and patterns of behavior.
- **Where it is now.** Current situations are critical to either modify if not acceptable or encourage if they are trending in the right direction.
- **And where it will be in the near future.** Being able to predict with surety the direction of the company is critical to sound planning and to creating sound business strategies.[36]

Business Intelligence

FIGURE 9.14

How BI Can Answer Tough
Customer Questions

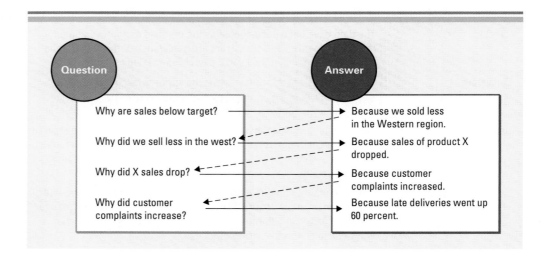

OPERATIONAL, TACTICAL, AND STRATEGIC BI

Claudia Imhoff, president of Intelligent Solutions, believes it is useful to divide the spectrum of data mining analysis and business intelligence into three categories: operational, tactical, and strategic. Two trends are displayed when viewing the spectrum from operational through tactical to strategic. First, the analysis becomes increasingly complex and ad hoc. That is, it is less repetitive, less predictable, and it requires varying amounts and types of data. Second, both the risks and rewards of the analysis increase. That is, the often time-consuming, more strategic queries produce value less frequently but, when they do, the value can be extraordinary. Figure 9.15 illustrates the differences between strategic, tactical, and operational BI.[37]

These three forms are not performed in isolation from each other. It is important to understand that they must work with each other, feeding results from strategic to tactical to promote better operational decision making. Figure 9.16 demonstrates this synergy. In this example, strategic BI is used in the planning stages of a marketing campaign. The results of these analytics form the basis for the beginnings of a new campaign, targeting specific customers or demographics, for example. The daily analyses of the campaign are used by the more tactical form of BI to change the course of the campaign if its results are not tracking where expected.

For example, perhaps a different marketing message is needed, or the inventory levels are not sufficient to maintain the current sales pace so the scope of marketing might be changed. These results are then fed into the operational BI for immediate actions—offering a different product, optimizing the sale price of the product, or changing the daily message sent to selected customer segments.

For this synergy to work, the three forms of BI must be tightly integrated with each other. Minimal time should be lost transporting the results from one technological environment to another. Seamlessness in terms of data and process flow is

FIGURE 9.15

Operational, Tactical,
Strategic BI

	Operational BI	Tactical BI	Strategic BI
Business focus	Manage daily operations, integrate BI with operational systems	Conduct short-term analysis to achieve strategic goals	Achieve long-term organizational goals
Primary users	Managers, analysts, operational users	Executives, managers	Executives, managers
Time frame	Intraday	Day(s) to weeks to months	Months to years
Data	Real-time metrics	Historical metrics	Historical metrics

FIGURE 9.16

The Three Forms of BI must
Work Toward a Common Goal

a must. TruServ, the parent company of True Value Hardware has used BI software to improve efficiency of its distribution operations and reap a $50 million reduction in inventory costs. The marketing department uses BI to track sales promotion results such as which promotions were most popular by store or by region. Now that TruServ is building promotion histories in its databases, it can ensure all stores are fully stocked with adequate inventory. TruServ was able to achieve a positive return on investment in about five to six months.[38]

BI's Operational Value

A leading risk insurance company allows customers to access account information over the Internet. Previously, the company sent paper reports and diskettes to all of its customers. Any errors in the reports would take one to two months to correct because customers would first have to receive the report, catch the mistake, and then notify the company of the error. Now customers spot the errors in real time and notify the insurance company directly through the extranet, usually within a couple of days.[39]

Richard Hackathorn of Bolder Technologies developed an interesting graph to demonstrate the value of operational BI. Figure 9.17 shows the three latencies that impact the speed of decision making. These are data, analysis, and decision latencies.

- **Data latency** is the time duration to make data ready for analysis (i.e., the time for extracting, transforming, and cleansing the data), and loading the data into the database. All this can take time depending on the state of the operational data to begin with.

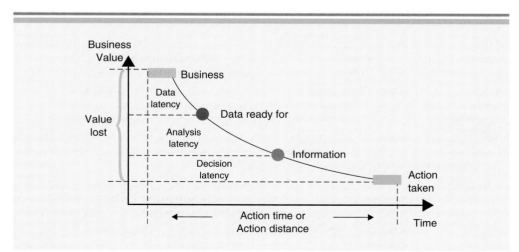

FIGURE 9.17

The Latency Between a
Business Event and an
Action Taken

- **Analysis latency** is the time from which data are made available to the time when analysis is complete. Its length depends on the time it takes a business to do analysis. Usually, we think of this as the time it takes a human to do the analysis, but this can be decreased by the use of automated analytics that have thresholds. When the thresholds are exceeded, alerts or alarms can be issued to appropriate personnel, or they can cause exception processes to be initiated with no human intervention needed.

- **Decision latency** is the time it takes a human to comprehend the analytic result and determine an appropriate action. This form of latency is very difficult to reduce. The ability to remove the decision-making process from the human and automate it will greatly reduce the overall decision latency. Many forward-thinking companies are doing just that. For example, rather than send a high-value customer a letter informing him of a bounced check (which takes days to get to the customer), an automated system can simply send an immediate email or voice message informing the customer of the problem.

The key is to shorten these latencies so that the time frame for opportunistic influences on customers, suppliers, and others is faster, more interactive, and better positioned. As mentioned above, the best time to influence customers is not after they have left the store or the website. It is while they are still in the store or still wandering around the website.

For example, a customer who is searching a website for travel deals is far more likely to be influenced by appropriate messaging actions then and there. Actions taken immediately, while customers are still in the site, might include:

- Offering customers an appropriate coupon for the trip they showed interest in while searching for cheap airfares.

- Giving customers information about their current purchase such as the suggestion that visas are needed.

- Congratulating them on reaching a certain frequent-buyer level and giving them 10 percent off an item.

A website represents another great opportunity to influence a customer, if the interactions are appropriate and timely. For example:

- A banner could announce the next best product to offer right after the customer puts an item in her basket.

- The customer could receive an offer for a product he just removed from his shopping basket.

- Appropriate instructions for the use of a product could come up on the customer's screen; perhaps warning a parent that the product should not be used by children under three.[40]

DATA MINING

At the center of any strategic, tactical, or operational BI effort is data mining. Ruf Strategic Solutions helps organizations employ statistical approaches within a large data warehouse to identify customer segments that display common traits. Marketers can then target these segments with specially designed products and promotions. **Data mining** is the process of analyzing data to extract information not offered by the raw data alone. Data mining can also begin at a summary information level (coarse granularity) and progress through increasing levels of detail (drilling down), or the reverse (drilling up). Data mining is the primary tool used to uncover business intelligence in vast amounts of data.[41]

To perform data mining, users need data-mining tools. **Data-mining tools** use a variety of techniques to find patterns and relationships in large volumes of information and infer rules from them that predict future behavior and guide decision making. Data mining uses specialized technologies and functionalities such as query tools, reporting tools, multidimensional analysis tools, statistical tools, and intelligent agents. Data mining approaches decision making with basically a few different activities in mind including:

- **Classification**—assign records to one of a predefined set of classes.
- **Estimation**—determine values for an unknown continuous variable behavior or estimated future value.
- **Affinity grouping**—determine which things go together.
- **Clustering**—segment a heterogeneous population of records into a number of more homogeneous subgroups.[42]

Sega of America, one of the largest publishers of video games, uses data mining and statistical tools to distribute its advertising budget of more than $50 million a year. Using data mining, product line specialists and marketing strategists "drill" into trends of each retail store chain. Their goal is to find buying trends that help them determine which advertising strategies are working best and how to reallocate advertising resources by media, territory, and time.[43]

Data-mining tools apply algorithms to information sets to uncover inherent trends and patterns in the information, which analysts use to develop new business strategies. Analysts use the output from data-mining tools to build models that, when exposed to new information sets, perform a variety of information analysis functions. The analysts provide business solutions by putting together the analytical techniques and the business problem at hand, which often reveals important new correlations, patterns, and trends. The more common forms of data-mining analysis capabilities include:

- Cluster analysis
- Association detection
- Statistical analysis.

Cluster Analysis

Data Mining

Cluster analysis is a technique used to divide an information set into mutually exclusive groups such that the members of each group are as close together as possible to one another and the different groups are as far apart as possible. Cluster analysis is frequently used to segment customer information for customer relationship management systems to help organizations identify customers with similar behavioral traits, such as clusters of best customers or onetime customers. Cluster analysis also has the ability to uncover naturally occurring patterns in information (see Figure 9.18).

Data-mining tools that "understand" human language are finding unexpected applications in medicine. IBM and the Mayo Clinic unearthed hidden patterns in medical records, discovering that infant leukemia has three distinct clusters, each of which probably benefits from tailored treatments. Caroline A. Kovac, general manager of IBM Life Sciences, expects that mining the records of cancer patients for clustering patterns will turn up clues pointing the way to "tremendous strides in curing cancer."[44]

A great example of cluster analysis occurs when attempting to segment customers based on zip codes. Understanding the demographics, lifestyle behaviors, and buying patterns of the most profitable segments of the population at the zip code level is key to a successful target marketing strategy. Targeting only those who have a high propensity to purchase products and services will help a high-end business cut its sales and marketing costs tremendously. Understanding each customer segment by zip code allows a business to determine the importance of each segment.[45]

Association Detection

Whirlpool Corporation, a $4.3 billion home and commercial appliance manufacturer, employs hundreds of R&D engineers, data analysts, quality assurance specialists, and customer service personnel who all work together to ensure that each generation of appliances is better than the previous generation. Whirlpool is an example of an organization that is gaining business intelligence with association detection data-mining tools.[46]

FIGURE 9.18

Cluster Analysis Example

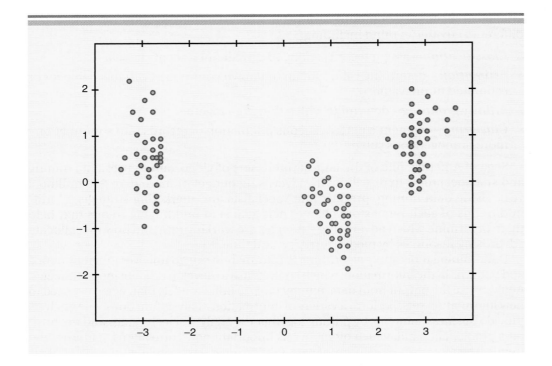

Association detection reveals the degree to which variables are related and the nature and frequency of these relationships in the information. Whirlpool's warranty analysis tool, for instance, uses statistical analysis to automatically detect potential issues, provide quick and easy access to reports, and perform multidimensional analysis on all warranty information. This association detection data-mining tool enables Whirlpool's managers to take proactive measures to control product defects even before most of its customers are aware of the defect. The tool also allows Whirlpool personnel to devote more time to value-added tasks such as ensuring high quality on all products rather than waiting for or manually analyzing monthly reports.[47]

Many people refer to association detection algorithms as *association rule generators* because they create rules to determine the likelihood of events occurring together at a particular time or following each other in a logical progression. Percentages usually reflect the patterns of these events; for example, "55 percent of the time, events A and B occurred together," or "80 percent of the time that items A and B occurred together, they were followed by item C within three days."

One of the most common forms of association detection analysis is market basket analysis. *Market basket analysis* analyzes such items as websites and checkout scanner information to detect customers' buying behavior and predict future behavior by identifying affinities among customers' choices of products and services (see Figure 9.19). Market basket analysis is frequently used to develop marketing campaigns for cross-selling products and services (especially in banking, insurance, and finance) and for inventory control, shelf-product placement, and other retail and marketing applications.

Statistical Analysis

Statistical analysis performs such functions as information correlations, distributions, calculations, and variance analysis. Data-mining tools offer knowledge workers a wide range of powerful statistical capabilities so they can quickly build a variety of statistical models, examine the models' assumptions and validity, and compare and contrast the various models to determine the best one for a particular business issue.

FIGURE 9.19

Market Basket Analysis

Kraft is the producer of instantly recognizable food brands such as Oreo, Ritz, DiGiorno, and Kool-Aid. The company implemented two data-mining applications to assure consistent flavor, color, aroma, texture, and appearance for all of its food lines. One application analyzed product consistency and the other analyzed process variation reduction (PVR).

The product consistency tool, SENECA (Sensory and Experimental Collection Application), gathers and analyzes information by assigning precise definitions and numerical scales to such qualities as chewy, sweet, crunchy, and creamy. SENECA then builds models, histories, forecasts, and trends based on consumer testing and evaluates potential product improvements and changes.

The PVR tool ensures consistent flavor, color, aroma, texture, and appearance for every Kraft product since even small changes in the baking process can result in huge disparities in taste. Evaluating every manufacturing procedure, from recipe instructions to cookie dough shapes and sizes, the PVR tool has the potential to generate significant cost savings for each product. Using these types of data-mining techniques for quality control and cluster analysis makes sure that the billions of Kraft products that reach consumers annually will continue to taste great with every bite.[48]

Forecasting is a common form of statistical analysis. Formally defined, ***forecasts*** are predictions made on the basis of time-series information. ***Time-series information*** is time-stamped information collected at a particular frequency. Examples of time-series information include web visits per hour, sales per month, and calls per day. Forecasting data-mining tools allow users to manipulate the time series for forecasting activities.

When discovering trends and seasonal variations in transactional information, use a time-series forecast to change the transactional information by units of time, such as transforming weekly information into monthly or seasonal information or hourly information into daily information. Companies base production, investment, and staffing decisions on a host of economic and market indicators in this manner. Forecasting models allow organizations to consider all sorts of variables when making decisions.

Nestlé Italiana is part of the multinational giant Nestlé Group and currently dominates Italy's food industry. The company improved sales forecasting by 25 percent with its data-mining forecasting solution that enables the company's managers to make objective decisions based on facts instead of subjective decisions based on intuition. Determining sales forecasts for seasonal confectionery products is a crucial and challenging task. During Easter, Nestlé Italiana has only four weeks to market, deliver, and sell its seasonal products. The Christmas time frame is a little longer, lasting from six to eight weeks, while other holidays such as Valentine's Day and Mother's Day have shorter time frames of about one week.

The company's data-mining solution gathers, organizes, and analyzes massive volumes of information to produce powerful models that identify trends and predict confectionery sales. The business intelligence created is based on five years of historical information and identifies what is important and what is not important. Nestlé Italiana's sophisticated data-mining tool predicted Mother's Day sales forecasts that were 90 percent accurate. The company has benefited from a 40 percent reduction in inventory and a 50 percent reduction in order changes, all due to its forecasting tool. Determining sales forecasts for seasonal confectionery products is now an area in which Nestlé Italiana excels.[49]

Today, vendors such as Business Objects, Cognos, and SAS offer complete data-mining decision-making solutions. Moving forward, these companies plan to add more predictive analytical capabilities to their products. Their goal is to give companies more "what-if" scenario capabilities based on internal and external information.

BUSINESS BENEFITS OF BI

Rapid innovations in systems and data-mining tools are putting operational, tactical, and strategic BI at the fingertips of executives, managers, and even customers. With the successful implementation of BI systems an organization can expect to receive the following:

Single Point of Access to Information for All Users   With a BI solution, organizations can unlock information held within their databases by giving authorized users a single point of access to data. Wherever the data reside, whether stored in operational systems, data warehouses, data marts and/or enterprise applications, users can prepare reports and drill deep down into the information to understand what drives their business, without technical knowledge of the underlying data structures. The most successful BI applications allow users to do this with an easy-to-understand, nontechnical, graphical user interface.

BI across Organizational Departments   There are many different uses for BI and one of its greatest benefits is that it can be used at every step in the value chain. All departments across an organization from sales to operations to customer service can benefit from the value of BI.

Volkswagen AG uses BI to track, understand, and manage data in every department—from finance, production, and development, to research, sales and marketing, and purchasing. Users at all levels of the organization access supplier and customer reports relating to online requests and negotiations, vehicle launches, and vehicle capacity management and tracking.[50]

Up-to-the-Minute Information for Everyone   The key to unlocking information is to give users the tools to quickly and easily find immediate answers to their questions. Some users will be satisfied with standard reports that are updated on a regular basis, such as current inventory reports, sales per channel, or customer status reports. However, the answers these reports yield can lead to new questions. Some users will want dynamic access to information. The information that a user finds in a report will trigger more questions, and these questions will not be answered in a prepackaged report.

While users may spend 80 percent of their time accessing standard or personalized reports, for 20 percent of their tasks, they need to obtain additional information not available in the original report. To address this need and to avoid frustration (and related report backlog for the IT team), a BI system should let users autonomously make ad hoc requests for information from corporate data sources.

For merchants of MasterCard International, access to BI offers the opportunity to monitor their businesses more closely on a day-to-day basis. Advertising agencies are able to use information from the extranet when developing campaigns for merchants. On the authorization side, a call center can pull up cardholder authorization transactions to cut down on fraud. MasterCard expects that in the long term and as business partners increasingly demand access to system data, the system will support more than 20,000 external users.[51]

Categories of BI Benefits

Management is no longer prepared to sink large sums of money into IT projects simply because they are the latest and greatest technology. Information technology has come of age, and it is expected to make a significant contribution to the bottom line.

When looking at how BI affects the bottom line, an organization should analyze not only the organization-wide business benefits, but also the various benefits it can expect to receive from a BI deployment. A practical way of breaking down these numerous benefits is to separate them into four main categories:

1. Quantifiable benefits.
2. Indirectly quantifiable benefits.
3. Unpredictable benefits.
4. Intangible benefits.

Quantifiable Benefits   Quantifiable benefits include working time saved in producing reports, selling information to suppliers, and so on. A few examples include:

BI Success

- Moët et Chandon, the famous champagne producer, reduced its IT costs from approximately 30 cents per bottle to 15 cents per bottle.

- A leading risk insurance company provides customers with self-service access to their information in the insurance company's database and no longer sends paper reports. This one benefit alone saves the organization $400,000 a year in printing and shipping costs. The total three-year ROI for this BI deployment was 249 percent.

- Ingram Micro, a wholesale provider of high-tech goods and technology solutions providers, is working to create a new BI extranet to deliver advanced information to the company's suppliers and business partners. Says Ingram Micro CIO Guy Abramo, "Today it's incumbent on us to provide our partners with sell-through information so they can see what happened once their PCs hit distribution. That's critical for them to do inventory planning and manufacturing planning—helping them to understand what products are selling to what segments of the marketplace."[52]

Indirectly Quantifiable Benefits   Indirectly quantifiable benefits can be evaluated through indirect evidence—improved customer service means new business from the same customer, and differentiated service brings new customers. A few examples include:

- A customer of Owens & Minor cited extranet access to the data warehouse as the primary reason for giving the medical supplies distributor an additional $44 million in business.

- "When salespeople went out to visit TaylorMade's customers at golf pro shops and sporting goods retail chains, they didn't have up-to-date inventory reports. The sales reps would take orders for clubs, accessories, and clothing without confidence that the goods were available for delivery as promised," Tom Collard, information systems director with TaylorMade, said. "The technology has helped TaylorMade not only reduce costs by eliminating the reporting backlog . . . it has eliminated a lot of wasted effort that resulted from booking orders that it couldn't fill."[53]

Unpredictable Benefits Unpredictable benefits are the result of discoveries made by creative users; a few examples include:

- Volkswagen's finance BI system allowed an interesting discovery that later resulted in significant new revenue. The customers of a particular model of the Audi product line had completely different behaviors than customers of other cars. Based on their socioeconomic profiles, they were thought to want long lease terms and fairly large upfront payments. Instead, the information revealed that Audi customers actually wanted shorter leases and to finance a large part of the purchase through the lease. Based on that insight, the company immediately introduced a new program combining shorter length of lease, larger upfront payments, and aggressive leasing rates, especially for that car model. The interest in the new program was immediate, resulting in over $2 million in new revenue.

- Peter Blundell, former knowledge strategy manager for British Airways, and various company executives had a suspicion that the carrier was suffering from a high degree of ticket fraud. To address this problem, Blundell and his team rolled out business intelligence. "Once we analyzed the data, we found that this ticket fraud was not an issue at all. What we had supposed was fraud was in fact either data quality issues or process problems," Blundell said. "What it did was give us so many unexpected opportunities in terms of understanding our business." Blundell estimated that the BI deployment has resulted in around $100 million in cost savings and new revenues for the airline.[54]

Intangible Benefits Intangible benefits include improved communication throughout the enterprise, improved job satisfaction of empowered users, and improved knowledge sharing. A few examples include:

- The corporate human resources department at ABN AMRO Bank uses BI to gain insight into its workforce by analyzing information on such items as gender, age, tenure, and compensation. Thanks to this sharing of intellectual capital, the HR department is in a better position to demonstrate its performance and contribution to the business successes of the corporation as a whole.

- Ben & Jerry's uses BI to track, understand, and manage information on the thousands of consumer responses it receives on its products and promotional activities. Through daily customer feedback analysis, Ben & Jerry's is able to identify trends and modify its marketing campaigns and its products to suit consumer demand.

OPENING CASE QUESTIONS

Customer First Awards

6. Explain the problems of gathering business intelligence from car accidents. How can BI solve this problem and help Progressive Insurance become more efficient and more effective?

7. Choose one of the three common forms of data-mining analysis and explain how Progressive Insurance can use it to gain BI.

8. How can Mini use tactical, operational, and strategic BI?

9. What types of ethical and security issues will companies face when using business intelligence?

Most corporations today are inundated with data—from their own internal operational systems, their vendors, suppliers, and customers and from other external sources such as credit bureaus or industry sales data. The problem with understanding where your company is going is not in the amount of data coming into it. The problem is that this tidal wave of data is not in a form that can easily be digested, comprehended, or even accessed. Ask simple questions like who are your best customers or what are your most profitable products and you will most likely get as many answers as there are employees. Not a comforting position to have in today's era of economic stress.

This is where business intelligence or BI comes in. The goal of BI is to provide the enterprise with a repository of "trusted" data—data that can be used in a multitude of applications to answer the questions about customers, products, supply and demand chains, production inefficiencies, financial trends, fraud, and even employees. It can be used to flag anomalies via alerts, provide visualization and statistical models, and understand the cause and effects of decisions upon the enterprise. Just about every aspect of an enterprise's business can benefit from the insights garnered from BI.

You, as a business student, must understand how technology can help you make intelligent decisions. But at the end of the day, how you interact with a customer face-to-face is the real test of your ability to foster and promote healthy customer relations.

KEY TERMS

Affinity grouping   339
Analysis latency   338
Analytical CRM   320
Association detection   340
Automatic call distribution   326
Business Intelligence   333
Call scripting system   327
Campaign management
      system   322
Classification   339
Cluster analysis   339
Clustering   339
Contact center (call center)   326
Contact management CRM
      system   323
CRM analysis technology   320
CRM predicting
      technology   320

CRM reporting technology   320
Cross-selling   322
Customer relationship
      management (CRM)   316
Data latency   337
Data mining   338
Data-mining tools   338
Decision latency   338
Employee relationship
      management (ERM)   331
Estimation   339
Forecasts   341
Interactive voice response
      (IVR)   326
List generator   326
Market basket analysis   346
Operational CRM   320

Opportunity management CRM
      system   324
Partner relationship
      management (PRM)   330
Personalization   328
Predictive dialing   326
Sales force automation
      (SFA)   323
Sales management CRM
      system   323
Statistical analysis   340
Supplier relationship
      management (SRM)   330
Time-series information   341
Up-selling   322
Web-based self service
      system   327

CLOSING CASE ONE

Calling All Canadians

With multiple communication channels available and so many CRM failures, many companies are concluding that the best method for providing customer service is good old-fashioned customer service provided by a real live person. At the same time that companies consider outsourcing their customer service departments to other countries in order to save money, many worry about foreign accents as well as time-zone issues related to offshore outsourcing.

Canada has become one of the primary targets for outsourcing customer service centers by U.S. companies. Not only are accent and time-zone issues nonexistent, but companies also receive a favorable exchange rate. The Bank of Canada estimates that over the past five years, the currency exchange rate between the United States and Canada favors Americans by 44 percent. For every dollar an American business spends in Canada, it receives over a dollar and a half in goods and services.

Additional factors that make Canada even more attractive include a high Canadian unemployment rate estimated at 7.5 percent in 2003, while the U.S. unemployment rate was 5.9 percent. Canadians also have high education rates with 63 percent of Canadians over the age of 15 being high school graduates. The country's predominantly rural population and strong work ethic along with a declining industrial base have made call center outsourcing an attractive solution for Canada, too.

Canada has been a leader in the call center industry for over a decade. Since the early 1990s, "the Canadian call center industry has grown at an annual rate of 20 percent," according to Steve Demmings, president of Site Selection Canada of Winnipeg, Manitoba. Site Selection Canada promotes and assists site selection for American and Canadian firms. Demmings estimated there are 14,000 call centers in Canada with six or more agents employing 500,000 people, contributing about $36 billion (Canadian) in annual salaries.

In 1994, two Canadian provinces—Manitoba and New Brunswick—made a concerted effort to develop a local call center industry, recognizing the area's high unemployment with little native industry, Demmings said. The other provinces soon followed. Then the call center industry "made a big move" to bring educational institutions on board. "Many colleges have set up call center training programs," Demmings reported. The result has been an established industry with an excellent skilled labor pool. "American companies come up here to go shopping and we need to have the tableware on the table," Demmings said.

What is important to outsourcing buyers is that many Canadian call center customer service representatives have made it their career. Consequently, there is a much lower turnover rate for call centers than in the United States. Demmings reported the CSR turnover rate in the Province of Ontario was 18.3 percent last year. Compare that to the United States, where call center staffing can be a problem. Christopher Fletcher, vice president and research director of CRM for the Aberdeen Group, stated, "It is tough to find people to staff a call center. Turnover ranges from 25 percent to 50 percent annually or above. The skill sets of the people you have available are often equivalent to McDonald's."[55]

Questions

1. What are the two different types of CRM and how can they be used to help an organization gain a competitive advantage?
2. Explain how a contact center (or call center) can help an organization achieve its CRM goals.
3. Describe three ways an organization can perform CRM functions over the Internet.
4. How will outsourcing contact centers (call centers) to Canada change as future CRM technologies replace current CRM technologies?

CLOSING CASE TWO

Fighting Cancer with Information

"The mission of the American Cancer Society (ACS) is to cure cancer and relieve the pain and suffering caused by this insidious disease," said Zachary Patterson, chief information officer, ACS.

The ACS is a nationwide voluntary health organization dedicated to eliminating cancer as a major health problem by supporting research, education, advocacy, and volunteer service.

Headquartered in Atlanta, Georgia, with 17 divisions and more than 3,400 local offices throughout the United States, the ACS represents the largest source of private nonprofit cancer research funds in the United States.

To support its mission, the ACS must perform exceptionally well in three key areas. First, it must be able to provide its constituents—more than 2 million volunteers, patients, and donors—with the best information available regarding the prevention, detection, and treatment of cancer. Second, ACS must be able to demonstrate that it acts responsibly with the funds entrusted to it by the public. "Among other things, that means being able to provide exceptional service when someone calls our call center with a question about mammography screening or our latest antismoking campaign," said Terry Music, national vice president for Information Delivery at the ACS. Third, ACS must be able to secure donations of time and money from its constituent base. Its success in this area is directly related to providing excellent information and service, as well as having an integrated view of its relationship with constituents. "To succeed, we need to understand the full extent of each constituent's relationship with us so we can determine where there might be opportunities to expand that relationship," Music said.

The ACS was experiencing many challenges with its current information. "Our call center agents did not know, for example, if a caller was both a donor and a volunteer, or if a caller was volunteering for the society in multiple ways," he said. "This splintered view made it challenging for American Cancer Society representatives to deliver personalized service and make informed recommendations regarding other opportunities within the society that might interest a caller."

The ACS chose to implement a customer relationship management solution to solve its information issues. Critical to the CRM system's success was consolidating information from various databases across the organization to provide a single view of constituents and all information required to serve them. After an evaluation process that included participation from individuals across the organization, the ACS chose Siebel Systems as its CRM solution provider. The society wanted to work with a company that could address both its immediate needs with a best-in-class ebusiness solution and its future requirements.

The Siebel Call Center is specifically designed for the next generation of contact centers, enabling organizations to provide world-class customer service, generate increased revenue, and create a closed-loop information flow seamlessly over multichannel sales, marketing, and customer service operations. Siebel Call Center empowers agents at every level by providing up-to-the-minute information and in-depth customer and product knowledge. This approach enables quick and accurate problem resolution and generates greater relationship opportunities. The ACS has received numerous benefits from the system including:

- Increased constituent satisfaction and loyalty by supporting personalized interactions between constituents and cancer information specialists.
- Improved productivity of cancer information specialists by consolidating all information required to serve constituents into a single view.
- Increased donations of time and money by helping call center agents identify callers who are likely to be interested in expanding their relationship with the ACS.[56]

Questions

1. How could the ACS's marketing department use operational CRM to strengthen its relationships with its customers?
2. How could the ACS's customer service department use operational CRM to strengthen its relationships with its customers?
3. Review all of the operational CRM technologies and determine which one would add the greatest value to ACS's business.
4. Describe the benefits ACS could gain from using analytical CRM.
5. Summarize SRM and describe how ACS could use it to increase efficiency in its business.
6. How could BI and data minning help fight cancer?

Intelligent Business: Is it an Oxymoron?

In a pilot program by the State of New York, suburban Rockland County announced that it had uncovered $13 million in improper Medicaid claims made over a 21-month period. Because the problems were discovered before the reimbursements were made, Rockland saved itself the headaches it would have faced if it had paid out the money first and asked questions later.

The credit goes not to a crew of hardworking sleuths but to search and analysis software created by IBM that automatically sorted through thousands of forms, plucked out key bits of information, and sized them up against Medicaid rules. Government officials believe that if the program were to be applied statewide, it could deliver $3.8 billion in savings per year. "This may change the Medicaid industry in New York," said Rockland County Supervisor C. Scott Vanderhoef.

This is just one example of a change in the way corporations and governments find and use information. Data are becoming much easier to access and vastly more useful.

Better Understanding

Organizations have huge amounts of data that pass through their computer systems as they place orders, record sales, and otherwise transact business. Much of this information is stored for future use and analysis. But advances in software and hardware make it easier for companies to analyze data in real time—when the data are first whizzing through their computers—and make them available to all kinds of employees.

Technological innovations also make it possible to analyze unstructured data, such as Rockland County's Medicaid claims, that do not easily fit into the tables of a traditional database. The result of all these changes: It is now possible for companies to understand what is happening in their businesses in a detailed way and quickly take actions based on that knowledge.

These improvements have come largely as a result of advances in business intelligence software. This software—a $3 billion segment growing at about 7 percent a year—gathers information in data warehouses where it can easily be reviewed, analyzes the data, and presents reports to decision makers. In the past, the reports had to be painstakingly assembled by tech-savvy business analysts and were typically made available only to top-tier people.

Personal Google

Information easily available to anybody in an organization is a phenomenon industry folks have dubbed "pervasive business intelligence." Companies are moving from a place where only the more technical people had access to information to more of a self-service situation. People can get information themselves, said Christina McKeon, global business intelligence strategist for software maker SAS Institute, based in Cary, North Carolina.

SAS and other BI software makers are reaching out to the masses in a variety of ways. Several of them have hooked up with search leader Google to give businesspeople easier access to those data warehouses via the familiar Google search bar. They have redesigned their business intelligence web portals so people who do Google searches get not only documents that include their keywords, but also others that are thematically related.

For instance, if a business-unit leader searches for first-quarter financial results, he might also get reports on the 10 largest customers in the quarter and the customers who deliver the most profits. "The data warehouse is starting to go mainstream," said analyst Mark Beyer of tech market researcher Gartner.

Directing Traffic

Business intelligence is also being added to other standard run-the-business applications, such as order fulfillment, logistics, inventory management, and the like. Consider a busy warehouse with a limited number of loading docks. Trucking companies do not want their rigs to wait in line for hours, so some of them charge fees for waiting time at the warehouse.

To avoid those costs, companies can build business intelligence into their logistics planning systems that lets them know when trucks are stacking up and directs supervisors in the warehouse to load the trucks that charge waiting fees before those that do not. The supervisors get this information via their PCs or handhelds on the warehouse floor. People are receiving the benefit of business intelligence without knowing it, said Randy Lea, vice president for product and services marketing at Teradata, a division of NCR, a leader in data warehousing software.

This kind of real-time, behind-the-curtains intelligence is even becoming available to end customers. Travelocity, one of the leading travel websites, has long used business intelligence software to help it analyze buying trends and segment customer types so new services can be tailored for them. Now it has rigged its vast data warehouse directly to its consumer website so it can gather and analyze information about what is going on as it is happening.

Computer Intuition

Travelocity links the profile of individual customers who are on the site to a monitor of their current activity and to information about available airplane flights, rental cars, and vacation packages. If a customer begins asking about flights to Orlando over the fourth of July weekend, Travelocity's system will understand that the customer is probably planning a family vacation and will place advertisements that are relevant to that kind of trip and even pitch special travel promotions. "If we want to, we could give every customer a custom offer," said Mark Hooper, Travelocity's vice president for product development.

What is next in easy-to-use business intelligence? Gartner has a concept it calls "Biggle"—the intersection of BI and Google. The idea is that the data warehousing software will be so sophisticated that it understands when different people use different words to describe the same concepts or products. It creates an index of related information—á là Google—and dishes relevant results out in response to queries.

In computer science, they refer to this capability as non-obvious relationship awareness. "Nobody's doing this yet," said Gartner's Beyer. Judging from the speed of recent advances in business intelligence, though, it may not be long before companies add the term "Biggling" to their tech lexicon.[57]

Questions

1. What is the problem of gathering business intelligence from a traditional company? How can BI solve this problem?
2. Choose one of the three common forms of data-mining analysis and explain how Travelocity could use it to gain BI.
3. How will tactical, operational, and strategic BI be different when applied to personal Google?
4. How is IBM's search and analysis software an example of BI?
5. What does the term *pervasive business intelligence* mean?
6. How could any business benefit from technology such as Personal Google?
7. How could a company use BI to improve its supply chain?
8. Highlight any security and ethical issues associated with Biggle.

1. Customer relationship management strategies

On average, it costs an organization six times more to sell to a new customer than to sell to an existing customer. As the co-owner of a medium-sized luggage distributor, you have recently been notified that sales for the past three months have decreased by an average of 17 percent. The reasons for the decline in sales are numerous, including a poor economy, people's aversion to travel because of the terrorist attacks, and some negative publicity your company received regarding a defective product line. In a group, explain how implementing a CRM system can help you understand and combat the decline in sales. Be sure to justify why a CRM system is important to your business and its future growth.

2. Comparing CRM vendors

As a team, search the Internet for at least one recent and authoritative article that compares or ranks customer relationship management systems. Select two packages from the list and compare their functions and features as described in the article(s) you found as well as on each company's website. Find references in the literature where companies that are using each package have reported their experiences, both good and bad. Draw on any other comparisons you can find. Prepare a presentation for delivery in class on the strengths and weaknesses of each package, which one you favor, and why.

3. Searching for employee loyalty

You are the CEO of Razz, a start-up web-based search company, which is planning to compete directly with Google. The company had an exceptional first year and is currently receiving over 500,000 hits a day from customers all over the world. You have hired 250 people in the last four months, doubling the size of your organization. With so many new employees starting so quickly you are concerned about how your company's culture will evolve and whether your employees are receiving enough attention. You are already familiar with customer relationship management and how CRM systems can help an organization create strong customer relationships. However, you are unfamiliar with employee relationship management and you are wondering what ERM systems might be able to offer your employees and your company. Research the web, create a report detailing features and functions of ERM systems, and determine what value will be added to your organization if you decide to implement an ERM solution.

4. Employee relationship management

All new employees at the Shinaberry Inn & Spa wear bathing suits during orientation to experience the spa's exfoliating showers and hot mineral baths. At the Shinaberry San Francisco, new employees get the same penthouse champagne toast the hotel uses to woo meeting planners. And at many properties, employees arriving for their first day have their cars parked by the valet or get vouchers for a free night's stay. This innovative orientation program, which lets employees experience what guests experience began two years ago after focus groups pointed to empathy as a service differentiator. As a result, the company added empathy to the attributes for which it screens and a training program that involves listening to recorded guest phone calls. Even its discounted employee travel program gives employees yet another way to understand the guest experience. Design an ERM system that would help Shinaberry further its employee-centered culture. The ERM system must consider all employee needs.

5. Increasing revenues with CRM

Cold Cream is one of the premier beauty supply stores in the metro New York area. People come from all over to sample the store's unique creams, lotions, makeup, and perfumes. The store is four stories high with each department located on a separate floor. The company would like to implement a CRM system to help it better understand its customers and their purchasing habits. Create a report summarizing CRM systems and detail how such a system can directly influence Cold Cream's revenues.

6. **Driving Up Profits with Successful Campaigns (or Driving Down?)**

The Butterfly Café is located in downtown San Francisco and offers specialty coffee, teas, and organic fruits and vegetables. The café holds a number of events to attract customers such as live music venues, poetry readings, book clubs, charity events, and local artist's night. A listing of all participants attending each event is tracked in the café's database. The café uses the information for marketing campaigns and offers customers who attend multiple events additional discounts. A marketing database company, InTheKnow.com, has offered to pay The Butterfly Café a substantial amount of money for access to its customer database, which it will then sell to other local businesses. The owner of the Butterfly Café, Mary Conzachi, has come to you for advice. Mary is not sure if her customers would appreciate her selling their personal information and how it might affect her business. However, the amount of money InTheKnow.com is offering is enough to finance her much needed new patio for the back of the café. InTheKnow.com has promised Mary that the sale will be completely confidential. What should Mary do?

7. **Supporting Customers**

Creative.com is an ebusiness that sells craft materials and supplies over the Internet. You have just started as the vice president of customer service, and you have a team of 45 customer service representatives. Currently, the only form of customer service is the 1-800 number and the company is receiving a tremendous number of calls regarding products, orders, and shipping information. The average wait time for a customer to speak to a customer service representative is 35 minutes. Orders are being cancelled and Creative.com is losing business due to its lack of customer service. Create a strategy to revamp the customer service center at Creative.com and get the company back on track.

APPLY YOUR KNOWLEDGE

1. Gaining Business Intelligence from Strategic Initiatives

You are a new employee in the customer service department at Premier One, a large pet food distributor. The company, founded by several veterinarians, has been in business for three years and focuses on providing nutritious pet food at a low cost. The company currently has 90 employees and operates in seven states. Sales over the past three years have tripled, and the manual systems currently in place are no longer sufficient to run the business. Your first task is to meet with your new team and create a presentation for the president and chief executive officer describing supply chain management and customer relationship management. The presentation should highlight the main benefits Premier One can receive from these strategic initiatives along with any additional added business value that can be gained from the systems.

2. Great Stories

With the advent of the Internet, when customers have an unpleasant customer experience, the company no longer has to worry about them telling a few friends and family; the company has to worry about them telling everyone. Internet service providers are giving consumers frustrated with how they were treated by a company another means of fighting back. Free or low-cost computer space for Internet websites is empowering consumers to tell not only their friends, but also the world about the way they have been treated. A few examples of disgruntled customer stories from the Internet include:

- **Bad Experience with Blue Marble Biking**—Tourist on biking tour is bitten by dog, requires stitches. Company is barred from hotel because of incident, and in turn it bars the tourist from any further tours.
- **Best Buy Receipt Check**—Shopper declines to show register receipt for purchase to door guard at Lakewood Best Buy, which is voluntary. Employees attempt to seize cart, stand in shopper's path, and park a truck behind shopper's car to prevent departure.
- **Enterprise Rent-A-Car Is a Failing Enterprise**—Enterprise Rent-A-Car did not honor reservations, did not have cars ready as stated, rented cars with nearly empty tanks, and charged higher prices to corporate account holders.

Project Focus

The Internet is raising the stakes for customer service. With the ability to create a website dedicated to a particular issue, a disgruntled customer can have nearly the same reach as a manufacturer. The Internet is making it more difficult for companies to ignore their customers' complaints. In a group, search the web for the most outrageous story of a disgruntled customer. A few places to start include:

- **Complain Complain** (complaincomplain.net)—provides professionally written, custom complaint letters to businesses.
- **The Complaint Department** (www.thecomplaintdepartment.ca)—a for-fee consumer complaint resolution and letter writing service.
- **The Complaint Station** (www.thecomplaintstation.com)—provides a central location to complain about issues related to companies' products, services, employment, and get rich quick scams.
- **Complaints.com Consumer Complaints** (www.complaints.com)—database of consumer complaints and consumer advocacy.
- **Baddealings.com** (www.baddealings.com)—forum and database on consumer complaints and scams on products and services.

3. JetBlue on YouTube

JetBlue took an unusual and interesting CRM approach by using YouTube to apologize to its customers. JetBlue's founder and CEO, David Neeleman, apologized to customers via YouTube after a very, very bad week for the airline: 1,100 flights canceled due to snow storms and thousands of irate passengers. Neeleman's unpolished, earnest delivery makes this apology worth accepting. But then again, we were not stuck on a tarmac for eight hours. With all of the new advances in technology and the many ways to reach customers, do you think using YouTube is a smart approach? What else could JetBlue do to help gain back its customers' trust?

Project Focus

You are the founder and CEO of GoodDog, a large pet food manufacturing company. Recently, at least 16 pet deaths have been tied to tainted pet food, fortunately not manufactured by your company. A recall of potentially deadly pet food has dog and cat owners studying their animals for even the slightest hint of illness and swamping veterinarians nationwide with calls about symptoms both real and imagined. Create a strategy for using YouTube as a vehicle to communicate with your customers as they fear for their pets' lives. Be sure to highlight the pros and cons of using YouTube as a customer communication vehicle. Are there any other new technologies you could use as a customer communication vehicle that would be more effective than YouTube?

4. Second Life CRM

The virtual world of Second Life could become the first point of contact between companies and customers and could transform the whole customer experience. Since it began hosting the likes of Adidas, Dell, Reuters, and Toyota, Second Life has become technology's equivalent of India or China—everyone needs an office and a strategy involving it to keep their shareholders happy. But beyond opening a shiny new building in the virtual world, what can such companies do with their virtual real estate?

Like many other big brands, PA Consulting has its own offices in Second Life and has learned that simply having an office to answer customer queries is not enough. Real people, albeit behind avatars, must be staffing the offices—in the same way having a website is not enough if there is not a call center to back it up when a would-be customer wants to speak to a human being. The consultants believe call centers could one day ask customers to follow up a phone call with them by moving the query into a virtual world.

Unlike many corporate areas in the virtual world, the National Basketball Association incorporates capabilities designed to keep fans coming back, including real-time 3-D diagrams of games as they are being played.[58]

Project Focus

You are the executive director of CRM at StormPeak, an advanced AI company that develops robots. You are in charge of overseeing the first virtual site being built in Second Life. Create a CRM strategy for doing business in a virtual world. Here are a few questions to get you started:

- How will customer relationships be different in a virtual world?
- What is your strategy for managing customer relationships in this new virtual environment?
- How will supporting Second Life customers differ from supporting traditional customers?
- How will supporting Second Life customers differ from supporting website customers?
- What customer security issues might you encounter in Second Life?
- What customer ethical issues might you encounter in Second Life?

5. Searching for BI

Imagine being able to Google customer phone requests for information, sort through the recorded files of customer complaint calls, or decipher the exact moment when an interaction between a customer and store employee went awry. Being able to query voice records using the same methods as querying textual ones would open up boundless areas of business opportunity. Web surfers can already search audio files and audio/video feeds, but now enterprise can use this technology to help employees search voice mails or recorded calls for keywords and phrases, and, in the end, to decode important customer concerns.

Project Focus

You have recently started your own marketing firm. You have built a BI tool that allows customers to query all of their unique data stores. Now all you need is to prepare your marketing materials to send to potential customers. Create a marketing pitch that you will deliver to customers detailing the business opportunities they could uncover if they purchase your product. Your marketing pitch can be a one-page document, a catchy tune, a video, or a PowerPoint presentation.

The Anatomy of Buzz. By Emanuel Rosen (New York: Double Day, 2000).

Today's consumers are skeptical, and they suffer from information overload. The result: They'll probably ignore the expensive television and print ads your marketing team creates. So how do people decide which car to buy, or which fashions fit the image they are looking for, or what new techno-appliance is a must for their homes? The first section of this book discusses how buzz spreads and the huge social networks to which we all belong and what we know about how buzz spreads through them.

The second section identifies two factors that need to be there for buzz to spread. First, the product must be "contagious" in some way. For example, the game Trivial Pursuit was contagious because people who played it were compelled to demonstrate their knowledge to others. But contagion needs to be accelerated. That is the second factor. The marketers of this game executed a massive grassroots campaign that let people in numerous social networks get "infected" by the game and tell others.

The third part of the book describes techniques that companies have used to encourage their customers to talk. How BMW created buzz about the Z3 Roadster through a "sneak preview" in a James Bond movie. How the founders of Powerbar spread the word about their energy food by working with "network hubs" such as coaches and leading athletes.[59]

Loyalty Rules! By Frederick F. Reichheld (Bain and Company, 2001).

Loyalty is at the heart of any company that boasts high productivity, solid profits, and sustained growth. For example, Harley-Davidson recovered from near bankruptcy by building loyal relationships with all stakeholders. And Southwest Airlines, which has never had a layoff, is the only consistently profitable major airline in the United States every year since 1973.

Frederick Reichheld, author of *Loyalty Rules!,* argues that loyalty is still the fuel that drives financial success—even, and perhaps especially, in today's volatile, high-speed economy—but that most organizations are running on empty. Why? Because leaders too often confuse profits with purpose, taking the low road to short-term gains at the expense of employees, customers, and, ultimately, investors. In a business environment that thrives on networks of mutually beneficial relationships, says Reichheld, it is the ability to build strong bonds of loyalty—not short-term profits—that has become the "acid test" of leadership.

Based on extensive research into companies from online start-ups to established institutions—including Harley-Davidson, Enterprise Rent-A-Car, Cisco Systems, Dell Computer, Intuit, and more—Reichheld reveals six bedrock principles of loyalty upon which leaders build enduring enterprises. Underscoring that success requires both understanding and measuring loyalty, he couples each principle with straightforward actions that drive measurement systems, compensation, organization, and strategy:

1. Play to win/win: Never profit at the expense of partners.
2. Be picky: Membership must be a privilege.
3. Keep it simple: Reduce complexity for speed and flexibility.
4. Reward the right results: Worthy partners deserve worthy goals.
5. Listen hard and talk straight: Insist on honest, two-way communication and learning.
6. Preach what you practice: Explain your principles, then live by them.

Providing tools for implementing the timeless principles of loyalty in a volatile economy, *Loyalty Rules!* is a practical guidebook for taking the high road in business—the only road that leads to lasting success.[60]

Enterprise Resource Planning and Collaboration Systems

CHAPTER OUTLINE

What's in IT for me?

Information is a powerful asset. It is a key organizational asset that enables companies to carry out business initiatives and strategic plans. Companies that manage information are primed for competitive advantage and success. Information technology is the key tool allowing access and flow of information across enterprises.

As a business student, you must understand how to give employees, customers, and business partners access to information. This includes taking advantage of newer technologies such as knowledge management, enterprise portals, and collaboration tools. Doing so facilitates completion of tasks while encouraging the sharing and generation of new ideas that lead to the development of innovations, improved work habits, and best practices.

This chapter showcases how information technology can help you capitalize upon the power of information by providing mechanisms for improved information access, sharing, and application. This includes access and use of structured information found in transactional database and data warehouses, unstructured information found in textual documents and email messages, and information that organizational employees possess.

Campus ERP

When Stefanie Fillers returned to college she needed to log in to the school's new online registration system to make certain that the courses she was taking would allow her to graduate. She also wanted to waive her participation in her college's health insurance plan. When the system crashed the day before classes began, Fillers, a senior, was annoyed. But at least she knew where her classes were—unlike most first-year students.

Several colleges around the country have experienced problems with nonfunctioning web portals that prevented students from finding out where their classes were. At one college, financial aid was denied to 3,000 students by a buggy new ERP system, even though they had already received loan commitments. The college provided short-term loans for the cash-strapped students while the IT department and financial aid administrators scrambled to fix the complex system.

Disastrous ERP implementations have given more than a few colleges black eyes. These campus meltdowns illustrate how the growing reliance on expensive ERP systems has created nightmare scenarios for some colleges. In every case, the new systems were designed to centralize business processes in what historically has been a hodgepodge of discrete legacy systems. College administrators are drawn to ERP systems offering integrated views of finance, HR, student records, financial aid, and more.

ERP implementations are difficult, even in very top-down corporate environments. Getting them to work in colleges, which are essentially a conglomeration of decentralized fiefdoms, has been nearly impossible. Staff members in the largely autonomous departments do not like the one-size-fits-all strategy of an ERP implementation. Plus, these nonprofit organizations generally lack the talent and financial resources to create and manage a robust enterprise system. Representatives from Oracle, which dominates the higher education market for ERP, say that much of the problem results from the inexperience of college IT departments and their tendency to rush implementations and inadequately test the new systems.

Standardizing at Stanford

Stanford University bought into the late 1990s enterprise software pitch and never slowed down its implementation engine. "In hindsight, we tried to do too much in too little time," said Randy Livingston, Stanford's vice president of business affairs and CFO.

Starting in 2001, Stanford implemented student administration systems, People-Soft HR, Oracle financials, and several other ancillary applications. Years later, users still complain that they have lower productivity with the new systems than with the previous ones, which were supported by a highly customized mainframe. Users also have had difficulty accessing critical information on a timely basis. Livingston said many transactions, such as initiating a purchase requisition or requesting a reimbursement, now take longer for users than with the prior legacy system.

Stanford has also not realized any of the projected savings the vendors promised. "We are finding that the new ERP applications cost considerably more to support than our legacy applications," Livingston said. He does not know how much it will cost to get the enterprise systems working at acceptable user levels.

Stanford's IT department found it difficult to get campuswide buy-in for the enterprise applications, which have necessitated new ways of doing business, which leads to nonuse of the new systems and costly customizations to keep all users satisfied. For example, Stanford's law school operates on a semester schedule, while the other six schools operate on a trimester schedule. "This means that every aspect of the student administration system needs to be configured differently for the law school," Livingston said. Within the schools, some faculty members are paid a 12-month salary; other schools pay by 9 months, 10 months, or 11 months. "The standard HR payroll system is not designed to handle all these unusual pay schedules," Livingston said.

To resolve the issues, Livingston reorganized the IT department to better manage the enterprise projects going forward. He also created a separate administrative systems group that reports directly to him, with responsibility for development, integration, and support of the major ERP systems.

The hurdles Stanford and other colleges face with ERP systems are largely cultural ones. For instance, lean staffs and tight budgets at most university campuses usually lead to a lack of proper training and systems testing. At Stanford, plenty of training was offered, but many users did not take it, Livingston said. He set up new training programs, including a group of trainers who sit side by side with users to help them learn how to do complex tasks; periodic user group meetings; website and email lists that offer more help; and expert users embedded in the various departments who aid their colleagues.

Stanford's IT was still struggling with integrating the enterprise systems when the newly launched PeopleSoft web portal (called Axess) crashed in 2004. Axess could not handle the load of all the returning students trying to log in to the untested web-based system at the same time, Livingston said. Stanford was able to fix those problems relatively quickly, but Livingston and his staff continue to struggle with the enterprise projects. The university's departments remain "highly suspicious and resistant" of his efforts to standardize and centralize business processes, Livingston said.[1]

INTRODUCTION

Enterprise resource planning (ERP) integrates all departments and functions throughout an organization into a single IT system (or integrated set of IT systems) so that employees can make decisions by viewing enterprisewide information on all business operations. Figure 10.1 highlights a few reasons ERP solutions have proven to be such a powerful force.

ERP as a business concept resounds as a powerful internal information management nirvana: Everyone involved in sourcing, producing, and delivering the company's product works with the same information, which eliminates redundancies, reduces wasted time, and removes misinformation.

Hot Topics

section 10.1 ENTERPRISE RESOURCE PLANNING

LEARNING OUTCOMES

10.1. Compare core enterprise resource planning components and extended enterprise resource planning components.

10.2. Describe the three primary components found in core enterprise resource planning systems.

10.3. Describe the four primary components found in extended enterprise resource planning systems.

10.4. Explain the business value of integrating supply chain management, customer relationship management, and enterprise resource planning systems.

10.5. Explain how an organization can use a balanced scorecard to measure ERP success.

ENTERPRISE RESOURCE PLANNING

Today's business leaders need significant amounts of information to be readily accessible with real-time views into their businesses so that decisions can be made when they need to be, without the added time of tracking data and generating reports. *Enterprise resource planning (ERP)* integrates all departments and functions throughout an organization into a single IT system (or integrated set of IT systems) so that employees can make decisions by viewing enterprisewide information on all business operations.

Many organizations fail to maintain consistency across business operations. If a single department, such as sales, decides to implement a new system without considering the other departments, inconsistencies can occur throughout the company. Not all systems are built to talk to each other and share data, and if sales suddenly implements a new system that marketing and accounting cannot use or is inconsistent in the way it handles information, the company's operations become siloed. Figure 10.2 displays sample data from a sales database, and Figure 10.3 displays samples from an accounting database. Notice the differences in data formats, numbers, and identifiers. Correlating this data would be difficult, and the inconsistencies would cause numerous reporting errors from an enterprisewide perspective.

FIGURE 10.1

Reasons ERP Systems Are Powerful Organizational Tools

Reasons ERP Systems Are Powerful Organizational Tools
ERP is a logical solution to the mess of incompatible applications that had sprung up in most businesses.
ERP addresses the need for global information sharing and reporting.
ERP is used to avoid the pain and expense of fixing legacy systems.

FIGURE 10.2

Sales Information Sample

OrderDate	ProductName	Quantity	Unit Price	Unit Cost	Customer ID	SalesRep ID
Monday, January 04, 2010	Mozzarella cheese	41.5	$ 24.15	$ 15.35	AC45	EX-107
Monday, January 04, 2010	Romaine lettuce	90.65	$ 15.06	$ 14.04	AC45	EX-109
Tuesday, January 05, 2010	Red onions	27.15	$ 12.08	$ 10.32	AC67	EX-104
Wednesday, January 06, 2010	Romaine lettuce	67.25	$ 15.16	$ 10.54	AC96	EX-109
Thursday, January 07, 2010	Black olives	79.26	$ 12.18	$ 9.56	AC44	EX-104
Thursday, January 07, 2010	Romaine lettuce	46.52	$ 15.24	$ 11.54	AC32	EX-104
Thursday, January 07, 2010	Romaine lettuce	52.5	$ 15.26	$ 11.12	AC84	EX-109
Friday, January 08, 2010	Red onions	39.5	$ 12.55	$ 9.54	AC103	EX-104
Saturday, January 09, 2010	Romaine lettuce	66.5	$ 15.98	$ 9.56	AC4	EX-104
Sunday, January 10, 2010	Romaine lettuce	58.26	$ 15.87	$ 9.50	AC174	EX-104
Sunday, January 10, 2010	Pineapple	40.15	$ 33.54	$ 22.12	AC45	EX-104
Monday, January 11, 2010	Pineapple	71.56	$ 33.56	$ 22.05	AC4	EX-104
Thursday, January 14, 2010	Romaine lettuce	18.25	$ 15.00	$ 10.25	AC174	EX-104
Thursday, January 14, 2010	Romaine lettuce	28.15	$ 15.26	$ 10.54	AC44	EX-107
Friday, January 15, 2010	Pepperoni	33.5	$ 15.24	$ 10.25	AC96	EX-109
Friday, January 15, 2010	Parmesan cheese	14.26	$ 8.05	$ 4.00	AC96	EX-104
Saturday, January 16, 2010	Parmesan cheese	72.15	$ 8.50	$ 4.00	AC103	EX-109
Monday, January 18, 2010	Parmesan cheese	41.5	$ 24.15	$ 15.35	AC45	EX-107
Monday, January 18, 2010	Romaine lettuce	90.65	$ 15.06	$ 14.04	AC45	EX-109
Wednesday, January 20, 2010	Tomatoes	27.15	$ 12.08	$ 10.32	AC67	EX-104
Thursday, January 21, 2010	Peppers	67.25	$ 15.16	$ 10.54	AC96	EX-109
Thursday, January 21, 2010	Mozzarella cheese	79.26	$ 12.18	$ 9.56	AC44	EX-104
Saturday, January 23, 2010	Black olives	46.52	$ 15.24	$ 11.54	AC32	EX-104
Sunday, January 24, 2010	Mozzarella cheese	52.5	$ 15.26	$ 11.12	AC84	EX-109
Tuesday, January 26, 2010	Romaine lettuce	39.5	$ 12.55	$ 9.54	AC103	EX-104
Wednesday, January 27, 2010	Parmesan cheese	66.5	$ 15.98	$ 9.56	AC4	EX-104
Thursday, January 28, 2010	Peppers	58.26	$ 15.87	$ 9.50	AC174	EX-104
Thursday, January 28, 2010	Mozzarella cheese	40.15	$ 33.54	$ 22.12	AC45	EX-104
Friday, January 29, 2010	Tomatoes	71.56	$ 33.56	$ 22.05	AC4	EX-104
Friday, January 29, 2010	Peppers	18.25	$ 15.00	$ 10.25	AC174	EX-104

Los Angeles is a city of 3.5 million, with 44,000 city employees, and a budget of $4 billion. Yet a few years ago each department conducted its own purchasing. That meant 2,000 people in 600 city buildings and 60 warehouses were ordering material. Some 120,000 purchase orders (POs) and 50,000 checks per year went to more than 7,000 vendors. Inefficiency was rampant.

FIGURE 10.3

Accounting Information Sample

OrderDate	ProductName	Quantity	Unit Price	Total Sales	Unit Cost	Total Cost	Profit	Customer	SalesRep
04-Jan-10	Mozzarella cheese	41	24	984	18	738	246	The Station	Debbie Fernandez
04-Jan-10	Romaine lettuce	90	15	1,350	14	1,260	90	The Station	Roberta Cross
05-Jan-10	Red onions	27	12	324	8	216	108	Bert's Bistro	Loraine Schultz
06-Jan-10	Romaine lettuce	67	15	1,005	14	938	67	Smoke House	Roberta Cross
07-Jan-10	Black olives	79	12	948	6	474	474	Flagstaff House	Loraine Schultz
07-Jan-10	Romaine lettuce	46	15	690	14	644	46	Two Bitts	Loraine Schultz
07-Jan-10	Romaine lettuce	52	15	780	14	728	52	Pierce Arrow	Roberta Cross
08-Jan-10	Red onions	39	12	468	8	312	156	Mamm'a Pasta Palace	Loraine Schultz
09-Jan-10	Romaine lettuce	66	15	990	14	924	66	The Dandelion	Loraine Schultz
10-Jan-10	Romaine lettuce	58	15	870	14	812	58	Carmens	Loraine Schultz
10-Jan-10	Pineapple	40	33	1,320	28	1,120	200	The Station	Loraine Schultz
11-Jan-10	Pineapple	71	33	2,343	28	1,988	355	The Dandelion	Loraine Schultz
14-Jan-10	Romaine lettuce	18	15	270	14	252	18	Carmens	Loraine Schultz
14-Jan-10	Romaine lettuce	28	15	420	14	392	28	Flagstaff House	Debbie Fernandez
15-Jan-10	Pepperoni	33	53	1,749	35	1,155	594	Smoke House	Roberta Cross
15-Jan-10	Parmesan cheese	14	8	112	4	56	56	Smoke House	Loraine Schultz
16-Jan-10	Parmesan cheese	72	8	576	4	288	288	Mamm'a Pasta Palace	Roberta Cross
18-Jan-10	Parmesan cheese	10	8	80	4	40	40	Mamm'a Pasta Palace	Loraine Schultz
18-Jan-10	Romaine lettuce	42	15	630	14	588	42	Smoke House	Roberta Cross
20-Jan-10	Tomatoes	48	9	432	7	336	96	Two Bitts	Loraine Schultz
21-Jan-10	Peppers	29	21	609	12	348	261	The Dandelion	Loraine Schultz
21-Jan-10	Mozzarella cheese	10	24	240	18	180	60	Mamm'a Pasta Palace	Debbie Fernandez
23-Jan-10	Black olives	98	12	1,176	6	588	588	Two Bitts	Roberta Cross
24-Jan-10	Mozzarella cheese	45	24	1,080	18	810	270	Carmens	Loraine Schultz
26-Jan-10	Romaine lettuce	58	15	870	14	812	58	Two Bitts	Loraine Schultz
27-Jan-10	Parmesan cheese	66	8	528	4	264	264	Flagstaff House	Loraine Schultz
28-Jan-10	Peppers	85	21	1,785	12	1,020	765	Pierce Arrow	Loraine Schultz
28-Jan-10	Mozzarella cheese	12	24	288	18	216	72	The Dandelion	Debbie Fernandez
29-Jan-10	Tomatoes	40	9	360	7	280	80	Pierce Arrow	Roberta Cross

"There was a lack of financial responsibility in the old system, and people could run up unauthorized expenditures," said Bob Jensen, the city's ERP project manager. Each department maintained its own inventories on different systems. Expense-item mismatches piled up. One department purchased one way, others preferred a different approach. Mainframe-based systems were isolated. The city chose an ERP system as part of a $22 million project to integrate purchasing and financial reporting across the entire city. The project resulted in cutting the check processing staff in half, processing POs faster than ever, reducing the number of workers in warehousing by 40 positions, decreasing inventories from $50 million to $15 million, and providing a single point of contact for each vendor. In addition, $5 million a year has been saved in contract consolidation.[2]

Figure 10.4 shows how an ERP system takes data from across the enterprise, consolidates and correlates the data, and generates enterprisewide organizational reports. Original ERP implementations promised to capture all information onto one true "enterprise" system, with the ability to touch all the business processes within the organization. Unfortunately, ERP solutions have fallen short of these promises, and typical implementations have penetrated only 15 to 20 percent of the organization. The issue ERP intends to solve is that knowledge within a majority of organizations currently resides in silos that are maintained by a select few, without the ability to be shared across the organization, causing inconsistency across business operations.[3]

Turner Industries grew from $300 million in sales to $800 million in sales in less than 10 years thanks to the implementation of an ERP system. Ranked number 369 on the Forbes 500 list of privately held companies, Turner Industries is a leading industrial services firm. Turner Industries develops and deploys advanced software applications designed to maximize the productivity of its 25,000 employees and construction equipment valued at more than $100 million.

The company considers the biggest challenges in the industrial services industry to be completing projects on time, within budget, while fulfilling customers' expectations. To meet these challenges the company invested in an ERP system and named the project Interplan. Interplan won Constructech's Vision award for software innovation in the heavy construction industry. Interplan runs all of Turner's construction, turnaround, shutdown, and maintenance projects and is so adept at estimating and planning jobs that Turner Industries typically achieves higher profit margins on

FIGURE 10.4

Enterprise Resource Planning System

projects that use Interplan. As the ERP solution makes the company more profitable, the company can pass on the cost savings to its customers, giving the company an incredible competitive advantage.[4]

Enterprise resource planning systems provide organizations with consistency. An ERP system provides a method for the effective planning and controlling of all the resources required to take, make, ship, and account for customer orders in a manufacturing, distribution, or service organization. The key word in enterprise resource planning is *enterprise* and there are two key components to ERP including:

- The Heart of ERP
- The Evolution of ERP

The Heart of ERP

Enterprise resource planning systems serve as the organization's backbone in providing fundamental decision-making support. In the past, departments made decisions independent of each other. ERP systems provide a foundation for collaboration between departments, enabling people in different business areas to communicate. ERP systems have been widely adopted in large organizations to store critical knowledge used to make the decisions that drive performance.

To be competitive, organizations must always strive for excellence in every business process enterprisewide, a daunting challenge if the organization has multi-site operations worldwide. To obtain operational efficiencies, lower costs, improve supplier and customer relations, and increase revenues and market share, all units of the organization must work together harmoniously toward congruent goals. An ERP system will help an organization achieve this.

One company that has blazed a trail with ERP is Atlanta-based United Parcel Service of America, Inc. (UPS). UPS has developed a number of web-based applications that track information such as recipient signatures, addresses, time in transit, and other shipping information. These services run on an ERP foundation that UPS customers can connect to using real-time ERP information obtained from the UPS website. Currently, 6.2 million tracking requests pass through the company's website each day. By automating the information delivery process, UPS has dramatically reduced the demand on its customer service representatives. Just as important, UPS has improved relationships with its business partners—in effect integrating its business with theirs—by making it easier for consumers to find delivery information without leaving the website of the merchant.[5]

The heart of an ERP system is a central database that collects information from and feeds information into all the ERP system's individual application components (called modules), supporting diverse business functions such as accounting, manufacturing, marketing, and human resources. When a user enters or updates information in one module, it is immediately and automatically updated throughout the entire system, as illustrated in Figure 10.5.

ERP automates business processes such as order fulfillment—taking an order from a customer, shipping the purchase, and then billing for it. With an ERP system, when a customer service representative takes an order from a customer, he or she has all the information necessary to complete the order (the customer's credit rating and order history, the company's inventory levels, and the delivery schedule). Everyone else in the company sees the same information and has access to the database that holds the customer's new order. When one department finishes with the order, it is automatically routed via the ERP system to the next department. To find out where the order is at any point, a user need only log in to the ERP system and track it down, as illustrated in Figure 10.6. The order process moves like a bolt of lightning through the organization, and customers get their orders faster and with fewer errors than ever before. ERP can apply that same magic to the other major business processes, such as employee benefits or financial reporting.[6]

ERP enables employees across the organization to share information across a single, centralized database. With extended portal capabilities, an organization can also involve its suppliers and customers in the workflow process, allowing ERP to

FIGURE 10.5

ERP Integration Data Flow

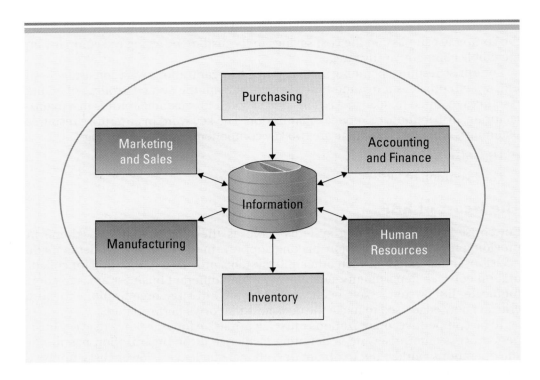

FIGURE 10.6

ERP Process Flow

ERP Success

penetrate the entire value chain, and help the organization achieve greater operational efficiency (see Figures 10.7 and 10.8).[7]

The Evolution of ERP

Originally, ERP solutions were developed to deliver automation across multiple units of an organization, to help facilitate the manufacturing process and address issues such as raw materials, inventory, order entry, and distribution. However, ERP was unable to extend to other functional areas of the company such as sales, marketing, and shipping. It could not tie in any CRM capabilities that would allow organizations to capture customer-specific information, nor did it work with websites or portals

FIGURE 10.7

The Organization before ERP

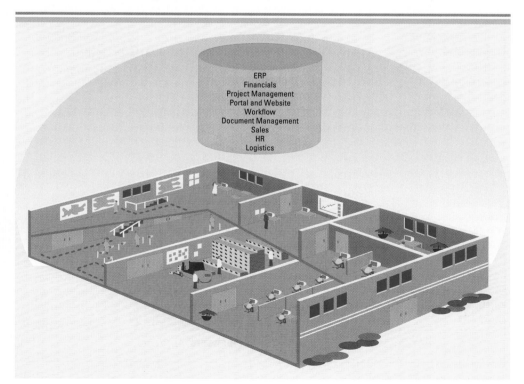

used for customer service or order fulfillment. Call center or quality assurance staff could not tap into the ERP solution, nor could ERP handle document management, such as cataloging contracts and purchase orders.[8]

ERP has grown over the years to become part of the extended enterprise. From its beginning as a tool for materials planning, it has extended to warehousing, distribution, and order entry. With its next evolution, ERP expands to the front office including CRM. Now administrative, sales, marketing, and human resources staff can share a tool that is truly enterprisewide. To compete on a functional level today, companies must adopt an enterprisewide approach to ERP that utilizes the Internet

FIGURE 10.8

ERP—Bringing the Organization Together

FIGURE 10.9

The Evolution of ERP

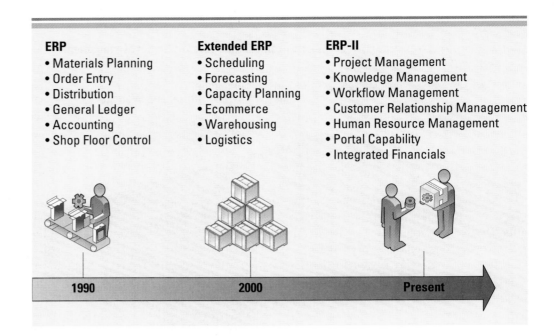

ERP
- Materials Planning
- Order Entry
- Distribution
- General Ledger
- Accounting
- Shop Floor Control

Extended ERP
- Scheduling
- Forecasting
- Capacity Planning
- Ecommerce
- Warehousing
- Logistics

ERP-II
- Project Management
- Knowledge Management
- Workflow Management
- Customer Relationship Management
- Human Resource Management
- Portal Capability
- Integrated Financials

1990   2000   Present

and connects to every facet of the value chain. Figure 10.9 shows how ERP has grown since the 1990s to accommodate the needs of the entire organization.[9]

ERP II: Core and Extended   Figure 10.10 provides an example of an ERP system with its core and extended components. *Core ERP components* are the traditional components included in most ERP systems and they primarily focus on internal operations. *Extended ERP components* are the extra components that meet the organizational needs not covered by the core components and primarily focus on external operations.

FIGURE 10.10

Core ERP Components and Extended ERP Components

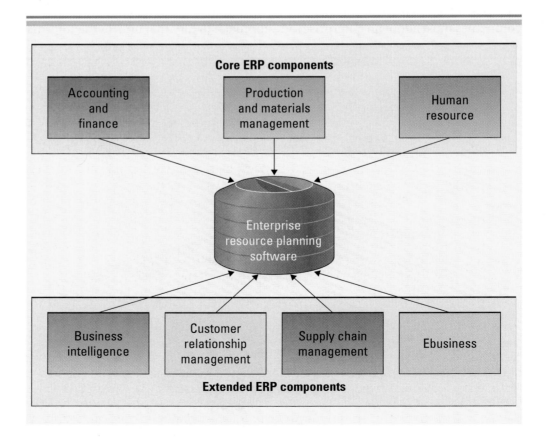

Core ERP components

| Accounting and finance | Production and materials management | Human resource |

Enterprise resource planning software

Extended ERP components

| Business intelligence | Customer relationship management | Supply chain management | Ebusiness |

CORE ERP COMPONENTS

The three most common core ERP components focusing on internal operations are:

1. Accounting and finance.
2. Production and materials management.
3. Human resources.

Accounting and Finance ERP Components

Deeley Harley-Davidson Canada, the exclusive Canadian distributor of Harley-Davidson motorcycles, has improved inventory, turnaround time, margins, and customer satisfaction—all with the implementation of a financial ERP system. The system has opened up the power of information to the company and is helping it make strategic decisions when it still has the time to change things. The ERP system provides the company with ways to manage inventory, turnaround time, and utilize warehouse space more effectively.[10]

Accounting and finance ERP components manage accounting data and financial processes within the enterprise with functions such as general ledger, accounts payable, accounts receivable, budgeting, and asset management. One of the most useful features included in an ERP accounting/finance component is its credit-management feature. Most organizations manage their relationships with customers by setting credit limits, or a limit on how much a customer can owe at any one time. The company then monitors the credit limit whenever the customer places a new order or sends in a payment. ERP financial systems help to correlate customer orders with customer account balances determining credit availability. Another great feature is the ability to perform product profitability analysis. ERP financial components are the backbone behind product profitability analysis and allow companies to perform all types of advanced profitability modeling techniques.

Production and Materials Management ERP Components

One of the main functions of an ERP system is streamlining the production planning process. *Production and materials management ERP components* handle the various aspects of production planning and execution such as demand forecasting, production scheduling, job cost accounting, and quality control. Companies typically produce multiple products, each of which has many different parts. Production lines, consisting of machines and employees, build the different types of products. The company must then define sales forecasting for each product to determine production schedules and materials purchasing. Figure 10.11 displays the typical ERP production planning process. The process begins with forecasting sales in order to plan operations. A detailed production schedule is developed if the product is produced, and a materials requirement plan is completed if the product is purchased.

Grupo Farmanova Intermed, located in Costa Rica, is a pharmaceutical marketing and distribution company that markets nearly 2,500 products to about 500 customers in Central and South America. The company identified a need for software that could unify product logistics management in a single country. It decided to deploy People-Soft financial and distribution ERP components allowing the company to improve customer data management, increase confidence among internal and external users, and coordinate the logistics of inventory. With the new software the company enhanced its capabilities for handling, distributing, and marketing its pharmaceuticals.[11]

Human Resources ERP Components

Human resources ERP components track employee information including payroll, benefits, compensation, and performance assessment, and assure compliance with the legal requirements of multiple jurisdictions and tax authorities. Human resources components even offer features that allow the organization to perform detailed analysis on its employees to determine such things as the identification of individuals who are likely to leave the company unless additional compensation or benefits are provided. These components can also identify which employees are

FIGURE 10.11

The Production Planning
Process

using which resources, such as online training and long-distance telephone services. They can also help determine whether the most talented people are working for those business units with the highest priority—or where they would have the greatest impact on profit.

EXTENDED ERP COMPONENTS

Extended ERP components are the extra components that meet the organizational needs not covered by the core components and primarily focus on external operations. Many of the numerous extended ERP components are Internet-enabled and require interaction with customers, suppliers, and business partners outside the organization. The four most common extended ERP components are:

1. Business intelligence.
2. Customer relationship management.
3. Supply chain management.
4. Ebusiness.

Business Intelligence ERP Components

ERP systems offer powerful tools that measure and control organizational operations. Many organizations have found that these valuable tools can be enhanced to provide even greater value through the addition of powerful business intelligence systems. The business intelligence components of ERP systems typically collect information used throughout the organization (including data used in many other ERP components), organize it, and apply analytical tools to assist managers with decisions. Data warehouses are one of the most popular extensions to ERP systems, with over two-thirds of U.S. manufacturers adopting or planning such systems.[12]

Customer Relationship Management ERP Components

ERP vendors are expanding their functionality to provide services formerly supplied by customer relationship management (CRM) vendors such as Oracle and Siebel. ***Customer relationship management*** involves managing all aspects of a customer's relationship with an organization to increase customer loyalty and retention and an organization's profitability. CRM components provide an integrated view of customer data and interactions allowing organizations to work more effectively with customers and be more responsive to their needs. CRM components typically include contact centers, sales force automation, and marketing functions. These improve the customer experience while identifying a company's most (and least) valuable customers for better allocation of resources.

Supply Chain Management ERP Components

ERP vendors are expanding their functionality to provide services formerly supplied by supply chain management vendors such as i2 Technologies and Manugistics. **Supply chain management (SCM)** involves the management of information flows between and among stages in a supply chain to maximize total supply chain effectiveness and profitability. SCM components help an organization plan, schedule, control, and optimize the supply chain from its acquisition of raw materials to the receipt of finished goods by customers.

ERP Solution

Ebusiness ERP Components

The original focus of ERP systems was the internal organization. In other words, ERP systems are not fundamentally ready for the external world of ebusiness. The newest and most exciting extended ERP components are the ebusiness components. **Ebusiness** means conducting business on the Internet, not only buying and selling, but also serving customers and collaborating with business partners. Two of the primary features of ebusiness components are elogistics and eprocurement. **Elogistics** manages the transportation and storage of goods. **Eprocurement** is the business-to-business (B2B) purchase and sale of supplies and services over the Internet.

Ebusiness and ERP complement each other by allowing companies to establish a web presence and fulfill orders expeditiously. A common mistake made by many businesses is deploying a web presence before the integration of back-office systems or an ERP system. For example, one large toy manufacturer announced less than a week before Christmas that it would be unable to fulfill any of its web orders. The company had all the toys in the warehouse, but it could not organize the basic order processing function to get the toys delivered to the consumers on time.

Customers and suppliers are now demanding access to ERP information including order status, inventory levels, and invoice reconciliation. Plus, the customers and partners want all this information in a simplified format available through a website. This is a difficult task to accomplish because most ERP systems are full of technical jargon, which is why employee training is one of the hidden costs associated with ERP implementations. Removing the jargon to accommodate untrained customers and partners is one of the more difficult tasks when web-enabling an ERP system. To accommodate the growing needs of the ebusiness world, ERP vendors need to build two new channels of access into the ERP system information—one channel for customers (B2C) and one channel for businesses, suppliers, and partners (B2B).[13]

INTEGRATING SCM, CRM, AND ERP

Applications such as SCM, CRM, and ERP are the backbone of ebusiness. Integration of these applications is the key to success for many companies. Integration allows the unlocking of information to make it available to any user, anywhere, anytime. Originally, there were three top ERP vendors—PeopleSoft, Oracle, and SAP. In December 2004, Oracle purchased PeopleSoft for $10 billion, leaving two main competitors in the ERP market—Oracle and SAP.

Most organizations today have no choice but to piece their SCM, CRM, and ERP applications together since no one vendor can respond to every organizational need; hence, customers purchase applications from multiple vendors. Oracle and SAP both offer CRM and SCM components. However, these modules are not as functional or flexible as the modules offered by industry leaders of SCM and CRM such as Siebel and i2 Technologies, as depicted in Figures 10.12 and 10.13. As a result, organizations face the challenge of

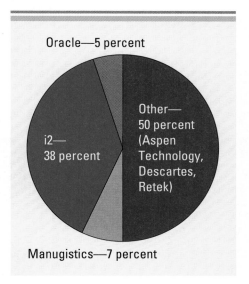

FIGURE 10.12

SCM Market Overview

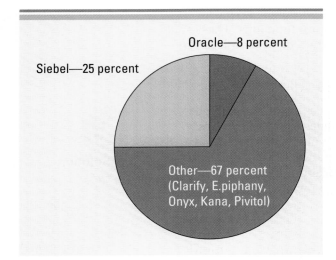

FIGURE 10.13

CRM Market Overview

integrating their systems. For example, a single organization might choose its CRM components from Siebel, SCM components from i2, and financial components and HR management components from Oracle. Figure 10.14 displays the general audience and purpose for each of these applications that have to be integrated.

From its roots in the California Gold Rush era, San Francisco-based Del Monte Foods has grown to become the nation's largest producer and distributor of premium quality processed fruits, vegetables, and tomato products. With annual sales of over $3 billion, Del Monte is also one of the country's largest producers, distributors, and marketers of private-label food and pet products with a powerful portfolio of brands including Del Monte, StarKist, Nature's Goodness, 9Lives, and Kibbles 'n Bits.

Del Monte's acquisition of StarKist, Nature's Goodness, 9Lives, and Kibbles 'n Bits from the H. J. Heinz Company required an integration between Del Monte's and H. J. Heinz's business processes. Del Monte needed to overhaul its IT infrastructure, migrating from multiple platforms including UNIX and mainframe systems and consolidating applications centrally on a single system. The work required integration of business processes across manufacturing, financial, supply chain, decision support, and transactional reporting areas.

The revamp of Del Monte's architecture stemmed from a strategic decision. Del Monte decided to implement an ERP system to support its entire U.S. operations, with headquarters in San Francisco, operations in Pittsburgh, and distribution centers and manufacturing facilities across the country. The company concluded that the only way it could unite its global operations and open its system to its customers, which are mainly large retailers, was through the use of an ERP system. Among other key factors was the need to embrace an ebusiness strategy. The challenge facing Del Monte was to select an ERP system to merge multiple systems quickly and cost effectively. If financial and customer service targets were to be achieved, Del Monte needed to integrate new businesses that more than doubled the size of the company.

FIGURE 10.14

Primary Users and Business Benefits of Strategic Initiatives

Since implementing the ERP system, customers and trading partners are now provided with a single, consistent, and integrated view of the company.[14]

Integration Tools

Effectively managing the transformation to an integrated enterprise is critical to the success of the 21st century organization. The key is the integration of the disparate IT applications. An integrated enterprise infuses support areas, such as finance and human resources, with a strong customer orientation. Integrations are achieved using *middleware*—several different types of software that sit in the middle of and provide connectivity between two or more software applications. Middleware translates information between disparate systems. ***Enterprise application integration (EAI) middleware*** represents a new approach to middleware by packaging together commonly used functionality, such as providing prebuilt links to popular enterprise applications, which reduces the time necessary to develop solutions that integrate applications from multiple vendors. A few leading vendors of EAI middleware include Active Software, Vitria Technology, and Extricity. Figure 10.15 displays the data points where these applications integrate and illustrates the underlying premise of architecture infrastructure design.

Companies run on interdependent applications, such as SCM, CRM, and ERP. If one application performs poorly, the entire customer value delivery system is affected. For example, no matter how great a company is at CRM, if its SCM system does not work and the customer never receives the finished product, the company will lose that customer. The world-class enterprises of tomorrow must be built on the foundation of world-class applications implemented today.

Coca-Cola's business model is a common one among well-known franchisers. Coca-Cola gets the majority of its $18 billion in annual revenue from franchise fees it earns from bottlers all over the world. Bottlers, along with the franchise, license Coke's secret recipe and many others including recipes for Odwalla, Nestea, Minute Maid, and Sprite. Now Coca-Cola hopes that bottlers will also buy into adopting common business practices using a service-oriented architecture (SoA) ERP system.

The target platform chosen by Coca-Cola is mySAP enterprise resource planning by SAP. If it works, Coca-Cola and its bottlers stand to make and save a lot of money, and SAP will be able to position itself as one of the dominant players in SoA-enabled ERP. Already, Coca-Cola and many of its bottlers use versions of SAP for finance, manufacturing, and a number of administrative functions. But Coca-Cola wants everyone to move to a "services" architecture environment.

FIGURE 10.15

Integrations between SCM, CRM, and ERP Applications

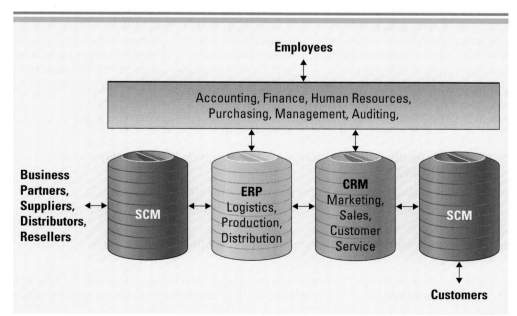

Coca-Cola hopes that this services standardization will make its supply chain more efficient and reduce costs. In explaining why a services approach is so vitally important, Jean-Michel Ares, CIO of Coca-Cola, stated, "That will allow bottlers to converge one step at a time, one process area at a time, one module at a time, at a time that's right for the bottler. We can march across the bottling world incrementally."[15]

MEASURING ERP SUCCESS

Measuring ERP success is extremely difficult. One of the best methods is the balanced scorecard. This approach to strategic management was developed in the early 1990s by Drs. Robert Kaplan of the Harvard Business School and David Norton. Addressing some of the weaknesses and vagueness of previous measurement techniques, the balanced scorecard approach provides a clear prescription as to what companies should measure in order to balance the financial perspective.[16]

The *balanced scorecard* is a management system, in addition to a measurement system, that enables organizations to clarify their vision and strategy and translate them into action. It provides feedback around both the internal business processes and external outcomes in order to continuously improve strategic performance and results. When fully deployed, the balanced scorecard transforms strategic planning from an academic exercise into the nerve center of an enterprise. Kaplan and Norton describe the innovation of the balanced scorecard as follows: "The balanced scorecard retains traditional financial measures. But financial measures tell the story of past events, an adequate story for industrial age companies for which investments in long-term capabilities and customer relationships were not critical for success. These financial measures are inadequate, however, for guiding and evaluating the journey that information age companies must make to create future value through investment in customers, suppliers, employees, processes, technology, and innovation."[17]

The balanced scorecard views the organization from four perspectives, and users should develop metrics, collect data, and analyze their business relative to each of these perspectives:

- The learning and growth perspective.
- The internal business process perspective.
- The customer perspective.
- The financial perspective (see Figure 10.16).[18]

Companies cannot manage what they cannot measure. Therefore, metrics must be developed based on the priorities of the strategic plan, which provides the key business drivers and criteria for metrics that managers most desire to watch. Processes are then designed to collect information relevant to these metrics and reduce it to numerical form for storage, display, and analysis. Decision makers examine the outcomes of various measured processes and strategies and track the results to guide the company and provide feedback. The value of metrics is in their ability to provide a factual basis for defining:

- Strategic feedback to show the present status of the organization from many perspectives for decision makers.
- Diagnostic feedback into various processes to guide improvements on a continuous basis.
- Trends in performance over time as the metrics are tracked.
- Feedback around the measurement methods themselves and which metrics should be tracked.
- Quantitative inputs to forecasting methods and models for decision support systems.[19]

One warning regarding metrics—do not go crazy. The trick is to find a few key metrics to track that provide significant insight. Remember to tie metrics to other financial and business objectives in the firm. The key is to get good insight without

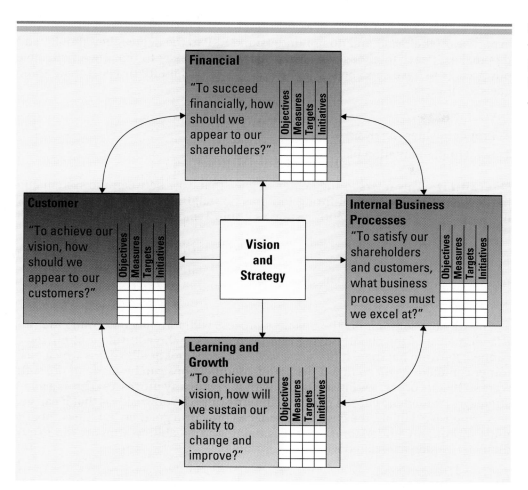

FIGURE 10.16

The Four Primary
Perspectives of the
Balanced Scorecard

becoming a slave to metrics. The rule of thumb is to develop seven key metrics, plus or minus two.[20]

CHOOSING ERP SOFTWARE

The many different ERP vendors on the market today each offer different ERP solutions. The core ERP functions for each vendor are the same and focus on financial, accounting, sales, marketing, human resource, operations, and logistics. ERP vendors differentiate themselves by offering unique functionality such as CRM and SCM systems.

Many customers find that their chosen ERP solution does not meet their expectations. Despite many improvements in the software, the industry itself is well aware that failed ERP implementations are still far too common. According to Gartner Research, the average failure rate for an ERP project is 66 percent. It is no wonder that some manufacturers view ERP as a necessary, strategic evil. The key word here though is *necessary*.[21]

Many companies strive to make good financial decisions by making smart investments. The best way to ensure a good investment in ERP is to understand why failure occurs and how to avoid it. The first challenge is that ERP is a product that comes in many flavors. Its main purpose is to provide support and automation to a business process. The business world has many different business models, and there are just as many ERP products available that serve them.

Finding the Right ERP Solution

A good ERP system will be highly reflective of the business process in place at the company. This means the software must perform many different tasks and that makes it complex. Most companies do not carry a high degree of ERP software expertise on their staff and do not understand ERP to the degree they should, and this makes it easy to choose the wrong package. The key to making an effective purchase is to have solid business processes. Successful ERP projects share three basic attributes:

1. Overall fit.
2. Proper business analysis.
3. Solid implementation plans.[22]

Overall Fit This refers to the degree of gaps that exist between the system and the business process. A well-fitting ERP has no major process gaps and very few minor ones. Think of a new ERP system as a suit. Typically, a customer buys a suit three ways:

1. Off the rack.
2. Off the rack and tailor it to fit.
3. Custom made.

The way the solution fits the business process will normally determine the satisfaction level of the client. Buying ERP off the rack is the equivalent of buying a canned software package. It fits some well, but some not at all. That is why a customer can tailor a suit so that it fits better. Modifications can be made to the software so that its processes line up better with the company processes. This is a good strategy, provided the chosen package supports this. The downside is that it can get very expensive. Finally, the custom system can provide a great fit, but the company must thoroughly understand what it is doing and be able to support the heavy financial burden associated with a custom-build.

Proper Business Analysis The best way to determine which fit strategy is right is to conduct a thorough business analysis. Successful companies normally spend up to 10 percent of the project budget on a business analysis. A proper analysis must result in a documented list of the business processes at work within the company. This will provide a basic tool that can measure vendor capability.

Solid Implementation Plans Like the installation of any successful process or piece of machinery, a plan is needed to monitor the quality objectives and timelines. It will also employ processes like workflow analysis and job combination to harvest savings.

A thorough implementation will transfer knowledge to the system users. When the project is complete the users of the new system must be capable of using the tools it provides. The users must also know what to do in cases when the process fluctuates. The majority of failed systems are the result of poor-quality implementation. It is important to remember that ERP is simply a tool. Tools that people do not know how to use can be as useless as having no tools at all.[23]

OPENING CASE QUESTIONS

Campus ERP

1. How could core ERP components help improve business operations at your college?

2. How could extended ERP components help improve business operations at your college?

3. How can integrating SCM, CRM, and ERP help improve business operations at your college?

10.6. Identify the different ways in which companies collaborate using technology.

10.7. Compare the different categories of collaboration technologies.

10.8. Define the fundamental concepts of a knowledge management system.

10.9. Provide an example of a content management system along with its business purpose.

10.10. Evaluate the advantages of using a workflow management system.

10.11. Explain how groupware can benefit a business.

TEAMS, PARTNERSHIPS, AND ALLIANCES

To be successful—and avoid being eliminated by the competition—an organization must constantly undertake new initiatives, address both minor and major problems, and capitalize on significant opportunities. To support these activities, an organization often will create and utilize teams, partnerships, and alliances because the expertise needed is beyond the scope of a single individual or organization. These teams, partnerships, and alliances can be formed internally among a company's employees or externally with other organizations (see Figure 10.17).

Businesses of all sizes and in all markets have witnessed the benefits of leveraging their IT assets to create competitive advantage. Whereas information technology efforts in the past were aimed at increasing operational efficiency, the advent and proliferation of network-based computing (the Internet being the most visible, but not only, example) has enabled organizations to build systems with which all sorts of communities can interact. The ultimate result will allow organizations to do business with customers, business partners, suppliers, governments and regulatory agencies, and any other community relevant to their particular operation or activity.

In the same way that organizations use internal teams, they are increasingly forming alliances and partnerships with other organizations. The **core competency** of an organization is its key strength, a business function that it does better than any of its competitors. Apple Computer is highly regarded for its strength in product design, while Accenture's core competency is the design and installation of information systems. A **core competency strategy** is one in which an organization chooses to focus

Solution People

FIGURE 10.17

Teams, Partnerships, and Alliances Within and External to an Organization specifically on what it does best (its core competency) and forms partnerships and alliances with other specialist organizations to handle nonstrategic business processes. Strategic alliances enable businesses to gain competitive advantages through access to a partner's resources, including markets, technologies, and people. Teaming up with another business adds complementary resources and capabilities, enabling participants to grow and expand more quickly and efficiently, especially fast-growing companies that rely heavily on outsourcing many areas of their business to extend their technical and operational resources. In the outsourcing process, they save time and boost productivity by not having to develop their own systems from scratch. They are then free to concentrate on innovation and their core business.

Information technology makes such business partnerships and alliances easier to establish and manage. An *information partnership* occurs when two or more organizations cooperate by integrating their IT systems, thereby providing customers with the best of what each can offer. The advent of the Internet has greatly increased the opportunity for IT-enabled business partnerships and alliances. Amazon developed a profitable business segment by providing ebusiness outsourcing services to other retailers that use Amazon's website software. Some well-known retailers partnering with Amazon include Office Depot and Target.[24]

COLLABORATION SYSTEMS

Heineken USA has shortened its inventory cycle time for beer production and distribution from three months to four weeks. By using its collaborative system to forecast demand and expedite shipping, the company has dramatically cut inventory levels and shipping costs while increasing sales.

Over the past few years most business processes have changed on various dimensions (e.g., flexibility, interconnectivity, coordination style, autonomy) because of market conditions and organizational models. Frequently, information is located within physically separated systems as more and more organizations spread their reach globally. This creates a need for a software infrastructure that enables collaboration systems.

A *collaboration system* is an IT-based set of tools that supports the work of teams by facilitating the sharing and flow of information. Collaboration solves specific business tasks such as telecommuting, online meetings, deploying applications, and remote project and sales management (see Figure 10.18).

FIGURE 10.18

Collaborative Business Areas

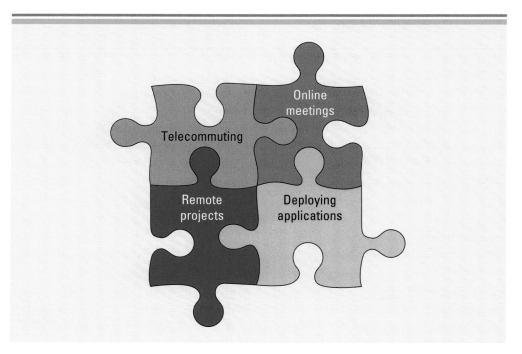

Collaboration systems allow people, teams, and organizations to leverage and build upon the ideas and talents of staff, suppliers, customers, and business partners. It involves a unique set of business challenges that:

- Include complex interactions between people who may be in different locations and desire to work across function and discipline areas.

- Require flexibility in work process and the ability to involve others quickly and easily.

- Call for creating and sharing information rapidly and effortlessly within a team.

Most organizations collaborate with other companies in some capacity. Consider the supplier-customer relationship, which can be thought of in terms of a continuous life cycle of engagement, transaction, fulfillment, and service activities. Rarely do companies excel in all four life cycle areas, either from a business process or from a technology-enabled aspect. Successful organizations identify and invest in their core competencies, and outsource or collaborate for those competencies that are not core to them. Collaboration systems fall into one of two categories:

1. **Unstructured collaboration** (sometimes referred to as **information collaboration**) includes document exchange, shared whiteboards, discussion forums, and email. These functions can improve personal productivity, reducing the time spent searching for information or chasing answers.

2. **Structured collaboration** (or **process collaboration**) involves shared participation in business processes, such as workflow, in which knowledge is hard-coded as rules. This is beneficial in terms of improving automation and the routing of information.

Collaboration

Regardless of location or format—be it unstructured or structured—relevant accurate information must be readily and consistently available to those who need it anytime, anywhere, and on any device. The integration of IT systems enables an organization to provide employees, partners, customers, and suppliers with the ability to access, find, analyze, manage, and collaborate on content. The collaboration can be done across a wide variety of formats, languages, and platforms.

Lockheed Martin Aeronautics Company's ability to share complex project information across an extended supply chain in real time was key in its successful bid of a $19 billion Department of Defense (DoD) contract to build 21 supersonic stealth fighters. New government procurement rules require defense contractors to communicate effectively to ensure that deadlines are met, costs are controlled, and projects are managed throughout the life cycle of the contract.[25]

In anticipation of the contract, the Fort Worth, Texas, unit of Lockheed Martin developed a real-time collaboration system that can tie together its partners, suppliers, and DoD customers via the Internet. The platform lets participants collectively work on product design and engineering tasks as well as supply chain and life cycle management issues. Lockheed will host all transactions and own the project information. The platform will let DoD and Lockheed project managers track the daily progress of the project in real time. This is the first major DoD project with such a requirement. The contract, awarded to the Lockheed unit and partners Northrop Grumman Corp. and BAE Systems, is the first installment in what could amount to a $200 billion program for 3,000 jet fighters over 40 years. The strengths of the collaboration process lie with the integration of many systems, namely:

- Knowledge management systems
- Content management systems
- Workflow management systems
- Groupware systems

KNOWLEDGE MANAGEMENT SYSTEMS

Knowledge management (KM) involves capturing, classifying, evaluating, retrieving, and sharing information assets in a way that provides context for effective decisions and actions. It is best to think of KM in the broadest context. Succinctly put,

KM is the process through which organizations generate value from their intellectual and knowledge-based assets. Most often, generating value from such assets involves codifying what employees, partners, and customers know, and sharing that information among employees, departments, and even with other companies to devise best practices. It is important to note that the definition says nothing about technology; while KM is often facilitated by IT, technology by itself is not KM.

Think of a golf caddie as a simplified example of a knowledge worker. Good caddies do more than carry clubs and track down wayward balls. When asked, a good caddie will give advice to golfers, such as, "The wind makes the ninth hole play 15 yards longer." Accurate advice may lead to a bigger tip at the end of the day. The golfer, having derived a benefit from the caddie's advice, may be more likely to play that course again. If a good caddie is willing to share what he knows with other caddies, then they all may eventually earn bigger tips. How would KM work to make this happen? The caddie master may decide to reward caddies for sharing their knowledge by offering them credits for pro shop merchandise. Once the best advice is collected, the course manager would publish the information in notebooks (or make it available on PDAs) and distribute them to all the caddies. The end result of a well-designed KM program is that everyone wins. In this case, caddies get bigger tips and deals on merchandise, golfers play better because they benefit from the collective experience of caddies, and the course owners win because better scores lead to repeat business.

KM in Business

Knowledge
Management

KM has assumed greater urgency in American business over the past few years as millions of baby boomers prepare to retire. When they punch out for the last time, the knowledge they gleaned about their jobs, companies, and industries during their long careers will walk out with them—unless companies take measures to retain their insights. In addition, CIOs who have entered into outsourcing agreements must address the thorny issue of transferring the knowledge of their full-time staff members, who are losing their jobs because of an outsourcing deal, to the outsourcer's employees.

Knowledge can be a real competitive advantage for an organization. Information technology can distribute an organization's knowledge base by interconnecting people and digitally gathering their expertise. The primary objective of knowledge management is to be sure that a company's knowledge of facts, sources of information, and solutions are readily available to all employees whenever it is needed.

Such knowledge management requires that organizations go well beyond providing information contained in spreadsheets, databases, and documents. It must include expert information that typically resides in people's heads. A ***knowledge management system (KMS)*** supports the capturing, organization, and dissemination of knowledge (i.e., know-how) throughout an organization. It is up to the organization to determine what information qualifies as knowledge.

Explicit and Tacit Knowledge

Not all information is valuable. Individual companies must determine what information qualifies as intellectual and knowledge-based assets. In general, intellectual and knowledge-based assets fall into one of two categories: explicit or tacit. As a rule, ***explicit knowledge*** consists of anything that can be documented, archived, and codified, often with the help of IT. Examples of explicit knowledge are assets such as patents, trademarks, business plans, marketing research, and customer lists.

Tacit knowledge is the knowledge contained in people's heads. The challenge inherent in tacit knowledge is figuring out how to recognize, generate, share, and manage knowledge that resides in people's heads. While information technology in the form of email, instant messaging, and related technologies can help facilitate the dissemination of tacit knowledge, identifying it in the first place can be a major obstacle. Shadowing and joint problem solving are two best practices for transferring or re-creating tacit knowledge inside an organization.

Shadowing With *shadowing,* less experienced staff observe more experienced staff to learn how their more experienced counterparts approach their work. Dorothy

Leonard and Walter Swap, two knowledge management experts, stress the importance of having the protégé discuss his or her observations with the expert to deepen the dialog and crystallize the knowledge transfer.

Joint Problem Solving   Another sound approach is *joint problem solving* by expert and novice. Because people are often unaware of how they approach problems or do their work and therefore cannot automatically generate step-by-step instructions for doing whatever they do, having a novice and expert work together on a project will bring the expert's approach to light. The difference between shadowing and joint problem solving is that shadowing is more passive. With joint problem solving, the expert and the novice work hand in hand on a task.[26]

Information is of little use unless it is analyzed and made available to the right people, at the right place, and at the right time. To get the most value from intellectual assets, knowledge must be shared. An effective KMS system should help do one or more of the following:

- Foster innovation by encouraging the free flow of ideas.
- Improve customer service by streamlining response time.
- Boost revenues by getting products and services to market faster.
- Enhance employee retention rates by recognizing the value of employees' knowledge.
- Streamline operations and reduce costs by eliminating redundant or unnecessary processes.

A creative approach to knowledge management can result in improved efficiency, higher productivity, and increased revenues in practically any business function. Figure 10.19 indicates the reasons organizations launch KMS.

Software is helping ChevronTexaco Corporation improve how it manages the assets in oil fields by enabling employees in multiple disciplines to easily access and share the information they need to make decisions. ChevronTexaco teams of 10 to 30 people are responsible for managing the assets, such as the drilling equipment, pipelines, and facilities, for a particular oil field. Within each team, earth scientists and various engineers with expertise in production, reservoir, and facilities work

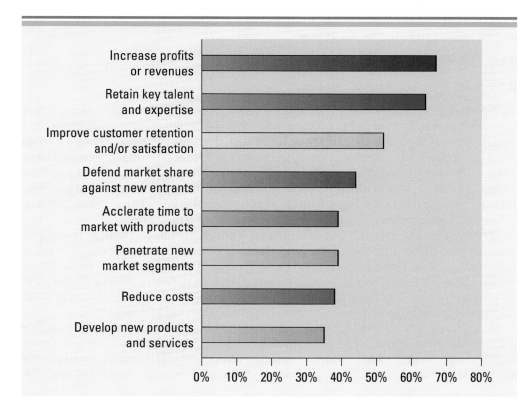

FIGURE 10.19

Key Reasons Organizations Launch Knowledge Management Systems together to keep the oil field up and running. Each member of the asset team needs to communicate with other members to make decisions based on the collection and analysis of huge amounts of information from various departments. Individual team members can look at information from the perspective of their own department.

This has helped ChevronTexaco achieve a 30 percent productivity gain, a 50 percent improvement in safety performance, and more than $2 billion in operating cost reductions. Through KMSs, ChevronTexaco has restructured its gasoline retailing business and now drills oil and gas wells faster and cheaper.[27]

Not every organization matches ChevronTexaco's success with KM. Numerous KM projects have failed over the past few years, generating an unwillingness to undertake—or even address—KM issues among many organizations. However, KM is an effective tool if it is tied directly to discrete business needs and opportunities. Beginning with targeted projects that deliver value quickly, companies can achieve the success that has proved elusive with many big-bang approaches. Successful KM projects typically focus on creating value in a specific process area, or even just for a certain type of transaction. Companies should start with one job at a time—preferably the most knowledge-oriented one—and build KM into a job function in a way that actually helps employees do their work better and faster, then expand to the next most knowledge-intensive job, and so on. Celebrating even small success with KM will help build a base of credibility and support for future KM projects.

KM Technologies

KM is not a purely technology-based concept. Organizations that implement a centralized database system, electronic message board, web portal, or any other collaborative tool in the hope that they have established a KMS are wasting both their time and money.

Although tools don't make a KMS, such a system does need tools, from standard, off-the-shelf email packages to sophisticated collaboration tools designed specifically to support community building and identity. Generally, KMS tools fall into one or more of the following categories:

- Knowledge repositories (databases).
- Expertise tools.
- Elearning applications.
- Discussion and chat technologies.
- Search and data mining tools.

KM and Social Networking

Companies that have been frustrated by traditional KM efforts are increasingly looking for ways to find out how knowledge flows through their organization, and social networking analysis can show them just that. ***Social networking analysis (SNA)*** is a process of mapping a group's contacts (whether personal or professional) to identify who knows whom and who works with whom. In enterprises, it provides a clear picture of how far-flung employees and divisions work together and can help identify key experts in the organization who possess the knowledge needed to, say, solve a complicated programming problem or launch a new product.

M&M maker Mars used SNA to identify how knowledge flows through its organizations, who holds influence, who gives the best advice, and how employees share information. The Canadian government's central IT unit used SNA to establish which skills it needed to retain and develop, and to determine who, among the 40 percent of the workforce that was due to retire within five years, had the most important knowledge and experience to begin transferring to others.[28]

SNA is not a replacement for traditional KM tools such as knowledge databases or portals, but it can provide companies with a starting point for how best to proceed with KM initiatives. As a component to a larger KM strategy, SNA can help companies identify key leaders and then set up a mechanism, such as communities of practice, so that those leaders can pass on their knowledge to colleagues. To identify experts in their organizations, companies can use software programs that track email and other kinds of electronic communication.[29]

CONTENT MANAGEMENT SYSTEMS

A *content management system* provides tools to manage the creation, storage, editing, and publication of information in a collaborative environment. As a website grows in size and complexity, the business must establish procedures to ensure that things run smoothly. At a certain point, it makes sense to automate this process and use a content management system to manage this effectively. The content management system marketplace is complex, incorporating document management, digital asset management, and web content management. Figure 10.20 highlights the three primary types of content management systems. Figure 10.21 lists the major content management system vendors.

Content management software is helping BMW Group Switzerland accelerate personalized, real-time information about products, services, prices, and events to its dealers countrywide. BMW uses a process that allows dealers to specify what information is seen by which employee, as well as to deliver marketing materials solely to members of the sales department, and technical specifications and support documents only to mechanics. That enhanced personalization eliminates the chance that information is sent to the wrong dealership or to the wrong individual, which provides higher quality customer service. The content management software also enables nontechnical employees to create pages using predefined layout templates, simplifying the web publishing process. More than 500 people use the solution daily, and all employees are able to publish information without calling on IT specialists, while maintaining the look and feel of the BMW brand.[30]

Working Wikis

Wikis are web-based tools that make it easy for users to add, remove, and change online content. *Business wikis* are collaborative web pages that allow users to edit documents, share ideas, or monitor the status of a project. Most people are familiar with Wikipedia, one of the largest online collaboration websites. Employees also use wikis to collaborate; for example, companies such as Intel, Motorola, IBM, and Sony use them for a host of tasks, from setting internal meeting agendas to posting documents related to new products. Many companies rely on wikis to engage

FIGURE 10.20

Common Types of Content Management Systems

Common Types of Content Management Systems	
Document management system (DMS)	DMS—Supports the electronic capturing, storage, distribution, archiving, and accessing of documents. A DMS optimizes the use of documents within an organization independent of any publishing medium (for example, the web). A DMS provides a document repository with information about other information. The system tracks the editorial history of each document and its relationships with other documents. A variety of search and navigation methods are available to make document retrieval easy. A DMS manages highly structured and regulated content, such as pharmaceutical documentation.
Digital asset management system (DAM)	DAM—Though similar to document management, DAM generally works with binary rather than text files, such as multimedia file types. DAM places emphasis on allowing file manipulation and conversion, for example, converting GIF files to JPEG.
Web content management system (WCM)	WCM—Adds an additional layer to document and digital asset management that enables publishing content both to intranets and to public websites. In addition to maintaining the content itself, WCM systems often integrate content with online processes like ebusiness systems.

FIGURE 10.21

Major Content Management
Systems Vendors

Vendors	Strengths	Weaknesses	Costs
Documentum www.emc.com	Document and digital asset management	Personalization features not as strong as competitors	Major components start at less than $100,000
FatWire www.fatwire.com	Web content management	May not scale to support thousands of users	SPARK, $25,000; Update Engine, $70,000 and up
InterWoven www.interwoven.com	Collaboration, enterprise content management	Requires significant customization	InterWoven 5 Platform, $50,000; average cost for a new customer, $250,000
Percussion www.percussion.com	Web content management	May not scale to support thousands of users	Rhythmyx Content Manager, about $150,000
Stellent www.stellent.com	Document conversion to web-ready formats	Engineering for very large implementations with thousands of users	Content and Collaboration Servers, $50,000 to $250,000 each
Vignette www.vignette.com	Personalization	Document management and library services are not as robust as others	V6 Multisite Content Manager, $200,000 and up; V6 Content Suite, $450,000 and up

customers in ongoing discussions about products. Wikis for Motorola and T-Mobile handsets serve as continually updated user guides. TV networks including ABC and CBS are creating fan wikis that let viewers interact with each other as they unravel mysteries from such shows as *Lost* and *CSI: Crime Scene Investigation*.[31]

A handful of tech-savvy employees at two very different European companies began dabbling in the use of wikis and witnessed a rapid spread of wikis at both companies—Finnish handset-maker Nokia and London- and Frankfurt-based investment bank Dresdner Kleinwort. Nokia estimates at least 20 percent of its 68,000 employees use wiki pages to update schedules and project status, trade ideas, edit files, and so on. "It's a reversal of the normal way things are done," says Stephen Johnston, senior manager for corporate strategy at Nokia, who helped pioneer the technology. Where Nokia once bought outside software to help foster collaboration, now "some of the most interesting stuff is emerging from within the company itself," says Johnston.

It is a similar tale at Dresdner Kleinwort. A few pioneers in the IT department at its London office sent a program called Socialtext to several groups to see how it might be used to facilitate different IT tasks. The wiki program spread so quickly that Dresdner Kleinwort decided to launch its own corporate wiki. By October 2006, the bank's 5,000 employees had created more than 6,000 individual pages and logged about 100,000 hits on the company's official wiki.

The experience of Nokia and Dresdner Kleinwort offer insight into how to nurture the use of a radically new technology to change the way organizations work. Clearly, not everyone recognizes the value of wikis right away. The initial efforts at Dresdner, for example, confused employees and had to be refined to make the technology easier to use. More important than tweaking the technology was a simple edict from one of the proponents: Do not send emails, use the wiki. Gradually, employees embraced the use of the wiki, seeing how it increased collaboration and reduced time-consuming email traffic.[32]

WORKFLOW MANAGEMENT SYSTEMS

A ***workflow*** defines all the steps or business rules, from beginning to end, required for a business process. Therefore, ***workflow management systems*** facilitate the automation and management of business processes and control the movement of work through the business process. Work activities can be performed in series or in parallel and involve people and automated computer systems. In addition, many workflow management systems allow the opportunity to measure and analyze the execution of the process because workflow systems allow the flow of work between individuals and/or departments to be defined and tracked. Workflow software helps automate a range of business tasks and electronically route the right information to the right people at the right time. Users are notified of pending work, and managers can observe status and route approvals through the system quickly.

There are two primary types of workflow systems: messaging-based and database-based. **_Messaging-based workflow systems_** send work assignments through an email system. The workflow system automatically tracks the order for the work to be assigned and, each time a step is completed, the system automatically sends the work to the next individual in line. For example, each time a team member completes a piece of the project, the system would automatically send the document to the next team member.

Database-based workflow systems store documents in a central location and automatically ask the team members to access the document when it is their turn to edit the document. Project documentation is stored in a central location and team members are notified by the system when it is their turn to log in and work on their portion of the project.

Either type of workflow system helps to present information in a unified format, improves teamwork by providing automated process support, and allows team members to communicate and collaborate within a unified environment.

New York City was experiencing a record number of claims, ranging from injuries resulting from slips on sidewalks to medical malpractice at city hospitals. The city processes over 30,000 claims and incurs $250 million in claim costs annually. Claims are generally filed with the Comptroller's Office, which investigates them and offers to settle meritorious claims. The New York City Comptroller's Office, with the assistance of its consultants Xerox and Universal Systems Inc., utilized a workflow management system to enhance revenues and decrease operating costs. With the implementation of the Omnibus Automated Image Storage Information System (OAISIS) for processing contracts and claims, New York City will save over $20 million.

Numerous city organizations were involved in the workflow management system, including Bureau of Law and Adjustment, Office of Contracts/Administration, Management and Accounting Systems, and Bureau of Information Systems.

In supporting all these New York City organizations, the system performs many functions that were previously labor-intensive and detracted from the quality and efficiency of investigations. The workflow management system screens claims to determine accordance with statutory requirements. Acknowledgment letters are generated automatically, with little or no resource allocation involved in assignment of claims or routing of claims to specific work locations. Status letters are automatically generated by the system for certain claim types, thus allowing the Comptroller's Office to keep claimants informed two months, five months, and one year from the date of their filing. All this is done automatically by the workflow management system.

Workflow management systems allow management to schedule individual systematic claim reviews without disrupting the investigation. Management can also see the entire claim process graphically and determine bottlenecks. Deployment of additional resources to needed areas occurs without a management analysis of a particular process problem.

GROUPWARE SYSTEMS

Groupware is software that supports team interaction and dynamics including calendaring, scheduling, and videoconferencing. Organizations can use this technology to communicate, cooperate, coordinate, solve problems, compete, or negotiate. While traditional technologies like the telephone qualify as groupware, the term

FIGURE 10.22

Groupware Systems

	Same time "Synchronous"	**Different time** "Asynchronous"
Same place "Co-located"	Presentation support	Shared computers
Different place "Distance"	Videophones, Chat	Email, Workflow

refers to a specific class of technologies relying on modern computer networks, such as email, newsgroups, videophones, and chat rooms. Groupware systems fall along two primary categories (see Figure 10.22):

1. Users of the groupware are working together at the same time (real-time or synchronous groupware) or different times (asynchronous groupware).

2. Users are working together in the same place (co-located or face-to-face) or in different places (non-co-located or distance).

The groupware concept integrates various systems and functionalities into a common set of services or a single (client) application. In addition, groupware can represent a wide range of systems and methods of integration. Figure 10.23 displays the advantages groupware systems offer an organization over single-user systems.

Lotus Notes is one of the world's leading software solutions for collaboration that combines messaging, groupware, and the Internet. The structure of Notes allows it to track, route, and manage documents. Systems that lend themselves to Notes involve tracking, routing, approval, document management, and organization.

Toyota developed an intranet system to promote information sharing within the company and to raise productivity. Unfortunately, the company's conventional email system became overloaded, generating problems. Users did not receive incoming messages and were not able to send messages. Individual departments had introduced their own email systems, which were not always compatible. Messages to other mail systems, including those outside the company, experienced delays. To deal with these difficulties, Toyota's information systems department reviewed the email system and restructured it so that email, now recognized as an important communication tool, is utilized more effectively in business transactions.[33]

FIGURE 10.23

Groupware Advantages

Groupware System Advantages
Facilitating communication (faster, easier, clearer, more persuasive)
Enabling telecommuting
Reducing travel costs
Sharing expertise
Forming groups with common interests where it would not be possible to gather a sufficient number of people face-to-face
Saving time and cost in coordinating group work
Facilitating group problem solving

Videoconferencing

A **videoconference** is a set of interactive telecommunication technologies that allow two or more locations to interact via two-way video and audio transmissions simultaneously. It has also been called visual collaboration and is a type of groupware. Videoconferencing uses telecommunications of audio and video to bring people at different sites together for a meeting. This can be as simple as a conversation between two people in private offices (point-to-point) or involve several sites (multipoint) with more than one person in large rooms at different sites. Besides the audio and visual transmission of people, videoconferencing can be used to share documents, computer-displayed information, and whiteboards.[34]

Simple analog videoconferences could be established as early as the invention of the television. Such videoconferencing systems consisted of two closed-circuit television systems connected via cable. During the first manned space flights, NASA used two radio frequency (UHF or VHF) links, one in each direction. TV channels routinely use this kind of videoconferencing when reporting from distant locations, for instance. Then mobile links to satellites using special trucks became rather common (see Figure 10.24 for an example of videoconferencing).

Videoconferencing is now being introduced to online networking websites to help businesses form profitable relationships quickly and efficiently without leaving their place of work. Several factors support business use of videoconferencing, including:[35]

FIGURE 10.24

Videoconferencing

- Over 60 percent of face-to-face communication is nonverbal. Therefore, an enriched communications tool such as videoconferencing can promote an individual's or a team's identity, context, and emotional situation.

- Fifty-six percent of business professionals waste an estimated 30 minutes a day using inefficient communication methods, costing businesses an estimated $297 billion annually.

- The latest technology is available with reliable and easy-to-use conferencing, fostering collaboration at meetings.

- Enterprises that fail to use modern communications technologies run the very real risk of falling behind their competition.[36]

FIGURE 10.25

Web Conferencing

Web Conferencing

Web conferencing blends audio, video, and document-sharing technologies to create virtual meeting rooms where people "gather" at a password-protected website. There, they can chat in conference calls or use real-time text messages. They can mark up a shared document as if it were a blackboard, and even watch live software demos or video clips.

Perhaps the biggest surprise about web conferencing is its simplicity. Users only need to set up an account and download a few small software files. The best part about a web conference is that attendees do not have to have the same hardware or software. Every participant can see what is on anyone else's screen, regardless of the application being used (see Figure 10.25 for an example of web conferencing).[37]

Even with its video features, web conferencing is not quite like being there—or like being in a sophisticated (and pricey) videoconferencing facility. Still, professionals can accomplish more sitting at their desks than in an airport waiting to make travel connections. A growing number of companies are offering web conferencing. Leaders in this industry include WebEx, SameTime 2, and Elluminate Live.

FIGURE 10.26

Instant Messaging
Application

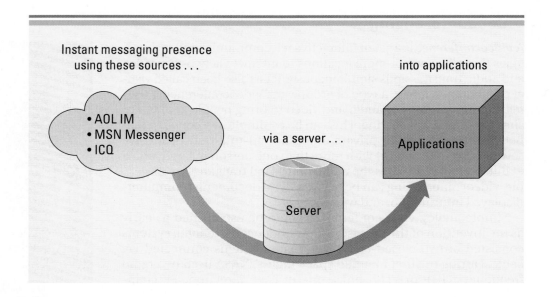

Instant Messaging

Email is by far the dominant collaboration application, but real-time collaboration tools like instant messaging are creating a new communication dynamic within organizations. *Instant messaging* (sometimes called *IM* or *IMing*) is a type of communications service that enables someone to create a kind of private chat room with another individual in order to communicate in real-time over the Internet. In 1992, AOL deployed IM to the consumer market, allowing users to communicate with other IMers through a buddy list. Most of the popular instant messaging programs provide a variety of features, such as:

- Web links: Share links to favorite websites.
- Images: Look at an image stored on someone else's computer.
- Sounds: Play sounds.
- Files: Share files by sending them directly to another IMer.
- Talk: Use the Internet instead of a phone to talk.
- Streaming content: Receive real-time or near-real-time stock quotes and news.
- Instant messages: Receive immediate text messages.

Commercial vendors such as AOL and Microsoft offer free instant messaging tools. Real-time collaboration, such as instant messaging, live web conferencing, and screen or document sharing, creates an environment for decision making. AOL, Microsoft's MSN, and Yahoo! have begun to sell enterprise versions of their instant messaging services that match the capabilities of business-oriented products like IBM's Lotus Sametime. Figure 10.26 demonstrates the IM application presence within IT systems.

IBM Lotus software has released new versions of its real-time collaboration platform, IBM Lotus Instant Messaging and IBM Lotus Web Conferencing, plus its mobile counterpart, IBM Lotus Instant Messaging Everyplace. These built-for-business products let an organization offer presence awareness, secure instant messaging, and web conferencing. The products give employees instant access to colleagues and company information regardless of time, place, or device.

The bigger issue in collaboration for organizations is cultural. Collaboration brings teams of people together from different regions, departments, and even companies—people who bring different skills, perceptions, and capabilities. A formal collaboration strategy helps create the right environment as well as the right systems for team members.

Campus ERP

4. How can a college campus achieve business success through the use of collaboration tools?

5. How can your college use knowledge management systems to improve operations?

6. How can your college use content management systems to improve operations?

7. How can a team of college students use a workflow management system to complete a group project?

8. If your college wanted to implement a groupware system, what would be its primary purpose?

SUMMARY OF KEY THEMES

This chapter discussed various ways that information technology can help organizations access, share, and use information. Organizations can leverage IT including ERP systems to provide employees with better access to the information they need, improved ways of sharing information with others, and a heightened means of turning information into knowledge.

Information comes in many different shapes and sizes and can be structured information found in databases or unstructured information found in documents, emails, and even in employees' heads. ERP systems can help organizations by combining all of the information into one core system.

Even though attempting to leverage such diverse information sources and implementing ERP systems can be challenging and difficult, there is a real payoff for organizations—employees are armed with the right information, at the right time, become empowered to turn that information into "action" by delivering innovations, forging best practices, and developing new products and services for the company.

You, as a business student, must understand the power of facilitating information access, promoting information sharing, and encouraging information use throughout your organization. Using technology can help your organization work collaboratively and promote knowledge generation, sharing, and use across the organization.

KEY TERMS

Accounting and finance ERP component 365
Balanced scorecard 370
Business intelligence 366
Business wiki 379
Collaboration system 374
Content management system 379
Core competency 373
Core competency strategy 373
Core ERP component 364
Customer relationship management (CRM) 366

Database-based workflow system 381
Digital asset management system (DAM) 379
Document management system (DMS) 379
Ebusiness 367
Elogistics 367
Enterprise application integration (EAI) middleware 369
Enterprise resource planning (ERP) 358
Eprocurement 367
Explicit knowledge 376

Extended ERP component 364, 366
Groupware 381
Human resources ERP component 365
Information partnership 374
Instant messaging (IM, IMing) 384
Knowledge management (KM) 375
Knowledge management system (KMS) 376
Messaging-based workflow system 381

CLOSING CASE ONE

DreamWorks Animation Collaboration

Hewlett-Packard (HP) and DreamWorks Animation SKG were the first to introduce a collaboration studio for simulating face-to-face business meetings across long distances. Vyomesh Joshi, executive vice president at HP, and Jeffrey Katzenberg, CEO of DreamWorks, officially unveiled the HP Halo Collaboration Studio in New York City in 2005. Halo enables people in different locations to communicate in a vivid, face-to-face environment in real time. Whether across a country or across the ocean, users can see and hear one another's physical and emotional reactions to conversation and information.

By giving participants the remarkable sense that they are in the same room, the Halo Collaboration Studio is already transforming the way businesses such as PepsiCo, Advanced Micro Devices, and DreamWorks communicate across the globe. Halo significantly increases team effectiveness, provides faster decision-making capabilities, and decreases the need for travel.

"The HP Halo Collaboration Studio enables remote teams to work together in a setting so lifelike that participants feel as though they are in the same room," Joshi said. "To create this experience, HP is harnessing its expertise in color science, imaging, and networking in this new category of innovation. It is something we believe will not only disrupt the traditional videoconferencing market, but will also change the way people work in a global market."

Early in the production of the animated film *Shrek 2,* DreamWorks realized a significant return on investment using the Halo technology. By connecting its California teams in Glendale and Redwood City, DreamWorks was able to speed up many aspects of the production.

"In 2002, while we were producing *Shrek 2,* we realized that DreamWorks needed face-to-face collaboration between key creative talent in different locations," Katzenberg said. "We weren't satisfied with the available videoconferencing systems, so we designed a collaboration solution that would fulfill our needs. HP took the system and turned it into Halo, which is now the only solution on the market that allows this kind of effective communication."

Halo Connection

To connect via Halo, organizations purchase at least two Halo rooms set up for six people each. Three plasma displays in each room enable participants to see those they are collaborating with in life-size images. The rooms come equipped with studio-quality audio and lighting, and participants use a simple on-screen user interface to begin collaborating with just a few mouse clicks.

An intricate software control system ensures Halo rooms work easily and seamlessly together. The control system also provides precise image and color calibration, so participants see each other as they appear in real life. A dedicated HP Halo Video Exchange Network provides a high-bandwidth experience with imperceptible delays between Halo studios worldwide.

To ensure a 24x7 connection and eliminate the need for enterprises to manage the operation and maintenance of a Halo room, services offered include network operations and management, remote diagnostics and calibration, concierge, equipment warranty, and ongoing service and repair.

Participants can easily share documents and data directly from their notebook PCs with individuals in other rooms using a collaboration screen mounted above the plasma displays. The rooms also contain a high-magnification camera that enables individuals to zoom in on objects on a table, revealing the finest of details and color shading, and a phone that opens a conference call line to those not in one of the Halo rooms.

"We believe there is a personal connection that comes with Halo that just clearly doesn't come from any other kind of technology we've used in the past," said Steve Reinemund, CEO of PepsiCo. "Halo is one of the best investments we've made to improve the effectiveness of our business and work/life balance for our people."[38]

Questions

1. How can companies use Halo to increase their business efficiency?
2. Explain how a company like PepsiCo can use Halo to gain a competitive advantage in its industry.
3. How can knowledge management be increased by using a product such as Halo?
4. Why would a company like DreamWorks, which is not IT focused, be interested in collaboration technology?
5. What are a few of the security issues surrounding this type of technology?

CLOSING CASE TWO

Enterprise Content Management at Statoil

Statoil is the world's third largest exporter of crude oil and a substantial supplier of natural gas to the European market. The company has approximately 25,500 employees in locations scattered over 34 countries. Based in Norway, Statoil is the leading operator on the Norwegian continental shelf and experiencing strong growth in international production.[39]

Since 2002, the company has adopted an ecollaboration strategy. The goal of the strategy is to create a corporate "knowledge reservoir" that provides global access to a common pool of digital assets and is used to support work processes and share information between Statoil and its customers, employees, and business partners.

Access to this knowledge reservoir is provided through an information portal and controlled through the assignment of end-user roles. For instance, a customer would have much more limited access to information housed in the knowledge reservoir than a Statoil employee would.

The need for this strategy arose from the information overload that burdened the company. Typical for many decentralized organizations, Statoil's information was scattered across a number of different storage media and applications. The total number of databases in 2002 exceeded 5,500.

The core foundation of the knowledge reservoir is content management. This involves the ability to support a content life cycle in the company that effectively deals with the capture, transformation, storage, security, distribution, retrieval, and eventual destruction of documents. Though Statoil is making great gains in facilitating such content management practices, it is also facing some challenges in getting there.

The largest problem is how content is currently maintained throughout the company. There are literally thousands of heterogeneous content databases involving stand-alone intranet and extranet applications and over 800 databases containing archived documents. Though technically all these are accessible across the enterprise, logically people are unaware of the availability of documents residing in those shared content areas, and hence, much of the material never gets loaded into a centralized, shared content management system. Having so much content resident outside of a shared, centralized content management system has negative implications on archiving, version management, publication, and workflow.

Another difficulty is that people still tend to use personal email folders to manage document attachments, rather than post documents once in a central location for others to use. Emailing attachments causes network congestion and chews up precious file storage space. If stored centrally, a document is stored just once and people can simply reference the document there if needed.

Another challenge is that the storage of files in their original production format makes retrieval of these items difficult after a few years. This is because content management system technologies change and the format of these production files do not. On the flip-side, updating the format to be compatible with content management system technologies may make these files unusable for retrieval by the original application that produced them. The best solution would be to store content in application-independent formats.

Difficulties also stem from the lack of embedded routines that could potentially delete unwanted information stored across production or archiving systems. This results in the redundant storage of information and the overaccumulation of content. To clean up content, Statoil has to issue "campaigns" to encourage employees to delete unnecessary information.

Another challenge pertains to search. No single integrated search facility can retrieve documents across the thousands of other heterogeneous content-based systems. This largely is a result of different business units utilizing different taxonomies to classify their content and storing their content in different physical structures. Hence, information retrieval across business units is problematic, despite the best intentions of the company.

Though these challenges are obstacles to the effective management of corporate content, Statoil is making great strides in overcoming them. To date, the ecollaboration strategy has yielded several successes for the company, including:

- A basic content management solution.
- Automatic archiving.
- Long-term storage of content with separate data indexes.
- Automatic security levels of information based on metadata.
- Integration of existing standard office tools.
- A corporate yellow pages.
- One common portal framework.
- Training services for the content management solution.
- Implementation of content management guidelines for use by third-party solution providers (i.e., for working on projects with partners).
- The establishment of required elearning modules for employees.

In this sense, Statoil is doing well in creating and managing information content, regardless of whether it is sourced internally within the organization or externally from information suppliers, and in automating the content life cycle, from creation to archival, with information delivered to the recipient independent of time, place, or media.[40]

Questions

1. Why do you think content management is such a critical part of Statoil's strategy?
2. Comment on the utility and importance of Statoil's use of an information portal to promote enterprisewide content management?

3. To what extent do you think Statoil's predicament of information overload is typical for organizations?

4. What lessons learned and insights from the chapter's discussion on collaboration tools could help promote Statoil's adoption and use of its content management initiative?

CLOSING CASE THREE

Shell Canada Fuels Productivity with ERP

Shell Canada is one of the nation's largest integrated petroleum companies and is a leading manufacturer, distributor, and marketer of refined petroleum products. The company, head-quartered in Calgary, produces natural gas, natural gas liquids, and bitumen. Shell Canada is also the country's largest producer of sulphur. There is a Canada-wide network of 1,809 Shell-branded retail gasoline stations and convenience food stores from coast-to-coast.

To run such a complex and vast business operation successfully, the company relies heavily on the use of a mission-critical enterprise resource planning (ERP) system. The use of such a system is a necessity in helping the company integrate and manage its daily operations—operations that span from wells and mines, to processing plants, to oil trucks and gas pumps.

For example, the ERP system has helped the company immensely in terms of reducing and streamlining the highly manual process of third-party contractors submitting repair information and invoices. On average, there are between 2,500 and 4,000 service orders handled by these contractors per month on a nationwide basis.

Before implementation of the ERP system, contractors had to send Shell Canada monthly, summarized invoices that listed maintenance calls the contractors made at various Shell gasoline stations. Each one of these invoices would take a contractor between 8 and 20 hours to prepare. Collectively, the contractors would submit somewhere between 50 and 100 invoices every month to Shell Canada. This involved each invoice being reviewed by the appropriate territory manager and then forwarded to the head office for payment processing. This alone consumed another 16 to 30 hours of labor per month. At the head office, another 200 hours of work was performed by data entry clerks who had to manually enter batch invoice data into the payment system.

And this would be the amount of time needed if things went smoothly! More hours of labor were required to decipher and correct errors if any mistakes were introduced from all the manual invoice generation and data reentry involved. Often errors concerning one line item on an invoice would deter payment of the whole invoice. This irritated the contractors and did not help foster healthy contractor relationships.

To make matters worse, despite the hours involved and the amount of human data-handling required, detailed information about the service repairs that contractors did was often not entered into the payment system. And if it were entered, the information was not timely—it was often weeks or even months old by the time it made it into the payment processing system. As a result, Shell was not collecting sufficient information about what repairs were being done, what had caused the problem, and how it had been resolved.

Fortunately, the ERP solution solved these inadequacies by providing an integrated web-based service order, invoicing, and payment submission system. With this tool, third-party contractors can enter service orders directly into Shell's ERP system via the web. When this is done, the contractors can also enter detailed information about the work that was performed—sometimes even attaching photos and drawings to help describe the work that was done. With the ERP system, it only takes a few minutes for a contractor to enter details about a service order. Further, this information can be transmitted through a wireless PDA to the appropriate Shell manager for immediate approval—shaving extra time off in unnecessary delays.

Another bonus of the ERP system is that the contractor's monthly, summarized invoices can now be generated automatically and fed directly into the ERP's system's account payables application for processing. No re-keying of data required! Even better, if there is an issue or concern with one invoice item, the other items on the invoice can still be processed for payment.

Shell Canada's ERP system also handles other operational tasks. For example, the system can help speed up maintenance and repair operations at the company's refineries. With the ERP system in place, rather than trying to utilize a variety of disparate internal systems to access blueprints, schematic, spare parts lists, and other tools and information, workers at the refineries can now use the ERP system to access these things directly from a centralized database.

An added benefit of the ERP system is its ease of use. Past systems used by refinery workers were complex and difficult to search for information. The ERP system in place now has a portal-like interface that allows refinery workers to access the functions and information they need to keep operations running. The web interface allows workers access to this information with one or two clicks of a mouse.

An important part of any successful ERP implementation is training end users to learn how to utilize the system and to teach them about the functions and abilities of the ERP system. Recognizing this, Shell Canada offered its personnel both formal and informal ERP training. These proved to be invaluable in teaching end users the mechanics of the system and raising awareness of the benefits of the system and the efficiencies that the ERP system could offer Shell Canada. This not only helped promote end-user acceptance of the ERP system, but also greatly increased employees' intentions to use the system in their daily work.

Shell Canada executives are pleased and optimistic about the advantages of the ERP system. With this new system, employees across the company have gained fast and easy access to the tools and information they need to conduct their daily operations.[41]

Questions

1. How did ERP help improve business operations at Shell?
2. How important was training in helping roll out the system to Shell personnel?
3. How could extended ERP components help improve business operations at Shell?
4. What advice would you give Shell if it decided to choose a different ERP software solution?
5. How can integrating SCM, CRM, and ERP help improve business operations at Shell?

MAKING BUSINESS DECISIONS

1. Implementing an ERP system

Blue Dog Inc. is a leading manufacturer in the high-end sunglasses industry, reaching record revenue levels of over $250 million last year. Blue Dog is currently deciding on the possibility of implementing an ERP system to help decrease production costs and increase inventory control. Many of the executives are nervous about making such a large investment in an ERP system due to its low success rates. As a senior manager at Blue Dog Inc. you have been asked to compile a list of the potential benefits and risks associated with implementing an ERP system along with your recommendations for the steps the company can take to ensure a successful implementation.

2. Most popular ERP component

Mackenzie Coombe is currently thinking about implementing an ERP solution in her online music company, The Burford Beat. The company is generating over $12 million in revenues and is growing by 150 percent a year. Create a one-page document explaining the advantages and disadvantages of ERP systems, why ERP systems include CRM and SCM components, and why the most popular ERP component in today's marketplace is the accounting and finance core component.

3. **Value-added ERP**

Pirate's Pizza is a large pizza chain that operates 700 franchises in 15 states. The company is currently contemplating implementing a new ERP system, which is expected to cost $7 million and take 18 months to implement. Once the system is completed, it is expected to generate $12 million a year in decreased costs and increased revenues. You are working in the finance department for the company and your boss has asked you to compile a report detailing the different financial metrics you can use to assess the business value of the new ERP system. Once your report is completed, the company will make a decision about purchasing the ERP system.

4. **Collaboration on intranets**

MyIntranet.com is a worldwide leader providing online intranet solutions. The MyIntranet .com online collaboration tool is a solution for small businesses and groups inside larger organizations that need to organize information, share files and documents, coordinate calendars, and enable efficient collaboration, all in a secure, browser-based environment. MyIntranet.com has just added conferencing and group scheduling features to its suite of hosted collaboration software. Explain why infrastructure integration is critical to the suite of applications to function within this environment.

5. **Gaining efficiency with collaboration**

During the past year, you have been working for a manufacturing firm to help improve its supply chain management by implementing enterprise resource planning and supply chain management systems. For efficiency gains, you are recommending that the manufacturing firm should be turning toward collaborative systems. The firm has a need to share intelligent plans and forecasts with supply chain partners, reduce inventory levels, improve working capital, and reduce manufacturing changeovers. Given the technologies presented to you in this unit, what type of system(s) would you recommend to facilitate your firm's future needs?

6. **Increasing revenues with ERP**

Cold Cream is one of the premier beauty supply stores in the metro New York area. People come from all over to sample the store's unique creams, lotions, makeup, and perfumes. The company receives its products from manufacturers around the globe. The company would like to implement an ERP system to help it better understand its customers and their purchasing habits. Create a report summarizing ERP systems and explain how an ERP system can directly influence Cold Cream's revenues.

APPLY YOUR KNOWLEDGE

1. Tying IT All Together

Jamie Ash is interested in applying for a job at a large software vendor. One criterion for the job is a detailed understanding of strategic initiatives such as SCM, CRM, and ERP and how the systems relate to each other and the risks and rewards such systems can provide to an organization and its employees.

Project Focus

Jamie has no knowledge of any of these initiatives and cannot even explain what the acronyms mean. Jamie has come to you for help. She would like you to compile a summary of the three initiatives including an analysis of how the three are similar and how they are different. You also need to include a section of how the systems relate to each other and the risks and rewards associated with the systems. Jamie would also like to perform some self-training via the web so be sure to provide her with several additional links to key websites that offer detailed overviews on these systems.

2. Classic Car Problems

Classic Cars Inc. operates high-end automotive dealerships that offer luxury cars along with luxury service. The company is proud of its extensive inventory, top-of-the-line mechanics, and especially its exceptional service, which even includes a cappuccino bar at each dealership.

The company currently has 40 sales representatives at four locations. Each location maintains its own computer systems, and all sales representatives have their own contact management systems. This splintered approach to operations causes numerous problems including customer communication issues, pricing strategy issues, and inventory control issues. A few examples include:

- A customer shopping at one dealership can go to another dealership and receive a quote for a different price for the same car.
- Sales representatives are frequently stealing each other's customers and commissions.
- Sales representatives frequently send their customers to other dealerships to see specific cars and when the customer arrives, the car is not on the lot.
- Marketing campaigns are not designed to target specific customers; they are typically generic, such as 10 percent off a new car.
- If a sales representative quits, all of his or her customer information is lost.

Project Focus

You are working for Customer One, a small consulting company that specializes in enterprisewide strategies. The owner of Classic Cars Inc., Tom Repicci, has hired you to help him formulate a strategy to put his company back on track. Develop a proposal for Tom detailing how an ERP system can alleviate the company's issues and create new opportunities.

3. Bean Integration

At Flavors, a premium coffee shop, customers receive more than just a great cup of coffee—they receive exposure to music, art, literature, and town events. Flavor's calendar for programs gives customers a quick view into this corner of the world—from live music and art displays, to volunteering or a coffee tasting. Flavors offers the following:

- Music center—Information to all live music events occurring in the area. The store also hosts an open microphone two nights a week for local musicians.
- Art gallery—A space in the store filled with great pieces from local artists.
- Book clubs—Customers can meet to discuss current and classic literature.
- Coffee sampler—Customers can sample coffees from around the world with the experts.
- Community events—Weekly meetings are held where customers can find ways to become more involved in their community.
- Brewing courses—The finer details of the brewing, grinding, and blending equipment for sale in Flavor stores—from the traditional press to a digital espresso machine. Also includes a trouble-shooting guide developed by brewing specialists.

Project Focus

Flavors' sales are great and profits are soaring; however, current operations need an overhaul. The owners of Flavors, J.P. Field and Marla Lily, built the business piece by piece over the last 12 years. The following offers a quick look at current operations.

- Flavors does not receive any information on how many of its customers attend live music events. Musicians typically maintain a fan email listing and CD sales records for the event; however, this information is not always provided to the store.
- Book club events are booked and run through the local book store, Pages Up. Pages Up runs a tab during the book club and provides Flavor with a check at the end of each month for all book club events. Flavors has no access to book club customer information or sales information.
- Artist gallery is run by several local artists who pay Flavors a small commission on each sale. Flavors has no input into the art contained in the store or information on customers who purchase art.
- Coffee sampler events are run through Flavors' primary operations.
- Community event information is open to all members of the community. Each event is run by a separate organization, which provides monthly event feedback to Flavors in a variety of formats from Word to Access files.
- Brewing and machine resource courses are run by the equipment manufacturer, and all customer and sales information is provided to Flavors in a Word document at the end of each year.

You have been hired as a consultant to Flavors. The owners want to revamp the way the company operates so it can take advantage of marketing and sales opportunities across its many different lines of business, such as offering customers who attend book club events discounts on art and brewing and machine resource courses. They also want to gain a better understanding of how the different events impact sales. For example, should they have more open microphone nights or more book clubs? Currently, they have no way to tell which events result in higher sales. Flavors would like you to create a CRM marketing strategy to help them gain visibility across their company.

4. Working Together

Upon execution of a business process, a workflow system dictates the presentation of the information, tracks the information, and maintains the information's status. For example, the following highlights the common steps performed during a team project:

1. Find out what information and deliverables are required for the project and the due date.
2. Divide the work among the team members.
3. Determine due dates for the different pieces of work.
4. Compile all the completed work into a single project.

One of the hardest parts of a team project is getting team members to complete their work on time. Often one team member cannot perform his or her work until another team member has finished. This situation causes work to sit idle waiting for a team member to pick it up to either approve it, continue working on it, or reformat it. Workflow systems help to automate the process of presenting and passing information around a team.

Project Focus

You have just received an assignment to work on a group project with 10 other students. The project requires you to develop a detailed business plan for a business of your choice. The types of activities you will need to perform include market analysis, industry analysis, growth opportunities, Porter's Five Forces analysis, financial forecasts, competitive advantage analysis, and so on. For your project, determine the following:

a. How could you use collaboration tools to facilitate the sharing of information and the completion of the project?
b. What advantages can your group gain from using groupware?
c. What advantages can your group gain from using IM?
d. How could you use a workflow system to manage the tasks for the group members?

e. Describe a few of the biggest issues you anticipate experiencing during the group project.

f. Identify ways that you can resolve these issues using collaboration tools.

5. Wiki Your Way

Wikis are web-based tools that make it easy for users to add, remove, and change online content. Employees at companies such as Intel, Motorola, IBM, and Sony use them for a host of tasks, from setting internal meeting agendas to posting documents related to new products.

Project Focus

Many companies rely on wikis to engage customers in ongoing discussions about products. Wikis for Motorola and T-Mobile handsets serve as continually updated user guides. TV networks including ABC and CBS are creating fan wikis that let viewers interact with each other as they unravel mysteries from such shows as *Lost* and *CSI: Crime Scene Investigation.* You would like to implement wikis at your new company, The Consulting Edge, a small computer consulting company catering to mid- and large-sized businesses. Answer the following questions:

- How can a wiki help you attract customers and grow your business?
- How can a wiki help your partners and employees?
- What ethical and security concerns would you have with the wiki?
- What could you do to minimize any concerns?

6. Blogging for Dollars

You have purchased a financial investment company, The Financial Level, that caters to individuals and families. You would like to develop a few blogs for your customers, employees, and partners. The goals for your customer blog is to gather honest feedback, provide a place for customers to interact, and help find new opportunities for your businesses. The goals for the employee blog is to gather knowledge, collect employment feedback, and offer a place where employees can post anonymous feedback for issues and concerns so you can better manage your staff.

Project Focus

a. Research the Internet and find several customer blogs and employee blogs.

b. Determine the top three blogs for customers and for employees and critique the blogs for content, ease of use, and overall value.

c. From these sites design a prototype customer blog and a prototype employee blog for The Financial Level using Word, PowerPoint, or a tool of your choice.

7. Sharptooth Incorporated

Stephen Kern is the founder and CEO of Sharptooth, a small business that buys and sells comic strips to magazines and newspapers around the country. Some of Sharptooth's artists have made it big and are syndicated in hundreds of magazines and newspapers, while others are new to the industry. Stephen started in the business as an artist and began contracting other artists when he realized he had a knack for promoting and marketing comic materials. Stephen's artistic background is great for spotting talented young artists, but not so great for running the business.

Project Focus

Stephen recently began selling comics to new forms of media such as blogs, websites, and other online tools. Stephen has hired you to build him a new system to track all online comic sales. You quickly notice that Stephen has a separate system for each of his different lines of business including newspaper sources, magazine sources, billboard sources, and now online sources. You notice that each system works independently to perform its job of creating, updating, and maintaining sales information, but you are wondering how Stephen operates his business as a whole. Create a list of issues Stephen will encounter if he continues to run his business with four separate systems performing the same operations. What could happen to Stephen's business if he cannot correlate the details of each? Be sure to highlight at least 10 issues where separate systems could cause Stephen problems.

8. Wiki Debate

Wikipedia is a multilingual, web-based, free content encyclopedia project. Wikipedia is written collaboratively by volunteers from all around the world. The name Wikipedia is a portmanteau of the words wiki (a type of collaborative website) and encyclopedia. Since its creation in 2001, Wikipedia has grown rapidly into one of the largest reference websites.

In every article, links guide users to associated articles, often with additional information. Anyone is welcome to add information, cross-references or citations, as long as they do so within Wikipedia's editing policies and to an appropriate standard. One need not fear accidentally damaging Wikipedia when adding or improving information, as other editors are always around to advise or correct obvious errors, and Wikipedia's software, known as MediaWiki, is carefully designed to allow easy reversal of editorial mistakes.

Project Focus

A group of people believe the end of Wikipedia is close as people use the tool to self-promote. Some believe that Wikipedia will fail in four years, crushed under the weight of an automated assault by marketers and others seeking online traffic. One law professor Eric Goldman, a professor at the Santa Clara University School of Law, argues that Wikipedia will see increasingly vigorous efforts to subvert its editorial process, much as Digg has seen. As marketers become more determined and turn to automated tools to alter Wikipedia entries to generate online traffic, Goldman predicts Wikipedians will burn out trying to keep entries clean. Goldman writes that Wikipedia will enter a death spiral where the rate of junkiness will increase rapidly until the site becomes a wasteland. Alternatively, to prevent this death spiral, Wikipedia will change its core open access architecture, increasing the database's vitality by changing its mission somewhat.

Create a paper discussing where you think the future of Wikipedia is headed.

9. Secure Collaboration

As the methods and modes of communication continue to evolve, challenges will mount for businesses trying to secure their data and for law enforcement looking to monitor communications as part of their investigations. That was the theme of the keynote that Sun Microsystems chief security officer and renowned cryptographer Whitfield Diffie delivered at the AT&T Cyber Security Conference.

The growth of virtual communities across the web as a communications channel creates a double-edged sword in this respect. Second Life and other virtual communities offer a growing abundance of information, although this information will ultimately need to be protected if virtual communities are to grow as meaningful channels of business-to-business and business-to-customer communication.

Diffie believes that with millions of people joining Second Life and companies building facilities there, it may be that virtual communities become the preferred medium of human communication. This growing volume of information opens the opportunity to use virtual communities as a source of intelligence, and communications will always be spied on.

Of course, the volume of businesses present in virtual communities such as Second Life will have to grow before they become a meaningful source of information. Once this happens, though, watch out. Diffie believes that communication always outstrips the ability to protect it. Do you wonder who would be interested in gathering intelligence floating through virtual communities? The answer is businesses, governments (domestic and foreign), and reporters—the same entities that have adapted every other form of communication preceding the web. Diffie believes the future will be a golden age for intelligence.

Project Focus

What is your answer to the following question: "As we create new and better ways to collaborate, what happens to information security?"

BUSINESS DRIVEN BEST SELLERS

The Tipping Point: How Little Things Can Make a Big Difference. By Malcolm Gladwell (New York: Back Bay Books, 2000).

This celebrated *New York Times* best seller is changing the way people think about selling products and disseminating ideas. The tipping point is that magical moment when an idea, trend, or social behavior crosses a threshold, tips, and spreads like wildfire. Just as a single sick person can start an epidemic of the flu, so too can a small but precisely targeted push cause a fashion trend, the popularity of a new product, or a drop in the crime rate. In this book, Malcolm Gladwell explores and brilliantly illuminates the tipping point phenomenon, changing the way people throughout the world think about selling products and disseminating ideas.

The Tipping Point is about change. In particular, it presents a new way of understanding why change so often happens as quickly and as unexpectedly as it does. For example, why did crime drop so dramatically in New York City in the mid-1990s? How does a novel written by an unknown author end up as a national best seller? Why do teens smoke in greater and greater numbers when every single person in the country knows that cigarettes kill? Why is word of mouth so powerful? What makes TV shows like *Sesame Street* so good at teaching kids how to read? Gladwell thinks the answer to all those questions is the same. It is that ideas and behavior and messages and products sometimes behave just like outbreaks of infectious disease. They are social epidemics. *The Tipping Point* is an examination of the social epidemics that surround us. [42]

Blink: The Power of Thinking Without Thinking. By Malcolm Gladwell (New York: Little, Brown & Company, 2005).

In his landmark best seller *The Tipping Point,* Malcolm Gladwell redefined how we understand the world around us. Now, in *Blink,* he revolutionizes the way we understand the world within. *Blink* addresses how we think without thinking, about choices that seem to be made in an instant—in the blink of an eye—that actually are not as simple as they seem.

Blink is about rapid cognition, about the kind of thinking that happens in a blink of an eye. When you meet someone for the first time, or walk into a house you are thinking of buying, or read the first few sentences of a book, your mind takes about two seconds to jump to a series of conclusions. Well, *Blink* is a book about those two seconds, because Gladwell thinks those instant conclusions that we reach are really powerful and really important and, occasionally, really good.

You could also say that *Blink* is about intuition. Gladwell does not like the word *intuition.* In fact, it never appears in *Blink.* Intuition strikes Gladwell as a concept people use to describe emotional reactions, gut feelings—thoughts and impressions that do not seem entirely rational. But Gladwell thinks that what goes on in that first two seconds is perfectly rational. It is thinking—it's just thinking that moves a little faster and operates a little more mysteriously than the kind of deliberate, conscious decision making that people usually associate with "thinking." In *Blink,* Gladwell tries to understand those two seconds. What is going on inside people's heads when they engage in rapid cognition? When are snap judgments good and when are they not? What kinds of things can individuals do to make the power of rapid cognition better? [43]

Developing Information Systems

This module describes the various ways information systems can be built to support 21st century global businesses, the challenges that come along with the process, and the beauty of how well things turn out if systems are built according to good design principles, sound management practices, and flexibility to support ever-changing business needs. This task not only requires extensive planning, but also incredible people skills to make it all happen. This is far easier said than done! Too often, information systems development projects are criticized for going over budget, being delayed, or lacking in desired functionality.

If a career in global business has crossed your mind, exploring global business and the impacts of competing in a global world is crucial. The United States is a market of about 290 million people, but there are over 6 million potential customers in the 193 countries that make up the global market. Perhaps more interesting is that approximately 75 percent of the world's population lives in developing areas where technology, education, and per capita income still lag considerably behind those of developed (or industrialized) nations such as the United States.

You, the business student, should be familiarized with the potential of global business, including its many benefits and challenges. The demand for students with training in global business is almost certain to grow as the number of businesses competing in global markets increases.

This module comprises two chapters. Chapter 11 provides an overview of how enterprise applications are developed using the traditional systems development life cycle. Chapter 12 dives into innovation and entrepreneurship along with how to compete in the 21st century where globalization is key.

MODULE ONE:
Business Driven Information Systems

MODULE TWO:
Essentials of Information Systems

MODULE THREE:
Enterprise Information Systems

MODULE FOUR:
Developing Information Systems

Module 4: DEVELOPING INFORMATION SYSTEMS

CHAPTER 11: Systems Development and Project Management

CHAPTER 12: Globalization, Innovation, and 21st Century Organizational Trends

CHAPTER

Systems Development and Project Management

What's in IT for me?

This chapter provides an overview of how organizations build information systems. You as a business student, need to know this because information systems are the underlying foundation of how companies operate. A basic understanding of the principles of building information systems will make you a more valuable employee. You will be able to identify trouble spots early and make suggestions during the design process that will result in a better delivered information systems project—one that satisfies both you and your business.

Building an information system is analogous to constructing a house. You could sit back and let the developers do all the design work, construction, and testing with hopes that the house will satisfy your needs. However, participating in the house building process helps to guarantee that your needs are not only being heard, but also being met. It is good business practice to have direct user input steering the development of the finished product.

The same is true for building information systems. Your knowledge of the systems development process will allow you to participate and ensure you are building flexible enterprise architectures that not only support current business needs, but also future business needs.

HP's Software Problems

With IT projects, pessimism—otherwise known as contingency planning—is the only way to keep small technology problems from becoming full-blown business disasters. Christina Hanger had little reason to be pessimistic in May 2004 when she was moving one of Hewlett-Packard's biggest North American divisions onto a centralized ERP system from SAP. As the leader of an IT consolidation project rooted in HP's acquisition of Compaq two years earlier, Hanger, HP senior vice president of Americas operations and IT, had an unbroken record of success migrating five product groups within the two former companies onto one of two SAP systems.

Hanger had every reason to believe that the sixth would go well too. Even so, she knew to be prepared for problems. At approximately $7.5 billion in annual revenue, the division involved with this latest project, Industry Standard Servers (ISS), was much larger than any of the others that Hanger had migrated to SAP to that point. Hanger took the contingency plan that her team had developed for the other five migrations and adjusted it to accommodate the ISS division's larger sales volume. She planned for three weeks of IT snafus, mostly focused on what might happen as a result of tweaking a legacy order-entry system to work with the new SAP system. The contingency plan addressed business impacts too. HP banked three weeks' worth of extra servers and took over an empty portion of an HP factory in Omaha to stand by for any overflow of orders that needed special configurations (for example, an unusual component or software combination) and could not be stockpiled ahead of time.

"We had a series of small problems, none of which individually would have been too much to handle. But together they created the perfect storm," stated Gilles Bouchard, CIO and executive vice president of global operations. Starting when the system went live at the beginning of June and continuing throughout the rest of the month, as many as 20 percent of customer orders for servers stopped dead in their tracks between the legacy order-entry system and the SAP system. As IT problems go, this was not too big: Some data modeling issues between the legacy system and the SAP system prevented the SAP system from processing some orders for customized products. These programming errors were fixed within four or five weeks. However, Hanger and her business colleagues from the ISS division who were on the project steering committee never envisioned the degree to which these programming glitches would affect the business.

Orders began to backlog quickly, and HP did not have enough manual work-arounds to keep servers flowing fast enough to meet customer demand. Angry customers picked up the phone and called HP—or worse, competitors Dell and IBM. In a commodity market such as servers, customer loyalty is built upon a company's ability to configure products to order and get them delivered on time. HP could do neither for much of the summer. In a third-quarter conference call on August 12, HP Chairman and CEO Carly Fiorina pegged the financial impact at $160 million: a $120 million order backlog that resulted in $40 million in lost revenue. That is more than the cost of the project itself, which AMR Research estimates to be $30 million.

The headlines all claimed an IT disaster, but in fact, HP's disaster resulted from a few relatively small problems in IT that snowballed into a much bigger problem for the business: the inability to cope with the order backlog. This was a disaster that could have been prevented—not by trying to eliminate every possibility for error in a major IT system migration, which is virtually impossible, but by taking a much broader view of the impact that these projects can have on a company's supply chain.[1]

INTRODUCTION

Every type of organization in business today, from farming to pharmaceutical to franchising, is affected by technology and the software developed to operate, improve, or innovate it. Companies are impacted by software solutions that enable them to improve their cost structure, manage people better, and develop and deliver new products to market. These organizational improvements help companies sustain their competitive advantage and position in the marketplace. They can solve complex problems, dislodge competitors, or create exciting opportunities to pursue. Organizations must learn and mature in their ability to identify, build, and implement systems to remain competitive.

Essentially, software built correctly can support nimble organizations and can transform as the organization and its business transforms. Software that effectively meets employee needs will help an organization become more productive and enhance decision making. Software that does not meet employee needs might have a damaging effect on productivity and can even cause a business to fail. Employee involvement along with using the right implementation methodology when developing software is critical to the success of an organization.

section 11.1 DEVELOPING ENTERPRISE APPLICATIONS

LEARNING OUTCOMES

11.1. Identify the business benefits associated with successful software development.

11.2. Describe the seven phases of the systems development life cycle.

11.3. Summarize the different software development methodologies.

11.4. Define the relationship between the systems development life cycle and software development.

11.5. Compare the waterfall methodology and the agile methodology.

Archtv2

DEVELOPING SOFTWARE

Nike's SCM system failure, which spun out of control to the tune of $400 million, is legendary. Nike blamed the system failure on its SCM vendor, i2 Technologies. Nike states that i2 Technologies' demand and supply planning module created serious inventory problems. The i2 deployment, part of a multimillion-dollar ebusiness upgrade, caused Nike CEO Philip Knight to famously say, "This is what we get for our $400 million?" The SCM vendor saw its stock plummet with the Nike disaster, along with its reputation. Katrina Roche, i2's chief marketing officer, asserted that Nike failed to use the vendor's implementation methodology and templates, which contributed to the problem.[2]

Software development problems often lead to high-profile disasters. Hershey's glitch in its ERP implementation made the front page of *The Wall Street Journal* and cost the company millions. Hershey said computer problems with its SAP software system created a backlog of orders, causing slower deliveries, and resulting in lower earnings. Statistics released in 2006 by the National Research Council show that U.S. companies spent $250 billion in 2005 to repair damage caused by software defects.[3]

If software does not work, the organization will not work. Traditional business risk models typically ignored software development, largely because most organizations considered the impact from software and software development on the business to be minor. In the digital age, however, software success, or failure, can lead directly to business success, or failure. Almost every large organization in the world relies on software, either to drive its business operations or to make its products work. As organizations' reliance on software grows, so do the business-related consequences of software successes and failures as displayed in Figure 11.1.[4]

Business-Related Consequences of Software Success and Failure

Increase or decrease revenues—Organizations have the ability to directly increase profits by implementing successful IT systems. Organizations can also lose millions when software fails or key information is stolen or compromised.

Nike's poorly designed supply chain management software delayed orders, increased excess inventories, and caused earnings to fall 24 percent below expectations.

Repair or damage to brand reputation—Technologies such as CRM can directly enhance a company's brand reputation. Software can also severely damage a company's reputation if it fails to work as advertised or has security vulnerabilities that affect its customers' trust.

H&R Block customers were furious when the company accidentally placed its customers' passwords and Social Security numbers on its website.

Prevent or incur liabilities—Technology such as CAT scans, MRIs, and mammograms can save lives. Faulty technology used in airplanes, automobiles, pacemakers, or nuclear reactors can cause massive damage, injury, or death.

The parent company of bankrupt pharmaceutical distributor FoxMeyer sued SAP for $500 million over ERP software failure that allegedly crippled its operations.

Increase or decrease productivity—CRM and SCM software can directly increase a company's productivity. Large losses in productivity can also occur when software malfunctions or crashes.

The Standish Group estimates that defective software code accounted for 45 percent of computer-system downtime and cost U.S. companies $100 billion in lost productivity in 2003 alone.

The lucrative advantages of successful software implementations provide significant incentives to manage software development risks. However, according to the Chaos report from the Standish Group, a Massachusetts-based consultancy, more than half the software development projects undertaken in the United States come in late or over budget and the majority of successful projects maintain fewer features and functions than originally specified. Organizations also cancel around 33 percent of these projects during development. Understanding the basics of software development, or the systems development life cycle, will help organizations avoid potential software development pitfalls and ensure that software development efforts are successful.[5]

THE SYSTEMS DEVELOPMENT LIFE CYCLE (SDLC)

The *systems development life cycle (SDLC)* is the overall process for developing information systems from planning and analysis through implementation and maintenance. The SDLC is the foundation for all systems development methodologies, and literally hundreds of different activities are associated with each phase in the SDLC. Typical activities include determining budgets, gathering system requirements, and writing detailed user documentation. The activities performed during each systems development project will vary.

The SDLC begins with a business need, followed by an assessment of the functions a system must have to satisfy the need, and ends when the benefits of the system no longer outweigh its maintenance costs. This is why it is referred to as a life cycle. The SDLC is comprised of seven distinct phases: planning, analysis, design, development, testing, implementation, and maintenance (see Figure 11.2).

Appendix D takes a detailed look at a few of the more common activities performed during the phases of the systems development life cycle along with common issues facing software development projects.

1. **Planning:** The *planning phase* involves establishing a high-level plan of the intended project and determining project goals. Planning is the first and most critical phase of any systems development effort an organization undertakes, regardless of whether the effort is to develop a system that allows customers to order products over the Internet, determine the best logistical structure for

FIGURE 11.2

The Systems Development
Life Cycle

The Systems Development Life Cycle

1: Planning
2: Analysis
3: Design
4: Development
5: Testing
6: Implementation
7: Maintenance

warehouses around the world, or develop a strategic information alliance with another organization. Organizations must carefully plan the activities (and determine why they are necessary) to be successful.

2. **Analysis:** The ***analysis phase*** involves analyzing end-user business requirements and refining project goals into defined functions and operations of the intended system. ***Business requirements*** are the detailed set of business requests that the system must meet in order to be successful. The analysis phase is obviously critical. A good start is essential and the organization must spend as much time, energy, and resources as necessary to perform a detailed, accurate analysis.

3. **Design:** The ***design phase*** involves describing the desired features and operations of the system including screen layouts, business rules, process diagrams, pseudo code, and other documentation.

4. **Development:** The ***development phase*** involves taking all of the detailed design documents from the design phase and transforming them into the actual system. In this phase the project transitions from preliminary designs to the actual physical implementation.

5. **Testing:** The ***testing phase*** involves bringing all the project pieces together into a special testing environment to test for errors, bugs, and interoperability and verify that the system meets all of the business requirements defined in the analysis phase.

6. **Implementation:** The ***implementation phase*** involves placing the system into production so users can begin to perform actual business operations with the system.

7. **Maintenance:** Maintaining the system is the final sequential phase of any systems development effort. The ***maintenance phase*** involves performing changes, corrections, additions, and upgrades to ensure the system continues to meet the business goals. This phase continues for the life of the system because the system must change as the business evolves and its needs change, demanding constant monitoring, supporting the new system with frequent minor changes (for example, new reports or information capturing), and reviewing the system to be sure it is moving the organization toward its strategic goals.

TRADITIONAL SOFTWARE DEVELOPMENT METHODOLOGY: WATERFALL

Today, systems are so large and complex that teams of architects, analysts, developers, testers, and users must work together to create the millions of lines of custom-written code that drive enterprises. For this reason, developers have created a number

FIGURE 11.3

The Traditional Waterfall
Methodology

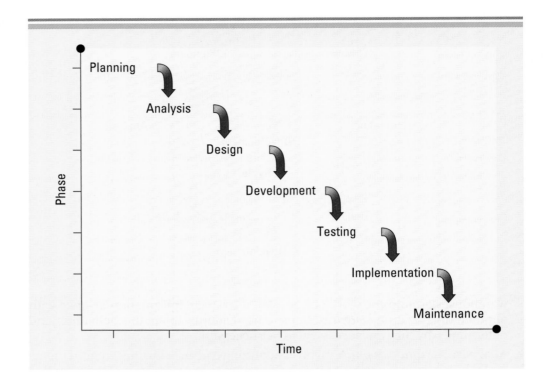

of different systems development life cycle methodologies. A ***methodology*** is a set of policies, procedures, standards, processes, practices, tools, techniques, and tasks that people apply to technical and management challenges. It is used to manage the deployment of technology with work plans, requirements documents, and test plans. It is also used to deploy technology. A formal methodology could include coding standards, code libraries, development practices, and much more.

Waterfall Methodology

The oldest of these, and the best known, is the waterfall methodology: a sequence of phases in which the output of each phase becomes the input for the next (see Figure 11.3). The traditional ***waterfall methodology*** is an activity-based process in which each phase in the SDLC is performed sequentially from planning through implementation and maintenance. The traditional waterfall method no longer serves most of today's development efforts. The success rate for software development projects that follow this approach is about 1 in 10. Paul Magin, a senior executive with Part Miner, a leading supplier of technical components, states, "Waterfall is a punishing technology. It forces people to be accurate when they simply cannot. It is dangerous and least desirable in today's development environment. It does not accommodate midcourse changes; it requires that you know exactly what you want to do on the project and a steady-state until the work is done; it requires guarantees that requirements will not change. We all know that it is nearly impossible to have all requirements up front. When you use a cascading method, you end up with cascading problems that are disastrous if not identified and corrected early in the process."[6]

Waterfall is inflexible, expensive, and requires rigid adherence to the sequentially based steps in the process. Figure 11.4 explains some issues related to the waterfall methodology.

Today's business environment is fierce. The desire and need to outsmart and outplay competitors remains intense. Given this drive for success, leaders push internal development teams and external vendors to deliver agreed upon systems faster and cheaper so they can realize benefits as early as possible. Even so, systems remain large and complex. The traditional waterfall methodology no longer serves as an adequate systems development methodology in most cases. Because this

Issues Related to the Waterfall Methodology	
The business problem	Any flaws in accurately defining and articulating the business problem in terms of what the business users actually require flow onward to the next phase.
The plan	Managing costs, resources, and time constraints is difficult in the waterfall sequence. What happens to the schedule if a programmer quits? How will a schedule delay in a specific phase impact the total cost of the project? Unexpected contingencies may sabotage the plan.
The solution	The waterfall methodology is problematic in that it assumes users can specify all business requirements in advance. Defining the appropriate IT infrastructure that is flexible, scalable, and reliable is a challenge. The final IT infrastructure solution must meet not only current but also future needs in terms of time, cost, feasibility, and flexibility. Vision is inevitably limited at the head of the waterfall.

FIGURE 11.4

Issues Related to the Waterfall Methodology

development environment is the norm and not the exception anymore, development teams use a new breed of alternative development methods to achieve their business objectives.

AGILE SOFTWARE DEVELOPMENT METHODOLOGIES

Standish Group's CHAOS research clearly shows that the smaller the project, the greater the success rate. The iterative development style is the ultimate in small projects. Basically, *iterative development* consists of a series of tiny projects. Iterative has become the foundation of multiple agile types of methodologies. Figure 11.5 displays an iterative approach.[7]

An *agile methodology* aims for customer satisfaction through early and continuous delivery of useful software components developed by an iterative process with a design point that uses the bare minimum requirements. Agile is what it sounds like: fast and efficient, small and nimble, lower cost, fewer features, shorter projects. Using agile methods helps refine feasibility and supports the process for getting

FIGURE 11.5

The Iterative Approach

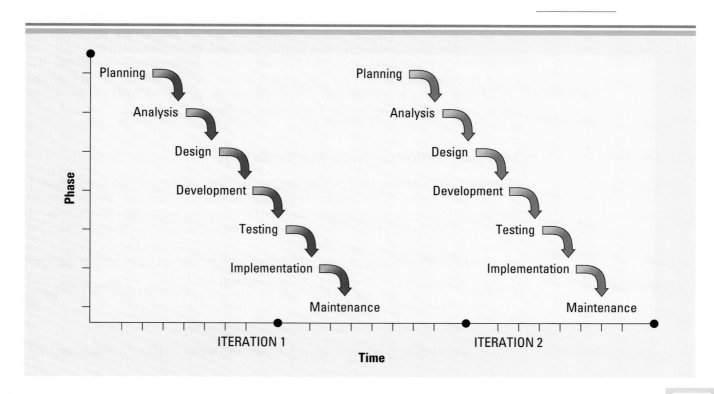

rapid feedback as functionality is introduced. Developers can adjust as they move along and better clarify unclear requirements.

Magin also states that the key to delivering a successful product or system is to deliver value to users as soon as possible—give them something they want and like early to create buy-in, generate enthusiasm, and, ultimately, reduce scope. Using agile methodologies helps maintain accountability and helps to establish a barometer for the satisfaction of end users. It does no good to accomplish something on time and on budget if it does not satisfy the end user. The primary forms of agile methodologies include:

- Rapid prototyping or rapid application development methodology.
- Extreme programming methodology.
- Rational unified process (RUP) methodology.
- SCRUM methodology.[8]

It is important not to get hung up on the names of the methodologies—some are proprietary brand names, others are generally accepted names. It is more important to know how these alternative methodologies are used in today's business environment and the benefits they can deliver.

Rapid Application Development (RAD) Methodology

Designer Development

In response to the faster pace of business, rapid application development has become a popular route for accelerating systems development. *Rapid application development (RAD)* (also called *rapid prototyping*) *methodology* emphasizes extensive user involvement in the rapid and evolutionary construction of working prototypes of a system to accelerate the systems development process. Figure 11.6 displays the fundamentals of RAD.[9]

A *prototype* is a smaller-scale representation or working model of the users' requirements or a proposed design for an information system. The prototype is an essential part of the analysis phase when using the RAD methodology.

PHH Vehicle Management Services, a Baltimore fleet-management company with over 750,000 vehicles, wanted to build an enterprise application that opened the entire vehicle information database to customers over the Internet. To build the application quickly, the company abandoned the traditional waterfall approach. Instead, a team of 30 developers began prototyping the Internet application, and the company's customers evaluated each prototype for immediate feedback. The development team released new prototypes that incorporated the customers' feedback every six weeks. The PHH Interactive Vehicle application went into production seven months after the initial work began. Over 20,000 customers, using a common browser, can now access the PHH Interactive site at any time from anywhere in the world to review their accounts, analyze billing information, and order vehicles.[10]

Extreme Programming Methodology

Extreme programming (XP) methodology, like other agile methods, breaks a project into tiny phases, and developers cannot continue on to the next phase until the first phase is complete. XP emphasizes the fact that the faster the communication or feedback the better the results. There are basically four parts: planning, designing,

FIGURE 11.6

Fundamentals of RAD

Fundamentals of RAD
Focus initially on creating a prototype that looks and acts like the desired system.
Actively involve system users in the analysis, design, and development phases.
Accelerate collecting the business requirements through an interactive and iterative construction approach.

coding, and testing. Unlike other methodologies, these are not phases; they work in tandem with each other. Planning includes user stories, stand-up meetings, and small releases. The design segment also stresses to not add functionally until it is needed. In the coding part, the user is always available for feedback, developers work in pairs, and the code is written to an agreed standard. In testing, the tests are written before the code. Extreme programming users are embedded into the development process. This technique is powerful because of the narrow communication gap between developers and users—it is a direct link. This saves valuable time and, again, continues to clarify needed (and unneeded) requirements.

One reason for XP's success is its stress on customer satisfaction. XP empowers developers to respond to changing customer and business requirements, even late in the systems development life cycle, and XP emphasizes teamwork. Managers, customers, and developers are all part of a team dedicated to delivering quality software. XP implements a simple, yet effective way to enable groupware-style development. Kent Beck, the father of XP, proposes conversation as the paradigm and suggests using index cards as a means to create dialog between business and technology. XP is a lot like a jigsaw puzzle; there are many small pieces. Individually the pieces make no sense, but when they are combined (again and again) an organization can gain visibility into the entire new system.[11]

Rational Unified Process (RUP) Methodology

The *rational unified process (RUP) methodology,* owned by IBM, provides a framework for breaking down the development of software into four gates. Each gate consists of executable iterations of the software in development. A project stays in a gate until the stakeholders are satisfied, and then it either moves to the next gate or is cancelled. The gates include:

- **Gate One: Inception.** This phase includes inception of the business case. This phase ensures all stakeholders have a shared understanding of the system.
- **Gate Two: Elaboration.** This phase provides a rough order of magnitude. Primary questions answered in this phase deal with agreed-upon details of the system including the ability to provide an architecture to support and build the system.
- **Gate Three: Construction.** This phase includes building and developing the product.
- **Gate Four: Transition.** Primary questions answered in this phase address ownership of the system and training of key personnel.[12]

Because RUP is an iterative methodology, the user can reject the product and force the developers to go back to gate one. Approximately 500,000 developers have used RUP in software projects of varying sizes in the 20 years it has been available, according to IBM. RUP helps developers avoid reinventing the wheel and focuses on rapidly adding or removing reusable chunks of processes addressing common problems.

Scrum Methodology

Another agile methodology, *Scrum methodology* uses small teams to produce small pieces of deliverable software using sprints, or 30-day intervals, to achieve an appointed goal. In rugby, a scrum is a team pack and everyone in the pack works together to move the ball down the field. Under this methodology, each day ends or begins with a stand-up meeting to monitor and control the development effort.

Primavera Systems, Inc., a software solutions company was finding it increasingly difficult to use the traditional waterfall methodology for development so it moved to an agile methodology. Scrum's insistence on delivering complete increments of business value in 30-day learning cycles helped the teams learn rapidly. It forced teams to test and integrate experiments and encouraged them to release them into production. Primavera's shift resulted in highly satisfied customers and a highly motivated, energetic development environment. Dick Faris, CTO of Primavera, said, "Agile programming is very different and new. It is a different feel to the way programming happens. Instead of mindlessly cranking out code, the process is one of team dialogue, negotiation around priorities and time and talents. The entire company commits to a 30-day sprint and delivery of finished, tested software. Maybe it is just one specific piece of functionality but it's the real thing, including delivery and client review against needs and requirements. Those needs and requirements, by the way, change. That is the strength we saw in the Scrum process."[13]

Implementing Agile Methodologies

Amos Auringer, an executive adviser for the prestigious Gartner Group, said, "Concepts such as agile, RAD, and XP are all various approaches to the same model—idea, production, delivery. These models represent consolidated steps, skipped steps for project size, and compressed steps to achieve the same result—a delivered product. Emerging process engineering models tend to focus on eliminating or reducing steps. The SDLC phases do not change—we just learn how to do our jobs better and more efficiently."[14]

If organizations choose to adopt agile methodologies, it is important to educate those involved. For an agile process to work, it must be simple and quick. The Agile Alliance is a group of software developers whose mission is to improve software development processes; the group's manifesto is displayed in Figure 11.7. Decisions must be made quickly without analysis paralysis. The best way to do this is to involve stakeholders, develop excellent communication processes, and implement strong project management skills. Understanding that communication is the most crucial aspect of a project is the core of collaborative development. Standish Group reports that projects in which users or user groups have a good understanding of their true needs have a better rate of return and lower risk. Strong project management is key to building successful enterprise applications and is covered in detail in the following section.

Successful
Software

DEVELOPING SUCCESSFUL SOFTWARE

Gartner Research estimates that 65 percent of agile projects are successful. This success rate is extraordinary compared to the 10 percent success rate of waterfall projects. The following are the primary principles an organization should follow for successful agile software development.[15]

Slash the Budget

Small budgets force developers and users to focus on the essentials. Small budgets also make it easier to kill a failing project. For example, imagine that a project that has already cost $20 million is going down the tubes. With that much invested, it is tempting to invest another $5 million to rescue it rather than take a huge loss. All too often, the system fails and the company ends up with an even bigger loss.

Jim Johnson, chairman of the Standish Group, says he forced the CIO of one Fortune 500 company to set a $100,000 ceiling on all software development projects.

FIGURE 11.7

The Agile Alliance Manifesto

The Agile Alliance Manifesto
Early and continuous delivery of valuable software will satisfy the customer.
Changing requirements, even late in development, are welcome.
Business people and developers must work together daily throughout the project.
Projects should be built around motivated individuals. Give them the environment and support they need, and trust them to get the job done.
The best architectures, requirements, and designs emerge from self-organizing teams.
At regular intervals, the team should reflect on how to become more effective, then tune and adjust its behavior accordingly.

There were no exceptions to this business rule without approval from the CIO and CEO. Johnson claims the company's project success rate went from 0 percent to 50 percent.[16]

If It Doesn't Work, Kill It

Bring all key stakeholders together at the beginning of a project and as it progresses bring them together again to evaluate the software. Is it doing what the business wants and, more important, requires? Eliminate any software that is not meeting business expectations. This is called triage, and it's "the perfect place to kill a software project," said Pat Morgan, senior program manager at Compaq's Enterprise Storage Group. He holds monthly triage sessions and says they can be brutal. "At one [meeting], engineering talked about a cool process they were working on to transfer information between GUIs. No one in the room needed it. We killed it right there. In our environment, you can burn a couple of million dollars in a month only to realize what you're doing isn't useful."[17]

Keep Requirements to a Minimum

Start each project with what the software must absolutely do. Do not start with a list of everything the software should do. Every software project traditionally starts with a requirements document that will often have hundreds or thousands of business requirements. The Standish Group estimates that only 7 percent of the business requirements are needed for any given application. Keeping requirements to a minimum also means that scope creep and feature creep must be closely monitored. **Scope creep** occurs when the scope of the project increases. **Feature creep** occurs when developers add extra features that were not part of the initial requirements. Both scope creep and feature creep are major reasons software development fails.[18]

Test and Deliver Frequently

As often as once a week, and not less than once a month, complete a part of the project or a piece of software. The part must be working and it must be bug-free. Then have the customers test and approve it. This is the agile methodology's most radical departure from traditional development. In some traditional software projects, the customers did not see any working parts or pieces for years.

Assign Non-IT Executives to Software Projects

Non-IT executives should coordinate with the technical project manager, test iterations to make sure they are meeting user needs, and act as liaisons between executives and IT. Having the business side involved full-time will bring project ownership and a desire to succeed to all parties involved. SpreeRide, a Salt Lake City market research outfit, used the agile methodology to set up its company's website. The project required several business executives designated full-time. The company believes this is one of the primary reasons that the project was successfully deployed in less than three months.[19]

OPENING CASE QUESTIONS

HP's Software Problems

1. Identify the business benefits associated with successful software development for HP.

2. Which of the seven phases of the systems development life cycle is most important to HP?

3. Which of the seven phases of the systems development life cycle is least important to HP?

4. Which of the different software development methodologies should HP use to implement successful systems?

5. Explain what might happen if HP used the waterfall methodology to develop its ERP system.

section 11.2 PROJECT MANAGEMENT

LEARNING OUTCOMES

11.6. Explain the triple constraint and its importance in project management.

11.7. Describe the project stakeholders' and executive sponsor's roles in choosing strategic projects.

11.8. Highlight the components of a project charter.

11.9. Describe the two primary diagrams most frequently used in project planning.

11.10. Identify the three primary areas a project manager must focus on managing to ensure success.

11.11. Explain the three different types of outsourcing.

INTRODUCTION

Digital
Domain

No one would think of building an office complex by turning loose 100 different construction teams to build 100 different rooms with no single blueprint or agreed-upon vision of the completed structure. Yet this is precisely the situation in which many large organizations find themselves when managing information technology projects. Organizations routinely overschedule their resources (human and otherwise), develop redundant projects, and damage profitability by investing in nonstrategic efforts that do not contribute to the organization's bottom line. Project management offers a strategic framework for coordinating the numerous activities associated with organizational projects. Business leaders face a rapidly moving and unforgiving global marketplace that will force them to use every possible tool to sustain competitiveness—project management is one of those tools.

MANAGING SOFTWARE DEVELOPMENT PROJECTS

Analysts predict investment in IT projects worldwide through 2010 will be over $1 trillion. This is a staggering amount, and even more staggering is that nearly 70 percent of it will be merely washed down the drain as a result of failed projects! In addition to lost earnings, companies from Nestlé to Nike have experienced additional consequences of failed projects—a damaged brand, lost goodwill, the dissolution of partnerships, lost investment opportunities, and the effects of low morale.[20]

According to the Standish Group, just 29 percent of IT projects were completed on time, within budget, and with features and functions originally specified by the customer to deliver business value. The grim reality of failed projects faces many businesses today.[21]

With so many skilled and knowledgeable IT professionals at the helm of IT projects, how can this happen? Every day, organizations adopt projects that do not align with mission-critical initiatives; they overcommit financial and human capital; they sign off on low-value projects that consume valuable and scarce resources; and they agree to support projects that are poorly defined from requirements to planning.

IT projects typically fail because, in most instances, they are complex, made even more so by poor planning and unrealistic expectations; they are rushed due to increasingly demanding market pressure; and their scope becomes too unmanageable. Because this is today's reality, it is important to apply solid project management techniques and tools to increase the success rate of IT projects.

The Triple Constraint

A project's vision needs to be clear, concise, and comprehensible, but it also has to be the same to all stakeholders. It is imperative that everyone be on the same page. From a business perspective, everyone has to be aligned with the direction of the overall business and the project's overall objectives. It is key for members of

FIGURE 11.8

Project Management
Interdependent Variables

an organization who desire to make meaningful contributions to understand the company's investment and selection strategy for projects and how it determines and prioritizes the project pipeline. Projects consume vast amounts of resources. It is imperative to understand how the organization allocates its scarce and valuable resources in order to get the big picture.

Figure 11.8 displays the relationships between the three primary variables in any project—time, cost, and scope. These three variables are interdependent. All projects are limited in some way by these three constraints. The Project Management Institute calls the framework for evaluating these competing demands the triple constraint.

The relationship between these variables is such that if any one of the three factors changes at least one other factor is likely to be affected. For example, moving up a project's finish date could result in either increasing costs to hire more staff or decreasing the scope to eliminate features or functions. Increasing a project's scope to include additional customer requests could result in extending the project's time to completion or increasing the project's cost—or both—in order to accommodate the new scope changes. Project quality is affected by the project manager's ability to balance these competing demands. High quality projects deliver the agreed upon product or service on time and on budget.

Project management is the science of making intelligent trade-offs between time, cost, and scope. All three of the factors combined determine a project's quality. Benjamin Franklin's timeless advice—by failing to prepare, you prepare to fail—applies to many of today's software development projects. A recent survey concluded that the failure rate of IT projects is much higher in organizations that do not exercise disciplined project management. Figure 11.9 displays the top six reasons IT projects fail, according to *Information Week's* survey of 150 IT managers. A successful project is typically on time, within budget, meets the business's requirements, and fulfills the customer's needs. The Hackett Group, an Atlanta-based consultancy, analyzed its client database, which includes 2,000 companies, including 81 Fortune 100 companies, and discovered:

- Three in 10 major IT projects fail.
- Twenty-one percent of the companies state that they cannot adjust rapidly to market changes.
- One in four validates a business case for IT projects after completion.[22]

FIGURE 11.9

Why IT Projects Fall Behind
Schedule or Fail

Poor planning or poor project management
Change in business goals during project
Lack of support from business management
Lack of resources
Lack of support from IT management
Change in technology during project

0% 20% 40% 60% 80%

PROJECT MANAGEMENT FUNDAMENTALS

The Project Management Institute (PMI) defines a ***project*** as a temporary endeavor undertaken to create a unique product, service, or result. ***Project management*** is the application of knowledge, skills, tools, and techniques to project activities to meet project requirements. Projects are short-term efforts such as removing old servers, developing a custom ecommerce site, or merging databases. Figure 11.10 provides an overview of PMI and its fundamental project management terms all managers should know and understand.[23]

Before its merger with Hewlett-Packard, Compaq decided to analyze and prioritize its system development projects. Knowing that the CIO wanted to be able to view every project, project management leaders quickly identified and removed nonstrategic projects. At the end of the review process, the company cancelled 39 projects, saving the organization $15 million. Most Fortune 100 companies are receiving bottom-line benefits similar to Compaq's from implementing a project management solution.[24]

Most business managers are not project managers, however, it is inevitable that all managers will be part of a project team. Therefore, it is important to understand how a business manages its project and how the culture supports the effort. The art and science of project management must coordinate numerous activities as displayed in

FIGURE 11.10

Project Management
Institute (PMI)

The ***Project Management Institute (PMI)*** develops procedures and concepts necessary to support the profession of project management (www.pmi.org). It has three areas of focus:

1. The distinguishing characteristics of a practicing professional (ethics).
2. The content and structure of the profession's body of knowledge (standards).
3. Recognition of professional attainment (accreditation).

Project deliverables are any measurable, tangible, verifiable outcome, result, or item that is produced to complete a project or part of a project. Examples of project deliverables include design documents, testing scripts, and requirements documents.

Project milestones represent key dates when a certain group of activities must be performed. For example, completing the planning phase might be a project milestone. If a project milestone is missed, then chances are the project is experiencing problems.

Project manager is an individual who is an expert in project planning and management, defines and develops the project plan, and tracks the plan to ensure the project is completed on time and on budget. The project manager is the person responsible for executing the entire project plan.

Project management office (PMO) is an internal department that oversees all organizational projects. This group must formalize and professionalize project management expertise and leadership. One of the primary initiatives of the PMO is to educate the organization on techniques and procedures necessary to run successful projects.

FIGURE 11.11

Project Management Roles

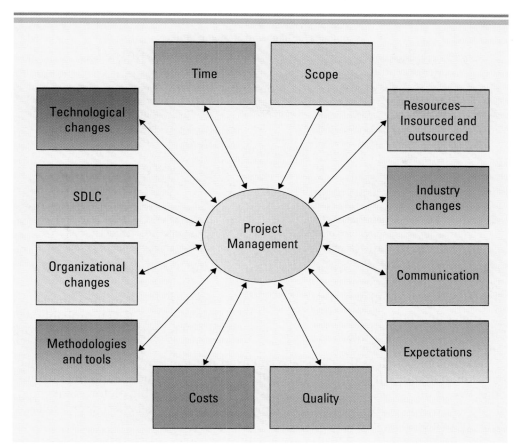

Figure 11.11. Project managers perform numerous activities. The remainder of this section focuses on four of these primary activities:

1. Choosing strategic projects.
2. Understanding project planning.
3. Managing projects.
4. Outsourcing projects.

CHOOSING STRATEGIC PROJECTS

One of the most difficult decisions organizations make is determining the projects in which to invest time, energy, and resources. An organization must identify what it wants to do and how it is going to do it. The "what" part of this question focuses on issues such as justification for the project, definition of the project, and expected results of the project. The "how" part of the question deals with issues such as project approach, project schedule, and analysis of project risks. Determining which projects to focus corporate efforts on is as necessary to projects as each project is to an organization.

Organizations also need to choose and prioritize projects in such a way that they can make responsible decisions as to which projects to eliminate. Jim Johnson, chairman of the Standish Group, has identified project management as the process that can make the difference in project success. According to Johnson, "Companies need a process for taking a regular look at their projects and deciding, again and again, if the investment is going to pay off. As it stands now, for most companies, projects can take on a life of their own." Figure 11.12 displays the three common techniques an organization can use to select projects.[25]

Project stakeholders are individuals and organizations actively involved in the project or whose interests might be affected as a result of project execution or

FIGURE 11.12

Techniques for Choosing
Strategic Projects

Techniques for Choosing Strategic Projects
1. **Focus on organizational goals**—Managers are finding tremendous value in choosing projects that align with the organization's goals. Projects that address organizational goals tend to have a higher success rate since they are important to the entire organization.
2. **Categorize projects**—There are various categories that an organization can group projects into to determine a project's priority. One type of categorization includes problem, opportunity, and directives. Problems are undesirable situations that prevent an organization from achieving its goals. Opportunities are chances to improve the organization. Directives are new requirements imposed by management, government, or some other external influence. It is often easier to obtain approval for projects that address problems or directives because the organization must respond to these categories to avoid financial losses.
3. **Perform a financial analysis**—A number of different financial analysis techniques can be performed to help determine a project's priority. A few of these include net present value, return on investment, and payback analysis. These financial analysis techniques help determine the organization's financial expectations for the project.

project completion. Stakeholders are not necessarily involved in the completion of project deliverables. For example, a chief financial officer (CFO) probably will not help test a new billing system, but she surely will be expecting the successful completion of the project.

Stakeholders, such as the CFO, also can exert influence over the project's objectives and outcomes. It is important for all stakeholders to understand the business objective of the project—once again, it is about getting the big picture. Stakeholders measure projects based on such factors as customer satisfaction, increased revenue, or decreased cost.

The project management team must identify stakeholders, determine their requirements and expectations, and, to the extent possible, manage their influence in relationship to the requirements to ensure a successful project. While all stakeholders are important, one stands out as having the most impact on the success or failure of a project. That person is the executive sponsor. PMI defines the ***executive sponsor*** as the person or group who provides the financial resources for the project. However, research has shown that the leadership strength of the executive sponsor has more to do with the success or failure of a project than any other critical success factor. In fact, the executive sponsor should be accountable to the project team for much more than the financial backing. The executive sponsor communicates up the chain on behalf of the project; he or she supports the project manager by championing the project to others sharing the vision and benefit of the successfully completed project; and the executive sponsor demonstrates the commitment and accountability necessary to survive a project! If a team has a hands-off sponsor who merely reviews invoices and inquires as to the status of a project, then that project surely is in trouble from the start.[26]

Another part of the equation is influence. If the executive sponsor has influence, he or she can use that influence to gain and direct essential resources needed to accomplish the project. A highly connected executive sponsor could mean the difference between success and failure. The executive sponsor should be committed to use this influence to ensure the health of the project. Executive management support influences the process and progress of a project. No matter what the case, the lack of executive support and input can place a project at a severe disadvantage.

UNDERSTANDING PROJECT PLANNING

Once an organization has selected strategic projects and identified its project manager it is time to build the critical component—the project plan. Building a project plan involves two key components:

- Project charter
- Project plan

Project Charter

Many project professionals believe that a solid project is initiated with documentation that includes a project charter, a scope statement, and the project management plan. A *project charter* is a document issued by the project initiator or sponsor that formally authorizes the existence of a project and provides the project manager with the authority to apply organizational resources to project activities. In short, this means someone has stepped up to pay for and support the project. A project charter typically includes several elements.

■ *Project scope* defines the work that must be completed to deliver a product with the specified features and functions. A project scope statement describes the business need, justification, requirements, and current boundaries for the project. The business need can be characterized by the problem the results of the project will satisfy. This is important in linking the project with the organization's overall business goals. The project scope statement includes constraints, assumptions, and requirements—all components necessary for developing accurate cost estimates.

■ *Project objectives* are quantifiable criteria that must be met for the project to be considered a success.

■ *Project constraints* are specific factors that can limit options. They include: budget, delivery dates, available skilled resources, and organizational policies.

■ *Project assumptions* are factors that are considered to be true, real, or certain without proof or demonstration. Examples include hours in a workweek or time of year the work will be performed.

The project objectives are one of the most important areas to define because they are essentially the major elements of the project. When an organization achieves the project objectives, it has accomplished the major goals of the project and the project scope is satisfied. Project objectives must include metrics so that the project's success can be measured. The metrics can include cost, schedule, and quality metrics along with a number of other metrics. Figure 11.13 displays the SMART criteria—useful reminders on how to ensure that the project has created understandable and measurable objectives.

- Specific
- Measurable
- Agreed upon
- Realistic
- Time framed

FIGURE 11.13

SMART Criteria for Successful Objective Creation

Project Plan

The *project plan* is a formal, approved document that manages and controls project execution. Figure 11.14 displays the characteristics of a well-defined project plan. The project plan should include a description of the project scope, a list of activities, a schedule, time estimates, cost estimates, risk factors, resources, assignments, and responsibilities. In addition to these basic components, most project professionals also include contingency plans, review and communications strategies, and a *kill switch*—a trigger that enables a project manager to close the project prior to completion.

A good project plan should include estimates for revenue and strategic necessities. It also should include measurement and reporting methods and details as to

Characteristics of a Well-Defined Project Plan
Easy to understand
Easy to read
Communicated to all key participants (key stakeholders)
Appropriate to the project's size, complexity, and criticality
Prepared by the team, rather than by the individual project manager

FIGURE 11.14

Project Plan Characteristics

how top leadership will engage in the project. A good plan informs stakeholders of the benefits of the project and justifies the investment, commitment, and risk of the project as it relates to the overall mission of the organization.[27]

An organization must build in continuous self-assessment, which allows earlier termination decisions on failing projects, with the associated cost savings. This frees capital and personnel for dedication to projects that are worth pursuing. The elimination of a project should be viewed as successful resource management, not as an admission of failure.

The most important part of the plan is communication. The project manager must communicate the plan to every member of the project team and to any key stakeholders and executives. The project plan must also include any project assumptions and be detailed enough to guide the execution of the project. A key to achieving project success is earning consensus and buy-in from all key stakeholders. By including key stakeholders in project plan development, the project manager allows them to have ownership of the plan. This often translates to greater commitment, which in turn results in enhanced motivation and productivity. The two primary diagrams most frequently used in project planning are PERT and Gantt charts.

PERT Chart A *PERT (Program Evaluation and Review Technique) chart* is a graphical network model that depicts a project's tasks and the relationships between those tasks. A *dependency* is a logical relationship that exists between the project tasks, or between a project task and a milestone. PERT charts define dependency between project tasks before those tasks are scheduled (see Figure 11.15). The boxes in Figure 11.15 represent project tasks, and the project manager can adjust the contents of the boxes to display various project attributes such as schedule and actual start and finish times. The arrows indicate that one task is dependent on the start or completion of another task. The *critical path* is a path from the start to the finish that passes through all the tasks that are critical to completing the project in the shortest amount of time. PERT charts frequently display a project's critical path.

FIGURE 11.15

PERT Chart Expert, a PERT Chart Example

FIGURE 11.16

Microsoft Project, a Gantt Chart Example

Gantt Chart A *Gantt chart* is a simple bar chart that depicts project tasks against a calendar. In a Gantt chart, tasks are listed vertically and the project's time frame is listed horizontally. A Gantt chart works well for representing the project schedule. It also shows actual progress of tasks against the planned duration. Figure 11.16 displays a software development project using a Gantt chart.

Managing Projects

MANAGING PROJECTS

Standish Group research clearly shows that projects are likely to be less challenged and more successful with a competent and skilled project manager on board. Again, a ***project manager*** is an individual who is an expert in project planning and management, defines and develops the project plan, and tracks the plan to ensure the project is completed on time and on budget. A project manager can, of course, bring enormous benefits to an organization such as reduced project expense, high company morale, and quicker time to market. A competent project manager sets the correct expectations early in the project with achievable milestones. Managing a project includes:

- Identifying requirements.
- Establishing clear and achievable objectives.
- Balancing the competing demands of quality, scope, time, and cost.
- Adapting the specifications, plans, and approach to the different concerns and expectations of the various stakeholders.[28]

In addition to managing these objectives, a successful project manager possesses a variety of hard and soft skills. Standish Group research also shows that successful project managers have basic business operational knowledge and good business skills. When a project manager has a good grasp of the business operations, he or she can improve critical communication among the designers, developers, user community, and top leadership. An experienced project manager should be able to minimize scope and create a better estimate. He or she knows how to say no without creating controversy. And a good project manager should have learned that a happy stakeholder is one who is underpromised and overdelivered! A project manager must focus on managing three primary areas to ensure success:

1. People
2. Communications
3. Change.

Managing People

Managing people is one of the hardest and most critical efforts a project manager undertakes. Resolving conflicts within the team and balancing the needs of the project with the personal and professional needs of the team are two of the challenges facing project managers. More and more project managers are the main (and sometimes sole) interface with the client during the project. As such, communication, negotiation, marketing, and salesmanship are just as important to the project manager as financial and analytical acumen. Many times, the people management side of project management makes the difference in pulling off a successful project.

Managing Communications

While many companies develop unique project management frameworks based on familiar project management standards, all of them agree that communication is the key to excellent project management. This is quite easy to state, but not so easy to accomplish! It is extremely helpful if a project manager plans what and how he or she will communicate as a formal part of the project management plan. Most often a document, it is referred to as a communications plan. A project manager distributes timely, accurate, and meaningful information regarding project objectives that involve time, cost, scope, and quality, and the status of each. The project manager also shares small wins as the project progresses, informs others of needed corrections, makes requests known for additional resources, and keeps all stakeholders informed of the project schedule.

Receiving Feedback   Another important aspect of a project management communications plan is to provide a method for continually obtaining and monitoring feedback from and for all stakeholders. This is not to say that a project manager needs to spend countless hours answering every email and responding to every question posed. Rather, the manager should develop a method for asking for specific feedback as part of the plan and responding to it in a timely, organized manner. Team members remain closest to the project and should be encouraged to share open and honest feedback. It is the project manager's role and responsibility to foster an environment of trust so that members feel safe to contribute their knowledge and ideas—even if it means relaying bad news or offering an opposing viewpoint.

Managing Change

Change, whether it comes in the form of a crisis, a market shift, or a technological development, is challenging for all organizations. Successful organizations and successful people learn to anticipate and react appropriately to change. Snap-on, a maker of tools and equipment for specialists such as car mechanics, is successful at managing change. The company recently increased profits by 12 percent while sales were down 6.7 percent. Dennis Leitner, vice president of IT, runs the IT group on a day-to-day basis and leads the implementation of all major software development initiatives. Each software development initiative is managed by both the business and IT. In fact, business resources are on the IT group's payroll, and they spend as much as 80 percent of their time learning what a business unit is doing and how IT can help make it happen. Leitner's role focuses primarily on strategic planning, change management, and setting up metrics to track performance.[29]

Dynamic organizational change is inevitable, and an organization must effectively manage change as it evolves. With the numerous challenges and complexities

FIGURE 11.17

Common Reasons Change Occurs

Common Reasons Change Occurs
1. An omission in defining initial scope
2. A misunderstanding of the initial scope
3. An external event such as government regulations that create new requirements
4. Organizational changes, such as mergers, acquisitions, and partnerships, that create new business problems and opportunities
5. Availability of better technology
6. Shifts in planned technology that force unexpected and significant changes to the business organization, culture, and/or processes
7. The users or management simply wanting the system to do more than they originally requested or agreed to
8. Management reducing the funding for the project or imposing an earlier deadline

that organizations face in today's rapidly changing environment, effective change management thus becomes a critical core competency. **Change management** is a set of techniques that aid in evolution, composition, and policy management of the design and implementation of a system. Figure 11.17 displays a few of the more common reasons change occurs.[30]

A **change management system** includes a collection of procedures to document a change request and define the steps necessary to consider the change based on the expected impact of the change. Most change management systems require that a change request form be initiated by one or more project stakeholders (systems owners, users, customers, analysts, developers). Ideally, these change requests are considered by a **change control board (CCB)** that is responsible for approving or rejecting all change requests. The CCB's composition typically includes a representative from each business area that has a stake in the project. The CCB's decision to accept or reject each change is based on an impact analysis of the change. For example, if one department wants to implement a change to the software that will increase both deployment time and cost, then the other business owners need to agree that the change is valid and that it warrants the extended time frame and increased budget.

Change is an opportunity, not a threat. Realizing that change is the norm rather than the exception will help an organization stay ahead. Becoming a change leader and accepting the inevitability of change can help ensure that an organization can survive and even thrive in times of change. Figure 11.18 displays the three important guidelines change leaders can follow to make change effective both inside and outside their organizations.[31]

OUTSOURCING PROJECTS

In the high-speed global business environment, an organization needs to maximize its profits, enlarge its market share, and restrain its ever-increasing costs. Businesses need to make every effort to rethink and adopt new processes, especially

FIGURE 11.18

Three Important Guidelines for Effective Change Management

Three Important Guidelines for Effectively Dealing with Change Management
1. Institute change management polices—Create clearly defined policies and procedures that must be followed each time a request for change is received.
2. Anticipate change—View change as an opportunity and embrace it.
3. Seek change—Every 6 to 12 months look for changes that may be windows of opportunity. Review successes and failures to determine if there are any opportunities for innovation.

FIGURE 11.19

Common Departments
Outsourced by Organizations

Percent of Functions Outsourced

Outsourcing

the prospective resources regarding insourcing and outsourcing. Two basic options are available to organizations wishing to develop and maintain their information systems—insourcing or outsourcing.

Insourcing (*in-house development*) is a common approach using the professional expertise within an organization to develop and maintain the organization's information technology systems. Insourcing has been instrumental in creating a viable supply of IT professionals and in creating a better quality workforce combining both technical and business skills.

Outsourcing is an arrangement by which one organization provides a service or services for another organization that chooses not to perform them in-house. In some cases, the entire information technology department is outsourced, including planning and business analysis as well as the installation, management, and servicing of the network and workstations. Outsourcing can range from a large contract under which an organization such as IBM manages IT services for a company such as Xerox to the practice of hiring contractors and temporary office workers on an individual basis. Figure 11.19 compares the functions companies have outsourced, and Figure 11.20 displays the primary reasons companies outsource.

In the early 1990s, British Petroleum (BP) began looking at IT outsourcing as a way to radically reduce costs and gain more flexible and higher-quality IT resources that directly improve the overall business. Over the past decade, all companies within the global BP Group have incorporated outsourcing initiatives in their business plans. BP's information technology costs were reduced by 40 percent globally over the first three years of the outsourcing engagement and have continued at a 10 percent reduction year after year, leading to hundreds of millions of dollars in savings to BP.[32]

Information technology outsourcing enables organizations to keep up with market and technology advances—with less strain on human and financial resources and more assurance that the IT infrastructure will keep pace with evolving business priorities (see Figure 11.21). Planning, deploying, and managing IT environments is both a tactical and a strategic challenge that must take into account a company's organizational, industrial, and technological concerns. The three different forms of outsourcing options a project must consider are:

1. *Onshore outsourcing*—engaging another company within the same country for services.

2. *Nearshore outsourcing*—contracting an outsourcing arrangement with a company in a nearby country. Often this country will share a border with the native country.

3. *Offshore outsourcing*—using organizations from developing countries to write code and develop systems. In offshore outsourcing the country is geographically far away.

FIGURE 11.20

Reasons Companies
Outsource

Tap outside sources of expertise
Concentrate resources on core business
Reduce head count and related expenses
Eliminate the need to reinvest in technology
Reduce costs
Better manage the costs of internal processes
Other

0% 10% 20% 30% 40% 50% 60% 70% 80%

Since the mid-1990s, major U.S. companies have been sending significant portions of their software development work offshore—primarily to vendors in India, but also to vendors in China, Eastern Europe (including Russia), Ireland, Israel, and the Philippines. The big selling point for offshore outsourcing is inexpensive good work. A programmer who earns as much as $63,000 per year in the United States is paid as little as $5,000 per year overseas (see Figure 11.22). Companies can easily realize cost savings of 30 to 50 percent through offshore outsourcing and still get the same, if not better, quality of service.[33]

Developed and developing countries throughout Europe and Asia offer some IT outsourcing services, but most are hampered to some degree by language, telecommunications infrastructure, or regulatory barriers. The first and largest offshore marketplace is India, whose English-speaking and technologically advanced population has built its IT services business into a $4 billion industry. Infosys, NIIT, Satyam, TCS, and Wipro are among the biggest Indian outsourcing service providers, each with a significant presence in the United States.[34]

Ever since Eastman Kodak announced it was outsourcing its information systems function in 1988 to IBM, DEC, and Businessland, large organizations have found it

FIGURE 11.21

Outsourcing Models and Cost Savings

Indirect

Offshore

Nearshore

Onshore

Direct

Close   Remote

Locations of outsourcing

Customer control

Developing Information Systems

FIGURE 11.22

Typical Salary Ranges for
Computer
Programmers

Country	Salary Range Per Year
China	$5,000–$9,000
India	6,000–10,000
Philippines	6,500–11,000
Russia	7,000–13,000
Ireland	21,000–28,000
Canada	25,000–50,000
United States	60,000–90,000

acceptable to transfer their IT assets, leases, and staff to outsourcers. In view of the changes in sourcing, the key question now is not "Should we outsource IT?" but rather "Where and how can we take advantage of the rapidly developing market of IT services providers?" Some of the influential drivers affecting the growth of the outsourcing market include:

- **Core competencies.** Many companies have recently begun to consider outsourcing as a means to fuel revenue growth rather than just a cost-cutting measure. Outsourcing enables an organization to maintain an up-to-date technology infrastructure while freeing it to focus on revenue growth goals by reinvesting cash and human capital in areas offering the greatest return on investment.

- **Financial savings.** It is typically cheaper to hire workers in China and India than similar workers in the United States. Technology is advancing at such an accelerated rate that companies often lack the resources, workforce, or expertise to keep up. It is close to impossible for an IT department to maintain a "best-of-breed" status, especially for small and medium-sized enterprises where cost is a critical factor.

- **Rapid growth.** A company's sustainability depends on both speed to market and ability to react quickly to changes in market conditions. By taking advantage of outsourcing, an organization is able to acquire best-practices process expertise. This facilitates the design, building, training, and deployment of business processes or functions.

- **Industry changes.** High levels of reorganization across industries have increased demand for outsourcing to better focus on core competencies. The significant increase in merger and acquisition activity created a sudden need to integrate multiple core and noncore business functions into one business, while the deregulation of the utilities and telecom industries created a need to ensure compliance with government rules and regulations. Companies in either situation turned to outsourcing so they could better focus on industry changes at hand.

- **The Internet.** The pervasive nature of the Internet as an effective sales channel has allowed clients to become more comfortable with outsourcing. Barriers to entry, such as lack of capital, are dramatically reduced in the world of ebusiness due to the Internet. New competitors enter the market daily.

- **Globalization.** As markets open worldwide, competition heats up. Companies may engage outsourcing service providers to deliver international services.[35]

Best Buy Co. Inc. is the number one U.S. specialty retailer for consumer electronics, personal computers, entertainment software, and appliances. Best Buy needed to find a strategic IT partner that could help the company leverage its IT functions to meet its business objectives. Best Buy also wanted to integrate its disparate enterprise systems and minimize its operating expenses. Best Buy outsourced these functions to Accenture, a global management consulting, technology services, and outsourcing company. The comprehensive outsourcing relationship that drove Best

FIGURE 11.23

Outsourcing Opportunities

Industry	Outsourcing Opportunities
Banking and finance	Check and electronic payment processing, credit report issuance, delinquency management, securities, and trades processing
Insurance	Claims reporting and investigation, policy administration, checkprocessing, risk assessment
Telecommunications	Invoice and bill production, transaction processing
Health care	Electronic data interchange, database management, accounting
Transportation	Ticket and order processing
Government	Loan processing, Medicaid processing
Retail	Electronic payment processing

Buy's transformation produced spectacular results that were measurable in every key area of its business, such as a 20 percent increase in key category revenue that translated into a $25 million profit improvement.[36]

According to PricewaterhouseCoopers' survey of CEOs from 452 of the fastest growing U.S. companies, "Businesses that outsource are growing faster, larger, and more profitably than those that do not. In addition, most of those involved in outsourcing say they are saving money and are highly satisfied with their outsourcing service providers." Figure 11.23 lists common areas for outsourcing opportunities across industries.[37]

Outsourcing Benefits

The many benefits associated with outsourcing include:

- Increased quality and efficiency of a process, service, or function.
- Reduced operating expenses.
- Resources focused on core profit-generating competencies.
- Reduced exposure to risks involved with large capital investments.
- Access to outsourcing service provider's economies of scale.
- Access to outsourcing services provider's expertise and best-in-class practices.
- Access to advanced technologies.
- Increased flexibility with the ability to respond quickly to changing market demands.
- No costly outlay of capital funds.
- Reduced head count and associated overhead expense.
- Reduced frustration and expense related to hiring and retaining employees in an exceptionally tight job market.
- Reduced time to market for products or services.[38]

Outsourcing Challenges

Outsourcing comes with several challenges. These arguments are valid and should be considered when a company is thinking about outsourcing. Many challenges can be avoided with proper research. The challenges include:

- **Contract length.** Most of the outsourced IT contracts are for a relatively long time period (several years). This is because of the high cost of transferring assets and employees as well as maintaining technological investment. The long contract causes three particular issues:
    1. Difficulties in getting out of a contract if the outsourcing service provider turns out to be unsuitable.

2. Problems in foreseeing what the business will need over the next 5 or 10 years (typical contract lengths), hence creating difficulties in establishing an appropriate contract.

3. Problems in reforming an internal IT department after the contract period is finished.

■ **Competitive edge.** Effective and innovative use of IT can give an organization a competitive edge over its rivals. A competitive business advantage provided by an internal IT department that understands the organization and is committed to its goals can be lost in an outsourced arrangement. In an outsourced arrangement, IT staff are striving to achieve the goals and objectives of the outsourcing service provider, which may conflict with those of the organization.

■ **Confidentiality.** In some organizations, the information stored in the computer systems is central to the enterprise's success or survival, such as information about pricing policies, product mixing formulas, or sales analysis. Some companies decide against outsourcing for fear of placing confidential information in the hands of the provider, particularly if the outsourcing service provider offers services to companies competing in the same marketplace. Although the organization usually dismisses this threat, claiming it is covered by confidentiality clauses in a contract, the organization must assess the potential risk and costs of a confidentiality breach in determining the net benefits of an outsourcing agreement.

■ **Scope definition.** Most IT projects suffer from problems associated with defining the scope of the system. The same problem afflicts outsourcing arrangements. Many difficulties result from contractual misunderstandings between the organization and the outsourcing service provider. In such circumstances, the organization believes that the service required is within the contract scope while the service provider is sure it is outside the scope and so is subject to extra fees.[39]

OPENING CASE QUESTIONS
HP's Software Problems

6. Review the project charter and explain how HP could benefit by using one.

7. Why is project management critical to HP's software development process?

8. Identify the three outsourcing options along with the pros and cons HP should consider if it chooses to outsource its systems development effort.

SUMMARY OF KEY THEMES

The purpose of this chapter was to provide you, the business student, with a detailed overview of the various ways in which organizations develop information systems. Major lessons raised in this chapter were:

■ Systems development encompasses a wide array of phases from initial planning right through to implementation and maintenance.

■ Companies have a variety of software development methodologies and insourcing/outsourcing options at their disposal.

- Due to the complexity and problems in designing systems, many organizations are widely choosing to follow good project management practices to better guarantee that the information systems they build are delivered on time, within budget, and meet user needs.

You, the business student, should now have sufficient knowledge of the systems development process so that you will be better able to participate and contribute to the successful development and implementation of information systems. The chapter also covered project management basics, which can lead a path to steer the successful completion of any project.

KEY TERMS

Agile methodology   405
Analysis phase   403
Business requirement   403
Change control board
   (CCB)   419
Change management   419
Change management
   system   419
Critical path   416
Dependency   416
Design phase   403
Development phase   403
Executive sponsor   414
Extreme programming (XP)
   methodology   406
Feature creep   409
Gantt chart   417
Implementation phase   403
Insourcing (in-house
   development)   420

Iterative development   405
Kill switch   415
Maintenance phase   403
Methodology   404
Nearshore outsourcing   420
Offshore outsourcing   420
Onshore outsourcing   420
Outsourcing   420
PERT (Program Evaluation and
   Review Technique) chart   416
Planning phase   402
Project   412
Project assumption   415
Project charter   415
Project constraint   415
Project deliverable   412
Project management   412
Project management office   412
Project manager   412, 417
Project milestone   412

Project objective   415
Project plan   415
Project scope   415
Project stakeholder   413
Prototype   406
Rapid application development
   (RAD) (rapid prototyping)
   methodology   406
Rational Unified Process (RUP)
   methodology   407
Scope creep   409
Scrum methodology   407
Systems development life cycle
   (SDLC)   402
Testing phase   403
Waterfall methodology   404

CLOSING CASE ONE

Disaster at Denver International Airport

One good way to learn how to develop successful systems is to review past failures. One of the most infamous system failures is Denver International Airport's (DIA) baggage system. When the automated baggage system design for DIA was introduced, it was hailed as the savior of modern airport design. The design relied on a network of 300 computers to route bags and 4,000 telecars to carry luggage across 21 miles of track. Laser scanners were to read bar-coded luggage tags, while advanced scanners tracked the movement of toboggan-like baggage carts.

When DIA finally opened its doors for reporters to witness its revolutionary baggage handling system the scene was rather unpleasant. Bags were chewed up, lost, and misrouted in what has since became a legendary systems nightmare.

One of the biggest mistakes made in the baggage handling system fiasco was that not enough time was allowed to properly develop the system. In the beginning of the project, DIA assumed it was the responsibility of individual airlines to find their own way of moving the baggage from the plane to the baggage claim area. The automated baggage system was not involved in the initial planning of the DIA project. By the time the developers of DIA decided to create an integrated baggage system, the time frame for designing and implementing such a complex and huge system was not possible.

Another common mistake that occurred during the project was that the airlines kept changing their business requirements. This caused numerous issues including the implementation of power supplies that were not properly updated for the revised system design, which caused overloaded motors and mechanical failures. Besides the power supplies design problem, the optical sensors did not read the bar codes correctly, causing issues with baggage routing.

Finally, BAE, the company that designed and implemented the automated baggage system for DIA, had never created a baggage system of this size before. BAE had created a similar system in an airport in Munich, Germany, where the scope was much smaller. Essentially, the baggage system had an inadequate IT infrastructure since it was designed for a much smaller system.

DIA simply could not open without a functional baggage system so the city had no choice but to delay the opening date for over 16 months, costing taxpayers roughly $1 million per day, which totaled around $500 million.[40]

Questions

1. One of the problems with DIA's baggage system was inadequate testing. Why is testing important to a project's success? Why do so many projects decide to skip testing?
2. Evaluate the different systems development methodologies. Which one would have most significantly increased the chances of the project's success?
3. How could more time spent in the analysis and design phase have saved Colorado taxpayers hundreds of millions of dollars?
4. Why could BAE not take an existing IT infrastructure and simply increase its scale and expect it to work?

CLOSING CASE TWO

Reducing Ambiguity in Business Requirements

The number one reason projects fail is bad business requirements. Business requirements are considered "bad" because of ambiguity or insufficient involvement of end users during analysis and design.

A requirement is unambiguous if it has the same interpretation for all parties. Different interpretations by different participants will usually result in unmet expectations. Here is an example of an ambiguous requirement and an example of an unambiguous requirement:

- Ambiguous requirement: The financial report must show profits in local and U.S. currencies.
- Unambiguous requirement: The financial report must show profits in local and U.S. currencies using the exchange rate printed in *The Wall Street Journal* for the last business day of the period being reported.

Ambiguity is impossible to prevent completely because it is introduced into requirements in natural ways. For example:

- Requirements can contain technical implications that are obvious to the IT developers but not to the customers.
- Requirements can contain business implications that are obvious to the customer but not to the IT developers.

- Requirements may contain everyday words whose meanings are "obvious" to everyone, yet different for everyone.
- Requirements are reflections of detailed explanations that may have included multiple events, multiple perspectives, verbal rephrasing, emotion, iterative refinement, selective emphasis, and body language—none of which are captured in the written statements.

Tips for Reviewing Business Requirements

When reviewing business requirements always look for the following words to help dramatically reduce ambiguity:

- *And* and *or* have well-defined meanings and ought to be completely unambiguous, yet they are often understood only informally and interpreted inconsistently. For example, consider the statement "The alarm must ring if button T is pressed and if button F is pressed." This statement may be intended to mean that to ring the alarm, both buttons must be pressed or it may be intended to mean that either one can be pressed. A statement like this should never appear in a requirement because the potential for misinterpretation is too great. A preferable approach is to be very explicit, for example, "The alarm must ring if both buttons T and F are pressed simultaneously. The alarm should not ring in any other circumstance."
- *Always* might really mean "most of the time," in which case it should be made more explicit. For example, the statement "We always run reports A and B together" could be challenged with "In other words, there is never any circumstance where you would run A without B and B without A?" If you build a system with an "always" requirement, then you are actually building the system to never run report A without report B. If a user suddenly wants report B without report A, you will need to make significant system changes.
- *Never* might mean rarely, in which case it should be made more explicit. For example, the statement "We never run reports A and B in the same month" could be challenged with, "So that means that if I see that A has been run, I can be absolutely certain that no one will want to run B." Again, if you build a system that supports a "never" requirement, then the system users can never perform that requirement. For example, the system would never allow a user to run reports A and B in the same month, no matter what the circumstances.
- Boundary conditions are statements about the line between true and false and do and do not. These statements may or may not be meant to include end points. For example, "We want to use method X when there are up to 10 pages, but method Y otherwise." If you were building this system, would you include page 10 in method X or in method Y? The answer to this question will vary causing an ambiguous business requirement.[41]

Questions

1. Why are ambiguous business requirements the leading cause of system development failures?
2. Why do the words *and* and *or* tend to lead to ambiguous requirements?
3. Research the web and determine other reasons for "bad" business requirements.
4. What is wrong with the following business requirement: "The system must support employee birthdays since every employee always has a birthday every year."

CLOSING CASE THREE

Staying on Track—Toronto Transit

Schedules are at the heart of Toronto Transit Commission's (TTC) celebrated transit system, which services over 1 million customers daily. More than 50 large engineering and construction projects are under way to expand, upgrade, and maintain Toronto's transit systems and structures. One such project is the Sheppard project, which consists of constructing the new six-kilometer line north of the city. Sheppard is estimated to take more than five years to complete, with a total cost of $875 million.

TTC's challenge is to keep its 50 individual projects, most of which fall within the $2 million to $100 million price range and span an average of five years, on schedule and under budget. Staying on top of so many multifaceted, multiyear, and often interdependent projects adds additional complexity for the company. TTC uses Primavera Project Planner (P3) to create a single master schedule for all of its engineering and construction projects.

TTC's 50 individual projects average 100 to 150 activities each, with some projects encompassing as many as 500 to 600 activities. "Seeing the big picture is important, not only for the 300 people who work in the engineering and construction branch of the TTC, but for the entire 9,000-person organization," said Vince Carroll, head scheduler for the engineering and construction branch. "Engineering managers need to see how other projects may impact their own. Materials and procurement managers need to track project progress. Senior managers need to be able to communicate with city government to secure funding. Marketing and public relations people need the latest information to set public expectations. And most important of all," Carroll said, "the operations group needs to stay informed of what is happening so that they can adjust the schedules that run the trains."

Carroll and his team of 25 people create, update, and publish a master schedule that summarizes the individual status of each project, shows the logical links between projects, and provides an integrated overview of all projects. The master schedule helps the team effectively and regularly communicate the status of all projects currently under way throughout the Toronto Transit system.

The master schedule organizes projects according to their location in the capital budget. For example, projects can be organized according to those that have been allotted funding for expansion, state of good repair, legislative reasons, or environmental reasons. Each project is organized by its logical flow—from planning, analysis, design, through the maintenance phase. The final report shows positive and negative balances for each project and a single overview of the status of all the engineering and construction projects. Carroll and his team use PERT charts to create time-scaled logic diagrams and then convert this information to bar charts for presentation purposes in the master schedule. TTC is currently linking its master schedule directly to its payroll system, enabling it to track the number of hours actually worked versus hours planned.[42]

Questions

1. Describe Gantt charts and explain how TTC could use one to communicate project status.

2. Describe PERT charts and explain how TTC could use one to communicate project status.

MAKING BUSINESS DECISIONS

1. Selecting a systems development methodology

Exus Incorporated is an international billing outsourcing company. Exus currently has revenues of $5 billion, over 3,500 employees, and operations on every continent. You have recently been hired as the CIO. Your first task is to increase the software development project success rate, which is currently at 20 percent. To ensure that future software development projects are successful, you want to standardize the systems development methodology across the entire enterprise. Currently, each project determines which methodology it uses to develop software.

Create a report detailing three system development methodologies that were covered in this text. Compare each of these methodologies to the traditional waterfall approach. Finally, recommend which methodology you want to implement as your organizational standard.

Be sure to highlight any potential roadblocks you might encounter when implementing the new standard methodology.

2. Understanding project failure

You are the director of project management for Stello, a global manufacturer of high-end writing instruments. The company sells to primarily high-end customers, and the average price for one of its fine writing instruments is about $350. You are currently implementing a new customer relationship management system and you want to do everything you can to ensure a successful systems development effort. Create a document summarizing the primary reasons why this project could fail, along with your strategy to eliminate the possibility of system development failure on your project.

3. Missing phases in the systems development life cycle

Hello Inc. is a large concierge service for executives operating in Chicago, San Francisco, and New York. The company performs all kinds of services from dog walking to airport transportation. Your manager, Dan Martello, wants to skip the testing phase during the company's financial ERP implementation. Dan feels that since the system came from a vendor it should work correctly. Draft a memo explaining to Dan the importance of following the SDLC and the ramifications to the business if the financial system is not tested.

4. Refusing to sign off

You are the primary client on a large extranet development project. After carefully reviewing the requirements definition document, you are positive that there are missing, ambiguous, inaccurate, and unclear requirements. The project manager is pressuring you for your sign-off since he has already received sign-off from five of your co-workers. If you fail to sign off on the requirements, you are going to put the entire project at risk since the time frame is nonnegotiable. What would you do? Why?

5. Saving failing systems

Crik Candle Company manufactures low-end candles for restaurants. The company generates over $40 million in annual revenues and has more than 300 employees. You are in the middle of a large multimillion-dollar supply chain management implementation. Your project manager has just come to you with the information that the project might fail for the following reasons:

- Several business requirements were incorrect and the scope has to be doubled.
- Three developers recently quit.
- The deadline has been moved up a month.

Develop a list of options that your company can follow to ensure the project remains on schedule and within budget.

6. Explaining project management

Prime Time Inc. is a large consulting company that specializes in outsourcing people with project management capabilities and skills. You are in the middle of an interview for a job with Prime Time. The manager performing the interview asks you to explain why managing a project plan is critical to a project's success. The manager also wants you to explain scope creep and feature creep and your tactics for managing them on a project. Finally, the manager wants you to elaborate on your strategies for delivering successful projects and reducing risks.

7. Applying project management techniques

You have been hired by a medium-sized airline company, Sun Best. Sun Best currently flies over 300 routes in the East. The company is experiencing tremendous issues coordinating its 3,500 pilots, 7,000 flight attendants, and 2,000 daily flights. Determine how Sun Best could use a Gantt chart to help it coordinate pilots, flight attendants, and daily flights. Using Excel, create a sample Gantt chart highlighting the different types of activities and resources Sun Best could track with the tool.

8. GUS software offshores

Founded in 2007, GUS Software provides innovative search software, website demographics, and testing software. All serve as part of its desktop and enterprise resource planning solutions for government, corporate, educational, and consumer markets. Website publishers, digital media publishers, content managers, document managers, business users, consumers, software companies, and consulting services companies use the Gus solutions. The company is currently thinking about offshore outsourcing its call center functions, ebusiness strategies, and application development. Describe how GUS could use outsourcing along with the potential advantages it might receive.

APPLY YOUR KNOWLEDGE

1. Methods Behind Methodologies

Signatures Inc. specializes in producing personalized products such as coffee mugs and pens with company logos. The company generates over $40 million in annual revenues and has more than 300 employees. The company is in the middle of a large multimillion-dollar SCM implementation, and it has just hired your project management outsourcing firm to take over the project management efforts.

Project Focus

On your first day, your team is told that the project is failing for the following reasons:

- The project is using the traditional waterfall methodology.
- The SDLC was not followed and the developers decided to skip the testing phase.
- A project plan was developed during the analysis phase, but the old project manager never updated or followed the plan.

Determine what your first steps would be to get this project back on track.

2. The Travel Store

In 2008, The Travel Store faced a dilemma. The retailer had tripled in size over a three-year period to $1 billion in sales, but it had done so despite operational deficiencies. The company's inability to evolve its business processes as it grew was causing problems. Within a year, sales and profits fell below expectations, and its stock price plummeted from approximately $10 a share to less than $2 a share.

Project Focus

The Travel Store is determined to take quick and decisive action to restore profitability and improve its credibility in the marketplace. One of its top priorities is to overhaul its inventory management system in an effort to create optimal levels of inventory to support sales demand. This would prevent higher-volume stores from running out of key sale items while also ensuring that lower-sales stores would not be burdened with excess inventory that could only be moved at closeout prices. The company would like to outsource this function but is worried about the challenges of transferring the responsibility of this important business function, as well as the issues surrounding confidentiality, and scope definition. List the competitive advantages outsourcing could give to The Travel Store, along with recommendations for addressing the company's outsourcing concerns.

3. GEM Athletic Center

First Information Corporation is a large consulting company that specializes in systems analysis and design. The company has over 2,000 employees and first-quarter revenues reached $15 million. The company prides itself on maintaining an 85 percent success rate for all project implementations. The primary reason attributed to the unusually high project success rate is the company's ability to define accurate, complete, and high-quality business requirements.

The GEM Athletic Center located in Cleveland, Ohio, is interested in implementing a new payroll system. The current payroll process is manual and takes three employees two days each month to complete. The GEM Athletic Center does not have an IT department and is outsourcing the entire procurement, customization, and installation of the new payroll system to First Information Corporation.

Project Focus

You have been working for First Information for a little over one month. Your team has just been assigned the GEM Athletic Center project and your first task is to define the initial business requirements for the development of the new payroll system.

a. Review the testimony of three current GEM Athletic Center accounting employees who detail the current payroll process along with their wish list for the new system. Use the files MaggieCleaver.doc, AnneLogan.doc, JimPoulos.doc.

b. Review the Characteristics of Good Business Requirements document (Business-Requirements.doc) that highlights several techniques you can use to develop solid business requirements.

c. After careful analysis, create a report detailing the business requirements for the new system. Be sure to list any assumptions, issues, or questions in your document.

Data Folder: AYK Chapters

4. Confusing Coffee

Business requirements are the detailed set of business requests that any new system must meet in order to be successful. A sample business requirement might state, "The system must track all customer sales by product, region, and sales representative." This requirement states what the system must do from the business perspective, giving no details or information on how the system is going to meet this requirement.

Project Focus

You have been hired to build an employee payroll system for a new coffee shop. Review the following business requirements and highlight any potential issues.

- All employees must have a unique employee ID.
- The system must track employee hours worked based on employee's last name.
- Employees must be scheduled to work a minimum of eight hours per day.
- Employee payroll is calculated by multiplying the employee's hours worked by $7.25.
- Managers must be scheduled to work morning shifts.
- Employees cannot be scheduled to work more than eight hours per day.
- Servers cannot be scheduled to work morning, afternoon, or evening shifts.
- The system must allow managers to change and delete employees from the system.

5. Picking Projects

You are a project management contractor attempting to contract work at a large telecommunications company, Hex Incorporated. Your interview with Debbie Fernandez, the senior vice president of IT, went smoothly. The last thing Debbie wants to see from you before she makes her final hiring decision is a prioritized list of the projects below. You are sure to land the job if Debbie is satisfied with your prioritization.

Project Focus

Create a report for Debbie prioritizing the following projects and be sure to include the business justifications for your prioritization.

- Upgrade accounting system.
- Develop employee vacation tracking system.
- Enhance employee intranet.
- Cleanse and scrub data warehouse information.
- Performance test all hardware to ensure 20 percent growth scalability.
- Implement changes to employee benefits system.
- Develop backup and recovery strategy.
- Implement supply chain management system.
- Upgrade customer relationship management system.
- Build executive information system for CEO.

6. Keeping Time

Time Keepers Inc. is a small firm that specializes in project management consulting. You are a senior project manager, and you have recently been assigned to the Tahiti Tanning Lotion account. The Tahiti Tanning Lotion company is currently experiencing a 10 percent success rate (90 percent failure rate) on all internal IT projects. Your first assignment is to analyze one of the current project plans being used to develop a new CRM system (see Figure AYK.1).

Project Focus

a. Review the project plan and create a document listing the numerous errors in the plan. Be sure to also provide suggestions on how to fix the errors.

b. If you have access to Microsoft Project, open the file BadProject.mpp. Fix the errors you found in question 1 directly to BadProject.mpp. (If you are new to using Microsoft Project, review the document MSProjectGuidelines.doc for an overview of several tips for using Microsoft Project.)

Data Folder: AYK Chapters

7. Growing, Growing, Gone

You are the founder of Black Pearl, a small comic book start-up. The good news is Black Pearl has found tremendous success. You have 34 employees in a creative, yet functional, office in downtown Chicago. The comics you produce are of extremely high quality. The artwork is unmatched and the story lines are compelling, gripping, and addictive, according to your customers. Your comics are quickly becoming a cult classic and Black Pearl customers are extremely loyal. You produce all of the comics and sell them in your store and via the Internet to individuals all over the United States.

Project Focus

You had vision when you started Black Pearl. You knew the potential of your business model to revamp the comic industry. You purchased high-end computers and customizable software to support your operations. Now, you are faced with a new dilemma. You have a large international following and you have decided to pursue international opportunities. You would like to open stores in Japan, France, and Brazil during the next year. To determine if this is possible, you need to evaluate your current systems to see if they are flexible and scalable enough to perform business internationally. You know that you are going to run into many international business issues. Create a list of questions you need to answer to determine if your systems are capable of performing international business.

FIGURE AYK.1

Sample Project Plan

A Survival Guide for Working with Humans. By Gini Graham Scott (New York: AMACOM, 2004).

To succeed in the workplace, good work relationships must be carefully developed and maintained. Although difficult people, back stabbers, whiners, know-it-alls, and others can make it hard to get through the workweek, many coping mechanisms can be put into place that can improve work relationships and improve productivity and communications. In *A Survival Guide for Working with Humans,* author and consultant Gini Graham Scott offers dozens of practical tools and examples that can help others resolve everyday conflicts and survive their jobs.

A Survival Guide for Working with Humans offers an eye-opening approach for coping with the idiosyncrasies and difficulties other people can present in the workplace. By focusing on specific work issues and providing relevant vignettes that describe the work issues involved, as well as a list of instructions to follow in similar circumstances, Scott takes the struggle out of conflicts and replaces it with strategy.[44]

Death March: The Complete Software Developer's Guide to Surviving "Mission Impossible" Projects. By Edward Yourdon (Upper Saddle River, NJ: Prentice Hall, 1997).

Today, IT projects are expected to achieve the impossible, overcome numerous constraints, deal with elevated stress levels and imperfect working conditions. In *Death March,* legendary software developer Edward Yourdon comes to the rescue. Yourdan developed the *Death March* project style quadrant as displayed here.

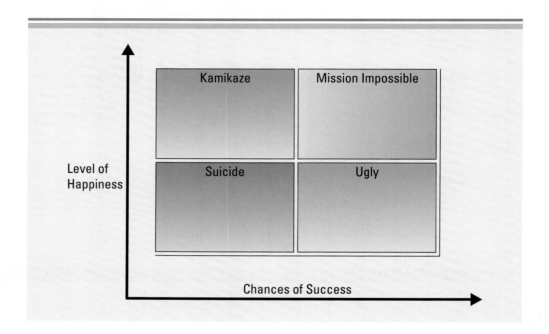

Yourdon takes direct aim at the projects that are "doomed to fail" presenting specific techniques for:

- Managing people and teams.
- Choosing the right processes.
- Making decisions about tools and technologies.
- Getting the flexibility you need to succeed.[43]

Globalization, Innovation, and 21st Century Organizational Trends

CHAPTER OUTLINE

What's in IT for me?

Have you ever dreamed of traveling to exotic cities like Paris, Tokyo, Rio de Janeiro, or Cairo? In the past, the closest many people ever got to working in such cities was in their dreams. Today, the situation has changed. Most major companies cite global expansion as a link to future growth. A recent study noted that 91 percent of the companies doing business globally believe it is important to send employees on assignments in other countries.

If a career in global business has crossed your mind, this chapter will help you understand the impacts of competing in a global world. The United States is a market of about 290 million people, but there are more than 6 billion potential customers in the 193 countries that make up the global market. Perhaps more interesting is that approximately 75 percent of the world's population lives in developing areas where technology, education, and per capita income still lag considerably behind those of developed (or industrialized) nations such as the United States.

You, the business student, should be familiar with the potential of global business, including its many benefits and challenges. The demand for students with training in global business is almost certain to grow as the number of businesses competing in global markets increases.

E-SPIONAGE

BusinessWeek magazine recently probed the rising attacks on America's most sensitive computer networks, uncovering startling security gaps. The email message addressed to a Booz Allen Hamilton executive was mundane—a shopping list sent by the Pentagon of weaponry India wanted to buy. But the missive was a brilliant fake. Lurking beneath the description of aircraft, engines, and radar equipment was an insidious piece of computer code, known as Poison Ivy, designed to suck sensitive data out of the $4 billion consulting firm's computer network.

The Pentagon had not sent the email. Its origin is unknown, but the message traveled through Korea on its way to Booz Allen. Its authors knew enough about the "sender" and "recipient" to craft a message unlikely to arouse suspicion. Had the Booz Allen executive clicked on the attachment, his every keystroke would have been reported back to a mysterious master at the Internet address cybersyndrome.3322.org, which is registered through an obscure company headquartered on the banks of China's Yangtze River.

The email aimed at Booz Allen paints a vivid picture of the alarming new capabilities of America's cyberenemies. On September 5, 2007, an email message appeared to be sent to John F. "Jack" Mulhern, vice president for international military assistance programs at Booz Allen. In the high-tech world of weapons sales, Mulhern's specialty, the email looked authentic enough. "Integrate U.S., Russian, and Indian weapons and avionics," the email noted, describing the Indian government's expectations for its fighter jets. "Source code given to India for indigenous computer upgrade capability." Such lingo could easily be understood by Mulhern. The 62-year-old former U.S. Naval officer and 33-year veteran of Booz Allen's military consulting business is an expert in helping to sell U.S. weapons to foreign governments.

The email was more convincing because of its apparent sender: Stephen J. Moree, a civilian who works for a group that reports to the office of Air Force Secretary Michael W. Wynne. Among its duties, Moree's unit evaluates the security of selling U.S. military aircraft to other countries. There would be little reason to suspect anything seriously amiss in Moree passing along the highly technical document with "India MRCA Request for Proposal" in the subject line. The Indian government had just released the request a week earlier, on August 28, and the language in the email closely tracked the request. Making the message appear more credible still, it referred to upcoming Air Force communiqués and a "Teaming Meeting" to discuss the deal.

But the missive from Moree to Jack Mulhern was a fake. An analysis of the email's path and attachment, conducted for *BusinessWeek* by three cybersecurity specialists, shows it was sent by an unknown attacker, bounced through an Internet address in South Korea, was relayed through a Yahoo! server in New York, and finally made its way toward Mulhern's Booz Allen in-box. The analysis also shows the code—known as malware, for malicious software—tracks keystrokes on the computers of people who open it. A separate program disables security measures such as password protection on Microsoft Access database files, a program often used by large organizations such as the U.S. defense industry to manage big batches of data.

Global Threats

The U.S. government and its sprawl of defense contractors have been the victims of an unprecedented rash of similar attacks recently, say current and former U.S. government officials. "It's espionage on a massive scale," said Paul B. Kurtz, a former high-ranking national security official. Government agencies reported 12,986 cybersecurity incidents to the U.S. Homeland Security Department in one fiscal year, triple the number from two years earlier. Incursions on the military's networks were up 55 percent, said Lieutenant General Charles E. Croom, head of the Pentagon's Joint Task Force for Global Network Operations. Private targets such as Booz Allen are just as vulnerable and pose just as much potential security risk. "They have our information on their networks. They're building our weapon systems. You wouldn't want that in enemy hands," Croom said. Cyber attackers "are not denying, disrupting, or destroying operations—yet. But that doesn't mean they don't have the capability."

The Monster We Created

BusinessWeek learned that the U.S. government launched a classified operation called Byzantine Foothold to detect, track, and disarm intrusions on the government's most critical networks. In some cases, the government's own cybersecurity experts are engaged in "hack-backs"—following the malicious code to peer into the hackers' own computer systems.

The government has yet to disclose the breaches discovered by the Byzantine Foothold. *BusinessWeek* learned that intruders managed to worm into the State Department's highly sensitive Bureau of Intelligence and Research, a key channel between the work of intelligence agencies and the rest of the government. The breach posed a risk to CIA operatives in embassies around the globe, said several network security specialists familiar with the effort to cope with what became seen as an internal crisis. Teams worked around the clock in search of malware, they said, calling the White House regularly with updates.

One member of the emergency team summoned to the scene recalled that each time cybersecurity professionals thought they had eliminated the source of a "beacon" reporting back to its master, another popped up. He compared the effort to the arcade game Whack-A-Mole. The State Department said it eradicated the infection, but only after sanitizing scores of infected computers and servers and changing passwords. Microsoft's own patch, meanwhile, was not deployed until August 2006, three months after the infection. A Microsoft spokeswoman declined to comment on the episode, but said: "Microsoft has, for several years, taken a comprehensive approach to help protect people online."

Poison Ivy

Commercial computer security firms have dubbed the malicious code hidden inside an email attachment Poison Ivy, and it has a devious—and worrisome—capability known as a RAT, a remote administration tool. RAT gives the attacker control over the host PC, capturing screen shots and perusing files. It lurks in the background of Microsoft Internet Explorer browsers while users surf the web. Then it phones home to its "master" at an Internet address currently registered under the name cybersyndrome.3322.org.

The digital trail to cybersyndrome.3322.org, followed by analysts at *BusinessWeek's* request, leads to one of China's largest free domain-name-registration and email services. Called 3322.org, it is registered to a company called Bentium in the city of Changzhou, an industry hub outside Shanghai. A range of security experts say that 3322.org provides names for computers and servers that act as the command and control centers for more than 10,000 pieces of malicious code launched at government and corporate networks in recent years. Many of those PCs are in China; the rest could be anywhere.

The founder of 3322.org, a 37-year-old technology entrepreneur named Peng Yong, says his company merely allows users to register domain names. "As for what our users do, we cannot completely control it," Peng said. The bottom line: If Poison Ivy infected Jack Mulhern's computer at Booz Allen, any secrets inside could be seen in China. And if it spread to other computers, as malware often does, the infection opens windows on potentially sensitive information there, too.

Internet Globalization: Good or Bad?

In just two years, thousands of highly customized attack emails have landed in the laptops and PCs of U.S. government workers and defense contracting executives. According to sources familiar with the matter, the attacks targeted sensitive information on the networks of at least seven agencies—the Defense, State, Energy, Commerce, Health and Human Services, Agriculture, and Treasury departments—and also defense contractors Boeing, Lockheed Martin, General Electric, Raytheon, and General Dynamics.

Many security experts worry the Internet has become too unwieldy to be tamed. New exploits appear every day, each seemingly more sophisticated than the previous one. The Defense Department, whose Advanced Research Projects Agency (DARPA) developed the Internet in the 1960s, is beginning to think it created a monster. "You don't need an Army, a Navy, an Air Force to beat the U.S.," said General William T. Lord, commander of the Air Force Cyber Command, a unit formed in November 2006 to upgrade Air Force computer defenses. "You can be a peer force for the price of the PC on my desk."

Adding to Washington's anxiety, current and former U.S. government officials say many of the new attackers are trained professionals backed by foreign governments. "The new breed of threat that has evolved is nation-state-sponsored stuff," said Amit Yoran, a former director of Homeland Security's National Cyber Security Division Added one of the nation's most senior military officers: "We've got to figure out how to get at it before our regrets exceed our ability to react."[1]

INTRODUCTION

Whether they are in Berlin or Bombay, Kuala Lumpur or Kansas City, San Francisco or Seoul, organizations around the globe are developing new business models to operate competitively in a digital economy. These models are structured, yet agile; global, yet local; and they concentrate on maximizing the risk-adjusted return from both knowledge and technology assets.[2]

Globalization and working in an international global economy are integral parts of business today. Fortune 500 companies to mom-and-pop shops are now competing globally, and international developments affect all forms of business.

section 12.1 GLOBALIZATION

LEARNING OUTCOMES

12.1. Explain the cultural, political, and geoeconomic challenges facing global businesses.

12.2. Describe the four global IT business drivers that should be included in all IT strategies.

12.3. Describe governance and compliance and the associated frameworks an organization can implement.

12.4. Identify why an organization would need to understand global enterprise architectures when expanding operations abroad.

12.5. Explain the many different global information issues an organization might encounter as it conducts business abroad.

12.6. Identify global system development issues organizations should understand before building a global system.

Rocketboom

GLOBALIZATION

According to Thomas Friedman, the world is flat! Businesses are strategizing and operating on a global playing field. Traditional forms of business are simply not good enough in a global environment. Recall the way the Internet is changing business by reviewing Figure 12.1. To succeed in a global business environment, cultural, political, and geoeconomic (geographic and economic) business challenges must be confronted.

Cultural Business Challenges

Cultural business challenges include differences in languages, cultural interests, religions, customs, social attitudes, and political philosophies. Global businesses must be sensitive to such cultural differences. McDonald's, a truly global brand, has created several minority-specific websites in the United States: McEncanta for Hispanics, 365Black for African-Americans, and i-am-asian for Asians. But these minority groups are not homogenous. Consider Asians: There are East Asian, Southeast Asian, Asian Indian, and, within each of these, divisions of national, regional, and linguistic nature. No company has the budget to create a separate website for every subsegment, but to assume that all Asian Americans fit into a single room—even a virtual room—risks a serious backlash. A company should ask a few key questions when creating a global website:

- Will the site require new navigational logic to accommodate cultural preferences?
- Will content be translated? If so, into how many languages?
- Will multilingual efforts be included in the main site or will it be a separate site, perhaps with a country-specific domain?

FIGURE 12.1

Examples of How Technology
Is Changing Business

Industry	Business Changes Due to Technology
Travel	Travel site Expedia.com is now the biggest leisure-travel agency, with higher profit margins than even American Express. Thirteen percent of traditional travel agencies closed in 2002 because of their inability to compete with online travel.
Entertainment	The music industry has kept Napster and others from operating, but $35 billion annual online downloads are wrecking the traditional music business. U.S. music unit sales are down 20 percent since 2000. The next big entertainment industry to feel the effects of ebusiness will be the $67 billion movie business.
Electronics	Using the Internet to link suppliers and customers, Dell dictates industry profits. Its operating margins rose from 7.3 percent in 2002 to 8 percent in 2003, even as it took prices to levels where rivals couldn't make money.
Financial services	Nearly every public efinance company remaining makes money, with online mortgage service LendingTree growing 70 percent a year. Processing online mortgage applications is now 40 percent cheaper for customers.
Retail	Less than 5 percent of retail sales occur online, but eBay was on track in 2003 to become one of the nation's top 15 retailers, and Amazon.com will join the top 40. Wal-Mart's ebusiness strategy is forcing rivals to make heavy investments in technology.
Automobiles	The cost of producing vehicles is down because of SCM and web-based purchasing. Also, eBay has become the leading U.S. used-car dealer, and most major car sites are profitable.
Education and training	Cisco saved $133 million in 2002 by moving training sessions to the Internet, and the University of Phoenix online college classes please investors.

- Which country will the server be located in to support local user needs?
- What legal ramifications might occur by having the website targeted at a particular country, such as laws on competitive behaviors, treatment of children, or privacy?[3]

Political Business Challenges

Political business challenges include the numerous rules and regulations surrounding data transfers across national boundaries, especially personal information, tax implications, hardware and software importing and exporting, and trade agreements. The protection of personal information is a real concern for all countries. For example, evidence from a national survey about citizen satisfaction with the Canadian government online services speaks to the importance of paying attention to privacy concerns. This highly publicized survey, known as Citizens First, was administered by the Institute for Citizen-Centered Service (ICCS) and the Institute for Public Administration in Canada (IPCA). Results from the survey indicate that although other factors help promote citizen satisfaction with the Internet, such as outcome, ease of finding information, sufficient information, site navigation, and visual appeal, the key driver that directly impacts whether citizens will conduct online transactions is their concerns over information security and privacy.

For security, there are high levels of concerns over information storage, transmission, and access and identity verification. For privacy and the protection of personal information, there are even stronger concerns about consolidation of information, unauthorized access, and sharing without permission.[4]

Global Geoeconomic Business Challenges

Geoeconomic refers to the effects of geography on the economic realities of international business activities. Even with the Internet, telecommunications, and air travel, the sheer physical distances covering the globe make it difficult to operate

FIGURE 12.2

Global IT Business
Management Areas

multinational business. Flying IT specialists into remote sites is costly, communicating in real-time across the globe's 24 time zones is challenging, and finding quality telecommunication services in every country is difficult. Skilled labor supplies, cost of living, and labor costs also differ among the various countries. When developing global business strategies, all of these geoeconomic challenges must be addressed.

Understanding the cultural, political, and geoeconomic business challenges is a good start to understanding global business, but the problems facing managers run far deeper. The remainder of this section focuses on business management issues that are central to all global business. Business managers must understand four primary areas—global IT business strategies, global enterprise architectures, global information issues, and global systems development—when running multinational companies (see Figure 12.2).

GLOBAL IT BUSINESS STRATEGIES

Global IT business strategies must include detailed information on the application of information technology across the organization. IT systems depend on global business drivers such as the nature of the industry, competitive factors, and environmental forces. For example, airlines and hotels have global customers who travel extensively and expect the same service regardless of location. Organizations require global IT systems that can provide fast, convenient service to all international employees who are servicing these customers. When a high-end hotel customer checks into a hotel in Asia she expects to receive the same high-end service as when she is checking into a hotel in Chicago or London. Figure 12.3 displays the global IT business drivers that should be included in all IT strategies.

Many global IT systems, such as finance, accounting, and operations management, have been in operation for years. Most multinational companies have global financial budgeting and cash management. As global operations expand and global competition heats up, pressure increases for companies to install global ebusiness applications for customers, suppliers, and employees. Examples include portals and websites geared toward customer service and supply chain management. In the past, such systems relied almost exclusively on privately constructed or government-owned telecommunications networks. But the explosive business use of the Internet, intranets, and extranets for electronic commerce has made such applications more feasible for global companies.

Global
Customers

FIGURE 12.3

Global IT Business Drivers

- Customers who travel anywhere or companies with global operations and global IT systems help provide fast, convenient, homogeneous service.

Global Customers

- Products are the same worldwide and global IT can help manage worldwide marketing, sales, and quality control.

Global Products

Global Collaboration

Global Operations and Resources

- The knowledge and expertise of colleagues in a global company can only be accessed, shared, and organized by global IT systems.

- Common equipment, facilities, assembly processes, and people are shared by a global company and IT can track shared resources, geographic flexibility, operations, and global supply chains.

Governance and Compliance

One fast-growing key area for all global business strategies includes governance and compliance. *Governance* is a method or system of government for management or control. *Compliance* is the act of conforming, acquiescing, or yielding. A few years ago the ideas of governance and compliance were relatively obscure. Today, the concept of formal IT governance and compliance is a must for virtually every company, both domestic and global. Key drivers for governance and compliance include financial and technological regulations as well as pressure from shareholders and customers.

Organizations today are subject to many regulations governing data retention, confidential information, financial accountability, and recovery from disasters. By implementing IT governance, organizations have the internal controls they need to meet the core guidelines of many of these regulations, such as the Sarbanes-Oxley Act of 2002.

IT governance essentially places structure around how organizations align IT strategy with business strategy, ensuring that companies stay on track to achieve their strategies and goals, and implementing good ways to measure IT's performance. Governance makes sure that all stakeholders' interests are considered and that processes provide measurable results. IT governance should answer key questions including how the IT department is functioning overall, what key metrics management requires, and what return the business is getting from its IT investment. Figure 12.4 displays the five key areas of focus according to the IT Governance Institute.[5]

Organizations can follow a few different IT governance frameworks, including:

- **CoBIT:** *Information Systems Audit and Control Association (ISACA)* is a set of guidelines and supporting tools for IT governance that is accepted worldwide and generally used by auditors and companies as a way to integrate technology to implement controls and meet specific business objectives.

FIGURE 12.4

IT Governance Institute Five
Focus Areas

STRATEGIC ALIGNMENT

Linking business and IT so they work well together. True alignment can occur only when the corporate side of the business communicates effectively with IT leaders about costs, reporting, and impacts.

VALUE DELIVERY

Ensuring the IT department delivers the promised benefits for every project or investment.

RISK MANAGEMENT

Instituting a formal risk framework that puts some rigor around how IT measures, accepts, and manages risk.

RESOURCE MANAGEMENT

Managing resources more effectively and efficiently. This allows organizations to deploy employees to various projects on a demand basis.

PERFORMANCE MEASURES

Putting structure around measuring business performance, such as a balanced scorecard, which uses both qualitative and quantitative measures.

- **ITIL:** The *Information Technology Infrastructure Library (ITIL)* is a framework provided by the government of the United Kingdom and offers eight sets of management procedures: (1) service delivery, (2) service support, (3) service management, (4) Information and Communication Technology (ICT) infrastructure management, (5) software asset management, (6) business perspective, (7) security management, and (8) application management. ITIL is a good fit for organizations concerned about operations.

- **COSO:** Developed by the *Committee of Sponsoring Organizations (COSO)* is key for evaluating internal controls such as human resources, logistics, information technology, risk, legal, marketing and sales, operations, financial functions, procurement, and reporting. This is a more business-general framework that is less IT-specific.

- **CMMI:** Created by a group from government, industry, and Carnegie Mellon's Software Engineering Institute, the *Capability Maturity Model Integration method (CMMI)* is a process improvement approach that contains 22 process areas. It is divided into appraisal, evaluation, and structure. CMMI is particularly well-suited to organizations that need help with application development, life cycle issues, and improving the delivery of products throughout the life cycle.[6]

GLOBAL ENTERPRISE ARCHITECTURES

An **enterprise architecture** includes the plans for how an organization will build, deploy, use, and share its data, processes, and IT assets. An organization must manage its global enterprise architecture to support its global business operations. Management of a global enterprise architecture is not only technically complex, but also has major political and cultural implications. For example, hardware choices are difficult in some countries because of high prices, high tariffs, import restrictions, long lead times for government approvals, lack of local service or replacement parts, and lack of documentation tailored to local conditions. Software choices also present issues; for example, European data standards differ from American or Asian standards, even when purchased from the same vendor. Some software vendors also refuse to offer service and support in countries that disregard software licensing and copyright agreements.

Threats

The Internet and the World Wide Web are critical to international business. This interconnected matrix of computers, information, and networks that reaches tens of millions of users in hundreds of countries is a business environment free of traditional boundaries and limits. Linking to online global businesses offers companies unprecedented potential for expanding markets, reducing costs, and improving profit margins at a price that is typically a small percentage of the corporate communications budget. The Internet provides an interactive channel for direct communication and data exchange with customers, suppliers, distributors, manufacturers, product developers, financial backers, information providers—in fact, with all parties involved in an international organization.[7]

The Paris-based organization Reporters without Borders notes that 45 countries restrict their citizens' access to the Internet. "At its most fundamental, the struggle between Internet censorship and openness at the national level revolves around three main means: controlling the conduits, filtering the flows, and punishing the purveyors. In countries such as Burma, Libya, North Korea, Syria, and the countries of Central Asia and the Caucasus, Internet access is either banned or subject to tight limitations through government-controlled ISPs. These countries face a lose-lose struggle against the information age. By denying or limiting Internet access, they stymie a major engine of economic growth. But by easing access, they expose their citizenry to ideas potentially destabilizing to the status quo. Either way, many people will get access to the electronic information they want. In Syria, for example, people go to Lebanon for the weekend to retrieve their email," said Virgini Locussol, Reporters Without Borders desk officer for the Middle East and North Africa.[8]

Figure 12.5 displays the top 10 international telecommunication issues as reported by the IT executives at 300 Fortune 500 multinational companies. Political issues dominate the listing over technology issues, clearly emphasizing their importance in the management of global enterprise architectures.[9]

Estimating the operational expenses associated with international IT operations is another global challenge. Companies with global business operations usually establish or contract with systems integrators for additional IT facilities for their subsidiaries in other countries. These IT facilities must meet local and regional computing needs, and even help balance global computing workloads through communications satellite links. However, offshore IT facilities can pose major problems in headquarters' support, hardware and software acquisition, maintenance, and security. This is why many global companies prefer to outsource these facilities to application service providers or systems integrators such as IBM or Accenture to manage overseas operations. Managing global enterprise architectures, including Internet, intranet, extranet, and other telecommunication networks, is a key global IT challenge for the 21st century.

GLOBAL INFORMATION ISSUES

While many consumer gadgets and software applications can benefit a company—for instance, by helping employees get their jobs done more efficiently—the security implications are legion, said Ken Silva, chief security officer at VeriSign, which

FIGURE 12.5

Top 10 Telecommunication Issues

Network

- Improving the operational efficiency of networks
- Dealing with different networks
- Controlling data communication security

Regulatory Issues

- Dealing with transborder data flow restrictions
- Managing international telecommunication regulations
- Handling international politics

Technology and Country-Oriented Issues

- Managing network infrastructure across countries
- Managing international integration of technologies
- Reconciling national differences
- Dealing with international tariff structures

specializes in network security software. "When we bolt those things onto corporate networks, we open up holes in the environment." Drugmaker Pfizer found this out the hard way. An employee's spouse loaded file-sharing software onto a Pfizer laptop at home, creating a security hole that appears to have compromised the names and Social Security numbers of 17,000 current and former Pfizer employees, according to a letter Pfizer sent to state attorneys general. Pfizer's investigation showed that 15,700 of those employees actually had their data accessed and copied.[10]

With war and terrorist attacks in many people's minds, security is a hot topic. For businesses, too, security concerns are widespread. Increasingly opening up their networks and applications to customers, partners, and suppliers using an ever more diverse set of computing devices and networks, businesses can benefit from deploying the latest advances in security technologies. These benefits include fewer disruptions to organizational systems, increased productivity of employees, and greater advances in administration, authorization, and authentication techniques.

Businesses must have the appropriate levels of authentication, access control, and encryption in place to ensure (1) that only authorized individuals can gain access to the network, (2) that they have access to only those applications for which they are entitled, and (3) that information cannot be understood or altered while in transit. Figure 12.6 displays a recent survey concerning both the level of physical security integration and the current security practices used by most organizations.[11]

FIGURE 12.6

Physical Security Integration and Best Security Practices

Yes 28%

No 72%

Is the organization's physical security integrated with IT security?

Network firewalls

User passwords

Virus protection

50 60 70 80 90 100%

Best security practices used today

Security breaches not only inconvenience business users and their customers and partners, but can also cost millions of dollars in lost revenues or lost market capitalization. The business cost of inadequate security does not stop at inconvenience and loss of revenues or market valuation. It can even force a business out of existence. For example, in early 2002 British Internet service provider Cloud-Nine Communications was the victim of a distributed denial-of-service (DDoS) attack that forced the company to close operations and to eventually transfer over 2,500 customers to a rival organization. While disruptive technologies can help a company to gain competitive advantage and market share (and avoid real business disruptions), lack of security can have the opposite effect, causing profitable companies to lose market share or even their entire business within hours or days of an attack.[12]

It is now more important than ever for an organization to have well-rehearsed and frequently updated processes and procedures to insure against a variety of adverse scenarios—Internet email and denial-of-service attacks from worms and viruses, loss of communications, loss of documents, password and information theft, fire, flood, physical attacks on property, and even terrorist attacks.

Rather than fight the trend, some companies are experimenting with giving employees more choice regarding the technology they use—so long as they accept more responsibility for it. In 2005, BP began a pilot project that gives employees about $1,000 to spend on productivity-enhancing tools in addition to standard-issue equipment, according to a report from the Leading Edge Forum. But before they can participate, employees must pass a test of their computer literacy skills.[13]

The company takes other steps to give employees free rein while mitigating risk. BP cordons off its network by letting employees link to the Internet via consumer connections, from outside the firewall, in the case of its 18,000 laptops. At the same time it beefs up security on those machines. This lets employees safely experiment with software such as Amazon's on-demand computing and storage services.

Deperimeterization occurs when an organization moves employees outside its firewall, a growing movement to change the way corporations address technology security. In a business world where many employees are off-site or on the road, or where businesses increasingly must collaborate with partners and customers, some say it's not practical to rely on a hardened perimeter of firewalls. Instead, proponents of deperimeterization say companies should focus on beefing up security in end-user devices and an organization's critical information assets.[14]

Information Privacy

For many years, global data access issues have been the subject of political controversy and technology barriers in global business environments. These issues have become more prevalent with the growth of the Internet and the expansion of ebusinesses. *Transborder data flows (TDF)* occur when business data flows across international boundaries over the telecommunications networks of global information systems. Many countries view TDF as violating their national sovereignty because transborder data flows avoid customs duties and regulations for the import or export of goods and services. Others view transborder data flows as violating their laws to protect the local IT industry from competition or their labor regulations from protecting local jobs. In many cases, the data flow issues that seem particularly politically sensitive are those that affect the movement out of a country of personal data in ebusiness and human resource applications.[15]

Many countries, especially those in the European Union (EU), may view transborder data flows as a violation of their privacy legislation since, in many cases, data about individuals are being moved out of the country without stringent privacy safeguards. Figure 12.7 highlights the key provisions of a data privacy agreement between the United States and the European Union. The agreement exempts U.S. companies engaging in international ebusiness from EU data privacy sanctions if they join a self-regulatory program that provides EU consumers with basic information about, and control over, how their personal data are used. Thus, the agreement is said to provide a "safe harbor" for such companies from the requirements of

FIGURE 12.7

U.S.–EU Data Privacy
Requirements

the EU's Data Privacy Directive, which bans the transfer of personal information on EU citizens to countries that do not have adequate data privacy protection.[16]

Information privacy concerns the legal right or general expectation of individuals, groups, or institutions to determine for themselves when and to what extent information about them is communicated to others. In essence, information privacy is about how personal information is collected and shared. To facilitate information privacy, many countries have established legislation to protect the collection and sharing of personal information. However, this legislation varies greatly around the globe.

Europe

On one end of the spectrum lies European nations with their strong information privacy laws. Most notably, all member countries of the European Union adhere to a directive on the protection of personal data. A directive is a legislative act of the European Union that requires member states to achieve a particular result without dictating the means of how to achieve that result.

The directive on the protection of personal data grants European Union members the following rights:

- The right to know the source of personal data processing and the purposes of such processing.
- The right to access and/or rectify inaccuracies in one's own personal data.
- The right to disallow the use of personal data.

These rights are based on key principles pertaining to the collection or storage of personal data. The directive defines personal data to cover both facts and opinions about an individual. Any organization processing personal data of a person living in the European Union must comply with these key principles as outlined in the directive; these state that the data must be:

- Fairly and lawfully processed.
- Processed for limited purposes.
- Adequate, relevant, and not excessive.
- Accurate.

- Not kept longer than necessary.
- Processed in accordance with the data subject's rights.
- Not transferred to countries without adequate protection.

This last right restricts the flow of personal information outside the European Union by permitting its transfer to only countries that provide an "adequate" level of privacy protection—adequate in the sense that these other countries have to offer a level of privacy protection equivalent to that of the European Union. When first implemented, this part of the directive caused some concerns since countries outside the EU had much weaker privacy protection laws. Organizations in the United States were greatly concerned because they were at a legal risk if the personal data of EU citizens were transferred to computer servers in the United States—a likely scenario in today's global world of ebusiness. This led to extensive negotiations. The result was the establishment of a "safe harbor" program in the United States. This program provides a framework for U.S. organizations to show evidence of compliance with the EU directive. In this way, American companies can self-declare their compliance with the key principles of the directive and do business with EU nations without worrying about EU citizens suing them.

The United States

On the other end of the spectrum lies the United States. Information privacy is not highly legislated nor regulated. There is no all-encompassing law that regulates the use of personal data or information. In many cases, access to public information is considered culturally acceptable, such as obtaining credit reports for employment or housing purposes. The reason for this may be historical. In the United States, the first amendment protects free speech, and in many instances the protection of privacy might conflict with this amendment.

There are some exceptions. Though very few states recognize an individual's right to privacy, California's constitution protects an inalienable right to privacy. The California legislature has enacted several pieces of legislation aimed at protecting citizen information privacy. For example, California's Online Privacy Protection Act, established in 2003, requires commercial websites or online services that collect personal information of California residents to clearly post a privacy policy on the website or online service and to comply with this policy. Other nationwide exceptions include the Children's Online Privacy Protection Act (COPPA) and the Health Insurance Portability and Accountability Act (HIPAA).[17]

COPPA is a federal law established in 1998 that applies to the collection of personal information from American children who are under 13 years of age. The act outlines what a website should include in its privacy policy, how to seek consent from a parent or guardian, and the responsibilities a website operator has to protect children's online safety and privacy. This law applies to any website that is perceived to be targeting American children. For example, if a toy company established in Canada wanted to sell toys in the United States, the company's website should have to comply with the collection and use of information as outlined in COPPA. To show compliance requires a substantial amount of paperwork. As a result, many websites disallow underage users to join online communities and websites. Not complying with COPPA can be costly. In September 2006, the website Xanga, an online community, was fined $1 million for violating COPPA legislation.

HIPAA was enacted by the U.S. Congress in 1996. Provisions in HIPPA establish national standards for the electronic data interchange of health care-related transactions between health care providers, insurance plans, and employers. Embedded in these standards are rules for the handling and protection of personal health care information.

Canada

Canada's privacy laws follow very closely to the European model. Canada as a nation is quite concerned about protecting the personal information of its citizens. Its primary privacy law is the Personal Information Protection and Electronic Document

Act (PIPEDA). The purpose of PIPEDA is to provide Canadians with a right of privacy with respect to how their personal information is collected, used, or disclosed by an organization. This is most important today, especially in the private sector, when information technology increasingly facilitates the collection and free flow of information.

Its precursor was the Privacy Act established in 1983 that restricted the handling of personal information within federal government departments and agencies only. This information concerned such things as pension and employment insurance files, medical records, tax records, and military records.

PIPEDA took effect in January 2001 and, like the Privacy Act, applied only to federally regulated organizations. By January 2004, PIPEDA's reach extended beyond government borders and applied to all other types of organizations, including commercial businesses. By doing so, Canada's PIPEDA law brought Canada into compliance with the European Union's directive on the protection of personal data. Hence, since January 2004, Canada no longer needed to implement safe harbor provisions for organizations wishing to collect and store personal information on European Union citizens.

GLOBAL SYSTEMS DEVELOPMENT

It is extremely difficult to develop a domestic information system, but the added complexity of developing a global information system quadruples the effort. Global information systems must support a diverse base of customers, users, products, languages, currencies, laws, and so on. Developing efficient, effective, and responsive information systems for multiple countries, differing cultures, and global ebusinesses is an enormous challenge for any organization. Managers should expect conflicts over local versus global system requirements and difficulties agreeing on common system features. For the project to succeed, the development environment should promote involvement and ownership by all local system users.

One of the most important global information systems development issues is the global standardization of data definitions. Common data definitions are necessary for sharing information among the parts of an international business. Difference in language, culture, and technology platforms can make global data standardization quite difficult. For example, what Americans call a "sale" may be called "an order booked" in the United Kingdom, an "order scheduled" in Germany, and an "order produced" in France. These are all referring to the exact same business event, but could cause problems if global employees have different versions of the data definition. Businesses are moving ahead to standardize data definitions and business processes. Many organizations are implementing corporate wikis where all global employees can post and maintain common business definitions.

Organizations can use several strategies to solve some of the problems that arise in global information systems development. First is transforming and customizing an information system used by the home office into a global application. This ensures the system uses the established business processes and supports the primary needs of the end users. Second, is setting up a multinational development team with key people from several subsidiaries to ensure that the system design meets the needs of all local sites as well as corporate headquarters. Third, an organization could use centers of excellence where an entire system might be assigned for development to a particular subsidiary based on its expertise in the business or technical dimensions needed for successful development. A final approach that has rapidly become a major development option is to outsource the development work to global or offshore development countries that have the required skills and experience to build global information systems. All of these approaches require development team collaboration and managerial oversight to meet the global needs of the business.

Integrating Global Systems

Information technology has penetrated the heart of organizations and will stay there in the future. The IT industry is one of the most dynamic in the global economy. As an

FIGURE 12.8

The Integration of Business and Technology

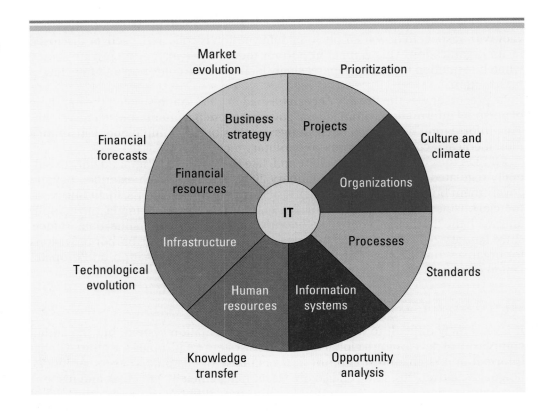

industry, it not only creates millions of high-level jobs, but also helps organizations to be more efficient and effective, which in turn stimulates innovation. The integration of business and technology has allowed organizations to increase their share of the global economy, transform the way they conduct business, and become more efficient and effective (see Figure 12.8).

The past few years have produced a confluence of events that has reshaped the global economy. Around the world, free-market competition has flourished and a new globally interdependent financial system has emerged. Reflecting these changes, core business relationships and models are dramatically changing, including shifts from:

- Product-centricity to customer-centricity.
- Mass production to mass customization.
- The value in material things to the value of knowledge and intelligence.

In concert with these trends, a new series of business success factors and challenges has emerged that is helping to determine marketplace winners and losers:

- Organization agility, often supported by a "plug and play" IT infrastructure (with a flexible and adaptable applications architecture).
- A focus on core competencies and processes.
- A redefinition of the value chain.
- Instantaneous business response.
- The ability to scale resources and infrastructure across geographic boundaries.

These developments add up to an environment that is vastly more complex than even five years ago. This in turn has resulted in organizations increasingly embracing new business models. The new environment requires organizations to focus externally on their business processes and integration architectures. The virtually integrated business model will cause a sharp increase in the number of business partners and the closeness of integration between them.

Never before have IT investments played such a critical role in business success. As business strategies continue to evolve, the distinction between "the business" and IT will virtually disappear.

section 12.2 21ST CENTURY ORGANIZATIONAL TRENDS

LEARNING OUTCOMES

12.7. Explain the six best practices of innovation.

12.8. Identify how energy consumption and recycling IT equipment can lead to greener IT.

12.9. Describe the three ways organizations can use social networking.

12.10. Explain virtual worlds and virtual workforces and their impact on business.

21ST CENTURY ORGANIZATION TRENDS

Many people have no idea how they would get any work done on business trips if they did not have a laptop. They simply cannot remember how they lived without their BlackBerry. Their cell phones might as well be surgically attached to their ear, it is so crucial to their job. It is hard to conceive of getting through the day without Google, or, if the person is under 40, text messaging or Facebook to stay in touch with an extended network of colleagues. In just a decade or less, technology has done a number on the way we work.

And in the next decade, the relentless march of computer power and Internet connection speeds will bring more profound changes to work than anything seen so far. Consider just a few of the breakthroughs technology visionaries think will occur in coming years. Picture Apple's slick iPhone shrunk to the size of a credit card. Then imagine it can connect not only to contacts on the latest social network, but also to billions of pea-sized wireless sensors attached to buildings, streets, retail products, and clothes—all simultaneously sending data over the Internet. This will allow tracking and managing more than static information; users will be able to track events in the physical world, from production on a factory floor to colleagues' whereabouts to how customers are using products. All that information will be much easier to view and analyze, using hand and arm gestures to control commands and viewing results with special glasses that make it seem as if the user is gazing at a life-size screen. Just imagine producing detailed prototypes of product or design ideas via a 3D printer that creates plastic models from computerized specs as easily as a paper printer spews out reports today.[18]

Organizations are facing technological changes and challenges more extensive and far reaching in their implications than anything since the modern industrial

Online Job Search Industry

revolution occurred in the early 1900s. Organizations that want to survive in the 21st century must recognize these technological changes and challenges, carry out required organizational changes in the face of it, and learn to operate in an entirely different way. Today's organizations focus on defending and safeguarding their existing market positions in addition to targeting new market growth. The primary changes and challenges organizations are focusing on in the 21st century include:

- Innovation: finding new.
- Social entrepreneurship: going green.
- Social networks: who's who.
- Virtual worlds: it's a whole new world.

INNOVATION: FINDING NEW

In the past, a company primarily focused on operational excellence, now innovation is driving the wheels of IT. **Innovation** is the introduction of new equipment or methods. The current impetus to innovate comes from the need to cut costs, while still creating a competitive advantage. Fundamental shifts in technology will make it possible for businesses to realize IT's promise of technology-enabled innovation, responsiveness, and speed.

Surfers from around the world converged on Maverick's at Pillar Point, just a few miles from San Francisco, to challenge each other on the big waves that have made this a legendary surfing destination. The sixth Mavericks Surf Contest had been announced only 48 hours earlier to ensure optimal wave conditions for the contestants. Surfers from as far away as Australia, Brazil, and South Africa scrambled to make their way to this invitation-only competition. It was magical to watch these athletes challenge 20-foot waves with an ease and grace that made it all seem so natural.

Beneath the surface, though, is a different story, one that contains important lessons for business executives. While all attention was on the athletes riding their surfboards, the technology and techniques used to master big-wave surfing have evolved over decades, driven by dedicated, perhaps even obsessed, groups of athletes and craftsmen. Executives can gain significant insight into the innovation process by looking at this sport and following the six best practices of innovation (see Figure 12.9).[19]

FIGURE 12.9

Six Best Practices of Innovation

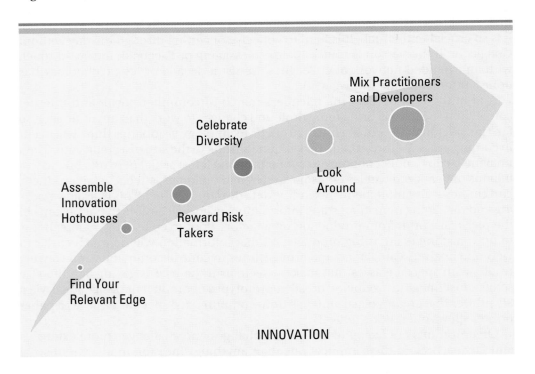

Find Your Relevant Edge

First, to push performance levels, organizations must find the relevant edge. In the case of big-wave surfers, there has been an ever-expanding search for the breaks that would produce bigger and rougher waves to test new board designs and surfing practices.

Following the lead of surfers, business executives need to find relevant edges that will test and push their current performance. For example, companies making diesel engines and power generators should be actively engaged in finding ways to more effectively serve lower-income customers in remote rural areas of emerging economies. These demanding customers could prompt significant innovation in both product design and distribution processes in an effort to deliver greater value at lower cost. The innovations resulting from these efforts on the edge could lead to significant improvements in product lines.

Assemble Innovation Hothouses

Second, attract motivated groups of people to these edges to work together around challenging performance issues. In the late 1950s, Waimea Bay, on the north shore of Oahu, became the test bed for athletes seeking to push the boundaries of big-wave surfing. In the isolation of the north shore, dedicated surfers spent 8 to 10 hours each day, every day, challenging themselves and each other on the big waves. The real advances in surfing technology and practices occurred at the breaks where surfers gathered and formed deep relationships over extended periods. They learned rapidly from each other and pushed each other to go to the next level.

Large companies have become very adept at establishing remote outposts in places like Beijing, Hyderabad, Haifa, and St. Petersburg to attract local talent and push forward challenging research and development projects. Often, though, these outposts either become disconnected from their parent companies or fail to establish deep links with other leading-edge participants in the area. The key challenge is to connect these company-owned facilities more effectively with their local environments as well as with each other through challenging and sustained innovation initiatives that build long-term, trust-based relationships. Performance improvement generally comes first in the form of tacit knowledge that is difficult to express and communicate more broadly. People have to be there to gain access to this tacit knowledge.

Reward Risk Takers

Third, recognize that the people who are likely to be attracted to the edge are big risk takers. This is a key reason the edge becomes such a fertile ground for innovation. It attracts people who are not afraid to take risks and to learn from their experiences. They relentlessly seek new challenges. Executives need to be thoughtful about how to attract these people, provide them with environments to support risk taking, and reward them for both successes and failures.

Celebrate Diversity

Fourth, recognize that the edge fosters not just risk taking, but very different cultures that are also edgy. The advances in big-wave surfing did not come from the casual surfers but from those who developed an entire lifestyle and culture, fostered by intense and even obsessive concentration on pushing the envelope. Executives need to find ways to protect and honor these edgy cultures, whether they are inhabited by tattooed web designers or the next generation of employees who learned how to innovate as members of guilds in World of Warcraft.

Look Around

Fifth, find ways to appropriate insights from adjacent disciplines and even more remote areas of activity. Early advances in surfing technology came from the aerospace industry because some of the employees in this industry were also avid surfers. Some of surfer Laird Hamilton's greatest insights came from his experiences as an expert windsurfer and his colleagues' experiences with snowboarding. By attracting diverse backgrounds and experiences to the edge, executives can foster creative breakthroughs.

Mix Practitioners and Developers

Sixth, bring users and developers of technology close together. It is no accident that the most innovative surfers also tended to be expert shapers of surfboards. These folks not only designed surfboards but also shaped the materials into the finished product and then took them out to life-threatening breaks to test and refine them. They were relentless tinkerers, integrating experience, intuition, and craft to come up with creative new boards. Technology and practice are intimately linked. Very little performance improvement comes directly out of the technology itself. It is only when seasoned practitioners engage with the technology, especially in close-knit communities, and evolve their practices to better use it, that the real performance breakthroughs occur.

SOCIAL ENTREPRENEURSHIP: GOING GREEN

Social responsibility implies that an entity whether it is a government, corporation, organization, or individual has a responsibility to society. *Corporate policy* is a dimension of social responsibility that refers to the position a firm takes on social and political issues. *Corporate responsibility* is a dimension of social responsibility that includes everything from hiring minority workers to making safe products. *Sustainable, or "green," IT* describes the manufacture, management, use, and disposal of information technology in a way that minimizes damage to the environment, which is a critical part of a corporation's responsibility. As a result, the term has many different meanings, depending on whether you are a manufacturer, manager, or user of technology. This section covers energy consumption, recycling IT equipment, and greener IT.

Energy Consumption

As a threat to operations and the bottom line, corporate computing's fast-growing power consumption is forcing companies to adopt green energy practices. Engineers at Hewlett-Packard made a startling realization about the servers running the company's computing systems. Surging power consumption, along with rising energy costs, will soon make it more expensive to keep a server going for a year than to acquire one in the first place. Left unchecked, costs like these interfere with HP's goal of cutting energy consumption 15 percent by 2010.[20]

When HP began constructing a new 50,000-square-foot building to house high-powered computers, it sought advice from Pacific Gas & Electric. By following the California power company's recommendations, HP will save $1 million a year in power costs for that data center alone, PG&E says.

Like HP, companies across the globe are adding equipment to keep up with surging computing needs—and then are forced to make substantial changes to curtail the leap in costs associated with running the big buildings, or data centers, housing all that gear. "Data centers use 50 times the energy per square foot than an office [does]," said Mark Bramfitt, principal program manager at PG&E. Figure 12.10 displays the breakdown of power usage in the typical data center.[21]

Industry experts say the power consumption of data centers is doubling every five years or so, making them one of the fastest-growing drags on energy in the United States. Figure 12.11 displays data center energy bills.[22]

With demand for computer power exploding, energy consumption by data centers doubled between 2000 and 2006, and could double again by 2011. So the pressure is on tech companies, utilities, and builders to come up with new ways of cutting energy consumption. Here are some of the ways they are responding.

Sun Microsystems: Throughput Computing   A decade ago, the chip industry had a single focus: making the digital brains of computers process data ever

FIGURE 12.10

Breakdown of Power Usage
in the Typical Data Center

faster. But Sun Microsystems chip architect Marc Tremblay saw a fatal flaw in that strategy. Faster chips would run hotter, and eventually they would burn out. So he designed what's known as a multicore chip, which has several processors on a single sliver of silicon, each of them running cooler and sucking less energy but collectively getting more work done. He also enabled each processor to perform more than one task at a time. The processors on Sun's Niagara server computers, based on Tremblay's designs, consumed just 70 watts of power, about one-third of a conventional microprocessor.[23]

Virtualization   It used to be possible to run only one application at a time on a given server. That meant if the application was not needed at any given time, the server just was not being used. Analysts estimate only 10 to 20 percent of the capability of a typical server is used. *Virtualization* is a framework of dividing the resources of a computer into multiple execution environments. Virtualization software allows

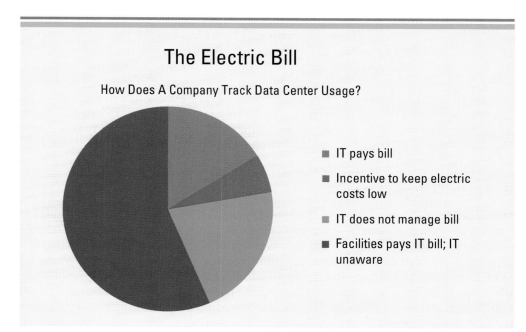

FIGURE 12.11

The Energy Bill

IT managers to easily load multiple programs on a single machine and move programs from one computer to another on the fly to make maximum use of a cluster of servers. This significantly reduces energy use because fewer servers are needed. Virtualization software has been used for decades on mainframe computers, but it only became popular on PC servers recently.[24]

Energy Rebate Programs   Pacific Gas & Electric's Mark Bramfitt saw virtualization as a great way to reduce energy use in Northern California's data centers, so he designed an innovative data center energy-saving program. Companies get rebates for reducing the number of servers they use in their data centers. In just one year, Bramfitt received more than 47 applications from data center operators and paid out four rebates. He is also urging other utilities to adopt similar programs. So far, three others have followed suit.[25]

Smart Cooling   Hewlett-Packard Research Fellow Chandrakant Patel came up with a new approach to data center energy use: Think of the data center as one giant machine. Out of that came HP's Dynamic Smart Cooling technology. Thousands of heat sensors monitor temperatures, and software directs the air-conditioning system to put the big chill on the places that need it most. Projected energy savings: 20 to 45 percent.[26]

Alternative Energy Sources   Web search giant Google, which operates some of the largest data centers in the world, has committed to using cutting-edge technologies to power and cool its data centers, including wind and solar power. It's already using wind to power a data center in the Netherlands, and there's speculation it may tap wind for a major new facility in Council Bluffs, Iowa.[27]

Energy

Biology Meets Chips   IBM researcher Bruno Michel and his team at IBM Zurich Research Laboratory are applying biological principles to deal with the heat problem in computing. Just as the human vascular system cools our bodies, Michel is designing devices that cool chips using liquid delivered through capillary-like circulation systems. Typically, the processors in server computers are air-cooled; chilled air is blown over metal caps on top of the chips, where tiny fins dissipate heat. One of Michel's inventions is a metal cap that fits over a processor and sprays jets of water out of 50,000 nozzles into microscopic channels etched in the metal. The channels behave like capillaries, circulating the liquid efficiently and cutting the energy required to pump the water.[28]

Government Involvement   The European Union has imposed limits on carbon emissions. Since 2005, the Emission Trading Scheme has required 12,000 iron, steel, glass, and power plants to buy CO_2 permits, which allows them to emit the gas into the atmosphere. If a company exceeds its limit, it can buy unused permits from other companies that have successfully cut their emissions. If they are unable to buy spare permits, however, they are fined for every excess ton of CO_2. Because IT contributes to the total carbon emissions in a company, carbon cap and trade or tax laws will impact how technology is managed. The EU and many U.S. states also have laws that require computer equipment, which contains many toxic substances, be recycled.[29]

Recycle IT Equipment

Sustainable IT disposal refers to the safe disposal of IT assets at the end of their life cycle. It ensures that *ewaste,* or old computer equipment, does not end up in a landfill, where the toxic substances it contains can leach into groundwater, among other problems. Many of the major hardware manufacturers offer take-back programs, so IT departments do not have to take responsibility for disposal. Some U.S. states and the European Union have laws requiring that ewaste be recycled. For example, Dell and Sony will take back any of their products for free and Toshiba will take back its laptops. Apple charges a fee, but will waive it if you are purchasing a new product.

HP also will charge you, but will give you a credit toward future HP purchases. For a complete list of recycling programs in the United States, visit the Computer Take-Back Campaign website (www.computertakeback.com). According to the Computer TakeBack Campaign, Maine, California, Texas, Oregon, Maryland, Washington, and Minnesota have ewaste laws. Some of these laws apply only to equipment manufacturers; others apply to end users. In 2007, ewaste bills were introduced in 23 states. Companies that mind their energy consumption and dispose of used equipment responsibly now will be better off when regulations are imposed.

Complying with ewaste regulations should become easier for IT managers due to new manufacturing regulations. The EU Directive on the Restriction of the Use of Certain Hazardous Substances in Electrical and Electronic Equipment, which took effect July 1, 2006, restricts the use of six hazardous materials in the manufacture of certain electronics: lead, mercury, cadmium, hexavalent chromium, polybrominated biphenyls, and polybrominated diphenyl ether (the last two are flame retardants used in plastics). Such requirements reduce the toxicity of electronics, and thus, the ewaste they produce.[30]

In 2006, obsolete desktops, laptops, and servers accounted for 18 billion pounds of electronic trash worldwide, but the major companies involved in ewaste recovery (Dell, HP, and IBM) recovered only 356 million pounds—about 2 percent.

Only about one-third of all U.S. companies have an IT asset disposal policy. The rest are either doing nothing or dumping them into municipal landfills. According to National Geographic's *The Green Guide,* 50 to 80 percent of recycled electronics end up in developing nations, where they are disassembled by untrained workers without the proper equipment. This exposes them to toxic substances such as mercury, cadmium, and lead. If the equipment is left in landfills, those same toxins end up in water sources.

Greener IT

At Sun Microsystems, OpenWork, the company's telecommuting program, provides employees with shared office space, home equipment, and subsidies for DSL and electricity, according to Dave Douglas, vice president of eco responsibility at Sun. More than 56 percent of Sun's employees are currently in the program. "In the last five years we have cut our office space by one-sixth and have saved over $60 million a year on space and power," Douglas said. Sun also saves an estimated 29,000 tons of CO_2 per year due to reduced employee commuting. That is equivalent to taking 5,694 cars off the road for one year, according to the EPA's carbon calculator.[31]

Dow Chemical's process control automation system will shut a plant down if it is not compliant with air and water emissions requirements. Dow also uses a monitoring system to measure the air and water emissions at its plants and is deploying an environmental reporting system to manage reporting of this data to state and federal authorities, said CIO and Chief Sustainability Officer David Kepler.

IT systems can also help save energy by controlling heat and air-conditioning in office buildings. Wireless sensors can be used to measure airflow and room occupancy. If the occupancy sensors (which turn lights on and off when people enter or leave a room) are networked to airflow sensors, the amount of air-conditioning used when people are not in a room can be reduced, said David Kepler. "The basic idea is to collect data on how the facility is using energy and use that information to define patterns that can help change what you are doing and reduce operating costs."

To keep up with its explosive growth, Google is building data centers off the beaten path, in places like Lenoir, North Carolina; Mount Holly, South Carolina, and Council Bluffs, Iowa. A 30-acre facility in The Dalles, Oregon, is the most recent of them to be completed and put into operations. The Dalles, a town of about 12,000, provided the perfect location for Google, with its hydroelectric dam, affordable land, and a 15-year tax incentive. An industrial-strength power grid connects the dam to Google's complex, where massive cooling systems rise above two data center buildings. Google spends approximately $600 million to build a major data center, requiring a staff of 100 to 200 operate. Figure 12.12 displays the current ways companies are choosing to go green.[32]

FIGURE 12.12

Ways To Go Green

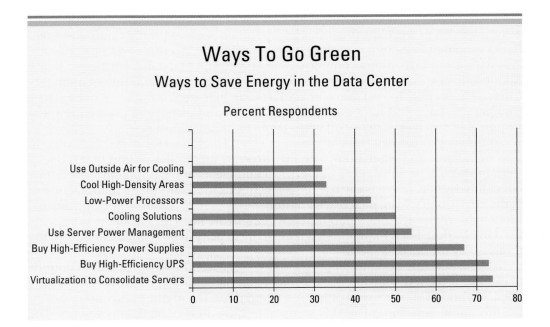

SOCIAL NETWORKS: WHO'S WHO

Encover Chief Executive Officer Chip Overstreet was on the hunt for a new vice president for sales. He had homed in on a promising candidate and dispensed with the glowing but unsurprising remarks from references. Now it was time to dig for any dirt. So he logged on to LinkedIn, an online business network. "I did 11 back-door checks on this guy and found people he had worked with at five of his last six companies," said Overstreet, whose firm sells and manages service contracts for manufacturers. "It was incredibly powerful."

So powerful, in fact, that more than a dozen sites like LinkedIn have cropped up in recent years. They are responding to a growing impulse among web users to build ties, communities, and networks online, fueling the popularity of sites such as News Corp.'s MySpace. As of April, the 10 biggest social-networking sites, including MySpace, reached a combined unique audience of 68.8 million users, drawing in 45 percent of active web users, according to Nielsen/NetRatings.[33]

Corporations and smaller businesses have not embraced online business networks with nearly the same abandon as teens and college students who have flocked to social sites. Yet companies are steadily overcoming reservations and using the sites and related technology to craft potentially powerful business tools. Figure 12.13 displays the three types of social networking an organization can implement: passive search, boomerangs, and marketing networks.

Passive Search

Recruiters at Microsoft and Starbucks, for instance, troll online networks such as LinkedIn for potential job candidates. Goldman Sachs and Deloitte run their own online alumni networks for hiring back former workers and strengthening bonds with alumni-cum-possible clients. Boston Consulting Group and law firm Duane Morris deploy enterprise software that tracks employee communications to uncover useful connections in other companies. And companies such as Intuit and Mini USA have created customer networks to build brand loyalty.

Many companies are leery of online networks. Executives do not have time to field the possible influx of requests from acquaintances on business networks. Employees may be dismayed to learn their workplace uses email monitoring software to help sales associates' target pitches. Companies considering building online communities for advertising, branding, or marketing will need to cede some degree of control over content.

FIGURE 12.13

Organizational Social
Networking

Passive Search

Boomerangs

Marketing
Networks

None of those concerns are holding back Carmen Hudson, manager of enterprise staffing at Starbucks, who said she swears by LinkedIn. "It's one of the best things for finding mid-level executives," she said.

The holy grail in recruiting is finding so-called passive candidates, people who are happy and productive working for other companies. LinkedIn, with its 6.7 million members, is a virtual Rolodex of these types. Hudson says she has hired three or four people this year as a result of connections through LinkedIn. "We've started asking our hiring managers to sign up on LinkedIn and help introduce us to their contacts," she says. "People have concerns about privacy, but once we explain how we use it and how careful we would be with their contacts, they're usually willing to do it."

Boomerangs

Headhunters and human resources departments are taking note. "LinkedIn is a tremendous tool for recruiters," said Bill Vick, the author of *LinkedIn for Recruiting*. So are sites such as Ryze, Spoke, OpenBc, and Ecademy. Many companies are turning to social networks and related technology to stay in touch with former employees. Consulting firm Deloitte strives to maintain ties with ex-workers and has had a formal alumni-relations program for years. It bolstered those efforts earlier this year, tapping business networking services provider SelectMinds to launch an online alumni network.

Ex-Deloitte employees can go to the site to browse 900 postings for jobs at a range of companies. They can also peruse open positions at Deloitte. The online network is an extension of an offline program that includes networking receptions and seminars.

Deloitte makes no bones about its aim to use the network to lure back some former employees, or so-called boomerangs. "Last year, 20 percent of our experienced hires were boomerangs," said Karen Palvisak, a national leader of alumni relations for Deloitte.

Boomerangs cost less to train than new hires and they tend to hit the ground running. As the labor market tightens, alumni become an increasingly attractive source of talent. Last year, 13 percent of employees who had previously been laid off were rehired by their former employers, according to a survey by Right Management Consultants of more than 14,000 displaced employees at 4,900 organizations.

Marketing Networks

Business-oriented networks help executives find employees, and they're increasingly useful in other areas, such as sales and marketing. When Campbell Soup Co. asked independent location booker Marilyn Jenett to select a castle in Europe for a promotion, she put a note on business networking site Ryze, offering a finder's fee to anyone who could suggest the right place.

Jenett got seven responses, including one pointing her to Eastnor Castle. She was so pleased with the location that she booked it again for another event. Jenett said Ryze also helped her develop another small business, a personal mentoring program called Feel Free to Prosper.

Social networks also help forge community with, and among, would-be customers. A group of Mini Cooper owners joined the company for its two-week cross-country car rally. Participants took part in company-sponsored events, such as the official wrap party overlooking the Hudson River and the Manhattan skyline in New Jersey.

But they also planned their own side events along the way with the help of the community forums on the Mini Owner's Lounge site, sponsored by Mini USA. Each month, about 1,500 to 2,000 new owners become active in the community. "Our very best salespeople are Mini owners, and they like to talk about their cars," said Martha Crowley, director of consulting for Beam Interactive, which provides various Internet marketing services for Mini USA.[34]

VIRTUAL WORLDS: IT'S A WHOLE NEW WORLD

Virtual is the theme of web 2.0. Two primary types of virtual must be considered when looking at the 21st century world. This includes virtual worlds and virtual workforces (see Figure 12.14).

Virtual Worlds

In the midst of the sprawling online virtual world Second Life, a new edifice recently surfaced, the digitized headquarters of *Wired* magazine on a one-acre lot. Garish neon-pink sliding doors lead to a conference room shaped like a Shuttle PC where as many as 50 people can sit on chairs that resemble circuit breakers and watch a screen that looks like a graphics card. *Wired,* meanwhile, unveiled its building in Second Life to kick off a package of stories on the game published Oct. 17. The company expects to use its new virtual building to let writers chat with one another and to host three or four virtual Q&A events a month with real-world as well as Second Life notables, says Chris Baker, senior associate editor at *Wired* magazine. "It's kind of a toe in the water for us," he said, adding that *Wired* is also actively looking to set up in other virtual worlds as well. "We are still not sure how to make use of this space; this is the test case."

Wired's virtual headquarters are right next to the offices of CNET Networks, which recently unveiled its own five-story office in Second Life. The building is an exact replica of the company's glass-and-brick headquarters in San Francisco, and it is set amid vast lawns overlooking Second Life's blue ocean.

Big media's land grab is well under way in Second Life, the online realm where real people, under the guise of avatars, mill and mingle and, in some cases, make a living. The game's audience, swiftly approaching 1 million, is growing at about 38 percent month over month, according to its creator,

FIGURE 12.14

It's a Whole New World

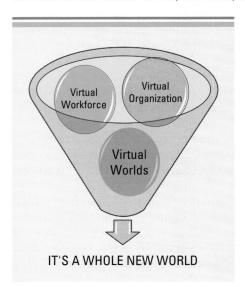

IT'S A WHOLE NEW WORLD

Linden Lab. The outfit added 200,000 to 250,000 new players—many of them the coveted younger early adopters—in one month alone. "Second Life is almost a phenomenon like YouTube, it's reached critical mass," said Baker.

Like so many other companies already setting up shop in Second Life, news organizations and other media outlets do not want to be left behind. As the virtual world grows up, it will get more attractive to companies that want to send a multimedia message. "Everyone's been searching for the killer broadband offering, and this is it," said Justin Bovington, CEO of Rivers Run Red, which helps companies like BBC Radio One create events and design buildings inside Second Life.

Companies as varied as Adidas, Sun Microsystems, and Toyota want to promote their products and ensure their brands are getting exposure amid the consumers, many of them young, who are spending increasingly long stretches not just on the Internet, but also immersed in virtual worlds. In-game advertising revenue in the United States was expected to rise from $186 million in 2005 to $875 million in 2009, according to Yankee Group.[35]

Media companies even face competition from virtual upstarts inside Second Life, including "New World Notes" and "SL Herald." Reuters commissioned its long-time tech reporter, Adam Pasick, to cover Second Life full-time and act as Reuters' Second Life bureau chief. Pasick's avatar sports a green shirt, a grim businesslike expression, and a press badge. One of his first stories reported on a U.S. congressional committee's investigation of online virtual economies like Second Life and Vivendi Universal's World of Warcraft and how virtual assets and income received in the games should be taxed.

Another Reuters story is an interview with the virtual president of Second Life's most popular bank, Ginko Financial. The Reuters site also offers a variety of market information, such as the exchange rate between the Linden dollar, a currency used in Second Life, and the U.S. dollar. Another table tracks the number of U.S. dollars ($404,063, at recent count) spent by players on Second Life in the past 24 hours. "Second Life is a really hot economy," said Pasick, who, in the game, goes under the name of Adam Reuters. "It was a natural for Reuters." "Second Life offers numerous features and options for businesses, and is a canvas that allows companies to do what they want to do in Second Life," said David Fleck, Linden's vice president of marketing. The following are a few examples of how businesses are using Second Life to compete in the global economy.[36]

CyberWorlds

Sun Microsystems   Sun Microsystems held a Second Life press conference with John Gage, chief scientist at Sun. The company created an area called Sun Pavilion, where a video blog of all of Sun's activities will be streamed. There were 60 avatars at the press conference—in Second Life terms, that's a full house.[37]

Warner Bros. Records   Warner Bros. promoted singer Regina Spektor's fourth album, *Begin to Hope,* by building a chic Manhattan loft within Second Life. As Spektor's music played, the loft's lighting and décor changed to roughly illustrate the song lyrics—a new marketing experience that was part video game, part music video.[38]

American Apparel   American Apparel launched a virtual store in Second Life in July 2006. The hip T-shirt maker is debuting styles before they are launched in the physical world and is offering cross-promotions. Visitors to the virtual store receive 15 percent off real-world purchases.[39]

Lego   Lego regularly visits university and corporate campuses to host events where new types of robots are built using Lego's popular Mindstorm Robotics Inventions kits. Recently, Lego hosted one such Big Robot on Campus gathering in Second Life, drawing robot makers from different locales to meet in cyberspace.[40]

Adidas   Adidas is working on selling virtual gym shoes in Second Life. The company hopes to test-market styles before rolling them out in the real world, tracking which color combos or designs prove popular among Second Lifers.[41]

Toyota Toyota's marketing plan for its hip, boxy Scion includes an art gallery in Los Angeles (Scion Space) and sponsored screenings of indie films (the Scion Independent Film Series). Now the pop-culture-aware carmaker is also a presence in Second Life, where it offers a virtual version of the Scion xB.[42]

Dartmouth College Educational institutions such as Dartmouth College are increasingly becoming a presence in the virtual world. In a Second Life version of Hanover, New Hampshire, where Dartmouth is located, the school's Institute for Security Technology Studies conducts emergency-response exercises in the virtual space.[43]

Major League Baseball Major League Baseball held a simulcast of its home-run derby within Second Life, with video streams of the event shown on screens within a digitized baseball stadium. Branching into Second Life made sense to MLB execs; MLB.com has a robust online community in its chat rooms.[44]

Virtual Hospital Palomar Pomerado Health opened a new state-of-the-art hospital—in Second Life. The opening of the virtual hospital followed the December 2007 groundbreaking for the health care provider's real-world $773 million, 600-bed Palomar Medical Center west in Escondido, California. With completion of the first phase of the hospital still three years away, PPH created the facility and all of its technology in the Second Life virtual world to show its 900,000 clients in Southern California what is to come. The Second Life hospital shows off operating rooms equipped with robotics technology and functional imaging systems that support medical procedures such as cardiovascular surgery. Using Second Life to receive user feedback is a cost-effective method—much better than just herding people into a room for a focus group.[45]

Virtual Workforce

Sunday morning and Tuesday afternoon are becoming completely the same, said KLM Chief Information Officer Boet Kreiken. At the same time, employees throughout organizations are becoming much more comfortable with a range of technologies.

In years past, employees might have had only a PC at home. Today they may juggle a network linking several PCs, printers, and backup devices connected to a high-speed Internet connection—in addition to a set-top box, gaming console, high-definition TV, and all manner of other web-based services such as YouTube and News Corp.'s MySpace. The benefits for businesses include lower costs and greater productivity, but figuring out how to communicate with off-site employees is crucial.

Traffic surrounding Microsoft headquarters in Redmond, Washington, has become so congested that Washington State Governor Chris Gregoire nearly missed a 9 a.m. speech at the company's main campus. Roads leading to the software maker simply were not designed to handle the 35,000 commuters who report for work there each day. The gridlock that greeted Gregoire was just the latest reminder that Microsoft needs to tackle its commuter crisis—and quickly.

Microsoft has embarked on a program aimed at getting more employees to work from home and other off-site locales, joining the growing ranks of companies to catch the virtual-workplace wave. About 17 percent of the U.S. workforce in 2009 was expected to get its job done at a home office more than two days per week, said Charlie Grantham, executive producer of consulting firm Work Design Collaborative. That is up from 11 percent in 2004.[46]

Letting employees work from outside the office keeps cars off the road, plus the practice can foster employee retention, boost worker productivity, and slash real estate costs. At IBM, about 42 percent of the company's 330,000 employees work on the road, from home, or at a client location, saving the computer company about $100 million in real estate-related expenses a year. VIPdesk, an employer of at-home customer-service reps, hangs onto 85 percent of its employees each year, compared with the 10 to 20 percent rate for traditional call centers, according to consulting firm IDC. And virtual workers are about 16 percent more productive than office workers, according to Grantham's research.

For all the benefits of freeing workers from the office, drawbacks abound. First, not everyone wants to leave. Some fear they will step off the corporate ladder, while others need a busy environment to stay productive. Some managers are reluctant to scatter direct reports because keeping tabs on a virtual workforce can be harder than managing those close at hand. Some virtual workers can feel lonely, isolated, or deprived of vital training and mentoring. And communication breakdowns can impede innovation, trust, job satisfaction, and performance.

Obstacles like these have prompted IBM, Sun Microsystems, and other companies to seek a host of creative solutions to the problems that virtual work presents. Some turn to a combination of mobile devices, email, instant messaging, and collaboration software to help colleagues stay in touch.

Tools for the Virtual Workforce   Mobility and wireless capabilities are the tools of the virtual workforce and include:

- *Mobile commerce (m-commerce),* the ability to purchase goods and services through a wireless Internet-enabled device.
- *Telematics,* the blending of computers and wireless telecommunications technologies with the goal of efficiently conveying information over vast networks to improve business operations. The most notable example of telematics may be the Internet itself, since it depends on a number of computer networks connected globally through telecommunication devices.
- *Electronic tagging,* a technique for identifying and tracking assets and individuals via technologies such as radio frequency identification and smart cards.

Other companies, including Microsoft, WebEx, and Citrix, also specialize in online conferencing and collaboration software that makes it easier for people in different locations to work together and conduct meetings. At Groove Networks, the company set a policy that if one person was operating virtually in a meeting, then everyone would sit in their offices and the entire meeting would be virtual. "Because there's a big sensory difference in that experience, it made sure that everyone was on a level playing field," she said. Another way to bridge the physical distance is to provide a worker with the tools needed to stay connected to colleagues.

For the virtual worker, a laptop, high-speed Internet access, and a personal digital assistant or mobile phone are required. But some companies go an extra mile to outfit virtual employees. IBM provides a universal messaging service that lets executives give a single phone number to clients and colleagues. The service then forwards calls to wherever that executive might be located, at home, on a cell phone, or in a so-called emobility center, one of the temporary offices set up by IBM in locations around the world. Patrick Boyle, director of health care and life-sciences sales at IBM, spends about half his time traveling, working from taxis, airport lounges, planes, and coffee shops. He is also a frequent user of emobility centers and considers headsets an essential tool of the trade.

OPENING CASE QUESTIONS

E-Spionage

7. How can the U.S. government and large organizations like Booz Allen use innovation to protect themselves from e-spionage?

8. Why would recycling IT equipment be a potential threat to a company or the U.S. government?

9. How could the U.S. government use social networking to combat e-spionage?

10. How could the U.S. government use virtual worlds such as Second Life to combat e-spionage?

Whether you aspire to be an entrepreneur, manager, or other type of business leader, it is increasingly important to think globally in planning your career. As this chapter points out, global markets offer many opportunities yet are laced with significant challenges and complexities including cultural, political, and geoeconomic issues, such as:

- Global business strategies.
- Global enterprise architectures.
- Global information issues.
- Global systems development.

Developing a global business perspective will help you reap the potential of global markets. New trends for the 21st century include:

- Innovation: finding new.
- Social entrepreneurship: going green.
- Social networks: who's who.
- Virtual worlds: it's a whole new world.

Capability Maturity Model Integration method (CMMI)   443
Committee of Sponsoring Organizations (COSO)   443
Compliance   442
Corporate policy   454
Corporate responsibility   454
Deperimeterization   446
Electronic tagging   463
Enterprise architecture   444

ewaste   456
Geoeconomic   440
Governance   442
Information privacy   447
Information Systems Audit and Control Association (ISACA)   442
Information Technology Infrastructure Library (ITIL)   443
Innovation   452

Mobile commerce (m-commerce)   463
Social responsibility   454
Sustainable IT disposal   456
Sustainable or green IT   454
Telematics   463
Transborder data flows (TDF)   446
Virtualization   455

Tata's Nano $2,500 Car

The announcement by Tata Motors of its newest car, the Nano priced at $2,500, was revealing on many levels. The announcement generated extensive coverage and commentary, but just about everyone missed the Nano's real significance, which goes far beyond the car itself.

At about $2,500 retail, the Nano is the most inexpensive car in the world. Its closest competitor, the Maruti 800, made in India by Maruti Udyog, sells for roughly twice as much. To put this in perspective, the price of the entire Nano car is roughly equivalent to the price of a DVD player option in a luxury Western car. The low price point has left other auto companies scrambling to catch up.

Thinking Outside the Patent Box

How could Tata Motors make a car so inexpensively? It started by looking at everything from scratch, applying what some analysts have described as "Gandhian engineering" principles-deep frugality with a willingness to challenge conventional wisdom. A lot of features that Western consumers take for granted—air conditioning, power brakes, radios, etc.—are missing from the entry-level model.

More fundamentally, the engineers worked to do more with less. The car is smaller in overall dimensions than the Maruti, but it offers about 20% more seating capacity as a result of design choices such as putting the wheels at the extreme edges of the car. The Nano is also much lighter than comparable models as a result of efforts to reduce the amount of steel in the car (including the use of an aluminum engine) and the use of lightweight steel where possible. The car currently meets all Indian emission, pollution, and safety standards, though it only attains a maximum speed of about 65 mph. The fuel efficiency is attractive—50 miles to the gallon.

Hearing all this, many Western executives doubt that this new car represents real innovation. Too often, when they think of innovation, they focus on product innovation using breakthrough technologies; often, specifically, on patents. Tata Motors has filed for 34 patents associated with the design of the Nano, which contrasts with the roughly 280 patents awarded to General Motors (GM) every year. Admittedly that figure tallies all of GM's research efforts, but if innovation is measured only in terms of patents, no wonder the Nano is not of much interest to Western executives. Measuring progress solely by patent creation misses a key dimension of innovation: Some of the most valuable innovations take existing, patented components and remix them in ways that more effectively serve the needs of large numbers of customers.

A Modular Design Revolution

But even this broader perspective fails to capture other significant dimensions of innovation. In fact, Tata Motors itself did not draw a lot of attention to what is perhaps the most innovative aspect of the Nano: its modular design. The Nano is constructed of components that can be built and shipped separately to be assembled in a variety of locations. In effect, the Nano is being sold in kits that are distributed, assembled, and serviced by local entrepreneurs. As Ratan Tata, chairman of the Tata group of companies, observed in an interview with The Times of London: "A bunch of entrepreneurs could establish an assembly operation and Tata Motors would train their people, would oversee their quality assurance and they would become satellite assembly operations for us. So we would create entrepreneurs across the country that would produce the car. We would produce the mass items and ship it to them as kits. That is my idea of dispersing wealth. The service person would be like an insurance agent who would be trained, have a cell phone and scooter and would be assigned to a set of customers."

In fact, Tata envisions going even further, providing the tools for local mechanics to assemble the car in existing auto shops or even in new garages created to cater to remote rural customers. With the exception of Manjeet Kripalani, BusinessWeek's India bureau chief, few have focused on this breakthrough element of the Nano innovation.

This is part of a broader pattern of innovation emerging in India in a variety of markets, ranging from diesel engines and agricultural products to financial services. While most of the companies pursuing this type of innovation are Indian, the U.S. engineering firm, Cummins (CMI) demonstrates that Western companies can also harness this approach and apply it effectively. In 2000 Cummins designed innovative "gensets" (generation sets) to enter the lower end of the power generator market in India. These modular sets were explicitly designed to lower distribution costs and make it easy for distributors and customers to tailor the product for highly variable customer environments. Using this approach, Cummins captured a leading position in the Indian market and now actively exports these new products to Africa, Latin America, and the Middle East.

Lessons Executives Should Learn

What are the broader lessons that Western executives should learn from this innovation story? Emerging markets are a fertile ground for innovation. The challenge of reaching dispersed, low-income consumers in emerging markets often spurs significant innovation. Western executives should be careful about compartmentalizing the impact of these innovations on the edge of the global economy. These innovations will become the basis for "attacker" strategies that can be used to challenge incumbents in more developed economies. What is initially on the edge soon comes to the core.

- Find ways to help customers and others on the edge to tinker with your products. Modular and open product designs help engage large numbers of motivated users in tailoring and pushing the performance boundaries of your products, leading to significant insight into unmet customer needs and creative approaches to addressing those needs.

- Pay attention to institutional innovation. Western executives often become too narrowly focused on product or process innovation. Far higher returns may come from investing in institutional innovation—redefining the roles and relationships that bring together independent entities to deliver more value to the market. Tata is innovating in all three dimensions simultaneously.

- Rethink distribution models. In our relentless quest for operating efficiency, we have gone for more standardization and fewer business partners in our efforts to reach customers. As customers gain more power, they will demand more tailoring and value-added service to meet their needs. Companies that innovate on this dimension are likely to be richly rewarded.[47]

Questions

1. How can cultural and political issues affect Tata Motor's Nano car?
2. How would governance and compliance affect Tata Motors?
3. Identify the different global system development issues Tata Motors might encounter as it deploys its Nano.
4. How did Tata Motors use innovation to develop the Nano?
5. How could Tata Motors use social networking to increase business?
6. How could Tata Motors use virtual worlds such as SecondLife to improve operations and increase sales?

CLOSING CASE TWO

Collective Innovation

Open innovation has been a hot management phrase for the past five years. So far, though, these collaborations have generally been focused on small-scale research and development or on technology ventures between giant global brands and smaller partners. Think Procter & Gamble's collaborations with universities and suppliers or IBM's embrace of an open-source software language that both saves the company money and provides it with a new revenue stream.

But what if you brought together design heads from some of the world's biggest global brands with the aim of stimulating innovation? That was the premise of the fifth annual Raymond conference in Rotterdam attended by 17 design managers from companies as diverse as Heineken, Philips, Lego, Airbus, and Hewlett-Packard. Designers are accustomed to working with external consultants and customers, but Raymond's aim is different: fostering cooperation between design teams at big global companies in radically different markets.

The conference is the brainchild of two Dutch design companies: Park Advanced Design Management and Eden, an interactive-experience design firm. Tired of attending crowded conferences dominated by endless speeches, they decided to start an invitation-only event where designers from noncompeting companies could freely share ideas with the aim of finding new ways to get more and better products out faster.

"Everyone talks about open innovation, but the design department is the place within a company most open to doing it," said Tim Selders, Raymond co-founder and Park director. Designers, especially those involved in corporate branding and product or service design, are accustomed to working with external partners and customers. "It's about finding new ways for companies to share design processes, resources, and tools," Selders said.

An Imaginary Global Firm

A recent Raymond conference followed an unusual format that led to some surprising insights and even a few potential commercial collaborations. Holed up together in a room for nearly two days, the attendees were asked to imagine they were part of a new global design company called design-Inc.com, with a team of some 1,200 designers.

Their mission, they were informed in a video presentation by the unseen "Raymond" (think Charlie from *Charlie's Angels*), was to deliver the best, fastest, and most inexpensive design solutions for a broad range of businesses across a variety of industries: medical, retail, toys, sports equipment, and clothing.

To do this, they had to figure out how to motivate staff to keep innovation fresh, which design tools and processes to use, how to benchmark their performance, and how to share knowledge of trends, materials, and technologies among designers. "Although we're all from different backgrounds and industries, we all face similar problems and we all have different ways of solving them," said Loe Limpens, a design manager for Dutch supermarket chain Albert Heijn.

The Spirit of a Collective Company

The process worked by asking six designers at a time to sit around a fictitious boardroom table to bat around ideas on how the new company would operate. Each board member was asked to contribute to the discussion on the three broad themes. While the participants brought their own experience to the exercise, the idea was to shed their own backgrounds in the spirit of creating a new company that would benefit from their collective expertise.

The experience got designers to break free from their own corporate silos and look at their businesses from another industry's perspective. So Clive Grinyer, director of product design at Orange France Telecom, was able to get designers from fashion retailer Mexx to see the mobile phone as more than just a fashion accessory. Instead of thinking in terms of a designer-branded phone, he said, a mobile phone company such as Orange could provide a fashion brand with access to a customer blog on street fashion, for instance, enabling both companies to get more detailed consumer insight from a target customer group. "These kinds of ideas may not pan out, but it's a great test-bed for innovation," Grinyer said.

On the second day of Raymond, designers created a marketplace, taking turns manning their own stalls, where they listed what they were willing to give another designer and what they would like to receive. Philippe Picaud, head of design at French sports retailer. Decathlon, invited designers from other companies such as Lego and high-end stroller manufacturer Bugaboo to visit his team (comprising 120 designers) in Lille to get a closer look at the company's internal design processes—including sharing some of the key metrics and processes he uses internally to measure design effectiveness. "These tools show design's added value to management, but they also act as an education tool for designers to better understand a company's values and what measurements drive management," Picaud said.

Picaud has used design to help transform Decathlon from a retailer that sold other sporting brands such as Nike and Adidas to a company where 60 percent of sales now come from Decathlon's 15 private-label brands. He'd like to send some of his designers to other companies on short-term exchanges. These, he said, "are a way for my team to get new ideas and develop new ways of dealing with various design problems."

Design-led companies such as Decathlon and Lego boast an impressive track record of innovation. But even they believe opening up their studios to other companies has real potential benefits. Lego's design director, Torsten Bjorn, plans to visit some of the design departments of companies that were at Raymond with the aim of seeing how they integrate different design functions. "We all have different cultures and processes, and sharing our experience can inspire you to think and work in a different way," he said.

Stretching the Mind of Design

It's a point of view shared by most of the participants. Orange's Grinyer offered to share online branding tools with designers from other industries. "When Orange and France Telecom's broadband provider Wanadoo came together we learned how to control 20 different websites within 20 different countries," he said. In exchange, Grinyer "bought" knowledge of Picaud's design metrics system. "This way I can go back and show management just how valuable my website tools are," he joked.

For others, such as Trevor Withell, director of innovation for Bugaboo, the main benefit of this open innovation exchange was discovering new ways to motivate his design team. "For designers, motivation isn't all about money," he said. He thinks the best way to keep designers motivated and innovation flowing is to open them up to new ideas and experiences. So he planned to send one of his head designers to a totally different type of company, such as a heavy engineering firm, to "really stretch the mind."

While Raymond reinforced the almost unlimited potential of open innovation in design, participants conceded the concept is not without challenges. As James Woudhuysen, professor of forecasting and innovation at De Montfort University in Leicester, England—who acted as an adviser at the event—points out, such ventures take time, money, and management commitment to develop and can lead to disputes about intellectual property. Still, Raymond showed open innovation is possible. "Getting 17 of the world's top corporate design directors in one room around a program of collaboration rather than egoism is already an achievement," Woudhuysen said. "To get, within two days, six agreements for pairs of design directors to embark on common projects is an even bigger success."[48]

Questions

1. Explain how the six best practices of innovation work at the Raymond conference.
2. How could social networking influence innovation?
3. How could innovation help create new forms of green IT?
4. How could a virtual world help innovation?
5. How could virtual workforces take advantage of innovation to create new products?
6. What ethical issues might a company find when pursing innovation?
7. If you were running a global innovation initiative what global issues might you encounter?

CLOSING CASE THREE

Confusing Carbon

To help shoppers make green choices, companies are slapping carbon labels on products. But even if the public can interpret the information, will it help reduce greenhouse gas emissions?

Next time you are in a shoe store, pick up a pair of clogs or leather walking shoes from Timberland. Inside, right by the heel, you will find a single number that tells you how "green" the shoe is. This number is explained in a card in the shoe box that provides a 0-to-10 carbon rating. A zero means less than 2.5 kilograms of carbon and other greenhouse gases were emitted when the shoe was produced and shipped. And a 10? That is a whopping 100 kg, roughly equal to the carbon released if you drive a car 240 miles.

There is a simple premise behind the new label. Everyday activities, whether making pancakes or jetting across the sky, are linked to the combustion of fuel, which releases gases that contribute to global warming. Timberland believes climate-conscious shoppers will buy shoes that help them cut their carbon count. And those same customers will feel more loyal to the brand because Timberland respects their wishes. Sixty different Timberland products sport such numbers. They reflect both the "carbon footprint" of the shoes and other factors, such as the quantities of harmful chemicals used to make them. By 2010, Timberland plans to put the labels on all its shoes and clothing, and other companies are set to follow its lead. The goal, said Timberland CEO Jeffrey Swartz, is "to arm consumers with as much information as we can."

But will shoppers really be able to interpret such information? And even if the tags catch on, will they make a difference in reducing greenhouse gases?

Experts are divided on these questions. Climate scholars point out that it is almost impossible to distill into a single number the intricacies of carbon chemistry, manufacturing processes, supply chains—and how they all affect global warming. And the very idea of doing so is controversial. Britain-based Tesco, the world's third-largest retailer, as announced plans to make public how much carbon is released in the production, transport, and consumption of all 70,000 products on its supermarket shelves. The plan immediately drew howls of protests from manufacturers, who thought the burden of measuring emissions would land on their shoulders. Global environmental groups declared labels a distraction from more important corporate efforts to improve energy efficiency. Shoppers, meanwhile, seemed confused by the first such tags that appeared on store shelves, except when they were part of a larger education campaign. "It requires leadership, commitment, and pressure to make something like this happen," said Edgar Blanco, a research associate at the Massachusetts Institute of Technology who has studied carbon labels. "The truth is, no one knows how to educate consumers about this, or how it will work." The skeptics certainly have a point. Yet many shoppers are eager to understand how their own activities affect the environment. In a survey last summer by AccountAbility, a nonprofit that advises corporations and governments on sustainable business practices, nearly half of 2,734 U.S. and British consumers polled said they wanted to know which products caused the least harm.

Pioneers like Tesco understand they are in the midst of a Europewide crackdown on greenhouse gas emissions, and that if they don't act on reducing carbon, they could get slammed with punitive regulations. Since 2005 major carbon emitters such as power plants and oil refineries within the European Union have been forced to curtail greenhouse gases. A climate change bill will make Britain the first country in the world to introduce legally binding CO_2 reduction targets. The new law, aimed at lowering Britain's emissions 20 percent by 2010, will extend the cap on carbon to large, nonenergy-intensive businesses such as retailers, hotel chains, and banks. Retailer Marks & Spencer, for one, has an ambitious plan to become carbon-neutral and send zero waste to landfills by 2012.

Carbon labels were a logical outgrowth of the crackdown on greenhouse gases, which is also playing out in Washington and many state capitals. Timberland, for example, is pushing other shoemakers to agree on an industry standard. But companies heading down this path might learn from the challenges encountered by the pioneers.

The highest hurdle is simply obtaining an accurate carbon count on different goods, a laborious process that may initially cost $10,000 or more per item. In most countries, each manufacturer figures out for itself how to gather the data that become the number on the label. Britain is trying to hash out a national standard for measuring the greenhouse gas associated with each product and service, working with the Carbon Trust, a government-funded nonprofit. That should bring down the cost of counting carbon over time.

Even with a standard, counting can involve mind-boggling complexity. Unilever, a top supplier of household products to Tesco, operates 260 factories in 70 countries and works with more than 10,000 subcontractors. With a supply chain like that, even labeling a line of packaged noodles is a chore. Say Unilever decides to shift production of the noodles from Poland to South Wales to save money. Because of fuel consumption and other factors, that change has a big impact on the carbon tally, even though the same recipe is used. Unilever worries that Tesco may ask it to recalculate the carbon footprint for such products each time it moves production, which might be as often as once a week. If asked, "we couldn't do it," said Gavin Neath, Unilever's senior vice president for global corporate responsibility. "Our supply chain is constantly changing."

Tesco admits there are difficulties to work out. Said David North, Tesco's director of government affairs, "We have to bring suppliers with us on this journey. It is early days." Once the labels are in place, companies find, it's hard to tell if consumers get the point. In a survey PepsiCo commissioned from researchers Populus, half of the 1,000 people interviewed said they were more likely to buy a product with a carbon label. But such numbers, while well-intended, may not convey much. "What does it mean to say a bag of chips contains 75 grams of carbon?" asks Steve Howard, CEO of the Climate Group in London. "I have a PhD in environmental physics, and it doesn't mean a thing to me."

There's another complication in labeling products: By focusing consumers' attention on this one issue, the retailer risks undercutting other store programs that are also socially responsible. When Tesco unveiled its carbon program, as an interim step it put little airplane stickers on products that were air-freighted, to alert shoppers that more fuel was burned in transport than for goods shipped by boat or truck. That prompted protests from governments of developing countries, including Uganda and Kenya, which felt Tesco's plans unfairly punished producers there. "The moment consumers looked at this sticker, they would stigmatize those products," said Abraham Barno, agricultural attaché at Kenya's embassy in Britain. Tesco has promised to work with developing countries to promote their products.

Despite the controversy surrounding labeling and the challenges in counting the carbon, defenders say there are big side benefits. In times of $100-per-barrel oil, most companies want to be more energy-efficient, and calculating a carbon footprint is one of the best ways to find where energy is wasted in the production and distribution network.[49]

Questions

1. How can companies help reduce carbon emissions?
2. How can finding alternative energy sources help reduce IT energy consumption?
3. How can labeling IT equipment green help promote green initiatives?
4. Why do global organizations need to be concerned with green or social entrepreneurship initiatives?
5. What ethical issues are associated with green technology?

MAKING BUSINESS DECISIONS

1. Transforming an organization

Your college has asked you to help develop the curriculum for a new course titled "Building a 21st Century Organization." Use the materials in this text, the Internet, and any other resources to outline the curriculum that you would suggest the course cover. Be sure to include your reasons why the material should be covered and the order in which it should be covered.

2. Buying green

You have recently been hired by Exclusive Recycling, an IT recycling company. The company is paid to pick up organizational IT equipment and safely dispose of the waste. After working for the company for a few weeks you realize that the company does not dispose of the majority of the equipment, instead it fixes or upgrades the equipment and then sells it on eBay. The firms paying to have their IT equipment recycled are not aware of this practice. Do you believe Exclusive Recycling is acting ethically? Why or why not?

3. Running the Glove

Running It is a collaborative social networking site for runners. It has tremendous success in the United State and has over 10 million members who use the site to pick runs, find running partners, register for marathons, discuss apparel, and so on. Running IT has hired you to help develop global websites in Europe, Asia, and Canada. What advice do you have for Running IT when it comes to expanding globally?

4. Building alternatives

IBM plans to invest $1 billion a year in products and services that will help reduce IT power consumption in data centers. By using new techniques, within the next three years IBM plans to double the computing capacity of its data centers—more than 8 million square feet worldwide—without increasing power consumption. Explain why all organizations should be interested in similar plans.

APPLY YOUR KNOWLEDGE

1. Connecting Components

Components of a solid enterprise architecture include everything from documentation to business concepts to software and hardware. Deciding which components to implement and how to implement them can be a challenge. New IT components are released daily, and business needs continually change. An enterprise architecture that meets your organization's needs today may not meet those needs tomorrow. Building an enterprise architecture that is scalable, flexible, available, accessible, and reliable is key to your organization's success.

Project Focus

You are the enterprise architect for a large clothing company called Xedous. You are responsible for developing the initial enterprise architecture. Create a list of questions you will need answered to develop your architecture. Below is an example of a few questions you might ask.

- What are the company's growth expectations?
- Will systems be able to handle additional users?
- How long will information be stored in the systems?
- How much customer history must be stored?
- What are the organization's business hours?
- What are the organization's backup requirements?

2. Peace of Mind

Virtual Margaret is the nickname for Margaret Hooshmand, an executive assistant at Cisco Systems who works in San Jose, California, even though she's physically located in Richardson, Texas. Margaret uses a so-called telepresence system made by Cisco, which provides real-time videoconferencing on 65-inch high-definition plasma screens. A life-sized screen that shows her working at her desk 1,600 miles away in Texas now sits in her cubicle in San Jose. But she can see and interact with her boss, Senior Vice President Marthin De Beer, and co-workers say it's almost like she's really there. Although these systems cost upwards of $80,000 today, another five to 10 years of chip and Internet connection price improvements could make systems like this common—and further erode the geographical limitations of any job that doesn't absolutely require physical presence.

Project Focus

Virtual Margaret is the first of many uses for Cisco's telepresence system. You have been hired by First Corporation as the Vice president of new business and your boss, Mark Wallburg, has asked you to develop other uses for telepresence systems. Be sure to compile your ideas in a PowerPoint presentation highlighting your ideas, including pictures or diagrams indicating how the system will work and look.

3. Virtual Work

Nearly every business that wants to look remotely hip is opening an outlet in Second Life, the online virtual world where people can interact via computer-generated avatars, or graphic representations of themselves. But a few companies are starting to go further, taking real work, not just marketing, into these strange new worlds. For instance, 1-800-Flowers.com opened a "virtual greenhouse" where customers can view flower arrangements and chat with 1-800-Flowers avatars. About a dozen telesalespeople are literally working inside Second Life now. Chief Executive Jim McCann, who helped pioneer the concept of telesales, thinks virtual worlds could change the nature of employment even further, by allowing customers to design their own arrangements more easily. "The line between our customers and our staff continues to blur," he says.

Project Focus

LivingLive is a start-up consulting company specializing in virtual worlds. You are a recent new hire and your boss would like you to spend a few hours familiarizing yourself with virtual worlds and how businesses are competing in this new environment. Search the Internet and find several examples of current companies that are using virtual worlds in new and exciting ways to promote, change, and enhance business.

4. Experimenting Virtually

Virtual worlds like Second Life are not just for games. Companies are experimenting with virtual environments for everything from training exercises to meeting spaces for remote workers. But the technology still has pitfalls. For emergency responders working along Interstate 95, accidents are not a game; they are a way of life. So it seemed odd to a group of firefighters, police, and medics, when researchers from the University of Maryland suggested it use a virtual world to collaborate on training for rollovers, multicar pileups, and life-threatening injuries. At first, the emergency responders who make up the I-95 Corridor Coalition didn't take seriously the idea of a virtual world as a training tool, said Michael Pack, director of research with the University of Maryland's Center for Advanced Transportation Technology. "It wasn't until we started to do elaborate demos that the first responders started to realize the true potential," said Pack, who has begun rolling out a virtual world pilot project that could accommodate training for hundreds of emergency workers.

Project Focus

Industry analysts and developers of virtual worlds believe that by immersing users in an interactive environment that allows for social interactions, virtual worlds have the potential to succeed where other collaborative technologies, like teleconferencing, have failed. Phone-based meetings begin and end abruptly. In a virtual world conversations between employees can continue within the virtual space—just like they do in company hallways after a meeting ends. Explain the value added by using a virtual world for interactive demonstrations and training. What other businesses in the 21st century could use virtual worlds for demonstrations and training.

5. IT Get's Its Say

CIOs need to speak the language of business to sell IT's strategic benefits. It is no secret that the most successful companies today are the ones that deliver the right products and services faster, more efficiently, more securely, and more cost-effectively than their competitors, and the key to that is a practical implementation of enterprise technology to improve business performance. IT executives and managers therefore must speak the languages of business to articulate how technology can solve business problems.

CIOs of tomorrow will focus on a number of changing dynamics: enabling the business to grow versus just optimizing performance, saying yes instead of no; allowing open innovation rather than closed, traditional R&D practices; creating a culture of strategic growth and innovation; and empowering the customer to make decisions that drive a heightened value proposition for both the customer and supplier. You have been charged with creating a slogan for your company that explains the correlation of business and IT. A few examples include:

- IT should no longer be viewed as just an enabler of somebody else's business strategy.
- The distinction between technology and business is antediluvian – it's gone.

Create a slogan that you can use to explain to your employees the importance of business and IT.

BUSINESS DRIVEN BEST SELLERS

How to Change the World. By David Bornstein (New York: Oxford University Press, 2004).

According to journalist David Bornstein, social entrepreneurs are people with powerful ideas to improve other people's lives who have implemented these ideas across cities, countries, and, in some cases, the world. These are the doctors, lawyers, engineers, teachers, journalists, and parents who solve social problems on a large scale and have a profound effect on society. Bornstein points out that they are usually not famous and are usually not politicians. They are the people who create a transformative force that addresses major problems in the pursuit of a vision, and they will not give up until they have spread their ideas as far as possible.

How to Change the World provides a close look at numerous people from several countries—including the United States, Brazil, Burkina Faso, Hungary, India, and Bangladesh—who have advanced systemic change and shifted behavior patterns and perceptions. They have ideas for attacking problems, Bornstein points out, and are unwilling to rest until they have spread their ideas throughout society.[50]

What Matters Most: How a Small Group of Pioneers Is Teaching Social Responsibility to Big Business, and Why Big Business Is Listening. By Jeffrey Hollender and Stephen Fenichell (New York: Basic Books, 2006).

While many people might assume that corporate social responsibility emerged with the Ben & Jerry's and The Body Shops of this world, the concept of a corporation having more responsibility than just making money for its owners is not new, as Jeffrey Hollender points out in this new book, *What Matters Most.* Hollender quotes Friedman's 1963 book *Capitalism and Freedom,* in which Friedman argued that "there is one and only one social responsibility of business—to use its resources and engage in activities designed to increase its profit so long as it stays within the rules of the game, which is to say, engages in open and free competition without deception or fraud." If corporations start believing that they have any responsibility to society, Friedman continues, the result can only be the end of freedom, for corporations will be ruled by "the iron fist of government bureaucrats."[51]

Management Challenges for the 21st Century. By Peter F. Drucker (New York: Harpercollins Publishers, 1999).

With the new millennium, much of what we have come to accept as true of business management is about to be challenged. The world is changing at a rapid pace, and only those who understand what those changes mean will be poised to prosper under the new rules. Old paradigms will be replaced by new ones.

This book summarizes which old assumptions are out. You will learn that management is not just business management and that there is no one ideal way to organize an enterprise. Nor, is there one way to manage people. In fact, the manager's role will not be to manage at all. Rather, the manager's job is to lead. National boundaries and even regional markets will no longer define an organization's boundaries.

The book also reveals the trends that will radically alter life and how companies are run. The developed world is experiencing a collapse of its birthrate, and an accompanying increase in the average age of its populations. The result will be political upheaval, a new emphasis on personal investment, and a substantial increase in the length of work life.[52]

The Leader of the Future: Visions, Strategies Practices, and for the New Era. By Leader to Leader Institute (San Francisco: Jossey-Bass, 2006).

Frances Hesselbein, Marshall Goldsmith, and Richard Beckhard are all connected with the Peter F. Drucker Institute for Nonprofit Management. They put out a call to their friends, today's leading business writers, for their thoughts on the leadership skills necessary to take advantage of the new century's challenges.

Over the past 50 years, Peter Drucker has discussed with hundreds of leaders their roles, goals, and performance. While there may be born leaders, there are far too few of them to depend on. Leadership, therefore, can and must be learned.[53]

If your students are looking for an introduction to MIS concepts and business concepts have them visit the Appendices that accompany this text. The following is an overview of the appendices and the associated topic areas. Appendices are located on this textbook's website at www.mhhe.com/baltzan.

Appendix	Description
A. Business Basics	■ Types of Business ■ Internal Operations of a Corporation ■ Accounting ■ Finance ■ Human Resources ■ Sales ■ Marketing ■ Operations/Production ■ Management Information Systems
B. Hardware and Software	■ Hardware Basics ■ Computer Categories ■ Software Basics
C. Networks and Telecommunications	■ Network Basics ■ Architecture ■ Topology ■ Protocols ■ Media ■ Ebusiness Networks
D. Systems Development Life Cycle	■ Systems Development Life Cycle ■ Plan ■ Analysis ■ Design ■ Development ■ Test ■ Implement ■ Maintain ■ Software Problems Are Business Problems

THE TECHNOLOGY PLUG-INS

The overall goal of the Technology Plug-Ins is to provide additional information not covered in the text such as personal productivity using information technology, problem solving using Excel, and decision making using Access. These plug-ins also offer an all-in-one text to faculty, avoiding need to purchase an extra book to support Microsoft Office. These plug-ins offer integration with the core chapters and provide critical knowledge using essential business applications, such as Microsoft Excel, Microsoft Access, and Microsoft Project with hands-on tutorials for comprehension and mastery. Plug-Ins T1 to T12 are located on this textbook's website at www.mhhe.com/baltzan.

Plug-In	Description
T1. Personal Productivity Using IT	This plug-in covers a number of things to do to keep a personal computer running effectively and efficiently. The 12 topics covered in this plug-in are: ■ Creating strong passwords. ■ Performing good file management. ■ Implementing effective backup and recovery strategies. ■ Using Zip files. ■ Writing professional emails. ■ Stopping spam. ■ Preventing phishing. ■ Detecting spyware. ■ Threads to instant messaging. ■ Increasing PC performance. ■ Using anti-virus software. ■ Installing a personal firewall.
T2. Basic Skills Using Excel	This plug-in introduces the basics of using Microsoft Excel, a spreadsheet program for data analysis, along with a few fancy features. The six topics covered in this plug-in are: ■ Workbooks and worksheets. ■ Working with cells and cell data. ■ Printing worksheets. ■ Formatting worksheets. ■ Formulas. ■ Working with charts and graphics.
T3. Problem Solving Using Excel	This plug-in provides a comprehensive tutorial on how to use a variety of Microsoft Excel functions and features for problem solving. The five areas covered in this plug-in are: ■ Lists ■ Conditional Formatting ■ AutoFilter ■ Subtotals ■ PivotTables
T4. Decision Making Using Excel	This plug-in examines a few of the advanced business analysis tools used in Microsoft Excel that have the capability to identify patterns, trends, and rules, and create "what-if" models. The four topics covered in this plug-in are: ■ IF ■ Goal Seek ■ Solver ■ Scenario Manager

(continued)

T5. Designing Database Applications	This plug-in provides specific details on how to design relational database applications. One of the most efficient and powerful information management computer-based applications is the relational database. The four topics covered in this plug-in are: ■ Entities and data relationships. ■ Documenting logical data relationships. ■ The relational data model. ■ Normalization.
T6. Basic Skills Using Access	This plug-in focuses on creating a Microsoft Access database file. One of the most efficient information management computer-based applications is Microsoft Access. Access provides a powerful set of tools for creating and maintaining a relational database. The two topics covered in this plug-in are: ■ Create a new database file. ■ Create and modify tables.
T7. Problem Solving Using Access	This plug-in provides a comprehensive tutorial on how to query a database in Microsoft Access. Queries are essential for problem solving, allowing a user to sort information, summarize data (display totals, averages, counts, and so on), display the results of calculations on data, and choose exactly which fields are shown. The three topics in this plug-in are: ■ Create simple queries using the simple query wizard. ■ Create advanced queries using calculated fields. ■ Format results displayed in calculated fields.
T8. Decision Making Using Access	This plug-in provides a comprehensive tutorial on entering data in a well-designed form and creating functional reports using Microsoft Access. A form is essential to use for data entry and a report is an effective way to present data in a printed format. The two topics in this plug-in are: ■ Creating, modifying, and running forms. ■ Creating, modifying, and running reports.
T9. Designing Web Pages	This plug-in provides a comprehensive assessment into the functional aspects of web design. Websites are beginning to look more alike and to employ the same metaphors and conventions. The web has now become an everyday thing whose design should not make users think. The six topics in this plug-in are: ■ The World Wide Web. ■ The unknown(s). ■ The process of web design. ■ HTML basics. ■ Web fonts. ■ Web graphics.
T10. Creating Web Pages Using HTML	This plug-in provides an overview of creating web pages using the HTML language. HTML is a system of codes that you use to create interactive web pages. It provides a means to describe the structure of text-based information in a document—by denoting certain text as headings, paragraphs, lists, and so on. The five topics in this plug-in are: ■ HTML(an introduction). ■ Creating, saving, and viewing HTML documents. ■ Applying style tags and attributes. ■ Using fancier formatting. ■ Creating hyperlinks. ■ Displaying graphics.

(continued)

T11.	Creating Web Pages Using Dreamweaver	This plug-in provides a tour of using Dreamweaver to create web pages. Dreamweaver allows anyone with limited web page design experience to create, modify, and maintain full-featured, professional-looking pages without having to learn how to code all the functions and features from scratch. The five topics in this plug-in are: ■ Navigation in Dreamweaver. ■ Adding content. ■ Formatting content. ■ Developing style sheets. ■ Creating tables.
T12.	Creating Gantt Charts with Excel and Microsoft Project	This plug-in offers a quick and efficient way to manage projects. Excel and Microsoft Project are great for managing all phases of a project, creating templates, collaborating on planning processes, tracking project progress, and sharing information with all interested parties. The two topics in this plug-in are: ■ Creating Gantt Charts with Excel. ■ Creating Gantt Charts with Microsoft Project.

NOTES

Chapter 1

1. "Apple Profit Surges 95 Percent on iPod Sales," Yahoo! News, http://news.yahoo.com/s/afp/20060118/bs_afp/uscompanyearningsit_060118225009, accessed January 18, 2005; "Apple's IPod Success Isn't Sweet Music for Record Company Sales," Bloomberg.com, http://quote.bloomberg.com/apps/news?pid=nifea&&sid=aHP5Ko1pozM0, accessed November 2, 2005; Peter Burrows, "How Apple Could Mess Up Again," BusinessWeek online, http://yahoo.businessweek.com/technology/content/jan2006/tc20060109_432937.htm, accessed January 9, 2006; www.apple.com/iphone, accessed June 7, 2007; news.com.com/NikeiPod+raises+RFID+privacy+concerns/2100-1029_3-6143606.html, accessed June 7, 2007.

2. Jon Surmacz, "By the Numbers," *CIO Magazine,* www.cio.com, accessed October 2004.

3. IT Centrix, "Optimizing the Business Value of Information Technology," www.unisys.com/products/mainframes/insights/insights__compendium, accessed December 10, 2004.

4. "IT Master of the Senate," *CIO Magazine,* www.cio.com, accessed May 1, 2004.

5. Glossary of Business Terms, www.powerhomebiz.com/Glossary/glossary-A.htm, accessed December 15, 2003; Financial Times, "Mastering Management," www.ft.com/pp/mfm, accessed December 15, 2003; "Glossary of Financial Terms," www.nytimes.com/library/financial/glossary/bfglosa.htm, accessed December 15, 2003; "Business Dictionary," www.glossarist.com/glossaries/business/, accessed December 15, 2003; and "Glossary of Business Terms," www.smallbiz.nsw.gov.au/smallbusiness/, accessed December 15, 2003.

6. Ibid.

7. "Integrating Information at Children's Hospital," *KMWorld,* www.kmworld.com/Articles/ReadArticle.aspx?ArticleID=10253, accessed June 1, 2005.

8. Dave Lindorff, "General Electric and Real Time," www.cioinsight.com/article2/0,3959,686147,00.asp, accessed March 1, 2004.

9. "IT Master of the Senate," *CIO Magazine,* www.cio.com, accessed May 1, 2004.

10. Cisco Press, www.ciscopress.com/index.asp?rl=1, accessed March 15, 2004.

11. "Integrating Information at Children's Hospital," *KMWorld.*

12. "Glossary of Business Terms," www.powerhomebiz.com/Glossary/glossary-A.htm, accessed December 15, 2003; Financial Times, "Mastering Management," www.ft.com/pp/mfm, accessed December 15, 2003; "Glossary of Financial Terms," www.nytimes.com/library/financial/glossary/bfglosa.htm, accessed December 15, 2003; "Business Dictionary," www.glossarist.com/glossaries/business/, accessed December 15, 2003; and "Glossary of Business Terms," www.smallbiz.nsw.gov.au/smallbusiness/, accessed December 15, 2003.

13. Ken Blanchard, "Effectiveness vs. Efficiency," Wachovia Small Business, www.wachovia.com, accessed October 14, 2003.

14. Lindorff, "General Electric and Real Time."

15. Cisco Press, www.ciscopress.com/index.asp?rl=1, accessed October 2003.

16. Ken Blanchard, "Effectiveness vs. Efficiency," Wachovia Small Business, www.wachovia.com, accessed October 14, 2003.

17. United Nations Division for Public Economics and Public Administration, www.un.com, accessed November 10, 2003.

18. Ibid.

19. EBay Financial News, "Earnings and Dividend Release," January 15, 2002.

20. "Sun and eBay Celebrate Record Uptime," www.sun.com/service/about/features/ebay.html, accessed January 14, 2004.

21. Michael E. Porter, *Competitive Strategy: Techniques for Analyzing Industries and Competitors.*

22. "Top 10 Bad Business Decisions," www.business20.com, accessed April 16, 2007.

23. Ibid.

24. "Innovative Managers," *BusinessWeek,* April 24, 2005.

25. www.thomaslfriedman.com, accessed September 2005.

26. Adam Horowitz and the editors of Business 2.0, *The Dumbest Moments in Business History: Useless Products, Ruinous Deals, Clueless Bosses, and Other Signs of Unintelligent Life in the Workplace.* By (New York: Portfolio, 2004).

27. Paul Ormerod *Why Most Things Fail: Evolution, Extinction, and Economics* (Hoboken, NJ: John Wiley & Sons, 2005).

28. Mark Eppler, *The Wright Way: 7 Problem-Solving Principles from the Wright Brothers That Can Make Your Business Soar,* (2004).

Chapter 2

1. Secondlife.com, accessed May 28, 2007; "Linden Lab to Open Source Second Life Software, Linden Lab (January 8, 2007)," secondlife.com/community/land-islands.php, accessed May 22, 2007; Irene Sege, "Leading a Double Life," *The Boston Globe,* October 25, 2006, accessed June 22, 2007; and James Harkin, "Get a (Second) Life," *Financial Times,* November, 17 2006, accessed June 15, 2007.

2. "1,000 Executives Best Skillset," *The Wall Street Journal,* July 15, 2003.

3. "The Visionary Elite," *Business 2.0,* December 2003, pp. S1–S5.

4. "Boston Coach Aligns Service with Customer Demand in Real Time," www-1.ibm.com/services/us/index.wss, accessed November 4, 2003.

5. "Industry Facts and Statistics," Insurance Information Institute, www.iii.org, accessed December 2005.

6. Neil Raden, "Data, Data Everywhere," *DSSResources .com,* February 16, 2003.

7. Ibid.

8. Ibid.

9. Christopher Koch, "How Verizon Flies by Wire," *CIO Magazine,* November 1, 2004.

10. Neil McManus, "Robots at Your Service," *Wired,* January 2003, p. 059.

11. "Put Better, Faster Decision-Making in Your Sights," www.teradata.com, accessed July 7, 2003.

12. Ibid.

13. S. Begley, "Software au Natural," *Newsweek,* May 8, 2005.

14. Beth Bacheldor, "Steady Supply," *InformationWeek,* November 24, 2003, www.informationweek.com, accessed June 6, 2003.

15. McManus, "Robots at Your Service."

16. "Put Better, Faster Decision-Making in Your Sights," www .teradata.com; "Neural Network Examples and Definitions," ece-www.colorado.edu/~ecen4831/lectures/NNdemo.html, accessed June 24, 2007; Begley, "Software au Natural"; McManus, "Robots at Your Service"; Santa Fe Institute, www.dis.anl.gov/abms/, accessed June 24, 2007; Michael A. Arbib, (ed. 1995). *The Handbook of Brain Theory and Neural Networks* L. Biacino and G. Gerla, "Fuzzy logic, continuity and effectiveness," *Archive for Mathematical Logic.*

17. Ibid.

18. www.columbiasportswear.com, accessed December 15, 2008.

19. "What Is BPR?" searchcio.techtarget.com/sDefinition/ 0,,sid182_gci536451,00.html, accessed October 10, 2005; BPR Online, www.prosci.com/mod1.htm, accessed October 10, 2005; Business Process Reengineering Six Sigma, www .isixsigma.com/me/bpr/, accessed October 10, 2005; and SmartDraw.com, www.smartdraw.com/, accessed October 11, 2005.

20. Ibid.

21. Ibid.

22. Ibid.

23. Michael Hammer, *Beyond Reengineering: How the Process-Centered Organization Is Changing Our Work and Our Lives* (New York: HarperCollins Publishers, 1996).

24. Richard Chang, "Process Reengineering in Action: A Practical Guide to Achieving Breakthrough Results (Quality Improvement Series)," 1996; H. James Harrington, *Business Process Improvement Workbook: Documentation, Analysis, Design, and Management of Business Process Improvement* (New York: McGraw-Hill, 1997); Hammer, *Beyond Reengineering;* Michael Hammer and James, Champy, "Reengineering the Corporation: A Manifest for Business Revolution," 1993; "Government Business Process Reengineering (BPR) Readiness Assessment Guide, General Services Administration (GSA)," 1996; Richard Chang, "Process Reengineering in Action: A Practical Guide to Achieving Breakthrough Results (Quality Improvement Series)," 1996. Michael Hammer, "Beyond Reengineering: How the Process-Centered Organization is Changing Our Work and Our Lives," 1997.

25. Ibid.

26. Ibid.

27. Ibid.

28. Ibid.

29. Ibid.

30. H. James Harrington, *Business Process Improvement: The Breakthrough Strategy for Total Quality, Productivity, and Competitiveness* (New York: McGraw-Hill, 1991); and Hammer, "Beyond Reengineering.

31. Ibid.

32. Ibid.

33. Ibid.

34. Bjorn Andersen, *Business Process Improvement Toolbox* (Milwaukee, WI: ASQ Quality Press, 1999).

35. "What is BPR?" searchcio.techtarget.com/sDefinition/ 0,,sid182_gci536451,00.html; SmartDraw.com, www .smartdraw.com/; BPR Online, www.prosci.com/mod1 .htm; and Business Process Reengineering Six Sigma, www.isixsigma.com/me/bpr/.

36. "What Is BPR?" searchcio.techtarget.com/sDefinition/ 0,,sid182_gci536451,00.html, accessed October 10, 2005; BPR Online, www.prosci.com/mod1.htm, accessed October 10, 2005; Business Process Reengineering Six Sigma, www.isixsigma.com/me/bpr/, accessed October 10, 2005; and SmartDraw.com, www.smartdraw.com/, accessed October 11, 2005.

37. "Darpa Grand Challenge," www.darpa.mil/grandchallenge/, accessed September 1, 2005.

38. www.investor.harley-davidson.com, accessed October 10, 2003; Bruce Caldwell, "Harley-Davidson Revs up IT Horsepower," *Internetweek.com,* December 7, 2000; "Computerworld 100 Best Places to Work in IT 2003," *Computerworld,* June 9, 2003, pp. 36–48; Leroy Zimdars, "Supply Chain Innovation at Harley-Davidson: An Interview with Leroy Zimdars," *Ascet 2,* April 15, 2000; "Customer Trust: Reviving Loyalty in a Challenging Economy," *Pivotal Webcast,* September 19, 2002; "Harley-Davidson Announces Go-Live: Continues to Expand Use of Manugistics Supplier Relationship Management Solutions," www.manugistics.com, May 7, 2002; and Roger Villareal, "Docent Enterprise Increases Technician and Dealer Knowledge and Skills to Maximize Sales Results and Customer Service," www.docent.com, August 13, 2002.

39. "The Incredible Lateness of Delta," *CIO Magazine,* www .cio.com, accessed February 15, 2003; "Can American Keep Flying?" *CIO Magazine,* www.cio.com, accessed February 15, 2003; Max Hopper, "Rattling Sabre," *Harvard Business Review,* October 2002; and John Helyar, "Delta's Chapter 11 Dogfight," *Fortune,* December 12, 2005, pp. 61–62.

40. Michael Hammer and James Champy *Reengineering the Corporation* (New York: Harper Collins Publishing, 2003).

41. Watkins, *The First 90 Days* (Boston: Harvard Business School Press, 2003).

42. Bossidy and Charan *Execution,* (New York: Random House, 2002).

Chapter 3

1. Beth Bacheldor, "From Scratch: Amazon Keeps Moving," *Information Week,* March 5, 2004; Gary Wolf, "The Great Library of Amazonia," *Wired,* October 23, 2003; "Amazon Company Information," *Forbes,* www.forbes .com, September 2005; and Rob Hof, "Amazon's Newest Product: Storage," *BusinessWeek,* March 13, 2006.

2. Cisco Press, www.ciscopress.com/index.asp?rl=1, accessed March 1, 2005.

3. Adam Lashinsky, "Kodak's Developing Situation," *Fortune,* January 20, 2003, p. 176.

4. www.wired.com, accessed November 15, 2003.

5. Lashinsky, "Kodak's Developing Situation."

6. Clayton Christensen, *The Innovator's Dilemma* (Boston: Harvard Business School, 1997).

7. Internet World Statistics, www.internetworldstats.com, January 2007.

8. info.cern.ch, accessed March 1, 2005.

9. "Internet Pioneers," www.ibiblio.org/pioneers/andreesen .html, accessed March 1, 2005.

10. Gunjan Bagla, "Bringing IT to Rural India One Village at a Time," *CIO Magazine,* March 1, 2005.

11. Tim O'Reilly, "What Is Web 2.0: Design Patterns and Business Models for the Next Generation of Software," www.oreillynet.com/pub/a/oreilly/tim/news/2005/09/30/ what-is-web-20.html, accessed June 25, 2007; and "Web 2.0 for CIOs," www.cio.com/article/16807, *CIO Magazine,* accessed June 24, 2007.

12. Ibid.

13. Ibid.

14. "The Complete Web 2.0 Directory," www.go2web20.net/, accessed June 24, 2007, and "Web 2.0 for CIOs," www .cio.com/article/16807.

15. Ibid.

16. Anne Zelenka, "The Hype Machine, Best Mashup of Mashup Camp 3," gigaom.com/2007/01/18/the-hype-machine-best-mashup-of-mashup-camp-3/, accessed June 14, 2007, and Webmashup.com, www.webmashup.com/ Insert New 25, accessed June 14, 2007.

17. Ibid.

18. Ibid.

19. Ibid.

20. "Info on 3.9M Citigroup," *Money,* June 6, 2005.

21. Amy Johnson, "A New Supply Chain Forged," *Computerworld,* September 30, 2002.

22. "Pratt & Whitney," *BusinessWeek,* June 2004.

23. "Let's Remake a Deal," *Business 2.0,* March 2004.

24. Laura Rohde, "British Airways Takes Off with Cisco," *Network World,* May 11, 2005.

25. www.t-mobile.com, accessed June 2005.

26. www.idc.com, accessed June 2005.

27. "A Site Stickier Than a Barroom Floor," *Business 2.0,* June 2005, p. 74.

28. www.emarketer.com, accessed January 2006.

29. Heather Harreld, "Lemon Aid," *CIO Magazine,* July 1, 2000.

30. Rachel Metz, "Changing at the Push of a Button," *Wired,* September 27, 2004.

31. www.hotel-gatti.com, accessed June 2003.

32. Frank Quinn, "The Payoff Potential in Supply Chain Management," www.ascet.com, accessed June 15, 2003.

33. www.oecd.org, accessed June 2005.

34. www.vanguard.com, accessed June 2005.

35. "Watch Your Spending," *BusinessWeek,* May 23, 2004.

36. Jack Welch, "What's Right About Wal-Mart," *CIO Magazine,* www.cio.com, accessed May 2005.

37. www.yankeegroup.com, accessed May 2005.

38. www.ingenio.com, accessed July 2005.

39. "E-Commerce Taxation," www.icsc.org/srch/government/ ECommerceFebruary2003.pdf, accessed June 8, 2004.

40. Robert Hof, "Pierre M. Omidyar: The Web for the People," *BusinessWeek,* December 6, 2004; Margaret Kane, "eBay picks up PayPal for 1.5 Billion," Cnet News, news.com.com, accessed July 8, 2002; John Blau, "Are eBay and Skype a Good Fit?" *Infoworld,* www.inforworld.com, accessed September 8, 2005; and "Better Ask: IRS May Consider eBay Sales as Income," *USA Today,* March 27, 2005.

41. "Success Stories," www.oracle.com, accessed June 2004 www.milliondollarhomepage.com, www .redpaperclip.com, accessed February 2007.

42. John Heilmann, "What's Friendster Selling?" *Business 2.0,* March 2004, p. 34.

43. Clayton Christensen, *The Innovator's Solution* (Boston: Harvard Business School Publishing, 2003).

44. Seth Godin, *Purple Cow* (New York: Penguin Group, 2003).

Chapter 4

1. "Sarbanes-Oxley Act," www.workingvalues.com, accessed March 3, 2004.

2. Michael Schrage, "Build the Business Case," *CIO Magazine,* www.cio.com, accessed November 17, 2003.

3. Scott Berianato, "Take the Pledge," *CIO Magazine,* www .cio.com, accessed November 17, 2003.

4. Ibid.

5. Ibid.

6. AMA Research, "Workplace Monitoring and Surveillance," www.amanet.org, accessed March 1, 2004.

7. Ibid.

8. Ibid.

9. Andy McCue, "Bank Boss Quits after Porn Found on PC," www.businessweek.com, accessed June 2004.

10. AMA Research, "Workplace Monitoring and Surveillance," www.amanet.org, accessed March 1, 2004.

11. www.vault.com, accessed January 2006.

12. AMA Research, "Workplace Monitoring and Surveillance."
13. "Health Information Management," www.gartner.com, accessed November 16, 2003.
14. "2005 CSI/FBI Computer Crime and Security Survey," www.gocsi.com, accessed February 20, 2006.
15. Ibid.
16. www.ey.com, accessed November 25, 2003.
17. "The Security Revolution," *CIO Magazine*, www.cio.com, accessed June 6, 2003.
18. "Losses from Identity Theft to Total $221 Billion Worldwide," www.cio.com, accessed May 23, 2003.
19. "Sony Fights Intrusion with 'Crystal Ball,'" *CIO Magazine*, www.cio.com, accessed August 9, 2003.
20. Mark Leon, "Keys to the Kingdom," www.computerworld.com, accessed August 8, 2003.
21. "Spam Losses to Grow to $198 Billion," *CIO Magazine*, www.cio.com, accessed August 9, 2003.
22. "Teen Arrested in Internet 'Blaster' Attack," www.cnn.com, accessed August 29, 2003.
23. www.norcrossgroup.com/casestudies.html, accessed October 2004.
24. "Hacker Hunters," *BusinessWeek*, May 30, 2005.
25. Alice Dragoon, "Eight (Not So) Simple Steps to the HIPAA Finish Line," *CIO Magazine*, www.cio.com, accessed July 7, 2003.
26. "What Is BPR?" searchcio.techtarget.com/sDefinition/0,,sid182_gci536451,00.html, accessed October 10, 2005; BPR Online, www.prosci.com/mod1.htm, accessed October 10, 2005; Business Process Reengineering Six Sigma, www.isixsigma.com/me/bpr/, accessed October 10, 2005.
27 Ibid.
28 Ibid.
29. Bethany McLean and Peter Elkind *The Smartest Guys in the Room.*
30. David D'Alessandro, *Career Warfare* (New York: McGraw-Hill, 2004).
31 Deborrah Himsel, Leadership Sopranos Style, (Chicago: Dearborn, 2004).

Chapter 5
1. "Virgin Mobile USA," www.bea.com/content/news_events/white_papers/BEA_VirginMobile_cs.pdf, accessed November 4, 2007.
2. Christine McGeever, "FBI Database Problem Halts Gun Checks," www.computerworld.com, accessed May 22, 2000.
3. www.cio.com, accessed November 2005.
4. "Distribution of Software Updates of Thousands of Franchise Locations Was Slow and Unpredictable," www.fountain.com, accessed October 10, 2003.
5. Christopher Koch, "A New Blueprint for the Enterprise," *CIO Magazine*, March 1, 2005.
6. "New Coalitions Increasing America's Crisis Preparedness," www.complianceexecutive.com, accessed November 29, 2007.

7. Ibid.
8. Bob Tedeschi, "*Protect Your Identity,*" pcworld.about.com/magazine/2212p107id118241.htm, accessed November 11, 2007.
9. "Password Management," www.fischerinternational.com, accessed December 1, 2007.
10. Martin Garvey, "Manage Passwords," *Information Week*, May 20, 2005.
11. Martin Garvey, "Security Action Plans," *Information Week*, May 30, 2005.
12. Ibid.
13. www.abercrombie.com, accessed November 29, 2008.
14. Erick Schonfeld, "Linux Takes Flight," *Business 2.0*, January 2003, pp. 103–105.
15. John Fontana, "Lydian Revs up with Web Services," *Network World*, March 10, 2004.
16. www.websidestory.com, accessed November 18, 2007.
17. Tim O'Reilly, "Open Source Paradigm Shift," tim.oreilly.com/articles/paradigmshift_0504.html, accessed January 11, 2008.
18. Julie Bort, "SOA Made Fast and Easy," *Network World*, October 22, 2007.
19. Dirk Slama, Robert Paluch, "Key Concepts of Service-Oriented Architecture," www.csc.com/cscworld/012006/web/web002.html, accessed on January 4, 2008.
20. Ibid.
21. "Achieving a Single Customer View," www.sun.com, accessed January 12, 2008.
22. "VMware—History of Virtualization," www.virtualization-works.com/Virtualization-History.asp, accessed January 23, 2008.
23. "EPA Report to Congress on Server and Data Center Energy Efficiency," www.energystar.gov/ia/partners/prod_development/downloads/EPA_Report_Exec_Summary_Final.pdf, accessed January 23, 2008.
24. Paul Krill, "Impending Death of Moore's Law Calls for Software Development Changes," *InfoWorld*, May 24, 2005.
25. Ibid.
26. Geoffrey Thomas, "Seeing Is Believing," *Air Transport World*, June 2007, p. 54.
27. Julie Bort, "Subaru Takes a Virtual Drive," *Network World*, September 25, 2006.
28. "Google Groans Under Data Strain," www.byteandswitch.com/document.asp?doc_id=85804, accessed January 30, 2008.
29. Alan Joch, "Grid Gets Down to Business," *Network World*, December 27, 2004.
30. Tim Wilson, "Don't Stop the Presses!," www.network-computing.com, accessed January 28, 2008.
31. www.usopen.org, accessed January 28, 2008.
32. Grant Gross, "Grids Help eBay Do Big Business," www.infoworld.com/article/06/09/12/HNebaygarids_1.html?GRID%20COMPUTING, accessed January 23, 2008.

33. Sandy Carter, "The New Language of Business: SOA & Web 2.0," safari.adobepress.com/013195654X, accessed February 1, 2008.

34. Nicholas Carr, "Does IT Matter?," www.nicholasgcarr .com/doesitmatter.html, accessed February 1, 2008.

Chapter 6

1. Daniel Pink, "The Book Stops Here," *Wired,* March 2005, pp.125–39; "Tapping the World's Brainpower with Wiki," *BusinessWeek,* October 11, 2004, p. 132; www .wikipedia.com, accessed November 2005; Robert Hoff, "Something Wiki This Way Comes," BusinessWeek online, accessed June 7, 2004; and www.wikipedia.org, accessed May 22, 2007.

2. "Google Reveals High-Profile Users of Data Search Machine," Reuters News Service, August 13, 2003, www .chron.com, accessed September 3, 2003.

3. Mitch Betts, "Unexpected Insights," *ComputerWorld,* April 14, 2003, www.computerworld.com, accessed September 4, 2003.

4. Ibid.

5. "Data Mining: What General Managers Need to Know," *Harvard Management Update,* October 1999.

6. Barbara DePompa Reimers, "Too Much of a Good Thing," *ComputerWorld,* www.computerworld.com, April 14, 2003.

7. Ibid.

8. "MSI Business Solutions Case Study: Westpac Financial Services," www.MSI.com, accessed August 4, 2003.

9. "Why Data Quality," www.trilliumsoft.com, accessed October 3, 2003.

10. Ibid.

11. Webopedia.com, www.webopedia.comTERM/d/database .html, accessed May 15, 2007; Oracle Database, www. oracle.com/database/index.html, accessed May 17, 2007.

12. Ibid.

13. Ibid.

14. Chicago Police Department, gis.chicagopolice.org/, accessed June 23, 2004.

15. Ford's Vision, donate.pewclimate.org/docUploads/Ford .pdf, accessed June 18, 2003.

16. Webopedia.com, www.webopedia.comTERM/d/database .html; Oracle Database, www.oracle.com/database/ index.html.

17. www.sitepoint.com/article/publishing-mysql-data-web, accessed May 16, 2007.

18. Ibid.

19. Oracle Success Stories, www.oracle.com/successstories/ army, accessed May 15, 2003.

20. Kathleen Melymuka, "Premier 100: Turning the Tables at Applebee's," *ComputerWorld,* www.computerworld.com, accessed February 24, 2003.

21. Julia Kiling, "OLAP Gains Fans among Data-Hungry Firms," *ComputerWorld,* January 8, 2001, p. 54.

22. Tommy Perterson, "Data Cleansing," *ComputerWorld,* www.computerworld.com, accessed February 10, 2003.

23. "Dr Pepper/Seven Up, Inc.," www.cognos.com, accessed September 10, 2003.

24. "Google Knows Where You Are," *BusinessWeek,* February 2, 2004; and www.google.com, accessed September 13, 2003.

25. Julie Schlosser, "Looking for Intelligence in Ice Cream," *Fortune,* March 17, 2003; Leslie Goff, "Summertime Heats Up IT at Ben & Jerry's," *Computer World,* July, 2001; and Customer Success Stories, www.cognos.com, accessed January 2005.

26. Meridith Levinson, "Harrah's Knows What You Did Last Night," May 2001; "Harrah's Entertainment Wins TDWI's 2000 DW Award," www.hpcwire.com, accessed October 10, 2003; Gary Loveman, "Diamonds in the Data Mine," *Harvard Business Review,* May 2003, p. 109; "NCR— Harrah's Entertainment, Inc.," www.ncr.com, accessed October 12, 2003; "Cognos and Harrah's Entertainment Win Prestigious Data Warehousing Award," www .cognos.com, accessed October 14, 2003; Kim Nash, "Casinos Hit Jackpot with Customer Data," www.cnn .com, accessed October 14, 2003; and Michael S. Malone, "IPO Fever," *Wired,* March 2004.

27. Bill Gates, *Business @ The Speed of Thought* (Grand Central Publishing, 1999).

28. Sydney Finkelstein *Why Smart Executive Fail.*

Chapter 7

1. www.ironman.com, accessed January 14, 2008.

2. www.sabreairlinesolutions.com/about/history.htm, accessed January 22, 2008.

3. "Rip Curl Turns to Skype for Global Communications," www.voipinbusiness.co.uk/rip_curl_turns_to_skype_for_ gl.asp July 07, 2006, accessed January 21, 2008.

4. "VoIP Business Solutions," www.vocalocity.com, accessed January 21, 2008.

5. www.skype.com, accessed February 15, 2008.

6. www.rei.com, accessed February 23, 2008.

7. Enrique De Argaez, "What You Should Know About Internet Broadband Access," www.internetworldstats .com/articles/art096.htm, accessed January 29, 2008.

8. "Broadband Technology Overview," www.corning.com/ docs/opticalfiber/wp6321.pdf, accessed February 1, 2008.

9. www.drpepper.com, accessed February 1, 2008.

10. "Navigating the Mobility Wave," www.busmanagement .com, accessed February 2, 2008.

11. www.mbia.com, accessed February 3, 2008.

12. Dan Nystedt, "Mobile Phones Grow Even More Popular," *PC World,* April 2006.

13. "How Do Cellular Devices Work," www.cell-phone101. info/devices.php, accessed February 9, 2008.

14. mobilementalism.com, accessed February 2, 2008.

15. V. C. Gungor, F. C. Lambert, "A Survey on Communication Networks for Electric System Automation, Computer Networks," *The International Journal of Computer and Telecommunications Networking,* May 15, 2006, pp. 877–897.

16. "CenterCup Releases PDA Caddy to Leverage Legalized Golf GPS," www.golfgearreview.com/article-display/1665.html, accessed February 3, 2008.

17. onstar.com, accessed February 10, 2008.

18. "Keeping Weeds in Check with Less Herbicide," www.ars.usda.gov/is/AR/archive/aug06/weeds0806.htm, accessed February 11, 2008.

19. www.gis.rgs.org/10.html, accessed February 7, 2008.

20. Coco Masters, "Bringing Wi-Fi to the Skies," www.time.com/time/specials/2007/article/0,28804,1665220_1665225,00.html, accessed February 20, 2008.

21. W. David Gardner, "McDonald's Targets Starbucks with Free Wi-Fi, Upscale Coffee Bars," *InformationWeek,* January 7, 2008.

22. "Security-Free Wireless Networks," www.wired.com, accessed February 11, 2008.

23. "Sprint Plans Launch of Commercial WiMAX Service in Q2 2008," www.intomobile.com, accessed February 10, 2008.

24. Deepak Pareek, "WiMAX: Taking Wireless to the MAX," CRC Press, 2006, pp. 150–51.

25. wimax.com, accessed February 9, 2008.

26. Mohsen Attaran, "RFID: an Enabler of Supply Chain Operations," *Supply Chain Management: An International Journal* 12 (2007), pp. 249–57.

27. Michael Dortch, "Winning RFID Strategies for 2008," *Benchmark Report,* December 31, 2007.

28. Ibid.

29. "RFID Privacy and You," www.theyaretrackingyou.com/rfid-privacy-and-you.html, accessed February 12, 2008.

30. "RFID Roundup," www.rfidgazette.org, accessed February 10, 2008.

31. Chris Silva, Benjamin Gray, "Key Wireless Trends That Will Shape Enterprise Mobility in 2008," www.forrester.com, accessed February 12, 2008.

32. "City of Logan, Utah," www.techrepublic.com, accessed February 2, 2008.

33. Kevin Shult. "UPS vs. FedEx: Battle of the Brands," www.bloggingstocks.com/2007/04/09/ups-vs-fedex-battle-of-the-brands/, accessed February 10, 2008.

34. Charles Waltner, "Florida Hospital Cuts Cord, Goes Wireless," newsroom.cisco.com, accessed February 1, 2008.

35. www.powerofmobility.com, accessed February 9, 2008.

36. www.amazon.com/Into-Leadership-Lessons-Westward-Expedition/dp/0814408168, accessed February 9, 2008.

Chapter 8

1. Bill Breen, "Living in Dell Time," *Fast Company,* November 2004, p. 86.

2. Norman E. Bowie, ed., *The Blackwell Guide to Business Ethics.* (Malden, MA: Blackwell, 2002).

3. Ibid.

4. Ibid.

5. Geoffrey Colvin, "Managing in the Info Era," *Fortune,* March 6, 2007, pp. F6–F9.

6. Christopher A. Bartlett and Sumantra Ghoshal, "Going Global: Lessons from Late Movers," *Harvard Business Review,* March–April 2000, pp. 132–34.

7. Stuart Crainer, *The Management Century* (New York: Jossey-Bass, 2000).

8. James Fitzsimmons and Mona Fitzsimmons, *Service Management,* 4th ed. (New York: McGraw-Hill Irwin, 2004).

9. Ibid.

10. William J. Hopp and Mark Spearman, *Factory Physics: Foundations of Manufacturing Management,* 2nd ed. (Burr Ridge, IL: Irwin, 2001).

11. Ibid.

12. Ibid.

13. Aasron Bernstein, "Backlash: Behind the Anxiety of Globalization," *BusinessWeek,* April 24, 2006, pp. 36–42. Terry Hill, *Manufacturing Strategy: Text and Cases* 3rd ed. (New York: McGraw-Hill, 2000).

14. Ibid.

15. Ibid.

16 Ibid.

17. Christopher A. Bartlett and Sumantra Ghoshal, "Going Global: Lessons from Late Movers," *Harvard Business Review,* March–April 2000, pp. 132–34.

18. Sharon Shinn, "What About the Widgets?" *BizEd,* November–December 2004, pp. 30–35.

19. Ibid.

20. James P. Womack, Daniel Jones, and Daniel Roos, *The Machine That Changed the World* (New York, Harper Perennial, 1991).

21. Ibid.

22. John Hagerty, "How Best to Measure Our Supply Chain," www.amrresearch.com, accessed March 3, 2005.

23. Andrew Binstock, "Virtual Enterprise Comes of Age," *InformationWeek,* November 6, 2004.

24. Mitch Betts, "Kinks in the Chain," *Computerworld,* December 17, 2005.

25. Walid Mougayar, "Old Dogs Learn New Tricks," *Business 2.0,* October 2000, www.Business2.com, accessed June 14, 2003.

26. "Creating a Value Network," *Wired,* September 2003, p. S13.

27. Fred Hapgood, "Smart Decisions," *CIO Magazine,* www.cio.com, accessed August 15, 2001.

28. "Creating a Value Network," *Wired.*

29. "Success Story," www.perdue.com, accessed September 2003.

30. "Creating a Value Network," *Wired.*

31. "The e-Biz Surprise," *BusinessWeek,* May 12, 2003, pp. 60–65.

32. Hagerty, "How Best to Measure Our Supply Chain."

33. Ibid.

34. Frank Quinn, "The Payoff Potential in Supply Chain Management," www.ascet.com, accessed June 15, 2003.

35. Mougayar, "Old Dogs Learn New Tricks."

36. Quinn, "The Payoff Potential," and William Copacino, "How to Become a Supply Chain Master," *Supply*

Chain Management Review, September 1, 2001, www .manufacturing.net, accessed June 12, 2003.

37. Ibid.
38. Kevin Kelleher, "BudNet: 66,207,896 Bottles of Beer on the Wall," *Business 2.0,* February 2004.
39. Jennifer Bresnahan, "The Incredible Journey," *CIO Enterprise Magazine,* August 15, 1998, www.cio.com, accessed March 12, 2004.
40. Kim Girard, "How Levi's Got Its Jeans into Wal-Mart," *CIO Magazine,* July 15, 2003.
41. Quinn, "The Payoff Potential," and William Copacino, "How to Become a Supply Chain Master," *Supply Chain Management Review,* September 1, 2001, www .manufacturing.net, accessed June 12, 2003.
42. Ibid.
43. Ibid.
44. Ibid.
45. Jim Collins, *Built to Last* (Collins Business Essentials, 1994).
46. Jim Collins, *Good to Great* (Collins Business Essentials, 2001).

Chapter 9

1. Secondlife.com, accessed May 28, 2007; "Linden Lab To Open Source Second Life Software. Linden Lab (January 8, 2007)," secondlife.com/community/land-islands.php, accessed May 22, 2007; Irene Sege, "Leading a Double Life," *The Boston Globe* October 25, 2006, accessed June 22, 2007; and James Harkin, "Get a (Second) Life," *Financial Times,* November 17, 2006, accessed June 15, 2007.
2. "Customer Success Stories," www.siebel.com, accessed November 12, 2003.
3. "Kaiser's Diabetic Initiative," www.businessweek.com, accessed November 15, 2003.
4. "Integrated Solutions—The ABCs of CRM," www.integrated-solutionsmag.com , accessed November 12, 2003.
5. Ibid.
6. "1800 flowers.com," *Business 2.0,* February 2004.
7. "The 'New' New York Times," *Business 2.0,* January 2004.
8. "New York Knicks—Success," www.jdedwards.com, accessed January 15, 2004.
9. "Barclays, Giving Voice to Customer-Centricity," crm .insightexec.com, accessed July 15, 2003.
10. "Customer Success—PNC Retail Bank," www.siebel .com, accessed May 5, 2003.
11. "California State Automobile Association Case Study," www.epiphany.com/customers/detail_csaa.html, accessed July 4, 2003.
12. www.salesforce.com, accessed June 2005.
13. "Vail Resorts Implements FrontRange HEAT," *CRM Today,* October 16, 2003, www.crm2day.com/news/crm/ EpyykllFyAqEUbqOhW.php, accessed December 2, 2003.
14. "3M Accelerates Revenue Growth Using Siebel eBusiness Applications," www.siebel.com, July 30, 2002, accessed July 10, 2003.
15. www.enterprise.com, accessed June 15, 2004.
16. "Avnet Brings IM to Corporate America with Lotus Instant Messaging," www.websphereadvisor.com/ doc/12196, accessed July 11, 2003.
17. Ibid.
18. Ibid.
19. www.nicesystems.com, accessed June 2005.
20. www.FedEx.com, accessed July 13, 2003.
21. "Documedics," www.siebel.com, accessed July 10, 2003.
22. Ibid.
23. Ibid.
24. "Customer Success—UPS," www.sap.com, accessed April 5, 2003.
25. Ibid.
26. "Customer Success—UPS."
27. "Supply Chain Planet," June 2003, http://newsweaver .co.uk/supplychainplanet/e_article000153342.cfm, accessed July 12, 2003.
28. "Customer Success—Cisco," www.sap.com, accessed April 5, 2003.
29. "Customer Success," www.costco.com, accessed June 2005.
30. "Customer Success," www.rackspace.com, accessed June 2005.
31. "Customer Success," www.siebel.com, accessed May 5, 2007.
32. "The Critical Shift to Flexible Business Intelligence," Used with Permission: Dr. Claudia Imhoff, Intelligent Solutions, Inc. "What Every Marketer Wants—And Needs—From Technology," Used with Permission: Dr. Claudia Imhoff, Intelligent Solutions, Inc. "Enterprise Business Intelligence," May 2006, Used with Permission: Dr. Claudia Imhoff, Intelligent Solutions, Inc. "The Business Case for Data Warehousing," Jill Dyche, 2005, (used with permission).
33. Ibid.
34. Ibid.
35. Ibid.
36. Ibid.
37. Ibid.
38. Ibid.
39. Ibid.
40. Ibid.
41. Ibid.
42. Ibid.
43. Ibid.
44. Ibid.
45. Ibid.
46. Ibid.
47. Ibid.
48. Ibid.
49. Ibid.
50. Ibid.
51. Ibid.
52. Ibid.
53. Ibid.
54. Ibid.
55. Ibid.

56. Ibid.
57. Steve Hamm, "Business Intelligence Gets Smarter," *BusinessWeek,* May 15, 2006.
58. Second Life, www.secondlife.org, accessed March 2008.
59. Emanuel Rosen, *The Anatomy of Buzz* Double Day.
60. Frederick F. Reichheld, *Loyalty Rules* Bain and Company.

Chapter 10

1. Thomas Wailgum, "Big Mess on Campus," *CIO Magazine,* May 1, 2005.
2. "Customer Success Story—Turner Industries," www.jdedwards.com, accessed October 15, 2003.
3. "Success Stories," www.sap.com, accessed April 2005.
4. "Customer Success Story—Turner Industries," www.jdedwards.com, accessed October 15, 2003.
5. Michael Doane, "A Blueprint for ERP Implementation Readiness," www.metagroup.com, accessed October 17, 2003.
6. "Amazon Finds Profits in Outsourcing," *CIO Magazine,* October 15, 2002, www.cio.com/archive/101502/tl_ec.html, accessed November 14, 2003.
7. "D-FW Defense Contractors Show Mixed Fortunes since September 11," www.bizjournals.com/dallas/stories/2002/09/09/focus2.htm, accessed June 8, 2004.
8. Steve Konicki, "Collaboration Is Cornerstone of $19B Defense Contract," www.business2.com/content/magazine/indepth/2000/07/11/17966, accessed June 8, 2004.
9. "Knowledge Management Research Center," *CIO Magazine,* www.cio.com/research/knowledge, accessed December 2005.
10. "Harley-Davidson on the Path to Success," www.peoplesoft.com/media/success, accessed October 12, 2003.
11. "Customer Success Story—Grupo Farmanova Intermed," www.jdedwards.com, accessed October 15, 2003.
12. "Customer Success Stories," www.jdedwards.com, accessed October 15, 2003.
13. Michael Doane, "A Blueprint for ERP Implementation Readiness," www.metagroup.com, accessed October 17, 2003.
14. Megan Santosus, "In The Know," *CIO Magazine,* January 2006.
15. Ibid.
16 The Balanced Scorecard, www.balancedscorecard.org, accessed February 2008.
17. Ibid.
18. Ibid.
19. Ibid.
20. Ibid.
21. "Speeding Information to BMW Dealers," www.kmworld.com/resources/featurearticles/index.cfm?action=readfea-ture&Feature_ID=337, accessed June 8, 2004.
22. "Toyota's One-Stop Information Shop," www.istart.co.nz/index/HM20/PC0/PV21873/EX236/CS25653, accessed June 8, 2004.
23. Ibid.
24. "Amazon Finds Profits in Outsourcing," *CIO Magazine,* October 15, 2002, www.cio.com/archive/101502/tl_ec.html, accessed November 14, 2003.
25. "D-FW Defense Contractors Show Mixed Fortunes since September 11," www.bizjournals.com/dallas/stories/2002/09/09/focus2.htm, accessed June 8, 2004.
26 Steve Konicki, "Collaboration Is Cornerstone of $19B Defense Contract," www.business2.com/content/magazine/indepth/2000/07/11/17966, accessed June 8, 2004.
27. "Knowledge Management Research Center," *CIO Magazine,* www.cio.com/research/knowledge, accessed December 2005.
28. Megan Santosus, "In The Know," *CIO Magazine,* January 2006.
29. Ibid.
30. "Speeding Information to BMW Dealers," www.kmworld.com/resources/featurearticles/index.cfm?action=readfeature&Feature_ID=337, accessed June 8, 2004.
31 Megan Santosus, "In The Know," *CIO Magazine,* January 2006.
32. Ibid.
33. "Knowledge Management Research Center," *CIO Magazine,* www.cio.com/research/knowledge, accessed December 2005.
34. Ibid.
35. Ibid.
36. Ibid.
37. Ibid.
38. "HP Unveils Halo Collaboration Studio," www.hp.com, December 12, 2005.
39. Bjorn Erik Munkvold, Tero Paivarinta, Anne Kristine Hodne, and Elin Stangeland, "Contemporary Issues of Enterprise Content Mananagement: The Case of Statoil," *Scandinavian Journal of Information Systems* 18, no. 2 (2006), pp. 69–100, accessible at www.cs.aau.dk/SJIS/jounral/volumes/volume19/no2/munkvoldetal18-2.pdf.
40. Ibid.
41. "IBM Helps Shell Canada Fuel New Productivity with PeopleSoft EnterpriseOne," case study, published August 8, 2005, validated February 5, 2007, available at www-306.ibm.com/software/success/cssdb.nsf.
42. Malcolm Gladwell, *The Tipping Point: How Little Things Can Make a Big Difference* (New York: Back Bay Books, 2000).
43. Malcolm Gladwell, *Blink: The Power of Thinking Without Thinking* (New York: Little Brown, 2005).

Chapter 11

1. "Overcoming Software Development Problems," www.samspublishing.com, accessed October 2005.
2. www.businessweek.com, accessed November 1, 2005.
3. "Software Costs," *CIO Magazine,* www.cio.com, accessed December 5, 2003.
4. "Defective Software Costs," *National Institute of Standards and Technology (NIST),* June 2002.
5. Ibid.

6. *CIO Magazine,* June 1, 2006, p. 55; "The Project Manager in the IT Industry," www.si2.com, accessed December 15, 2003; www.standishgroup.com, accessed December 12, 2003; Jim Johnson, "My Life Is Failure," p. 46; and .Gary McGraw, "Making Essential Software Work," *Software Quality Management,* April 2003, www.sqmmagazine .com, accessed November 14, 2003.

7. Ibid.

8. Ibid.

9. Ibid.

10. "Customer Success Story—PHH," www.informatica.com, accessed December 12, 2003.

11. *CIO Magazine,* June 1, 2006; "The Project Manager in the IT Industry"; www.standishgroup.com; Johnson, "My Life Is Failure"; and McGraw, "Making Essential Software Work."

12. Ibid.

13. Ibid.

14. Ibid.

15. "Building Events," www.microsoft.com, accessed November 15, 2003.

16. Agile Alliance Manifesto, www.agile.com, accessed November 1, 2003.

17. "Software Metrics," *CIO Magazine,* www.cio.com, accessed December 2, 2003.

18. "Building Software That Works," www.compaq.com, accessed November 14, 2003.

19. "Software Metrics," *CIO Magazine.*

20. www.agile.com, accessed November 10, 2003.

21. "Python Project Failure," www.systemsdev.com, accessed November 14, 2003.

22. *CIO Magazine,* June 1, 2006; "The Project Manager in the IT Industry"; www.standishgroup.com; Johnson, "My Life Is Failure"; and McGraw, "Making Essential Software Work."

23. Ibid.

24. McGraw, "Making Essential Software Work."

25. *CIO Magazine,* June 1, 2006; "The Project Manager in the IT Industry"; www.standishgroup.com; Johnson, "My Life Is Failure"; and McGraw, "Making Essential Software Work."

26. Ibid.

27. "Top Reasons Why IT Projects Fail," *InformationWeek,* www.infoweek.com, accessed November 5, 2003; www.calpine.com, accessed December 14, 2003; "The Project Manager in the IT Industry," www.si2.com, accessed December 15, 2003, www.standishgroup.com, accessed December 12, 2003; and www.snapon.com, accessed December 13, 2003.

28. Ibid.

29. Ibid.

30. Ibid.

31. Ibid.

32. Ibid.

33. www.standishgroup.com, accessed November 14, 2003.

34. Ibid.

35. www.microsoft.com, accessed November 16, 2003.

36. "REI Pegs Growth on Effective Multi-channel Strategy," *Internet Retailer,* www.internetretailer.com, accessed February 17, 2005, and Alison Overholt, "Smart Strategies: Putting Ideas to Work," *Fast Company,* April 2004, p. 63.

37. *CIO Magazine,* June 1, 2006; "The Project Manager in the IT Industry"; www.standishgroup.com; accessed December 12, 2003; Johnson, My Life Is Failure"; and McGraw, "Making Essential Software Work."

38. Ibid.

39. Ibid.

40. "Baggage Handling System Errors," www.flavors.com, accessed November 16, 2003.

41. www.microsoft.com, accessed November 16, 2003.

42. "Staying on Track at the Toronto Transit Commission," www.primavera.com, accessed December 16, 2003.

43. Edward Yourdon, *Death March: The Complete Software Developer's Guide to Surviving "Mission Impossible" Projects* (Pearson Education).

44. Gini Graham Scott, *A Survival Guide for Working with Humans* (New York: Amacom).

Chapter 12

1. Brian Grow, Keith Epstein and Chi-Chu Tschang; E-Spionage, *BusinessWeek,* April 10, 2008.

2. *BusinessWeek: Innovation,* http://www.businessweek .com/innovate/, accessed February 15, 2008.

3. —46. Ibid.

47. Harold Sirkin, "Tata's Nano: An Ingenious Coup," *BussinessWeek,* February 14, 2008.

48. Kerry Capell, "Building Expertise Through Collective Innovation," *BusinessWeek,* March 5, 2008.

49. Heather Green and Kerry Capell, "Carbon Confusion," *BusinessWeek,* March 6, 2008.

50. David Bornstein *How to Change the World.*

51. Jeffrey Hollender and Stephen Fenichell *What Matters Most, The Future of Corporate Social Responsibility,*

52. Peter F. Drucker *Management Challenges for the 21st Century.*

53. Peter F. Drucker Foundation *The Leader of the Future: Visions, Practices, and Strategies for a New Era.*

APPENDIX A (at www.mhhe.com/baltzan)

1. Julie Schlosser, "Toys 'R'Us Braces for a Holiday Battle," *Money,* December 22, 2003.

2. Glossary of Business Terms, www.powerhomebiz .com/Glossary/glossary-A.htm, accessed December 15, 2003 Financial Times, Mastering Management, www .ft.com/pp/mfm, accessed December 15, 2003 Glossary of Financial Terms, www.nytimes.com/library/financial/glos-sary/bfglosa.htm, accessed December 15, 2003 Business Dictionary, www.glossarist.com/glossaries/business/, ac-cessed December 15, 2003 Glossary of Business Terms, www.smallbiz.nsw.gov.au/smallbusiness/, accessed December 15, 2003.

3. Ibid.

4. Ibid.
5. Alison Overholdt, "The Housewife Who Got Up Off the Couch," Fast Company, September 2004, p. 94.
6. Glossary of Business Terms, www.powerhomebiz.com/Glossary/glossary-A.htm, accessed December 15, 2003 Financial Times, Mastering Management, www.ft.com/pp/mfm, accessed December 15, 2003 Glossary of Financial Terms, www.nytimes.com/library/financial/glossary/bfglosa.htm, accessed December 15, 2003 Business Dictionary, www.glossarist.com/glossaries/business/, accessed December 15, 2003 Glossary of Business Terms, www.smallbiz.nsw.gov.au/smallbusiness/, accessed December 15, 2003.
7. Ibid.
8. Ibid.
9. Ibid.
10. Ibid.
11. Ibid.
12. Adrian Danescu, "Save $55,000," CIO Magazine, December 15, 2004, p. 70.
13. Glossary of Business Terms, www.powerhomebiz.com/Glossary/glossary-A.htm, accessed December 15, 2003 Financial Times, Mastering Management, www.ft.com/pp/mfm, accessed December 15, 2003 Glossary of Financial Terms, www.nytimes.com/library/financial/glossary/bfglosa.htm, accessed December 15, 2003 Business Dictionary, www.glossarist.com/glossaries/business/, accessed December 15, 2003 Glossary of Business Terms, www.smallbiz.nsw.gov.au/smallbusiness/, accessed December 15, 2003.
14. Ibid.
15. Ibid.
16. "Can the Nordstroms Find the Right Style?" BusinessWeek, July 30, 2001.
17. Geoff Keighley, "Will Sony's PSP Become the iPod of Gaming Devices?" Business 2.0, May 2004, p. 29.
18. Glossary of Business Terms, www.powerhomebiz.com/Glossary/glossary-A.htm, accessed December 15, 2003 Financial Times, Mastering Management, www.ft.com/pp/mfm, accessed December 15, 2003 Glossary of Financial Terms, www.nytimes.com/library/financial/glossary/bfglosa.htm, accessed December 15, 2003 Business Dictionary, www.glossarist.com/glossaries/business/, accessed December 15, 2003 Glossary of Business Terms, www.smallbiz.nsw.gov.au/smallbusiness/, accessed December 15, 2003.
19. Ibid.
20. "From the Bottom Up," Fast Company, June 2004, p. 54.
21. Glossary of Business Terms, www.powerhomebiz.com/Glossary/glossary-A.htm, accessed December 15, 2003 Financial Times, Mastering Management, www.ft.com/pp/mfm, accessed December 15, 2003 Glossary of Financial Terms, www.nytimes.com/library/financial/

glossary/bfglosa.htm, accessed December 15, 2003 Business Dictionary, www.glossarist.com/glossaries/business/, accessed December 15, 2003 Glossary of Business Terms, www.smallbiz.nsw.gov.au/smallbusiness/, accessed December 15, 2003.
22. Ibid.
23. "Harley-Davidson: Ride Your Heritage," Fast Company, August 2004, p. 44. "Ford on Top," Fast Company, June 2004, p. 54.
24. Michael Hammer, Beyond Reengineering: How the Process-Centered Organization Is Changing Our Work and Our Lives (New York: HarperCollins Publishers, 1997).
25. Progressive Insurance, Business Week, March 13, 2004.
26. "Toy Wars," www.pbs.org, accessed December 23, 2003.
27. "Innovative Managers," Business Week, April 24, 2005.

APPENDIX B (at www.mhhe.com/baltzan)

1. "Electronic Breaking Points," PC World, August 2005.
2. Tom Davenport, "Playing Catch-Up," CIO Magazine, May 1, 2001.
3. "Hector Ruiz, Advanced Micro Devices," BusinessWeek, January 10, 2005.
4. www.powergridfitness.com, accessed October 2005.
5. Denise Brehm, "Sloan Students Pedal Exercise," www.mit.edu, accessed May 5, 2003.
6. Margaret Locher, "Hands That Speak," CIO Magazine, June 1, 2005.
7. www.needapresent.com, accessed October 2005.
8. Aaron Ricadela, "Seismic Shift," Information Week, March 14, 2005.
9. www.mit.com, accessed October 2005.
10. "The Linux Counter," counter.li.org, accessed October 2005.

APPENDIX C (at www.mhhe.com/baltzan)

1. Timothy Mullaney and Arlene Weintraub, "The Digital Hospital," BusinessWeek, March 28, 2005, and Michelle Delio, "How Secure Is Digital Hospital," Wired, March 28, 2001.
2. Eva Chen, "Shop Talk," CIO Magazine, October 15, 2004.
3. www.perrio.com, accessed November 2005.
4. Chris Murphy, "RIM Settles BlackBerry Suit," InformationWeek, March 6, 2006.

APPENDIX D (at www.mhhe.com/baltzan)

1. "Python Project Failure," www.systemsdev.com, accessed November 14, 2003.
2. Gary McGraw, "Making Essential Software Work," Software Quality Management, April 2003, www.sqm-magazine.com, accessed November 14, 2003.
3. www.standishgroup.com, accessed November 14, 2003.

GLOSSARY

A

acceptable use policy (AUP)   A policy that a user must agree to follow in order to be provided access to a network or to the Internet.

accounting   Analyzes the transactional information of the business so the owners and investors can make sound economic decisions.

accounting and finance ERP component   Manages accounting data and financial processes within the enterprise with functions such as general ledger, accounts payable, accounts receivable, budgeting, and asset management.

accounting department   Provides quantitative information about the finances of the business including recording, measuring, and describing financial information.

adware   Software that generates ads that install themselves on a computer when a person downloads some other program from the Internet.

affinity grouping   Determination of which things go together.

agile methodology   Aims for customer satisfaction through early and continuous delivery of useful software components.

analysis latency   The time from which data is made available to the time when analysis is complete.

analysis phase   Analyzing end-user business requirements and refining project goals into defined functions and operations of the intended system.

analytical CRM   Supports back-office operations and strategic analysis and includes all systems that do not deal directly with customers.

analytical information   Encompasses all organizational information, and its primary purpose is to support the performing of managerial analysis tasks.

anti-spam policy   States that email users will not send unsolicited emails (or spam).

application architecture   Determines how applications integrate and relate to each other.

application programming interface (API)   A set of routines, protocols, and tools for building software applications.

application service provider (ASP)   A company that offers an organization access over the Internet to systems and related services that would otherwise have to be located in personal or organizational computers.

application software   Used for specific information processing needs, including payroll, customer relationship management, project management, training, and many others.

arithmetic/logic unit (ALU)   Performs all arithmetic operations (for example, addition and subtraction) and all logic operations (such as sorting and comparing numbers).

artificial intelligence (AI)   Simulates human intelligence such as the ability to reason and learn.

As-Is process model   Represents the current state of the operation that has been mapped, without any specific improvements or changes to existing processes.

asset   Anything owned that has value or earning power.

associates program (affiliate program)   Businesses can generate commissions or royalties from an Internet site.

association detection   Reveals the degree to which variables are related and the nature and frequency of these relationships in the information.

attribute   Characteristics or properties of an entity class.

authentication   A method for confirming users' identities.

authorization   The process of giving someone permission to do or have something.

automatic call distribution   A phone switch routes inbound calls to available agents.

availability   Addresses when systems can be accessed by users.

B

backdoor program   Viruses that open a way into the network for future attacks.

backup   An exact copy of a system's information.

backward integration   Takes information entered into a given system and sends it automatically to all upstream systems and processes.

balance sheet   Gives an accounting picture of property owned by a company and of claims against the property on a specific date.

balanced scorecard   A management system (not only a measurement system) that enables organizations to clarify their vision and strategy and translate them into action.

bandwidth   The difference between the highest and the lowest frequencies that can be transmitted on a single medium, and it is a measure of the medium's capacity.

banner ad   Small ad on one website that advertises the products and services of another business, usually another dot-com business.

benchmark   Baseline values the system seeks to attain.

benchmarking   The process of continuously measuring system results, comparing those results to optimal system performance (benchmark values), and identifying steps and procedures to improve system performance.

binary digit (bit)   The smallest unit of information that a computer can process.

biometric The identification of a user based on a physical characteristic, such as a fingerprint, iris, face, voice, or handwriting.

black-hat hacker Breaks into other people's computer systems and may just look around or steal and destroy information.

blog Website in which items are posted on a regular basis and displayed in reverse chronological order.

Bluetooth A telecommunications industry specification that describes how mobile phones, computers, and personal digital assistants (PDAs) can be easily interconnected using a short-range wireless connection.

bookkeeping The actual recording of the business's transactions, without any analysis of the information.

break-even point The point at which revenues equal costs.

brick-and-mortar business A business that operates in a physical store without an Internet presence.

broadband High-speed Internet connections transmitting data at speeds greater than 200 kilobytes per second (Kbps), compared to the 56 Kbps maximum speed offered by traditional dial-up connections.

bullwhip effect Occurs when distorted product demand information passes from one entity to the next throughout the supply chain.

business continuity planning (BCP) A plan for how an organization will recover and restore partially or completely interrupted critical function(s) within a predetermined time after a disaster or extended disruption.

business-critical integrity constraint Enforces business rules vital to an organization's success and often requires more insight and knowledge than relational integrity constraints.

business facing process Invisible to the external customer but essential to the effective management of the business and includes goal setting, day-to-day planning, performance feedback, rewards, and resource allocation.

business intelligence Refers to applications and technologies that are used to gather, provide access to, and analyze data and information to support decision-making efforts.

business process A standardized set of activities that accomplish a specific task, such as processing a customer's order.

business process improvement Attempts to understand and measure the current process and make performance improvements accordingly.

business process management (BPM) Integrates all of an organization's business processes to make individual processes more efficient.

business process model A graphic description of a process, showing the sequence of process tasks, which is developed for a specific purpose and from a selected viewpoint.

business process modeling (or mapping) The activity of creating a detailed flow chart or process map of a work process showing its inputs, tasks, and activities, in a structured sequence.

business process reengineering (BPR) The analysis and redesign of workflow within and between enterprises.

business requirement The detailed set of business requests that the system must meet in order to be successful.

business wiki Collaborative web pages that allow users to edit documents, share ideas, or monitor the status of a project.

business-to-business (B2B) Applies to businesses buying from and selling to each other over the Internet.

business-to-business (B2B) marketplace An Internet-based service that brings together many buyers and sellers.

business-to-consumer (B2C) Applies to any business that sells its products or services to consumers over the Internet.

buyer power High when buyers have many choices of whom to buy from and low when their choices are few.

byte Group of eight bits represents one natural language character.

C

cache memory A small unit of ultra-fast memory that is used to store recently accessed or frequently accessed data so that the CPU does not have to retrieve this data from slower memory circuits such as RAM.

call scripting system Accesses organizational databases that track similar issues or questions and automatically generates the details for the customer service representative who can then relay them to the customer.

campaign management system Guides users through marketing campaigns performing such tasks as campaign definition, planning, scheduling, segmentation, and success analysis.

capability maturity model integration method (CMMI) A process improvement approach that contains 22 process areas.

capacity planning Determines the future IT infrastructure requirements for new equipment and additional network capacity.

capital Represents money whose purpose is to make more money, for example, the money used to buy a rental property or a business.

central processing unit (CPU) (or microprocessor) The actual hardware that interprets and executes the program (software) instructions and coordinates how all the other hardware devices work together.

change control board (CCB) Responsible for approving or rejecting all change requests.

change management A set of techniques that aid in evolution, composition, and policy management of the design and implementation of a system.

change management system Includes a collection of procedures to document a change request and define the steps necessary to consider the change based on the expected impact of the change.

chief information officer (CIO)   Responsible for (1) overseeing all uses of information technology and (2) ensuring the strategic alignment of IT with business goals and objectives.

chief knowledge officer (CKO)   Responsible for collecting, maintaining, and distributing the organization's knowledge.

chief privacy officer (CPO)   Responsible for ensuring the ethical and legal use of information within an organization.

chief security officer (CSO)   Responsible for ensuring the security of IT systems and developing strategies and IT safeguards against attacks from hackers and viruses.

chief technology officer (CTO)   Responsible for ensuring the throughput, speed, accuracy, availability, and reliability of an organization's information technology.

classification   The assignment of records to one of a predefined set of classes.

click-and-mortar business   A business that operates in a physical store and on the Internet.

clickstream   Records information about a customer during a web surfing session such as what websites were visited, how long the visit was, what ads were viewed, and what was purchased.

clickstream data   Exact pattern of a consumer's navigation through a site.

click-through   A count of the number of people who visit one site and click on an advertisement that takes them to the site of the advertiser.

click-to-talk   Buttons allow customers to click on a button and talk with a customer service representative via the Internet.

client   Computer that is designed to request information from a server.

client/server network   A model for applications in which the bulk of the back-end processing, such as performing a physical search of a database, takes place on a server, while the front-end processing, which involves communicating with the users, is handled by the clients.

cluster analysis   A technique used to divide an information set into mutually exclusive groups such that the members of each group are as close together as possible to one another and the different groups are as far apart as possible.

clustering   Segmentation of a heterogeneous population of records into a number of more homogeneous subgroups.

coaxial cable   Cable that can carry a wide range of frequencies with low signal loss.

cold site   A separate facility that does not have any computer equipment, but is a place where employees can move after a disaster.

collaboration system   An IT-based set of tools that supports the work of teams by facilitating the sharing and flow of information.

collaborative demand planning   Helps organizations reduce their investment in inventory, while improving customer satisfaction through product availability.

collaborative engineering   Allows an organization to reduce the cost and time required during the design process of a product.

commercial off-the-shelf (COTS)   A software package or solution that is purchased to support one or more business functions and information systems.

committee of sponsoring organizations (COSO)   Evaluates internal controls such as human resources, logistics, information technology, risk, legal, marketing and sales, operations, financial functions, procurement, and reporting.

communication device   Equipment used to send information and receive it from one location to another.

competitive advantage   A product or service that an organization's customers place a greater value on than similar offerings from a competitor.

complex instruction set computer (CISC) chip   Type of CPU that can recognize as many as 100 or more instructions, enough to carry out most computations directly.

compliance   The act of conforming, acquiescing, or yielding.

computer   Electronic device operating under the control of instructions stored in its own memory that can accept, manipulate, and store data.

computer-aided software engineering (CASE)   Software suites that automate systems analysis, design, and development.

confidentiality   The assurance that messages and information are available only to those who are authorized to view them.

consolidation   Involves the aggregation of information and features simple roll-ups to complex groupings of interrelated information.

consumer-to-business (C2B)   Applies to any consumer that sells a product or service to a business over the Internet.

consumer-to-consumer (C2C)   Applies to sites primarily offering goods and services to assist consumers interacting with each other over the Internet.

contact center (call center)   Customer service representatives (CSRs) answer customer inquiries and respond to problems through a number of different customer touchpoints.

contact management CRM system   Maintains customer contact information and identifies prospective customers for future sales.

content filtering   Occurs when organizations use software that filters content to prevent the transmission of unauthorized information.

content management system   Provides tools to manage the creation, storage, editing, and publication of information in a collaborative environment.

control unit   Interprets software instructions and literally tells the other hardware devices what to do, based on the software instructions.

cookie   A small file deposited on a hard drive by a website containing information about customers and their web activities.

copyright The legal protection afforded an expression of an idea, such as a song, video game, and some types of proprietary documents.

core competency An organization's key strength or business function that it does better than any of its competitors.

core competency strategy When an organization chooses to focus specifically on what it does best (its core competency) and forms partnerships and alliances with other specialist organizations to handle nonstrategic business processes.

core ERP component Traditional components included in most ERP systems and they primarily focus on internal operations.

corporate policy A dimension of social responsibility that refers to the position a firm takes on social and political issues.

corporate responsibility A dimension of social responsibility that includes everything from hiring minority workers to making safe products.

corporation (also called, **organization, enterprise,** or **business**) An artificially created legal entity that exists separate and apart from those individuals who created it and carry on its operations.

counterfeit software Software that is manufactured to look like the real thing and sold as such.

cracker A hacker with criminal intent.

critical path A path from the start to the finish that passes through all the tasks that are critical to completing the project in the shortest amount of time.

critical success factor (CSF) A factor that is critical to an organization's success.

CRM analysis technologies Help organizations segment their customers into categories such as best and worst customers.

CRM predicting technologies Help organizations make predictions regarding customer behavior such as which customers are at risk of leaving.

CRM reporting technologies Help organizations identify their customers across other applications.

cross-selling Selling additional products or services to a customer.

cube The common term for the representation of multidimensional information.

customer facing process Results in a product or service that is received by an organization's external customer.

customer relationship management (CRM) Involves managing all aspects of a customer's relationship with an organization to increase customer loyalty and retention and an organization's profitability.

cyberterrorist Seeks to cause harm to people or to destroy critical systems or information and use the Internet as a weapon of mass destruction.

D

data Raw facts that describe the characteristics of an event.

database Maintains information about various types of objects (inventory), events (transactions), people (employees), and places (warehouses).

database management system (DBMS) Software through which users and application programs interact with a database.

database-based workflow system Stores documents in a central location and automatically asks the team members to access the document when it is their turn to edit the document.

data-driven website An interactive website kept constantly updated and relevant to the needs of its customers through the use of a database.

data flow diagram (DFD) Illustrates the movement of information between external entities and the processes and data stores within the system.

data latency The time duration to make data ready for analysis, i.e., the time for extracting, transforming, and cleansing the data, and loading it into the database.

data mart Contains a subset of data warehouse information.

data mining The process of analyzing data to extract information not offered by the raw data alone.

data-mining tool Uses a variety of techniques to find patterns and relationships in large volumes of information and infer rules from them that predict future behavior and guide decision making.

data model A formal way to express data relationships to a database management system (DBMS).

data warehouse A logical collection of information—gathered from many different operational databases—that supports business analysis activities and decision-making tasks.

decision latency The time it takes a human to comprehend the analytic result and determine an appropriate action.

decision support system (DSS) Models information to support managers and business professionals during the decision-making process.

demand planning system Generates demand forecasts using statistical tools and forecasting techniques.

denial-of-service attack (DoS) Floods a website with so many requests for service that it slows down or crashes the site.

dependency A logical relationship that exists between the project tasks, or between a project task and a milestone.

deperimeterization Occurs when an organization moves employees outside its firewall, a growing movement to change the way corporations address technology security.

design phase Involves describing the desired features and operations of the system including screen layouts, business rules, process diagrams, pseudo code, and other documentation.

development phase Involves taking all of the detailed design documents from the design phase and transforming them into the actual system.

digital asset management system (DAM) Though similar to document management, DAM generally works with binary rather than text files, such as multimedia file types.

digital Darwinism Organizations that cannot adapt to the new demands placed on them for surviving in the information age are doomed to extinction.

digital dashboard Integrates information from multiple components and tailors the information to individual preferences.

digital divide When those with access to technology have great advantages over those without access to technology.

digital wallet Both software and information—the software provides security for the transaction and the information includes payment and delivery information (for example, the credit card number and expiration date).

disaster recovery cost curve Charts (1) the cost to the organization of the unavailability of information and technology and (2) the cost to the organization of recovering from a disaster over time.

disaster recovery plan A detailed process for recovering information or an IT system in the event of a catastrophic disaster such as a fire or flood.

disruptive technology A new way of doing things that initially does not meet the needs of existing customers.

distributed denial-of-service attack (DDoS) Attacks from multiple computers that flood a website with so many requests for service that it slows down or crashes.

distribution management system Coordinates the process of transporting materials from a manufacturer to distribution centers to the final customer.

dividend A distribution of earnings to shareholders.

document management system (DMS) Supports the electronic capturing, storage, distribution, archival, and accessing of documents.

drill-down Enables users to get details, and details of details, of information.

E

ebusiness The conducting of business on the Internet, not only buying and selling, but also serving customers and collaborating with business partners.

ebusiness model An approach to conducting electronic business on the Internet.

ecommerce The buying and selling of goods and services over the Internet.

effectiveness IT metric Measures the impact IT has on business processes and activities including customer satisfaction, conversion rates, and sell-through increases.

efficiency IT metric Measures the performance of the IT system itself including throughput, speed, and availability.

egovernment Involves the use of strategies and technologies to transform government(s) by improving the delivery of services and enhancing the quality of interaction between the citizen-consumer within all branches of government.

elogistics Manages the transportation and storage of goods.

electronic bill presentment and payment (EBPP) System that sends bills over the Internet and provides an easy-to-use mechanism (such as clicking on a button) to pay the bill.

electronic catalog Presents customers with information about goods and services offered for sale, bid, or auction on the Internet.

electronic check Mechanism for sending a payment from a checking or savings account.

electronic data interchange (EDI) A standard format for exchanging business data.

electronic marketplace, or emarketplace Interactive business communities providing a central market space where multiple buyers and suppliers can engage in ebusiness activities.

electronic tagging A technique for identifying and tracking assets and individuals via technologies such as radio frequency identification and smart cards.

elevation of privilege Process by which a user misleads a system into granting unauthorized rights, usually for the purpose of compromising or destroying the system.

email privacy policy Details the extent to which email messages may be read by others.

emall Consists of a number of eshops; it serves as a gateway through which a visitor can access other eshops.

employee monitoring policy States how, when, and where the company monitors its employees.

employee relationship management (ERM) Provides employees with a subset of CRM applications available through a web browser.

encryption Scrambles information into an alternative form that requires a key or password to decrypt the information.

enterprise application integration (EAI) middleware Represents a new approach to middleware by packaging together commonly used functionality, such as providing prebuilt links to popular enterprise applications, which reduces the time necessary to develop solutions that integrate applications from multiple vendors.

enterprise architect (EA) Person grounded in technology, fluent in business, a patient diplomat, and provides the important bridge between IT and the business.

enterprise architecture Includes the plans for how an organization will build, deploy, use, and share its data, processes, and IT assets.

enterprise resource planning (ERP) Integrates all departments and functions throughout an organization into a single IT system (or integrated set of IT systems) so that employees can make decisions by viewing enterprisewide information on all business operations.

entity   In the relational database model is a person, place, thing, transaction, or event about which information is stored.

entity-relationship diagram (ERD)   A technique for documenting the relationships between entities in a database environment.

entry barrier   A product or service feature that customers have come to expect from organizations in a particular industry and must be offered by an entering organization to compete and survive.

environmental scanning   The acquisition and analysis of events and trends in the environment external to an organization.

epolicies   Policies and procedures that address the ethical use of computers and Internet usage in the business environment.

eprocurement   The B2B purchase and sale of supplies and services over the Internet.

estimation   Determine values for an unknown continuous variable behavior or estimated future value.

eshop (estore or etailer)   A version of a retail store where customers can shop at any hour of the day without leaving their home or office.

ethernet   A physical and data layer technology for LAN networking.

ethical computer use policy   Contains general principles to guide computer user behavior.

ethics   Principles and standards that guide our behavior toward other people.

ewaste   Old computer equipment where the toxic substances it contains can leach into groundwater, among other problems.

executive information system (EIS)   A specialized DSS that supports senior-level executives within the organization.

executive sponsor   The person or group who provides the financial resources for the project.

expense   Refers to the costs incurred in operating and maintaining a business.

expert system   Computerized advisory programs that imitate the reasoning processes of experts in solving difficult problems.

explicit knowledge   Consists of anything that can be documented, archived, and codified, often with the help of IT.

extended ERP component   The extra components that meet the organizational needs not covered by the core components and primarily focus on external operations.

extensible markup language (XML)   A markup language for documents containing structured information.

extraction, transformation, and loading (ETL)   A process that extracts information from internal and external databases, transforms the information using a common set of enterprise definitions, and loads the information into a data warehouse.

extranet   An intranet that is available to strategic allies (such as customers, suppliers, and partners).

extreme programming (XP) methodology   Breaks a project into tiny phases, and developers cannot continue on to the next phase until the first phase is complete.

F

failover   A backup in which the functions of a computer component (such as a processor, server, network, or database) are assumed by secondary system components when the primary component becomes unavailable through either failure or scheduled downtime.

fair use doctrine   In certain situations, it is legal to use copyrighted material.

fault tolerance   A computer system designed that in the event a component fails, a backup component or procedure can immediately take its place with no loss of service.

feasibility study   Determines if the proposed solution is feasible and achievable from a financial, technical, and organizational standpoint.

feature creep   Occurs when developers add extra features that were not part of the initial requirements.

fiber optic (optical fiber)   The technology associated with the transmission of information as light impulses along a glass wire or fiber.

finance   Deals with the strategic financial issues associated with increasing the value of the business while observing applicable laws and social responsibilities.

financial accounting   Involves preparing financial reports that provide information about the business's performance to external parties such as investors, creditors, and tax authorities.

financial cybermediary   Internet-based company that facilitates payments over the Internet.

financial EDI (financial electronic data interchange)   Standard electronic process for B2B market purchase payments.

financial quarter   A three-month period (four quarters per year).

financial statement   Written records of the financial status of the business that allow interested parties to evaluate the profitability and solvency of the business.

firewall   Hardware and/or software that guards a private network by analyzing the information leaving and entering the network.

first-mover advantage   An organization can significantly impact its market share by being first to market with a competitive advantage.

Five Forces model   Helps determine the relative attractiveness of an industry.

flash memory   A special type of rewriteable read-only memory (ROM) that is compact and portable.

for-profit corporations   Primarily focus on making money and all profits and losses are shared by the business owners.

forecast   Predictions made on the basis of time-series information.

foreign key A primary key of one table that appears as an attribute in another table and acts to provide a logical relationship between the two tables.

forward integration Takes information entered into a given system and sends it automatically to all downstream systems and processes.

fuzzy logic A mathematical method of handling imprecise or subjective information.

G

Gantt chart A simple bar chart that depicts project tasks against a calendar.

genetic algorithm An artificial intelligence system that mimics the evolutionary, survival-of-the-fittest process to generate increasingly better solutions to a problem.

geoeconomic The effects of geography on the economic realities of international business activities.

geographic information system (GIS) Designed to work with information that can be shown on a map.

gigabyte (GB) Roughly 1 billion bytes.

gigahertz (GHz) The number of billions of CPU cycles per second.

global inventory management system Provides the ability to locate, track, and predict the movement of every component or material anywhere upstream or downstream in the production process.

global positioning system (GPS) Is a constellation of 24 well-spaced satellites that orbit the Earth and make it possible for people with ground receivers to pinpoint their geographic location.

goal-seeking analysis Finds the inputs necessary to achieve a goal such as a desired level of output.

governance A method or system of government for management or control.

graphical user interface (GUI) The interface to an information system.

grid computing An aggregation of geographically dispersed computing, storage, and network resources, coordinated to deliver improved performance, higher quality of service, better utilization, and easier access to data.

groupware Software that supports team interaction and dynamics including calendaring, scheduling, and video-conferencing.

H

hacker People very knowledgeable about computers who use their knowledge to invade other people's computers.

hactivist Person with philosophical and political reasons for breaking into systems and will often deface the website as a protest.

hard drive Secondary storage medium that uses several rigid disks coated with a magnetically sensitive material and housed together with the recording heads in a hermetically sealed mechanism.

hardware Consists of the physical devices associated with a computer system.

hardware key logger A hardware device that captures keystrokes on their journey from the keyboard to the motherboard.

help desk A group of people who respond to internal system user questions.

hierarchical database model Information is organized into a treelike structure that allows repeating information using parent/child relationships, in such a way that it cannot have too many relationships.

high availability Refers to a system or component that is continuously operational for a desirably long length of time.

hoaxes Attack computer systems by transmitting a virus hoax, with a real virus attached.

hot site A separate and fully equipped facility where the company can move immediately after a disaster and resume business.

human resource ERP component Tracks employee information including payroll, benefits, compensation, and performance assessment, and assures compliance with the legal requirements of multiple jurisdictions and tax authorities.

human resources management (HRM) Includes the policies, plans, and procedures for the effective management of employees (human resources).

hypertext transfer protocol (HTTP) The Internet standard that supports the exchange of information on the WWW.

I

identity theft The forging of someone's identity for the purpose of fraud.

implementation phase Involves placing the system into production so users can begin to perform actual business operations with the system.

income statement (also referred to as **earnings report, operating statement,** and **profit-and-loss (P&L) statement**) Reports operating results (revenues minus expenses) for a given time period ending at a specified date.

information Data converted into a meaningful and useful context.

information accuracy Extent to which a system generates the correct results when executing the same transaction numerous times.

information architecture Identifies where and how important information, like customer records, is maintained and secured.

information cleansing or scrubbing A process that weeds out and fixes or discards inconsistent, incorrect, or incomplete information.

information ethics Concerns the ethical and moral issues arising from the development and use of information technologies, as well as the creation, collection, duplication, distribution, and processing of information itself (with or without the aid of computer technologies).

information granularity Refers to the extent of detail within the information (fine and detailed or "coarse" and abstract information).

information integrity A measure of the quality of information.

information partnership Occurs when two or more organizations cooperate by integrating their IT systems, thereby providing customers with the best of what each can offer.

information privacy Concerns the legal right or general expectation of individuals, groups, or institutions to determine for themselves, when, and to what extent, information about them is communicated to others.

information privacy policy Contains general principles regarding information privacy.

information reach Refers to the number of people a business can communicate with, on a global basis.

information richness Refers to the depth and breadth of information transferred between customers and businesses.

information security A broad term encompassing the protection of information from accidental or intentional misuse by persons inside or outside an organization.

information security plan Details how an organization will implement the information security policies.

information security policy Identifies the rules required to maintain information security.

information systems audit and control association (ISACA) A set of guidelines and supporting tool set for IT governance that is accepted worldwide.

information technology (IT) A field concerned with the use of technology in managing and processing information. Information technology can be an important enabler of business success and innovation.

information technology infrastructure library (ITIL) A framework provided by the government of the United Kingdom offering eight sets of management procedures.

information technology monitoring Tracking people's activities by such measures as number of keystrokes, error rate, and number of transactions processed.

infrastructure architecture Includes the hardware, software, and telecommunications equipment that, when combined, provide the underlying foundation to support the organization's goals.

innovation The introduction of new equipment or methods.

input device Equipment used to capture information and commands.

insider Legitimate users who purposely or accidentally misuse their access to the environment and cause some kind of business-affecting incident.

insourcing (in-house development) A common approach using the professional expertise within an organization to develop and maintain the organization's information technology systems.

instant messaging (IM or IMing) A type of communications service that enables someone to create a kind of private chat room with another individual in order to communicate in real-time over the Internet.

integration Allows separate systems to communicate directly with each other.

integrity constraint The rules that help ensure the quality of information.

intellectual property Intangible creative work that is embodied in physical form.

intelligent agent A special-purpose knowledge-based information system that accomplishes specific tasks on behalf of its users.

intelligent system Various commercial applications of artificial intelligence.

interactive voice response (IVR) Directs customers to use touch-tone phones or keywords to navigate or provide information.

interactivity Measures the visitor interactions with the target ad.

intermediary Agents, software, or businesses that bring buyers and sellers together that provide a trading infrastructure to enhance ebusiness.

international organization for standardization (ISO) A nongovernmental organization established in 1947 to promote the development of world standards to facilitate the international exchange of goods and services.

Internet A global public network of computer networks that pass information from one to another using common computer protocols.

Internet service provider (ISP) A company that provides individuals and other companies access to the Internet along with additional related services, such as website building.

Internet use policy Contains general principles to guide the proper use of the Internet.

interoperability Capability of two or more computer systems to share data and resources, even though they are made by different manufacturers.

intranet An internalized portion of the Internet, protected from outside access, that allows an organization to provide access to information and application software to only its employees.

intrusion detection software (IDS) Searches out patterns in information and network traffic to indicate attacks and quickly responds to prevent any harm.

inventory management and control system Provides control and visibility to the status of individual items maintained in inventory.

iterative development Consists of a series of tiny projects.

J

joint application development (JAD) A session where employees meet, sometimes for several days, to define or review the business requirements for the system.

K

key logger, or key trapper, software A program that, when installed on a computer, records every keystroke and mouse click.

key performance indicator (KPI) Measures that are tied to business drivers.

kill switch A trigger that enables a project manager to close the project prior to completion.

kiosk Publicly accessible computer system that has been set up to allow interactive information browsing.

knowledge management (KM) Involves capturing, classifying, evaluating, retrieving, and sharing information assets in a way that provides context for effective decisions and actions.

knowledge management system (KMS) Supports the capturing, organization, and dissemination of knowledge (i.e., know-how) throughout an organization.

L

liability An obligation to make financial payments.

limited liability Means that the shareholders are not personally liable for the losses incurred by the corporation.

limited liability corporation (LLC) A hybrid entity that has the legal protections of a corporation and the ability to be taxed (one time) as a partnership.

limited partnership Much like a general partnership except for one important fundamental difference; the law protects the limited partner from being responsible for all of the partnership's losses.

list generator Compiles customer information from a variety of sources and segments the information for different marketing campaigns.

local area network (LAN) Designed to connect a group of computers in close proximity to each other such as in an office building, a school, or a home.

location-based services (LBS) Wireless mobile content services that provide location-specific information to mobile users moving from location to location.

logical view Focuses on how users logically access information to meet their particular business needs.

logistics The set of processes that plans for and controls the efficient and effective transportation and storage of supplies from suppliers to customers.

loose coupling The capability of services to be joined together on demand to create composite services, or disassembled just as easily into their functional components.

loss Occurs when businesses sell products or services for less than they cost to produce.

loyalty program Rewards customers based on the amount of business they do with a particular organization.

M

magnetic medium Secondary storage medium that uses magnetic techniques to store and retrieve data on disks or tapes coated with magnetically sensitive materials.

magnetic tape Older secondary storage medium that uses a strip of thin plastic coated with a magnetically sensitive recording medium.

mail bomb Sends a massive amount of email to a specific person or system resulting in filling up the recipient's disk space, which, in some cases, may be too much for the server to handle and may cause the server to stop functioning.

maintenance The fixing or enhancing of an information system.

maintenance phase Involves performing changes, corrections, additions, and upgrades to ensure the system continues to meet the business goals.

maintenance, repair, and operations (MRO) materials (also called indirect materials) Materials necessary for running an organization but do not relate to the company's primary business activities.

malicious code Includes a variety of threats such as viruses, worms, and Trojan horses.

management information system (MIS) A general name for the business function and academic discipline covering the application of people, technologies, and procedures—collectively called information systems—to solve business problems

managerial accounting Involves analyzing business operations for internal decision making and does not have to follow any rules issued by standard-setting bodies such as GAAP.

market basket analysis Analyzes such items as websites and checkout scanner information to detect customers' buying behavior and predict future behavior by identifying affinities among customers' choices of products and services.

marketing The process associated with promoting the sale of goods or services.

marketing communication Seeks to build product or service awareness and to educate potential consumers on the product or service.

marketing mix Includes the variables that marketing managers can control in order to best satisfy customers in the target market.

market segmentation The division of a market into similar groups of customers.

market share Calculated by dividing the firm's sales by the total market sales for the entire industry.

mashup editor WYSIWYG (What You See Is What You Get) for mashups.

mass customization Ability of an organization to give its customers the opportunity to tailor its products or services to the customers' specifications.

materials requirement planning (MRP) system Uses sales forecasts to make sure that needed parts and materials are available at the right time and place in a specific company.

megabyte (MB or M or Meg) Roughly 1 million bytes.

megahertz (MHz) The number of millions of CPU cycles per second.

memory card   Contains high-capacity storage that holds data such as captured images, music, or text files.

memory stick   Provides nonvolatile memory for a range of portable devices including computers, digital cameras, MP3 players, and PDAs.

messaging-based work-flow system   Sends work assignments through an email system.

methodology   A set of policies, procedures, standards, processes, practices, tools, techniques, and tasks that people apply to technical and management challenges.

metropolitan area network (MAN)   A large computer network usually spanning a city.

microwave transmitter   Uses the atmosphere (or outer space) as the transmission medium to send the signal to a microwave receiver.

middleware   Different types of software that sit in the middle of and provide connectivity between two or more software applications.

mobile commerce, or **m-commerce**   The ability to purchase goods and services through a wireless Internet-enabled device.

model   A simplified representation or abstraction of reality.

modeling   The activity of drawing a graphical representation of a design.

multitasking   Allows more than one piece of software to be used at a time.

N

nearshore outsourcing   Contracting an outsourcing agreement with a company in a nearby country.

net income   The amount of money remaining after paying taxes.

network   A communications, data exchange, and resource-sharing system created by linking two or more computers and establishing standards, or protocols, so that they can work together.

network database model   A flexible way of representing objects and their relationships.

network operating system (NOS)   The operating system that runs a network, steering information between computers and managing security and users.

network topology   Refers to the geometric arrangement of the actual physical organization of the computers (and other network devices) in a network.

network transmission media   Various types of media used to carry the signal between computers.

neural network (an artificial neural network)   A category of AI that attempts to emulate the way the human brain works.

nonrepudiation   A contractual stipulation to ensure that ebusiness participants do not deny (repudiate) their online actions.

not-for-profit (or **nonprofit**) **corporation**   Usually exists to accomplish some charitable, humanitarian, or educational purpose, and the profits and losses are not shared by the business owners.

O

offshore outsourcing   Using organizations from developing countries to write code and develop systems.

online ad   Box running across a web page that is often used to contain advertisements.

online analytical processing (OLAP)   The manipulation of information to create business intelligence in support of strategic decision making.

online service provider (OSP)   Offers an extensive array of unique services such as its own version of a web browser.

online training   Runs over the Internet or off a CD-ROM.

online transaction processing (OLTP)   The capturing of transaction and event information using technology to (1) process the information according to defined business rules, (2) store the information, and (3) update existing information to reflect the new information.

onshore outsourcing   The process of engaging another company within the same country for services.

open source   Any program whose source code is made available for use or modification as users or other developers see fit.

open system   A broad, general term that describes non-proprietary IT hardware and software made available by the standards and procedures by which their products work, making it easier to integrate them.

operating system software   Controls the application software and manages how the hardware devices work together.

operational CRM   Supports traditional transactional processing for day-to-day front-office operations or systems that deal directly with the customers.

operational planning and control (OP&C)   Deals with the day-to-day procedures for performing work, including scheduling, inventory, and process management.

operations management (OM)   The management of systems or processes that convert or transform resources (including human resources) into goods and services.

opportunity management CRM system   Targets sales opportunities by finding new customers or companies for future sales.

opt-in   Implying that a company will contact only the people who have agreed to receive promotions and marketing material via email.

output device   Equipment used to see, hear, or otherwise accept the results of information processing requests.

outsourcing   An arrangement by which one organization provides a service or services for another organization that chooses not to perform them in-house.

owner's equity   The portion of a company belonging to the owners.

P

packet-switching Occurs when the sending computer divides a message into a number of efficiently sized units called packets, each of which contains the address of the destination computer.

packet tampering Altering the contents of packets as they travel over the Internet or altering data on computer disks after penetrating a network.

partner relationship management (PRM) Focuses on keeping vendors satisfied by managing alliance partner and reseller relationships that provide customers with the optimal sales channel.

partnership Similar to sole proprietorships, except that this legal structure allows for more than one owner.

partnership agreement A legal agreement between two or more business partners that outlines core business issues.

peer-to-peer (P2P) network Any network without a central file server and in which all computers in the network have access to the public files located on all other workstations.

performance Measures how quickly a system performs a certain process or transaction (in terms of efficiency IT metrics of both speed and throughput).

personalization Occurs when a website can know enough about a person's likes and dislikes that it can fashion offers that are more likely to appeal to that person.

PERT (Program Evaluation and Review Technique) chart A graphical network model that depicts a project's tasks and the relationships between those tasks.

phishing Technique to gain personal information for the purpose of identity theft, usually by means of fraudulent email.

physical view The physical storage of information on a storage device such as a hard disk.

pirated software The unauthorized use, duplication, distribution, or sale of copyrighted software.

planning phase Involves establishing a high-level plan of the intended project and determining project goals.

podcasting Distribution of audio or video files, such as radio programs or music videos, over the Internet to play on mobile devices and personal computers.

polymorphic virus and worm Change their form as they propagate.

pop-under ad Form of a pop-up ad that users do not see until they close the current web browser screen.

pop-up ad Small web page containing an advertisement that appears on the web page outside of the current website loaded in the web browser.

portal A website that offers a broad array of resources and services, such as email, online discussion groups, search engines, and online shopping malls.

predictive dialing Automatically dials outbound calls and when someone answers, the call is forwarded to an available agent.

primary key A field (or group of fields) that uniquely identifies a given entity in a table.

primary storage Computer's main memory, which consists of the random access memory (RAM), cache memory, and the read-only memory (ROM) that is directly accessible to the CPU.

privacy The right to be left alone when you want to be, to have control over your own personal possessions, and not to be observed without your consent.

private exchange A B2B marketplace in which a single buyer posts its need and then opens the bidding to any supplier who would care to bid.

process modeling Involves graphically representing the processes that capture, manipulate, store, and distribute information between a system and its environment.

product life cycle Includes the four phases a product progresses through during its life cycle including introduction, growth, maturity, and decline.

production The creation of goods and services using the factors of production: land, labor, capital, entrepreneurship, and knowledge.

production and materials management ERP component Handles the various aspects of production planning and execution such as demand forecasting, production scheduling, job cost accounting, and quality control.

production management Describes all the activities mangers do to help companies create goods.

profit Occurs when businesses sell products or services for more than they cost to produce.

project A temporary endeavor undertaken to create a unique product, service, or result.

project assumption Factors that are considered to be true, real, or certain without proof or demonstration.

project charter A document issued by the project initiator or sponsor that formally authorizes the existence of a project and provides the project manager with the authority to apply organizational resources to project activities.

project constraint Specific factors that can limit options.

project deliverable Any measurable, tangible, verifiable outcome, result, or item that is produced to complete a project or part of a project.

project management The application of knowledge, skills, tools, and techniques to project activities to meet project requirements.

project management institute (PMI) Develops procedures and concepts necessary to support the profession of project management (www.pmi.org).

project management office (PMO) An internal department that oversees all organizational projects.

project manager An individual who is an expert in project planning and management, defines and develops the project plan, and tracks the plan to ensure all key project milestones are completed on time and on budget.

project milestone   Represents key dates when a certain group of activities must be performed.

project objective   Quantifiable criteria that must be met for the project to be considered a success.

project plan   A formal, approved document that manages and controls project execution.

project scope   Defines the work that must be completed to deliver a product with the specified features and functions.

project stakeholder   Individuals and organizations actively involved in the project or whose interests might be affected as a result of project execution or project completion.

protocol   A standard that specifies the format of data as well as the rules to be followed during transmission.

prototype   A smaller-scale representation or working model of the user's requirements or a proposed design for an information system.

public key encryption (PKE)   Encryption system that uses two keys: a public key that everyone can have and a private key for only the recipient.

pure-play (virtual) business   A business that operates on the Internet only without a physical store.

R

radio frequency identification (RFID)   Technologies using active or passive tags in the form of chips or smart labels that can store unique identifiers and relay this information to electronic readers.

random access memory (RAM)   The computer's primary working memory, in which program instructions and data are stored so that they can be accessed directly by the CPU via the processor's high-speed external data bus.

rapid application development (RAD) (also called rapid prototyping) methodology   Emphasizes extensive user involvement in the rapid and evolutionary construction of working prototypes of a system to accelerate the systems development process.

rational unified process (RUP) methodology   Provides a framework for breaking down the development of software into four gates.

read-only memory (ROM)   The portion of a computer's primary storage that does not lose its contents when one switches off the power.

real simple syndication (RSS)   Family of web feed formats used for web syndication of programs and content.

real-time information   Immediate, up-to-date information.

real-time system   Provides real-time information in response to query requests.

recovery   The ability to get a system up and running in the event of a system crash or failure and includes restoring the information backup.

reduced instruction set computer (RISC) chip   Limits the number of instructions the CPU can execute to increase processing speed.

redundancy   The duplication of information, or storing the same information in multiple places.

reintermediation   Using the Internet to reassemble buyers, sellers, and other partners in a traditional supply chain in new ways.

relational database model   A type of database that stores information in the form of logically related two-dimensional tables.

relational integrity constraint   The rules that enforce basic and fundamental information-based constraints.

reliability   Ensures all systems are functioning correctly and providing accurate information.

requirements definition document   Contains the final set of business requirements, prioritized in order of business importance.

response time   The time it takes to respond to user interactions such as a mouse click.

revenue   Refers to the amount earned resulting from the delivery or manufacture of a product or from the rendering of a service.

reverse auction   An auction format in which increasingly lower bids are solicited from organizations willing to supply the desired product or service at an increasingly lower price.

rivalry among existing competitors   High when competition is fierce in a market and low when competition is more complacent.

router   An intelligent connecting device that examines each packet of data it receives and then decides which way to send it onward toward its destination.

S

sales   The function of selling a good or service and focuses on increasing customer sales, which increases company revenues.

sales force automation (SFA)   A system that automatically tracks all of the steps in the sales process.

sales management CRM system   Automates each phase of the sales process, helping individual sales representatives coordinate and organize all of their accounts.

satellite   A big microwave repeater in the sky; it contains one or more transponders that listen to a particular portion of the electromagnetic spectrum, amplifying incoming signals, and retransmitting them back to Earth.

scalability   Refers to how well a system can adapt to increased demands.

scope creep   Occurs when the scope of the project increases.

script kiddies or script bunnies   Find hacking code on the Internet and click-and-point their way into systems to cause damage or spread viruses.

scrum methodology   Uses small teams to produce small pieces of deliverable software using sprints, or 30-day intervals, to achieve an appointed goal.

search engine optimization (SEO) Set of methods aimed at improving the ranking of a website in search engine listings.

secondary storage Consists of equipment designed to store large volumes of data for long-term storage.

secure electronic transaction (SET) Transmission security method that ensures transactions are secure and legitimate.

secure socket layer (SSL) (1) Creates a secure and private connection between a client and server computer, (2) encrypts the information, and (3) sends the information over the Internet.

selling chain management Applies technology to the activities in the order life cycle from inquiry to sale.

semantic web An evolving extension of the World Wide web in which web content can be expressed not only in natural language, but also in a format that can be read and used by software agents, thus permitting them to find, share, and integrate information more easily.

sensitivity analysis The study of the impact that changes in one (or more) parts of the model have on other parts of the model.

server Computer that is dedicated to providing information in response to external requests.

service A business task.

service level agreement (SLA) Defines the specific responsibilities of the service provider and sets the customer expectations.

service-oriented architecture (SOA) A business-driven IT architectural approach that supports integrating a business as linked, repeatable tasks or services.

shareholder Another term for business owners.

shopping bot Software that will search several retailer websites and provide a comparison of each retailer's offerings including price and availability.

sign-off The system users' actual signatures indicating they approve all of the business requirements.

slice-and-dice The ability to look at information from different perspectives.

smart card A device that is around the same size as a credit card, containing embedded technologies that can store information and small amounts of software to perform some limited processing.

smartphone Combines the functions of a cellular phone and a PDA in a single device.

sniffer A program or device that can monitor data traveling over a network.

social engineering Using one's social skills to trick people into revealing access credentials or other information valuable to the attacker.

social networking analysis (SNA) A process of mapping a group's contacts (whether personal or professional) to identify who knows whom and who works with whom.

social responsibility Implies that an entity, whether it is a government, corporation, organization, or individual, has a responsibility to society.

software The set of instructions that the hardware executes to carry out specific tasks.

sole proprietorship A business form in which a single person is the sole owner and is personally responsible for all the profits and losses of the business.

solvency Represents the ability of the business to pay its bills and service its debt.

source document Describes the basic transaction data such as its date, purpose, and amount and includes cash receipts, canceled checks, invoices, customer refunds, employee time sheets, etc.

spam Unsolicited email.

spamdexing Uses a variety of deceptive techniques in an attempt to manipulate search engine rankings, whereas legitimate search engine optimization focuses on building better sites and using honest methods of promotion.

spoofing The forging of the return address on an email so that the email message appears to come from someone other than the actual sender.

spyware Software that comes hidden in free downloadable software and tracks online movements, mines the information stored on a computer, or uses a computer's CPU and storage for some task the user knows nothing about.

statement of cash flow Summarizes sources and uses of cash, indicates whether enough cash is available to carry on routine operations, and offers an analysis of all business transactions, reporting where the firm obtained its cash and how it chose to allocate the cash.

statement of owner's equity (also called **the statement of retained earnings or equity statement**) Tracks and communicates changes in the shareholder's earnings.

statistical analysis Performs such functions as information correlations, distributions, calculations, and variance analysis.

strategic business units (SBUs) Consist of several stand-alone businesses.

strategic planning Focuses on long-range planning such as plant size, location, and type of process to be used.

structured collaboration (or process collaboration) Involves shared participation in business processes, such as work flow, in which knowledge is hard coded as rules.

supplier power High when buyers have few choices of whom to buy from and low when their choices are many.

supplier relationship management (SRM) Focuses on keeping suppliers satisfied by evaluating and categorizing suppliers for different projects, which optimizes supplier selection.

supply chain Consists of all parties involved, directly or indirectly, in the procurement of a product or raw material.

supply chain event management (SCEM) Enables an organization to react more quickly to resolve supply chain issues.

supply chain execution (SCE) system Automates the different steps and stages of the supply chain.

supply chain management (SCM) Involves the management of information flows between and among stages in a supply chain to maximize total supply chain effectiveness and profitability.

supply chain planning (SCP) system Uses advanced mathematical algorithms to improve the flow and efficiency of the supply chain while reducing inventory.

supply chain visibility The ability to view all areas up and down the supply chain.

sustainable, or "green," IT The manufacture, management, use, and disposal of information technology in a way that minimizes damage to the environment, which is a critical part of a corporation's responsibility.

sustainable IT disposal The safe disposal of IT assets at the end of their life cycle.

sustaining technology Produces an improved product customers are eager to buy, such as a faster car or larger hard drive.

switching cost The costs that can make customers reluctant to switch to another product or service.

system availability Number of hours a system is available for users.

systems development life cycle (SDLC) The overall process for developing information systems from planning and analysis through implementation and maintenance.

system software Controls how the various technology tools work together along with the application software.

system virtualization The ability to present the resources of a single computer as if it is a collection of separate computers ("virtual machines"), each with its own virtual CPUs, network interfaces, storage, and operating system.

T

tacit knowledge The knowledge contained in people's heads.

tactical planning Focuses on producing goods and services as efficiently as possible within the strategic plan.

telecommunication system Enables the transmission of data over public or private networks.

telematics The blending of computers and wireless telecommunications technologies with the goal of efficiently conveying information over vast networks to improve business operations.

terabyte (TB) Roughly 1 trillion bytes.

test condition The detailed steps the system must perform along with the expected results of each step.

testing phase Involves bringing all the project pieces together into a special testing environment to test for errors, bugs, and interoperability and verify that the system meets all of the business requirements defined in the analysis phase.

threat of new entrants High when it is easy for new competitors to enter a market and low when there are significant entry barriers to entering a market.

threat of substitute products or services High when there are many alternatives to a product or service and low when there are few alternatives from which to choose.

throughput The amount of information that can travel through a system at any point in time.

time-series information Time-stamped information collected at a particular frequency.

To-Be process model Shows the results of applying change improvement opportunities to the current (As-Is) process model.

token Small electronic devices that change user passwords automatically.

transaction Exchange or transfer of goods, services, or funds involving two or more people.

transaction processing system The basic business system that serves the operational level (analysts) in an organization.

transaction speed Amount of time a system takes to perform a transaction.

transactional information Encompasses all of the information contained within a single business process or unit of work, and its primary purpose is to support the performing of daily operational tasks.

transborder data flow (TDF) Business data flows across international boundaries over the telecommunications networks of global information systems.

transformation process Often referred to as the technical core especially in manufacturing organizations and is the actual conversion of inputs to outputs.

Transmission Control Protocol/Internet Protocol (TCP/IP) Provides the technical foundation for the public Internet as well as for large numbers of private networks.

transportation planning system Tracks and analyzes the movement of materials and products to ensure the delivery of materials and finished goods at the right time, the right place, and the lowest cost.

Trojan-horse virus Hides inside other software, usually as an attachment or a downloadable file.

twisted-pair wiring A type of cable composed of four (or more) copper wires twisted around each other within a plastic sheath.

U

unstructured collaboration (or information collaboration) Includes document exchange, shared whiteboards, discussion forums, and email.

up-selling Increasing the value of a sale.

user documentation Highlights how to use the system.

utility software Provides additional functionality to the operating system.

V

value-added The term used to describe the difference between the cost of inputs and the value of price of outputs.

value-added network (VAN)   A private network, provided by a third party, for exchanging information through a high-capacity connection.

value chain   Views an organization as a series of processes, each of which adds value to the product or service for each customer.

videoconference   A set of interactive telecommunication technologies that allow two or more locations to interact via two-way video and audio transmissions simultaneously.

viral marketing   Technique that induces websites or users to pass on a marketing message to other websites or users, creating exponential growth in the message's visibility and effect.

virtualization   A framework of dividing the resources of a computer into multiple execution environments.

virtual private network (VPN)   A way to use the public telecommunication infrastructure (e.g., Internet) to provide secure access to an organization's network.

virus   Software written with malicious intent to cause annoyance or damage.

voice over IP (VoIP)   Uses TCP/IP technology to transmit voice calls over long-distance telephone lines.

volatility   Refers to RAM's complete loss of stored information if power is interrupted.

W

waterfall methodology   Activity-based process in which each phase in the SDLC is performed sequentially from planning through implementation and maintenance.

web 2.0   A set of economic, social, and technology trends that collectively form the basis for the next generation of the Internet—a more mature, distinctive medium characterized by user participation, openness, and network effects.

web-based self-service system   Allows customers to use the web to find answers to their questions or solutions to their problems.

web conference   Blends audio, video, and document-sharing technologies to create virtual meeting rooms where people "gather" at a password-protected website.

web content management system (WCM)   Adds an additional layer to document and digital asset management that enables publishing content both to intranets and to public websites.

web log   Consists of one line of information for every visitor to a website and is usually stored on a web server.

web mashup   A website or web application that uses content from more than one source to create a completely new service.

web service   Contains a repertoire of web-based data and procedural resources that use shared protocols and standards permitting different applications to share data and services.

web traffic   Includes a host of benchmarks such as the number of page views, the number of unique visitors, and the average time spent viewing a web page.

what-if analysis   Checks the impact of a change in an assumption on the proposed solution.

white-hat hacker   Works at the request of the system owners to find system vulnerabilities and plug the holes.

wide area network (WAN)   Spans a large geographic area, such as a state, province, or country.

wiki   Web-based tools that make it easy for users to add, remove, and change online content.

WiMAX   The Worldwide Interoperability for Microwave Access is a telecommunications technology aimed at providing wireless data over long distances in a variety of ways, from point-to-point links to full mobile cellular type access.

wireless fidelity (wi-fi)   A means of linking computers using infrared or radio signals.

wireless Internet service provider (WISP)   An ISP that allows subscribers to connect to a server at designated hotspots or access points using a wireless connection.

wireless media   Natural parts of the Earth's environment that can be used as physical paths to carry electrical signals.

wire media   Transmission material manufactured so that signals will be confined to a narrow path and will behave predictably.

workflow   Defines all the steps or business rules, from beginning to end, required for a business process.

workflow management system   Facilitates the automation and management of business processes and controls the movement of work through the business process.

workshop training   Set in a classroom-type environment and led by an instructor.

World Wide Web (WWW)   A global hypertext system that uses the Internet as its transport mechanism.

worm   A type of virus that spreads itself, not only from file to file, but also from computer to computer.

Chapter 1

Cut 1.1A, page 3, © McGraw-Hill Companies/Jill Braaten, photographer.

Cut 1.1B, page 3, The McGraw-Hill Companies, Inc./Lars A. Niki, photographer.

Cut 1.1C, page 3, The McGraw-Hill Companies, Inc./Christopher Kerrigan, photographer.

Figure 1.1, page 8, Paige Baltzan.

Figure 1.10, page 14, www.cio.com, accessed August 2005.

Figure 1.11. page 14. "What Concerns CIOs the Most?" www.cio.com. Accessed November 17, 2003.

Figure 1.12, page 15, www.cio.com, accessed August 2005.

Figure 1.13, page 18, United National Division for Public Economics and Public Administration, www.un.com, accessed November 10, 2003.

Figures 1.17, 1.18, 1.19, 1.21, 1.22, 1.23, pages 22–26, Porter, Michael E., Competitive Strategy: Techniques for Analyzing Industries and Competitors, The Free Press, 1998.

Figure 1.20 top left, page 25, Photo courtesy Hyundai Motor America.

Figure 1.20 top right, page 25, Photo courtesy Audi of America.

Figure 1.20 bottom left, page 25, Courtesy Kia Motors American, Inc.

Figure 1.20 bottom right, page 25, Courtesy General Motors.

Chapter 2

Cut 2.1A, page 43, Courtesy of Linden Labs.

Cut 2.1B, page 43, Courtesy of Linden Labs.

Cut 2.1C, page 43, Courtesy of Linden Labs.

Figure 2.3, page 49, Google Analytics, www.google.com/analytics, accessed July 13, 2007.

Figure 2.4, page 49, Google Analytics, www.google.com/analytics, accessed July 13, 2007.

Page 56 (left), Alexander Heimann/AFP/Getty Images.

Page 56 (center), AP/Wide World.

Page 56 (right), Jeff Greenberg/Photoedit.

Figure 2.9, page 54, www.visualmining.com, accessed June 24, 2005.

Figure 2.10, page 54, www.visualmining.com, accessed June 24, 2005.

Figures 2.13, 2.14, 2.15, 2.16, Michael Hammar and James Champy, *Beyond Reengineering, How the Process-Centered Organization Is Changing Our Work and Our Lives, New York:* HarperCollins, Publisher, 1996.

Figures 2.18, 2.19, 2.20, 2.22, 2.23, 2.24, 2.25, pages 66–71, www.smartdraw.com, accessed June 24, 2004.

Chapter 3

Cut 3.1A, page 85, Macduff Everton/Corbis.

Cut 3.1B, page 85, Jack Kurtz/The Image Works.

Cut 3.1C, page 85, AP/Wide World.

Figure 3.1, page 88, Adam Lashinsky, "The Disrupters," *Fortune,* August 11, 2003, pp. 62–65.

Figures 3.3, 3.4, pages 89–90, www.internetworldstats.com/stats.htm, accessed January 2006.

Figure 3.5, page 90, www.expedia.com, accessed October 13, 2003; www.apple.com, accessed October 13, 2003: www.dell.com, accessed October 13, 2003; www.lendingtree.com, accessed October 13, 2003: www.amazon.com, accessed October 13, 2003: www.ebay.com, accessed October 13, 2003; www.cisco.com, accessed October 13, 2003.

Figure 3.9, page 93, Tim O'Reilly, "What Is Web 2.0: Design Patterns and Business Models for the Next Generation of Software", 9/30/2005.

Figure 3.10, page 93, Tim O'Reilly, "What Is Web 2.0: Design Patterns and Business Models for the Next Generation of Software", 9/30/2005.

Figure 3.32, 3.35, pages 113 and 115, "E-Commerce Taxation," www.icsc.org/srch/ government/ECommerceFebruary2003.pdf, accessed June 8, 2004.

Chapter 4

Cut 4.1A, page 130, PhotoLink/Getty Images.

Cut 4.1B, page 130, PhotoLink/Getty Images.

Cut 4.1C, page 130, Janis Christie/Getty Images.

Figure 4.2, page 133, Scott Berianato, "Take the Pledge," www.cio.com, accessed November 17, 2003.

Figures 4.13, 4.14, 4.15, pages 142, 144, AMA Research, "Workplace Monitoring and Surveillance," www.amanet.org, April 2003, accessed March 1, 2004.

Figure 4.18, page 147, "2004 CSI/FBI Computer Crime and Security Survey."

Figure 4.19, page 139, "2005 CSI/FBI Computer Crime and Security Survey," www.usdoj.gov/criminal/cybercrime/FBI2005.pdf.

Figure 4.21, page 150, "The Security Revolution," www.cio.com, accessed June 6, 2003.

Figure 4.22, 4.23, pages 151–152, "Losses from Identity Theft to Total $221 Billion Worldwide," www.cio.com, May 23, 2003.

Figure 4.24, 4.27, 4.28, pages 154–156, "Spam Losses to Grow to $198 Billion," www .cio.com, accessed August 9, 2003.

Chapter 5

Cut 5.1A, page 168, Royalty Free/Corbis.

Cut 5.1B, page 168, Royalty Free/Corbis.

Cut 5.1C, page 168, Royalty Free/Corbis.

Figure 5.1, page 171, *BusinessWeek,* January 10, 2005.

Figure 5.2, page 171, *InformationWeek,* August 9, 2004.

Chapter 6

Page 201 (left) Digital Vision/Getty Images.

Page 201 (center), Banana Stock/PictureQuest.

Page 201 (right), Jason Reed/Getty Images.

Figure 6.8, page 216, Webopedia.com, www.webopedia.comTERM/d/database.html, accessed May 15, 2007; Oracle Database, www.oracle.com/database/index.html, accessed May 17, 2007; www.sitepoint.com/article/publishing-mysql-data-web, accessed May 16, 2007.

Chapter 7

Cut 7.1A, page 237, Getty Images.

Cut 7.1B, page 237, Getty Images.

Cut 7.1C, page 237, Getty Images.

Figure 7.13, page 253, AP/Wide World.

Chapter 8

Cut 8.1A, page 278, C. Sherburne/PhotoLink/Getty Images.

Cut 8.1B, page 278, Digital Vision/Getty Images.

Cut 8.1C, page 278, Ryan McVay/Getty Images.

Figures 8.11, 8.12, 8.15, 8.16, 8.17, pages 291–296, William Copacino, "How to Become a Supply Chain Master," Supply Chain Management Review, September 1, 2001, www.manufacutirng.net, accessed June 12, 2003.

Chapter 9

Cut 9.1A, page 313, Stockbyte/Punchstock Images.

Cut 9.1B, page 313, Steve Cole/Getty Images.

Cut 9.1C, page 313, The McGraw-Hill Companies, Inc./Lars A. Niki, photographer.

Figure 9.10, page 328, "Finding Value in the Real-Time Enterprise," *Business 2.0,* November 2003, pp. S1–S5.

Figure 9.11, page 329, "Finding Value in the Real-Time Enterprise," *Business 2.0,* November 2003, pp. S1–S5.

Figure 9.12, page 332, www.donotbuydodge.ca, accessed April 2007.

Figure 9.13, 9.16, pages 335–337, used with permission, Claudia Imhoff and Richard Hackathorn, April 2007.

Chapter 10

Cut 10.1A, page 356, Doug Menuez/Getty Images.

Cut 10.1B, page 356, Patrick Clark/Getty Images.

Cut 10.1C, page 356, Jules Frazier/Getty Images.

Figure 10.1, page 358, "ERP Knowledge Base," www.cio.com, accessed July 2005.

Figures 10.4, 10.5, 10.6, 10.7, 10.8, pages 360–363, Exact Software, "ERP-II: Making ERP Deliver On Its Promise to the Enterprise",

jobfunctions.bnet.com/whitepaper.aspx?docid = 144338, accessed July 25, 2007.

Figure 10.9, page 364, Michael Doane, "A Blueprint for ERP Implementation Readiness," www.metagroup.com, accessed October 17, 2003.

Figure 10.10, page 364, Kaplan, Robert, Norton, David, "The BSC: Translating Strategy into Action" (Vintage Books: 1998) The Balanced Scorecard Institute, www.balancedscorecard.org/, accessed May 15, 2007.

Figure 10.12, 10.13, pages 367–368, www.sap.com.

Figure 10.16, page 371, Supply Chain Metrics.com, www.supplychainmetric.com/, accessed June 12, 2007.

Chapter 11

Cut 11.1A, page 399, The McGraw-Hill Companies, Inc./Christopher Kerrigan, photographer.

Cut 11.1B, page 399, Getty Images.

Cut 11.1C, page 399, The McGraw-Hill Companies, Inc./Christopher Kerrigan, photographer.

Figure 11.1, page 402, "Software Costs," CIO Magazine, www.cio .com, accessed December 5, 2003.

Figure 11.7, page 408, Agile Alliance Manifesto, www.agile.com, accessed November 1, 2003.

Figure 11.12, page 414, "Top Reasons Why IT Projects Fail," InformationWeek, www.infoweek.com, accessed November 5, 2003.

Figure 11.19, page 420, Deni Connor, "IT Outlook Declines Due to Outsourcing, Offshoring," www.nwfusion.com/careers/2004/0531manside.html, accessed June 8, 2004.

Figure 11.22, page 422, Todd Datz, "Outsourcing World Tour," *CIO Magazine,* July 15, 2004, pp. 42–48.

Chapter 12

Cut 12.1A, page 436, © Getty Images.

Cut 12.1B, page 436, © Royalty-Free/CORBIS.

Cut 12.1C, page 436, Royalty-Free/CORBIS.